SPEAK·TRUTH·TO·POWER

COMMANDER
STEVEN HAINES
ROYAL NAVY

AGAINST WAR AND EMPIRE

THE LEWIS WALPOLE SERIES IN EIGHTEENTH-CENTURY CULTURE AND HISTORY

The Lewis Walpole Series, published by Yale University Press with the aid of the Annie Burr Lewis Fund, is dedicated to the culture and history of the long eighteenth century (from the Glorious Revolution to the accession of Queen Victoria). It welcomes work in a variety of fields, including literature and history, the visual arts, political philosophy, music, legal history, and the history of science. In addition to original scholarly work, the series publishes new editions and translations of writing from the period, as well as reprints of major books that are currently unavailable. Though the majority of books in the series will probably concentrate on Great Britain and the Continent, the range of our geographical interests is as wide as Horace Walpole's.

AGAINST WAR AND EMPIRE

Geneva, Britain, and France in
the Eighteenth Century

Richard Whatmore

Yale

UNIVERSITY
PRESS
New Haven & London

Published with assistance from the Annie Burr Lewis Fund.

Yale University Press books may be purchased in quantity for educational,
business, or promotional use. For information, please e-mail
sales.press@yale.edu (U.S. office) or sales@yaleup.co.uk (U.K. office).

Set in Electra type by IDS Infotech Ltd., Chandigarh, India.
Printed in the United States of America.

Whatmore, Richard.
Against war and empire : Geneva, Britain, and France in the eighteenth century /
Richard Whatmore.
p. cm.—The Lewis Walpole series in eighteenth-century culture and history
Includes bibliographical references and index.
ISBN 978-0-300-17557-8 (alk. paper)
1. Geneva (Republic)—History—18th century. 2. Republicanism—Geneva
(Republic)—History—18th century. 3. Geneva (Republic)—Foreign relations—France.
4. France—Foreign relations—Geneva (Republic). 5. Geneva (Republic)—Foreign
relations—Great Britain. 6. Great Britain—Foreign relations—Geneva (Republic).
I. Title.
DQ140.G3 W53 2012
949.4′51605—dc23   2012006776

A catalogue record for this book is available from the British Library.

This paper meets the requirements of ANSI/NISO Z39.48–1992
(Permanence of Paper).

10 9 8 7 6 5 4 3 2 1

To my wife,
Ruth Woodfield,
and our three boys,
Jess, Kim, and Davy Whatmore

It is not to be expected, among Men, that a superior Power will contain itself within the Bounds of an exact Moderation, and it will not employ its Force to obtain, for itself, what Advantages it can, by oppressing the Weaker. Or if this Power should happen to be for some time harmless in the hands of an Excellent Prince, who could hear such Prosperity so well, the Wonder 'tis likely would cease with his Reign.
—*François de Salignac de la Mothe-Fénelon,* Two Essays on the Ballance of Europe *(London, 1720), 6–7*

Wars and the administration of public affairs, are the principal subjects of history; but the number of persons interested in these busy scenes, is very different, according to the different condition of mankind. In great monarchies, millions of obedient subjects pursue their useful occupations in peace and obscurity. The attention of the Writer, as well as the Reader, is solely confined to a court, a capital, a regular army, and the districts which happen to be the occasional scene of military operations. But a state of freedom and barbarism, the season of civil commotions, or the situation of petty republics, raises almost every member of the community into action, and consequently into notice. The irregular divisions, and the restless motions, of the people of Germany, dazzle our imagination, and seem to multiply their numbers. The profuse enumeration of kings and warriors, of armies and nations, inclines us to forget that the same objects are continually repeated under a variety of appellations, and that the most splendid appellations have been frequently lavished on the most inconsiderable objects.
—*Edward Gibbon,* The History of the Decline and Fall of the Roman Empire, *vol. 1 (London, 1776), 2nd ed., 241*

CONTENTS

PREFACE

The two epigraphs at the beginning of this book suggest its contents. The first epigraph comes from François Fénelon, the great French Catholic theologian and moralist, in an essay originally written as a note to the *Examen de conscience sur les devoirs de la royauté*, expressing his view that powerful states could not be expected to limit their ambitions to their own domains. Any prince within a strong state that refrained from subduing his neighbors might be considered "the ornament of history," but the key fact was that his like should "not be looked for again." Fénelon's writings were popular throughout the eighteenth century in part because his views resonated with the fact that so many of the states that formed Europe, a continent then comprising a multitude of states of different kinds, believed their independence to be increasingly under threat. In the second epigraph the historian Edward Gibbon makes the argument that "the most inconsiderable objects" were worthy subjects of historical study, including the "petty republics" whose "irregular divisions" and "restless motions" might "dazzle our imagination." The subject of *Against War and Empire* is Geneva, until 1798 one of the smallest republics in Europe, and this book relates the complicated story of the attempts by some inhabitants of this city-state to maintain its independence in the face of the overwhelming power and influence of France and Britain, the great empires of western Europe then locked in a struggle for international supremacy that led to a series of conflicts stretching from the War of the Grand Alliance (1688–1697) to the culmination of the Napoleonic Wars in 1815.

The particular case of Geneva serves to illustrate the wider political concerns of the age that were generated by the fighting empires, namely the fears about perpetual war and the possible descent into a new dark age, the corruption of commerce, the rise of luxury, the challenge to established religion, and the collapse of civilization. The more general story developed from the difficulties experienced by Europe's small states in the early modern world, after they discovered that they could no longer stand militarily against commercial monarchies, and above all against France. Problems for small states became acute because of the gulf in power by comparison with larger states: from the early eighteenth century onward, a small state could be defined as one that did not have the resources or desire to aspire to empire. With increasing commerce becoming central to the funding of national defense, the size of a state began to be of greater importance. Large states supported extensive national markets and offered opportunities to organize national commerce in a manner that aspired to guarantee expenditure on defense; equally, such expenditure might underwrite the expansion of empire. Small republics more especially could not, it was widely argued, cope with luxury, could not defend themselves against larger states, and had been in terminal decline for two centuries because of their unstable and corrupt internal politics. Many observers expected small republics to fall to predatory enterprises, as appeared to be happening across Europe by the 1760s. Traditional survival strategies for small republics, ranging from defensive alliances and incorporation into federal republics to economic specialization and reliance upon the republican patriotism generated by civic virtue, appeared to have fallen out of date, such was the disparity between their own resources and those of their potential imperial enemies.

One traditional survival strategy, often associated with Machiavelli, was to turn a small state into a large empire. One of the great questions for eighteenth-century republicans was whether their ideas about politics could be applied to large as well as to small states, without the kinds of war associated with Machiavelli's advised imperial policy. For many commentators this was the fundamental intellectual barrier that needed to be overcome if republics were to survive. Europe had to become peaceful for small states to remain intact. If peace was to become the norm for a continent embroiled in war for every decade bar the 1720s, a common view among republicans held that republics had to become large or large monarchies had to become small. The transition mechanism to such a state of perpetual peace was much discussed. Imagining Europe as an altered political entity was often the consequence of debate about the means to peace in perpetuity.

The Genevan contribution to the broader controversy over the future of small states came to a head in 1782. Geneva had enjoyed relative political stability since Calvin's Reformed ecclesiastical and civil constitution was established in the sixteenth century. A link was often presumed between Protestantism and political liberty, and equally between Protestantism, political liberty, and the growth of commerce. As such Geneva was seen to be among the most successful of republics surviving into the modern world. While the riches of Venice and Genoa were waning, and while other small states followed the Florentine and Milanese models and became dukedoms or were aggrandized into larger empires, Geneva remained free despite its position between France, Savoy, and the reputedly powerful Swiss confederation. Many Genevans saw this continued independence as providential, a sure sign that God was confirming in history the truth of the founding myths of the republic. Geneva was not Swiss in the eighteenth century, being an allied neighbor rather than a canton. The Treaty of Soleure (1579) ratified French support for Swiss protection of Geneva, in return for the free passage of troops in times of necessity. In October 1584 Zurich made a perpetual alliance with Geneva, and the triple alliance between Bern, Zurich, and Geneva was renewed in 1642. The rulers of Savoy, who had become kings of Sardinia under Victor Amadeus II (1666–1732), renounced their claim to Geneva and acknowledged its existence as a free state only in 1754. Genevans inherited a strong sense of the value of independence, partly from Calvin's Geneva-based Reformation, and partly from the legacy of the great Swiss military exploits of the Renaissance period. Swiss military capacity had been so great that small states across western Europe, and particularly across the Holy Roman Empire, considered "turning Swiss" by establishing confederations for self-defense against monarchical dominion. Only echoes of such times remained.

The history of Geneva in the eighteenth century was characterized by what contemporaries, and famously Voltaire, called a civil war. Defenders of an oligarchic constitution of small executive councils, increasingly dominated by members of particular families, faced citizens who accused the ruling magistrates of abandoning popular sovereignty and of being corrupted by francophone libertinism. The *représentant* or reformist movement sought to alter the laws of the city: "représentant" signified someone who brought concerns about violations of law to the General Council of all bourgeois and citizens, deeming this body to be sovereign. The représentants were opposed to the oligarchy of rich citizens, considered the morals of the citizenry to be in jeopardy from them, and in consequence were concerned about the possibility of national economic collapse. For such reasons the reformers challenged the magistracy directly by means of public demonstrations, which, in the 1730s and 1760s, required the intervention of Swiss and French mediators to establish several short-lived constitutional compromises.

The view of the représentants by the 1770s was that Geneva survived only through an alliance with Switzerland and with France, and as time wore on was becoming a Protestant enclave in a Catholic French empire, maintaining a show of independence for reasons of state: it was easier for France to rule de facto, paying lip service to the Calvinist and republican heritage for reasons to do with commerce, the Huguenot faction within France, and international relations across the continent. In Geneva a national revival was sought that was both Calvinist and republican. The events of 1782 were a response to this demand and set the seal on a much longer debate about the accuracy of the founding myths of the state. One of Calvin's most significant legacies was the belief that political or moral transformation was possible by embracing reform to its fullest extent, enabling purposive change to occur over a short period. This perspective remained powerful within représentant circles.

The acts of rebellion culminated in the uprising of 1782. A circle of young Genevan lawyers, merchants, and pastors, many of them disaffected friends or followers of Jean-Jacques Rousseau, had begun in the 1760s to contemplate more radical reforms than Rousseau had envisaged for Geneva. Among them, Jean-André Deluc, Etienne Clavière, Jean-Louis de Lolme, and Jacques-Antoine du Roveray were leaders of the représentants in the later 1760s. In 1782 Clavière, Du Roveray, and another young lawyer named François d'Ivernois led the initially successful rebellion against the ruling magistrates, managed to pacify the city, and initiated the process of creating a new constitution for the republic, before the old magistrates returned via a French-led army's entry into the city. These men, and their compatriot Etienne Dumont, who soon followed them into exile, were led gradually to the view that Europe's large monarchies had to be reformed constitutionally and economically if small states across the continent were to survive and if peace was to be more than a fleeting experience. Democratic reform at Geneva, they argued, would be possible only if the major powers of Europe ceased to be directly involved in the republic's affairs. More specifically, the French "guarantee" of the constitution, which provided the perfect pretext for interference, was seen as the main impediment to reform on the grounds that the other guaranteeing powers, Zurich and Bern, had declined in power relative to France.

The French invasion of 1782 was anathema to Geneva's représentants because French dominion signaled a loss of sovereignty and the death of the international Calvinism that so many représentants saw as the only real link between Protestants in modern times. When the French invaders expelled the leaders of the représentants, it confirmed to them that Geneva could no longer rely for its continued independence on civic virtue or manliness, leagues of Protestant states and republics, or a balance of power among Savoy, France, and the Swiss cantons. Alternative strategies for national survival had to be developed, entailing a moral philosophy erected on a foundation other than virtue and a politics that went beyond the acceptance of decline, as well as being capable of challenging the supremacy of commercial monarchies in Europe as presently constituted, or at least of erecting a system of international relations that promised to put an end to the rapaciousness of modern monarchy with regard to smaller or lesser states. In short, it required the commercial monarchies to abandon empire as traditionally conceived.

Three strategies were developed by the exiled représentants in the years between 1782 and the outbreak of the French Revolution in 1789. The first was to support a cosmopolitan and commercial alliance between Britain and France that would rid the world of mercantile empire. The second was to persuade Britain, which was perceived as the only state capable of challenging France, to become the protector of popular republics. Britain's empire was widely considered more moderate in its imperial designs than France. The counterargument was that Britain might prove to be more successful in acquiring dominion over small states because its mercantile system destroyed the trade of competitor states by brutal economic competition, which could be a prelude to political subjection, veiled or open. The third option was to reform France domestically, with the object of making that state more amenable to the existence of democratic republics. The argument initially deployed by the Genevan représentants was that, if commercial practices were reformed in Britain and France by abandoning aristocratic, state, or corporate controls over trade, what Adam Smith had called "the natural progress of opulence" would be reestablished internationally, making it irrational to undertake wars entailing the invasion of fellow commercial states. Forms of "patriotic commerce," a term Smith himself would never have used, compatible with public virtue and devoted to sustaining national independence, were described as the linchpins of Europe's planned pacific future. Such forms of patriotism were expected by the Genevan représentants to define an individual self-interest compatible with the common good of humankind. The Genevan exiles sought to persuade British ministers to dismantle the "mercantile system" of economic controls over imperial trade. The culmination of the campaign was the Anglo-French Commercial Treaty of 1786, which was seen as a major step in protecting the interests of small commercial republics by uniting the economic interests of Britain and France. Commercial empires were expected to become compatible with national independence. Indeed, their reform was intended to help establish perpetual peace in Europe.

The commencement of the French Revolution opened up new opportunities for the transformation of the prospects of Europe's small states. The

Genevan représentants continued to be interested in cosmopolitan empire and in schemes to transform both Britain and France by banishing jealousy of trade and reason of state: amoral doctrines for imperial aggrandizement or economic dominion were held to be the major impediments to small state security. The alternative was to inaugurate an era of perpetual peace. Revolutionary France was expected to take the lead. Some radical Genevans, and preeminently Clavière, despite becoming an Irish subject, were ever faithful to the cosmopolitan critique of Britain's empire. His compatriots de Lolme and Deluc, by contrast, believed that Britain's parliamentary monarchy was capable of ensuring that the mercantile system would not translate into reason-of-state politics. England's successful and mutually beneficial union with Scotland provided proof. The small Scottish state had gained from free trade and from security. A similar union was advocated for Ireland. Du Roveray, d'Ivernois, and Dumont only gradually became convinced that a free Europe entailed the destruction of France's empire and Britain becoming the dominant power on mainland Europe. They agreed that such a project would be successful only if the British mercantile system were abolished. In short, the course of the Revolution caused the représentants to divide and to begin to develop contrasting visions for peace and empire.

Attempts have been made before to narrate the remarkable tale of the Genevan représentants. Two authors deserve particular mention. The first is Otto Karmin, whose pioneering biography *Sir Francis d'Ivernois* appeared posthumously in 1920; the author, then in his late thirties, was an early victim of the influenza epidemic that followed World War I. The second is the Catholic priest Jean Bénétruy and his magisterial *L'atelier de Mirabeau: Quatre proscrits Genevois dans la tourmente révolutionnaire* of 1962. Large debts must equally be signaled to other scholars, including Bronisław Baczko, Cyprian Blamires, Jean-Daniel Candaux, Clarissa Campbell Orr, Graham Gargett, Eric Golay, André Gür, Marc Lahmer, Ralph Leigh, Derek Jarrett, Linda Kirk, Marc Neuenschwander, Cristina Pitassi, Michel Porret, Jennifer Powell-McNutt, Jean-Marc Rivier, Barbara Roth-Lochner, Helena Rosenblatt, Gabriella Silvestrini, and Jean Starobinski, all of whom have illuminated little-known aspects of Genevan political life.

All authors to date, however, have underplayed the Genevan radicals' contribution to European power politics and more particularly the contemporary politics of empire in Britain and in France. *Against War and Empire* is the first intellectual history of the leading représentants. It considers the substantial development of the movement in London and Paris from their engagement with the tradition of radical politics at Geneva and with Rousseau in the 1760s.

It goes on to study the reform politics the représentants developed up to Dumont's edition of Bentham's *Political Tactics* of 1816, which was intended to supersede the représentant movement at Geneva as traditionally conceived. The story of the attempt to transform France and Britain for the betterment of small republics like Geneva was the initial subject of Etienne Dumont's autobiography, commenced at Bath in 1799, which was posthumously published as *Souvenirs sur Mirabeau* in 1832. It was, as Dumont and his subsequent editors confessed, never finished. The most ambitious aim of this work is to present a fuller account.

Acknowledgments

This book has taken a long time to write, and numerous debts need to be recorded. The first is to my colleagues at the Sussex Centre for Intellectual History, and especially Knud Haakonssen and Donald Winch, who have ceaselessly toiled to improve this book and its author; the failings of course have nothing to do with them. Former colleagues, the late John Burrow and Brian Young, also influenced the argument to a significant extent. I learned a great deal from the "New Work in Intellectual History" series of symposia created by Knud Haakonssen, and especially those devoted to the work of John Robertson, Istvan Hont, Maria Rosa Antognazza, and Stefan Collini. Special thanks go to Cyprian Blamires, Clarissa Campbell Orr, Béla Kapossy, and Michael Sonenscher for reading and commenting on the book and for helping me to frame it. Cyprian deserves particular mention for his pathbreaking book on Dumont and Bentham, as well as for his unfailing generosity in sharing ideas and sources. Jean-Marc Rivier, who revealed his work on Clavière to me at an early stage, was equally generous.

I could not have written the book without the work of scholars who have investigated states, empires, and Geneva in the eighteenth century, including Manuela Albertone, David Armitage, Keith Baker, Jimmy Burns, Clarissa Campbell Orr, Emmanuelle de Champs, William Doyle, Graham Gargett, Rachel Hammersley, Tim Hochstrasser, Istvan Hont, Ian Hunter, Jonathan Israel, Béla Kapossy, Johnson Kent Wright, Linda Kirk, Marc Lahmer, Jim Moore, Isaac Nakhimovsky, Cristina Pitassi, John Pocock, Michel Porret, Allan Potofsky, Jennifer Powell-McNutt, John Robertson, Fred Rosen, Helena Rosenblatt, Philip Schofield, Gabriella Silvestrini, Michael Sonenscher, Koen Stapelbroek, and Gareth Stedman-Jones. Others who've acted, whether intentionally or not, as sources of guidance and inspiration at different times are Maria Rosa Antognazza, Richard Bourke, Loïc Charles, Stefan Collini, Aurelian Craiutu, Cesare Cuttica, Robert Darnton, Jeremy Jennings, Duncan Kelly, Colin Kidd, Paschalis Kitromilides, Catherine Larrère, David Lieberman, Jim Livesey, Jon Parkin, Nick Phillipson, Steve Pincus, Isabel Rivers, Emma Rothschild, Ruth Scurr, John Shovlin, Quentin Skinner, Mark Somos, Céline Spector, Tim Stanton, Philippe Steiner, Sandy Stewart, Ann Thomson, Edoardo Tortarollo, Keith Tribe, Norman Vance, Georgios Varouxakis, Katia Visconti, and David Wykes. Aid from intellectual history students at Sussex needs to be recognized, including from Sophie Bisset, Kris Grint, Andy Mansfield, Amanda McKeever, Peter Price, Amy Smith, and Emma Veitch. Ken Goodwin and Lucie Ragosy provided a huge amount of help over many years, and continue to do so. Yvonne Santacreu's and Åsa Söderman's labors were indispensable in keeping the Sussex Centre afloat, and without such work this book would not have been written.

Librarians at the British Library, London Library, National Archives, National Library of Ireland, Bibliothèque Nationale, Bibliothèque de l'Arsenale, and University of Sussex Library were extremely helpful. Barbara Roth-Lochner and her staff at the Bibliothèque de Genève deserve special thanks for endless bibliographic services. I would also like to thank Chris Rogers, Laura Davulis, Christina Tucker, Phil King, Duke Johns, and the staff of Yale University Press for seeing the book through the production process (and two anonymous referees for useful comments on the original manuscript). I would equally like to thank the editors of *Modern Intellectual History* and *The Historical Journal* for comments on articles I published with them in 2006 and 2007, respectively. The odd section from those articles can be found in this book and I'm grateful to the editors and publishers for permission to publish them. Last but not least, I would like to thank the Arts and Humanities Research Council, the British Academy, and the School of Humanities/History, Art History and Philosophy Research Fund at Sussex for funding parts of this project.

The book is dedicated to my wonderful wife, to whom I owe the most of all, and to our children.

Part One

INTRODUCTION

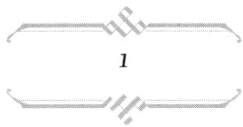

1782 AND AFTER

ENLIGHTENMENT GENEVA

A rebellion against the government of Geneva occurred in April 1782.[1] It was deemed necessary by the représentants because of the overweening power of France in the affairs of the state. Situated at the southwest end of Lake Leman, Europe's largest freshwater lake, and between France, Savoy, and Switzerland, forty-five miles north of Chambéry, thirty-four miles southwest of Lausanne, and seventy-two miles southwest from Bern, Geneva in 1782 was a walled city-state of "about three miles compass."[2] It was said that only Bordeaux and Constantinople could challenge the beauty and natural advantages of Geneva's geographical location.[3] The city was divided by the river Rhone, which ran in two channels between the sides of Geneva, forming an island of barely half a mile between them, all of which were connected by two bridges. The southern or left-hand side of the city, looking south from the island, was called "Geneva" by its inhabitants and encompassed a lower part comprising houses on a flat plain and an upper town on the hill, where the better-off citizens and burghers tended to live. On the north or right side of the Rhone stood "Saint-Gervais," deemed rougher, less wealthy, less orthodox, and less austere.[4] Geneva was, of course, a Rome for Protestants. The Genevan Academy, established in 1558, provided one of the most rigorous training regimes for Protestant ministry and civil education. By 1760 there were eleven professors, each elected by the Venerable Company of Pastors: three of theology and ecclesiastical history, one of oriental languages, two of natural and civil law, one of German law, two of philosophy, one of mathematics, and one of belles lettres.[5] It was said that the academy "hath spread the name and fame of Geneva all over the world, whereas it was before that, hardly known beyond the limits of Switzerland and Savoy."[6]

If the history of the independent republic of Geneva was intertwined with religion, it was equally concerned with trade. It was at Geneva that the major trade routes crossed from Marseille to Lyon and to southern Germany, and from Milan to St. Bernard to Paris. This continued into the eighteenth century, with the city acting as a hub for the exchange of goods between Italy, the Swiss cantons, France, and the German states, having particularly good road and commercial connections with Lyon, Strasbourg, and Frankfurt. Genevans were well known for their manufactures and especially for "silks, gold and silver lace, thread-lace, pistols, shammy leather, watches, and printing of books."[7] They were increasingly well known for banking, with the dynasties of the Lullins, Gallatins, and Boissiers being followed by the de Tournes, Neckers, Thellusons, and Vernets among others.[8] The compatibility of wealth and virtue was always questioned at Geneva.[9] This was why luxury was forbidden, manners were monitored and supervised, and estates were divided between children equally at death in order to prevent the growth of excessive riches.

Geneva had always had "jealous and potent neighbours," and historically had subsisted "like a bone 'twixt three mastiffs," the Holy Roman emperor, the French king, and the dukes of Savoy. The crucial point was that none of the surrounding powers "dare touch it singly, for fear that the other two would fly upon him."[10] Geneva had remained into the eighteenth century "acknowledged as a free, sovereign State by all the Princes of Europe, even the greatest, as the King of France, Louis XIV . . . hath sometimes used the expression, *We desire and pray the Republick of Geneva.*"[11] Proof of a direct relationship between godliness and national survival was seen as manifest in the greatest event in the history of Genevan patriotism, the "Escalade" of 1602. The Escalade followed the decision of Charles Emmanuel, son of Philibert the Duke of Savoy, to attack Geneva at night with a body of over a thousand troops, two hundred of whom used ladders (*escalades*) to scale the bastions. Fortunately for the town, an alarm was called. Portcullises closed before the invaders could open the gates with a petard, and the citizens managed to repulse the invasion with courage and self-sacrifice. Sixteen Genevans died in addition to more than two hundred Savoyard troops. A tradition of republican valor and a reputation for self-defense was thenceforth created, and the Escalade was celebrated every subsequent 11 December. One observer recalled, "Some body at that time happily enough found out the Word VENGEE [reveng'd] in that of Genève."[12] The aged academy rector Théodore de Bèze had slept through the agitation of the Escalade, but he returned to the pulpit on 12 December and preached a sermon during which Psalm 124 was sung. The psalm became an emblem of popular patriotism, with its plain message that Genevans had thrown back the invaders because of "the Lord who was on our side." There could be no more direct example of the beneficial relationship between Calvinism, republicanism, and liberty. Calvinism generated patriotism. When fused with republican *virtus*, the survival of the little republic was assured.

Such a view was challenged in the eighteenth century because of the extent of the difference in power between Geneva and the states surrounding it. In the late 1730s the Marquis d'Argens expressed the opinion that fortune alone could explain the survival of Geneva. The city had not been incorporated into a larger empire only because the jealous powers surrounding it would interpret the destruction of the city as a slight upon their own status:

> Two reasons oblige France and the Swiss to protect Geneva; in the first place, it is no doubt the interest of the former to prevent the Savoyards and Piedmontese from extending their dominion on this side of the Alps; and next it is no less the interest of the Protestant cantons to prevent the destruction or subduing of a city which may be looked upon as the metropolis of the Calvinist religion.[13]

D'Argens pointed out that the Genevan government's investment in extended fortifications earlier in the century had been foolish, because they would never deter invasion. He deemed them also dangerous, because the existence of advanced fortifications threatened to upset the delicate balance that maintained Genevan independence:

> To give a man, whose heart is easily inflamed, an opportunity of gazing upon a beautiful woman whom he may find means to gain, is a dangerous step. A day may perhaps come, when the people of Geneva will repent their having dressed out and adorned their city like a new bride. Some King of France may happen to fall in love with her and even force her into an irregular marriage.[14]

For many Genevan représentants, exactly this came to pass in 1782. Geneva was on the edge of a precipice because of the likelihood of its becoming part of a French empire.

THE GENEVAN REVOLUTION

The représentants believed that Geneva was in decline, and that the only hope for the future moral and economic health of the city lay in democratic reform. They recognized that France was unlikely to accept such reform but attempted to persuade the court at Versailles to support them. The Genevan représentants hoped that France might view events at Geneva in the same fashion as the republican rebellion against Britain's North American colonies. Following the logic of the reformist ministry of Anne-Robert-Jacques Turgot between 1774 and 1776, the belief was widespread that France had abandoned its historic development of an imperial and mercantile empire, had turned its back on Colbert's legacy, and was instead pursuing a new policy based on free trade and international peace. Such a strategy had been advocated, without the expectation by its author that it could be realized, in Adam Smith's *Wealth of Nations* (1776) and dovetailed with the ideas of the second generation of French physiocrats such as André Morellet and Pierre-Samuel Dupont de Nemours.

It was in expectation that the French foreign minister Charles Gravier, comte de Vergennes, might be willing to apply his North American policy to Europe that the leading représentants Etienne Clavière and Jacques-Antoine du Roveray met him in 1781. Instead, Vergennes warned them that the security of France with respect to all of the powers of Europe depended on Geneva, and that "such a place would be ill defended by a democracy." Vergennes also referred to the ancient French guarantee of Geneva's constitution, and instructed the représentants that the guarantee allowed France to put down any rebellion at Geneva, on the grounds of preventing Genevans from "imposing" laws to do with the reconstitution of the state. This was a reference to a committee established to revise the laws of Geneva, in which Clavière and Du Roveray were prominent, and which in September 1779, having failed to agree upon a new code of law, was refused leave to continue its labors by the executive Council of Two Hundred. The result was a stalemate that left, according to some observers, a French-led governing aristocracy facing a factious group of democrats supported by Britain.[15]

Du Roveray had united the représentants in 1780 with radical members of the "natif" party: residents of the city who had been born at Geneva but whose parents were neither bourgeois nor citizens, and who in consequence enjoyed limited civil and commercial rights. Complaints were sent to the executive Council of Two Hundred regarding the excessive power of the French *résident* (legate) at Geneva, and the existence of paid spies serving the French interest rather than the public good.[16] Vergennes demanded that Du Roveray lose his citizenship. In order to placate France the magistrates at Geneva removed him from the office of *procureur général*.[17] In response some of the représentants and natifs decided to seize the government of the state. This came to pass on 5 February 1781, when a tumult followed a gathering of antagonistic parties of natifs arguing about revisions to the constitution. After the commander of the arsenal accidentally killed two supporters of magistracy, having mistaken them for violent représentants, disorder spread, and quickly the party of représentants took control of the town.[18] They demanded greater civil rights for the natifs and, more significantly, that the government should "renounce all interference whatever of foreign powers," which amounted to a renunciation of the constitutional guarantee of France and the Swiss cantons.[19]

The prevarication of the magistrates after the revolt of the natifs led directly to the revolution of 8–9 April 1782, which once again saw the représentants begin to govern the city. This time the magistrates were locked up, deaths occurred during battles for two of the gates of the city, and order was restored only with difficulty.[20] Clavière, writing to his friend the banker Théophile Cazenove at London, had hopes that France would rely on negotiation, avoiding military intervention because of its consequences for international relations; in other words, he hoped that some shame would be felt by a France countenancing intervention at Geneva, having supported liberty in North America, and that this would prevent military involvement in the affairs of the small republic.[21] Clavière was then using his friend Pierre-Marc Bourrit to present the perspective of the représentants directly to Vergennes, and was seeking to persuade other intermediaries, such as Jean-André Deluc, to do the same.[22] He was altogether mistaken about Vergennes's intentions, and the reaction of France caused Clavière to believe that he might be assassinated. He anticipated "our unfortunate republic becoming a theater for the most appalling desolation."[23] Louis XVI reportedly told Vergennes:

> While the political differences at Geneva were confined to matters of mere dispute, it was to be doubted whether France had any right to take notice of them. But now, when all principles, destructive of society, have established there one set of people, who tyrannise over and imprison the other; now that this usurpation has seized on an authority disputed by all classes; I owe it to the Genevese government, whose ally and protector I am, as my ancestors have ever been, to give them relief and assistance in their distress.[24]

Opponents of the représentants were writing that they would prefer to become French subjects rather than be "governed by such men as Du Roveray, Clavière, Vieusseux and the like," who would leave the magistrates "at the mercy of the devil."[25] Vergennes promised to intervene "to banish the sources of division from the republic and to fix the rights and powers of each of the bodies that form the state."[26] From London, Willoughby Bertie, 4th Earl of Abingdon, was reputedly already negotiating with François d'Ivernois about British assistance to the rebels. In 1766 he had been living at Geneva, and he sought to involve William Pitt the Elder, then prime minister, in the affairs of the republic. Abingdon's dispatches of 1766 never reached their destination because they were intercepted and confiscated by the magistrates. They were said to contain his will and an expression of his desire to die beside the représentants in defense of their city.[27]

Due to such links, in 1782 emissaries were sent to London by the représentants, who were encouraged by the prominence of their British supporters. Du Roveray led the delegation. Abingdon then gave d'Ivernois the bad news that "the fleets of England were the speaking trumpets of justice to the whole world," but Britain was now "no longer in a capacity to speak to the enemies of the liberties of mankind in its wonted tone of authority."[28] Du Roveray reportedly met Charles-James Fox, then minister of foreign affairs in the Rockingham ministry, in May 1782, and was offered the meager support of Britain's putting pressure on Savoy not to intervene at Geneva.[29] Samuel Romilly noted that the British ministers, while vocally ardent in favor of Geneva, were as likely to go to the aid of the city as to help an oppressed nation on the moon.[30] Related appeals to Holy Roman Emperor Joseph II, who was asked to behave in the manner of his forefather Charles V and to save Geneva as had occurred in 1540, came to nothing.[31]

The représentant emissaries then traveled to Turin, which was clearly a more important court for them than London, but were equally unsuccessful. Lord John Mount Stuart, British ambassador to Savoy, had been receiving information about Geneva from the représentants since 1779.[32] He resigned his position at Turin because of his opposition to the sending of Savoyard troops under the Count de la Mormora to put down the rebels.[33] The troops—over ten thousand of them—were led by the French general Charles-Léopold, Marquis de Jaucourt, who, in addition to the Savoyards and his own regiment, also headed a body of Bernese soldiers under Steiger de Watieville de Bels.[34] The philosophe Jacques-Pierre Brissot, traveling to Neuchâtel and curious to see Geneva, despite "the state of this poor town today," observed work being undertaken upon the ramparts of the city and noted that the inhabitants had hopes of a general peace because of the goodwill of the mediating powers.[35] This was not forthcoming. Arriving at the city on 29 June 1782, the three generals demanded the reinstatement of the magistrates and the delivery of all arms to the invading troops, offering five hours for surrender, which was increased to a whole day at the request of the insurgents.[36] D'Ivernois later noted the irony that Jaucourt's troops included a regiment newly returned from North America, underscoring the gulf in French policy between the continents. Geneva had suffered "a universal abandonment."[37]

FRENCH DOMINION

According to the historian Jean-Louis Giraud Soulavie, in the defense of the city wives were seen "exhorting their husbands, and mothers their children, to expire on the ramparts." Gunpowder was amassed in two central houses of the aristocratic quarter of the city and also placed in the center of the cathedral of Saint-Pierre. The représentant pastor Isaac Salomon Anspach asked his fellow citizens to "embrace our oppressors—but let it be the embrace of Samson, to crush them in the last ruins and ashes of our temples."[38] Another représentant, Jacques Grenus, proclaimed that it was better to die at the hands of the invaders rather than being hung in the aftermath. Religious songs were sung through the ramparts by the defenders.[39] It was said that there was not a single voice raised against the desire to die for the country.[40] Such was the ardor of the populace that the poor beyond the city, and women within it, joined the defensive body:

> The peasants of the territory flocked of their own accord, and without pay, to mount guard, and to work at the fortifications; women, of all ranks, crowded to the ramparts, as to a place of public amusement; encouraging and animating the men to persevere in their labour; and some even sharing in their fatigue assisted in transporting burdens or in planting cannon on the bastions . . . about eighty women and girls, dressed in uniforms, offered to form themselves into a company, for the purpose of defending the country. The committee of safety accepted their services, and placed them in a barrack, which by its situation was covered from the cannon of the besiegers. These amazons, with a spirit above their sex, refused a station that was not sufficiently exposed.[41]

From beyond the city, représentants such as Jean Roget, safely ensconced at Lausanne, exhorted their fellows to sacrifice themselves rather than accept a tyranny, even if it entailed the destruction of the sacred city.[42] Attempts by the Consistory to negotiate with the invaders failed.[43]

On the evening of 1 July 1782, the heads of the political circles who were organizing the resistance resolved to allow the hostages to leave the city and then to defend it to the last man. During the night, however, while the French batteries were being assembled, discussion began to center on the likely losses of up to two thousand people during a siege lasting two days, and the effects of the constant bombardment by French guns. The members of the government then decided that opposition to the troops would serve only to destroy the town and its populace. Proposals to bring the hostages to the ramparts were rejected. On the night of 1–2 July 1782, fifty-seven of the leading rebels voted for capitulation, while forty continued to support resistance. Gradually, amid the fear and panic, the argument was accepted that it was better to save "the effusion of so much blood from virtuous men," and that liberty might be enjoyed "in another country, which [Genevans] could no longer expect to find in their own."[44] The old magistrates were then released, the cannons disabled, and other weapons broken. The generals were invited to enter the town. Some of the représentants, having gone to sleep in the anticipation of an honorable death in the name of liberty, awoke to find that the city had been handed over to foreign troops.[45]

The leaders of the représentants chose to flee. Du Roveray, Clavière, and d'Ivernois, among others, left by boat, rowing across the lake to safety at Cologny. They were fired at by their supporters in the city and chased by a French brig.[46] At Cologny someone attempted to put a sword through Du Roveray.[47] Genevan opponents of the représentants were in the vanguard of the invading powers on their entrance into the city. They marched "with drums beating and colors flying." The former magistrates were "reestablished in their several charges to the sound of martial music." The only trouble within the city came when a former defender tried to fire a cannon at the invaders, but he failed in his attempt.[48] A public proclamation by the French general Jaucourt offered an amnesty to all rebels, with the exception of the twenty-one leaders of the représentants and radical natifs:

> So much lenity . . . would prove detrimental to the republic, and would exceed the limits of what every free state owes to itself, and the rights of all sovereigns, were it extended to all the authors of the commotion in Geneva. It is therefore indispensably necessary that Jacob Vernes, pastor, and Isaac-Salomon Anspach, minister and regent, be deposed from their offices of pastor and of regent; that Julian Dentand, elder syndic, Jacques Vieusseux, Jean Flournoy, and Etienne Clavière, members of the grand council, Jacques-Antoine Du Roveray, François d'Ivernois, advocates, and Marc-François Rochette, notary, be banished for ever; and that our sovereigns should engage with the republic not to allow them to reside in their territories, or within forty miles of their frontier: that Jacques Grenus, David Chauvet, Jean Janot, Guillaume Ringler, Jean-Jacques Breusse la Motte, members of the general council; Jean-Antoine Thuillier, citizen, Ésaïe Gasc, pastor, and Jean-Louis Schraidl, natives, be also exiled; but that at the end of ten years, by petitioning the grand council, promising to submit to its laws, and to live like peaceable citizens, they may return to Geneva, if a majority of three-fourths of the votes in the council shall so allow; it being nevertheless understood that they can never become members of the council of two hundred, nor fill the office of adjuncts: that Jean-Jacques Bonnet, formerly a

captain in the service of his most Christian majesty, be also exiled and incapable of returning within this city or its territory, without the consent of the said majority.[49]

Vergennes reported to Louis XVI that "the insurgents whom I expel from Geneva are the agents of England; the insurgents of America have long since been the friends of France. I have acted towards them not with any view to their political opinions, but according as I have found them disposed toward France. Such is my reason of state."[50] Soulavie argued that this view was confirmed because "scarcely had the twenty-one exiles quitted Geneva, when they named six commissaries: d'Ivernois, Clavière, Grenus, Ringler, Du Roveray, and Gasc, who set out for London, and joined Siordet, La Roche, and others, who already besieged the public offices."[51] In fact, Clavière had requested and received permission on 19 August 1782 to reside at Neuchâtel. It was only in January 1783 that he joined the exiles who had headed for Britain, having explored the possibility of permanent settlement in the German states.[52] Meanwhile, at Geneva over two thousand troops from France, Savoy, and Bern were garrisoned in the city. Around two thousand représentants were said to have left Geneva on the eve of the surrender and during the following day.[53] The invaders oversaw the inauguration of a new constitution that gave more power to the magistrates than they had enjoyed since the Reformation.

In determining not to sacrifice themselves, and in abandoning the city, the exiled représentants provided to their critics, and many of their ashamed followers who remained within Geneva, an exact illustration of the gulf between ancient republican valor and modern republican manners. Only the leaders of the Consistory considered the saving of the city to have been providential rather than shameful.[54] Catherine Roget noted that the exiles "were abused in almost every place they have traveled." There were, she wrote, no contemporary Saint Eustaces, referring to the former Roman general who had allowed himself to be roasted alive with his wife and children for his Christian faith. Du Roveray and d'Ivernois were reputed to have favored self-sacrifice during the discussion of the councils that formed on the eve of the surrender.[55] D'Ivernois, with others, likened Geneva's position to that of Saguntum facing Hannibal, the added anticipated parallel being that this siege had sparked the Second Punic War. Another example cited was Messina, the Sicilian state sacked by the Cathaginians and subsequently enslaved by a Rome to which it had looked for protection.[56] Clavière was stated to be the leader of those who had advocated a cowardly retreat.[57] It was noted that "the defenders of the people finished by becoming their victims. The celebrated Clavière and du Roveray are today the sad proof.

They were cursed by the citizens, for whom they have sacrificed their wealth, their talents, and even their lives."[58]

In the aftermath of the revolution, supporters of the traditional constitution, called "constitutionnaires" or "négatifs," were returned to power. They put an end to radical resistance through the passage of a "black act," the *édit noir* incorporated into the *Edit du 21 novembre 1782*, which stifled dissent and banished in perpetuity the leaders of the représentants.[59] The latter were declared dead in law. The journalist Jacques Mallet du Pan, supporting the edict, was reputed to have said "there is no law of the peoples for the factious."[60] Isaac Cornuaud, a natif who was paid by the magistrates to defend their cause, considered the settlement just and helped arrange the passage of the edict through a General Council greatly reduced in membership by the exclusion of the représentants.[61] All parties recognized that the ultimate arbiter of the situation was Vergennes, who could not tolerate a democratic republic on his borders.[62] When the leaders of the représentants attempted to create a "New Geneva" at Waterford in Ireland, their initial intention was to transport the Genevan Academy with them, on the grounds that Geneva had become amoral and was unsuited to learning.[63] Clavière wrote that the virtue of the people could be salvaged only if an asylum could be found. It had to be an asylum through which "we will give to men of all countries the courage to resist despotism."[64]

DUMONT AND BOWOOD

Etienne Dumont was too young to have been a leader of the représentants in 1782, having been born at Geneva on 18 July 1759 to the jeweler Abraham David Dumont and educated at the Genevan Academy.[65] Rather than choosing to flee the city in 1782, as so many of his subsequent associates did, Dumont remained and was ordained as a pastor of the Genevan Reformed Church on 2 December 1783. Yet he remained a représentant. His first public sermon, on 28 March 1784, attacked the policies of the governing magistrates and pronounced dire warnings about the future from the growth of luxury and corruption at Geneva.[66] After being heavily criticized in consequence, Dumont left Geneva for St. Petersburg.[67] In July 1784 he became pastor to the Reformed community there. Eighteen months later, in January 1786, he traveled to England to enter the household of William Petty, formerly 2nd Earl of Shelburne and, after 1784, 1st Marquis of Lansdowne, who had served as prime minister between 1782 and 1783. At Bowood House near Calne in Wiltshire or at Shelburne House in London, Dumont became Shelburne's resident intellectual, replacing Joseph Priestley in this role, and was in part responsible for the education of Shelburne's younger son, Henry Petty.[68] Dumont thus entered one of the most imaginative and influential political circles of the latter half of the eighteenth century.

Identifying the "real" nature of the British constitution was one of the obsessions of the members of Shelburne's broader circle of politicians and philosophers, the members of the "Bowood circle." Jeremy Bentham had attracted the attention of Shelburne after publishing his *Fragment on Government* in 1776, and Samuel Romilly became acquainted with Shelburne because of his *Fragment on the Constitutional Power and Duties of Juries*.[69] Bowood writers tended to believe in the excellence of the British constitution by comparison with the constitutions of comparable monarchies, but also in its limitations by reference to political principle and current practice. Reform was possible, and it entailed modernizing underlying constitutional strengths. Romilly, for example, was always seeking out corruption and bad laws, but he ultimately believed in "some general and permanent system, founded upon the principles of our ancient constitution."[70] In consequence, successfully altering monarchical constitutions in other nations necessitated spreading knowledge of a reformed version of Britain's. Shelburne had long been aware that financial crisis might push France toward Britain's example, and his hope, at times strong and at times questioned in the later 1780s and early 1790s, was that a new and pacific system of international relations would emerge in which France would join Britain in an alliance for free trade and political reform. When in London, Dumont became prominent in that city's growing Genevan exile community. He associated with the leaders of the Genevan revolution of 1782: the lawyer d'Ivernois, the politician Du Roveray, and the merchant Clavière. Furthermore, Dumont began to espouse their radical politics.

Over ten years later, at Bath in 1799, Dumont drafted a memoir of his experiences with the Genevan exiles, focusing particularly upon activities at France and Geneva in the early 1790s. These, left in manuscript form after Dumont's death in 1829, were edited by Jacob-Louis Duval, Dumont's nephew and literary executor, and appeared in 1832 as *Souvenirs sur Mirabeau et sur les deux premières assemblées législatives*.[71] On its appearance, Dumont's *Souvenirs* was accepted as among the most significant histories of the early French Revolution.[72] Dumont's original plan had been for a far more extensive book, amounting to an outline history of the aspirations and plots of Clavière, Du Roveray, and d'Ivernois, among others, who were known to contemporaries as the leaders of Geneva's représentants. Their quest was to make the modern world of commerce and empire, dominated by the commercial monarchies of Britain and France, safe for small republics.

Having lived in Paris for a year from March 1789, in the Bath manuscript Dumont described the formation of the influential Genevan workshop, the "atelier de Mirabeau," comprising Dumont, Clavière, Du Roveray, and another Protestant pastor, Etienne-Salomon Reybaz. Writing at times as individuals and sometimes collaboratively, they were responsible for many of the great orator Honoré-Gabriel Riquetti de Mirabeau's speeches in the National Assembly, in addition to writing his newspaper, the *Courier de Provence*.[73] Clavière and Du Roveray first met Mirabeau at Neuchâtel immediately after their banishment from Geneva in 1782. Mirabeau was in Switzerland in order to sell two of his manuscripts, the "Lettres de cachet" and "L'espion dévalisé," to Samuel Fauche, his Neuchâtelois editor.[74] As was so often the case, Mirabeau was short of money. Pierre-Alexandre Du Peyrou must have introduced Mirabeau to the exiles. He was a long-standing friend of Rousseau and the représentants, and Clavière was staying with Du Peyrou from the end of July 1782. The Genevans no doubt paid Mirabeau to promote their cause, knowing that one of his correspondents was Vergennes.[75] Mirabeau put his name to a memorandum on Geneva and sent it to Vergennes; the author may well have been Du Roveray.[76] It amounted to a last-ditch attempt to persuade France to abandon its historic policy of antagonism toward radical movements in Europe's small states.[77] The memorandum was followed by more popular works that appeared through the 1780s, such as *Considérations sur l'ordre de Cincinnatus* (1784) and *Doutes sur la liberté de L'Escaut réclamée par l'empereur; sur les causes & sur les conséquences probables de cette réclamation* (1785), concerned directly or indirectly with reform politics in Britain and in France, and all of which were linked in one way or another to the Genevans.

A similar relationship was established by the Genevan exiles with the aspiring philosopher Jacques Pierre Brissot, who in the autumn of 1782 was meeting his publisher Frédéric Samuel Ostervald, director of the Société typographique de Neuchâtel, and was speculating about which writing project might make his name and fortune.[78] Brissot had been in contact with François d'Ivernois earlier in the year, having received one of d'Ivernois's works about Genevan politics.[79] Both men had an interest in the establishment of civil liberty, and Brissot had completed a large number of tracts and books outlining a program of anti-Christian skepticism and institutional reform for the French state. He was an advocate of the improvement of manners on the basis of widespread humanitarian reforms, and criminal legislation more particularly.[80] In 1782, after being enlightened about politics by Clavière, Brissot declared that his own ideas had been "rather French," making him "a slave to existing prejudices rather than an apostle of truth."[81] What Brissot meant by "rather French" is indicated in his published works up to that date, where he had praised patriot rulers, among whom he included Catherine the Great, Joseph II, Frederick II, and Louis XVI, and in which he attacked republics and republican ideology.[82] Clavière gradually supplied a second education, having "an inexhaustible stock of new ideas."[83] The exiles evidently paid Brissot to write the *Philadelphien à Genève* (1782) in defense of the représentants.[84]

The représentants clearly contributed to the composition of Mirabeau's letter to Vergennes and Brissot's *Philadelphien*, ensuring that they faithfully expounded the perspective of the représentants. Dumont himself became involved with Mirabeau at Paris from 1788, because the latter's ascent in French politics was gradually recognized to have become the surest path to transforming Geneva. Building on the Anglo-French Commercial Treaty (1786) that promised to lay the foundations of a permanent peace between Britain and France, there was an expectation that France would play a more supportive role for small states, as it had so famously done during the American Revolution, and was continuing to do during the Dutch Patriot Revolt (1785–1787). Britain's support for the stadtholder against the patriots, however, signaled a return to more polarized international relations.[85] The French Revolution was important to the Genevans because they hoped it might presage the establishment of international relations devoid of amoral schemes for empire.

DUMONT AND BENTHAM

In the main, the fame of the published version of Dumont's *Souvenirs* was due to masterful portraits of the Revolution's principal personalities, and more particularly its firsthand description of Mirabeau's appropriation of the works of others in his speeches and writings. Dumont described Mirabeau's authorial practice when recalling the host of projects he had in mind at London in the mid-1780s. "Having become acquainted with a geographer, whose name I forget, he also meditated writing a universal geography. Had anyone offered him the elements of Chinese grammar, he would, no doubt, have attempted a treatise on the Chinese language. He studied a subject whilst he was writing upon it, and he only required an assistant who furnished matter."[86]

The *Souvenirs* also provide evidence of Dumont's growing interest in Jeremy Bentham's science of legislation, entailing a new approach to jurisprudence. Bentham's shadow needs to be recalled when reading Dumont's memoirs, which were written in the midst of the first of their author's mammoth editorial labors on Bentham's behalf, soon to appear in the latter's name as *Traités de législation civile et pénale* in 1802.[87] After the success of the *Traités* and later of the *Souvenirs*, Dumont became known for his relationship both with Mirabeau and with Bentham, and a resulting minor industry has scrutinized his contribution to the oeuvre of each.[88] With regard to the *Souvenirs*, however, in supplying the title *Souvenirs sur Mirabeau* Duval was inadvertently confining his uncle's opinions to the debate about the greatness of Mirabeau as a French national icon.[89] Duval left out chapters of the draft memoir concerning Dumont's activities at Geneva, particularly after Mirabeau's death in April 1791. For readers this was unfortunate, as only hints remained in the published text of 1832 regarding Geneva and Dumont's actual intentions during the turbulent years of the French Revolution.

Dumont embraced Benthamism as the successor to republican ideology, which by the late 1790s he deemed bankrupt because of the new large-state republicanism that had developed in France. Bentham was also to Dumont a modern successor to Calvin, in having developed an antidote to materialism and irreligion; Dumont's view of Bentham will of course strike modern scholars as rather odd. For the rest of his life, Dumont continued to view Benthamism, if not the mature views of Bentham himself, as key to the progress of global morality and cosmopolitanism.[90] As his nephew noted, he was praising Bentham's principle of utility shortly before his death in 1829, and calling Bentham a successor to François Fénelon:

> What I most admire is the manner in which Mr Bentham has laid down his principle, the development he has given to it, and the rigorous logic of his inductions from it. The first book of the *Treatises on legislation* is an art of reasoning upon this principle, of distinguishing it from the false notion which usurps its place, of analysing evil, and of showing the strength of the legislator in the four sanctions, natural, moral, political and religious. The whole is new, at least with regard to the method and arrangement, and they who have attacked the principle generally, have taken good care not to make a special attack upon the detailed exposition of the system. Egotism and materialism! How absurd! Nothing but vile declamation and insipid mummery! Look into the catalogue of pleasures, for the rank which the author assigns to those of benevolence, and see how he finds in them the germ of all social virtues! His admirable *Treatise* upon the indirect means of preventing crime, contains, among others, three chapters sufficient to pulverise all those miserable objections. One is on the cultivation of benevolence, another on the proper use of the motive of honour, and the third on the importance of religion when maintained in a proper direction; that is to say of that religion which conduces to the benefit of society. I am convinced Fénelon himself would have put his name to every word of this doctrine.[91]

Bentham's writings, mostly received in manuscript form in the mid-1790s, fascinated Dumont. They addressed issues that had obsessed him as a young pastor at Geneva, and which also figured prominently in the writings of Dumont's early mentor Pastor Jacob Vernes, another rebel of 1782: social structures, popular morals, international justice, legitimate commercial practice, and the prospects for states involved in competition for international supremacy by trade and war.[92]

In turning to Bentham, Dumont was acknowledging that the Geneva radical movement in which he had served had failed. He no longer had any hope of influencing parliaments and kings; as he put it in his final days, "Mr Bentham's ensign leads neither to riches nor to power"; directly moderating executive power had been his and his compatriots' goal from the Genevan radicals' response to Rousseau in the 1760s until the Terror in France in 1793. But from another perspective, Bentham's *Treatises*, the great manual for reform and moral practice for individuals in every station of life, registered the shift of focus of long-standing Genevan reform aspirations from the legislator to the individual, and from politicians and statesmen to humankind. There was another continuity. Bentham's draft project of an international law capable of providing perpetual peace, which Dumont commented on at length but failed to publish, was another attempt to reform the European states system and to maintain the independence of petty sovereignties: the project that had obsessed Genevan représentants since the 1760s.

Reconstructing the représentant perspective is the goal of the following chapters, beginning with eighteenth-century views of the nature of the Genevan city-state, its link with Calvinism, and the legacy of its republican past.

Part Two

THE CRISIS OF THE REPUBLIC, 1698–1786

2

GENEVA AND FRANCE, 1698–1754

When France was recognized to be infinitely stronger than the Swiss cantons or Savoy, the international balance of power, which Geneva had relied upon for external stability since Calvin's death, collapsed. One clear consequence of French greatness was widespread fear for the future of Protestant states within France's sphere of influence. After Louis XIV took Protestant Strasbourg by force of arms in 1681; closed the Huguenot academies of Sedan in 1681, of Die in 1684, and of Saumur and Montauban in 1685; and inaugurated a period of domestic persecution for Protestants by revoking the Edict of Nantes in 1685, neighboring states were flooded with refugees who wanted to avoid forced conversion to Catholicism. Geneva was particularly concerned at the destruction of Protestant temples in the Pays de Gex by French troops, as this brought the Catholic threat very close to the city.[1] At certain times in the late 1680s, up to a thousand refugees per week were finding their way to Geneva. Many sought and obtained permanent residence, boosting the population by a third and "bringing opulence and disquiet."[2]

An altered relationship between Geneva and France was discernible from the second half of the seventeenth century. Genevan awareness of its dependent status was signaled by the magistrates' keenness in the 1650s to renew the terms of the 1579 Treaty of Soleure (between France, Bern, and Soleure), which was perceived to have protected Geneva during Europe's wars of religion. It was achieved as a clause within the renewed alliance between France and the Protestant cantons in 1658. In 1659 the Council of Two Hundred punished pastors whose sermons had likened France and Spain to Herod and Pontius Pilate.[3] In 1660 the syndic André Pictet was sent to Paris to congratulate Louis XIV on the Treaty of the Pyrenees, which ended the war with Spain, and on his marriage contract with the Spanish infanta Marie-Thérèse. In an oration Pictet called the king the keeper of peace in Europe, "ever victorious and invincible."[4] In 1666 Genevan soldiers began to serve in French regiments, a practice that became a vocation for many families and one that continued until the Napoleonic Wars.[5]

Proof of a different international relationship had come in 1679, when several prominent Genevans were soliciting the French court for the position of chargé d'affaires at the city, and Louis XIV decided to appoint a permanent ambassador or *résident*.[6] The issue illustrated the dilemmas facing Geneva with respect to external policy. When the Sieur de Chauvigny arrived from France, he was lauded by the magistrates and given permission to celebrate mass at his house. This was remarkable, especially as even Lutheranism was not then tolerated in Geneva. The populace mobbed the property of the résident, and the magistrates shut the gates of the city to prevent foreign Catholics from attending on holy days.[7] This became a particular problem, as Chauvigny encouraged up to thirty persons to celebrate mass at his residence. One historian noted that when the populace saw "their cruel enemies," the monks and priests, arriving for mass "they shook with fear."[8]

While the magistrates felt obliged to facilitate the résident, the view of the general citizenry was that the religious identity of the city was being challenged, and its history as a free and Protestant state betrayed. In spite of this, the magistrates consistently adhered to a policy of bowing to France. Attempts by the syndic Jean de Normandie to protect Geneva from France by joining the Swiss confederation as a canton were rebuffed by the executive councils in the 1680s and 1690s.[9] In 1689 William of Orange's request to send an English ambassador to Geneva was refused by the magistrates, and similar rejections were issued in 1694, 1710, and 1715. Nor would Geneva agree to become part of an Anglo-Dutch Protestant alliance, despite the strong links with the Protestant world that developed while Jean-Alphonse Turrettini was the leading pastor.[10] The executive councils equally attempted to quell popular celebration at Anglo-Dutch victories over the French in 1694, during which bonfires were lit outside the house of the résident.[11] At the same time, permission was refused to the résident to extend his chapel to accommodate yet more celebrants in 1695. When, in the same year, popular enthusiasm in the city after William of Orange's capture of Naumur was deemed excessive by the résident, Louis XIV forbade Genevan trade with France. He declared that his ambassador's house in the city was part of France and not subject to local authority. Although they continued to refuse to extend the chapel, Genevan magistrates visited Versailles to apologize to the king.[12] Such action was a sign of the weakness of Geneva and of the strength of France. Genevans could not rely on an anti-French alliance led by England/Britain, which was struggling with the dilemma of support for the Holy Roman Empire against France, the price of which was reduced support from the states antagonistic to Austria, including Holland and Prussia.

While Savoy no longer challenged France, the threat from Savoy to Geneva actually strengthened in the aftermath of the Nine Years' War (1688–1697) because of the growing imperial ambitions of this rising state, with its efficient bureaucracy and prominence within the Counter-Reformation movement.[13] It added to the growing paranoia in early-eighteenth-century Geneva that a Catholic state would invade and annex the city. The refortification of Geneva initiated in the 1660s, when funds were secured from the Dutch for the construction of a new bastion, was speeded up when rumors circulated of an alliance between France, Savoy, and the Catholic cantons during the regency of Louis XV.[14] At the beginning of the War of the Austrian Succession (1740–1748), it was said that French ministers had agreed to allow Savoy to take Geneva, in return for an end to the Sardinian alliance with Austria.[15] When Savoy was invaded by Spanish troops in 1743, bringing Catholic soldiers to within miles of Geneva's gates, the magistrates sat in permanent session and cannons were brought to the ramparts; hundreds of militiamen were added to the normal guard for the following fifteen months.[16] Such worries raised dilemmas as to whether the proper policy was being pursued in international affairs.

As in the mid–seventeenth century, a view became commonplace in diplomatic circles that Geneva had, above all other goals, to remain on friendly terms with France. One sign of this was the magnificent fête held in the town hall by the résident in 1725 to celebrate the marriage of Louis XV, followed by the discharge of a hundred cannons from the ramparts.[17] Prior to this it was significant that the sometime syndic Antoine Tronchin sought to limit discussion of recent conflicts with France in his contribution to an official history of the state.[18] Isaac Thellusson, the Genevan ambassador at Paris between 1730 and 1744, followed this line, being paranoid about angering French ministers, and perpetually fearful of the possibility of a French alliance with Savoy leading to the collapse of the state.[19] One significant sign of altered times was that in 1744 Geneva accepted French demands that no books from the city be sent to French Reformed churches, and it was also willing to counter the clandestine book trade of anti-French works.[20] France continued to play upon the fears of Genevans and to some extent encouraged them, as evinced by the erection of a competitor city to Geneva at Versoix during the tenure of Etienne François, duc de Choiseul, as Louis XV's foreign minister (1758–1770). Between 1769 and 1770 the current résident, Pierre-Michel Hennin, was said to be planning to attract artisans by declaring freedom of religion in the proposed new city.[21] For Genevans, the fundamental question became whether it was better to embrace France as a protector, even if this entailed the renunciation of an active Protestant identity in international politics. Luminaries of the Genevan Academy and magistrates such as Jean-Jacques Burlamaqui, confident that their study of modern natural law revealed a clearheaded politics, advocated exactly this policy.

It is significant that, during the civil turbulence that marred the first decade of the eighteenth century, Geneva's magistrates turned to the cantons of Bern and Zurich in requesting mediators rather than to France.[22] Visitors still noted that the link with Bern was the key to Geneva's security, because "it can easily put in a matter of days 50,000 men in the field."[23] One argument that was made in 1707 was that a formal alliance (*combourgeoisement*) existed with the cantons and not with France, and accordingly there would never be a need to involve France directly in local affairs.[24] The magistrates, however, acknowledged a need to inform the French court about Genevan circumstances and called on Swiss diplomacy to this end.[25] Switzerland was then engulfed, in 1712, by the intermittent religious war between the Protestant cantons of Bern and Zurich and the Catholic cantons of Uri, Lucerne, Schwyz, Unterwalden, and Zug.[26] Times had changed radically by the 1730s. Using the excuse of the "guarantee" of the Genevan constitution, France was from this decade onward more often and more directly involved in Genevan politics. The French résident, in conjunction with the eminent and usually military mediators appointed by the king, took the lead in negotiations between opposing parties in the city and naturally dominated mediators from the fellow guaranteeing powers of Bern and Zurich.[27]

Popular disturbances at Geneva were stopped by France between 1734 and 1738 and in 1767–1768. In 1737 the French went so far as to censure all writings contrary to their resolutions for the reestablishment of civil order.[28] As Frederick II of Prussia put it in 1736, the French, "our modern Romans," were moving beyond Roman policy in demanding to be the arbiter of local politics: "whether from corrupt or other motives, the citizens of Geneva have thrown themselves into her arms."[29] Geneva was considered by French authorities to require particular attention and, on the grounds of not wanting to see the city "tear itself apart," intervention was justified "to reestablish peace, secure the form of government, respect the law, conserve the liberties of the people, and maintain the independence of the state."[30] In 1766–1767 France blockaded Genevan trade in order to pressure the populace to reject the ideas of those deemed unruly radicals. The "guarantee" was equally relied upon to justify the invasion of Geneva in 1782.[31]

The concern of those opposed to Geneva's closer relationship with France was that life under the skirts of a more powerful and Catholic neighbor would have an impact upon popular morals and religious beliefs. As early as 1697 the councils ruled against the excessive length of wigs for men and for women, which were deemed to be an undesirable sign of luxury, commonplace because of the influence of French culture.[32] Concerns about the future of the republic were compounded by worries about the effects of increasing commerce and, especially as the century wore on, of being a creditor to Europe's major monarchies. Speculation was rife about the future of Protestantism in relation to commerce and debt, for the obvious reason that such forces determined the outcome of wars. The question was acute because of a widespread impression that militant Catholicism continued to rise in the eighteenth century and was the inevitable corollary to ultimate French success in arms. John Brown, the English essayist and clergyman, summarized the fears of many Protestants when he wrote that "enthusiastic religion leads to conquest; rational religion leads to rational defence; but the modern spirit of irreligion leads to rascally and abandoned cowardice."[33]

Brown's fundamental concern was that Catholicism was more suited to a degenerate age, being in his view a religion of passion and fury rather than of reason, and might well overwhelm Protestantism in consequence.[34] This view had long been shared by certain pastors within the Genevan Consistory, some of whom were accused of being "furiously" anti-French. In the eighteenth century such views added to divisions within the city.[35] Any Protestant league had to be led by Britain, given the decline of the Swiss and the Dutch.[36] The critics of magistracy at Geneva debated what the British might do to defend Protestantism and whether Genevan bankers ought to support British interests only in their foreign financial investments. Despite the claims of Catholic observers, there was not a "Protestant bank" but rather a wide-ranging discussion of whether institutions providing credit and developing commerce should organize themselves internationally to foster Protestantism and the interests of the states that adhered to this creed.[37]

Taking Geneva closer to France in politics and in culture was never going to receive the support of the people of the city, whose Protestantism remained strong. Critics of magisterial policy were convinced that independence was being lost just as national identity was being undermined. As opposition to France lay within the General Council of citizens, it became necessary for pro-French magistrates to limit the power of that body. The democratic element of the state had to be sacrificed for peaceful international relations, or, as the magistrates saw it, democracy had to be sacrificed to maintain independence. The contrary view of the critics of Francophilia was of course that independence had already been lost. This became the great split in Genevan politics in the eighteenth century. It was tied up with the issue of the formal structure of the citizenry, because widening access to citizenship was expected to generate further Francophobia. It was equally tied to the question of whether the form of government at Geneva was now the major impediment to national survival; the accusation was leveled increasingly as the eighteenth century wore on that the existing structure of government had allowed the magistrates to transfer sovereignty to France.

CITIZENSHIP AND GOVERNMENT

In the 1757 *Encyclopédie* article "Genève," Jean Le Rond d'Alembert identified five social orders among Genevan males: "subjects" (*sujets*), "inhabitants" (*habitants*), "natives" (*natifs*), "burgesses" (*bourgeois*), and "citizens" (*citoyens*). These groups were subject to different taxes and levels of taxation. A "lods" taxed the exchange of property and varied from 12 to 16 percent depending upon status; a "gardes" tax was levied on personal fortunes; the "halles" or customs duty also depended upon status, as did the "gabelle" upon salt, meat, and wine.[38] The sujets lived within or beyond the city and lacked political rights, being simply "Protestants who have no other benefit than that of living under a mild government."[39] The sujets paid the distinctive *taille* and *cens* taxes until the passing of the so-called Code Bénévolent of 1781, when their rights became equivalent to those of habitants and they began to pay general taxes called *gardes de la campagne*. During the 1790s they gained full civic rights. The habitants were foreigners who had purchased the right to live in the city, enjoyed no political rights, and had only restricted rights to engage in commerce. With their children they formed the largest group in the state, being approximately twice in number to the body of citizens and bourgeois.

The natifs were the children of habitants, and they too were not allowed to become members of the sovereign General Council. Like their parents, they paid a double tax on marketable goods, a third higher rate on transfers of real estate, and an annual "protection" to engage in commerce and upon marriage, measured against their potential cost to the state if they or their families became reliant upon public charity through ill health or poverty. Only after 1737 were the natifs allowed to practice the master crafts, and after 1782 began to be taxed at the same rate as citizens. The bourgeois were individuals who had purchased greater civic rights or were citizens of the first generation. Their numbers were restricted because the price of citizenship rose sharply in the eighteenth century to 5,000 florins, well beyond the ambition of any but the singularly wealthy. The children of a first-generation bourgeois or citizen alone enjoyed full civic rights and alone could serve as magistrates or in the executive councils. Admission to the executive Council of Two Hundred was also confined to the wealthy, however, as high taxes had to be paid to become eligible for membership. Geneva has in consequence been described as "an oligarchy, nominally ruled by the fourth of its inhabitants who composed the citizenry, but effectively governed by the Patrician Haute Bourgeoisie who comprised less than six per cent of the total population."[40]

In the first book of his *Contrat social,* Rousseau acknowledged the veracity of d'Alembert's observation that republics such as Geneva were founded upon a graduated status system. Rousseau underlined the importance of the fact that "only two [social orders] compose the Republic," signifying at Geneva the distinction between bourgeois and citizens, who enjoyed political rights, and the other classes who were disallowed from serving the state. In recognizing the reliance of republics upon ranks, "no other French writer, to my knowledge, has understood the real meaning of the word citizen."[41] Citizenship could be associated with wisdom and virtue, but it could also be passive rather than always being active, involving all of the people in political life. The latter notion, which Rousseau opposed, was later said to summarize the view of the French revolutionaries ("the French are the only people who take on themselves the name of citizens indiscriminately"), by contrast with that of early modern republican states.[42]

For several leading theorists of politics of the early modern era, there was a natural relationship between such a civic hierarchy and aristocratic government. In his *Six livres de la république,* Jean Bodin described Geneva as a state aristocratic in form, on the grounds that a council of two hundred citizens sat in perpetuity as a sovereign body. At the same time, he noted that there was a popular bridle upon this sovereignty because the general body of citizens gathered together could remove magistrates, had to confirm laws, and determined decisions of war and peace. According to Bodin, this division of power explained the remarkable stability of the polity:

> [In 1528 the Genevese] changed their Pontifical monarchy into a Popular state, governed in manner of an Aristocracy. And albeit that the Towne long time before pretended itself not to be subject unto the laws either of the Duke of Savoy or of the Pope, but to be free from them both; yet the citizens

thought it not best for them to attempt any thing, until that discord about the Sovereignty was risen not only between the Duke and the Bishop, but even betwixt the bishop and the people also: at which time they took hold upon the occasion then presented unto their desires for the changing both of their Religion and state. Wherefore their Commonweal now set at liberty, they established a Council of two hundred citizens, with sovereign and perpetual power; but that the people still reserved to themselves the confirmation of laws, the election of their Syndics and other great magistrates, and the treaties of peace and war; all which belong unto the right of Sovereignty, as we have before declared. Now out of this great Council of two hundred, they made choice of a perpetual Senate of threescore persons: and out of that Senate, they take five and twenty to be of the prime Council for ever, chosen all by the great Council, and the four Syndics chosen every year for sovereign Magistrates, beside the other Judges and ordinary magistrates . . . the great Council of Geneva, the Senate, and the prime council are once chosen for ever: yet lo, as that the censuring of every one of them every year is still reserved unto the Citizens: which is most straightly looked into; whereby it comes to pass, that the Commonweal of Geneva is more firm, and less subject unto alteration or seditious innovation.[43]

Two of Bodin's judgments attracted particular attention and near universal agreement. The first was that Geneva became a free and independent republic only with the decision of the General Council to detach the state from the Roman Catholic Church in favor of Calvin's Reformed Church.[44] The second was that Geneva had always been a popular state governed aristocratically.[45] The problem was that the precise division of governmental powers established during the period of the Reformation became contested from the final decades of the seventeenth century, paralleling Louis XIV's imperial ambitions for France and for the Gallican church.[46]

The central disputed issue was the relationship between the General Council of all citizens and bourgeois, and the smaller councils of state, the Council of Two Hundred (Conseil des deux cents or Grand conseil), and the executive Council of Twenty-Five (known as the Petit conseil, Conseil des vingt-cinq, Conseil étroit, or Sénat).[47] The dispute concerned the location of sovereignty: whether it existed in the General Council alone or in the three councils combined, on the grounds that the General Council could not summon itself, never debated issues, and only consented to or rejected propositions put to it by the smaller executive councils. It was accepted that Geneva had originally been governed democratically, in the sense that in the ancient constitution the General Council elected the officers of government (the syndics or procurators), considered issues of concern, and delegated to a *conseil ordinaire* the administration of the state.[48]

THE ANCIENT CONSTITUTION IN THE EIGHTEENTH CENTURY

Two narratives emerged in the eighteenth century concerning this democratic legacy. The first, which became prominent at times of political crisis, held that the ancient constitution needed to be revived in order to protect the liberty of the citizens and the independence of the republic:[49]

> At the period of the Reformation . . . every affair, whether important or trifling, was laid before the general assembly. This assembly, consisting of the heads of families, constituted a sovereign, deliberating and acting body, that always left the cognizance of details to four syndics or procurators, reserving to itself the discussion and decision of all weighty matters. The more entire this species of democracy, the fewer jealousies and distrusts were perceived; external dangers kept alive the flame of patriotism, and continually cemented the general union: the city was annually governed by two procurators of its own election; they were responsible for their administration; and their administration, truly paternal, then presented Geneva under the image of one family.[50]

The view came to be expressed that neither Calvin nor Theodore Beza after him had properly fixed the city's constitutional laws. As François d'Ivernois wrote in the 1780s, by relying on the purity of the manners of the people rather than the certainty of the laws at the time of the Reform, the popular element in the constitution came to be questioned. Calvin had been a republican inclined to popular government, and only later conspiracies among the magistrates had caused the loss of political liberty that marred the recent history of the city:

> The corruption of the clergy gradually introduced the reformation; and the hatred of the people to the bishop and his officers, could not but be favourable to a doctrine tending to their legal expulsion. Calvin appeared, and his genius . . . gained him an influence which he exerted for the advantage of the public liberty. A mortal foe to ecclesiastical hierarchy, it would have ill become him to oppose the equality of civil right, and besides, what probability was there, that the Genevese would rest contented with bartering a religious for a political yoke? Calvin's legislation was therefore a republican work. . . . Calvin imagined that he had left the Democracy still better settled on the basis of the manners he found established, than on that of the laws framed by him and accepted by the people. He was deceived: the

manners of the chiefs were preserved in their primitive purity, only to the beginning of the seventeenth century. When these were changed, the chiefs sought to overturn the laws, or at least to lull them to sleep, to evade and explain away their meaning, by contesting the sense even of the plainest terms.[51]

The conclusion of such a perspective was that, however impressive the ancient constitution had been, the constitutional laws of the state required reformulation.

Against such perspectives, a second narrative supported the various edicts that changed the nature of republican government at Geneva beginning in the 1530s, arguing that democracy was curtailed and an efficient government capable of maintaining the state was created by adapting politics and diplomacy to the interests of France. The constitutional revisions were made in the Edicts of 1543, 1568, and 1570, by which the General Council agreed to give up many of its rights to the Council of Two Hundred and the Council of Twenty-Five. The latter councils in the 1530s had established the right to elect each other's members annually, and acquired the further right in 1543 to determine the issues brought to the General Council.[52] With the Edict of 1543, four syndics continued to be elected annually by the General Council every January, but these four syndics could only be chosen from a list of eight candidates presented by the smaller councils. Following the election, the syndics would summon the Council of Two Hundred and confirm in their offices or reject the members of the Council of Twenty-Five (this process was called *le grabeau*). Those who had lost their offices would be replaced from a list of candidates submitted for selection to the Council of Two Hundred by the Council of Twenty-Five. Once the Council of Twenty-Five was reconstituted, it would similarly confirm or replace the members of the Council of Two Hundred.

In 1568 the smaller councils asserted their judicial authority in criminal cases, and in 1570 they gained the collective right to raise public revenues and to establish new taxes without having to consult the General Council.[53] By such means the sovereignty of the General Council was not deemed to have been abandoned but to have begun to be shared with the small councils, and in significant matters of policy delegated to them.[54] To the advocates of popular sovereignty in the later eighteenth century, while the person of Calvin was sacred, the sixteenth-century edicts were invalid because they contradicted the Genevan magna carta known as *Les franchises*, established by Bishop Adhémar Fabri in 1387, which confirmed in perpetuity the liberties of the citizens, their power to elect syndics who were judges in criminal matters, and the authority of the citizens to consent to taxation.[55]

At the beginning of the eighteenth century, elections continued to be conducted through the gathering of the General Council of approximately 1,500 citizens and bourgeois, which met at Saint-Pierre Cathedral twice a year to elect the magistrates, to set the wine tax, to consent to laws proposed by the smaller councils, and to approve proposals concerning alliances and international relations.[56] The magistracy comprised the four syndics, who were elected on the first Sunday in the new year from the Council of Twenty-Five, presided over the councils, held their office for a year, and could not be reelected for a further four years; a *lieutenant de police* responsible for public order, also from the Council of Twenty-Five; six *auditeurs du droit* from the Council of Two Hundred, who aided the lieutenant and served for three years, with two of the six losing their posts annually; and the *procureur-général*, who served for three years, could be reelected for a further term, and whose role was to observe and superintend the rights and laws of the state and to identify abuses— crucially, not ex officio but by order of the Council of Twenty-Five. All offices other than the syndics were elected each November.

The General Council did debate proposals until the Edit de la Médiation of 1738, after which it could simply reply "aye or no, approve or reject."[57] Its power was limited to the election of the principal magistrates and to approving or rejecting laws and executive decisions concerning war, peace, and alliances. The process of electing the principal magistrates was singular. On the morning of an election, the members of the General Council met in the Saint-Pierre Cathedral and heard a sermon preached by the oldest minister. A printed list of candidates (provided by the smaller councils), usually twice the number of the available positions, was then given to each citizen or bourgeois, who walked past the members of the Council of Twenty-Five, laid their hands upon a large open Bible, and retired one by one into a small closet to sign against the name of the desired candidate. The ballots were then put into a box, votes counted, and those elected determined. For other votes four secretaries, two from the General Council and two from the Council of Two Hundred, sat before the magistrates with a paper divided into columns for "approbation" or "disapprobation," and a piece of curtain around their heads so that they could not see who was voting. Each member of the General Council whispered their choice into the ear of the secretary and observed his writing it down in the proper column. Such processes were designed to prevent corruption and the growth of faction.[58]

As nominations for office continued to be made by the executive Council of Two Hundred and Council of Twenty-Five, most observers considered sovereignty to be shared or divided. Many considered the Council of Two Hundred to be the supreme court of justice, having the power to pardon and also to be the source of deliberation about propositions for the General Council. The Council of Two Hundred met on the first Monday of each month. The Council of Twenty-Five also claimed rights to judge criminal cases, dealt with civil disputes, had the right to summon the Two Hundred and to create bourgeois and administer national finances, and functioned as the everyday executive government of the state. Regular meetings made decisions by majority vote. One difference in the constitution evident by the eighteenth century was that these councils were increasingly dominated by members of a small number of Geneva's leading families, such as the Pictet, Lullin, Du Pan, Trembley, and Rilliet houses, and the rich families of Italian origin, the Callandrini, Turrettini, Gallatini, and Minotali.[59] Laws of consanguinity were established in the first decade of the eighteenth century, allowing only a father and two sons, three brothers, or six members of the same name and family to serve in the Council of Two Hundred; in the Council of Twenty-Five, fathers and sons or two brothers could not be members conjointly. George Keate praised such laws for preventing "particular families from becoming too considerable in the state . . . that proved destructive to Florence, and which has occasioned the ruin of so many flourishing commonwealths."[60] Such laws were Pierre Fatio's central legacy at Geneva. Fatio was the first citizen who demanded more popular government as the sole means to the continued independence of the state and its Protestantism.

FATIO'S REBELLION

At the beginning of the eighteenth century, when the outcome of the War of the Spanish Succession was unclear across Europe, the need for improved fortifications raised the issue of the justice of higher taxes to pay for them and the burden of taxation, particularly on grain and wine, across the classes of Genevan society.[61] Controversy over taxation led to demands for the General Council to assert its sovereignty against the smaller councils, to defend the citizens against unjustly levied and unfairly distributed taxes. Divisions were highlighted in February 1704 when the lawyer Marc Revilliod opposed a decision by the Council of Two Hundred to sell to the Turrettini family an exclusive right to hunt in the land surrounding the Château des Bois. Revilliod's argument was that only the General Council, as the state's sovereign body, could sell such a right.[62] In December 1706 the Council of Twenty-Five was made aware by its procureur-général Jean du Pan that a document was circulating demanding the reform of voting procedure within the General Council by instituting a secret ballot, rather than whispers into the ear of a secretary. Pierre Fatio led this reform movement.

Fatio was a prominent lawyer, holding a doctorate in law from the University of Basel, and having been educated at Valence and Montpellier; he had been a member of the Council of Two Hundred since 1688. He was concerned about the loss of justice in politics, as the city became more oligarchic. From Fatio's perspective, the growth of aristocracy could be likened to foreign dominion, in that nobility was alien to the free history of the city; furthermore, aristocratic magistrates would be more likely to acquiesce in French encroachment. Reform, in combating oligarchy, would secure national independence. Fatio was a devout Calvinist and argued that Geneva would survive only if the clerical culture that had been established in tandem with political liberty was maintained. This complicated any civic humanist or classical republican heritage. The exercise of conscience defined Calvin's faith in Fatio's view, and independence of mind was the central characteristic of a culture that provided religious and political health.

It was within the Council of Two Hundred that the issue of voting procedure was first raised by Fatio.[63] In January 1707 reform proposals to reduce family membership within the executive councils, to introduce ballot papers when voting, to annually consider changes to the law at a specially convened General Council, and to publish a revised code of public edicts concerning the government of the state were put forth by François de La Chana within the General Council.[64] After debate was refused on the grounds that the smaller councils had not discussed the issues beforehand, La Chana drew up a memorandum and presented it to the first syndic, Jean de Normandie, who publicly burned the document. This resulted in gatherings of up to five hundred citizens critical of the syndic's actions. In consequence a commission was established, with members such as Fatio, La Chana, and Revilliod from the reform party and magistrates who opposed them, including the prominent second syndic and former Academy rector Jean-Robert Chouet.[65] No agreement could be reached.[66]

Within the Council of Two Hundred, Fatio began to argue in favor of a new law intended to resolve political disputes. It was proposed that documents on particular political subjects supported by three members of the Council of Twenty-Five, ten members of the Council of Two Hundred, or fifty citizens should always be considered by the executive councils, and the conclusions of these councils would be met with a yes or no response from the General Council within two weeks. By such means the sovereignty of the General Council would be guaranteed, and the citizens directly and regularly involved in political decision making. The bolstering of patriotism and civic virtue was anticipated.

In February 1707 the magistrates accepted the need to publish the constitutional edicts that governed the state and promised to respond to verbal representations from discontented citizens within a month, but refused to alter the voting system or to increase the role of the General Council. Popular clamor then forced the magistrates to agree to an extraordinary meeting of the General Council, to convene in May. The magistrates called for mediators from the allied cantons of Bern and Zurich, on the basis of needing support in a battle against domestic sedition.[67] The magistrates also ensured that the clergy "inveighed bitterly from the pulpit against all abettors of unrestrained liberty" and "joined the cause of religion to that of magistracy."[68]

The second syndic, Chouet, with the intention of ending the civic discord, took the opportunity to outline the magistrates' perspective on Genevan government in a series of discourses that culminated in an address to the General Council on 5 May 1707. He acknowledged the sovereignty of the General Council with respect to "law-making, the appointment of magistrates, the right to go to war and to make peace, striking coins, granting pardons to criminals, raising capital and imposing taxes on the populace." Accordingly he called the government of the state "purely democratic," in the sense that sovereignty belonged to the citizens and bourgeois who formed the political state. A distinction had to be made, however, between the right of sovereignty and its exercise, in order to maintain a working and stable democracy. The exercise of sovereignty had been delegated to the smaller executive councils who ruled on behalf of the citizens. This was the practice followed by "all the wisest and most prudent democracies" and was vital to retain decorum, confidentiality, and diligence. Chouet envisaged Geneva as being divided into social groups or orders and the General Council as a conglomeration of these distinct corporations forming the state.[69] This perspective underlined the necessity of the delegation of sovereignty, as it would have been unjust to allow a single corporation, such as the body of the citizens, to act as sovereign without reference to fellow orders. Unity was the central aspiration of statesmen and citizens; the alternative was faction, which would undermine public manners and lead to national collapse.[70]

Chouet likened Geneva's General Council to England's Parliament, where powers were balanced and the national will peaceably expressed.[71] England was not a "true democracy" but a democracy tempered to secure order, peace, and the rule of the wise. Geneva likewise had instituted its own parliament in the form of the Council of Two Hundred:

Firstly, Magnificent and Sovereign Lords, I humbly beseech Your Lordships to consider that the form of government under which we have lived so contentedly since the establishment of our Edicts up to the present time is founded not only on reason alone but also on the example of the most eminent democracies in Europe. I could put forward those of Holland, those of Germany and the greater part of those of Switzerland but I will content myself with citing the sole example of a nation which, because of the goodwill and wisdom of its government, is admired by all the others, I speak of course, of England. For although she has a monarch, at her head, all the most famous writers maintain that she is a true democracy, and at least we can agree with other very celebrated and disinterested authors that she does certainly have a mixed government, that is to say, a mixture of the monarchic and the democratic forms. Therefore it suffices to say that in this case the Prince and the people share the rights of sovereignty between them. However, the people in question does not govern directly by itself and it is never assembled either for making laws, for levying taxes, or for the exercise of any other of its sovereign rights. It has to do all that it has to through a less numerous assembly on which it relies. It acts through the Parliament which is not the whole nation, but which is only composed of members of Parliament, who represent the people and act in their name. Our government, Magnificent and Sovereign Lords, is obviously similar to that of the English. Here, we have the whole body of citizens and bourgeois, who make up the General Council, to whom belong all rights of sovereignty. It is, however, this same General Council, as we have already said, which has not worked in this way for a long period of years so as to exercise its rights itself and assemble for the purpose. It has handed the exercise of these rights to another less numerous gathering, in this case, the Council of the Two Hundred, which represents it and which acts in its name and under its authority. It did this because everyone thought that in the imitation of other democratic governments lay the well-being and security of the State.[72]

Chouet was certain that Geneva, in yielding up to the Council of Two Hundred the exercise of sovereignty, had secured itself by adopting a less popular form of government from the time of the Reformation onward. Direct democracy always "exposed the state to inevitable ruin." Alliance had been possible with similarly constituted Swiss states, which would never have supported a properly democratic Geneva.[73]

Chouet's argument was contentious for many magistrates in acknowledging the right of the General Council to act as a sovereign body. The magistrates issued a public letter that was less forgiving of their critics, employing the Ciceronian argument that secret ballots were detrimental to patriotism and national unity, and warning of the dire consequences of popular rule, which they believed explained the collapse of the once great republics of Athens, Rome, and Florence, because the rule of popular passion and ignorance replaced that of law.[74] The letter was followed up by Jacob de Chapeaurouge's *Lettre d'un Citoyen à un Citoyen*, which circulated after 20 April.[75] Like Fatio and Chouet, Chapeaurouge acknowledged that the General Council was sovereign, but he stated that, because the people could never govern themselves, the Council could only be expected to convene itself when the magistrates had become tyrannical, something altogether alien to Geneva since the Reformation. Chapeaurouge equally used the examples of Athens, Florence, and Rome when making the general claim that popular government led to rule by caesars. Factions weakened the state, and the divisions generated by popular passions encouraged foreign invasion:

> These examples [of Athens, Rome and Florence] should make us tremble and so much more so as these perils are infinitely more to fear for our State, than they seemed to be for those Republics. We are by comparison much smaller. We have only one town to lose and we are surrounded on all sides by very powerful neighbors and with whom we have had all too often conflicting interests. Who will then be able to guarantee us that none of these powers will ever take advantage of these combined forces unleashed by trouble and emotion, excited perhaps by their own creatures to take us by surprise and leave us bereft of assistance?[76]

By contrast, the "solid, legitimate and well-regulated liberty" to be found in the city, where the citizens sanctioned the laws and elected magistrates, and where the magistrates and clergy lived exemplary lives, amounted almost to perfection in politics. Proof lay in national prosperity, particularly the numbers of the moderately wealthy, and above all in the fact that the magistrates had avoided involvement in the wars of Europe for a century.[77] Chapeaurouge went so far as to condemn limitations on familial membership of the executive councils on the grounds that such people were among the best educated and able in the state, could not be corrupted, and always put the interest of the state before that of the family.[78] Another argument employed in the General Council was that, because religion remained pure at Geneva and while the Academy continued to instruct Europe's Protestants, there was no need for popular involvement in political life because religion ensured the best possible rule and the election of the most able and the most wise.[79]

Against such claims Fatio argued in favor of an active and regularly convened General Council in which citizens and bourgeois would be able to make
law and to check on the activities of the smaller councils. God was described as
the author of the liberty of the General Council and equally the source of the
right reason that led citizens to deliberate properly in large assemblies.
Preventing the growth of oligarchy necessitated a right to censure measures of
the smaller councils, by the exercise of a vote by written ballot, an end to the
mutual election of members of the smaller councils, and limits on members
of the same family serving in the small councils. Fatio also used the examples of
Rome and Athens, arguing that they owed their glory to the involvement of
their citizens in government and had managed to couple order with convening
large popular assemblies.[80] He equally claimed that the ancient constitution of
the Genevan state had been violated in allowing 120 years to pass since the
General Council had deliberated upon the laws of the state. Fatio held that
article 168 of the Ecclesiastical Ordinances of 1576 demanded that the General
Council read the statutes of the church every five years and consider amendments to them from the smaller councils.[81]

Debate in the General Council on 10 May was ended when the magistrates
demanded that the oath of citizenship be recited by every citizen. This was supportive of the existing constitutional arrangements because the oath included a
promise "to observe the ways, customs, edicts, statutes and ordinances of the
city."[82] It was attacked on the grounds that sovereign bodies cannot take any
oath that might constrain them. Fatio spoke against the presence of the Swiss
envoys in the General Council, on the grounds that "the precedent would at
any time authorize the envoys of France to insist on the same privilege."[83] The
level of confusion and disagreement about procedure caused the assembly to be
adjourned until 12 May. When similar problems plagued this assembly, a third
meeting was declared for 26 May. Here Fatio successfully instituted periodic
legislative assemblies to meet every five years, a mode of voting entailing the
delivery of votes to four secretaries from the magistracy and the citizenry, and
limited, to not more than three, family memberships of the executive councils.
At the same assembly, direct voting by ballot on separate issues was rejected.
Popular disturbances followed, and the magistrates asked for three hundred
troops to be sent from the cantons to help maintain order.[84]

An innkeeper named Christian Brochet, hitherto a member of the reforming
party, then claimed before the Council of Twenty-Five on 17 August 1707 that
Fatio's associates were planning an insurrection to remove the Swiss troops and
the magistrates who opposed their views. One of the leaders of the reform party
stated to be in charge of the coup, named Nicolas Le Maître, was put to the rack

and publicly strangled. The magistrates' justification drew a parallel between Le Maître's refusal to acknowledge guilt and the "false honor" of serving one's party unto death, which was stated to have marred the history of England.[85] Another reformer, Jean-Antoine Piaget, was hung in effigy after he drowned in attempting to flee the city. La Chana was banished for life for fomenting popular disturbances and for criticizing the magistrates and the pastors.

Fatio was convinced that he was going to be poisoned and "abstained from all food except eggs."[86] In fact he was arrested on the grounds that among his papers was a document by La Chana demanding that the General Council control the admittance of foreign troops and institute other measures to limit magisterial powers. Fatio was then charged with sedition and illegal assembly and condemned to public decapitation. His brother, a member of the Council of Twenty-Five, argued in favor of private execution by shooting, on the grounds of not wanting to bring ignominy on the family (the actual grounds were no doubt a desire to avoid further public disturbance). Fatio was therefore told of the sentence only a short while before it was carried out. No public bell tolled for the event, the "batons of the syndics" were sent privately to the prison, and "the ministers [went] thither disguised in secular dress."[87] Before he died, Fatio opened a Bible and read the first verse of the 58th Psalm ("Are your minds set upon righteousness, O ye congregation: and do ye judge the things that are right, O ye sons of men?"). He then calmly blindfolded himself, declared his innocence, and asked for power from above to forgive his persecutors, all the while professing that he had always dedicated himself to his duties as a Christian and a citizen.[88] In so doing Fatio became the foremost national martyr, Geneva's first Gracchi (with negative parallels being drawn between Fatio's brother and the second of the Gracchi).[89] Christian and classical ideals of self-sacrifice were in evidence at Fatio's death. A visitor at the time stated that only the arrival of hundreds of troops from the cantons prevented a much greater insurgency, and the price was "the liberty of the bourgeoisie":[90]

> Its government is a mixture of Aristocracy and Democracy; but as the principal and most ancient families use their utmost endeavours to derogate from, and by slow degrees destroy the privileges of the citizens, in order to draw the power over to themselves, and perpetuate themselves in their posts, this practice is attended with frequent murmurings, and in these last times an insurrection had began, which would have broken out into a great fire, if Zurich and Bern had not sent wise and able deputies to extinguish it, and afterwards a good number of troops to garrison the city, which at present seems to keep quiet, though with evident prejudice to the liberty of its citizens.[91]

The conduct of the Councils toward the accused citizens was condemned by the British, the Prussians, and the Holy Roman emperor, although (significantly) not by France or by Bern.[92] When on 10 December 1712 the periodic general assembly was convened to discuss legislative reform, its first act was to repeal Fatio's edict and to annul itself. Certain pastors, most prominently Antoine Léger, professor of philosophy and theology at the Academy, continued to defend the separation of church and state and to demand that the General Council assert the independence of the Consistory against the magistrates' attempts to make the pastors serve the Councils. Léger was the author of the *Lettres anonymes* of 1718, which followed Fatio in describing Geneva as historically being a "free city," where the magistrates were ministers of the General Council rather than a distinct order that shared or directly exercised sovereignty.[93] As in 1707, the magistrates called on leading pastors, including Benedict Pictet and Jean-Alphonse Turrettini, who promised to do "all that might depend on them to back the councils."[94]

MICHELI DU CREST'S POLITICAL THOUGHT

Fatio became an icon for the rebellious bourgeoisie and in subsequent commentary was seen to have toiled to resurrect the city's ancient liberties, which the magistrates were seeking to overturn. Fatio had questioned Geneva's independence, particularly with respect to overreliance upon Switzerland, but the limitations of his reform program were equally evident to contemporaries. Fatio's followers were concerned about levels of taxation and their distribution, but they did not address the claim that if Geneva was to remain independent new fortifications were vital. In consequence, reform proposals that sidelined the broader issue of the economic foundation of a reformed state rang hollow. Fatio's supporters lamented the growth of luxury and excessive wealth, but they did not formulate proposals to address such problems. Seeking to restore lost liberty also necessitated dealing with the likely initial negative consequences for domestic security, because a more popular government at Geneva would alter its relationship with allies and enemies; antagonism could be anticipated from the aristocratically governed cantons and from monarchical France. Chapeaurouge's argument—that the magistrates had saved Geneva from involvement in Europe's major wars, erected a government respected across the continent, and called for higher taxes only in cases of absolute necessity—could be challenged only with difficulty. A narrative of Geneva's success with respect to international security came to the fore in the decades after Fatio's murder. Within this narrative a polarity became commonplace between naive bourgeois reformers and security conscious, realistic magistrates.

In 1730 civil strife intensified after the syndic Jean Trembley proposed that the militia be controlled by the mercenary garrison. The pastor Michel Léger, son of Antoine Léger, composed a list of grievances as *Représentations des citoyens et bourgeois de Genève*, which were submitted to the executive councils in 1734. These proposals demanded the restoration of the sovereign rights of the General Council. When Trembley was further accused of disabling artillery in the city by spiking twenty-two cannons with wooden pegs, potentially prefiguring military action against the citizens, disturbances became commonplace, particularly because of rumors that troops would be arriving from the cantons to restore order.[95] On 21 August 1737 the militia took control of the garrison, leading to eleven deaths. By this date, Louis XV had decided to intervene. Mediators were called from France, Zurich, and Bern, an action stated to be in accordance with the Treaty of Soleure. The leading mediator was the comte de Lautrec, then lieutenant general of the French province of Guyana, who arrived in the city in October 1737.[96] In 1738 he imposed the compromise called the Règlement or Médiation.[97] The prior disorder was distinctive in part because the party critical of magistracy found a spokesman of genius in Jacques-Barthélemy Micheli du Crest, who addressed the lacunae in Fatio's arguments.[98] It is significant that, although many of the bourgeois rebels called themselves "Michelistes" during these years, they refused to embrace his reform program in its entirety.

Micheli du Crest is remembered today as a polymath.[99] He invented the universal thermometer, provided the first scientific cartographic panorama of the Alps, and was influential through his work on fortification, instrument making, and surveying.[100] His scientific work was widely publicized, and he was at different times identified as a "bon ingénieur"; more controversially, he was called "bon patriote" and "apôtre de la démocratie."[101] Micheli's family were originally Tuscan, and his ancestor Francesco Micheli, on becoming Protestant, moved from Lucca to Geneva in 1556. The Micheli family subsequently became one of the most prominent in Genevan political and religious life; Micheli du Crest's first cousin was Jean-Alphonse Turrettini. Micheli du Crest was born at Geneva in 1690 and educated at the Collège de Genève; for a short time he studied theology at the Academy. Following the example of many young Genevan men, he served as a captain in the French Besenval regiment, and it was his military experience that caused him to criticize the government's fortification plans of 1716.[102] Micheli entered the Council of Two Hundred in 1721, and by 1727 was a member of a *Commission des conseils* that examined the issues raised in renewing the cities' fortifications. The story goes that because Micheli lost his voice in the General Council of January 1728 he decided to compose a *Mémoire* advocating a policy of commercial development combined with the refortification of a vastly expanded city and the redirection of the river Rhone.[103]

Micheli was different from Fatio in that security was his first concern. His sense of the loss of independence was also more acute. Like Fatio a committed Calvinist, he was certain that a democratic state had to be able to defend itself to maintain republican and religious mores. This explained his plan for the rebuilding of Geneva and its development as a leading commercial entrepôt. Micheli envisaged Geneva as a miniature modern Carthage, acquiring fame for trade and for self-defense. In his *Mémoire* of 1728 and in an earlier outline reform program, the *Question politique, savoir s'il convient, en 1716, d'entreprendre un grand projet de fortification pour Genève*, Micheli argued against the view he claimed to be commonplace, that Geneva was "never in a situation . . . to resist the King of France if he attacked Geneva, but that one would, so to speak, have to open the gates on receipt of just a simple letter from his Majesty." Rather, neither a France addicted to foreign warfare nor cantons prone to civil war could be relied upon to act permanently as protectors of Geneva. In consequence it was necessary to "work constantly to increase [Geneva's] resources to enable it to stand alone, and make [the fortifications] truly superior to those of its allies." Micheli argued that Geneva should aim to be able to put eight thousand soldiers in arms at short notice, and this necessitated a great extension of the city to near double its present size, creating a refuge for Protestants, devotees of republican liberty, and tradesmen. Such a city could withstand even French arms, as Barcelona had for several months in 1714, being constructed so that any enemy "would face fire from five different directions on a wide front."[104]

Micheli argued that democracy was the natural form of government for Geneva. An aristocratic republic governed by a small number of families would be unable to generate the popular patriotism that was vital to the preservation of small states, "binding the citizens together" to survive "periods of public calamity." Geneva had to look to the greatest examples of Roman and Athenian civic self-sacrifice and imitate them.[105] But he also envisaged a democracy in which constitutional and criminal laws were fixed. What he called "true equality" would be established when the laws applied to all classes of citizens. Micheli's republic was not egalitarian. Rather, the different capacities of individual citizens meant that a civic hierarchy based on merit ought always to emerge. The institution of noble families was "an institution founded not only on nature and upon justice, but is advantageous to a state since it tends to procure prestige in the eyes of foreigners." Aristocracy was a necessary aspect of every society and the basis of good government.[106] Representation ensured the emergence of a patrician class, since the people tended to elect the rich and eminent.[107] The resulting "equality of distinction" was vital "to engender emulation in republics in order to reward those who have greatly served the state."[108] Rome and Athens were equally model republics in this respect. What Micheli termed "democracy of distinction" and absolute monarchy were the two forms of government that deserved praise in the modern world.[109] In the former case, citizens would be attracted to such a state because of the justice of its laws and the fact that it was a well-organized hierarchical republic defending free government.

At Geneva the key would be to check aristocratic government by a citizen body responsible for the making of law, led by syndics in the manner of Roman tribunes, and making the people counter the aristocracy by being the ultimate court of appeal in criminal cases. A better future could be established if the General Council asserted its sovereignty over the smaller councils, making executive power wholly dependent on the will of the citizen body.[110] A constitutional refounding in the name of the sovereign populace was essential in the 1730s to prevent the magistrates, the pastors, or the mediating powers, from overturning reform by reference to an ancient constitution. Citing Machiavelli, Micheli argued that the political body, like the human, "requires regular purgation": frequent upheavals were like "winds dispelling unhealthy air to rouse people from their natural indolence, leaving them free to glimpse the abuses that have crept in and remedy them before they become too deeply entrenched."[111] Geneva, by contrast, had become a tyranny, ruled by an "aristo-anarchique" faction.[112]

MICHELI AND THE MAGISTRATES

Micheli fell foul of the magistrates in November 1728, when copies of his plans, outlined in the *Mémoire*, were seized on their appearance at Geneva. Printed copies had been sent by Micheli to fifty members of the councils, and he was called a traitor for writing about the defensive weaknesses of the city. On 7 December 1728 the work was censored by the Council of Two Hundred, and a request was made for Micheli to return all copies in addition to his private papers.[113] Micheli, now back with his regiment stationed at Strasbourg, asked for a copy of the judgment against him and an ultimate verdict from the General Council. The Council of Two Hundred demanded that Micheli present himself before its members on 18 March 1729. Micheli refused on the grounds that his case could be determined only by the sovereign. The accusation was subsequently leveled that Micheli had become a democrat only because of the negative verdict of the Council of Two Hundred.[114] On 9 May 1729 Micheli was removed from membership of this council, lost his bourgeois status, and had his land and his goods at Geneva confiscated. He in turn declared this judgment forfeit and once more, on 24 September 1729, called for the General Council to hear his case. Friends within Geneva, such as Jean Joly and Toussaint-Pierre Lenieps, corresponded with Micheli and sent him the leading works on the office of "tribune" at Geneva, Jacob de Chapeaurouge's *Mémoire concernant la charge de Procureur Général et ses prérogatives* (Geneva, 1715) and Louis Lefort's *Réponse au Mémoire de Monsieur le Conseiller de Chapeaurouge par Louis Lefort* (Geneva, 1715).[115] It was the receipt of such works that inspired the writing of the *Discours sur le gouvernement de Genève*, which began to circulate in manuscript in 1735.

On 2 June 1731 Micheli was declared a traitor and sentenced, on 8 June, in his absence, to perpetual imprisonment.[116] He was charged with seeking to "alter the fundamental constitution of the state" and having "disturbed public tranquility with all the ardor and malignity possible."[117] Among his followers, Lenieps was banished from Geneva for life, while Joly was exiled for five years.[118] For embracing Micheli's ideas, Lenieps was accused of "seeking to turn the republic upside down and initiating a deadly war between Magistrates and people."[119] In his later account, Lenieps refuted the accusation that he and Micheli had committed treason in seeking to justify civil war, the abolition of the executive councils in favor of direct democracy, or the sovereign rule of elected syndics. Rather, he presented himself as an avid reader of Plutarch and René-Aubert Vertot and a seeker after the ideal republican constitution, who did not accept that the Edicts of 1570 represented the fundamental constitution of the state, and who simply wanted to persuade the magistrates to adhere to the laws of the state.[120]

Micheli became certain that his plans for reform had been undermined by the Council of Two Hundred. Although forbidden from setting foot in Geneva himself, Micheli inspired the party critical of magistracy in the 1730s to demand convocation of the General Council to consent to or reject all taxes. Unlike Micheli, they did not go so far as to demand revisions to the form of government:

> His party at Geneva became gradually so formidable [in 1734], that in order to obviate greater disorders, the council found it necessary to commute the

tax imposed for carrying on the fortifications into a voluntary contribution. Notwithstanding this mitigation, the citizens often met in consultation; and eight hundred of them came to the *procureur-général*, with a petition, in which they remonstrated against all taxes hitherto levied; animadverted upon certain decisions of the senate, which they deemed partial; and prayed for the immediate convocation of the general assembly. The senate maintained, that according to the records, and especially a formal edict of the preceding century [1570], all contested points were left to the decision of the council. The citizens, far from acquiescing in this, became more clamorous, and threw out some menaces. The General Council assembled on the seventh of June: on the twenty-third the citizens delivered to the syndics and the *procureur-général* a declaration, in which they protested, that they by no means wished or demanded any change in the form of government, but that they merely desired some explanation concerning the taxes, and the fortifications.[121]

In May 1735, when he was living at Château-Blanc in Savoy, Micheli was visited by nearly eight hundred citizens who asked for his views of Geneva's government.[122] In September he published the *Requetes, avertissement, plaçet et mémoire du Sieur Micheli du Crest*. As a result the Council of Twenty-Five condemned him to death by decapitation, and this was undertaken in effigy while his writings were burned. On 20 November 1735 many citizens and bourgeois in the General Council were supportive of Micheli, although in January 1736 Micheli failed in his plan to attend the General Council. Once again Micheli's supporters were imprisoned or exiled. In truth, Micheli's own status at Geneva never became a key issue in the bourgeois cause, which underlines the fact that, however indebted they were to him for particular arguments, there was no predominant Micheliste party among the critics of magistracy. Even those who had been exiled, such as Lenieps, adopted a moderate tone with regard to anticipated reform. In a letter to Jacques-François Deluc of 1736, Lenieps summarized the reform program as strengthening the powers of the General Council as sovereign, ensuring a popular garrison that served the council, increasing lay influence within the Consistory, and restating the ancient constitution of the state. He expected the magistrates to quickly return to their role as fathers of the people, the pastors to the regulation of manners, and artisans and merchants to increasing the wealth of the state. Harmony would then characterize the polity, enable it to preserve itself, and become the "envy of our neighbors."[123] Geneva had originally been a perfect democracy, but the modifications of 1568 had been sensible. Since that time the magistrates had usurped some of the powers of the sovereign General Council, particularly in 1604, 1707, and 1712. It was time to restore the law and end the risk of anarchy or loss of the state, which would be the product of reliance upon foreign troops.[124]

It is significant that in 1734, Micheli, now living in Paris, had high hopes that France might be persuaded to support his case and the bourgeois rebels. As a French officer Micheli dedicated his *Requetes* to the bastard prince Louis-Auguste de Bourbon, duc du Maine, the grandson of Louis XIV. Initially this proved fruitful, as Micheli obtained support from the Parlement de Paris, which concluded by an *avis de droit* that the judgments against Micheli at Geneva were null and void because of uncertainty about the right of the Council of Two Hundred to judge criminal cases, because Micheli's accusers were also his judges, and because the procureur-général at Geneva had not pronounced the necessary "réquisitoire" in the trial of 1728–1729. The *Requetes* commenced with a "Consultation de messieurs les avocats au Parlement de Paris soussignés." Dated 6 February 1734, the document stated that "under a government purely democratic, such as the Republic of Geneva, the General Council of citizens and bourgeois assembled are sovereign." Parallel sentiments were being expressed by the bourgeoisie at Geneva. Many of them believed that the French résident Pierre Cadiot de la Closure was sympathetic to their views.[125] Micheli petitioned French ministers and courtiers to defend the General Council at Geneva against usurpation. While the first syndic, Louis Lefort, had invited representatives of the cantons to help resolve disputes within the city in December 1734, he did not then invite or involve parties from France.[126]

One of the ironies of Micheli's campaign was that it led to closer links between the governments at Geneva and Paris. As Micheli and the bourgeois were petitioning France, the magistrates were following suit, ensuring, for example, that six hundred copies of Michel Léger's *Relation des troubles* at Paris were confiscated.[127] A much stronger antireform movement developed in consequence, led by magistrates and the pastors, academicians, and natural lawyers who supported them.[128] These figures demanded more active protection from France on the grounds of public order, warning of the dire consequences for France of a democratic and more assertively Protestant republic on its borders.[129] The response of the French was express willingness to provide assistance to put down the "awful sedition."[130]

MICHELI, THE NATURAL JURISTS, AND THE MÉDIATION

In 1731 Micheli had discovered how decidedly opposed to him modern natural jurists were. He had requested an opinion on his case from Jean Barbeyrac, *professeur en droit* at Groningen. Barbeyrac was famous for his opposition to civil oppression and for his advocacy of religious toleration; he had once called France "that seat of tyranny and the kingdom of darkness."[131] Nevertheless, the reply of Europe's foremost natural lawyer was altogether negative. He took the view that Micheli had endangered the republic by his publications, and thereby supported the accusation of treachery. He argued that the Council of Two Hundred did not need to provide Micheli with details of its deliberations and was correct to bring proceedings because of his continued disobedience. Furthermore, Barbeyrac condemned the view that the General Council be more greatly involved in the business of the state and accepted that matters of justice had properly been delegated to the smaller councils.[132] He affirmed that Geneva was a tempered democracy:

> Let the people of Geneva be the sovereign power as much as you like, they do not exercise acts of sovereignty on their own except in cases that they reserve unto themselves. Certain matters are left in the hands of two [executive] councils. . . . I have no need to tell you that the Republic of Geneva, as I perceive it, is a state where democracy is tempered by aristocracy. . . . All history testifies that a republic in which the people are the masters or have too much power can hardly result in anything but a continual parade of riots, seditions, upheavals and injustices. . . . there is no edict in the Republic of Geneva which gives to its citizens the right to appeal to the General Council against the judgments made by the Council of Two Hundred.[133]

Barbeyrac concluded that it was vital "for peace and public tranquility" to "make some sacrifice of liberty." Soon after he published an essay defending the authority of the state over the church. While condemning ecclesiastical inquisitions, he emphasized the honor due to magistrates and the necessity of civil obedience.[134]

Barbeyrac's views accorded with those of Jean-Jacques Burlamaqui, who had graduated in law at the Genevan Academy in 1716, married Jacob de Chapeaurouge's daughter in 1717, and was made honorary professor of the Academy in 1720 by the Council of Twenty-Five and professor of natural law in 1723.[135] Prior to the latter appointment, he responded "yes" to the question of "whether supreme power in religious matters belongs to the prince, at least in all that regards the human domain."[136] This view was reiterated when Burlamaqui served on the commission to respond to the *Représentations* of 1734, concluding that a contract had been made with Geneva's people in 1568 that transferred sovereignty in perpetuity, so long as the government was not tyrannical, to the executive councils. While a contract existed between the populace and its government, through which the former could be said to be sovereign, the exercise of sovereignty was delegated to the smaller councils.[137] The best form of government was an elective aristocracy in republics.[138] The greatest threat to them was excessive liberty and government by the people, as the ancient histories underscored, in addition to the modern experiences of Poland, Genoa, and Florence.[139] Sermons by Turrettini, Jean-Louis Lullin, and Jacob Vernet emphasized the duties of the citizen toward the magistrates and the necessity of order in a free state that could not afford insurgency.[140]

The French résident La Closure and his compatriot the French-appointed mediator the comte de Lautrec were the key figures in the formulation of the *Règlement de l'Illustre Médiation pour la pacification de la République de Genève* of 7 April 1738, which was ratified by the General Council on 8 May. The first paragraph of the Règlement stated that it had been inspired by "His most Christian Majesty being informed of the extreme danger in which the republic found itself." Geneva had "always honored [Louis XV's] benevolence and had sought mediation from him" through the historic alliance between these states. The document satisfied the bourgeoisie in asserting the sovereignty of the General Council in articles 3 and 4; the General Council was ruled to have to validate all new laws and to consent as a body to any changes in the constitutional laws of the state. At the same time there was no sense of popular sovereignty, because the state was held to be composed of five orders: the General Council, the four syndics, the Council of Twenty-Five, the Council of Sixty, and the Council of Two Hundred. Articles 5 and 6 stated that anything set before the General Council had to be "traité & approuvé" by the Council of Two Hundred, whose own deliberations had in turn to be approved by the executive Small Council. The mutual election of the executive councils was maintained, and convening the General Council continued to be contingent upon the agreement of the smaller councils. While militia control over the garrison was asserted, militia companies were not allowed to take up arms without government permission. In the light of all parties agreeing to the Règlement, further political discussion was censored.

Most subsequent commentators accepted that the compromise of the Règlement brought the city a period of peace and prosperity, lasting until the outbreak of the Seven Years' War.[141] When Geneva sent envoys to France, Zurich, and Bern to thank these states for their intervention, it was widely noticed that at Paris the syndic Du Pan called Louis XV "the perfect image of divinity."[142] In March 1739 Geneva's magistrates agreed to demands from France to renounce all correspondence with Protestants in the kingdom, to send no books into France concerning religion, and to censure a work entitled "l'histoire des papes."[143] The challenge to Genevan mores was equally signaled in the fact that, despite the reaffirmation of the long-standing ban on theatrical entertainment in the Sumptuary Laws of 1732, a French troupe was given permission to perform for the comte de Lautrec during the period of the Médiation and until 1739.[144] French involvement was accepted to the extent that Lenieps himself appealed for justice directly to the comte de Lautrec, whom he had met prior to the latter's departure from Paris. In a brief memoir he explained that neither he nor Micheli had ever sought anything other than "that the fundamental laws of the state remain firm and stable."[145]

GENEVA AFTER FRENCH INTERVENTION

One consequence of the Médiation was division among the critics of magistracy. Micheli repudiated the Médiation and added to his notoriety by arguing that Geneva's magistrates were no longer independent.[146] Micheli, like the bourgeois reformers within the city, had trusted France. He belatedly concluded this to have been a great error and considered himself to have been betrayed by the French mediators.[147] England was the model republic to follow, having a gradation of citizens that was barely noticed, and where the people were ultimately sovereign because the king could never rule independently, making England in Micheli's eyes a democracy of distinction.[148] By contrast, Geneva lay like Rome when the patricians' corruption infected "all the republic"; like the Romans, the citizens of Geneva did not realize that the next step would be "the loss of liberty and the destruction of all the noble families under the emperors who would follow."[149] Micheli turned to the cantons for support but received none.

Many in Geneva turned against Micheli in consequence. Jacques-François Deluc, the leader of the critics of magistracy in the city after 1738 and a watchmaker of the rue Basse, had been a Micheliste in the mid-1730s; as Lenieps later related, Deluc had been one of the few citizens entrusted with copies of the letters of Micheli's friends in the city (and had denied this when pressed by the magistrates in 1731).[150] In 1738, however, he embraced the Médiation, became particularly close to the comte de Lautrec, and persuaded many among the bourgeois opponents of the magistrates to follow him.[151] In 1747 Deluc avowed his conversion to a more moderate political line, composing a *Réfutation des erreurs de Mr. Micheli du Crest*, which circulated in manuscript. In this he called the Médiation providential and justified the censorship of Micheli's writings.[152] Deluc held the constitution of 1738 to have confirmed the sovereignty of the General Council over the garrison, taxes, and membership of the smaller councils.[153] He saw the Médiation as a sacred text, God's own work, and as such a reaffirmation of Calvin's Reform. By contrast, the older leader of those opposed to Geneva's magistrates, Michel Léger, only reluctantly agreed to the Médiation.

After attacking the Médiation, in 1744 Micheli was confined at Neuchâtel at the request of Geneva's government. In 1747, despite being deprived of writing material, he composed his despondent *Maximes d'un Républicain* on the back of a set of playing cards. Although imprisoned, he was allowed visitors, and this led to him being charged as an enemy of stable government for his involvement in the anti-Bernese Henzi conspiracy in 1749.[154] He was then held by Bern at the fortress of Aarbourg until just before his death in 1766.[155] In the *Maximes* he expressed the view that well-ordered republics were now all but extinct: "Nothing is rarer today than a well-ordered republic where liberty reigns to a very high degree, one in which the people make the law, and the liberty of the great is curtailed."[156] Genevan radicals later recalled the bitter experience of "the unfortunate Micheli" at Aarbourg when they passed the prison.[157]

In August 1749, at the end of the War of the Austrian Succession, a treaty was signed between the General Council at Geneva and Louis XV, establishing free trade between France and Geneva, resolving all boundary disputes, allowing the practice of Catholicism in some of the villages outside the city, reaffirming the ancient alliance, and guaranteeing that Geneva would not allow troops hostile to France to cross its territory.[158] The treaty praised the "zeal and affection" with which France had protected Geneva in the past.[159] On 3 June 1754 Geneva signed a treaty with Charles Emmanuel, "King of Sardinia, Cyprus and Jerusalem" (Savoy to the modern reader), determining all boundaries and resolving all disputes between the states. The treaty concluded with Savoy acknowledging Geneva as a free state and renouncing all claims to its sovereignty.[160] Geneva was paying off all debts, "and all things seemed at this period to cooperate toward its prosperity." Burlamaqui's *Principes du droit politique* appeared in 1751, and the magistrates' perspective on politics was further bolstered with the appearance of the first volume of Pastor Jacob Vernet's *Instruction chrétienne* in the same year.[161] Vernet was by this time the city's leading theologian.[162] In 1756 a "Discours d'un Patriote Genevois" stated that the greatest threat to modern states was luxury but argued that luxury was rendered impotent within Christian Geneva by the control of mores; Geneva was fortunate in seeing "Military virtues cede their place to talent and great men be replaced by great geniuses."[163] The article, characteristic of the *Journal helvétique*, was followed by similarly optimistic accounts of Geneva's present circumstance and prospects.[164] Wealth at Geneva was growing, and both residents and foreigners were purchasing stately houses in surrounding areas.[165]

When d'Alembert's article "Genève" caused a storm within the city, it was significant that the general response was patriotic unity against an anti-Christian philosophe movement rather than domestic discord.[166] D'Alembert's leading critic within the city, Jacob Vernet, emphasized the health of public culture and ensured that no connection was made between the accusation that Geneva was no longer Calvinist and its strong political links with France.[167] This was no mean achievement. Vernet had spent most of the 1720s as a tutor in France and had met Voltaire as early as 1733.[168] His views had long been recognized to have moved far beyond the orthodox, and indeed to have challenged traditional Calvinism in favor of a "reasonable Christianity" whose foundation was utilitarian and whose Christology was anti-Trinitarian.[169] Yet Vernet presented himself as an orthodox Calvinist and slighted patriot. D'Alembert was derided for having displayed invidious behavior characteristic of a deist or atheist rather than the actions of a Frenchman.[170]

Rousseau was one of the few authors who responded to d'Alembert's article by identifying the latter's views as archetypically French, and by arguing that Geneva's government could not long stand once "Parisian" mores had entered the city.[171] He accused the philosophes of self-interest in desiring a theater and advised the Genevans to respond by being "men and citizens until your final breath."[172] Although Vernet and others praised Rousseau's work, they were careful to ensure that the controversy did not result in more general Francophobia. Vernet's letter to Rousseau praised the latter's concern about "the stupid imitation of great cities and the manners of a monarchy." Yet, rather than blaming France, Vernet used the debate to reaffirm the traditional constitutional and cultural values at Geneva, and presumed Rousseau's agreement: "You make clear with justice that with respect to the constitution of a state everything is connected. In our case, for example, a moral and religious regime is vital. We rely upon sumptuary laws, Ecclesiastical discipline, simple customs and a regular domestic and social life, military exercises and such like, no theater, dances but no masques, the play of commerce but no gambling."[173]

The strategy was successful if the evidence of foreign observers is considered. Voltaire initially had hopes that he could bring the parties together, writing to the young pastor Jacob Vernes that "[I am] much grieved that our philosopher of Paris [d'Alembert], [is] at odds with my philosopher of Geneva. Since you did not offend him willfully, I'll write to him he ought not take offense. Men who think like you and he, should be friends."[174] But in practice d'Alembert was shocked that his article was interpreted as a bitter attack on the faith of Geneva pastors and that he was accused of saying that the Genevans were no longer Christians.[175] George Keate, a travel writer and friend of Voltaire, wrote at the beginning of the 1760s that a visitor could expect to see at Geneva "a republic founded in wisdom and virtue . . . a people happy and free, yet who have defended themselves with bravery on every occasion." Geneva was the most philosophic nation, where "philosophy is more studied than the sword."[176] In 1761 Jean-Robert Tronchin, then procureur-général of the republic, published a discourse in the *Journal helvétique* praising Geneva as enjoying the most moderate of governments and being the most governed by law. Genevans had discovered legal means to tame the passions and relied on law, rather than dangerous institutions such as the tribunes of the plebs that had brought down Rome, to maintain tranquility.[177] Voltaire, by contrast, wrote that he was advising his friends "not to go to Geneva, because only small fools and petty tyrants dwell there."[178] For other visitors the continued existence of the most austere Calvinist morals remained evident.[179]

Whether liberty had been sacrificed was one consequent issue. As the historian Joseph Planta noted, the Médiation, in adding the declaration of the guarantee of the mediating powers, entailed "a fatal blow no doubt to the independence of the republic, since it authorized at all times the interference of preponderating neighbours."[180] From a longer perspective, the price of French involvement in Genevan politics was a comparative loss of order: Andrew Lemercier had noted at the beginning of the century that he could identify only two public disorders at Geneva in the two hundred years before 1707.[181]

THE FORMATION OF THE REPRÉSENTANTS

Jacques-François Deluc continued to lead the bourgeois radicals within Geneva in the 1750s and the early 1760s. Deluc, like many of the critics of magistracy of the lower town (the rue Basse), was a master watchmaker who had thrived since 1738. In 1751 he was pleased with the signing of the treaty with Savoy. He accepted the modus vivendi by which France was given a powerful voice in the councils of the republic in return for military protection and closer economic ties. All radicals asserted the sovereignty of the General Council, but for Deluc it was the keystone of an imagined status quo, itself guaranteed by the mediators' ultimate power to impose a constitutional settlement. Democracy necessitated the division of sovereignty enshrined in 1738. The Règlement of 1738 guaranteed the supremacy of the bourgeois in the economic sphere and provided means for them to prevent competition from natifs or habitants. The constitutional innovations demanded by the Michelistes would, in his eyes, have threatened internal peace and prosperity by giving the natifs an opportunity to demand civic equality.

The 1750s, however, saw the watchmaking fraternity challenged by demands for higher taxes to continue the magistrates' policy of fortification and for the repair of the cathedral of Saint-Pierre.[182] In less auspicious economic conditions, the bourgeois were also concerned by the growing demands of the natifs to alleviate constraints on their economic activities: the natifs lacked political and economic rights because they had been born in Geneva to habitants, persons from beyond the city who had become residents. When a sympathetic ear was lent to the natifs by the magistrates, the watchmaking fraternity, led by Deluc, became especially concerned. It is significant that they did not initially fall back to Micheli's position. Deluc's preferred strategy entailed successive *représentations*, or appeals to the magistrates and the annual General Council, "to place our Magistrates in the happy position of being required to better observe our laws."[183] It was at this time that Deluc's followers began to call themselves représentants. The représentants were formed into clubs (*cercles*) that formulated written attacks on the oligarchic practices and francophone manners of the ruling magistracy.

Deluc was unclear about how to reach agreement with the magistrates "without troubling peace and public tranquility." He repeatedly asserted in représentations that the historic rights of the citizens had been clear since the *Franchises* of Bishop Adhémar Fabri.[184] Given that the magistrates claimed equal clarity for a different reading of the ancient constitution, stalemate was the likely outcome.[185] What perplexed the magistrates was that Deluc relied on privileges and rights dating back to 1387 at the same time as he claimed to be defending the settlement of 1738.[186] In practice Deluc was dividing the représentants by refusing any compromise, setting his defense of the General Council in articles 3 and 4 of the Médiation against the magistrates' support for articles 5 and 6.[187] Since the council had accepted French intervention in the 1730s, the only prospect for reform was for a further mediation, in which it was hoped that France would be more sympathetic to the bourgeois cause. As long as the French guarantee of the constitution was accepted, the reformers had little room for maneuvering.[188]

It was in this context of lack of clarity about the best strategy for the représentants to follow that Deluc became involved with Jean-Jacques Rousseau. Rousseau's relationship with Deluc père, his two sons Jean-André and Guillaume-Antoine, and Jean-André's wife, Françoise Vieusseux, developed in the summer of 1754, during Rousseau's four-month return to

Geneva, culminating in a six-day boat trip around the lake in September.[189] Although Rousseau returned to Paris in October, Deluc sought to involve Rousseau in Genevan politics from this time onward, probably because he considered Rousseau to have expressed représentant opinions in the *dédicace* to Rousseau's *Discours sur l'origine de l'inégalité*.[190] In 1758 he promoted Rousseau's *Lettres sur les spectacles* as an assault on patrician culture alongside his own comments in the *Journal helvétique*.[191] In turning to Rousseau, Deluc probably intended to reinforce his policy of shaming the magistrates and thereby "maintaining by the exercise of wisdom our happy constitution."[192] Deluc was certain that Rousseau had a divine mission and was equally convinced that his own role was to guide it. This was why he sought to restore Rousseau to the true Calvinist faith, by personal visits (a technique he had also used with Voltaire), through the sending of his own and other orthodox theological tracts, and via letters.[193] What happened in practice was that Rousseau's involvement with Geneva after the publication of *Émile* and the *Contrat social* in 1762 underscored the bankruptcy of Deluc's policy, presenting the représentants with the choice of supporting a Geneva dominated by France or of developing new strategies for small state survival.

3

ROUSSEAU AND GENEVA

ROUSSEAU AND THE REPUBLIC

Rousseau's writings in the 1750s made him the archcritic of modern European society and the clearest expositor of a jeremiad view of the prospects for commercial states small and large.[1] But he had not written directly about Geneva's political situation and present circumstances, and had not formulated a plan for the représentants to revivify themselves and secure the long-term stability and independence of the state. This needs to be borne in mind when considering Rousseau's relationship with Geneva. This chapter charts Rousseau's relationship with the représentants prior to 1762, his composition of the *Lettres écrites de la montagne* (which addressed the problems Geneva faced), and the subsequent rejection of his political ideas by the représentants.[2]

The story begins with two banned books, both of which could be interpreted as commenting directly upon Geneva. At the behest of the governing Council of Twenty-Five in June 1762, both *Émile* and the *Contrat social* were burned in the city as anarchical and heretical books destructive of religion and all government.[3] Rousseau had asserted in the *Contrat social* that no man has a natural authority over his neighbor; the only legitimate political authority was consequently that to which one submitted oneself. Sovereignty resided in the people, was inalienable, and could not be conferred upon another body. What Rousseau called the general will, emanating from the assembled citizenry, was alone the source of law. The general will was identical with the common good of all and derived from their shared interests. It was the motor behind the social body.[4] The particular will of individuals or groups with separate interests from the commonality was the great threat to a legitimate polity. Government was a delegated power. When governments challenged the principles of political right, the people effectively became slaves who had renounced their independence. Political relationships returned to those of the state of nature. The message for small republics was that the sovereignty of all the members of a state, being the fundamental principle of political right, needed to be continually reaffirmed in order to maintain liberty.[5]

Such claims frightened the ruling magistrates at Geneva. Rousseau appeared to be aligning himself with the increasingly vociferous représentants' demand that taxes be reassessed by the sovereign General Council. The *Contrat social* could be read as rejecting the right of the smaller councils to reject propositions critical of the magistrates prior to any consideration by the assembled citizens. As one historian put it, while *Émile* contained "passages derogatory to the Christian religion," in the *Contrat social* "the most unlimited democracy meets a warm encomium."[6] Eminent Genevans such as the physician Théodore Tronchin called *Émile* "a complete code of deism" and "wished this unfortunate man dead."[7] As Tronchin later put it, "If Rousseau is a Christian then Cicero is a Catiline."[8] The natural philosopher Charles Bonnet attacked Rousseau for finding Christianity incompatible with government, and for viewing "republic and Christianity as contradictory terms."[9] For another reader, Rousseau "attacks government, the kings are idiots, the priests little knaves. He attacks revealed religion with an unequaled liberty and passion."[10] By contrast, the pastor Antoine-Jacques Roustan called Rousseau "Demosthenes and Fénelon," and likened the impact of his work to those of the great republican theorists of recent times, asking "How many citizens has Montesquieu made?" and "How many republicans have Vertot or Rollin made among us?"[11] The Genevan magistrates' decision to condemn Rousseau's books was justified in Procureur-Général Jean-Robert Tronchin's *Lettres écrites de la campagne* that appeared in September 1763.[12] Tronchin had initially reported on Rousseau's work for the governing councils and had concluded that he was a skeptic, an advocate of "extreme liberty," of "periodic assemblies," and of making constitutional law "always revocable."[13] The later *Lettres* developed these arguments, directly associating Rousseau's books with the représentants, and indeed lambasted the latter for excessive involvement with such an anarchic author.

The timing of the appearance of Rousseau's two books was of fundamental importance to their contemporary understanding. French failure in the Seven Years' War was clear by 1762 and raised questions about the alignment of Geneva with France rather than with Britain and Prussia. The decline of France also raised questions about investments by banking families tied to the magistrates in the finances of the French state. Characteristically, Rousseau went much further than those who were fearful about a future Europe in which the French played a lesser role than the Anglo-Saxons and the Germans. He predicted the collapse of Europe's commercial monarchies in *Émile,* and in the *Contrat social* warned of the threat posed by the oriental despotisms of the East.[14] As a result, many read the *Contrat social* as a description of a postapocalyptic world, where public finance was irrelevant because it had fostered the destruction of the old state system and where commerce was limited to the provision of primary products and necessities.

Such a vision would not have been deemed unrealistic in 1762, as the war between Britain and France engulfed so many nations, and the prospect of a second decline and fall of European civilization was widely deemed to be imminent. Rousseau wrote that the *Contrat social* "was not a book made for France."[15] It was not a book made for monarchies or commercial states either. As certain critics recognized, Rousseau refused sovereignty to kings.[16] Regarding Britain, he notoriously called its representative government a vestige of feudal tyranny, illegitimate when evaluated against the republican maxim that "Any law which the People has not ratified in person is null; it is not a law."[17] He was of the opinion that monarchies as traditionally conceived across Europe would have to give way to small republics if the renewal of successive barbarian invasions was to be avoided.

Generations of historians have argued that the *Contrat social* emerged from engagement with an early-eighteenth-century Genevan milieu that had sought to return this state to its democratic constitutional origins.[18] Rousseau's work has in consequence been viewed within a tradition of republican reform politics that responded to the international dominion of European commercial monarchies by demanding more popular control over lawmaking and the public purse, and a larger and more aggressively civic militia.[19] Historians have equally united around a second claim. Représentants associated with Rousseau in the early 1760s, such as Etienne Clavière, Jacques-Antoine du Roveray, and Jacques Vieusseux, found themselves in Paris, having been banished after the failed revolution at Geneva of 1782. Their involvement in the republican movement in France before 1792 provides support for portrayals of Rousseau as an ideological cause of the French Revolution.[20]

Such claims are only partly justifiable. In the *Contrat social* Rousseau was seeking to remake the science of politics, and considered himself to be replacing what he held to be Montesquieu's justifications of existing positive laws with a return to foundational principles. The latter would legitimize and promote small polities and republics more particularly. The first problem in aligning Rousseau with the radicalism at Geneva is that by the 1750s it was clear that représentant politics, as articulated by Jacques-François Deluc, were befuddled.

The magistrates' perspective was simply more convincing. Rousseau had acknowledged this in the dédicace to the *Discours sur l'origine de l'inégalité*, where he wrote, "the more I reflect on your political and civil situation, the less can I imagine that the nature of human things could admit of a better":

> Your sovereignty, acquired or recovered at sword's point, and maintained for two centuries by dint of valour and wisdom, is at last fully and universally recognised. Honourable treatises fix your boundaries, insure your rights, and confirm your security. Your constitution is excellent, dictated by the most sublime reason and guaranteed by friendly and respectable powers; your state enjoys tranquillity, you have neither wars nor conquerors to fear; you have no other masters than wise laws, made by yourselves, administered by the upright Magistrates of your choosing; you are neither so rich as to become enervated by softness and lose the taste for true happiness and solid virtues in vain delights, nor so poor as to need more foreign assistance than your industry provides; and it costs you almost nothing to preserve the precious freedom which great nations can maintain only by means of exorbitant taxes.[21]

Rousseau may have been inspired by such figures as Micheli du Crest, but his goal of reversing the decline of the small republics was far grander than any vision deriving from Geneva.[22] Furthermore, he considered the politics of Micheli and other contemporary republican luminaries to be inadequate, in that they lacked a general program for republican reform derived from engagement with the classic works of Hugo Grotius.[23]

The second problem with linking Rousseau to Genevan reform politics prior to the 1750s was that the *Contrat social* was not a finished work. Rousseau justified republics but did not explain how they might defend themselves or engage with contemporary instabilities in domestic politics and international relations. In a pamphlet published in 1790, the comte d'Antraigues claimed to have a manuscript from Rousseau's own hand that completed the *Institutions politiques*, of which the *Contrat social* formed a part. It revealed, d'Antraigues claimed, "the means by which small states can exist beside great powers, through the formation of confederations." He also stated that he would never publish it because it threatened "to weaken and perhaps to destroy royal authority."[24] If the *Contrat social* was a work for an altered European future this was explicable. But for contemporary republicans engaged in battles with magistrates and concerned about the power of larger states and interfering courts, Rousseau did not provide a practical manual. Famously, he then did so: for Geneva in 1764, for Corsica in the *Projet de constitution pour la Corse* (1763), and for Poland in the *Considérations sur le gouvernement de Pologne* (1772).

In the Genevan case, with the publication of his response to Tronchin, the *Lettres écrites de la montagne*, Rousseau refuted the republican reform politics of both Deluc and Micheli. He recommended a policy that many représentants rejected, including all of the radicals later involved in the revolution of 1782 at Geneva and the revolution of 1789 at Paris.

ROUSSEAU AT GENEVA

It has been claimed that Rousseau knew little of Genevan politics because he enjoyed an apolitical upbringing prior to leaving the city at the age of sixteen in 1728.[25] In fact, Rousseau's association with Genevan criticisms of magistracy can be presumed from his early life. The upheavals of 1718 surrounding the publication of the *Lettres anonymes* occurred at a time when he moved from the wealthy upper town to the Saint-Gervais district, which was distinguished by watchmaker agitation.[26] It is also significant that David Rousseau, his grandfather, lost the post of *dizenier* or moral censor for the Grand-Mézel district of Geneva because he had supported Pierre Fatio. Rousseau's father Isaac may have shared such politics.[27] Rousseau described him as a committed patriot, and it is significant that he fled Geneva after unsheathing his sword in a quarrel with the patrician Pierre Gautier.[28] Rousseau's knowledge can be documented from the late 1730s, when he was trying to obtain information about his uncle Gabriel Bernard's papers, which included Micheli du Crest's *Mémoire pour le magnifique Conseil des Deux Cents de Genève*.[29] Rousseau admitted in his *Confessions* that he had committed an act of treason in later passing Micheli's essay to Pierre-Louis-Clément Cocelli, then *directeur du service de la péréquation* at Chambéry, and thence to the Savoy authorities.[30]

Rousseau briefly visited the city in 1737, on his twenty-fifth birthday, to claim his inheritance, and recounted in the *Confessions* his shock at seeing members of the same family take up arms against one another. His interest in Genevan politics then appears to have waned. It was reignited in 1754, when he returned to Geneva and its church, assisting in the General Council, which was irregularly convened in July to swear in the syndic Pierre Mussard, and agreeing to pay the civic *taxe des gardes*.[31] The dédicace to the *Discours sur l'origine de l'inégalité* has sometimes been read as the first salvo in a long war between Rousseau and Geneva's government.[32] The *Confessions* noted that the dédicace "brought me enemies within the Council and jealousies among the bourgeoisie."[33] This was far from clear to contemporaries. As has been noted, Rousseau's dédicace could equally be read as a eulogy, with its question, "Does anyone of you know anywhere in the universe a more upright, more enlightened, or more respectable body than your magistracy?"[34] It was welcomed as such by leading magistrates, and Rousseau sent a copy to the first syndic Jean-Louis Chouet with the expectation of a positive response.[35] Rousseau was worried about the reaffirmation of his citizenship but was initially pleased at the reception of the dédicace.[36] His self-portrait as a "citizen of Geneva" was fraudulent, because he had abjured the faith that the civic oath was designed to uphold.[37] Rousseau hoped for rehabilitation without punishment, and above all to avoid the normal practice of a public renunciation of Catholicism. The Consistory was ultimately more generous with Rousseau than with other apostates.[38] He employed every art to ensure that the dédicace did not complicate a prodigal's return.

In the 1750s Rousseau's theological views were deemed more contentious than his uncertain politics, because he was perceived in the *Discours sur l'inégalité* to have questioned divine providence.[39] The magistracy were aware that Rousseau had friends among the citizens and bourgeois who called Geneva an oligarchy in decline. The political consequences of such connections have often been described as being confirmed in the *Lettre à d'Alembert sur les spectacles* of 1758. Jacques-François Deluc certainly wanted to ally Rousseau with the bourgeois critique of Voltaire-led *incrédules* responsible for loosening popular morals and weakening the state. Voltaire had even called the theatrical performances he organized from his house the "anticonsistoire."[40] Among the latter cabal Deluc identified Diderot's *Pensées philosophiques* and François-Vincent Toussaint's *Les moeurs* as particularly damaging.[41] Yet despite the dire warnings in the *Lettre* of the consequences of the Frenchification of Geneva, Rousseau did not in that text put forward any proposals for reform, explicitly support the représentants, or damn the magistrates.

The controversy was not in any case polarized between magistrates and représentants. Notable citizens supportive of the magistracy, such as Théodore Tronchin, were wary of the threat posed to traditional mores by popular entertainment. Tronchin wrote to Rousseau in praise of his writing but warned him that the days of the Greek republics were gone, as the modern division of labor and reliance upon trade meant that states could no longer provide a civic education and expect it to create dedicated citizens. Instead, the patrol of manners had become key in modern policy to prevent the excesses of a commercial age.[42] Notable pastors believed that Rousseau was simply defending Geneva's Consistory from d'Alembert's accusations.[43] Rousseau warned the Genevans against Voltaire and was praised for his defense of free will and the immortality of the soul.[44] It is equally significant that Tronchin was instrumental in offering Rousseau the position of librarian to the Bibliothèque de Genève as late as February 1757.[45] This would not have happened if Rousseau had already been identified as a party man. It was equally the case that supporters of the bourgeois cause did not necessarily accept Rousseau's position.[46] In March 1758, when Jacques-François Deluc sent Rousseau a copy of Michel Roset's *Chroniques de Genève*, a staple of représentant political argument, Rousseau replied that he was unsure why he had been presented with it.[47] A year later, he was pleased to receive for comment Pastor Jacob Vernes's manuscript copy of a *Histoire de Genève* that he was writing with Pastor Antoine-Jacques Roustan.[48] Both men were sympathetic to the représentant cause at this time. Before 1759, therefore, Rousseau and the représentants were not deemed by contemporaries to be natural bedfellows.

ROUSSEAU THE REPRÉSENTANT

In the aftermath of the War of the Austrian Succession, Genevans were for-mulating radical reform policies that engaged directly with the political divide in the city. One of the most notorious of the 1750s was Georges-Louis Le Sage's *L'esprit des lois*, which came to the notice of the magistrates at Geneva in February 1752, when it was circulating in manuscript. Le Sage was a habitant who had come to Geneva from France in the 1680s. His religious and political views were extreme. Le Sage was of the opinion that Protestantism was distin-guished among Christian denominations as a nondogmatic religion, and as such was suited to toleration and freedom of expression. He envisaged individu-als working out an independent relationship with God and living peacefully alongside those of different faiths in a single community. He hated aristocracy, blaming the social hierarchy at Geneva for the fact that his son could not be trained in medicine because of his status. He saw the voice of the people as the voice of God and traced the troubles of the 1730s to unwillingness among the magistrates to accept that the first natural law was the equality of persons. The root cause of the magistrates' unwillingness was their support for the gross and growing economic inequality within the city. Le Sage viewed the Médiation as promoting magisterial hegemony, by enabling them to continue to rule without recourse to an active General Council. The Médiation allowed the magistrates to divide and rule the city's social groups. Le Sage predicted the economic collapse of Geneva under pressure from the greater economic powers of Britain and France. He blamed the selling of citizenship to rich fam-ilies such as the Neckers, whom he detested as false patriots, enemies of the people, and a danger to the state in their belief that their wealth was concordant with their reason.[49] Such views went far beyond Rousseau's in linking perspec-tives on natural religion and natural equality to critiques of Calvinism, natural jurisprudence, and aristocracy. But they were also impractical, as they did not formulate a reform program that might stand as an alternative to those of Deluc or Micheli. Nevertheless, Le Sage's pamphlet was censored, and he was forbidden from writing about politics by the magistrates.

It was the enemies of the représentants at Geneva who identified Rousseau as the true leader of the movement. In arguing that Rousseau's *Émile* and *Contrat social* were direct attacks upon republicanism as traditionally conceived and a profound challenge to the magistrates at Geneva, Jean-Robert Tronchin turned Rousseau into the spokesman of the représentants. Tronchin's pamphlet ridiculed représentant aspiration to popular government in the small city-republic. The procureur-général called the arguments of the représentations confused in claiming that Rousseau had not been properly judged because of the necessity of syndics presiding over criminal tribunals.[50] Tronchin claimed that the views of the représentants were at odds with the history of the republic and more particularly with the Edicts of 1738.[51] Furthermore, their ideas were dangerous in that they risked overturning the state and creating "a race of Sophists." He accused the représentants of seeking to violate the vital balance of the Genevan constitution, which had made it as successful as Britain in generating domestic stability.[52] The central pillar of Tronchin's text was a defense of the *droit négatif*, the right of the Council of Twenty-Five to veto proposals that were put to it, rather than having all proposals evaluated by the General Council, including the représentants' représentations:

> Under our constitution the Small Council is accorded the right to undertake any examination [of claims about the meaning of law] and has as a result the right to approve or reject proposals that are put to it. This right has undoubtedly been conferred upon it because, being charged with responsibility for the various parts of the government, it is more able to evaluate proposals, examining their consequences, and judging the overall relationship that emerges between the constituent parts [of the state] and the whole. Be that as it may, this right is accorded to [the Small Council] by Articles 5 & 6 of the Edict of 1738, which amplifies the Edict of 1568. This law is both clear and fundamental. It underpins the order and the very structure of the constitution.[53]

Tronchin also justified the banning of Rousseau's books, "which cast doubt on the most important principles of government and of religion," and the decree that Rousseau be arrested for having "attacked religion itself."[54] By the publication of *Émile* and the *Contrat social*, "religion and government are delivered into the hands of their most audacious critic." Rousseau had "written against the Gospel," sought to demolish "prophets and miracles," "rejects prayer as useless," and "declares that religion is incompatible with liberty, that is to say, with the happiness of civil society, and is only made for despots and slaves." Banning such books was essential because the "first duty of the Syndics and Council is to maintain the pure religion."[55] Tronchin claimed that "there is not any other people who enjoy more security over the use that the government is able to make of the power that has been confided within it." The alternative was direct democracy, in which all notions of moderation, prudence, and government vanished.[56] The oath of the bourgeoisie obliged them to prevent "any machinations or undertakings against the Holy Evangelical Reformation." In consequence they were ceasing to be Genevans in supporting Rousseau.[57] Tronchin's *Lettres* facilitated the electoral success of magisterial candidates to every office of state in January 1764. In his speech to the Council of Two Hundred, he reiterated his warning against those who tied religious and political enthusiasm together, stating that Genevans faced a choice between rabid democracy or government in accordance with religion, virtue, and liberty.[58]

Rousseau decided to respond to Tronchin after being appealed to for help by the représentants, who had turned to Rousseau in the autumn of 1763.[59] The publication of Rousseau's response, the *Lettres écrites de la montagne*, was carefully orchestrated by the représentants, appearing in the city on 18 December in order to influence the election of chief magistrates (syndics) in January 1765. Hitherto the composition of Rousseau's *Lettres* had been a closely guarded secret, referred to in correspondence as "les airs de Mandoline."[60] With his sons and François-Henri d'Ivernois, Deluc furnished material for Rousseau to facilitate the composition of the *Lettres*.[61] A secret journey was undertaken to Môtiers-Travers on 22 November 1763 by Jean-André Deluc with papers and books requested by Rousseau. Rousseau returned two cases of material, mistaking their contents after Jean-André Deluc became ill: they were successfully sent again at the end of the year.[62] Other représentant writings emanating from the Deluc circle were passed on to Rousseau for comment during this period.[63] Perhaps unsurprisingly, Deluc and his sons had nothing but praise for Rousseau's *Lettres*. Jean-André Deluc described the first letters as the work "of a Christian who deserves to be happy and who will be because his soul is disposed to enjoy celestial benefits and is waiting for them."[64] François-Henri d'Ivernois told Rousseau he was the savior of his country.[65]

The response of the magistrates to the *Lettres* was to reinforce Tronchin's policy of presenting Rousseau as the most deadly représentant of all. As a result the *Lettres* were condemned with even more vitriol than had been directed toward the *Contrat social* and *Émile*. Théodore Tronchin wrote that they were written "for Milton's demons by the most demonic demon of all."[66] Jacob Vernet, another sometime friend to Rousseau, identified the *Lettres* as "the farewell of Medea." A year and a half after renouncing his citizenship, Rousseau "condemns our government and claims that it is a tyrannical aristocracy."[67] Vernet was convinced that Rousseau was making a reality of d'Alembert's accusation in fomenting Socinianism and deism in the manner of Marie Huber's *Lettres sur la religion essentielle à l'homme* (1739).[68] The Council of Twenty-Five castigated Rousseau publicly on 12 February 1765 for the ideas of liberty and virtue contained in the *Lettres*.[69] The Consistory equally condemned the book as destructive of Christianity and public order.[70] Concurrently, leading magistrates had acquired damaging information concerning Rousseau's private life and had passed it on to Voltaire. Within a week of the publication of the *Lettres*, Voltaire revealed to the world that the author of *Émile* had abandoned his children.[71] Voltaire also joined the throng labeling Rousseau a heretic and an anarchist, accusing him both of undermining Christianity in *Émile* by teaching deism and of causing insurrection at Geneva.[72] The magistrates sought directly to tarnish Rousseau's reputation and only indirectly to confute his political ideas.[73] Rousseau believed that the source of the libel was Geneva's Consistory and wrongly identified the représentant Jacob Vernes as its author.[74] The persecution mania that dogged Rousseau's final years began to take hold. He was soon writing to the représentant François-Henri d'Ivernois that he would have no further contact with Genevan politics.[75]

GENEVA AS ROUSSEAU'S MODEL FOR EUROPE

In many respects Rousseau adhered in the *Lettres écrites de la montagne* to the foundational claim of all the critics of magistracy at Geneva in the eighteenth century, namely that the sovereignty of the General Council needed to be asserted. He advocated the involvement of citizens more directly in the making of law and demanded that general councils become a more assertive check on the executive arm of government. In the sixth of his *Lettres*, Rousseau responded to the question, "In what does the unity of the state consist?"

> In the union of its members. And whence arises this union of its members? From the mutual obligations which unite them; so far then we are agreed. But what is the basis of this obligation? Here authors are divided. According to some, it is force; according to others, paternal authority; and again, according to others, the will of God. Each party maintains its own principle, and controverts those of the others. I myself have done the same; and, adopting the most salutary sentiments of those who have discussed these subjects,

have laid down the convention of its members, as the foundation of the body politick, and have refuted the contrary opinions. This principle, independent of its truth, is preferable to all others for the solidity of the basis it lays down: for what more certain foundations can be devised for any obligation among men than the voluntary engagement of those who are bound? Every other principle will admit of some dispute; but this will admit of none.[76]

From the principle that the convention of the members of a body politic was the sole legitimate foundation of political society, Rousseau proceeded to describe the resulting social contract as "an engagement of a singular kind . . . in that it binds the contracting parties, without reducing any one to a state of subjection," making "the will of All" the "supreme rule, being general and personified [and] what is called the Sovereign." Rousseau argued that it followed from this that sovereignty had to be "indivisible, unalienable, and essentially invested in all the members of the body." Law became a public and solemn emanation from the sovereign body and as such identified with what Rousseau called "the general will." In this and other sections of the sixth letter, Rousseau made plain his intention to restate and defend the perspective on the body politic outlined in the first two books of the *Contrat social* and at the close of *Émile*.[77] In describing the constitution of Geneva as an inspiration for the *Contrat social*, and both works as defenses of the pure and ancient stable polity Geneva had once been, he could condemn the decision to burn the *Contrat social* while refuting Tronchin's accusation that his ideas were corrosive of Geneva's present government:

> I have taken your own constitution, which I thought a fine one, for the model of political institutions, and by proposing it as an example to the rest of Europe, was so far from endeavouring to subvert it, that I pointed out the very means of preserving it. Even this constitution, good as it is, is not without its defects; the alterations it hath suffered might be corrected indeed, to preserve it from the danger it is in at present. I foresaw this danger; I foretold it, and pointed out the preservatives. Was it endeavouring to subvert a Government, to point out the means of its preservation? My attachment to your constitution made me desirous that nothing should alter it. This is my whole crime. I have, perhaps, been wrong. But if a love for my country hath blinded me, as to this particular, ought I to be punished for it?[78]

Rousseau always maintained that one of his intentions as an author was to make Geneva's constitution a model for European states, and he did this most explicitly in the *Lettres*.[79]

Rousseau's view of Geneva was distinctive. He coupled his defense of the représentants with more critical reflections about bourgeois politics and the magistrates, and came to the conclusion that a new mediation was vital for the state. Rousseau expected the représentants to embrace his ideas. Many of them indeed praised the *Lettres* and attacked the magistrates' response to them as being characteristic of tyrants.[80] They were clearly in agreement with Rousseau's foundational political principles and his defense of the sovereignty of the General Council. Yet the représentants took a decision not to cite the *Lettres* in subsequent polemics. Instead they were inspired by the arguments of a book published in January 1765, written in the main by Jean-André Deluc and Jacques Vieusseux, entitled *Réponse aux Lettres écrites de la campagne*. Unlike Rousseau's *Lettres*, the *Réponse* "contained rather a candid exposition of the facts that Tronchin had urged in favour of his thesis, than a regular system." Jean-André Deluc and Vieusseux had decided that the best policy was "to present a simply historical view of the encroachments of the councils on the people's rights."[81] A sentiment expressed in one contemporary commentary was characteristic: Rousseau in the *Lettres* had gone beyond the confines of acceptable political argument.[82]

Rousseau was profoundly unhappy about the représentants' neglect of the *Lettres*.[83] He enlarged upon this point in his *Confessions*:

> The remonstrating party, far from complaining of the odious declaration [against the *Lettres*], acted according to the spirit of it, and instead of making a trophy of the Letters from the Mountain, which they veiled to make them serve as a shield, were pusillanimous enough not to do justice or honour to that work, written to defend them, and at their own solicitation. They did not either quote or mention the Letters, although they tacitly drew from them all their arguments, and by exactly following the advice with which they conclude, made them the sole cause of their safety and triumph. They had imposed on me this duty: I had fulfilled it, and unto the end had served their cause and their country. I begged of them to abandon me, and in their quarrels, to think of nobody but themselves. They took me at my word, and I concerned myself no more about their affairs, further than constantly to exhort them to peace.[84]

As early as February 1765 Rousseau was asking François-Henri d'Ivernois why he was not being directly contacted by représentants.[85] In the same month he received a letter from an anonymous Genevan who declared himself a follower of Rousseau's "at a time when all the world wishes to throw stones [at you]."[86] Rousseau later claimed that in the years between 1764 and 1767 he had only had personal correspondence with d'Ivernois among the représentants. In these letters he had never discussed politics at Geneva, such was his sense of distance from all parties.[87]

In Rousseau's eyes, Geneva's historic constitution was valuable because it provided an example of a workable distinction between sovereignty and government. From his perspective, contemporary Geneva was in crisis because Tronchin and his fellow magistrates were threatening to overturn the established division of power between citizens and the executive by challenging the sovereignty of the General Council. As worrying in Rousseau's view, however, was the policy of the représentants, which threatened to destroy the existing distinction between sovereignty and government by making the government democratic. Rousseau believed that the republican reform politics of the représentants and the historic critics of magistracy were destabilizing Genevan political life. One of the aims of the *Lettres* was to underline the bankruptcy of représentant politics with regard to reforming the constitution. Rousseau foresaw the need for a new treaty of peace in domestic politics. His own version of the required compromise, a revised Médiation, was in fact outlined in the *Lettres*, and he believed that it would establish political concord at Geneva by reinforcing the existing distinction between sovereignty and government that was at the heart of the *Contrat social*.

Rousseau also attracted criticism among the représentants because of his religious heterodoxy. When Geneva's Council of Twenty-Five condemned *Émile* and the *Contrat social* as heretical books advocating political anarchy, Jacques-François Deluc, to Rousseau's surprise, was initially silent.[88] He was not among those, led by Lieutenant-Colonel Charles Pictet, who questioned why the magistrates were condemning Rousseau's character as well as his books, while being lenient toward more dangerous freethinkers such as Voltaire.[89] Nor was he involved in Rousseau's relatives' request for a copy of the *arrêt*.[90] Deluc's private view was that Rousseau had attacked Christianity in *Émile* and the *Contrat social*.[91] In consequence, as a devout Calvinist, Deluc found it difficult to challenge the verdict of the magistrates. As Pastor Paul-Claude Moultou, Rousseau's closest friend at this time, reported concerning Deluc's lack of activity, "He sees in you a citizen and regrets the fact that he does not see a Christian."[92]

Moultou's perspective is significant in providing a sense of the more general responses to Rousseau's politics, as well as the perceived danger of his theology. Moultou argued that *Émile* and the *Contrat social* proved Rousseau to be "superior to Montesquieu himself," for having revealed how to be truly free "amidst the servitude of nations." At the same time he underscored the damage that Rousseau had done to the radical Calvinists who otherwise favored his politics: "what you have said concerning religion has hurt those among your compatriots who you like the most, although they seek to excuse and to defend you."[93] Moultou advised a work of clarification that praised both Christianity and Calvinism, in the manner of Montesquieu's *Défense de l'Esprit des Loix* of 1750. If such a labor was not undertaken, Moultou warned, many of Rousseau's supporters would be blinded by his religious opinions.[94] Moultou saw Rousseau's *Lettre à Christophe de Beaumont*, then archbishop of Paris, as exactly this.[95] He subsequently defended Rousseau against the accusation that he was not a Christian. Foremost among the objecting représentants was the pastor Jacob Vernes, who claimed that Rousseau was seeking to destroy Christian institutions.[96] Moultou's response was that it was pointless to seek orthodoxy among divines as diverse as Bénédict Pictet, Jean-Alphonse Turrettini, Vernet, Jean-Frédéric Ostervald, or Vernes himself, and far more important to link Rousseau's positive message about the human capacity for freedom and toleration to the reform of "social institutions."[97] After the *Lettre à Christophe de Beaumont*, Rousseau presented himself as "tolerant by principle because I am a Christian," an opinion that was shared by a small group of Genevan pastors, including Moultou, Antoine-Jacques Roustan, Théophile Abauzit, and David Chauvet.[98] Despite their attraction to Rousseau's theology, it is significant that even Roustan could not defend the separation of church and state envisaged in the final chapter of the *Contrat social*.[99]

At some point in the summer of 1762, Deluc decided that Rousseau *could* be defended against the charge of heresy and began to battle those who called him unchristian.[100] In his long-winded *Observations sur les savants incrédules*, appearing at this time, Deluc distinguished between Rousseau and the dangerous freethinkers in league with Voltaire.[101] He had hopes that Rousseau could be made to see "sense" and return to orthodox Calvinism, commenting to Moultou that the impious passages of *Émile* and the *Contrat social* "would not have been written had he read my own book."[102] The product of such misplaced confidence was that by September 1762 Deluc had begun to plot anew to use Rousseau's private letters, and those of Pastor Frédéric-Guillaume de Montmollin, who had given Rousseau communion in Neuchâtel, to prevent Jean-Robert Tronchin's reelection as procureur-général.[103] Deluc also tried to persuade Rousseau to return to Geneva at Christmas of this year to reaffirm his commitment to the church.[104]

Rousseau renounced his citizenship on 12 May 1763 after the Council of Twenty-Five, under pressure from the French résident, Etienne-Jean de Guimard des Rocheretz, baron de Montpéroux, stopped the sale of the *Lettre à*

Christophe de Beaumont.[105] Deluc was responsible for the subsequent intensification of local opposition to Rousseau's perceived illegal treatment by the magistrates, whom he accused of violating article 88 of the *Ordonnances ecclésiastiques:* the Consistory of Geneva ought to have judged *Émile* and the *Contrat social* prior to the verdict of the Council of Twenty-Five. He persuaded Rousseau to follow his advice in writing to Marc Chappuis the famous letter later heralded as "le tocsin de la sédition."[106] It was followed by the drafting and delivery of représentations on 18 June, 8 August, and 29 September. These combined a defense of Rousseau with rejection of the magistrates' claim to have a right to reject représentations: the so-called droit négatif, or "negative right," which justified the rejection by the Council of Twenty-Five of proposals intended for the General Council.

The magistrates held the droit négatif to have been confirmed by the Médiation of 1738; article 6 stated that anything laid before the General Council had to be "traité & approuvé" by the Council of Two Hundred. Deluc argued that the balance of the constitution was being destroyed by the droit négatif, which was a deadly constitutional innovation because it gave the magistrates means to control the sovereign and thereby placed them above the citizens.[107] Geneva was on the verge of becoming an oligarchy dependent on the importation of luxuries from France, turning its back on natural law and its foundation, Holy Scripture. Evidence for this came from the friendship offered by the magistrates to Voltaire, the author of books "against Providence, against the immortality of the soul, against the religion of the Jews, against Sacred history, and in which religion is treated as satirical."[108] Deluc lacked a comprehensive reform program, but he used the condemnation of Rousseau's books to be more confrontational. Such accusations were the immediate cause of the writing of Tronchin's *Lettres écrites de la campagne.*

ROUSSEAU AGAINST JACQUES-FRANÇOIS DELUC

It is notable that, on the few occasions when Rousseau adopted Deluc's adversarial approach to Genevan politics, as in the case of the letter to Marc Chappuis of May 1763, he quickly drew back, arguing that his intentions had been mistaken.[109] He came to see it as another example of his being treated by Deluc as a political weapon.[110] Rousseau had long been critical of the policy of directly confronting the Council of Twenty-Five and the practice of successive représentations.[111] He recognized that continued opposition meant civil war, with the likely consequence of invasion by France. Deluc's policy was self-defeating, because the basis of his attack on the magistrates was their violation of the agreement of 1738, yet in refusing to countenance their interpretation of constitutional law he was destroying the very Médiation he held to be sacred. This was why Rousseau considered Deluc a good man but of limited intelligence.[112] In the first of the *Lettres écrites de la montagne*, Rousseau affirmed: "My advocates [at Geneva] were silent when they should have spoken, and have spoken when they should have remained silent. I foresaw the inutility of their remonstrances, as well as the consequences of them: I apprehended their inevitable effects must either disturb the public tranquillity, or alter the constitution of the state. The event hath too fully justified these apprehensions; and you [représentants] see yourselves reduced to the alternative I feared."[113]

When a meeting was held at Thonon in the first week of August 1764 to discuss the publication of the *Lettres*, divisions of opinion were confirmed.[114] It is remarkable that at Thonon Rousseau did not share the contents of the *Lettres* with the représentants, despite the work then being complete.[115] When the Deluc circle sent their *Réponse aux Lettres écrites de la campagne* to Rousseau for comment on 12 October 1764, the brief reply was scathing.[116] The *Réponse* largely reinforced Deluc's policy of limiting représentant argument to refuting Tronchin point by point. But there were also signs that the représentants were beginning to embrace ideas associated with Micheli. The *Réponse* sketched a possible solution to the dispute, in defending the promotion of a syndic who would lead the citizens and bourgeois against the magistrates.[117] Rousseau had anticipated that the représentants might return to Micheli's constitutional viewpoint.[118] The *Lettres* explained why Micheli's program of reform was no longer an option for long-term stability.

The singular fact evident to Genevan readers of Rousseau's *Lettres* was the continued assertion of the need to separate the theological and political elements of the state. Yet the relationship between the church and the state was the cornerstone of the ideology of the Deluc circle, for whom the threat to liberty came from the magistrates and not the Consistory; Deluc wanted to increase the powers of the Consistory and the General Council, in order to establish a clear division of sovereignty and to increase control over manners. Rousseau's point of departure from this position was twofold. First, he did not believe that the democratic constitution established at Geneva could be maintained if it rested upon the division of sovereignty envisaged by Deluc. Rousseau believed that democratic constitutions had not been properly studied or understood by philosophers or statesmen, making such a form "nothing but a Government without a Government."[119] Democratic governments were one of the most dangerous political forms, and Deluc risked establishing an unstable popular government through his uncertain political speculations. Nor did

Deluc's formal représentations offer solutions to the issue of the magistrates' usurpation of sovereignty. The specific problem at Geneva was that involving the General Council or the Consistory more directly in everyday politics was unsustainable, because the General Council or any other popular representative body had no leverage over the smaller councils. The finances of the state were such that the magistrates were not dependent on the General Council with respect to public revenue. Although there was an appearance of free election, "[citizens] are so restrained on every side, that you cannot choose a first Syndic, nor a Syndic of the guard."

> In short, though you [citizens and bourgeois] are sovereign Lords when assembled, you are afterwards nothing. Subordinate Sovereigns four hours a year, you are subjects the rest of your lives, and given up, without reserve, to the discretion of others. It hath happened to you, Gentlemen, as it hath happened to all Governments like yours. The legislative and executive powers, which constitute the Sovereignty, were not at first distinct. The people, being sovereign, had a will of their own, and by their own act executed that will. But the inconvenience of the general concurrence of all to every thing, presently obliged the people to make choice of particular members to execute their will. . . . By degrees these commissions became frequent, and at length permanent. Thus a body was insensibly formed, whose action was constant. A body whose action is permanent and constant, cannot give an account of each single act: it accounts only for the principal; and presently arrives at such a pitch, as to account for none at all. The more active the executive power is, the more it enervates the legislative power. . . . After this there remains in the state only one acting power, which is the executive. Now the executive power is nothing but force; and where force only is nothing but force; and where force only prevails the State is dissolved. This, Sir, is at length the final dissolution of all democratical States.[120]

Rousseau concluded that the history of Geneva since the Reformation might have been foretold by a "clear-sighted politician." To such a figure it would have been evident that the constitution then established was "proper for the first establishment of public liberty, but improper for its preservation."[121] Accordingly, the problems Geneva had experienced since Fatio were to be expected in part because of uncertainties about how to establish and maintain democratic states. Rather than being an organized plot seeking to plunder popular liberty, the experience of civil war at Geneva could be explained by reference to the generic problem of democracy, and could be addressed by reasserting the ancient distinction between sovereignty and government. Despite his personal involvement, Rousseau was sure that by making this position clear more even-handed solutions would emerge, because the existing government at Geneva was capable of reform. Although they behaved like tyrants, he did not believe that Geneva's leaders *were* tyrants, at least so long as the laws of the state retained some authority.

This perspective was complicated by the second factor governing Rousseau's analysis. Geneva's peculiar history could not be ignored if a serious attempt was to be made to keep the state both free and independent. Naturally the Reformation, and Calvin's role in it, loomed large. Rousseau's major claim, in the first of the *Lettres*, was that the constitutional battle of the 1760s could be resolved only by a reassessment of this seminal event. This reflected his belief that the actions of the magistracy condemning him and his books had been taken in league with the Consistory. A spirit of fanaticism and superstition had infected leading pastors. In the first letter, Rousseau said that no religion would be better than "to have one that is cruel and persecuting, and which, being tyrants over the laws themselves, is not compatible with the moral obligations of the people." Such arguments derived from Rousseau's study of the history of the Genevan church.[122]

Rousseau's view of the process of historical change influenced his view of the dangerous role played by the church in Geneva. Free states were largely the product of accident and fortune; and the greatest of historical developments, rather than being the product of legislative vision or individual action, were in the main the result of gradual, directionless, and piecemeal change. Geneva's history was no exception. At one point in the *Lettres*, Rousseau made a claim that any Calvinist or patriot would have found particularly unpalatable. It was that Geneva had enjoyed liberty under the bishops as a city within the Holy Roman Empire, and that it was only under the Protestant magistrates that this liberty began to be eroded.[123] Rousseau had in fact toned down this argument. A fuller examination of the relationship between liberty and the Reform was contained in his *Histoire de Genève*, drafted concurrently with the *Lettres*. The original plan had been to publish the *Lettres* at the end of 1764, largely restricted to a self-defense against Tronchin's accusations, and then to follow them a year later with the *Histoire*.[124] The latter would "serve as an instructive memoir for the Judges"—the mediators Rousseau expected to have been called upon by 1766. The project was abandoned before March 1764, no doubt because the views expressed in the *Histoire* were too extreme for contemporaries of any political persuasion.[125]

The manuscript notes of the *Histoire* that remain demonstrate that liberty in Geneva was an accidental product of the conflict between the bishop and the duke of Savoy. The bishop gave privileges to the citizens and bourgeois of the city in order to maintain their support for the church, and in order to create a bulwark against invasion. The city was, in the fifteenth century, "much more free than it had been when it became a republic."[126] Furthermore, liberty had been maintained only because of the support of the cantons of Bern and Fribourg. With respect to liberty in Geneva, "religion played no part in its becoming free."[127] Such evidence led Rousseau to conclude that "every element of the present constitution was established before the Reformation." Far from being part of the same historical process, "the prior establishment of liberty was the source of that liberty established at the Reform." Having tasted independence, Genevans had turned their gaze to the church. They had conveniently forgotten that a Catholic bishop had granted the city its original freedom.

Taking this manuscript into account clarifies Rousseau's argument in the first *Lettres*. In his view, the Reformation was a liberation movement against the intolerance, fanaticism, and superstition of Catholicism. In the name of "raison et l'Évangile," strictly in order of priority, the Reform had affirmed "we are Christians each in our own manner."[128] Reiterating the ideas outlined at the end of the *Contrat social*, Rousseau attacked those who had sought to establish Christianity as a national religion or to involve Christ in worldly affairs ("they have sullied His celestial purity").[129] One of his targets was Calvin. Despite his greatness in throwing off the Catholic yoke, Calvin was cited as proof that no man can avoid subjection to the passions. Pride caused him, and "the majority of his associates," to become dogmatic and arrogant. The result was a new theological orthodoxy, which to Rousseau was the antithesis of Protestantism. The Genevan church stood for toleration and evangelical liberty. As such, it could have no profession of faith.[130]

In the fifth letter, Rousseau praised the ordinary clergy of Geneva who, "without attaching themselves to a merely speculative doctrine, refer all to morality, and the proper discharge of the duties of man and the citizen."[131] Certain pastors made Rousseau optimistic about the possibility of reaffirming the message of the true Reform at a time of declining religious belief. He was thinking of his friends Paul-Claude Moultou, Antoine-Jacques Roustan, and Théophile Abauzit. Rousseau believed himself to be contributing to the abbé de Saint-Pierre's project of closing the schools of theology while sustaining religion. This had been the intention behind the Savoyard "profession de foi" in *Émile*, Rousseau argued, in fostering faith without disputation, reason without impiety, philosophical toleration, Christian charity, few dogmas, many virtues, and zeal without fanaticism. The result would be no great alteration in the form of religious worship but an enormous change in their interrelationship and consequently in national culture.[132]

The choice for Geneva was therefore either a purely civil religion of fundamental dogmas useful to society or the reaffirmation of what Rousseau called pure Christianity, "in its true manifestation," as opposed to "dogmatic Christianity."[133] Each necessitated the absolute separation of church and state. It is clear that Rousseau favored the second option in Geneva. An end would be made to the role of the Consistory in the executive councils, the civic sermon would change, and as a result, Rousseau claimed, no further arbitrary punishments would sully Christianity or Geneva. Public tribunals would address religious questions only indirectly, when the faith of individuals became a matter of national or domestic security.[134] Pastors playing politics had corrupted the city. To be useful to public morality, they had to abandon the political arena and focus upon the reform of manners and combating luxury and immorality.

For Deluc and the majority of Genevan représentants, it was scandalous to link their dispute with the magistracy with a reordering of the theological institutions of the state. Deluc's orthodox Calvinism entailed a confessional state in which the Consistory was a branch of the executive.[135] Deluc never hid his opposition to Rousseau's religious heterodoxy, which he blamed on living too long among "the heretical and the superstitious." In a letter of September 1762 he warned Rousseau of the harm he had done to Christianity.[136] Early in their relationship, Rousseau had offered to have Deluc's sons' observations on glaciers published in the *Encyclopédie*. Nothing could have been more shocking to Deluc, who replied that his sons' work sought to establish "a theory of the world conforming to Genesis, and founded upon the most advanced natural philosophy."[137] When Deluc advised him to soften the tone of the *Lettre à Christophe de Beaumont*, in order to make it acceptable to the Consistory, Rousseau responded that "my friends are not my masters."[138] Deluc held firm to the view that Rousseau should recant the chapter on civil religion.[139] He and his friends' own refutation of Tronchin acknowledged accordingly that one of their intentions was to insulate Rousseau's ideas from représentant politics with respect to the Genevan church, stating that they "had never adopted all that they had found in the books of Mr. Rousseau."[140] The *Lettres* were in consequence treated as a refutation of Tronchin, rather than being addressed as Rousseau's imaginative solution to Geneva's political and religious problems. By February 1765 Rousseau had tired of the Genevan représentants' refusal to link protestation with political reform.[141] To Guillaume-Antoine and Jean-André Deluc he announced the end of an epistolary relationship with their family.[142] Guillaume-Antoine Deluc refused to accept Rousseau's desire and continued to express the view to Rousseau that God was a représentant, that Rousseau's work had enlightened everyone at Geneva, and that the (purported) policy developed between Rousseau and his father was beginning to bear fruit.[143]

ROUSSEAU AGAINST MICHELI

Through the medium of another exile, a distant relative named François Mussard, Rousseau began to associate with the jeweler and sometime banker Toussaint-Pierre Lenieps while at Paris in the 1750s.[144] As previously mentioned, in 1731 Lenieps had been banished from Geneva for life, in addition to being fined and losing his bourgeois status, for having corresponded with Micheli du Crest.[145] Having decamped to Paris, Lenieps continued to be a staunch Micheliste. In a letter of 14 February 1737, which circulated in Geneva before being censored, he reaffirmed his belief that "The General Council when assembled states and declares that all powers not expressed in the Edicts are reserved to it, and that it only confers the exercise of power to the Syndics and Councils when it is confident that they will faithfully fulfill their duties; the General Council has the authority to return to itself all powers whenever it sees fit."[146] When Micheli died in the fortress of Aarbourg in 1766, Lenieps wrote that "no one better understood the nature of the Republic than him, and all that he said [about Geneva] has been confirmed."[147] In the early 1760s Jacques-François Deluc came to share Micheli's view, against his own *Réfutation*, that tribunals without syndics were illegal, and that the General Council ought to be the ultimate court of appeal in criminal cases.[148] He then attempted to heal the ancient rift with Lenieps. Deluc urged Rousseau to inform Lenieps that he was willing to petition the magistrates for the latter's return to Geneva. Rousseau appears to have been aware that such conciliatory approaches were futile, as he did not pass on Deluc's offer and falsely reported to Deluc Lenieps's rejection.[149] It is certain that Lenieps continued to despise Deluc and that the central division between them continued to be the Médiation.[150] Lenieps rejected the Médiation and the excessive reliance of Geneva upon France. He believed that a constitutional refounding remained essential for the city, and that this would only occur if the leaders of the radical party committed themselves to Micheli's reform program.

There can be no doubt that Lenieps perceived Rousseau to be expressing political ideas related to his own and derived from Micheli's. On reading the *Contrat social*, he commented, "I had viewed sovereignty and government just as you have, but I have never seen this relationship expressed and justified with so much truth and force." He also praised the chapter on civil religion; priests "are everywhere similar to women as when one attacks one of them you attack them all." Although the power of the religious authorities was limited in Protestant states, Lenieps noted that the pastors were never friends to the people, as was evident from the troubles of Geneva in the 1730s.[151] With regard to *Émile*, he wrote, "I read and re-read the Confession of your Savoyard Vicar, and I discover something each time that moves me and that elevates the soul."[152] He expressed sympathy for Rousseau in experiencing civil and ecclesiastical condemnation. More pertinently, he likened Rousseau to Micheli, but a Micheli for a new generation.[153] In July 1763 Lenieps wrote that he read only Rousseau's books: "all the rest are insipid to me." In Rousseau he found the need for a reformation of manners most fully justified, and the philosophy that "without virtue there is not true happiness."[154]

When Rousseau became more directly involved with the représentants in 1764, Lenieps furnished him with material concerning the recent political history of Geneva, including his own perspective on Geneva's history and politics.[155] Lenieps's *Réponse aux cinq lettres écrites de la campagne* reaffirmed Micheli's claim that Geneva had become an aristocratic oligarchy because the General Council's sovereignty had been usurped by the smaller councils. Lenieps attacked the droit négatif at Geneva as the central means of aristocratic control, stating that the only legitimate veto in politics was exercised to protect the people, as illustrated by the tribunes at Rome. He accused the magistrates of seeking, since the first decade of the century, to model Geneva's constitution upon that of aristocratic Bern. He noted the increasing links between Bern and Geneva, at the expense of close relations with the more democratic Zurich.[156] He also took pains to refute Jean-Robert Tronchin's parallel between the balance of power at Geneva and British liberties. Lenieps argued that the constitutions of the two states were altogether at odds, because the British "have granted the King the liberty to adhere to the public good, and tied his hands to prevent wrongdoing." The surest example concerned taxes and finance, for which a British king depended upon Parliament, while the Genevan magistrates controlled the public purse. He warned Genevans that "it is through seas of blood that the English have acquired and conserved their liberty. If they had allowed Charles 1st to remain, can you believe that this state would today enjoy its empire of the sea, its riches, commerce, and have so many citizens?"[157]

Rousseau's relationship with Lenieps was different from his relationship with Deluc. This was because of Rousseau's greater respect for Lenieps as a person, and because of the concordance in their attitudes toward religion. When Jacques-François Deluc initiated the représentations defending Rousseau in June 1763, it was to Lenieps that Rousseau complained of their lateness and futility.[158] When Lenieps advised Rousseau not to live among the English ("a people full of pride, unsociable, divided and intolerant"), he did so without the patronizing or imploring characteristic of Deluc's epistles. Rousseau was not for Lenieps an object of political value. Being fellow exiles with little hope of return, it was easier to exchange their views of Geneva: "Pitiful country, a new Jerusalem that destroys its prophets. . . . We are in the greatest of days but sense that we live in winter."[159] Rousseau also had greater respect for Lenieps's politics. When Lenieps informed him that he had mistaken the nature of Geneva's political *cercles* in his *Lettre à d'Alembert sur les spectacles*, Rousseau was quick to confirm his involuntary error; he bowed to Lenieps's superior knowledge of "the true state of our manners and of our republic."[160] Some commentators have argued in consequence that Micheli, through the medium of Lenieps, was a major influence on Rousseau's politics and particularly on the notion of sovereignty and government in the *Contrat social*.[161] In the *Lettres écrites de la montagne*, however, Rousseau developed a critique of the Micheli/Lenieps solution to Geneva's constitutional impasse.[162]

Rousseau recognized Micheli's demand that popular syndics be elected as tribunes, with authority to challenge the permanent magistrates in the executive councils. This was expected to lead to a more direct form of democracy, with citizens and bourgeois exercising an individual right to call general councils. Rousseau's rejection of this position was due in part to his view of history, in which innovation by constitutional fiat was more often than not a failure. More significant still was Geneva's particular history since the rule of the bishops. A free constitution had been established and maintained. This was owing to the excellence of constitutional law from the time of Adhémar Fabri's *Franchises*, which Rousseau likened to the Magna Carta.[163]

Rousseau saw no reason to challenge what he saw as the fundamental laws of Genevan politics, founded upon a balance of power between citizens and magistrates, that had developed over the centuries and largely maintained civil concord. Micheli, like Deluc, threatened to collapse the established distinction between sovereignty and government. Against Micheli, Rousseau praised the Médiation of 1738, stating that it was "the salvation of the Republic."[164] However servile Geneva's current condition, "nothing is more free than your state legitimately constituted."[165] A compromise between magistrates and people was essential, rather than an open-ended constitutional revolution that, in following Micheli, would simply replace a tyrannical magistracy with a tyrannical populace. This reflected the key difference between them. Rousseau was as opposed to the people combining executive and legislative power as he was to the magistrates doing so.[166]

According to Rousseau, there was no need for a legislator to intervene in Genevan politics. The quality of the existing laws meant that the most important goal of any opponent of oligarchy was to restore the sovereignty of the laws. This was the task Rousseau set himself in the second half of the *Lettres*. The truly shocking element to the représentants was his support for the droit négatif. The right of the magistrates to prevent the people from making new constitutional laws was described as being necessary in present circumstances. In a statement that must have horrified the représentants, Rousseau wrote that Tronchin's defense could not be bettered.[167] Any proposal to the General Council would be assessed for its novelty by the magistrates. The difference between Rousseau and Tronchin was that the former favored a double-edged droit négatif. Balancing the magistrates' veto, the citizens and bourgeois were to enjoy a similar power, being able to censure the magistrates for innovation. Rousseau envisaged the exercise of this right in two distinct ways. The first was by means of bourgeois and citizens gathered together into companies. Such groups, if they concurred with a proposition that the law had been broken, would have the right to make a représentation to the General Council for redress. The magistrates could prevent a représentation only if they chose to respond immediately to the accusation, thereby confirming that they were acting as a government conforming to the general will.[168] The alternative or second way was to reestablish periodic general councils of all the citizens. These would have the power to act not as sovereigns but as supreme magistrates or dictators, interpreting the law and if necessary coercing the members of the councils to follow the laws.

Such a constitutional balance underlined the difference between Rousseau's politics and those of the représentant community in Geneva or in Paris. Rousseau refused to criticize the Médiation for giving too much power to the magistrates; its mistake had been not to acknowledge sufficiently a similar power for the citizens.[169] He differed from the représentants because he knew the consequences of taking away too much of the magistrates' power and refused to do so. Magisterial abuse of authority did not mean that any other group of citizens or bourgeois would better define the general will. Democratic states confirmed their decline when they responded to the rise of oligarchy by giving excessive authority to the people as a body.

The people, Rousseau reminded his readers, were always poor judges, and would either elect a despot or continue to abuse liberty themselves.[170] Neither the people, the pastors, nor the magistrates could sufficiently control the passions and be trusted sufficiently to exercise authority without checks upon their actions. The only legitimate check was law, and the only successful

constitutional settlement in Geneva would be one by which the law became
more certain and more authoritative. Whatever their form of government, the
people were free "when those who govern appear only as the organs of the
law."[171] Rousseau was confident that he had discovered a middle way to resolve
two seemingly intractable problems. First was the preservation of religion as the
foundation of morals. He believed this position could be defended against
evangelical Catholic or Protestant clerics in addition to the *incrédules* of
Voltaire's persuasion.[172] Second was the maintenance of peace for the magistrates and liberty for the people, entailing aristocracy as the best of governments
and the worst of sovereigns.[173] If his ideas were put into practice, he predicted,
the government of Geneva would be the best that ever existed.[174]

Despite the complaints in his letters and the verdict of the *Confessions*, there
is evidence that Rousseau did not expect his ideas to be embraced. No democratic states could avoid decline once fundamental laws had begun to be abro-
gated. Unlike some représentants, he refused to blame France for Geneva's ills.
Rousseau accepted that the position and size of Geneva made France the dominant mediator in any dispute. He accordingly ended the *Lettres* with the statement that the Genevans "were more in need of concord than consultation."[175]
France was straightforwardly too powerful to be crossed. In the *Confessions* he
stated that the essence of the *Lettres* was a "stoical moderation." His message
had been "to constantly exhort [the Genevans] to peace," as this was the only
means to avoid "being crushed by France."[176] Micheli's desire to make Geneva
an international power was utterly futile. Rousseau identified the greater problem for European states to be the rise of oriental despotism. States such as
China, which pursued a policy of being harsher on their aristocrats than on
their people, were growing in power and population. In Europe, by contrast,
where the monarchs and magistrates blamed the populace for the problems of
the state, population was, he believed, declining by 10 percent every thirty
years.[177] Until the great collapse of commercial monarchies, there was little that
could be done.

The argument that the modern world was simply too corrupt to be reformed
was often associated with Rousseau's writings. One of Rousseau's Genevan correspondents offered this verdict in 1765: "nature has been turned upside down,
there are hardly any animals or living things that have conserved their primitive
state, and we live today only through prejudice and error. You have seen what
an immense work would be necessary to restore things to their natural state."
Rousseau had done much in his writings to point the way back to nature,
but "corruption is too great, prejudice too deeply rooted, kings too engorged
with glory and power, priests too attached to their incomes and the vanity

that accompanies the direction of consciences, the rich too in love with their gold."[178]

Rousseau was sincere in describing the *Contrat social* as a history of Genevan government, and Geneva itself as a political model for Europe. What he meant was that the distinction between sovereignty and government established at Geneva was worthy of enquiry. He did not mean that the existing *government* of Geneva ought to be seen as a model, or that the représentant plans for a revised constitution were worthy of support. The dominant narratives of Genevan history that had emerged since the founding of the republic were mistaken, and Rousseau wanted to use the *Lettres* as the basis of a new mediation that would more clearly define the relationship between sovereignty and government. The *Lettres* accordingly support the portrayal of Rousseau as an arch-critic of contemporary republican and magisterial politics, and one opposed to founding political associations in Christian or philosophic notions of sociability. Rousseau wanted citizens to agree to create a disembodied sovereign, ideally synonymous with the laws themselves, establishing a form of government that put the general will above individuals. He was, however, pessimistic about the possibility of realizing such an enterprise, considering it akin to squaring the circle; it could not be found "between the most austere democracy and a perfect Hobbism."[179]

Rousseau's view of Genevan history led his profoundly heterodox perspective on its institutions to be widely contested. The reform theology that derived from his historical research could never have been embraced by représentants who were also Calvinists, most clearly in the sense of the *Consensus Helveticus* of 1674, but also of the revised theology of Jean-Robert Chouet, Jean-Alphonse Turrettini, and even Jacob Vernet at his least orthodox.[180]

As an enemy of political conflicts centering on a disputed "ancient" constitution, and as an opponent of democratic republicanism in small states, Rousseau appeared to be seeking to move beyond Swiss republican reform politics. His emphasis upon the stability of law and the necessity of political authority properly constrained by established law, itself embodied by a political culture distinguished from the institutions of the church, underscores the differences between Rousseau and the représentants in the 1760s. For the représentants, Rousseau's distinction between sovereignty and government was suspect, in that a preference for a wise aristocracy appeared to justify the Council of Twenty-Five. It is significant that Rousseau's friends the pastors Moultou and Roustan responded to the constitutional disputes of the later 1760s in a manner that paralleled Rousseau's own position in the *Lettres*. Moultou expressed shock to his friend Pastor Leonhard Usteri at Zurich concerning the line the représentants in Geneva had adopted: "Some will think that the people enjoy the right to carry to the General Council all of the questions that agitate them, and it can be imagined what kind of anarchy we would then fall into."[181] Moultou called Rousseau's political writings "masterpieces of patriotism" but stated that the response of the représentants to Rousseau had led him to the judgment, "Geneva is no longer anything to me."[182]

NÉGATIFS AND REPRÉSENTANTS AFTER ROUSSEAU'S *LETTRES ÉCRITES DE LA MONTAGNE*

In February 1763 a représentant named Robert Covelle was accused of seducing and impregnating a young unmarried woman named Catherine Ferboz. He refused to kneel before the Consistory on the grounds that he was willing to bow only before God. Voltaire took up Covelle's cause. The resulting poem provided a portrait of a successful commercial city whose religious mores were barbarous, being akin to a modern inquisition:

> Beneath an hill, which time has render'd bare
> Geneva rises—city rich, and fair;
> Her habitants, of many a furnace proud
> Plung'd in accounts, a money-getting crowd.
> Silver, not sense, they valuable hold
> And here refine, nor wit, but sterling gold.
> In this dull land, no smile-creating mirth
> Was heard—no comedy had ever birth.
> Rameau's sweet airs are utterly unknown,
> Talk but of dancing, and the people groan.
> The mangled hymns, indeed, of Israel's king
> Geneva chants, but never dares to sing;
> As if the pow'r, who rules the realms of light,
> In execrable verse could take delight:
> Their priests, a rigid, melancholy race
> Have stampt austerity on every face.
> Presumptuous Calvin here receiv'd his call,
> That vile interpreter of holy Paul.
> Here he maintain'd, that virtue's heav'nly food
> Helps not the Christian to his final good.
> Still the harsh doctrine preach his mongrel crew
> That God does all, and man has nought to do.[183]

Voltaire accused the pastors of cursing "the people in the name of God" and delighted in drawing a parallel between Catholic and Calvinist strategies for persecution: "Geneva mimics Rome, as monkeys men." Fortunately, the example of Covelle showed that contemporary manners had sufficiently developed to disdain historic dread of damnation.[184]

Voltaire also commented upon the political situation at Geneva in the later 1760s. While praising the moderation of the now aged Jacques-François Deluc, he stated that Geneva had been close to ruin because the représentants had become a democratic party in the state, allowing lessons to be gleaned from ancient and modern republics facing related threats:

> Geneva's sovereign and magnificent lords
> Are almost bound in slavery's rigid cords.
> In former times thus Athens sunk to shame,
> So fell the Tyrian and the Punic name.
> So Greece, who led her thousands to the fight,
> Became a desert, shocking to the fight.
> Thus Rome was taken in St. Peter's net
> Thus St. Marino was of late beset.[185]

Voltaire ended his poem on the optimistic note that a "golden age" was being revived at Geneva because "the people to their wits return again"; he was referring to the Edict of 11 March 1768 that resolved the constitutional disputations after two years, during which Geneva had been on the brink of civil war.[186] He took the opportunity to warn the Genevans against future troubles. He stated that the philosophic manners that would destroy Calvinism came from France and needed to be fostered at Geneva. This was necessary because fanatical Calvinism was the greatest danger to the republic. The fundamental message was that the stability of the republic remained in consequence a product of Genevan friendship with France.[187] During the troubles of the 1760s he had reminded the French diplomats several times that "the happiness of our little country of Geneva is in your hands."[188]

Voltaire's argument would have been appreciated at Versailles, which was taking an ever-growing interest in Geneva throughout the 1760s. This development paralleled the rise to prominence in French politics of César Gabriel de Choiseul, duc de Praslin, who was foreign minister between 1761 and 1766, and his cousin Etienne-François, duc de Choiseul, who served in most of the major offices of state until 1770. The duc de Praslin and the duc de Choiseul took a much firmer line against the représentants, a policy that was reiterated in diplomatic correspondence from 1765 onward. Charles Bonnet noted that France was becoming keenly involved in the city; the results of all elections at Geneva were immediately transmitted to Paris.[189] The French résident, the baron de Montpéroux, blamed Rousseau for the instabilities of Genevan political life, arguing that Rousseau's *Lettres écrites de la montagne* "attacks the religion of the pastors and the conduct of the magistrates, who are portrayed as tyrants."[190] Montpéroux informed the Council of Twenty-Five on 16 March 1765 that France would continue to guarantee the existing constitution at Geneva.[191] At the same time, the duc de Praslin informed Geneva's magistrates, via their ambassador Jean-Pierre Crommelin, that "You recognise the friendship of the King towards your republics and be assured you can rely upon this at all times."[192] The dispatches of the duc de Praslin to Montpéroux were made public, informing Genevans that "the king would not behold with a serene eye the violations of the mediation edict, and the overthrow of a compact intended to secure perpetually liberty and prosperity to Geneva."[193]

When Pierre-Michel Hennin was appointed to replace Montpéroux after the latter's death in 1765, he reminded the Genevans that for two centuries they had relied on France for peace, and he praised the city for having "joined simplicity and opulence, modesty and authority, and subordination and liberty."[194] He too was convinced that Rousseau lay behind all of the troubles of the city, being "the apple of discord," and wrote as much to the duc de Praslin, calling Rousseau "professor of democracy" and noting that the leaders of the représentants had been seduced by "the principles of the *Contrat social*."[195] Geneva was corrupt and factious, and France had to resolve the problem before civil war commenced.[196] French magistrates asked Jacques-François Deluc, "Is not peace and tranquillity preferable to all of these discussions? . . . you have too much sense not to recognise the problems that follow an excess of democracy."[197]

Deluc's leadership of the représentants, however, was giving way to a younger and more radical generation, including his son Jean-André Deluc. Jean-André was initially given training as a merchant but excelled in the natural and mathematical sciences. From 1754, with his brother Guillaume-Antoine, he studied the fossil record while exploring the Alps and the Jura mountains. By 1760 he was working on improvements to the thermometer and hygrometer, and soon after invented the portable barometer. At Geneva after 1765 he came to prominence through politics.

Dispute about Geneva's constitution continued between représentants and magistrates, who were now termed "négatifs" because they continued to defend the right of the Council of Twenty-Five to reject représentations. The latter were brought to the General Council by the bourgeois to determine the

magistrates' powers with respect to taxation and criminal law.[198] For the négatifs, as articulated in their combative *Lettres populaires*, Geneva was a mixed
state whose orders shared sovereignty, while the bourgeois wanted to turn the
city into a democracy, something suited only to semisavage states and which
made no sense in a rich and commercial city.[199] In their eyes, their opponents
had become pawns of Rousseau, who had not understood the nature of liberty
at Geneva and who dishonored Calvinism and the inviolable principle of societal subordination.[200] Overtures from Voltaire to make peace between the parties were rejected, and the authors of the *Lettres populaires* were publicly
thanked for expressing their views.[201] Rousseau's public quarrel with David
Hume was also cited as evidence of the madness of the représentant cause, the
foolish neuroticism of their mentor having been unmasked.[202] For the représentants Geneva was becoming a corrupt aristocracy and losing its independence,
like Denmark, whose parliament had voluntarily surrendered to royal absolutism in 1760. Geneva too might fall from a state of liberty to become an absolute
monarchy.[203] The right to reject représentations, the représentants argued, was
an innovation that proved such assertions, derived from misunderstanding the
term "approuvé" in the Médiation of 1738.[204]

The représentants then exercised what became known as the "right of new
election," by refusing all of the candidates presented for the leading magistracies during seven successive general councils, beginning in November 1765.
Stalemate was ultimately reached in January 1766, when the bourgeois in the
General Council once again refused all of the candidates proposed to the office
of syndic by the Council of Twenty-Five.[205] In such circumstances members of
the Council of Twenty-Five requested intervention by the guaranteeing powers.
On 14 December 1765 the Council of Twenty-Five had written to the cantons
of Bern and Zurich that "the republic was in so melancholy a situation as to be
unable to remedy her dissensions by herself." The ills of the state were ascribed
to a "secret council" organized by "a few popular leaders."[206] More significantly,
the French were contacted for aid on the grounds that the rebellious citizens
were seeking to establish "a pure democracy."[207] Antagonism resulted in prepa-
rations for a new mediation commencing in 1766. For the représentants, the
fact that the mediation was called for by the Council of Twenty-Five in a state
of pique against the sovereign acts of the General Council made it illegal. The
duc de Choiseul wanted to have the leaders of the représentants arrested and
exiled, a supportive vote in the General Council secured by any means necessary, and a visual warning given to the city by the movement of French troops
to Geneva's French border.[208] The secret goal of the résident Hennin was to
allow Genevans free trade with France through the Pays de Gex, as a prelude to

making them subjects of Louis XV. Writing to Voltaire, whom he believed shared such a goal, he stated that he was convinced that "where there is treasure, there also is the heart." The Genevans would gradually become French and thereby benefit from stability and prosperity.[209] Voltaire called Hennin "the angel of peace."[210]

Once more the mediation was to be led by France, again including mediators from Bern and Zurich. The plenipotentiaries gathered at Geneva in March 1766. The négatifs presented themselves as continuing Jean-Robert Tronchin's argument of the *Lettres écrites de la campagne* that Geneva's long-established balanced constitution relied upon particular elements of the state having particular powers ("droits & attributions particulières"), all of which guaranteed that the resulting policy would be synonymous with the public good. In challenging the droit négatif, the représentants were attempting to establish an "anarchic democracy." They had been led astray by Rousseau, who was a devotee of Thomas Hobbes's view that humans were involved in a war of all against all and "had no worse enemies than our superiors." Rousseau differed from Hobbes only in justifying the resulting necessary absolute sovereignty in the people as a whole rather than in a hereditary monarch. Both authors in consequence were advocates of despotism.[211] Geneva was rather a state like Venice, whose citizens and bourgeois formed a hereditary aristocracy, some of whom were elected to the highest offices of state.[212] This entailed "new laws" and a different form of government, and one opposed to the historic Edicts of 1568 and the Règlement of 1738. Change was necessary because of the national interest in commerce and peace.[213] The représentants argued that the mediation was illegal because the sovereign General Council had not agreed to it, but they nevertheless accepted the need to negotiate.[214] Early in 1766 they organized themselves into twelve clubs or *cercles*, each of which elected two members, who became the commissaries responsible for negotiation with the mediators and the magistrates.[215]

THE REPRÉSENTANTS AND THE CANTONS

Prior to their arrival at Geneva to join the mediation, the state of Zurich praised the Genevan magistrates' "sage moderation [and] patriotic and paternal intentions," and with the leaders of the delegation from Bern described the mediation as being necessary to reaffirm the Genevan constitution.[216] The leader of the French delegation, Pierre de Buisson, chevalier de Beauteville, drew up a peace plan in July 1766 that was supportive of the magistrates, who were called "moderate and paternal." Beauteville followed the advice of the

Bernese to remove the right of the General Council to reject candidates by the process of scrutiny called the *grabeau*, which was the basis for the policy of rejecting magisterial candidates that the représentants had adopted in 1765.[217] Beauteville made his position clear in writing to Rousseau that the latter was responsible for the ills of the city.[218] The peace plan itself condemned the "atrocious calumnies" directed against the magistrates by Rousseau's *Lettres écrites de la montagne*.[219] All opponents of magistracy, whether in Geneva or the cantons, he condemned as partisans of Rousseau.[220] Beauteville also intended the right to present représentations to be limited, advised the establishment of a tribunal dominated by magistrates to resolve future disputation, and further censored constitutional discussion.[221] Just prior to the peace plan, the French court had demanded the punishment of the twenty-four commissaries of the représentants for their injudicious reports of 24 June to the mediators.[222]

The peace proposal was published on 23 November 1766. The duc de Praslin warned the représentants that a rejection of the plan would be followed by a ban upon commerce between France and Geneva and the prevention of the movement of représentants into France. Voltaire was affected by the blockade and loudly complained in consequence.[223] This was after the threat was carried out by means of a cordon of soldiers at the frontier, after the General Council rejected the French "Règlement de pacification" on 15 December 1766. At the same time the person the French court held to be instigating représentant opposition to France, Toussaint-Pierre Lenieps, was taken to the Bastille; this act was conceived as a warning to the leaders at Geneva, and Lenieps's papers were reported as providing evidence of a représentant plot to undermine the Médiation of 1738.[224] During this time the représentants remained united in the face of acute opposition from the magistrates and from France.[225] The British government obtained evidence of a speech delivered by Hennin on 15 December 1766 to the twenty-four représentant deputies, reprimanding them and accusing them of seeking to overthrow the government at Geneva. All of them were forbidden to enter France on pain of the confiscation of their property, and told to compromise with the magistrates.[226] It was at the same time reported that, should peace not return, France would demand "the heads of nine commissaries," including Jean-André Deluc, François-Henri d'Ivernois, and Etienne Clavière.[227] In April 1767 the policy was reinforced by Praslin's decision to build a new commercial town and port to compete with Geneva at Versoix. Versoix was to be established as a free port enjoying religious toleration.[228] Many négatifs expressed surprise and horror at the loyalty of the people toward the leading représentants.[229]

The représentants rejected the Beauteville plan on the grounds that the General Council had a right to reject magisterial candidates for office, had a right to receive représentations, and could not rely on mediating powers for the resolution of internal discord.[230] In private they called the plan "abominable" for putting an end to the right to make représentations and in consequence any sense of political liberty, and referred to Beauteville as "the angel Gabriel."[231] Voltaire wrote that, in rejecting the pacification, the représentants had become more malign than Rousseau himself.[232] The représentants were accused of becoming anti-French.[233] This would be going too far. Jean-André Deluc traveled to Paris in October 1766 to plead their cause, in the hope of persuading Versailles that Beauteville's plan would not secure peace, and that a stable représentant Geneva would better suit France's interest in security and trade. Although the plan failed, Deluc continued to try to influence the French court. His correspondence with the banker Jacques Necker, soon to be appointed the Genevan ambassador at Paris (1768), is singularly revealing in this respect. Necker shared an interest in natural history with Jean-André Deluc, and both men were devout Calvinists. Deluc tried to convince Necker that the représentants would never be so foolish as to want to anger French ministers or to oppose French policy.[234] Necker was sympathetic to Deluc but at the same time warned that the damage to French relations done by Rousseau, Voltaire, and their followers meant that peace was likely to arrive only by the abandonment of the grabeau—the représentants could not alter the constitution without French support, and that would not be forthcoming in present circumstances.[235] Indeed, all Genevans who lived in Paris were warned that if Beauteville's plan was rejected by the General Council they would be forced to leave France.[236]

In the spring of 1766 a group of représentants was elected by the bourgeois political circles to be among twenty-four commissaries involved in the process of mediation. Jean-André Deluc, Etienne Clavière, Jacques Vieusseux, Gédéon Flournoy, and Théodore Rilliet began to lead the représentants.[237] Of Flournoy little is known. Vieusseux had been a prominent représentant and friend to Rousseau since the early 1760s, was renowned as a devout Calvinist and good citizen, and was related to Deluc, Clavière, and Rilliet by marriage.[238] Clavière had been born at Geneva in January 1735 to Jean-Jacques Clavière, a linen merchant originally from Dauphiné, and Marthe Louise Garnier, herself the daughter of a Genevan citizen, Jean-Louis Garnier. Clavière's mother was significant in being a devotee of Count Zinzendorf's Moravian Brethren, who sought to revivify Protestantism through pietism and who favored the union of Protestants on the basis of common tenets. The Moravians were necessarily critical of Lutheran and Calvinist orthodoxies.

Although he had been born into a prosperous family at Geneva, Clavière had second-order "bourgeois" status rather than being a "citizen," because his father only purchased bourgeois status for himself just after his son's birth. As a bourgeois, Clavière had full rights to exercise commerce in the city, was a member of the sovereign General Council, and could be elected to the executive Council of Two Hundred, but he could not serve in the highest magistracies of the state. Clavière's father had emigrated from France in the aftermath of Louis XIV's persecution of the Huguenot minority in the 1680s, and chose Geneva as a commercial entrepôt and safe haven for Protestant refugees. The younger Clavière was apprenticed to the Bavarian merchant firm of Christian-Erlangen and then worked in the trade and banking business part owned by his family, Cazenove, Clavière et Fils. This firm had interests in the British East India Company, a fact which often brought Clavière to Britain and led him to become fluent in English. He was successful in commerce from the first. He was also dedicated to political reform. After Jean-André Deluc's departure from Geneva, Clavière became the leader of the représentants, remaining in this position into the 1780s. It was said of Clavière, by the représentant pastor Esaïe Gasc, that "he loves liberty for the sake of liberty," a fact proven by the fact that, despite his wealth and personal happiness, after 1768 he continued to dedicate himself to politics. Jean-Pierre Bérenger, the historian of Geneva and leader of the natifs, equally identified Clavière as the most innovative political thinker among the représentants.[239]

Théodore Rilliet was of a prominent family, being the son of the citizen Louis Rilliet (1695–1755) and Jeanne Esther de Saussure (1708–1773). After studying at the Académie de Genève he became a lawyer in 1751 and subsequently became one of the représentants' most accomplished pamphleteers and the author of the manifesto, *Solution générale ou lettres à Monsieur Covelle le fils, citoyen de Genève* (1765). Clavière may have been involved in the writing of the text: he was cited in Voltaire's poem as a significant supporter of Covelle's cause. The policy of the *Solution générale* and other texts was to chart a history of magisterial tyranny and violations of the sovereignty of the General Council. Rilliet argued that the Consistory's attempt to force genuflection on Covelle was an instance of the magistrates using the church to oppress the people. Genuflection, he wrote, was a papal innovation at odds with core Christian teaching and an attempt to plant monarchical mores in Geneva's republican soil.[240] The magistrates had a mistaken view of the constitution and were attempting to turn Geneva into an oligarchy of the rich governed de facto by France.[241] Regarding the mediation, Rilliet and the other représentants argued that it was taking the role of the sovereign at Geneva, the General Council, in setting itself up as the highest authority in political affairs and in allowing the magistrates to behave like oriental despots.[242]

The strategy of the new generation was twofold. With regard to external policy, they turned to the cantons. In the winter of 1766, and more emphatically in the summer of 1767, Jean-André Deluc and Rilliet visited Bern and Zurich to "plead the cause of their compatriots." In the aftermath of the rejection of the Beauteville peace plan, the représentants were concerned that the guaranteeing powers would impose a settlement by force of arms; they carried with them a document stating that such an act would "wound the independence of the republic."[243] Measures continued to be taken to influence French policy, by means of Necker or the Genevan merchants at Paris. Little was expected, however, and the negotiations with the Swiss were conducted in secret; indeed, the représentants were paranoid about the response at Versailles should the full extent of their diplomatic maneuvers be revealed.[244] In fact the duc de Choiseul was fully apprised of représentant activities, having been told that Bernese councils included factions that were "Zurichois, anti-French, *représentants*, and followers of Rousseau," and that the party of "Rousseau and the *représentants* was particularly strong."[245] The représentants did not expect the cantons to oppose France openly. Although the chevalier de Beauteville was convinced that Zurich was wholly committed to the représentants, who in that city were supported by the British ambassador to the cantons, the sovereign councils in both cities remained pro-French.[246] The représentants hoped that the Bernese would persuade France to continue to negotiate and ideally remove the cordon around Geneva blocking commerce. They also expected the cantons to prevent France from crushing Geneva, in the event that the General Council continued to reject Beauteville's peace plans.[247] The représentants were of the opinion that only the cantons' willingness to slow down the process of mediation had saved them.[248] As the stalemate continued, the représentants sought to use claims about the loss of Swiss liberty to persuade the mediators from Bern and Zurich to counter French diplomacy, and thereby reaching a settlement that could be presented to the French as acceptable to the représentants as well as the less extreme négatifs. As Etienne Clavière wrote, "our cause is also that of all of the Swiss republics."[249] Attempts to involve the British and the Dutch came to nothing.[250]

The first step was to persuade the Bernese not to ratify Beauteville's peace plan. Arriving at Bern, Jean-André Deluc wrote, "It is impossible to provide an idea of the ignorance, even of those who are our supporters, about the key issues we face." The représentants were portrayed as seeking "a pure democracy" that was akin to "a state of anarchy."[251] Rilliet wrote that few recognized that "to pronounce against Geneva is to forge manacles for Switzerland," and in any case, "Those who are our friends are not the leaders."[252] To counter this Rilliet composed a list of reasons why the Swiss should reject Beauteville's peace plan. The first was that it reinforced the aristocratic nature of the Council of Twenty-Five, and in doing so would "increase the constancy and fortitude of the citizens in pursuing their unique goal, which is the recovery of their rights and their liberty." The second was that Genevan sovereignty, the essence of which was the right of the General Council to make legislation, was being impugned, the parallel being a challenge to the sovereignty of the Council of Two Hundred at Berne. Third, the peace plan, in replacing law with force, would lead to civil war. Fourth, it was necessary to show the Catholic king of France that the Protestant cantons valued their independence; otherwise, he would take advantage of their weakness at a future time. Finally, the représentants, in being willing to martyr themselves, deserved to be heard across Switzerland.[253] Partly because of the great strength of France in diplomatic terms, and the straightforward opposition of the Bernese to popular politics at Geneva, représentant diplomacy failed. The Bernese accepted the peace plan on 18 July 1767, despite being told that they were "imitating the despotism at Geneva." Instead they were sure that time would destroy the représentants' enthusiasm for virtue.[254]

At Zurich the représentants fared as badly. Rilliet reported that "the lack of knowledge [of Genevan affairs] is even more striking than it was at Bern." At Zurich there was a far greater fear of France and a sense of the risk that would be taken in opposing French policy. The représentants were several times advised to "trust France," on the grounds that as a state it was beneficent rather than ferocious.[255] Deluc wrote to his father Jacques-François that the basic fear across Switzerland was that the French could destroy their markets by banning trade through Geneva and at the same time erecting commercial towns on the model of Versoix.[256] In consequence, the state of Zurich followed Bern in supporting Beauteville. Rilliet wrote to Clavière that the response of the représentants to such setbacks had to be "to fortify our union."[257] Although their direct goal failed, the fact that the cantons took so long to come to a decision enabled the représentants "to acquaint Europe with their rights, the misfortunes they suffered, and those they were threatened with." The duc de Choiseul was reported as seeking to bring the twenty-four commissaries to Paris in manacles prior to their execution.[258]

The représentant strategy with respect to policy within Geneva was more successful. It rested on the continued espousal of moderation throughout 1767, while refusing to bow to French demands for a settlement favoring the magistracy.[259] As Clavière put it after the failure of negotiations with the Swiss, "In the name of God my dear Rilliet, be moderate."[260] Accordingly, the représentants, after the représentation of 16 October, which was later called "the master piece of the représentants," refused to give in to the négatifs or the mediators but rejected increasing moves among the populace toward violence and reiterated their willingness to negotiate a peaceful settlement.[261] Many of the more extreme négatifs abandoned Geneva during the long period of proposal and counterproposal, as Jean-Pierre Bérenger noted: "The project of conciliation has just been rejected, and the anger of a powerful king is directed against us, his ambassador has abandoned us, rich citizens and even magistrates have abandoned their country, as if daggers were being used against them, as if enemy soldiers were advancing to destroy us, astonishment is on their faces, fear in their heart, timidity and weakness yield bloody and awful pictures, and the courageous man is silent."[262]

Despite their outward unity the représentants were constantly discussing the form that popular government should take in the city. Some were happy simply to strengthen the bourgeois check upon the magistrates by maintaining the grabeau in the form of the "line of new election," which had allowed them to reject members of the Council of Twenty-Five on an annual basis. Others wanted the représentants to replace the magistrates through the election of the members of the smaller councils by the General Council. Clavière saw the election of magistrates as a natural right, derived from the ability of citizens to act in accordance with their consciences, and in consequence to be accepted as sacred in any settlement.[263] Jean-André Deluc prudently advocated a compromise entailing the removal of the grabeau and the maintenance of the droit négatif for new laws. At the same time the right of représentations would be maintained, as the Council of Sixty would judge représentations claiming that existing laws had been violated. The représentants were to be strengthened by giving the General Council a right to elect half of the members of the Council of Sixty.[264] Civil war was recognized by all parties to be close, with représentants such as d'Ivernois sending their families away from the city for their safety.[265]

By November 1767 the négatifs retained hope of winning out, advising the Venerable Company of Pastors to continue to pray for peace—but not for the plenipotentiaries of the guaranteeing powers, because their role was deemed finished.[266] When the représentants once again stood firm, negotiations began with the négatifs, with Jean-André Deluc, Vieusseux, and Clavière leading the former party. In the tortuous negotiations that followed for the next three months, the négatifs attempted several times to outmaneuver the représentants by making proposals, such as the election of a quarter of the Council of

Two Hundred by the General Council, intended to divide the représentant opposition and its leadership. The last attempt was made as late as 28 February 1768.[267] Leading négatifs continued to see Rousseau behind the unstable policy of attacking the institutions of magistracy.[268] From the other side, some représentants now advocated what was termed "pure democracy," entailing the election of over half of the Council of Two Hundred, a grabeau over all magisterial candidates, and increased salaries for office holders, so that the poor might serve as well as the rich. Above all they favored increasing the numbers of bourgeois by reducing the price of ascent to citizen status, and by annually making at least ten natifs freemen of the city.[269]

Fortunately for the représentants, Bern's leaders now advocated a revised peace settlement, and in a series of letters to the Council of Twenty-Five they advised continued negotiation.[270] An additional factor was the more active role played by prominent pastors such as Jacob Vernes, who marshaled the Venerable Company to promote renewed negotiation and a settlement acceptable to both sides.[271] The représentants remained divided between those who continued to see their role as being to check the magistrates constantly, by means of a grabeau over both the Council of Two Hundred and the Council of Twenty-Five, and those for whom it was vital to get the bourgeois class into government by means of the election of at least half of the Council of Two Hundred by the General Council. Théodore Rilliet and the young lawyer Jean-Louis de Lolme famously debated these options at the end of January 1768, after which the decision was taken that the représentants must henceforth share government with the magistrates.[272] As François d'Ivernois later wrote, "the cause was between aristocracy and democracy."[273]

Agreement was reached early in March and ratified on 11 March 1768. The bourgeois lost the right in the General Council to refuse to elect candidates put forward by the Council of Twenty-Five (the right of new election), but in return the General Council would elect half of the members of the Council of Two Hundred and also obtained a right to exclude four members of the Council of Twenty-Five annually. The Council of Twenty-Five retained the right to convoke the other councils, to elect half the Council of Two Hundred, and to make proposals to the General Council. In characteristically moderate Genevan fashion, these rules were to be gradually introduced over a period of five years.[274] Jean-André Deluc, in a speech on 11 March before the Town House to the populace and the magistrates, said a lasting peace had been established because unity had been restored to the republic. The Council of Twenty-Five then instructed all individuals in the republic to go to church and thank God for the new peace: "All the church bells rang, and the *représentants*, intermingled with the *négatifs*, went to give thanks to the supreme being, and to entreat his blessing on that happy day."[275]

The foreign mediators accepted the settlement despite their successive condemnations of représentant policy.[276] Former négatifs also accepted the settlement, although one of the negotiators for the magistracy, Gédéon Turrettini, recognized that, in giving the people a greater constitutional role, a new balance would have to be determined. He equally asserted that Geneva's future depended upon French policy and particularly on whether it remained directly antagonistic toward the représentants.[277] The great fear among the magistrates was that the relationship with France—"which has been for us for two centuries a friendly and beneficent power, and treats us [Genevans] in this beautiful kingdom as its own subjects"—would be lost.[278] Others lamented the remarkable unity of the représentants in the General Council and the fire that Rousseau was seen to have spread across the republic.[279] The Council of Twenty-Five thanked the duc de Choiseul for "securing the peace" on 14 March; in his reply he stated that he was pleased that peace had returned and would not look closely at the concessions made to the représentants, the implication being that these had been too great.[280]

ROUSSEAU AND THE REPRÉSENTANTS AFTER THE *LETTRES ÉCRITES DE LA MONTAGNE*

Rousseau's role in the new représentant politics of the later 1760s was complicated by his view of France. Within Geneva, supporters of the magistrates were afraid that he had such an influence over French ministers that he might be called upon to choose future mediators.[281] By contrast, Rousseau blamed "all my misfortunes" on a passage of the *Contrat social* that was conceived as a eulogy to the duc de Choiseul but which was read as a direct insult upon the minister.[282] Rousseau always accepted that French involvement at Geneva was inevitable. He called the act of mediation "a noble function."[283] The fact that his message for the représentants had become ambiguous was underscored in an exchange of letters with François-Henri d'Ivernois in early 1767. D'Ivernois wrote to inform him that after Lenieps had been taken to the Bastille—on the orders of the duc de Choiseul and because of his politics—his papers were found to contain Rousseau's plan "to reverse the constitution [of Geneva] and establish a pure democracy." Rousseau's reply was genuine shock that the représentants had not understood him. Did d'Ivernois know him so little and fail to recognize that in the *Contrat social* he "had never approved of democratic government"?[284]

D'Ivernois was at the same time seeking Rousseau's view of recent developments. Rousseau initially refused the bait, praising the courage of the représentants as historic, but cautioning, "This is the first time and the last time that I will have allowed myself to speak of your affairs since Thonon [meetings with the représentants in August 1764]."[285] In another letter he refused to comment on a political memoir sent by d'Ivernois, except for expressing a desire for peace between Geneva's parties.[286] It was only on 9 February 1768, in a letter to d'Ivernois but directed to the committee of leading représentants, that Rousseau gave his verdict.

Rousseau once more reiterated the view that Geneva's difficulties resulted from both parties. The Council of Twenty-Five tended toward "a harsh aristocracy," while représentant policy entailed "not the excess but the abuse of democracy." A body had to be established that would act as an intermediary authority. In Rousseau's eyes this had to be the Council of Two Hundred, but the problem was that at present it acted as the "slave of the Council of Twenty-Five." Rousseau had no faith in the représentant policy of using the grabeau to remove magisterial candidates; rejection by the assembled citizenry of magisterial candidates prior to the process of election he considered a practice akin to inquisition and likely to sow division. The grabeau ought to be abolished. He also denied that the key problem was the lack of power of the General Council. Rather, the relationship between the three councils that formed the government—the Council of Twenty-Five, the Council of Two Hundred, and the all-but-redundant Council of Sixty—had to be reworked. In short, aristocracy at Geneva had to be accepted as necessary and the aspiration made to establish "a mixed government . . . where the people are free without being masters, and where the magistrate commands without being tyrannical."[287]

Rousseau wanted the Council of Sixty to provide new candidates for magisterial positions whenever the General Council rejected those proposed by the Council of Twenty-Five. The Council of Sixty was to be elected by the General Council, and as such individuals would also be members of the Council of Two Hundred. Thereby a popular source of future magistrates would be established. Reviving the powers of the Council of Sixty was an idea that Rousseau ascribed to the mediators, and he praised them for it, although Jean-André Deluc had favored such a policy in 1766. Rousseau rejected the proposal of représentants to elect half of the Council of Two Hundred on the grounds that this would establish permanent divisions between the parties. Indirect election was a better policy for the people to embrace. He also wanted the General Council to abandon the right claimed by the représentants for it to judge représentations. This right properly belonged to the Council of Two Hundred.

As in the *Lettres écrites de la montagne*, Rousseau defended the magistrates' droit négatif. He opposed the foundations of représentant policy on the grounds that they were trying to turn a sovereign body into an arm of government. Pursuing such a line would make Geneva a democracy that would suffer the fate of Athens. But he wanted the représentants to compromise speedily, advising them, "make peace my friends, make peace." Even if it took a further generation for the représentant cause to triumph, it was better to capitulate than to become disunited or fall prey to civil war.[288]

In another letter of February 1767 Rousseau reminded François Coindet, then a clerk in Isaac Vernet's bank, of the représentants' distance from his views. He warned that Geneva was too commercial to be a democracy, with "too many rich people and where everyone is employed [by commerce]." Equally, an aristocratic Geneva "would not survive for twenty years without being depopulated and ruined." When agreement was reached, he was delighted with the compromise, on the grounds that he saw "subordination and confidence" restored; the veneration of magistrates was the essence of republican glory.[289] To Moultou he wrote how much he regretted being involved in Geneva's disputes, how little he was valued by the représentants, and how the latter's patriotic zeal would undo them. He had come to the conclusion that peace was more important than liberty in Geneva's case.[290] Ironically, his position was seen by some bourgeois to be near to that of Voltaire, who had also been appealed to as a mediator in Genevan affairs, a "protector of humanity" and an opponent of the "droit négatif oriental."[291] Moultou was of this opinion, writing to Voltaire a letter full of praise for Choiseul and sensible of the parties being unable to resolve their ongoing conflict: "We are still very much divided here. The council sincerely wishes for peace, but the citizens wish to impose terrible conditions; they are not satisfied with electing half the two hundred and the little council. They wish further to *grabeller* [scrutinize and if necessary reject candidates for] the two hundred every year. But when each citizen is the judge of his magistrates, it seems to me, sir, that no one will wish to be a magistrate; the role of citizen will be preferable. In truth, I do not know how it will all finish, but the manner in which the conflict is being carried on proves that nothing is expected from the guaranteeing powers."[292]

Rousseau's pacific advice was given at a time when his religious opinions remained controversial among the représentants. Jean-André Deluc was still being advised in 1765 that "it is necessary to agree that *Émile* and especially the *profession du Vicaire Savoyard* . . . could not be tolerated in any Christian community."[293] Deluc's mature position was that Rousseau was a theist who saw the goal of religion as the betterment of humanity; he "would have been a Christian if he had not had an excessive penchant for independency." This independency led him to question revelation, following the *Théorie de la terre*, the book by Georges-Louis Leclerc, comte de Buffon, that Rousseau believed had refuted Mosaic history. Buffon was often wrong, but Rousseau clung to his ideas and "unfortunately meditated upon these subjects in his celebrated works, the *Contrat social* and *Émile*, in which he attempted to establish the principles of morality independently of revelation."[294]

Négatifs continued to call Rousseau an advocate "of equality and pure democracy."[295] But it was hugely significant that Rousseau's politics began to draw ire from the new and more radical représentant generation. The final letters to d'Ivernois, Moultou, and Coindet of 1767 and 1768 damaged Rousseau's reputation. Hitherto some représentants described his ideas as "the basis for our conduct" and used writings such as the *Discours sur l'économie politique* to attack the magistrates.[296] It became common to describe Rousseau as someone for whom tranquility was more precious than liberty. The then young lawyer François d'Ivernois noted that Rousseau "sometimes carried too far his contempt for the rich." Although the *Lettres écrites de la montagne* amounted to a "masterly sketch," it "errs in circumstantial details, because [Rousseau] was not in possession of particular facts." D'Ivernois described the *Réponse aux Lettres écrites de la campagne*, to which his father had contributed, as the real inspiration for représentant policy, because it revealed the discrepancy between the historical constitutional edicts of Geneva and the copies manipulated by the Council of Twenty-Five.[297] It was noticeable that by April 1765 leading magistrates were describing the *Réponse* as the more dangerous book, in part because of its justification of periodic general councils and its more general reading of the history of Geneva as a progressively developing tyranny.[298] D'Ivernois traced Rousseau's apostasy to February 1768, when he had advised the représentants to yield to the patricians or leave their homeland. D'Ivernois's verdict was damning: "Unfortunate man! Instead of fanning the fire of discord among [his fellow citizens], an imputation he did not escape, he employed in his correspondence with [F.-H.] d'Ivernois all the arts of eloquence and friendship to persuade the représentants that tranquility was yet more precious than liberty, and that they ought to think themselves happy to purchase peace by any sacrifice."[299]

The représentants rejected Rousseau's politics because they had come to the conclusion that Geneva could become a more popular state at the same time as it remained commercial, domestically stable, and independent with regard to its more powerful neighbors. If Geneva had become an aristocratic tyranny, means had to be worked out for abolishing aristocracy and for moving the state toward a stable democracy. This was the clear premise of two of the most radical tracts published by the représentants in the late 1760s: the *Purification des trois points de droit souillés par un anonyme ou réponse à l'Examen des trois points de droit traités dans les Mémoires des Représentans du 19 mai et 16 octobre*, a virulent attack on Beauteville's peace plan, and *Réflexions politiques et critiques, par un citoyen représentant, sur le Projet d'arrangement*, which equally condemned négatifs' attempts to compromise with the représentants.[300] Their author was Jean-Louis de Lolme. De Lolme was born at Geneva into a family of citizens and studied law at the Collège de Genève. By the 1760s he had become a notary and soon after an advocate. The *Purification* accused the magistrates of going beyond oriental despotism in invoking "a monarchical spirit" to justify the sovereignty of the Council of Twenty-Five. In fact, de Lolme argued, the sovereign General Council could do what it liked, being the legislative power in the state, and having greater authority than any monarch, who was only the representative of the people; the General Council, limited by neither history nor the executive, was "sovereign, nation, and law." The magistrates were commissioners of the General Council and enjoyed a limited and short-term authority delegated to them by the collected body of the people.[301] De Lolme did not speculate about the means of maintaining a democratic Geneva, but this became the imperative political issue. The *Purification* was condemned by the magistrates, and de Lolme was banished from the city. He left with funds supplied by Clavière.[302]

Rousseau's work continued to inspire writers such as de Lolme, but his name and ideas were used selectively. Despite the message of abnegation in Rousseau's letters to François-Henri d'Ivernois of 1767 and 1768, the patriotic republican element of a final letter praising the March 1768 compromise was cited in later représentant writing: "You seek peace my worthy friend, and by uniting wisdom with courage you have taken the sole measures capable of overcoming force. Whatever the condition of men, we are always free when we know how to die."[303] Selective memory was equally evident in recollections of Rousseau. One associate wrote to Rousseau that his name had ceased to generate any passion in the city.[304] Jacques-Pierre Brissot, on meeting Jacob Vernes in 1782, noted that Vernes shed tears when recalling his friend Rousseau; no reference was made to the fact that the two had become enemies by 1763. At the same time Brissot noted that Vernes "was openly a democrat."[305] In fact the democratic, anti-French, and antiaristocratic elements of représentant thought had made Rousseau's ideas of little relevance. Such ideas clashed with the policy of the *Lettres écrites de la montagne*. The politics of compromise that Rousseau had always advised—which entailed trusting the magistrates to control the government—were increasingly abhorrent to self-professed democrats advocating the sovereignty of the General Council, and who in 1768 secured a sharing of power between représentants and négatifs. For such men Rousseau was not a republican reformer. The new questions were how to sustain a more democratic Geneva and whether such a state necessitated an altogether different policy of international relations. The latter led the représent-ants to speculate about the nature of Britain's empire and of British policy toward small states.

4

Geneva and Britain

PROTESTANT CONSPIRACY AT GENEVA

In the *Journal de Paris* of Wednesday, 26 June 1782, the Abbé Jean-Louis Giraud Soulavie wrote a short article describing "the plans of England for erecting our Southern Protestant Provinces into a Republic." Soulavie had come to public notice because of his *Histoire naturelle de la France méridionale*, which appeared in eight volumes between 1780 and 1784. The work attracted criticism within the Gallican church.[1] More especially, the *Histoire naturelle* was attacked by the Abbé Augustin Barruel, on the grounds that Soulavie's description of a fossil record shaped by different climates and terrain, rather than geographical locations in accordance with sacred history, questioned biblical truth.[2] But Soulavie continued his ascent in the church, becoming *vicaire general* at Châlons-sur-Marne in 1788. During the Revolution he embraced the civil constitution of the clergy and served the ministry of foreign affairs, becoming French résident at Geneva from June 1793 until September 1794. Spending a year in prison after the fall of Robespierre, Soulavie then abjured his revolutionary credentials, returned to Catholicism, and was reconciled with the Abbé Barruel, to whom he reputedly made a personal retraction.[3]

Soulavie continued to speculate on the origins of the Revolution and became convinced, in the final years of the century, that a Protestant plot fueled by British funds had brought down the Old Regime, finally succeeding where it had failed in previous centuries. Soulavie believed the key fact of the eighteenth century was the sometimes open but more often concealed Anglo-French conflict, which he likened to that of Rome against Carthage. In his *Historical and Political Memoirs of the Reign of Louis XVI* he traced "the secret war carried on between the French and English cabinets." It was here that he

exposed another perceived conspiracy, based on British support for "the anar-
chists at Geneva," who were employed to undermine the finances of Old
Regime France and ultimately to destroy the state.[4]

In the fifth volume of his *Historical and Political Memoirs*, Soulavie recalled
that his friend Benjamin Franklin, then the United States ambassador to Paris,
had recommended that he publish the details of the English plot, which was
deemed to have been ongoing for a hundred years from the 1620s, because "a
party had arisen in the heart of France inimical to the American war, and
Dr Franklin was of opinion that this publication would show them the necessity
of retaliating on England."[5] Soulavie showed Vergennes his work and was
praised for doing so.[6] The third volume of Soulavie's *Histoire naturelle de la
France méridionale* was the subject of the discussion with Franklin, who was
reportedly fascinated by the parallel between the rise and fall of the sea in different locations across the globe and related turbulence within "the moral
world." One continent, he stated to Soulavie, "becomes old, another rises into
youth and perfection" and "will in its turn correct the other." Similarly, "monarchies, by way of restoration, become republics; republics sink into monarchies." Franklin was thinking of events in North America, but he asked Soulavie,
"Who is the natural enemy you mention of the French monarchy that wished
to raise a protestant republic in the heart of your southern mountains?" The
review of Soulavie's volume in the royal propaganda sheet the *Courier de
l'Europe* had equally raised the question of "the state of the rebellion" by
Protestants against France.[7]

Soulavie went on to explain to Franklin that, although the French Protestants
were "now quiet and live peaceably," there were "protestants of another kind,"
either lowly in society and seeking change because of the burden of taxes, or
philosophers actively plotting revolution. The Catholic clergy were aware of
this dual challenge to France and "said officially to Louis XV, before his death,
that a revolution was preparing in the state, similar to the English one of 1688."
The first step of the planned revolution was to act against the first estate of the
clergy, and Soulavie stated that the eminent natural philosopher Georges-Louis
Leclerc, comte de Buffon, had "advised me [as a priest] to take care of myself"
as early as December 1778. Franklin replied that he was sure France "will long
resist the spirit of innovation that overturns governments" and that the
Protestants "would hardly expose their frail existence to the danger of a
sedition." Soulavie was far less optimistic. In somber terms he explained that
the Protestant plot was supported by Britain and that distinct means to
establish British supremacy had been developed since 1628, when an English
assault upon the Ile de Rhé had been defeated. Afterward Cromwell and then

William III had paid for emissaries, such as Pierre Jurieu, to make fanatic republicans in the Cevennes region and begin the war of the Camisards:

> In the memorable reign of the king you mention [Louis XIV], so devoted to the Jesuits, and so violent against the protestants, it was the chiefs of the latter party that England employed for the purpose of a revolt in the Cevennes. The prophet Jurieu, in 1689; the English emissaries in 1702; Cavalier, the leader of the Camisards in 1703; Ravanel in 1705; Dupont, four years afterwards, and Justet of Vals, received and distributed the sums set apart by England for encouraging the armed insurrections that ensued. The disturbances at Vernoux, in 1740, had the same origin; but, under Louis XIV, it was the insurrection and independence of republicans that was aimed at.[8]

Soulavie advised Franklin to read the *Année littéraire* to find evidence from the clergy in general, and the Archbishop of Paris in particular, "of the gradual decline of religion and the increase of a spirit of independence and republicanism."[9]

It was at Geneva that Soulavie identified "a universal dissent from all the doctrines of Europe." Rousseau was the source: "disliking all existing social institutions, [he] approved of none but the ideal government he had himself conceived and created in his *Social Contract,* a work which began to operate a revolution in the public mind." It was, oddly, stated to be the banker and magistrate Jacques Necker who "executed, as far as was in his power, the theories of his countryman Rousseau; and he organised in France all the revolutions attempted by England at Geneva."[10] The Genevan model of government was characterized by opposition to constitutional checks and balances. It equally lacked intermediary powers between political institutions capable of reconciling the opposed forces of the patricians and the citizens. Soulavie was convinced that the English had taken advantage of the popular party at Geneva and used it to engender revolt in this French sphere of Europe by "three times in the space of a century . . . paying its leaders" to foment revolt. The consequences by the last decade of the century were devastating for France:

> Unfortunately for the repose of surrounding governments, the Genevese, with their system founded in nature and democracy, diffused everywhere maxims tending to disorganise all established societies. Blotted from the list of military states, they possessed a tactic of opinions and a philosophical theory more dangerous and destructive than the canon of warlike nations. The whole of the eighteenth century passed at Geneva either in open revolutions or in intervals in which they were dreaded; and these alternate situations produced polemic writings, which, spread over Europe, contributed,

like the works of Montesquieu, Mably, and Voltaire, to corrupt our manners and national genius, to introduce into the greatest empire of Europe the frail constitution of Geneva, to establish it in France, as on the borders of the Leman lake, on the ruins of the priesthood, nobility, and monarchy, and to subject it to all kinds of dangers and conspiracies, like that of Geneva, the original model of all organised anarchy in government.[11]

Soulavie supplied a history of Geneva (in the years before 1789) in which a magisterial or patrician party was devoted to France, and a popular party of représentants followed Britain in seeking to remove French influence over the republic. The représentants were accused of seeking to destroy France's empire of influence and replace it with that of Britain. It was illustrative that the magistrates refused a request from George III at the beginning of his reign to send a minister to reside at Geneva on the grounds of a fear of antagonizing France.[12] The leaders of the party antagonistic to France's empire Soulavie identified as Etienne Clavière, Jacques-Antoine du Roveray, and François d'Ivernois. As agents of Britain and rabid democrats seeking to overturn monarchy, church, and aristocracy, Soulavie blamed the activities of these men at Geneva, Paris, and London between 1778 and 1792 for leading "the city of Geneva to its ruin."[13]

REVOLUTION AT GENEVA AS A MODEL FOR FRANCE

Soulavie was not the first writer during the final decades of the eighteenth century to link Geneva with the French Revolution. Earlier observers had focused on the conspiratorial element of the Genevan radical vision. In the 1780s the Genevan représentants were described as fools for seeking "to assimilate themselves to the republics of Athens and Rome: they will have difficulty in doing this because such times are no more. We can find today many Philips but few Lycurguses and Numas."[14] It later became commonplace to blame the Genevans for the Revolution. The French engineer Achille-Nicolas Isnard in 1789 warned that the modern Epicurean Jean-Jacques Rousseau who, like his ancient precursors, denied the truths of natural law, had formulated the principle that caused the separation of North America from Britain and the revolution at Geneva in 1782, and that was capable of "cutting France from the House of Bourbon."[15] The principle, formulated in the *Contrat social*, which Isnard considered the most dangerous book of the age, was that "the law is the act or expression of the general will." This principle could overturn states when the general will was deemed to derive solely from the sovereign people and when there was no executive constraint upon legislation, because legislative power emanated from the people gathered together in democratic assemblies.

In 1794 the Bernese politician and soldier François Rodolphe de Weiss expressed his agreement about the Genevan origins of the French Revolution: "[It was] from the nidus of Rousseaus, or Neckers, &c. proceeded every germ of revolution. Geneva, the most enlightened city in Europe, a city where public spirit has long been in unison with these new principles [of liberty and equality]. Geneva has incessantly been agitated with internal complaints and accusations." It was easy for Weiss to attack the Genevans as latter-day Spartans and as false republicans. The Spartans were "futile and irrelevant" because they had "kings, a scanty population, with helots for slaves, and history informs us they were far from happy, because they deviated too much from the ordinary course of nature."[16]

Still wilder descriptions of the activities of the Genevan radicals could be found in Abbé Augustin Barruel's *Mémoires,* describing the "fifth step of the conspiracy against kings: the democratic essay at Geneva": "All Europe is acquainted with the troubles which agitated Geneva from the year 1770 till 1782. The public prints were filled with accounts of the disordered state into which the constitution of Geneva had been thrown; but the public prints have been entirely silent as to the part which the Sophisters took in it, and which it will be the particular object of our Memoirs to reveal. We shall lay open those intrigues and secret artifices, by which they hoped to establish an absolute Democracy according to the system of Jean-Jacques Rousseau."[17] Barruel ascribed to Montesquieu and Rousseau the foundational ideas of the Genevan représentants but claimed that Voltaire had also "fallen into such democracy" in arguing that "civil government is the will of all, executed by one or many, by virtue of laws which all have enacted." Barruel argued that the physiocrat Pierre-Samuel Dupont de Nemours had supported the Genevan "leveling sect" in the popular journal *Ephémérides du citoyen,* and together they promoted the antimonarchical revolution that manifested itself in France "more efficaciously than the frantic rebels of Holbach's Club." It was no surprise that men such as Clavière "continued his revolutionary career at Paris."[18]

Soulavie's *History* appeared after these works became notorious, but he provided the most detailed argument that the Genevan représentants, said to be led by Du Roveray, Clavière, and d'Ivernois, were the authors of the extremism that destroyed the French monarchy and had also led to the Terror at Geneva in 1794. He repeated time and time again the claim that these Genevans were highly significant opponents of French conceptions of government and empire, in the pay of the British state. His interpretation of the revolution at Geneva in 1782 derived from the view that it was different from other civil commotions that had marred the city in the eighteenth century, because it was a direct and organized attack upon France. Soulavie argued that because the friends of the radicals at Geneva, Jean-André Deluc and Jean-Louis de Lolme, were already "in places of the utmost trust and confidence in England," there was direct evidence of a systematic plot that emanated from London against the interests of France. He claimed that the British government subsequently paid d'Ivernois, Clavière, and Du Roveray £50,000 in 1783 to foment revolution at Paris. The result, he believed, was a clear connection between the failed Genevan and successful French revolutions, both of which were founded on a desire to exterminate France as a major international power, to challenge Gallican Catholicism, and to transform states like France and Geneva into egalitarian Protestant states owing allegiance to Britain.

Some modern historians have been convinced by Soulavie's view, leading to the judgment that Geneva deserved particular attention as the "petit théâtre" of the French Revolution.[19] But this chapter charts British interest in Genevan politics in a less lurid way. More particularly, the chapter focuses upon the work of the first Genevan représentants who exiled themselves to Britain, Jean-Louis de Lolme and Jean-André Deluc. It reveals imaginative and cosmopolitan aspirations for relations between Britain and France, for the protection of small states, and for the development of pacific empires, rather than subversive plots for civil war in France coupled with British dominion in Europe.

BRITISH PERSPECTIVES ON GENEVA

In Britain, concern for Europe's small republics was necessarily tied to arguments about the proper extent of Britain's involvement with mainland European politics and about the impact of small states upon the intensifying economic, and sometimes military, competition between Britain and France. In his *Droit des gens* (1757), Emer de Vattel was calling for more direct British involvement in mainland Europe in response to what he called "the last war," which was that of the Austrian Succession, during which British regiments had opposed the French invasion of the Austrian Netherlands. It was also recognized during this war (appropriately termed "King George's War" domestically) that Britain would stand as the protector of Hanover and related German states. Prussian and British troops later asserted the combined interests of these states against France and Austria with remarkable effect during the Seven Years' War. Moving more directly against France on mainland Europe, and seeking to do so in the aftermath of war, was a different matter. Such a step would necessarily challenge British perceptions of their historic success as a state because of their distance from European power politics. It would also go directly against the sense of Britain as a seaborne empire first and foremost. In the case of Geneva, the step would have been still greater because the city republic was France's neighbor, was allied to France, and was accepted as being within France's historic sphere of influence. Accordingly, however much British authors supported Protestant union, a Protestant league of states, or wanted Britain to play a more active role in European politics on the grounds of extending liberty or justice, no author called for direct British intervention in Geneva. Nevertheless, there was a growing interest in events at Geneva, and recognition that this republic did have a role to play in Anglo-French relations. This becomes clear by studying the attitudes to Geneva among British politicians, diplomats, and commentators.

At the diplomatic level a pattern can be discerned that developed in tandem with the rise of British power. British ministers were neither interested in nor involved with the internal controversies at Geneva in the first decade of the eighteenth century. There was a flurry of activity in 1717, when members of James Francis Edward's Jacobite retinue were arrested in the city, but this exception proved the rule.[20] By the 1730s the sense of distance had perceptibly changed. Partly this was due to Geneva's position on any grand tour, and also to the fact that wealthy Englishmen had begun to purchase houses in the vicinity of the city.[21] British writers had also begun to comment on a state that surprised because of its rigid mores and distinctive national character, despite its evident military weakness:

> Geneva is a pretty town, but of no great extent. It is well fortified on all sides, and entertains a garrison of about seven hundred men, which, however, in case of an assault, would be found not near sufficient to man the walls. It is true that the little republic depends chiefly for its security on the mutual jealousy of the French king and the Duke of Savoy. The city is built on a rising ground in the middle of a fine plain, agreeably diversified with vineyards, meadows, and little villas. . . . As all public spectacles are forbidden, our amusements are few. These honest burghers lead a plain, uniform life, which, if it is not enlivened by many pleasures, is not ruffled by strong passions; a little commerce, a little love, and a very little gallantry, make up the business and ambition of the place. The whole town dines regularly at half an hour after twelve. About two they form themselves into parties, which they call societies, for cards, where, if a man is in an ill run of fortune, he may lose three or four shillings. This continues till six; and then all the little beau monde of Geneva appears either on the bastions of their fortifications or in a public walk which they call the Treille. The women simper at the men, and the men say silly things to the women, till half an hour after seven,

when every one returns to his own home to supper and to bed. The women (who are neither handsome nor ugly) dress disagreeably, though against their own inclination, for the mode is fixed by a reform of the commonwealth, which forbids them likewise to wear any gold or silver lace on their clothes. But that fashionable superfluity is indulged to strangers, because the inhabitants find their account in it.[22]

Diplomatic exchanges in the late 1730s were more directly about power relations. The British were concerned about French involvement at Geneva and the possibility that they might annex the state by taking advantage of the domestic unrest. Cardinal Fleury, then French foreign minister, took pains to reassure his British counterpart, the Duke of Newcastle, that France would respect the independence of Geneva and protect the state against Savoy.[23] By means of the sometime diplomat Luke Schaub, the British warned the French that they expected Swiss neutrality to be respected more generally, and would oppose unjustified favoritism toward the Catholic cantons in any negotiations concerning Switzerland or Geneva. Reports were received of the overweening behavior of the French during the Médiation at Geneva of 1738, but once again French diplomats informed the British minister that they trusted the resolution of the disorders at Geneva was satisfactory.[24] The syndics and councils wrote to James Waldegrave, the British ambassador at Paris, to thank him for his good work in reaching the settlement.[25] Despite such indirect activity, there was no sense that the British supported the radicals at Geneva, were seeking to counter the involvement of France within the city, or had visions of Geneva becoming part of the British sphere of influence. Indeed, Louis Lefort, one of the opponents of the magistrates in the 1730s, had accused the comte de Marsay, the British ambassador to the cantons, of encouraging Bern and Zurich to intervene directly in Geneva to support the magistrates and restore order. An apology was subsequently issued to the British, during a dispute in which French diplomats characteristically acted as go-betweens.[26]

In most respects little had changed by 1766. British ministers were equally concerned that France might annex Geneva by taking advantage of the uncertain civil situation. As in the 1730s, they warned the French not to do so via Charles Lennox, the British ambassador at Paris, and received the reply that the French would take offense at such an insinuation being raised directly, while being happy to refute it via private correspondence. The British minister Henry-Seymour Conway then took a decision to allow the French free reign, unless troops were moved toward Geneva.[27] When the French proposed to do exactly this in June 1766, prior warning was given to the British that the French were only concerned with restoring order and supporting their mediator, the chevalier de Beauteville. Significantly, the British were advised that if they became involved the result would be a victory for the "democrats at Geneva," the presumption being that neither large state would support such an outcome. Accordingly, and as the troops, although paid for by France, came from Bern, the British accepted French policy, and more specifically the advice to "trust Choiseul." Britain was informed once again that direct questioning would be ignored because Geneva was France's concern, but that in practice France would inform the British of what was happening in order to prevent diplomatic embarrassment.[28] In effect the policies of the two great states were identical. When the British learned that their chargé d'affaires Colonel Jean Pictet might use Britain's name in support of the représentant party he favored, he was brusquely ordered not to interfere in internal politics.[29]

What was different by 1766 was that the Genevans themselves had begun to petition the British to become more directly involved in the affairs of the city. Abraham Trembley, the renowned botanist, advised Charles Lennox that Geneva was on the brink of anarchy and requested British involvement to prevent this from happening.[30] Another change was that British observers began to call for a moral foreign policy defensive of liberty, envisaging Britain as the scourge of tyrants wherever found. The Scottish geologist James Hutton made an impassioned appeal along these lines to William Petty, 2nd Earl of Shelburne, who from July 1766 until October 1768 was serving in the ministry of William Pitt the Elder, 1st Earl of Chatham, as secretary of state for the Southern Department. Hutton expressed the view that Geneva was on the verge of ruin, was being dominated by France, could not trust the cantons to defend Genevan independence, and in consequence had only Britain to turn to for rescue:

> My neighbour's house, the finest house of its size in Europe is on fire, I beg your Lordship to send as many engines as you can to help extinguish it, and that your Lordship will pardon my thus breaking in upon you. . . . Your Lordship's noble and humane mind always a friend of legal liberty will value that virtuous people of Geneva whose beautiful state is on fire if I may use the term. . . . I am sorry that the Magistrates, who are most of them my good friends and whom I love and Honour have brought this French misery on their own Country. . . . I will only add the Swiss will never defend Geneva against France, only against Savoy for which they are more than a match, and want France to uphold them in the Pays de Vaud which they formerly conquered from Savoy and therefore will never disoblige France when France is at Peace with Savoy. My poor Heart will bless your Lordship & every friend of Geneva.[31]

Hutton went on to argue that it was a general principle of liberty "that no weak state in Europe shall be overturned by any strong power," adding that Britain's merchants did not want to lose Geneva's trade, and Britain did not want to see such a fortified city under French command.[32] Another appeal identified Shelburne as someone "known [for his] compassion for the oppressed assertors of their privileges and independence, in the ingenious, industrious, once flourishing protestant little republic of Geneva."[33] Pastor Antoine-Jacques Roustan, who was close to the leaders of the représentants, appealed to Britain's commercial interests in preventing France from becoming dominant across Switzerland.[34] Shelburne dined with the représentant Jean-Pierre Trembley, who wanted to negotiate with him, but it led to nothing.[35]

That the British favored the magistrates rather than the représentants was equally evident in the involvement of the Stanhope family, who resided at Geneva throughout the crises of the 1760s. Philip Stanhope, 2nd Earl Stanhope, had brought his family to Geneva in the early 1760s in the hope of having his son Philip's tuberculosis cured by Théodore Tronchin. When this failed, his son having died in 1763, they remained at Geneva for the good health of their second son, Charles, until 1774. From the first the Stanhopes were interested in Britain's relationship with Geneva. They disliked Colonel Pictet, and sought to bypass him on the grounds that he was too antagonistic toward the magistrates.[36] They also detested Rousseau as an extremist with dangerously radical and impractical politics.[37] Philip Stanhope was involved in the constitutional crisis of 1766–1768. In 1766 he was sending a copy of the *Edits de Genève* to his cousin, the prime minister William Pitt. He was also negotiating with Jean-Robert Tronchin, who remained procureur-général, to establish peace in the city. This was conducted in secret because of fear that, if the French became aware, there might be adverse consequences for members of the Tronchin family living at Paris.[38] By means of William Norton, the British ambassador to the cantons at Bern, Philip Stanhope then proposed to make Geneva a canton and sought to involve Pitt to this end.[39] His rationale to Pitt was that France was dominating the republic and that Britain needed to counter such a development. He stated that the twenty-four représentant commissioners supported his view, having seen other measures for pacification fail.[40] The key fact is that neither Pitt nor his minister Shelburne supported such an initiative, and they pursued the policy of allowing France to sort out Geneva's internal difficulties, as the French recognized.[41] Philip Stanhope was too anti-French for their liking, and dividing France from the cantons was too dangerous a suggestion for contemporary Anglo-French relations. By 1768 the British were convinced that France was not going to invade, and they allowed the mediation to proceed without further interference.[42] The more characteristic voice was that of the English Catholic priest and botanist John Turberville Needham, who wrote to his friend the négatif Charles Bonnet that he hoped the foreign mediators would add justice to the virtuous magisterial cause.[43]

Rousseau's fame, the celebrity of Voltaire's residence near Geneva, and growing British visitations increased the British public's interest in events at Geneva. In the 1760s, mirroring the diplomatic perspective, the main theme of public and private British commentary on Geneva was the extent of domestic unrest. Boswell summed up much of this in a humorous note to John Wilkes, on the latter's impending visit to the city: "At Geneva you will be very well received. The malcontents will flock around you, and borrow some of that fire which has blazed with such violence. As far as I can judge, the Geneva opposition is better founded than that in a certain great kingdom."[44] Rousseau was frequently blamed for fomenting the unrest. Thomas Gray's verdict on the *Lettres écrites de la montagne* was characteristic: "Excepting the *Contract Social*, it is the dullest performance he ever published. It is a weak attempt to separate the miracles from the morality of the Gospel: the latter (he would have you think) he believes, was sent from God, & the former he very explicitly takes for an imposture. . . . his intention in this is plainly to raise a tumult in the city, & to be revenged on the *Petit Conseil*, who condemned his writings to the flames."[45] David Hume seconded Gray's opinion.[46]

Equally commonplace was the expression of difference between the British constitution and that of Geneva. The view was frequently put forward that Britons were fortunate in being subjects of a mixed state rather than citizens of an anarchic democracy:

> The contrast between the liberty enjoyed by the British nation, and the arbitrary power under which so great a part of the world at present groans, is not only very striking, but of all the species of political liberty known, none is so truly desirable as that. The subjects of republics are generally governed with no small severity, and universally labour under the misery of the executive authority being lodged by turns in the hands of certain individuals who are naturally prone to tread too much on their fellows: In aristocratical republics the people are slaves, and, perhaps, of the worst species. But the executive part of government lying in a mixed monarchy in the hands of the king, and he possessing no other power but what is given by the people, this evil is at once prevented. And in whatever other points the companion is made, the superiority will be found to reside infinitely on the fide of the mixed monarchy, or the British constitution.[47]

It was significant that the figure of "a factious burgher of Geneva" became recognizable in political commentary. Lord Lyttleton derided Lord Camden as such for his support of North American liberties in a speech to the House of Lords. Lyttleton distinguished between republican government motivated by "that levelling principle, which pulls down every thing, and sets up nothing . . . which rises against all order and subordination," and the constitution of England, which "abhors all despotism . . . of one man, and the tyranny of the uncounted multitude." Freedom in Britain was, by contrast with that in more popular republics, "guarded and governed by law under the control and protection of the three powers of the state, king, lords, and commons, in parliament assembled."[48]

Charles Stanhope, later to become 3rd Earl Stanhope but at the time known as Lord Mahon, was distinctly un-British in having been brought up at Geneva, much more directly opposed to French involvement in the republic, and supportive of the représentant cause.[49] In 1771 Mahon was given bourgeois status, elected to the Council of Two Hundred, and made commander of the *tir de l'arc*, or company of archers.[50] As head of the archers, he opposed the Genevans visiting the theater, and in 1773, when the alterations to the constitution agreed to in 1768 were introduced, he favored the reelection of all the magistrates by the General Council. This would be an act of moderation and would also confirm the sovereignty of the latter body.[51] By this time there were substantial numbers of British persons within the city; Adam Ferguson noted that "we are a numerous colony of English amounting when all are reckoned to near a hundred."[52] Ferguson was shocked at the peace and quiet of the city when he visited in 1774 and was convinced that the turmoil was a thing of the past:

> The silence of politics here and in the Aristocratical Cantons of Switzerland is amazing: government does not think itself safe but by keeping out of sight. Notwithstanding the democratical dash which this little republic has lately received all deliberations are secret, elections never heard of till the day & then made in profound silence. Even the doors of the presbetery are shut, so that all idle expectations of being sometimes amused with republican debates are entirely disappointed. D'Alembert passed some weeks here a few years ago, chiefly at Voltaires, when some of the younger clergy in haste to show their enlarged views talked a little freely & he was idle enough to put in his that they are all Socinians. This raised a great ferment in the Church of Calvin that is but now in some measure appeased.[53]

During the following decade, public perceptions of the republic altered. Partly because of the views of well-connected individuals such as Mahon, because of continued travel between the countries, and above all because of a growing desire for Britain to develop a foreign policy defending Europe's oppressed, sympathy with the représentants was increasingly expressed. British diplomats in 1776 noted that Geneva was seeking to be included in the renewal of the Franco-Swiss alliance that was then being negotiated.[54] When unrest in the city in 1781 turned into revolution in 1782, the information relayed to the British public was perceptibly different from that supplied in the past. It focused on the union between the magistrates and the French court and generally portrayed the rebels as seekers after a liberty being denied them by the over-weening power of France.[55] By May 1782 reports were arriving from Turin of 6,000 French troops and 4,500 Sardinian soldiers marching toward Geneva, with the intention of restoring order and establishing a settlement guaranteed by these two powers, if necessary by massacre.[56] On 6 July 1782 it was reported that French, Sardinian, and Bernese troops had reinstated magistrates who had held their posts before the représentant uprising of 7 April, had poured eight hundred barrels of gunpowder into the Rhone, collected fourteen thousand armaments from the populace, imposed martial law, and forced those who had been granted bourgeois status since the revolution to return their liberty docu-ments. Provisions were said to be scarce, and half the trees had been cut down "under the pretence of protecting a freedom, which is now but an empty name."[57] According to the *British Magazine and Review*, nothing of relevance happened across Europe in December 1782 "except the total submission of Geneva to her new guardians."[58] Another observer lamented that "a greater part of Geneva, once so flourishing, now affords little better than the dreary representation of a desert."[59]

Individuals linked to Geneva, such as the lawyer Samuel Romilly, provided a portrait of Genevan sufferings in the press. He was asked by his brother-in-law Jean Roget to "fill the English papers with the reasons why a weak, innocent and oppressed people are being sacrificed to the pride, tyranny and injustice of the powers that surround them."[60] It was reported among British diplomats that King George III had been personally concerned about occurrences at Geneva. Moral opinion aside, what was especially noteworthy was that in allying with Savoy and in bringing Savoyard troops to France, the French foreign minister Vergennes was signaling that the old Franco-Swiss guarantee of Geneva's con-stitution was no longer required to justify intervention. The status quo was no longer to be maintained by France. Rather, Geneva had become a pawn in European power politics, whose future could be determined by larger powers acting together. France could bolster an alliance with Savoy by involving Geneva's historic enemy in the affairs of the city. Indeed, the fact that Bernese troops were involved, but neither mediators nor troops from Zurich, was significant. Acting without the support of Zurich, the coguarantor of Geneva's constitution, confirmed that France was willing to break historic treaties when carrying out its Geneva policy.

While British diplomats and statesmen were well aware of the shift in policy, and while England's newspapers endlessly commented upon the negative consequences of the alliance between France and Savoy, the European political situation precluded direct British involvement. In 1782 Britain was losing the war in the North American colonies, was heavily in debt, lambasted as an enemy to liberty, and widely seen to be falling behind France in the competition for international supremacy. Willoughby Bertie, the 4th Earl of Abingdon, attempted to involve the British after the représentant commissioners asked him for additional help on 10 June 1782. He ultimately reported that there was nothing the British could do because of their present situation, "rent by divisions at home, and surrounded by enemies abroad."[61]

Britain did act in the aftermath. It became a "matter of serious consideration whether anything or how much could be done for them [the exiles]." Negotiations were begun with François d'Ivernois to "secure a favourable reception for such families as were determined to quit Geneva, and not only a favourable reception but such positive encouragement & support as might reimburse their expenses, & lay the foundation of an establishment in this country."[62] Such activity occurred despite the complaints of the Genevan magistrates.[63]

When the exiles arrived in Ireland, there was a feeling that a blow had been struck against tyranny and also a point made against the French. Expectations were high that another Huguenot diaspora might do for the Irish economy what had been done for the English at the end of the seventeenth century. Similarly, France's economic power would be weakened with the decline of Geneva. Although the Genevans in Ireland were given permission to write their own constitution, there was no sense of adapting the ideas of the représentants for Britain in general. The British had become interested in the représentant exiles' cause, but few were interested in their political philosophy, with its democratic ideals for small states. In that sense, the intellectual engagement between the states remained one way. Since 1770 the représentants had, however, been evaluating Britain's constitutional arrangements, the history of the state, and its lessons for Europe's small republics. The reason was that new ideas were recognized to be required in the aftermath of the 1768 settlement, to prevent future French intervention should further domestic unrest at Geneva occur. The first Genevan représentant to formulate a full response to this question was Jean-Louis de Lolme.

DE LOLME AND THE HISTORY OF REPUBLICS

Jean-Louis de Lolme (1740–1806) was among the first Genevan représentants to abandon his place of birth for London, arriving in 1768 after his banishment. Why he chose London as his destination is uncertain. As has been noted,
there were close links between England and Geneva at this time. It is possible
that such links led de Lolme to Britain; his first book was dedicated to the Earl
of Abingdon, with whom he had become acquainted at Geneva.[64] Another possibility is that de Lolme was simply looking for the best market for a writer, the
profession he had determined upon rather than that of law, in which he had
been trained.[65] What is certain is that, as a committed reformer of a republican
constitution, he was keen to understand the working of the system deemed to
provide the greatest civil liberties in modern history. De Lolme's study of Britain
made his name across Europe, appearing as *Constitution d'Angleterre ou État
du gouvernement anglais, comparé avec la forme républicaine et avec les autres
monarchies de l'Europe* in Amsterdam in 1771.[66] The *Constitution d'Angleterre*
was hailed as a superior study of the working of the British constitution, worthy
of placement beside Montesquieu's eleventh book of *L'esprit des lois* (1748) and
William Blackstone's *Commentaries on the Laws of England* (1765–1769).[67] De
Lolme's first publication in English followed, the *Parallel between the English
Government and the former Government of Sweden* (1772), and in 1775 a revised
and expanded English edition of the *Constitution d'Angleterre* appeared in
London as *The Constitution of England or an Account of the English Government;
in which it is compared with the republican form of government and occasionally
with the other monarchies in Europe.* De Lolme continually added to his work,
and further editions in English appeared in 1777, 1781, and 1784, which as the
fourth edition incorporated the most extensive reworking of the text.

De Lolme's *Constitution of England* has never been read in the light of his
représentant politics. In the introduction to every edition, de Lolme stated that
"even the great disproportion between the republic of which I am a member
(and in which I formed my principles) and the British empire, has perhaps only
contributed to facilitate my political enquiries."[68] In the advertisement to the
revised third London edition of 1781, de Lolme acknowledged that he had
gained an insight into "the first real principles of governments" from being "late
a witness of the broils which had for some time prevailed in the republic in
which I was born, and of the revolution by which they were terminated." De
Lolme took seriously Montesquieu's comment that Britain was a republic hid-
ing beneath the form of a monarchy. De Lolme's intention in writing was in
large part to explain exactly what Montesquieu must have meant. In de Lolme's

view, Britain was distinguished as a state because of "the solidity of the power of the crown." The key fact was that "all the monarchs that ever existed" had required "regular forces at their constant command" to "maintain their ground against certain powerful subjects (or a combination of them)." The power of the British monarch was "equal to what has ever been related of the most absolute Roman emperors," despite having a guard of no "more than a few scores of men." Britain was unique because of the role of the nobility within the polity. This had also been the view of Montesquieu, who had claimed that Britain's noble class had been destroyed during the civil turbulence of the seventeenth century. But while Montesquieu drew the conclusion that contemporary Britain was less stable in consequence and might ultimately fall prey to an ambitious Caesar figure, de Lolme came to exactly the opposite conclusion. He also came to exactly the opposite verdict to Montesquieu on the potential stability and survival of republics. De Lolme remained a republican, but his book was intended to underline the fact that Britain was the only republic worth this name in the modern world. His commentary on Geneva, and historic republics more generally, served as a necessary background to the full statement of this radical argument.

De Lolme was clearly proud of his représentant heritage and argued that représentations by the people alone had saved Genevan liberty:

> This right of publicly discussing political Subjects, is alone a great advantage to a People who enjoy it; and if the Citizens of Geneva, for instance, have preserved their liberty better than the people have been able to do in the other Commonwealths of Switzerland, it is, I think, owing to the extensive right they possess of making public remonstrances to their Magistrates. To these remonstrances the Magistrates, for instance the Council of Twenty-five, to which they are usually made, are obliged to give an answer. If this answer does not satisfy the remonstrating Citizens, they take time, perhaps two or three weeks, to make a reply to it, which must also be answered; and the number of Citizens who go up with each new remonstrance increases, according as they are thought to have reason on their side. Thus, the remonstrances which were made some years ago, on account of the sentence against the celebrated M. Rousseau, and were delivered at first by only forty Citizens, were afterwards often accompanied by about nine hundred. This circumstance, together with the ceremony with which those remonstrances (or Representations, as they more commonly call them) are delivered, has rendered them a great check on the conduct of the Magistrates: they even have been still more useful to the Citizens of Geneva, as a preventative than as a remedy; and nothing is more likely to deter the Magistrates from

taking a step of any kind than the thought that it will give rise to a Representation.[69]

He went on to praise the settlement of 1768 at Geneva, noting that an uncommon spirit of union and perseverance had arisen and that the représentants had succeeded "in a great measure, to repair the injuries which they had been made to do to themselves for two hundred years and more."[70]

At the same time, de Lolme was vitriolic in his critique of Geneva's magistrates, portraying them as straightforwardly seeking to divest power from the citizenry and using ruses of a base kind to do so. The example he gave was of the decision of 1707 by the General Council to hold regular assemblies to assess the fundamentals of the constitution, which was repealed at the very first meeting in 1712. De Lolme claimed that the magistrates ensured that the citizens removed power from themselves by proposing a measure to abolish such assemblies and corruptly interpreting the votes of the populace as follows: "when a citizen said approbation, he was understood to approve the proposal of the magistrates; when he said rejection, he was understood to reject the periodical assemblies." Another example was drawn from the experience of the Médiation of 1738, when de Lolme claimed that liberty was lost because the magistrates slipped the word "approved" into the Règlement, enabling them to reject représentations prior to their consideration by the General Council. He also noted that the election of syndics was gradually restricted to the membership of the executive councils, further underlining the loss of liberty.[71]

De Lolme's judgment of Geneva's experience was not that it should serve as a model for free states, and that small republics ought to be forever challenging their magistrates and seeking to establish a democracy. Rather, he altogether rejected traditional republican practices for securing liberty, and historic claims about the necessary link between republican or democratic government and liberty itself. The latter claim was a general one, and de Lolme intended it to be devastating. Much of the *Constitution d'Angleterre* in consequence was concerned with the history of republics, with the intention of revealing the limited extent to which they could be described as free states or as models revealing lessons for the defense of liberty. De Lolme stated that there was only one kind of liberty: "private liberty," of the greatest importance as it secured the protection of the individual from abuse: "Private liberty, according to the division of the English lawyers, consists first, of the right of property, that is, of the right of enjoying exclusively the gifts of fortune, and all the various fruits of one's industry; secondly, of the right of personal security; thirdly, of the locomotive faculty, taking the word liberty in its more confined sense."[72]

De Lolme argued that the great mistake in the history of thinking about politics was that there was another kind of liberty, public liberty, synonymous with an individual voting on laws for himself, and more generally participating directly in the formulation of legislation for the state. In a series of paragraphs that were among the most important in his book, de Lolme made a mockery of and refuted such a claim:

> What then is Liberty? Liberty, I would answer, so far as it is possible for it to exist in a Society of Beings whose interests are almost perpetually opposed to each other, consists in this, that, every Man, while he respects the persons of others, and allows them quietly to enjoy the produce of their industry, be certain himself likewise to enjoy the produce of his own industry, and that his person be also secure. But to contribute by one's suffrage to procure these advantages to the Community, to have a share in establishing that order, that general arrangement of things, by means of which an individual, lost as it were in the crowd, is effectually protected, to lay down the rules to be observed by those who, being invested with a considerable power, are charged with the defence of individuals, and provide that they should never transgress them, these are functions, are acts of Government, but not constituent parts of Liberty.
>
> To express the whole in two words: To concur by one's suffrage in enacting laws, is to enjoy a share, whatever it may be, of Power: to live in a state where the laws are equal for all, and sure to be executed (whatever may be the means by which these advantages are attained) is to be free.
>
> But are those writers in the right? A Man who contributes by his vote to the passing of a law, has himself made the law; in obeying it, he obeys himself, he therefore is free. A play on words, and nothing more. The individual who has voted in a popular legislative Assembly, has not made the law that has passed in it; he has only contributed, or seemed to contribute, towards enacting it, for his thousandth, or even ten thousandth share: he has had no opportunity of making his objections to the proposed law, or of canvassing it, or of proposing restrictions to it, and he has only been allowed to express his assent, or dissent. When a law is passed agreeably to his vote, it is not as a consequence of this his vote that his will happens to take place; it is because a number of other Men have accidentally thrown themselves on the same side with him: when a law contrary to his intentions is enacted, he must nevertheless submit to it.[73]

Numerous reasons could be given why directly voting or participating in politics was not identical with the express will of an individual. Honesty had to be presumed, along with being well informed and able to express one's opinions, the fairness of the calculation of votes, and an outcome concordant with the views of individuals whose opinions had become collective. In practice the people had neither the leisure to defend themselves nor sufficient understanding and abilities. As a body, "the multitude, in consequence of their being a multitude, are incapable of coming to any mature resolution."[74] Popular assemblies did not reason. Rather, they were prey to the ambitious, the domineering, and the cunning. When the people give a majority vote, "it is finally proclaimed as the general will of all; and it is at bottom nothing more than the effect of the artifices of a few designing men, who are exulting among themselves."[75] De Lolme concluded that "laws would be wiser, and more likely to procure the advantage of all, if they were to be made by drawing lots, or casting dice, than by the suffrages of a multitude."[76] For such reasons de Lolme described popular participation in legislation as "acts of government, but not constituent parts of liberty."

De Lolme's stated opponent was Rousseau. The philosopher was taken to task for having "cried up the governments of Sparta and Rome, as the only ones fit for us to imitate." Assembling the people "was an illusory ceremony," as the history of every republic revealed that it was "the few who really governed."[77] Rousseau had been misled because he had ignored a fact evident in the history of every republic: that in trusting to magistrates who then formed an aristocracy, all republics became tyrannies. They ultimately collapsed because the magisterial aristocracy succeeded in permanently removing popular liberty, or because the people in rebelling replaced the aristocrats with kings: "If we can turn our eyes on all the states that ever were free, we shall see that the people ever turning their jealousy, as it was natural, against the executive power, but never thinking of the means of limiting it, so happily prevalent in England, never employed any other expedients beside the obvious one of trusting that power to magistrates, whom they appointed annually, and these magistrates sooner or later would rebel against the people and take their sovereignty."[78]

When a state was small and poor there was a possibility of survival as a free state because the ambition of the magistrates would be limited. Equally, republican valor and patriotism, evident when a republic was in the process of becoming an empire, could delay aristocratic dominion. But the day always arose "when the legislature is badly informed and the magistrates can promote their private views easily, they accumulate honours, and become masters while the people do not realise what has happened." Either the aristocrats won out or "the people at length succeed in forming somewhere a centre of union," appointing a popular leader who presented himself as a protector of liberty before betraying his supporters: "Power produces its wonted effects; and the protector becomes a tyrant."[79] Proof lay in "what everyone knows" of the Athenian tyrants Pisistratus and Megacles; of Gaius Marius and Lucius Cornelius Sulla, both popular generals at Rome who became tyrants; and of Julius Caesar and Gnaeus Pompeius Magnus, who initiated the civil war that led to Caesar's dominion over the Roman Senate. Machiavelli's *History of Florence* (1525) was then cited as revealing that aristocratic factions always undermined republican liberty and the public good in the modern world, just as it had in antiquity.[80]

De Lolme was convinced that power within republics could never be limited over time, and that aristocracies would always arise to dominate. This was "the necessary consequence of the communicability of power, a circumstance essentially inherent in the republican form of government, it is impossible for it ever to be restrained within certain rules." Those who were called upon to defend republican liberty always aimed higher.[81] This was clear from the history of the reputedly most democratic state, Athens: "And in Athens itself, which is the only one of the ancient Commonwealths in which the people seem to have enjoyed any degree of real liberty, we see the Magistrates proceed nearly in the same manner as they now do among the Turks: and I think no other proof needs to be given than the story of that Barber in the Piraeus [from Plutarch's *Life of Nicias*], who having spread about the Town the news of the overthrow of the Athenians in Sicily, which he had heard from a stranger who had stopped at his shop, was put to the torture, by the command of the Archons, because he could not tell the name of his author."[82]

At Rome, de Lolme argued, it was not luxury that had destroyed the republic but the fact that the executive and supreme power resided in the Senate, a body which had always dominated the people. Rome had always served "the ambition and avarice of a few."[83] The lesson was that "it is a contradiction, that the people should act, and at the same time retain any real power." If the people did retain power they became "the clients of a certain number of patrons."[84] Proof that democracy should never be embraced was, according to de Lolme, provided by England's experience during the Interregnum of 1649–1660. Power simply shifted in the name of the people from Parliament to Protector to bodies of soldiers, while more general subjection increased: "An attempt to establish liberty in a great nation, by making the people interfere in the common business of government, is, of all attempts, the most chimerical: that the authority of all, with which men are amused, is, in reality no more than the authority of a few powerful individuals, who divide the republic among themselves."[85]

Democracy thus was a false form of government. The people never had real power but always existed in "but a disguised, and the worst of aristocracies."[86]

Rousseau had been mistaken about British liberty, having been misled by his study of the history of Rome: "For a Man to decide that a State with whose Government and interior administration he is unacquainted, is a State in which the People are slaves, are nothing, merely because the Comitia [the Roman assemblies that enjoyed the legislative power] of ancient Rome are no longer to be met with in it, is a somewhat precipitate decision."[87] With regard to the représentants at Geneva, it was an illusion to think that a lasting compromise could be established between the magistrates and the citizens. Like Rousseau, de Lolme accepted that it was "useful and perhaps even necessary" to have an executive who proposed laws for the assembled people to accept or reject. This was stated to have been the case in the "first times of the Roman republic, at Venice and at Bern, and at Geneva." The problem was that it also caused an enmity to develop between the legislature and the executive, which always resulted in domestic upheaval and ultimately in changing the state's form of government.[88] Britain was fortunate in having a system whereby the peoples' representatives proposed legislation in the House of Commons.

THE HISTORY OF EUROPEAN MONARCHY

Just as de Lolme was fascinated particularly by Roman history as exemplifying the nature of republican government, in France he found the exemplar of European monarchy. His argument once more was that Britain was altogether different and superior from the perspective of liberty and order. Gallic monarchy, de Lolme claimed, had first been established in the aftermath of the barbarian invasions of the Roman Empire. At this time monarchies were democratic. The German nations that conquered Roman Gaul were led by princes who "had no other title to their power but their own valour and the free election of the people." Their followers were "companions in conquest." After the spoils of war were divided, kings continued in the main to be elected. This was certainly the case in France, de Lolme argued, drawing upon the authority of François Hotman's *Franco-Gallia*, until Hugh Capet "established the hereditaryship of fiefs as a general principle."[89] In doing so "the lords who gave their suffrages to Hugh Capet forgot not their ambition." Rather, they became independent, refusing royal jurisdiction and exercising a right to wage war. This meant that the Capetian kings enjoyed only "a nominal superiority over the number of sovereigns who then swarmed in France." In consequence "the lords were everything. And the bulk of the nation were accounted nothing." Although revolts occurred as the people were "wearied out by sufferings and rendered desperate by oppression," these were always crushed. The people were "trained to obedience," and "the spirit of union was lost, or rather had never existed." When the provinces of France gradually came under the authority of the crown, the term "re-union" was employed to signify "immediate dependence." Reunion became "a yoke of subjection."

De Lolme's view was that in the majority of European states the existence of an active and powerful nobility prevented the people from enjoying true liberty. France was characteristic in that the nobility was so pervasive that the people looked to regal power for solutions to the problems of the state, and in consequence gradually saw representative assemblies decline. In France the only bodies that were left were the *parlements*, which de Lolme considered "too dangerous a body of nobles" and capable of expressing only the interests of this class.[90] Spain had like France been divided into regions and then relied upon royal power for reunion. As in France the people had come to be dominated by grandees and ecclesiastics. Representation had been sacrificed to a desire to reduce the overweening power of the nobility.[91] Germany was different because of the emergence of an elective monarchy that was dependent on the nobility. This prevented the kind of reunion prevalent elsewhere, and thereby prevented Germany from becoming an empire. The authority of the Holy Roman emperor remained feudal in consequence. Accordingly, Europe could be divided into states where "feudal tyranny" remained and where "a more regular kind of despotism" had developed.[92]

De Lolme arrived at a judgment that the excessive power of noble classes undermined liberty and order in republican states and in monarchies. They were the reason that Europe had arrived at an age of absolute monarchy, which was always an enemy to liberty. De Lolme paid particular attention to Sweden, because this state had recently undergone a revolution that saw the replacement of mixed government with absolute monarchy. Sweden fascinated British observers because of the widespread and worried expectation that a similar process would occur in the most prominent mixed state. De Lolme's first book written in English appeared as *A parallel between the English constitution and the former government of Sweden* in 1772, and its findings were incorporated in the English editions of the *Constitution d'Angleterre* from 1775.

Against the majority of observers, de Lolme's view was that liberty was lost in Sweden because the monarchy was too weak, rather than because it was aggrandizing and overpowerful. The fundamental problem was the excessive power of a Senate that convoked and controlled the more popular element of the constitution: the estates of the realm. The Swedish Senate had authority over peace, war, and taxes. Its members owned much of the landed property of the state and were able to use their influence over the clergy to limit the power of the burghers who were elected to the estates from the cities. This "immense preponderance" of the nobility created a government that was "merely aristocratical."[93]

Rather than drawing parallels between Britain and Sweden, de Lolme argued that the real parallel lay with Europe's monarchies and republics in which a noble class was overpowerful or had historically reduced or removed the rights of the people. Where the nobles held sway, government became a "petty tyranny," and Sweden had become a state farcically governed by a corrupt aristocracy, like Venice and Genoa.[94] Rome and France, the greatest of republics and the greatest of modern monarchies, both harbored the same fault. Sweden was following a European-wide trend in experiencing a contest between nobles and monarch, in which the latter emerged victorious and in which the sufferers were the people: "Hence the endless revolutions of the Greek and Sicilian Republics: the perpetual uneasiness of the Roman people, and the continual terrors of the Senate. Hence the facility with which the kings of France have established their uncontrolled authority. Hence the revolution that, a century since, threw all the government of Denmark into the hands of the king. Hence the late revolution in Sweden."[95]

De Lolme was certain that the "current trend" was for "dominant kings" and that Sweden would follow France and reduce its *parlements* to impotence. Equally like France, Europe's states would veer between "an uncontrolled king and dominant nobles."[96] Sweden had had an opportunity to become a state like Britain, de Lolme argued, in 1720, but it opted to give too much power to the nobles and too little legal protection to the people. In doing so Sweden moved to the commonplace trajectory of national European experience. Britain was different. The nobility in this state were fellow subjects, and the representatives of the people proposed laws. Union was established by the power and majesty of the crown. The people were the most patriotic in the history of the world, de Lolme maintained, enjoying both the greatest liberty in history and the most order.[97] He advised Hume not to seek the perfect commonwealth anywhere but at home. All other states bore the defect of a noble class that could arise and destroy the state. In failing to recognize this, Hume's work was flawed.

De Lolme saw religion as an important factor in European history, but it was insignificant compared to the kind of constitutional rules that determined the operation of governments and the balance of social power that they expressed. Accordingly he claimed that the Protestant religion "brought with it more freedom and toleration." He opposed Catholicism "not because it tended to establish in England the doctrines of transubstantiation and purgatory, doctrines in themselves of no political moment, but because the unlimited power of the sovereign had always been made one of its principal tenets."[98] Anglicanism was the best of Christian denominations not for its doctrinal or liturgical elements but because it was an exact representation of the kind of mixed government that had developed in England, in the sense that the church assembled acted like a parliament but was dependent upon the crown; the king was head of the church but "can neither alter the established religion, or call individuals to an account for their religious opinions."[99]

When English monarchs moved against the national model, with respect either to the church or to the state, they were acting in a "European" fashion. De Lolme's perception of the Tudors was of a family seeking to impose continental practices upon an alien soil. Charles I had equally been a European in seeking to promote absolutism. Consequently the events of the seventeenth century were "the effects of particular circumstances" derived from the effects of established European prejudices that "could not be shaken off but by a kind of general convulsion."[100] The victory of Parliament and the reestablishment of limited monarchy made Britain's constitution in the eighteenth century "the only constitution which is fit for a great state and a free people; I mean that in which a chosen number deliberate, and a single hand executes; but in which, at the same time, the public satisfaction is rendered, by the general relation and arrangement of things, a necessary condition of the duration of government."[101]

The British alone had learned how to separate power and liberty.[102] How they had managed to do so was the central message of the *Constitution d'Angleterre*.

BRITAIN AS A MODERN REPUBLIC

In the *Constitution d'Angleterre* de Lolme sought to explain "why, of two neighbouring nations, situated almost under the same climate, and having one common origin, the one has attained the summit of liberty, the other has gradually sunk under an absolute monarchy."[103] Liberty could be seen to be all but dead within France by the fact that at Saint-Maur on 29 October 1465, Louis XI of France had shared his power with the princes and peers of France yet "not a word was inserted in favour of the people."[104] In short, by the fifteenth century France was a tyranny. By contrast, de Lolme developed the argument that liberty in Britain was an unintended consequence of the importation of French despotism. Britain's distinctive history centered upon the role of the nobility within the state. De Lolme traced this to the history of England. The key event was the Norman Conquest: "If the conquest had never taken place, which, by an immense as well as unusual power on the head of the feudal system, compelled the nobility to contract a lasting and sincere union with the people, it is very probable that the English government would at this day be the same as that which long prevailed in Scotland (where the king and nobles jointly, or by turns, engrossed the whole power of the state), the same as in Sweden, the same as in Denmark, countries whence the Anglo-Saxons came."[105]

While feudal government across the continent of Europe had been established "through a long series of slow successive events," in England it was "established by dint of arms, and all at once." William of Normandy had divided England into military fiefs controlled by the crown, taxed as a he saw fit, and by means of the Aula Regis tribunal, which he presided over, "kept the first noblemen in the kingdom under the same control as the meanest subject."[106] The great irony of English history was that it was the seemingly unlimited power of the king that made England free, "because it was this very excess that gave rise to the spirit of union and of concerted resistance."[107] The king had "crushed at pleasure the most powerful barons in the realm." Only by "close and numerous confederacies" had the nation learned to resist monarchical tyranny. This had forced a noble class that otherwise would have remained self-serving and tyrannical to become patriotic. The lesson of the conquest was that power "is nothing more than the right of the strongest, and may be repressed by the exertion of a similar right." This meant that "the principle of primeval equality became everywhere diffused and established. A sacred principle, which neither injustice nor ambition can erase; which exists in every breast, and, to exert itself, requires only to be awakened among the numerous and oppressed classes of mankind. . . . The lord, the vassal, the inferior vassal, all united. They even implored the assistance of the peasants and cottagers; and the haughty aversion with which on the continent the nobility repaid the industrious hands that fed them, was, in England, compelled to yield to the pressing necessity of setting bounds to the royal authority."[108] This was the product of equal subordination before the king. The sheer power of the Norman kings caused the nobility and the people to become "partners of public liberty." The conquest equally ensured that England "was not like France, an aggregation of a number of different sovereignties: it formed but one state, and acknowledged but one master, one general title."[109]

As the people insisted that "every individual should be entitled to the protection of the law," laws intended to constrain the crown ended up limiting the powers of the nobility. This came to pass after weaker kings, from Henry I onward, recognized that their authority derived from "gaining the satisfaction of his subjects." Henry I abolished the worst of the taxes upon the poor. Under Henry II, trial by jury was established. The Magna Carta under John enshrined equality under the law. Edward I was "the English Justinian" who, in order to raise subsidies, invited towns and boroughs to send representatives to Parliament. This meant that the king was not so dependent upon a small body of magistrates, but it also led to the establishment of a right to consent to taxes (by the statute *de tallagio non concedendo*), which, with the Magna Carta, de Lolme said "forms the basis of the English constitution."[110] As a result, when the first two Stuart kings acted like Tiberius against the Roman Senate, Parliament was able to continue to control subsidies and stand firm. It was the pattern set in medieval times which ensured that the Petition of Right condemned Charles I's raising of taxes without parliamentary approval and confirmed the right of parliamentary consent to subsidies of any kind.[111] In 1689 habeas corpus and a royal oath against standing armies in peacetime were enshrined, taxes without parliamentary consent were declared illegal, all subjects were allowed to petition the king through the Bill of Rights, and the liberty of the press became "the keystone . . . to the arch." With regard to liberty of the press, de Lolme argued that this was a better means of preventing the abuse of authority or the corruption of manners than any form of public censorship. He claimed that Britain's refusal to contemplate a censorial tribunal was wise, despite such an institution being popular in so-called free states, being defended by Montesquieu and by Rousseau, and of course being the prerogative of the Consistory at Geneva.[112] Overall, Britain's peculiar constitution was a development of ancient principles established in the aftermath of the conquest.[113]

The fundamental principle from which the uniqueness of Britain's modern constitution derived was giving legislative power to Parliament: "The basis of the English constitution, the capital principle on which all others depend, is, that the legislative power belongs to parliament alone; that is to say, the power of establishing laws, and of abrogating, changing, or explaining them."[114] The major annual legislative act was agreement to the proposals for the public purse put forward by the ministers of the monarchy. Money bills were the concern of the House of Commons, making this body superior to the House of Lords. More significantly, having the power to limit the crown's ability to raise funds made the monarch a real executive power, his or her actions being constrained to the execution of the law. Such a right was "the ultimate and lawful resource against the violences of power."[115] Furthermore, its result was that a British monarch acting in an executive capacity "is no more than a magistrate."[116] A monarch could bestow a place but not pay a salary, could declare war but not carry it on, could coin money but not alter the standard, could pardon individuals but was unable to exempt them from paying compensation to their victims.[117] "In a word, the royal prerogative, destitute as it is of the power of imposing taxes, is like a vast body, which cannot of itself accomplish its motions; or, if you please, it is like a ship completely equipped, but from which the parliament can at pleasure draw off the water, and leave it aground, — and also set it afloat again, by granting subsidies."[118]

In limiting the power of the crown, Britons acted like a number of peoples who had sought liberty in history. The great difference was that Britain had become and remained a free state by not becoming a republic. De Lolme's most controversial and challenging argument for contemporaries was that British liberty derived from the office of the crown. The stability and success of the state was equally dependent upon the figure of the monarch: "By making one great, one very great man in the state, has an effectual check been put to the pretensions of those who otherwise would strive to become such; and disorders have been prevented, which, in all republics ever brought on the ruin of liberty, and, before it was lost, obstructed the enjoyment of it."[119] While fellow free states were undone by the people falling prey to generals, were beguiled by dictators, or collapsed internally because of the ambition of their magistrates, British monarchs prevented such disorders by their very majesty: "By diminishing the power, or rather actual exercise of the power of the people, and making them share in the legislative only by their representatives, the irresistible violence had been avoided of those numerous and general assemblies, which, on whatever side they throw their weight, bear down upon every thing. Besides, as the power of the people, when they have any kind of power, and know how to use it, is at all times really formidable, the constitution has set a counterpoise to it; and the royal authority is this counterpoise."[120]

The delicate balance that had been established between the monarch and the people gave the crown the right to dismiss legislative assemblies and to reject the laws they proposed. But the restricted power of the monarch over national resources ensured that his or her authority was limited. The essential fact that made Britain different was that limited power was combined with unlimited majesty. The monarch was regal in every sense of the term. Popular reverence reduced disorders, while hereditary office made the nobility play a role defending the public good between monarch and people, rather than being a self-interested and potentially independent power in the realm: "Amidst all the agitations which are the unavoidable attendants of liberty, the royal power, like an anchor that resists both by its weight and the depth of its hold, ensures a salutary steadiness to the vessel of the state.[121] . . . The essential advantage of the English government over all those that have been called free, and which in many respects were but apparently so, is, that no person in England can entertain so much as a thought of ever rising to the level of the power charged with the execution of the laws."[122]

Standing so far above even the greatest noble in the realm avoided accumu-
lations of power that had been "the ruin of so many republics." Aristocratic tyranny was prevented "by rendering it impossible for any citizen to rise to any
dangerous greatness."[123] High birth might result in an administrative position
serving the king, and such office had become the highest aspiration. De Lolme
was struck by the fact that with public office in Britain came "a kind of ostracism." No Hannibal could have carried on a war against Rome against the will
of the British Parliament, and he had done without permission of the
Carthaginian Senate. No Caesar could have done what he did in Gaul had he
been a servant of the British crown. Proof lay in the experience of Marlborough
after the War of the Spanish Succession; despite his great victories, popular
acclaim, and universal commendation, he was easily "removed from his
employments."[124] The fact that all public servants, including the prime minister, knew that they would one day lose their place ensured that an interest arose
to limit their own power and to constantly respect popular liberties.[125] It was
fitting that de Lolme provided a "Dedication to the King" with the edition of
the *Constitution d'Angleterre* from 1784. This stated that de Lolme was "subject
by choice." Earlier editions had identified the author as "advocate" and "citizen
of Geneva."

Ostracism was a tool developed by ancient republicans, but de Lolme's argument was that it worked much better in the kind of monarchy that Britain had
become. It was one of a number of constitutional practices derived from republics, in de Lolme's opinion. The capacity of Parliament to impeach the ministers of the crown for malpractice was an expedient "so highly useful, that it is to
the want of the like that Machiavel attributes the ruin of his republic."[126] The
fact that, at the end of each monarch's reign, the "the civil list, and consequently that kind of independence which it procured, are at an end" was
deemed by de Lolme to be equivalent to an advantage "that all free states have
sought to procure for themselves; I mean of a periodical reformation."[127] While
sumptuary laws "to restore that equality which is the essence of a democratical
government" were a disaster in Rome, and similarly the practice of *ripigliar il
stato* or "recovering the state" had negative consequences at Florence, in
Britain it was otherwise. The end of a reign signaled national continuity but
also an end to any abuses that might have arisen.

Dividing legislative assemblies was described by de Lolme as necessary for
a free state to avoid foolish laws, such as those passed by the sometimes all-
powerful popular assemblies of the ancient republics, who wanted to make sure
particular laws became permanent and so added a clause "that made it death to
propose the revocation of it."[128] De Lolme criticized the tribunes at Rome, so

praised by Micheli and other modern writers, for being ineffective guardians of the people, because they so rarely led the people and because their own aim in so many cases was higher office for themselves. By contrast, the representatives in Parliament were active on behalf of the British people directly and were the most devoted patriots, seeing themselves as having risen to one of the most important roles in the state.[129] De Lolme claimed that there were few patriots in the history of Rome, and those who could be identified, such as Tiberius Gracchus, Gaius Gracchus, and Marcus Fulvius Flaccus, had ended up losing their office and dying for a lost cause. Representatives within the British Parliament were also better for representing the whole body of the nation, unlike the deputies of the United Provinces or the Swiss Cantons, who were elected to defend a particular locality only. Britain's representatives had also fostered rational rules of procedure within the assemblies, which were lacking in other free states.[130]

The combination of a unified executive power and a divided legislative power was the surest means to stability. For such reasons Britain's republican monarchy was infinitely less prey to disorder than other free states: "A representative Constitution places the remedy in the hands of those who feel the disorder; but a popular Constitution places the remedy in the hands of those who cause it; and it is necessarily productive, in the event, of the misfortune, of the political calamity, of trusting the care and the means of repressing the invasions of power, to the Men who have the enjoyment of power."[131] This argument was becoming more commonplace as the wars of the previous century receded in popular and political memories, but de Lolme was aware that contemporary luminaries of the science of politics were making exactly the opposite claim. He had read Hume's *Essays Moral and Political* and wanted to refute any note of pessimism about Britain's prospects contained therein. He equally named Adam Smith as an author insufficiently aware of the history of republics, given his defense of standing armies in the fifth book of *The Wealth of Nations* on the grounds of their increasing national security. Britain, as a free state, had to beware of the possibility of an army becoming an aristocratic force within the state, and also of setting up a martial law for the sake of a despotically inclined monarch.[132] Despite such engagements, de Lolme's major opponents were Montesquieu and Rousseau, for having predicted the decline of Britain and, for the former author, foreseeing its inevitable demise as a free state.[133]

This was most evident in the major claim that formed the final section of the *Constitution d'Angleterre*, where de Lolme made the argument that Britain was unique among free states in that its upheavals had resulted in improvements in popular liberty and in national stability, while in the history of every other free state the opposite had been the case: "[In the history of free states] we shall see that the public dissentions that have taken place in them have constantly been terminated by settlements in which the interests only of a few were really provided for, while the grievances of the many were hardly, if at all, attended to. In England the very reverse has happened; and we find revolutions always to have been terminated by extensive and accurate provisions for securing the general liberty."[134]

De Lolme reinforced this argument by attending to each of the fellow free states that he compared Britain to. In each case he found them wanting:

> I have been somewhat explicit on the effects produced by the different Revolutions that have happened in the Roman Republic, because its History is much known to us, and we have either in Dionysius of Halicarnassus, or Livy, considerable monuments of the more ancient part of it. But the History of the Grecian Commonwealths would also have supplied us with a number of facts to the same purpose. That Revolution, for instance, by which the Pisistratidae were driven out of Athens, that by which the Four hundred, and afterwards the Thirty, were established, as well as that by which the latter were in their turn expelled, all ended in securing the power of a few. The Republic of Syracuse, that of Corcyra, of which Thucydides has left us a pretty full account, and that of Florence, of which Machiavel has written the History, also present us a series of public commotions ended by treaties, in which, as in the Roman Republic, the grievances of the People, though ever so loudly complained of in the beginning by those who acted as their defenders, were, in the issue, most carelessly attended to, or even totally disregarded.[135]

The same generalization could also be applied to other forms of state, with de Lolme noting that "the Revolutions which have formerly happened in France, have all ended like those above mentioned. . . . The same facts are also to be observed in the History of Spain, Denmark, Sweden, Scotland, &c." In short, Britain was not only the most free state in history but was also the most stable, and one in which when domestic disorder did occur it happened in the interests of the public good. The contemporary constitution was a "political wonder."[136] For contemporaries, de Lolme's remarkable optimism about the future of Britain was the most distinctive theme of his book. It clashed with the prominent contemporary jeremiad literature. Some readers were fearful that "our ruin has been concealed from us."[137]

The weakness of Britain's constitution identified by de Lolme was the empire. The nature of the empire as he saw it in the 1770s allowed de Lolme once again to draw a distinction between Britain's experience and that of Rome. The British, unlike the Romans, had not become simply conquerors: "The Roman people were not, in the latter ages of the common-wealth, a people of citizens but of conquerors. Rome was not a state, but the head of a state. By the immensity of its conquests it came in time to be in a manner only an accessory part of its own empire. Its power became so great, that, after having conferred it, it was at length no longer able to resume it; and from that moment it became itself subjected to, for the same reason that the provinces were so."[138] Rome's empire brought forms of commerce that corrupted manners, which caused an aristocracy to develop from which the emperors who destroyed liberty emerged. De Lolme's conclusion was that Rome had always been too imperial a state: "Rome was destined to lose her liberty when she lost her empire; and she was destined to lose her empire, whenever she should begin to enjoy it."[139] Britain remained stable, having no concentrated power in one point, but de Lolme drew the lesson from the experience of Rome that the pursuit of empire might be fatal to British liberties, when the crown "by the acquisition of foreign dominions, acquire a fatal independency on the people."[140] His greatest fear was that the crown might be supplied directly by the empire. This had been a real possibility in North America, and a reason why the loss of the colonies was of benefit to the domestic constitution.[141] De Lolme wanted free states to model themselves on Britain, but he envisaged a Britain ever limited in size and able to abandon parts of the empire that threatened to alter the nature of the state.

DE LOLME'S MESSAGE FOR SMALL STATES

De Lolme's financial difficulties were revealed in an advertisement to the fourth edition of *The Constitution of England*, which stated that the English edition had been completed years before its appearance in 1775 but had been delayed by the lack of an eminent patron or supportive printer and bookseller. Despite the praise the work received, De Lolme appears to have undertaken a variety of literary labors in order to survive. In 1777 he reworked Jacques Boileau's *Historia flagellantium* (1700) as *The History of the Flagellants; or the advantages of the Discipline; being a Paraphrase and Commentary on the Historia Flagellantium of the Abbé Boileau, Doctor of the Sorbonne, Canon of the Holy Chapel etc. by somebody who is not Doctor of the Sorbonne*. Four editions of this work were followed by its revision and republication as *Memorials of Human Superstition; Being a Paraphrase and Commentary on the Historia Flagellantium* (1784 and 1785). The work was clearly undertaken for monetary reward, although it allowed de Lolme to warn against the false search for virtue and forms of religious discipline that would bring neither salvation nor secular benefit, as well as to express opposition to the more esoteric branches of contemporary Catholicism. Such labor did not bring de Lolme financial solvency. In the following years the Royal Literary Fund provided some financial support to him, although he retained a reputation for being slovenly and ill-kempt because of his poverty.[142]

After the appearance of *The History of the Flagellants*, de Lolme worked on a restatement of his core political beliefs, which appeared in their most developed theoretical form as *Essay on Constitutional Liberty, wherein the necessity of frequent elections of parliament is shewn to be superseded by the unity of the executive power* (1780). While the *Constitution d'Angleterre* had largely engaged with Rousseau and with Montesquieu, the *Essay on Constitutional Liberty* revealed a de Lolme seeking to engage with more domestic luminaries, particularly Locke, whom he considered a utopian thinker, but more particularly the three major republican theorists who he believed had set the tone for contemporary critics of government: James Harrington; Henry St. John, 1st Viscount Bolingbroke; and Adam Ferguson. De Lolme was clearly concerned about the impact of contemporary republican doctrines calling for the reform of Parliament and a widening of the suffrage, and he underlined the message of the *Constitution d'Angleterre* that republicanism was a doctrine for backward states; in the modern world it would lead to domestic disorder and ultimately the collapse of a state.[143] In Britain's case it would cause "a reiteration of the scenes of Charles the First's time."

The danger was that "our modern demagogues attempt to reconcile things in their nature incompatible."[144] Rational republicans, and seekers after liberty more generally, were once again advised to become monarchists on the grounds that "the power of our kings was the original cause of general liberty."[145] States such as Poland, if they wanted a government supportive of the public good, had to follow England and create a powerful monarchy, capable of causing the nobility and the people to unite in defense of popular liberty.[146] De Lolme was most impressed with Harrington among republican theorists, and he attacked Montesquieu's description that Harrington had "built a Chalcedon, though he had a Byzantium before his eyes." Harrington had been honest in demanding the abolition of ranks as the prerequisite for republicanism. While de Lolme could not conceive of such a scheme in Britain, where manners and opinions were too diverse, he nevertheless accepted that it was possible in small states with a homogeneous populace.[147] Despite such praise for Harrington, de Lolme emphasized the fact that he was no longer a republican in any traditional sense. Furthermore, he was no longer a représentant, warning "that the equality requisite to constitute a perfect republic is entirely chimerical: it exists in no society that has made the smallest progress in the arts of life."[148] This was no doubt why in 1781 he was blind to attempts by the représentants to gain his support in publications supporting their rebellion against France, which they hoped might appear in the *Courier de l'Europe*.[149] In the war with the colonies, de Lolme supported the British cause and opposed American independence.

The British were advised by de Lolme to maintain their current constitution, which had served them so well. Arguments against corruption might have some purchase, but corruption was not endemic and was to be expected in any large empire. Equally, the crown might be powerful, but reducing the influence of the crown would either set up the House of Commons as a potential republican government or upset the balance of the constitution in other ways. De Lolme confessed that he could see no means of reducing the power of the crown. He went so far as to support the system of public credit erected in the late 1690s as necessary for war and supported by taxes that were agreed upon by the representatives of the people. An alternative system would require too great an upheaval and would not necessarily procure the great benefits contemporary Britain enjoyed:

> The petitioners complain of the increase of taxes, and of the influence of the crown, as dangerous to liberty. The system of finance now followed, is that which was established immediately after the Revolution. That many objections may be made to it, does not escape me; but I believe that every one who has thought upon the subject, will allow, that to frame another without the imperfections of the present, and which will answer the exigencies of state equally well, is a matter of no small difficulty. Taxes have always increased when we have been engaged in war. If, therefore, the new taxes are not injudiciously laid, which is not pretended, there can be no ground of complaint, while parliament approves of the ends for which they are levied.[150]

There was insufficient virtue or "love of country" in the modern world to create an alternative. Britain was fortunate in having largely abandoned "republican whimsies."[151]

De Lolme managed to address the major weakness of the *Constitution d'Angleterre* in another essay of the 1780s. In condemning empire and in praising Britain as a model state in its present form, he had not sufficiently considered international relations, and more precisely the likely future of Europe given the ongoing war between Britain and France. The argument against empire was problematic because without empire it was widely recognized that Britain would be defeated by France, however great the popular liberty that existed within Britain. De Lolme dealt with these issues in an essay of 1786 on Britain, the union with Scotland, and the prospective union with Ireland. This appeared as *An Essay containing a few strictures on the Union of Scotland with England; and on the present situation of Ireland* in 1787 but was first published as an introduction to a new edition of Daniel Defoe's *History of the Union* (1786). An extended edition also appeared in 1787, significantly entitled *The British Empire in Europe* (1787). This work provided a clear and unequivocal message to contemporary republicans, as well as citizens and subjects in small states.

De Lolme's optimistic tone was tempered in this *Essay . . . on the Union of Scotland with England*. Britain had, he acknowledged, been degraded both in terms of power and in reputation by its recent defeats in war against France and the United States. The union with Scotland had proceeded smoothly, he claimed, only because "the formidable strength of England, owing to a success-ful foreign war, or rather a continued series of the most brilliant victories, enabled her government to carry her point, however unpalatable the union might have been to a great part of the Scottish nation."[152] De Lolme's intention was to show that the union between England and Scotland had been of enor-mous benefit to both states, and to advocate the full union of the British Isles by the incorporation of Ireland. The essay, like the *Constitution d'Angleterre*, was steeped in history and employed largely historical arguments to illustrate the disaster of neighboring states perpetually at war with one another. In the case of both Scotland and Ireland, the great benefit to England was domes-tic security. In the case of Scotland, the union of 1707 prevented "the renewal of those scenes which had attended the struggles between the Houses of York and Lancaster."[153] In the case of Ireland, the threat presented by Spain and France might have been reduced since the time of James II, but it remained, and it was in Britain's interest to make the colony a part of the state.[154] An additional reason was to put an end to "restlessness and violent national jealousy":

> Since the beginning of the present century, Ireland has acquired great importance as a separate kingdom and nation. Ireland is equal, in the num-bers of her inhabitants, to Scotland, and possesses some superior advantages in regard to climate and goodness of soil: still, reasons have existed, which have prevented there, till these later times, the rise, or at least the exertions, of that spirit of restlessness and violent national jealousy which used to take place in Scotland, and has constantly been manifested by those nations who, being possessed of considerable internal power, have been precluded from being the seat of the government.[155]

The other benefit to Ireland was commercial. De Lolme refuted the argument that the poor state of Ireland would undercut British commerce because of the cheapness of its labor, noting that "it has been demonstrated, and is a truth generally received, that a poor nation can never carry away from a rich one, those manufactures, the cheapness of which depends chiefly on large capitals." The Irish and British in commerce would be "like bees labouring for the same hive, they will no longer look upon each other as belonging to a swarm of interlopers, but range the vast fields of ocean with concord and unanimity, gathering the riches of all-bounteous nature, wheresoever industrious enterprise shall point them out.[156] Scotland "has continually augmented her opulence," and Ireland would be able to exchange "the residence of idle country gentlemen, for a numerous race of industrious farmers, manufacturers, merchants, and sailors."[157] The result would be a stronger British empire, larger markets for goods, reduced taxation, and greater resources made available for the conduct of future wars.

De Lolme's message to small states was that they should seek means of joining greater empires. The histories of Scotland and Ireland he related were stories of turbulence and crisis or futile religious disputation, poverty, and war. The British Empire might not be as great as it had been at the time of the composition of the *Constitution d'Angleterre*, and the theme of a supreme state with few difficulties had disappeared, but the lesson to be drawn was that both states would benefit by the incorporation in the Commons and the Lords of representatives from the former colony. With regard to France, de Lolme did express a note of optimism. He argued that where union was impracticable, as in the case of Britain and France, commercial treaties should be fostered. De Lolme praised the recently passed Eden Treaty despite a more substantial treaty being prevented because of lobbying by mercantile interests.[158]

In 1788 de Lolme outlined a series of proposals for domestic reform that would not entail constitutional alteration, attacked window taxes, and attracted attention for a commentary on the Regency crisis then engulfing court politics after the beginning of George III's mental illness (*The Present National Embarrassment considered*).[159] The latter text opposed making a regent of the Prince of Wales on the ground that the members of Parliament, having "the King's trust," were already endowed with all the necessary powers of government. De Lolme's point was that Britain's existing constitution was capable of maintaining national unity throughout the tumultuous challenges of the late 1780s.[160] No more stable state existed; no other state was more trustworthy in international relations or more capable of happy union with smaller nations. This view was at odds with de Lolme's représentant friends, who followed him in abandoning Geneva in the 1770s and 1780s. For them, France could not simply be described as an abhorrent absolute monarchy whose policies were the essence of self-interest or amoral reason of state. Rather, France might be a new kind of empire. Such views were explored by the représentants during the turbulent decade that followed France's 1778 entry—soon to be followed by Spain and the Dutch republic—into the war of the thirteen North American states against British rule.

Part Three

THE CRISIS OF THE EMPIRES, 1782–1802

5

COSMOPOLITAN VERSUS MERCANTILE EMPIRE

JEAN-ANDRÉ DELUC AND BRITAIN

Jean-André Deluc arrived in Britain seven years later than de Lolme. Having come to the forefront of représentant politics in the 1760s, and having speculated about Geneva becoming a canton through his strong links with Bern and Zurich, Deluc had become the foremost author of the compromise of 1768, being the leading negotiator for the représentants and consistently the voice of moderation. Jean-André Deluc believed that the représentants together with the négatifs could bring unity and peace to Genevan government. The powers of the democratically minded, made manifest in the sovereign legislative General Council, balanced the necessarily aristocratic government of the magistrates in the Council of Twenty-Five. The two parties came together in the Council of Two Hundred to air and resolve grievances but ultimately to express the united will of the state. Deluc believed that Calvinism held the Genevan polity together and that Providence directed the singular destiny of the city toward a pacific future. Jean-Robert Chouet's perspective of 1707 echoed powerfully in Deluc's vision.

Religion had always united the diverse parties of the city and had helped to keep them from violence throughout the 1760s; into the future, Deluc expected religious commitment to prevent civil war and to counter the threat posed by base commercial manners. Like so many of his generation, Deluc was obsessed with defending the purity of manners against the widespread forces of corruption. He followed Rousseau and a host of Swiss authors in describing the benefits of Alpine life to avid readers interested in places that appeared to have avoided the perils of urban living and amorality.[1] Calvinism was among the most successful forms of Protestantism because it taught the practice of Christian duty in so direct a fashion.[2] Deluc clung to the belief that Jesus had been sent to link together the nations of the world in knowledge of the true God. Jesus had made plain the duties owed to God and had justified the exercise of similar duties toward one's neighbors. Such knowledge was part of the natural religion shared by humanity and accessible through the act of conscience.[3] The fact that négatifs such as Charles Bonnet were as evangelical in their Calvinism as Deluc himself indicated that the political divisions of the city could be overcome.[4]

Although Deluc entered the Council of Two Hundred in 1770, he had been badly affected by the death of his wife in 1768, and faced financial difficulties with the decline of the watchmaking trade in the city.[5] He decided to leave Geneva for England in 1773, initially hoping to secure a teaching position within one of the many émigré Swiss or Genevan Protestant banking families.[6] The représentant Charles Stanhope returned to England in 1774 and probably acted as the link between Deluc and such eminent figures in British society as Lord Shelburne. Deluc visited the latter's country seat, Bowood House in Wiltshire, in the same year.[7] Rather than assuming a modest teaching position, Deluc found that his abilities as a natural philosopher secured an alternative mode of life. He published a new edition of his *Recherches sur les modifications de l'atmosphère, contenant l'histoire critique du Baromètre & du Thermomètre* at Paris in 1774. The first edition of 1772 had become well known because it revealed the instruments necessary to a scientific geological study of the Alps, and Deluc undertook this research in a comprehensive fashion. As a result, he was elected a fellow of the Royal Society and given the role of reader to Queen Charlotte at Windsor in 1774.[8] His international profile in science was subsequently raised by the appearance of his *Lettres physiques et morales, sur l'histoire de la terre et de l'homme*, which appeared in six volumes dedicated to the British queen between 1779 and 1780, with the intention of establishing a concordance between Mosaic history and the latest developments in natural philosophy. Through his work at court, the contemporary significance of his scientific research, his reputation for probity, and his devout Protestantism, Deluc became the most elevated of the représentants abroad in the 1780s.

His *Lettres physiques et morales, sur les montagnes et sur l'histoire de la terre et de l'homme*, which initially appeared in one volume in 1778, is revealing because, natural philosophy aside, it espoused the beliefs that he had manifested as a leader of the représentants during the 1760s. Some readers described the book as reading like a sentimental novel.[9] The ideal state for humanity was under a gentle government, where manners were simple and luxuries forbidden, where a moderate state of wealth was the norm, and where commerce was valued as a product of skill and a generator of happiness, without becoming the dominant mode of life or being detrimental to the satisfaction of fundamental need via agriculture. Such a life was in accordance with the teaching of the gospel, and provided a worldly tranquility akin to that experienced by the inner being through devotion. Enjoying in peace the product of one's labors and loving one's government, while forever contemplating religious duty in both this life and the next, expressed an ideal of equanimity that was manifest in the rustic Swiss communities of the Alpine valleys but which ought to be aspired to everywhere.[10]

The more expansive *Lettres physiques et morales, sur l'histoire de la terre et de l'homme* provided a fuller picture. Divided into eleven parts, they sought to confirm the truths of biblical revelation and the book of Genesis, in part by showing that "our continents are not of a very ancient date." Positing religion as the foundation of morals and the basis for all proper conduct, Deluc's *Lettres* were equally an attempt to define a Calvinist enlightenment. He perceived himself to be refuting the party of the philosophes, which he saw as being led by Voltaire and Claude Adrien Helvétius. Deluc was concerned that Joseph Priestley's Unitarian camp in Britain was inadvertently supporting the philosophes by justifying a materialist doctrine that Deluc believed would destroy societies, being akin in its effects to the atheism of the philosophes. Deluc defended free speech, a free press, and religious toleration at length. He sketched out a portrait of an ideal reasoner and defended the morality of agricultural communities and of Calvinist sects, such as the Moravians, and the communities they had founded. He was praised by readers as "one of the first natural philosophers of our time," having made the subject "more interesting to humanity" by linking his scientific ideas to the life of "the moralist, the citizen, [and] the friend of man." He had spoken "the language of wisdom to the peasant, the artist, the legislator, and the sovereign, and appreciates with sensibility, truth, and precision, the genuine source of human felicity."[11] Such views were of course expressive of the moderation that Deluc believed he manifested in every aspect of his political life, and which had guided him to what he termed "the happy revolution" of 1768.[12] This was particularly clear to his readers among the représentants, for whom the praise of George III's Britain was noteworthy; the central belief that human beings were good and could be turned from evil made the book "infinitely precious, useful, consoling and destined to be epoch-making."[13]

FRANCE AND THE NATIFS

Deluc had abandoned Geneva but retained a definite interest in Genevan politics and international relations. Well into the 1770s he continued to be viewed as the person most likely to be trusted by all parties as a mediator. As his friend Clavière put it to Deluc in 1773, "there will always be for you the resource of government. I will go so far as to affirm that [Geneva] has need of you, and whenever you are ready to work you will not have to wait for the offer of a [magisterial] position."[14] Geneva had by this time become an experiment in politics by which two wholly antagonistic factions, the négatifs and the représentants, were forced to share power. An added difficulty was the position of the natifs, the sons born in the city to foreign parents, whose commercial and political privileges were restricted and whose political rights were null. As François d'Ivernois wrote, Geneva's population would have collapsed without the constant influx of immigrants, but "it would have been dangerous to introduce indiscriminately all these new-comers into the legislative body" because "the distinction of rank was more necessary at Geneva than elsewhere."[15]

The natifs, the largest body of people within the city by the 1760s, formed an organized group at the time of the mediation and had been clamoring for greater political rights from the mid-1760s.[16] The Edict of 1738 had allowed them access to all trades except particular "liberal professions" such as surgery and medicine, and the artisanal class that developed was of fundamental importance to the prosperity of the city. The price of obtaining bourgeois status was greatly increasing. Far fewer natifs were made "free men" without payment during the eighteenth century. Their right to receive welfare remained limited, while membership in the militia and involvement in politics continued to be forbidden. Such factors explain why demands for improvement were increasingly voiced. The settlement of 1768 allowed greater access to the professions and removed other outstanding commercial restrictions, but it did not address the political status of the natifs and did not establish civil equality.[17] Indeed, a natif who proclaimed that he ought to enjoy all the rights of a citizen was banished for a decade during the time of the mediation.[18] Deluc's own diary revealed the extent to which the représentant commissaries had attempted to ameliorate the condition of the natifs, the main means of which was by incorporating ever larger numbers of them into the ranks of bourgeoisie. Many natifs agreed with this policy. They also stated that if the city became more reliant upon the more lucrative financial trades associated with the richer magisterial families, foreign powers would become more jealous of Geneva and more likely to challenge its independence. Equally, as the French were developing commercial centers to compete with Geneva and offering freedom of religion and an equality of status, the natifs warned all parties that it would be easy for them to abandon the city for richer pastures in France or Savoy.[19]

Many natifs worked for Voltaire at Ferney, and in consequence the great philosophe was especially interested in their cause.[20] His friend the French résident Hennin was equally struck by the condition of the natifs, noting in 1770 that it was proper to encourage them to leave for France, so piteous was their condition at Geneva.[21] The natifs argued that the original constitution at Geneva had not distinguished between civic ranks; that they had at least as much right to citizenship as the rich foreign families such as the Neckers, who quickly purchased a political voice; and that they could be trusted within the polity, being permanent residents. More particularly, they argued that making the natifs members of the General Council would have no impact upon international relations, and a positive impact upon the economic health of the state. Furthermore, in removing a class that could be used in the political balance by unstable alliances with the négatifs or the représentants, and in linking political activity and economic liberty, freeing the natifs would help to remove corruption from the state.[22]

When the natifs continued to demand political rights, in a campaign that came to a head in a violent demonstration on 15 February 1770, Voltaire expressed horror at the intransigence of the représentants and the négatifs, neither of whom then contemplated a more democratic constitution.[23] The genuine concern of both parties was that Geneva, having established a balance between two opposed groups, could not withstand the addition of a third party to political life. At the same time both représentants and négatifs paid lip service to the natifs and sought their support, without committing themselves to greater civil equality and while refusing political equality. Matters were decided on 22 February 1770, when the eight leading natifs were banished in perpetuity for sedition. Their fellow supporters were forced to take an oath in favor of the existing polity, in return for greater commercial privileges and a small number being granted bourgeois status.[24] On abandoning Geneva, it was said that Versoix and Ferney became "an asylum for a very large number" of natifs.[25] Voltaire actively sought the development of both settlements and went so far as to offer the natifs a domicile much farther afield, under the protection of Tsarina Catherine of Russia.[26] Before he left for Britain, Deluc once more acted as a pacifier, seeking to bring all the parties together without violence.[27] Attempts at establishing a more permanent compromise failed. Young natifs, such as Jacques Mallet du Pan, began to condemn the représentants for lack of principle.[28]

The subsequent unhappiness of the natifs and their ongoing campaign for political rights indicated that Deluc's vaunted post-1768 era of peace was proving impossible to sustain. The antagonisms generated during the 1760s died hard, not least with regard to external relationships with foreign powers. With relish at the irony, Voltaire noted that "the subjects of the King [of France] are every day insulted at Geneva, whilst the Genevans are received with the greatest courtesy in the [French] Pays de Gex."[29] In another letter to Hennin, Voltaire observed "the lack of affection at Geneva for France, which is compatible with the Genevans' extreme obsession with French Louis d'ors."[30] One of the great themes of politics in the city during the 1770s was the relationship between France and Geneva in the aftermath of the mediation. The attitude of France was complicated by the change of position signaled by covert support for the natifs. Whether this meant that France was no longer wedded to the magistrates was one question. Another was whether France, should trouble recommence within the city, would continue to intervene so directly using the justification of the guarantee. Choiseul's activities in Corsica, which many Genevans perceived as a prelude to their own annexation, formed part of the commonplace contemporary notion of France as a modern imperial Rome. But France was undergoing a decade of experimentation in policy during the 1770s. Part of the reason was the rise of physiocratic ideas within France, which came to a head with the ministry of Anne-Robert-Jacques Turgot.

Although Turgot's ministry was short-lived (August 1774–May 1776), its impact was remarkable in freeing trade and in imagining "certain fixed fundamental principles of law, commerce, morality and politics comprehensive enough to embrace all religions and all countries."[31] The French résident Hennin had long favored physiocratic ideas. The question for Genevans was what they entailed. Two perspectives on small states could be discerned within physiocracy. The first was to maintain the freedom and independence of such states. The physiocrats believed that there was a natural progress of opulence for humanity, moving through hunter-gathering, pastoral farming, and arable farming stages, toward a commercial society dedicated to the satisfaction of true need, through the commercialization of agriculture in conditions of free trade. This natural order of things had been upset in Europe by the history of war and empire. War was not a natural state for humankind, because it threatened the attainment of the most basic and fundamental human necessities.

Turgot was of exactly this opinion, opposing French intervention in North America on such grounds and much preferring the policy of waiting until free trade had done its work and restored the natural economic health of a nation, rather than actively breaking up systems restrictive of commerce. In Turgot's opinion, if France remained at peace, a much stronger nation would emerge and surpass a much weaker Britain, the latter being artificially bloated in trade by its mercantile system.[32] In a significant memoir written when the Anglo-American troubles were intensifying in 1776, Turgot prefigured Jeremy Bentham's later (1793) call for nations to "emancipate their colonies."[33] When

North America became independent, Turgot anticipated "a complete revolution in the political and economic relationships between Europe and America,"
whereby "all the imperial states will be forced to abandon their empire over
their colonies, allow them an entire liberty of commerce with all nations, and
content themselves with participating in this liberty with others, conserving
with their former colonies links of friendship and fraternity."[34] Turgot advised
the Spanish to prepare for this new relationship with their colonies and for both
states to watch the British exhaust themselves, while developing the French
navy. He also advised the creation of plans for the invasion of England and of
India, should the British determine to initiate another war in defense of their
unsustainable mercantile system.[35] He then vociferously argued that, whatever
the outcome of further war, states that had abandoned imperial designs, such as
the Swiss, enjoyed the consumption of as many products as imperial states like
France but at a much reduced cost, and did not lose in terms of military reputation but rather could enjoy the huge benefits of long-standing peace. If
the rebellion of the North American colonies could show the world that new
times had come, instructing Europe's states to abolish what Turgot called "the
jealousy of commerce," an era of perpetual peace might be initiated.[36]

The second physiocratic approach to small states was more active, and
potentially more aggressive, in seeing large agricultural markets as the key to
economic success and the best means of bolstering French trade in the creation
of vast provincial markets for French goods. Such an approach might entail the
incorporation of Geneva into a French empire, with the rationale of expanding
markets for both states' benefit. Physiocrats such as Pierre-Samuel Dupont de
Nemours believed that France could reduce its national debt by increasing
economic activity in the provinces, establishing free trade across the nation and
across national boundaries.[37] Dupont de Nemours, who served as Turgot's secretary during his ministries and the editor of his papers after he died in 1781,
wrote a significant paper on Geneva in the physiocratic journal *Ephémérides du
citoyen* in 1770. Here he candidly expressed his lack of comprehension at the
survival strategies of such small states. The physiocratic movement had revealed
to the world that states thrived only by developing their agricultural markets
and using these as the basis for a more varied commercial sector in conditions
of peace and natural liberty. States such as Geneva with no extensive hinterland
made no sense. Dupont wrote that it was a paradox he found difficult to com-
prehend that some republicans ascribed their survival to the maintenance of
political forms of liberty once vaunted in distant classical times but of no relevance at all to modern political economy.[38] Where the profit from commercial
activities, which the physiocrats called the net product, was going to be limited,

Dupont could see the benefits of a democratic constitution. Democracy was suited to poor states; citizens openly determined the distribution of the net product together, and this facilitated peace. Dupont equally accepted that such a form of government was prey to anarchic enthusiasm and was sustainable only where inequality was kept to a minimum, and where an industrious poverty was the norm.[39] Dupont described Geneva as an aristocratic republic because the division of the citizenry into ranks was clear, and the two distinct classes of bourgeois and citizens ruled the state and divided the net product. His fear was that, despite their numbers, the people (by which he meant the natifs) counted for nothing. In consequence, a less stable state than Geneva, despite its reputation for learning, could not be found.[40]

Turgot's more passive position of encouraging competition between Geneva and the French Pays de Gex and Ferney was initially more representative of physiocratic policy.[41] Hennin knew that allowing the Pays de Gex to trade freely with every region of France would entail difficult negotiations with the existing pays d'état such as Burgundy, Grenoble, and Provence, but he was equally convinced that a liberated Pays de Gex would both overwhelm Geneva commercially and raise vast revenues for the French state. During Turgot's ministry Hennin worked to secure this goal and promised Vergennes, who had been ambassador to Sweden since 1771 and became Louis XVI's foreign minister in 1774, that rich rewards could be expected from this policy.[42] The beauty of the French policy was that there was no longer a perceived need for direct intervention at Geneva, because a Geneva weakened commercially would have to rely upon France for protection from Savoy. Alternatively, an economically successful Geneva, recognizing the limited significance of national boundaries and their limitation of trade, might follow the argument of Victor Riquetti de Mirabeau's "friend of mankind" of the 1750s, with his cosmopolitan vision of a France ensuring justice across Europe. Geneva, seeking large markets, would ultimately become part of a union in which national boundaries were of limited significance.[43] In this vision, Britain would fall prey to economic corruption, excessive debt, and national bankruptcy.

FRANCE AND NORTH AMERICA

Perspectives on France at Geneva were influenced by the rise of physiocracy. They were altered by the decision of France and Spain in 1778 to enter the war against Britain being carried on by the United States. This move shocked contemporaries in Europe's republics, not least because France was supporting the foundation of a coalition of small republics in another part of the world, raising the possibility of similar support for the little republics of Europe. Visions of a less imperial France, less motivated by reasons of state and more disposed to the will of the people in allied states, became widespread, increasingly contrasted with descriptions of the British violating liberties and fighting wars because of their lust for trade and desire to protect their monopoly of law, politics, and commerce. The state of Ireland, whose industries were tied to the welfare of the imperium and whose populace lacked full civil and political rights, was an example often cited to underscore the likely fate of the North Americans under permanent British rule.[44] The question this raised for the Genevan représent-ants was whether their old grievances against France ought to be set aside. Had France become a cosmopolitan power, willing to rely upon free trade to secure the French empire and in consequence to play the role of Europe's policeman? Would France act fairly in international disputes? Above all, was France a pater-nal state desirous of maintaining existing national boundaries and the current division of states?

By the time of the victory of 1768, the représentants had become confident about the future of Geneva. A short pamphlet by Jacques-Antoine du Roveray, *Traduction des thèses philosophiques sur la patrie*, is indicative. Du Roveray's grandfather had been a coalman in the city with bourgeois status, and his father, François du Roveray, to whom the pamphlet was dedicated, was one of the twenty-four représentant commissaries of the later 1760s. Du Roveray was being educated in law at the Collège de Genève when he wrote the *Traduction des thèses philosophiques sur la patrie*. He qualified as an advocate in 1771 and sub-sequently rose to prominence within représentant circles, becoming respected as a passionate leader without guile but also known as "obstinate, hot-tempered and violent."[45] The young Du Roveray of 1767 described the nation (*patrie*) as the father of the people, being derived from the collected will of the citizens, contracting together for mutual benefit, and formulating law that became the expression of the public will (*volonté publique*). For such a society to flourish, the magistrates had to ensure civil equality. They had to secure person and property. They were advised to favor industry and the arts. Du Roveray advocated a just price for goods. He supported the exercise of religion and the prevention of superstition. If religion was not tied to the practice of public vir-tue, despotism would quickly ensue.[46] Furthermore, the government ought to prevent extremes of inequality, combat luxury, and simplify manners: "[The magistrates] should direct opinions in a fashion to prevent the extreme inequal-ity of fortune, repress luxury, and encourage the happy simplicity of manners that is the firmest support of law and the constitution. The chiefs should nour-ish in every heart the love of glory, and ensure that this passion is so active and venerated that it turns all the time to the common good. [The magistrates] should themselves provide an edifying example of the virtues, as it is the surest means to draw praise upon themselves, and to ensure the respect of their compatriots."[47]

Following Horace, Du Roveray believed the security of the state depended upon the capacity of the citizens to defend themselves, and he recommended training in war, relying on their virtue to defend themselves, and a willingness to sacrifice oneself, rather than any reliance upon "vile mercenaries." Phocion ought to be the model for citizens, and Coriolanus "a monster to your eyes." Every citizen had to be taught that "virtue governs the world."[48] Du Roveray's text might strike any reader as jejune given the recognized dissimilarities between Geneva and the classical republics he adored. But the ideals of moderate wealth, artisan-based trade that would not foster luxury, a stable religion teaching good morals, and a real patriotism based on the national past and associated with its manifest destiny were widely espoused by représentants at this time. For some représentants, including Du Roveray, the reformation of Calvinism toward a natural and simple religion of shared moral ideals was also necessary.[49] For other more devout men, such as the pastors Isaac-Salomon Anspach, Esaïe Gasc, and Etienne-Salomon Reybaz, Calvinism was the only form of Christianity capable of fostering the reformation of manners and of countering luxury.[50] The question was how to square reform with the overweening power of France, seemingly so interested in being involved in everyday politics within the republic.

The issue of French relations tortured the représentants throughout the 1770s. This is revealed by Etienne Clavière's correspondence with Jean-André Deluc. With Deluc abroad, Clavière became the leader of the représentants, despite not being a full citizen. Speculation about the future was necessarily tied to political economy, and in the case of Clavière and Deluc discussion usually began with the merits of particular individual investments that might make either man better off. As a merchant, Clavière traveled regularly to the main commercial capitals and was increasingly interested in speculation on government stocks, and more particularly the French issue of *rentes viagères*, or life annuities, claiming that the returns promised were secure, in part because of the health of the Genevan maidens to whose lives the annuities were tied.[51] Clavière was, in 1773, confident about the stability of the French economy, and he recommended such investments to Deluc, noting in passing that "I esteem Necker greatly, especially for his beneficent qualities."[52] But he remained concerned about relations between France and Geneva and had come to the conclusion that "the friendship of Britain has become precious to us." Clavière had been treated in England for deafness in the 1750s, knew the language, and had excellent contacts. One of them, James Hutton, had attempted to link Clavière with Shelburne in 1767.[53] In the 1770s Clavière believed that Geneva needed Britain not simply to secure the independence of the republic but also to protect the international grain market, should states like Savoy suddenly constrain it. The difficulty was that British ministers were inconsistent in policy, not least in failing to support their accredited résident Colonel Jean Pictet, whom the magistrates were refusing to acknowledge on the grounds that he was too close in his politics to the représentants. Religion no longer appeared to be a bond between the two states. The choice for Geneva was between an excessively interested natural enemy and an uninterested natural friend.[54] France seemed to be rising, paying its debts, and benefiting from the experience of a new and good king who loved the simple life.[55]

Clavière wrote to Deluc in 1774 that "the republic is as you left it, governed in my view as if it was about to collapse." Decadence was the order of the day, and Clavière was full of disdain for the magistrates who lived distant lives from the populace and whose politics were so at odds with the general desire for moderate wealth and honest industry. The excessive wealth of the négatifs was his great fear, since the rich "in general carry on a cruel war against the happiness of the poor." Clavière believed that, rather than there being a necessary reciprocity between the parties, "the rich have a great need of the poor, while the poor can live without the rich." The magistrates at Geneva would continue to conspire against the citizens until corruption had created a state of oppression or had been challenged. Clavière once more praised the British for their laws, guaranteed by an honest and wise noble class, but he could see no linkage with Geneva. He was concerned by the likely consequences for international relations across Europe of British antagonism toward the North American colonies. Britain's reputation was being tarnished, and the worst elements of the mercantile system appeared to be dictating policy.[56]

France's experiences were altogether different. Success in the war against Britain appeared to have reversed the sense of national insecurity and decline established by the Peace of Paris in 1763. A new role was being developed for France in the cabinets of Europe and beyond. In May 1784 Vergennes enunciated this role in a memoir summarizing the policies of the young King Louis XVI during the first decade of his reign. Vergennes praised Louis XVI as the foremost peacemaker, having prevented both the War of the Bavarian Succession and the Russo-Turkish War from becoming general European conflagrations.[57] France's long-term interest was above all in maintaining peace, according to Vergennes, allowing it to become Europe's premier commercial power, holding the balance between less stable but more ambitious polities:

> Wars [for empire] are no less dangerous to the political body than a compli-
> cated disease is to the human frame. The war that ended in 1763 is certain
> proof, and I appeal to your Majesty never to lose sight of this fact. France is
> in so many respects the center of Europe, drawing strength from the size and
> linked nature of our regions, from the wealth of our soil and agricultural
> population. France is surrounded by fortifications that protect our frontiers,
> and by neighbors who, taken in isolation, have no capacity to attack us.
> France has no need to expand or to undertake conquests. The policy and
> interest of France should be directed toward the maintenance of public
> order, and in preventing the different states that form Europe's equilibrium
> from being destroyed.[58]

Vergennes advised his king accordingly to distinguish between those states that wanted to overturn the existing division of powers across Europe and those that were willing to help maintain it. Among the former Vergennes placed Austria, and advised using a Franco-Prussian alliance to limit Emperor Joseph II's overweening ambition, even if the outcome was the end of France's alliance with Austria, and the price the sacrifice of an allied Bourbon state such as Naples. Vergennes expected Europe's monarchies to recognize that only France could secure their thrones and that the only other global power, Britain, would never be willing to do so.[59] By maintaining alliances with Prussia, Holland, Sweden, Turkey, and Russia, France would become aligned with the more conservative powers, those least likely to cause war. Such a federal alliance would be able to cope with the eccentric times when a ruler came to the fore with irrational imperial ambitions, as in the case of Tsarina Catherine. A French-led grand alliance would help to put an end to the greatest problem facing modern Europe: Britain's lust for mercantile empire. It was vital "to repress Britain's pride, and to labor to bring low this state." Britain would always prepare for war with France, and the fight would ultimately mean the degradation of either power. Vergennes advised Louis XVI to act as Europe's moderator and arbiter, a paternal power devoted to peace, but to prepare the French navy and the armies of France and allied states for an end to the peace. British policy made little sense from the perspective of international politics traditionally understood, being a state "so jealous of France" that national ruin was a price worth paying.[60] The question was how paternal and peaceful French foreign policy under Vergennes would be when faced with a further outbreak of disorder at Geneva.

VERGENNES, CORNUAUD, AND THE CONSTITUTIONNAIRES

For Clavière, a crisis point was once more approaching by 1775. The négatifs remained disconcerted by the capacity of the General Council to remove them from office "which they considered as a species of ostracism."[61] Reports were being circulated of a secret council of négatifs seeking means of reversing the settlement of 1768. Clavière was more concerned that the public finances of the state were in a poor condition. The magistrates were not corrupt in a pecuniary sense, but they believed that they could spend public funds without accounting for them to the sovereign of the state, and no system existed to provide an annual account of expenditures and receipts. Clavière particularly opposed indirect taxes, such as that favored by the Council of Twenty-Five upon lanterns, on the grounds that the rich did not feel them, and the poor paid such a high proportion of their income in taxes that their capacity to satisfy basic needs was threatened. He asked why the members of a republic could not live like brothers, since in civic terms they were supposed to be fraternally connected, and pay in proportion to income.[62] Such sentiments reflected a broader concern that "manners conserve states with particular constitutions and the corruption of manners equally lies behind their collapse." While the malady was not yet incurable at Geneva, it was difficult to lead the people toward stable commercial manners because of the excessive power of the rich and the destructive nature of their mores.

Clavière was also concerned about resolving the problem of the natifs, which he believed required the rewriting of the constitution rather than simply a domestic resolution to alter marginally the existing division of powers. The question was whether the guaranteeing powers would countenance constitutional innovation.[63] To Deluc's advice to turn to the cantons for aid, Clavière replied, "but where today can one find the good Swiss? They furnish mercenaries to foreign powers, and sell their country to any who would command them." To become a canton was to become docile and dominated by magistrates.[64] It was also to establish a further bulwark against French dominion. When Deluc's friend Gédéon Turrettini proposed to make Geneva a canton in 1779, during negotiations for the renewal of the Franco-Swiss alliance, he was recalled by the Council of Twenty-Five and castigated.[65] By 1775 Clavière, like Turrettini, but without any faith in making Geneva a canton, was moving toward a position that rejected the 1768 settlement as a failure and sought to explore new means of securing Genevan independence.

By 1777 the central dividing line between the représentants and the négatifs had become the new law code for Geneva, determined upon in 1768 and initially taken up by both parties as a means of ending the constitutional controversies. As the membership of the reforming commission was shared equally, division was the outcome, with the représentants seeking a new order and the négatifs the protection of what they believed defined Geneva's ancient constitution. In Clavière's eyes, a new code was the last hope for reform, because corruption was "attacking and destroying that which must be conserved," and more especially the manners that lay behind stable politics. The central issue was the response of the guaranteeing powers to the proposed new law code, a draft of which was published on 7 April 1779. On 1 September 1779 the Council of Two Hundred rejected the draft and declared that the committee to revise the laws was dissolved. The négatifs, led by Joseph des Arts and Jean-Jacques Chapeaurouge, then began to call themselves *constitutionnaires*, on the grounds that the Règlement of 1738 was being challenged and the ancient constitution undermined by the représentants and their code. A defense of established constitutional laws was required against the innovating and enthusiastic faction seeking to overturn the state.[66]

The new French résident Gabard de Vaux, appointed in 1778, had received a letter from Vergennes stressing that the représentants were troublemakers who lacked the support of the populace for their proposed innovations, and that the view of the Council of Two Hundred needed to be respected. Its members were "the elite of the state," being those with the greatest property and accordingly the most devoted to the public good. Any attempt to revise the Règlement was to be prevented by France.[67] To coincide with the rejection of the code by the Council of Two Hundred, the letter was dated 1 September. This underlined the union of strategies between Vergennes and the constitutionnaires. Clearly Vergennes believed that the pacific policy of Louis XVI did not extend to the states directly bordering France, which ought to be protectorates and never critical of or a challenge to French authority. He had long been warned that the représentants were demagogues, and a particular danger as their numbers were growing in the aftermath of 1768.[68]

The fact was that the représentants, in refusing to give the natifs equal political rights, had allowed the counsels of a growing body of their critics among the natifs to prevail. The latter were led by Isaac Cornuaud, who gradually rose to parity with Jean-Pierre Bérenger, the leader of the natifs exiled in 1770. Bérenger always remained close to the représentants, favoring increasing numbers of natifs joining the ranks of the bourgeoisie and an assertion of the authority of the General Council.[69] His *Histoire de Genève*, completed in exile, appeared in six volumes between 1772 and 1773 and provided historical support for his advocacy of moderate reform and the gradual expansion of the bourgeoisie, whom he continually praised in his portrait of eighteenth-century politics.[70] Cornuaud, a case maker and bookkeeper, chose a very different course. He had been involved in the disturbances of 1770, had been disarmed and seen his wife harassed, and harbored an inveterate antagonism toward the représentants for failing to treat the natifs as equals. His strategy was to ally the natifs with the constitutionnaires in return for giving the natifs full civil but not political rights. By the late 1770s Cornuaud had become the leader of a large body of natifs. He had used long-standing links with Voltaire to be introduced to the leading magistrates, prominent among whom was Joseph des Arts, who closely allied himself with Cornuaud after January 1778. Des Arts was willing to accept civil equality for natifs as the necessary price of the defeat of the représent-ants, and he formed a secret committee of négatifs, modeled on the représent-ant commissaries of the 1760s, to maintain the constitution by means of a new mediation.[71] The concessions Cornuaud won, the praise he received from France, his manner of keeping peace in the city by means of patrolling circles of natifs, and his ceaseless stream of publications praising the magistrates and ridiculing the représentants undermined représentant strategy.[72]

The central claim of the représentants was always to be the authentic voice of the people, capable in consequence of bringing the people together against the magistrates when necessary. Cornuaud made a mockery of such a claim in publications such as *La Voix publique* of January 1780, which underscored the extent to which the popular element of Geneva's polity was divided.[73] He identified the représentants as just another faction within the city and accused their leaders of being aspiring aristocrats and self-servers, whose central goal was the replacement of the magistrates by their own party. He called the représent-ants avaricious, a mercantile aristocracy supportive of the kinds of luxury associ-ated with rentes viagères, and favoring a political system "absolutely democratic" and "purely demagogic." The code for the revision of the laws, he claimed, was in fact a strategy for bringing the représentants to power and subjecting the city to chaos.[74] The représentants were a force for corruption in Genevan life, being dedicated to the Rousseauist subversion of social and political hierarchy. Cornuaud worked with the constitutionnaires and the French court to blacken the public reputation of the représentant leaders, associating them with extreme, foolhardy, and amoral politics and political economy; the représent-ants presented themselves as lovers of liberty, but this translated in practice to a lust for self-serving dominion.[75] Cornuaud presented his followers, by contrast, as advocates of neutrality and moderation.[76] Great damage was done to the représentant relationship with the natifs when, in a speech of 1779 to the Council of Two Hundred, Du Roveray called the latter "tenants" by comparison with the citizen and bourgeois "proprietors." By contrast, after February 1780 the constitutionnaires explicitly favored the natifs and praised Cornuaud's group.[77]

Fortunately for the représentants, an appeal by the constitutionnaires to bring back the guaranteeing powers was refused by the cantons of Bern and Zurich, after hurried appeals to the Swiss from both Clavière and Du Roveray. When both men went to Paris to seek to improve relations with the French court, in January 1780, it was made clear to them that Vergennes believed he was dealing with an enthusiastic faction seeking to turn Geneva into a democracy. Therefore they concentrated upon modernizing the traditions embodied by the Règlement of 1738. In February 1780 Clavière wrote to Vergennes, arguing that the revision of the law code had been demanded by the Règlement itself and that the goals of the revision were to sanctify the division of powers between the legislative and executive councils of the state, and above all to end disputation about the ancient constitution of Geneva and the meaning of particular and sometimes circumstantial laws concerned with political authority. The revision was also intended to update particular laws, such as those governing grain stores, and to ensure that the poorest members of the community did not carry an unfair burden of taxation. Rather than being innovators, Clavière contended, the représentants were conserving the essence of the Règlement and bringing it up to date. He denied that the représentants were democrats wishing to transfer all powers to a représentant-controlled General Council. He claimed to be advocating limits to liberty and a constitution that prevented both aristocracy and democracy from arising, stating that it was in the interest of all of Geneva's neighbors to see industry flourishing within the city, which would be put at risk if the internal disputations continued.[78]

Acknowledging that France had the power to "dissolve our little republic," Clavière requested that Vergennes better understand the internal controversy, which was not a threat to the state and did not require the intervention of external mediators. Calling Vergennes "a just and wise man and a friend of truth," he ended the letter with the statement that, according to the Règlement, France could not interfere with Genevan affairs alone by reference to existing political conventions and treaties, and ought always to work with the cantons. Clavière's tone was desperate. Vergennes was acknowledged to have misunderstood Genevan politics and to have been misled by parties in the city. In refusing to blame Vergennes, the letter was redolent of Renaissance "mirror for princes" literature based on appeals to the monarch to exercise justice, and relying upon reason alone to this end. Cornuaud's later memoirs underscored the hopelessness of Clavière's cause, as he was known as "the demagogue par excellence," and as his private letters, including a memoir from Bérenger attacking the role of France within the republic, were being intercepted and circulated.[79]

Cornuaud, working with Gabard de Vaux and Hennin, summarized the natifs' demands as the return of the exiles of 1770, civil equality, admission to military ranks, partial admission to the bourgeoisie, and the ratification of these reforms by the guaranteeing powers.[80] Cornuaud was paid by the magistrates for supporting the constitutionnaire cause, starting with the winter of 1780.[81] Given the positive response both of the constitutionnaires and France, the représentants appeared to have been outmaneuvered by des Arts and Cornuaud.[82] With the Bernese unwilling to cause further disturbance at Geneva by overtly favoring the représentants, the latter's cause was widely held to have been defeated. Although numbers of citizens at Zurich supported the représentants, the magistrates there were unwilling to move against either Bern or France. Many Swiss observers condemned the représentants as demagogues and supported French-led intervention. By the autumn of 1780 Vergennes was reported to be furious with the cantons for failing to support France's position decisively. Reports were circulated that he wanted to bring Savoy into negotiations with the constitutionnaires, to establish a new guarantee, to reduce the power of the représentants in the Council of Two Hundred, and to create a new tribunal at Geneva capable of maintaining civil concord.[83] Many représentants were beginning to acknowledge that there was no possibility of national unity with three parties within the state detesting one another. French government bonds had made so many individuals rich that "equality, the foundation of the happiness of our republic, has been destroyed absolutely . . . luxury increases ceaselessly and idleness accompanies it, vanity, excess, the love of pleasure, the collapse of the soul all come to the rich, and the poor seek only to imitate them."[84]

FRANCE AS A PATERNAL EMPIRE

It was in such circumstances that Clavière, Du Roveray, and a new generation of représentants decided to go on the offensive in the winter of 1780. In a series of représentations to the General Council, they attacked France for intervening in Genevan politics, and they coordinated public demonstrations of opposition to the guaranteeing powers' involvement in the city's political affairs.[85] At the same time they appealed to their old friend Jean-André Deluc for advice. Deluc had maintained excellent contacts with the représentant community abroad.[86] Vergennes was also at this time soliciting Deluc's opinion. Remarkably, Deluc had by 1780 come to the view that the French court should be trusted to maintain order at Geneva, and that the role of the représentants should be straightforwardly to support peace.

After 1768 Deluc was sure that France could be relied upon to act as a paternal power, so long as Geneva remained close to the Protestant cantons. He believed he had established a settlement that was durable, because it forced each party in the state to commit to peace and to compromise to maintain it, and because his personal negotiations with the representatives of the cantons were the basis for a new and more positive relationship between Geneva and the Swiss, which the French would always respect. He clung to the view that it was irrational for the négatifs to embrace the natifs, as the latter were democrats while the former favored aristocracy, and that alliance between them would ruin their respective causes. In short, the représentants had little to fear from the natifs and should continue to allow them to become bourgeois without making Geneva into a more popular state.[87] Politics was a matter of prudence, and if conducted with the moderation exemplified in 1768, civil war could be avoided and the unity of the state maintained.

Like so many of his generation, Deluc had substantial faith in Jacques Necker, initially as Geneva's ambassador to Paris and more especially as head of the royal treasury at Paris from 22 October 1776 and as *directeur général des finances* from 29 June 1777, in which office he served until 19 May 1781.[88] Furthermore, Deluc expressed the view that the duc de Choiseul had never been a puppet master with malign designs on Geneva.[89] A France in which Necker governed the finances would never, Deluc believed, do anything against Genevan independence. Deluc's "profession of political faith" stated that "the councils [Council of Twenty-Five and Council of Two Hundred] could not imprison without proper legal process, that representations had to be addressed, and that limits needed to be accepted upon the General Council's refusal to elect magistrates." Equally fundamental was his continued opinion that "the guaranteeing powers can resolve our difficulties." Deluc believed that because France and the cantons would prevent civil war, the représentants should continue to labor to maintain national unity, to oppose the spirit of faction, and to prevent democracy, which would threaten the very existence of private property and destroy the state. What he called "mutual love" alone could serve as the basis of political life at Geneva.[90]

Despite the strife that once more divided Geneva as the 1770s wore on, Deluc continued to put his faith in France and in what he saw as the principles of 1768. Other prominent représentants of the 1760s came to the same view. Théodore Rilliet, for example, now argued that Geneva could never stand against France and needed above all else to cultivate a healthy relationship with that great state. France was on the way to becoming Europe's superpower, and Rilliet advised the utmost extension of public credit by France to win the necessary wars to such an end.[91] Deluc, like Rilliet, maintained a correspondence with the leaders of the représentants but increasingly was aware that they were rejecting his counsel, particularly after a visit to Geneva in 1776, during which time he advised his old friends to leave the refusal to elect magistrates "in reserve in the arsenal of liberty."[92] One of his friends and fellow naturalists, the pastor and représentant Pierre-Gédéon Dentand, was reported to have died of a broken heart because "the sovereignty of this country has been sold to France."[93] Yet Deluc adhered to his beliefs, and in 1781 he published his perspective on Geneva in a letter to Vergennes, which called upon the latter to reject the recent policies of his former représentant associates. As the title indicated, Deluc had visited Paris and enjoyed a series of meetings with Vergennes.[94] In these he outlined the view that power could continue to be shared at Geneva by giving the right to propose legislation to the Council of Twenty-Five, the right of deliberation to the Council of Two Hundred, and the right to accept or reject propositions to the General Council. The role of the Council of Twenty-Five would then become the executive function of ensuring that laws were enacted and adhered to. In failing to follow these wise constitutional rules, both the représentants and the négatifs were at fault. Both parties had to be prevented from establishing an aristocratic regime or a democracy, both of which were wholly at odds with Geneva's mixed constitutional heritage.[95]

Vergennes had proposed a tribunal of two hundred citizens over forty years of age to resolve the political impasse, but Deluc feared that the magistrates would dominate elections to this body, and he believed that what was required was an intermediary power that could stand above the warring factions. Deluc's solution was to force représentant candidates for a peace-making tribunal to be vetted by the Council of Twenty-Five, and the leading magistrates' candidates similarly vetted by the bourgeoisie. Forcing each party to accept candidates for office from their opponents would, he believed, create a tie of interest and mutual esteem, which, if bolstered by shared religious belief and enforced from Paris, would restore peace in the manner of the 1768 settlement. A tribunal constituted in such a fashion would be trusted and could deal directly with issues brought to public attention in the form of représentations.[96] Deluc was full of praise for France's role, and more particularly the position of Vergennes. Through reason, he believed, his fellow citizens could be persuaded to embrace the counsel of moderation, which was that of true patriots such as himself. Deluc denied that he any longer supported any party in the republic. His views were advocated by other moderates, including the venerable magistrate Gédéon

Turrettini.[97] Cornuaud refuted them on the grounds that they would permanently give an excess of power to the bourgeoisie.[98] The leaders of the représentants were so incensed that they published Deluc's private journal of the events
of 1768, which had been sent to François-Henri d'Ivernois and must have been
copied by his son François. This embarrassing document for the Deluc of 1780
revealed the extent to which his younger self had been scathing about France
in the 1760s, placing his faith in the cantons just as he now relied upon France.[99]

FRANCE AS A COSMOPOLITAN EMPIRE

Clavière's rejection of the 1768 settlement was favored by a younger generation of représentants, prominent among whom were Jacques-Antoine du
Roveray and François d'Ivernois. The three men were behind a series of publications that formulated a new strategy for the représentants in the winter of
1780, in direct opposition to the views of Deluc. Du Roveray had risen through
the study of the law and by 1770 was serving as a member of the commission
established to provide a new law code for the city. In 1775 he became a member
of the executive Council of Two Hundred, sitting alongside magistrates seeking
to defend the status quo. Du Roveray was elected to one of the leading magisterial positions, that of *procureur général*, seen to be the office of "the defender of
the liberties of the people," on 19 December 1779. It was from this office that he
launched a représentation, on 20 October 1780, that attacked Vergennes specifically for challenging the independence of Geneva.[100] The représentation
warned that "in a century as enlightened as ours" it had become clear that economic prosperity was directly tied to liberty and to the state of independence
first and foremost. France ought to act in a cosmopolitan fashion following this
rule but was instead plotting, through Vergennes and Gabard de Vaux, to
destroy the settlement of 1768 and to challenge the right of the General Council
to demand or refuse foreign involvement in Genevan affairs. Louis XVI, being
just and honest, would not want to intervene at Geneva, and accordingly a plot
could be identified within Versailles to create a self-defeating imperial policy.[101]

Du Roveray's first remonstrance followed on 15 November, asserting that
Geneva's right to invoke the guarantee was being disputed by Vergennes, who
was in turn seeking to overturn the constitutional settlement of 1768.[102] It was as
if the British Act of Parliament fixing the royal succession in the house of
Brunswick-Hanover was being challenged by the guaranteeing powers of the
Peace of Utrecht. In such a case, the external powers would recognize that it
was an act of war to challenge a decision about a settlement domestically agreed
upon by an act of the sovereign. In the case of Geneva, it was shocking that

France was doing exactly this in challenging the agreements made and ratified in 1768. Du Roveray warned France that aggression during the 1760s toward Geneva had simply tarnished the reputation of a great state. He reiterated his view that the right to elect half of the Council of Two Hundred, and a proportion of the Council of Twenty-Five, would improve the stability of the state and bring moderate government appreciative of popular liberties.[103] While the magistrates at Geneva wanted to turn the small council into a Roman-style Senate, the people at Geneva gathered in the General Council remained sovereign, and their will was to modify the 1768 settlement by giving greater political rights to the natifs but not to overturn the agreement that put an end to the dreadful disputes of the 1760s.

François d'Ivernois had been born at Geneva on 9 April 1757. His father's family were from Neuchâtel; François-Henri d'Ivernois had become a habitant in 1746 but purchased bourgeois status two years later. François-Henri d'Ivernois was, as previously discussed, a leading représentant and merchant throughout the turmoil of the 1760s. He had an intense love of and faith in Rousseau and always considered himself a close friend of Jean-Jacques, one of the few whose relations with him were consistently cordial. Had he lived to see them, François-Henri would, accordingly, have been shocked by Rousseau's disparaging remarks about him in the posthumously published *Confessions*.[104] François d'Ivernois's mother was Marianne Dehors, from a family of habitants who had come to Geneva from Elbeuf in Normandy. The d'Ivernois family had eight children, six of whom reached adulthood. François was the fifth child and fourth and final son. One of his brothers, Philippe-Charles, following his Neuchâtelois heritage, became a Prussian general. François was educated in law at the Collège de Genève until 1777 and completed his studies to become an advocate in 1781. On his father's death in 1778, however, he established, with Pierre Boin and Jean-François Bassompierre, a publishing firm (the Société typographique de Boin, d'Ivernois et Bassompierre). Their goal was to publish a complete edition of Rousseau's writings, including manuscripts left in the possession of his widow, Thérèse Levasseur, and of his friends the soldier René-Louis Girardin, siegneur-vicomte d'Ermenonville, the Genevan citizen Paul Moultou, and Pierre-Alexandre Du Peyrou of Neuchâtel. The venture continued until it was liquidated in 1784, and, despite the project being dogged by pirate editions and lack of capital, the "Geneva" edition of Rousseau's works was the outcome.[105] By the time the first books were appearing in 1779, d'Ivernois's attention had turned to politics. He wrote on behalf of the représentants and directly against Vergennes in November 1780. D'Ivernois's *Lettre à son excellence le Comte de Vergennes* of 3 November, which was composed as a preface to the receipt at Versailles of the représentation of 20 October, was followed up by what became known as Du Roveray's *Fameuse Remonstrance* of 11 December 1780. Together the texts became manifestos for the représentant movement, making abundantly clear the shift in représentant policy. The négatifs called d'Ivernois "the seditious subaltern."[106]

D'Ivernois's *Lettre à son excellence le Comte de Vergennes* appealed to the interests of France and the true nature of the French state. The message was both negative and positive. He stated baldly that "no state could interfere with [Geneva's] troubles, without harming its true interest, without violating justice, and without abusing its power."[107] Challenging Geneva's "happy obscurity" risked European war, because it would draw in first the cantons and Savoy and then other powers in domino fashion. France was in fact a cosmopolitan empire—Vergennes had himself "aided America"—and the fundamental doctrine of any cosmopolitan creed was to maintain the independence of free states. Even if Geneva became "the most absolute democracy," intervention was not justified, because any externally imposed shackle upon liberty would increase unrest and prevent the "gentle and moderate government" that the représentants promised. D'Ivernois declared that an aristocracy was being established in Geneva by the constitutionnaires against "the will of the greatest number." In seeking to support aristocracy at Geneva, in the vain hope of establishing a government akin to its own, France would face armed defenders and the outcome of either a ruined reputation for France or a ruined Geneva. If the focus was rather that "the greatest number are happy," then the interest of France as a monarchy was at one with ideas about the public good to be found in any republic.

A large monarchy that found small republics on its boundaries was singularly fortunate, d'Ivernois held, because it "had no need of a rampart for itself," being able to rely upon "the invincible garrison" of patriotic citizens who did not aspire to empire but only wanted to live in harmony with their neighbors and to maintain the existing division of territory in the vicinity.[108] Vergennes would never want Geneva to turn into Strasbourg, whose decline had followed its loss of independence as a free imperial city at the orders of Louis XIV. Any attempt to violate Genevan independence would be at odds with the spirit of the constitutional guarantee signed by France, Bern, and Zurich in 1738. The guarantee was established not to set up a foreign power as overlord nor to enforce the will of an aristocratic faction, but rather to maintain the independence of the state and the sovereignty of the General Council.[109]

D'Ivernois rejected the accusation that the représentants were democrats in any radical sense of the term, claiming that "extreme democracy" was "incompatible with our actual mores," being suited "to a society of farmers or soldiers uniquely concerned with defense." Geneva was not this kind of state. A society that was "tranquil, industrious and commercial" was necessarily characterized by "the talents of ambition and the virtues of equality," but it could not be a "tumultuous democracy," which existed where the populace lacked work and was ignorant and superstitious. The need to labor and to be productive in order to satisfy basic needs prevented popular governance. Nor could an industrious state be an aristocracy, because such forms of government were incompatible with commerce and the arts, rendering the citizens docile and constraining the citizens' commercial enterprises through hierarchical codes and rules. Above all, an aristocratic republic was weak and unable to defend itself because its citizens lacked verve and a willingness to sacrifice themselves for the good of all. A society based on labor and civil equality, by contrast, was likely to be one where patriotism, honesty, knowledge, and a commitment to social duties defined public virtue: this was exactly the kind of society aspired to by the représentants, who were happy to honor their magistrates and help them maintain both order and liberty.[110] Magistrates, however, had to be the delegates of the people, in order to prevent them from becoming aristocrats serving interests other than those of the state. The représentants were the people. As a majority within the General Council they determined issues of national sovereignty. The basic issue was independence. It was illegal and ill-advised to be ruled by foreign powers, and this was why the cantons were so wise in refusing direct involvement at Geneva. The second issue was the need for far greater scrutiny of the magistrates by the people. The law of reelection, which allowed the General Council to reject magistrates on an annual basis, had to be asserted as the only means of preventing the current disturbances, which could be traced to an aristocratic faction that had become too rich and self-serving. Preventing corruption in commercial societies entailed the scrutiny of magistrates and their removal where tendencies of aristocracy were proven. The lack of such a law had, d'Ivernois claimed, ruined Britain's Parliament, which was famously corrupt.[111]

Du Roveray's *Fameuse Remonstrance*, a vocal attempt to shame Vergennes, to unite the représentants and the natifs, and to restore the committee established for a new code of laws, was presented as a means of asserting national independence and of restoring domestic peace. Like d'Ivernois, Du Roveray described a cosmopolitan France dedicated to maintaining the constitution of Geneva, having signed a document with the cantons to secure the independence of the state, and benefiting from the peace and wealth a stable Geneva brought. Previous French foreign ministers, and most notably Choiseul himself in 1767, became involved at Geneva only when the General Council and the smaller councils together asked for aid; they acted only in concert with the cantons and relied on a formal correspondence between the magistrates and the French résident.[112] Du Roveray went much further than d'Ivernois in blaming Vergennes for supporting a faction within the city, which was contrary to historic practice, violated the existing guarantee, and was at odds with the established law of nations.[113]

Proof lay in a letter of 29 November from the résident Gabard de Vaux to several leading constitutionnaires and natifs (with Cornuaud prominent among the latter party), expressing support for a new mediation and seeking to coordinate the strategies of Geneva's French supporters to this end. Du Roveray laid this information before the Council of Twenty-Five pompously, as a patriot who had discovered a plot by a foreign power to "reverse the constitution." The implication was that the supporters of Vergennes within the city were traitors, the pawns of a foreign state who had abandoned their patriotic duty to sustain Geneva's independence.[114] Du Roveray pushed his message home by stating that French policy should never be conducted by means of private messages toward "simple individuals" who were neither representative of the will of the people nor synonymous with the state. It was farcical that France, "an immense monarchy," should be so interested in the politics of a minority in the city, he argued, inviting Vergennes to cease acting as a schismatic.[115] Du Roveray, who unlike d'Ivernois wanted to draw upon Britain as a positive example, asked whether the House of Lords would idly stand by if the monarch's opinion was associated with a faction within the House.[116] Geneva's situation was likened to the position of a woman in a world dominated by men: the virtue of the female sex, like the independence of a small state, had to be scrupulously respected and upheld, as it could so easily be lost.[117]

Du Roveray traced Vergennes's conspiracy against Genevan independence to the beginning of 1780, when he and Clavière had noted attempts to circulate a claim that "there was no justice at Geneva" and to denigrate the party of représentants as wild democrats. The most damaging accusation that Du Roveray made was that Vergennes had coordinated the rejection of the new law code with the constitutionnaires in the Council of Two Hundred. The goal of France appeared to be the establishment of a servile aristocratic republic, incorporated de facto into a French empire.[118] Du Roveray's depiction of French intentions reiterated d'Ivernois's portrait of a society of simple manners, which sustained industry, commerce, and the arts, made compatible with the virtue of frugality. Du Roveray cited Rousseau, "our immortal compatriot," whose description of Geneva in the preface to the *Discours sur l'inégalité* as a city of virtue and dedicated magistrates could be restored by the représentants.[119] Du Roveray called the représentants the true constitutionnaires, being dedicated to maintaining a constitution based on the laws of 1738 and 1768. This was disingenuous, given that he also appealed to the natifs to join with the représentants in creating a constitution based on civil and political equality, which would guarantee order through their combined majority in a larger General Council and by means of the annual scrutiny of elected magistrates.[120] Du Roveray, Clavière, and d'Ivernois were asserting the need for a state governed by the représentants, rather than any division of power with an increasingly hereditary magistracy, which had been attempted and had failed after 1768. Du Roveray ended his speech with praise of Bern, "our faithful ally," whose resolution not to support a new mediation was an example of "glorious justice and salutary for [Geneva]." Fellow représentants recognized that refusing mediation was vital, on the grounds that "it went against the law of nations for two opposed parties to bring in a third party as a mediator, who secretly favored one of them." Reliance upon the cantons was equally essential.[121] The bullying tactics of Choiseul had been defeated in the later 1760s, and the situation was now the same under a different minister.[122]

Du Roveray's strategy of "j'accuse" against Vergennes, and his confident assertion that a union of natifs and représentants could resolve all of Geneva's difficulties, was based on the expectation that Vergennes might be replaced as foreign minister. Necker, now *directeur général des finances* at Versailles, was in the background. The représentants, their correspondence makes clear, were gambling that Necker might soon have greater influence over foreign as well as domestic policy and would always oppose French dominion over Geneva. Rumors of Vergennes's "disgrace" were commonplace.[123] When d'Ivernois visited Vergennes at Paris in October 1780, presenting him with some of the texts that formed the *Offrande à la liberté*, Vergennes asked Gabard de Vaux if the visit was in any way official. The negative response confirmed the représentants in their opposition and formed the background to the subsequent denunciations of Vergennes's policies.[124] As a result, Necker's fall from power in May 1781 was a real blow to the représentants, particularly as he was seen as their "illustrious protector." Clavière wrote that his fall was "a great error of [political] calculation."[125] In 1782 it was said that Necker would never have allowed the armed intervention by France to go ahead.[126]

In an angry letter to Bern and Zurich of 24 December 1780, Vergennes accused the représentants of seeking to ruin Geneva and of violating the 1738 Règlement.[127] He condemned Du Roveray more particularly to Gabard de Vaux at the end of the year, making clear his desire to see the représentant punished for slandering the minister and for disrespect toward France.[128] Genevans learned of this in the New Year, when a letter of 4 January 1781 delivered to the magistrates by Gabard de Vaux demanded that Du Roveray be removed from his position as a magistrate for libeling both France and her foreign minister.[129] The magistrates took the decision to do exactly that on 17 January. Cornuaud called Du Roveray "the Caius Gracchus of the bourgeoisie," sneering as he fell.[130] Du Roveray lost his place within the Council of Two Hundred, and the *Fameuse Remonstrance* was lacerated and burned before the Hotel de Ville.[131] In consequence there was great agitation within the city, and residents worried that Genevan sovereignty might be at an end if France could remove individual magistrates. Du Roveray's removal was "death to the heart of all true patriots," and hundreds were said to be ready to martyr themselves for liberty.[132]

Vergennes, in a further letter, criticized the cantons for failing to support France, declared that he was willing to act alone in using force against Geneva, and demanded that Du Roveray be banished and his *Fameuse Remonstrance* publicly burned again. Vergennes also placed individuals such as Cornuaud under the protection of France, treating them in effect as French subjects.[133] The historic Franco-Swiss guarantee was seen to have been abandoned.[134] The représentants decided to take control of the city after a popular disturbance among the natifs on 5 February 1781. A period of calm followed, during which the représentants ameliorated the condition of the natifs in an edict of 10 February, which allowed the exiles of 1770 to return, gave one hundred natifs immediate bourgeois status, guaranteed all natifs bourgeois status from the third generation, promised to elevate eight further natifs per year to the bourgeoisie, allowed them to be officers in the militia, and supplied full commercial and civil privileges alongside those enjoyed by the citizenry.[135] At the same time the law of reelection established in 1768 was confirmed.

It was acknowledged that the defiance of the représentants relied wholly on the support of the cantons. The Swiss moved in two contradictory directions. Against the représentants, Swiss mediators problematically declared the edict of 10 February null.[136] Against the négatifs, the Swiss refused to abandon the guarantee of the constitution. They also sought to pacify Vergennes by including France in a new settlement based on the concords of 1738 and 1768.[137] Vergennes was willing to let the Swiss make peace, but he continued to declare that the basis for any peace had to be the repression of the représentants.[138] He was at the same time preparing for the transfer of natifs into France.[139] The great hope of the représentants was that Vergennes would be so concerned with other issues, and more particularly the war with Britain, that he would leave Geneva alone, allowing the peaceful establishment of a bourgeois state and the permanent abolition of the guarantee.[140] Jean Roget, writing to his brother-in-law Samuel Romilly in London, praised the moderation of the représentants in government but reminded him that "we live in the century of Poland's dismemberment and Corsica's enslavement."[141] Letters from Frederick the Great also accused the représentants of leading Geneva to the precipice.[142]

During the summer and autumn of 1781, France refused to behave as a cosmopolitan empire and instead continued to show the représentants the more brutal face of "reason of state."[143] Plenipotentiaries from France and the cantons met at Soleure, chosen because it was the seat of the French ambassador to Switzerland, but could not find common ground concerning the fate of Geneva. Vergennes now used Deluc against his former allies, meeting him at Versailles in September and October 1781 and again in February 1782, gaining his support for French policy.[144] Cornuaud, after July living in Ferney, argued that civil liberty was of greater significance than political liberty, that the extension of the latter would cause the collapse of the republic, and that the February 1781 edict, in extending political liberty, directly countered the mixed nature of the state.[145] In a letter to Geneva's magistrates, Vergennes formally abandoned the guarantee of the constitution, declaring that the cantons were now released from the Règlement of 1738, once more threatening armed intervention if "tumultuous democracy" was established at Geneva, and warning the Swiss to restore peace quickly because the French king had "taken all of the orders of the state under his protection."[146] He again accused the représentants of fomenting civil war and demanded that their leaders be severely punished.[147]

Cornuaud accused Clavière and Du Roveray of setting themselves up as Geneva's caesars. He encouraged emigration to Ferney and demanded foreign intervention. For Joseph des Arts the représentants were advocates of an anarchic democracy.[148] Vergennes stated that he would punish the représentants should any individual suffer the loss of life or of liberty. Jean Roget called this a revolution in French policy. A letter from Vergennes followed to the cantons on 28 September 1781, in which he attacked their "constant opposition," claimed that they had been infected by Geneva's radicals, told them to pacify the city, and baldly stated that, if Geneva's government degenerated into a democracy, France would intervene.[149] A regiment of French troops was marched into the Pays de Gex. In a représentation of 24 October, a final appeal was made by the représentants to the cosmopolitan Louis XVI, hoping that the king would put an end to the plots of his mistaken minister.[150] This gambit failed. By the end of the year Vergennes was calling the leaders of the représentants to the house of Jean-Baptiste-Gédéon de Curières de Castelnau, the new French résident, to be informed that they would be held personally responsible for the outbreak of either violence or democracy.[151] Castelnau wrote to his master that the pastors Etienne-Salomon Reybaz and Jacob Vernes were especially culpable, that Clavière was "a nasty man in the full sense of the term," and that Du Roveray, while not as bad as Clavière, "had abominable traits."[152] The constitutionnaires and Cornuaud's natifs continued to demand French intervention on the grounds that only its constant involvement was capable of restoring and maintaining peace in Geneva.[153]

Tranquility was the basis of commerce, and inequality had to be maintained at the city to prevent the establishment of a warlike democracy destructive of peace and trade. Cornuaud called the leaders of the représentants terrorist advocates of a constitution at odds with tradition in general and more specifically with the Règlement of 1738.[154] His party was now abetted by the polemicist Jacques Mallet du Pan, who attacked the représentants and praised Vergennes in the pages of the *Annales politiques, civiles et littéraires*, which he was editing while its usual editor, Simon-Nicholas-Henri Linguet, was in the Bastille.[155] Castelnau was soon being described as "the conductor of the négatifs."[156]

By contrast, the représentants continued to seek to shame Vergennes by the example of more pacific ministers, claiming that their party alone could restore peace but was being prevented from doing so by a francophone cabal within Geneva. The intervention of France, they argued, lay behind the refusal of the Council of Twenty-Five to ratify the edict of 10 February and the continued refusal to reinstate Du Roveray.[157] They warned of the dreadful economic consequences of a Geneva made bankrupt by French intervention, and of the loss of French reputation when Europe saw the city of Calvin reduced to rubble over the bodies of self-sacrificing citizen patriots. They also maintained hopes that Necker would return to power or that Louis XVI himself would see reason and replace Vergennes with a minister in the mold of Turgot.[158] Against the constitutionnaires' portrayal of a commercial city based on a clear civic hierarchy and economic inequality, living under the skirts of France and integrated within the French economy, the représentants were advocating a commercial society based on moderate wealth and the virtues associated with sobriety, frugality, and industry. More popular government was tied to economic success, the avoidance of the dangers of luxury, and international independence, while recognizing the overwhelming power of France: the great claim was that France would benefit more from an economic powerhouse of industrious patriots than it would from luxury-loving aristocrats. When the représentants took control of the government, Jean Roget was delighted that the Consistory was encouraged to return to its ancient role of the police of manners, in a more rigorous fashion than in recent times. Sumptuary laws were enforced and the excessively rich encouraged to leave the city: "equality is being reborn, and with equality there is less luxury, less corruption, and less pride."[159] It was highly significant that during 1781 the leaders of the représentants rarely considered appealing to Britain. They recognized that "Britain, humiliated and defeated, has already experienced so many reverses of her own, that she could never even consider preventing ours."[160]

All of these arguments could be found in François d'Ivernois's *Offrande à la liberté et à la paix,* the représentants' refutation of Deluc, which appeared at the end of 1781. D'Ivernois argued that Geneva could become "the asylum of the virtuous and the refuge of the oppressed," a "monument to liberty," enjoying a thriving economy and stable popular government. Deluc was accused of having changed his mind about Geneva, as he now advocated the feudal model of sovereignty shared between hierarchical social groups. A tribunal that sought to govern conflict in such a system, d'Ivernois claimed, would only replicate social division and thereby aggravate societal antagonisms.[161] By contrast, Geneva was a modern form of state in which sovereignty was unified in the General Council and government was delegated to an aristocracy of the able and the wise. This "democracy wisely tempered" was based on the assertion of popular institutions within the republic and modeled on the political circles that had governed the représentant movement throughout the 1760s. Discussion within those circles, and the responsiveness of the leaders of the movement to ordinary members, created ties that could be replicated on a national basis within a small state, creating a populace exceptional for its political wisdom, its faith in its magistrates, its patriotism, and its dedication to the public good. D'Ivernois stated that he was indebted to the Marquis d'Argenson for the idea that "popular administration under the authority of a sovereign does not diminish public authority, but augments it, and can be the source of the happiness of peoples."

What d'Ivernois called "democracy in appearance" reduced the risk of anarchy or turmoil in government by tying the magistrates directly to the sovereign and thereby to the express will of the people, allowing the removal of magistrates in a legal fashion rather than by upheaval or other wild acts of discontent. In short, democratic sovereignty created the best of governments: an aristocracy supported by the people. The law established in 1768, which allowed the General Council to remove four magistrates from the Council of Twenty-Five annually, was not only akin to the law of ostracism "that prevented violence at Athens" and the law of destitution that allowed the removal of unpopular magistrates across the cantons, but it also paralleled the act of a monarch in removing his ministers. The right to remove ministers allowed the British to combat corruption and explained the survival of the republics of Lucca, Ragusa, Hamburg, and the majority of the free imperial cities of the Holy Roman Empire. Such laws were vital to prevent aristocratic government from degenerating into tyranny. Geneva had managed to create a republic that could be stable once its hereditary aristocracy recognized that election, removability, and balance were the watchwords of the 1768 settlement.[162]

D'Ivernois argued that he was following the counsel of both Machiavelli and of Montesquieu in the claim that large councils could be relied upon to be wise. In exercising such a right, large councils would always elect the prominent and the wealthy. Ironically, democratic sovereignty at Geneva would be likely to see the election of the same magistrates, with the difference that they would be trusted by the people and closer to them, and hence less likely to be led astray by the corruption of excessive wealth or of excessive self-regard. By contrast, hereditary aristocracy was a hydra that fomented civil war and would itself create the tumultuous democracy that its supporters promised they could avoid.[163] Civil liberty had to be made secure, as the lack of proper penal laws lay behind so much of the antagonism of the Genevan people toward their magistrates. Equally, the excessive concentration of power in the Council of Twenty-Five had to be diffused by ensuring that the General Council exercised the powers granted to it in 1768. D'Ivernois argued that no political body in Europe had as much power as the Council of Twenty-Five. For such claims he relied most of all upon Montesquieu, but he also liberally cited Machiavelli, de Lolme, Bodin, Blackstone, Vattel, and d'Argenson.[164] Once peace had been established at Geneva, a system of national education in civic knowledge would be needed in order to entrench patriotism and ensure that the members of all councils were informed about the nature and workings of the state.[165]

Deluc replied that d'Ivernois was a wild democrat who misunderstood the constitution of Geneva and the division of sovereignty between the different orders of the polity. He accused the représentants of wanting to follow the masters of political theory—he named Pufendorf, Montesquieu, and Rousseau—in founding an ideal republic, rather than being interested in solving the problems of an existing state by restoring its long-established and accepted constitutional foundations. The result of a sovereign populace exercising power in a General Council would be anarchy and ultimately the rule of a caesar.[166] So great had Deluc's antagonism toward the représentants become that he was reputed to be advising the British government not to support the exiles when they arrived in the winter of 1782.[167] Meanwhile, Du Roveray underlined the populist credentials of the représentant movement in his advice to the canton of Fribourg, whose citizens were rebelling against a magisterial oligarchy in 1781. He advised the rebels that small cantons, cities, or states were best governed democratically and that the usurpations of an illegitimate aristocracy threatened to destroy the economy of Fribourg. Because the social contract had been broken by the institution of a corrupt and hereditary magistracy, the right to resist had to be exercised.[168] For Clavière, the négatifs had become violent usurpers of popular authority. The représentants were the only true republicans at Geneva.[169]

POLITICAL THOUGHT IN 1782

On 18 March 1782 the représentants made a représentation requesting the confirmation of the law passed in the aftermath of the February upheaval the previous year. They claimed that an organized plot led by France was seeking to overturn the constitution established in 1768, and that the sovereignty of the General Council was once more being challenged. In seeking to implement the 10 February 1781 edict, which was "graven on their hearts in indelible characters," the représentants claimed they were following the will of the General Council. For peace to be maintained, it was vital to institute forms of civic education that would further unite the population. If this were achieved, a new era of prosperity would be inaugurated.[170] The representation ended with thirty-five pages of documentation reiterating the evidence for the sovereignty of the General Council, from Rozet's *Chronique de Genève* and Jean-Robert Chouet's 1707 discourse to Jean-Robert Tronchin's *Lettres écrites de la campagne* and numerous more contemporary speeches, agreements, declarations, and commentaries.

The Council of Twenty-Five replied, on 7 April 1782, that "government is neither willing nor able to ratify the edict" (of 10 February 1781).[171] This sparked further unrest among the natifs. A call to arms was issued, and a battle raged for control of the city, which was won by the représentants. The dispute between the parties was likened to that between the houses of Lancaster and York in fifteenth-century England.[172] Making the decision to remove the existing magistrates, the représentants took some négatifs hostage. The edict of 10 February was finally confirmed. A security committee was established with eleven members responsible for public order, for guarding the hostages, and for national defense. An appeal was made to the syndics to support the newly established national unity and the prudence and moderation that would now characterize national government. If this was rejected, the threat was made that the représentants were willing to perish "as free men and virtuous citizens," should Providence so will it.[173] Clavière hoped that the smallness of Geneva (relative to the larger context of current international turbulence) would save the state from foreign intervention.[174]

Bern and Zurich condemned the new représentant government as founded on usurpation and violence, amounting to the rule of a faction rather than of the people. Jacques Vieusseux was in turn revolted at the attitude of the Bernese, horrified that they would capitulate to France so readily.[175] Vergennes "returned unopened the dispatches of the new Senate."[176] The résident Castelnau left Geneva on 10 April. Frederick the Great wrote to the Bernese giving his support for intervention to restore "the ancient form of government." Neither Austria's Joseph II nor the Dutch, however, were interested in Geneva.[177] Vergennes wrote to the cantons that a shared interest existed in "establishing tranquility by restoring legitimate government."[178] Clavière was the person deemed to be the most dangerous leader of the représentants and the most deserving of reprisals.[179] Roget later noted that France might not have intervened had Vergennes been aware of the defeat, on 12 April 1782, of the Comte de Grasse's flotilla by British Admiral George Rodney at the Battle of the Saintes, which prevented the French invasion of Jamaica.[180] Geneva was merely a pawn in an international power game, the problem being that in 1782 the strength of France was at a peak unparalleled since the 1680s. Using the pretense that the legitimate magistrates were requesting French aid, Vergennes stated that it was the duty of France to intervene. Vergennes cited his letter of 28 September 1781 to the magistrates, claiming that, while the Règlement of 1738 had given twenty-five years of prosperity, that of 1768, because France had been less involved, had put an end to political stability.[181] The Bernese were soon reputed to be seeking to chase Genevans from their territories, clearly wanting to follow the lead of France.[182] Attempts by the Consistory to persuade Bern to defend the représentants came to nothing.[183] Cornuaud now demanded French intervention more vociferously than ever, accusing the représentants of atrocious crimes against their négatif hostages and of an organized plot to initiate a civil war, with the intention of establishing an extreme democracy led by "factious tyrants."[184] Republics that ceased to be mixed states would always see "ambitious or fanatic demagoguery," in which amour propre replaced patriotism, and as such the représentants' extremism was the natural logic of their republican politics. The likely republican self-sacrifice, so vaunted in the final days of the defense, was proof of the ill effects of democracy and of the cancer that the représentants had brought to the body politic.[185]

Jean Roget, viewing the situation from Lausanne, feared that Geneva would suffer the fate of Denmark and become a "despotic monarchy." He reminded Samuel Romilly that Vergennes had been behind the last revolution in Sweden, in 1771, which, as in Denmark, had established an absolute sovereign. With a French garrison supporting the négatifs, "what aristocracy could be more secure, what government more iniquitous and more odious than that of Geneva?"[186] For other observers it was simply the case that France needed to replace Geneva's government with one more conducive to French economic and political needs, manners and values having moved away from the kinds of republican fortitude that clashed with commerce and luxury.[187] The représent-ants defended themselves by identifying the aristocratic cabal at Geneva intent on destroying the settlement of 1768 and of making Geneva into a Venice or a Bern. In the case of Geneva the aristocratic strategy was deadly because the magistrates, whether they called themselves constitutionnaires or négatifs, were "indifferent by their wealth to the rights of commerce and of industry" and unable to recognize the economic benefits that would accompany the provi-sion of full civil and political rights to the natifs.[188]

Calling on the Roman maxim *Salus populi suprema lex esto* to justify their defense of the state, the représentants argued that they alone—and not the "aristocratic league" led by Vergennes—could bring peace to the republic. The origins of Geneva, like so many republics, had been "happy and tranquil under a democratic government." The magistrates had lived with and served the peo-ple "with simple manners and mores" and in consequence had been able to rule as "fathers of the family." Since that time the natural order of republican states had been perverted across Europe, and Geneva was only the last in a long line of states to suffer the desire of a self-styled aristocratic faction to separate itself from the people while retaining an exclusive right to rule. War by the magistrates against a state's own populace was the consequence, sometimes conducted behind a veil of legitimacy. The resulting replicated history across so many small states explained why there was so much domestic turmoil at Geneva. The fact that aristocratic factions could mask their intentions by becoming imperial powers equally explained why so many wars were occurring internationally in modern Europe. Such an explanation for Geneva's ills was later transplanted to the history of France, with Vergennes portrayed as repre-senting a body of nobles seeking to do to France what he had done to Geneva.[189]

When the city fell on 2 July 1782, without resistance, to the combined armies of France, Bern, and Savoy, Roget wrote that "Geneva is dead, and if I had ever doubted the existence of hell, this is the moment when I would begin to believe in it."[190] The subsequent justification for joint intervention was that Geneva had been saved "from anarchy and oppression," that the intervening powers were the saviors of the independence of the state, and that a violent plot had been prevented, whose instigators had to be removed in perpetuity from the city.

Stretching from the Consistory to the lawyers and on to the Council of Two Hundred, the conspirators had sought to create a new state at odds with historic tradition, the interest of the city, and the existing and legitimate magistracies.[191] With the passage of the "Edit noir" of 21 November 1782, the power of the General Council to remove magistrates annually from the Council of Twenty-Five was removed. The right of the General Council to elect half of the members of the Council of Two Hundred was equally annulled. The right of représentation was transferred to a body of thirty-six citizens chosen by lot. Due to their lack of power, this body was derided as "the shadows." The Council of Two Hundred alone henceforth exercised the grabeau that confirmed the membership of the Council of Twenty-Five. All political gatherings, the *cercles*, were forbidden. The militia was abolished. No citizen was permitted to bear arms.[192] Cornuaud and other opponents of the représentants such as Jean-Louis Mallet argued that the "black act" was necessary to remove democratic elements from Geneva.[193] Paul Moultou wrote of the sadness that "our leaders have abandoned us, the foreigners are in the town." This said, he stated that the saving of Geneva from destruction was a providential miracle, necessary because the enthusiasm of the citizens for liberty had become excessive.[194] From Paris, Necker was held to have condemned the oath now required of all citizens to support the new constitution. He was believed to have had meetings with Clavière after the latter's escape from the city. Evidence was also supplied to Vergennes that "Turgot, when he was a minister, intrigued with the demagogues [at Geneva]."[195] Charles Stanhope, Lord Mahon, wrote to the magistrates to have his name stricken from the list of bourgeois and citizens.[196] Jacques Vieusseux wrote that his only crime as a représentant had been "fidelity to the laws and the constitution," and that their only goal had been the introduction of new laws, amounting to a system of national education, to fight "luxury, the corruption of manners, and irreligion." Without such laws Geneva would decline.[197] In the aftermath of the 1782 revolution, Cornuaud claimed that Geneva became richer and more polite, and that with peace science and the arts thrived. He called Vergennes the ultimate cosmopolitan, on the grounds that he had spent vast sums of money on thousands of troops to keep Geneva free and independent.[198] Vergennes gave Cornuaud a pension in September 1782 by appointing him *directeur des messageries de France*. He was granted bourgeois status at Geneva in 1784.[199] It was claimed that the reestablishment of order was a huge success and that a peaceful Geneva had been created, characterized by national unity.[200] By contrast, Albanis Beaumont, a visitor from Savoy, noted that sumptuary laws "have now fallen into disuse, and been so totally neglected, that there was no more resemblance in 1788 between a Genevese of that time [the Reformation], and one at the commencement of the present century, than between an Athenian and a Lacadæmonian." He traced the decline to the establishment of a theater and coffee-houses, and the arrival of too many foreigners, who "have introduced a taste for luxury and fashion heretofore unknown among the Genevese."[201] Madame Roland, another visitor, seconded this view, adding her view of the incompatibility of democracy with trade in a republic:

> The active and industrious people [of Geneva] are no longer any thing but a collection of workmen and shopkeepers, between whom fortune alone establishes any difference. Its leading men are become aristocrats; today oppressors and tomorrow oppressed, they accelerate corruption, by means of which they have enslaved their fellow citizens. Geneva is a French town: language and manners, every thing assimilates it to our nation. It has a theatre, a citadel, barracks and luxury. . . . Trade, which enlivens and enriches Geneva, is incessantly militating against republican austerity, and must have contributed to make it disappear; it may be considered as the first and preparatory cause of the last revolution. A democratic and at the same time trading state, is a moral contradiction, the existence of which cannot long be maintained; for the essence of democracy is incompatible with that of commerce; they necessarily destroy each other.[202]

It was significant that the Venerable Company of Pastors were informed in the aftermath of the revolution that the Council of Two Hundred henceforth enjoyed the right to determine the frequency of church services and the content of the sermons. The number of pastors in the city was cut from thirteen to nine in 1786.[203]

Jean Roget wrote that he was ashamed of the exiled leaders of the représentants, who had failed to ask the people of Geneva whether they wanted to surrender, had abandoned the city, and had been casuistic in their arguments for opening the city gates. Each of them in retrospect, he reported, wished they had died rather than having fled in such disorder. Clavière was castigated particularly. His position above Du Roveray was emphasized by Roget, who pointed out that Du Roveray's fortune, based on ownership of French government bonds, was entirely the product of Clavière's own investments.[204] Despite their sullied reputation, invitations to create a "new Geneva," a trading community of watchmakers, came to the exiled représentants from the Elector of Palatine, the Prince of Baden-Durlach, the Countess of Neustadt, the Landgrave of Hesse-Homburg, from Holland, and from the grand duchy of Tuscany.[205] These were followed by offers from North America and from the Ukraine.[206] Seventeen families were given permission by Joseph II, in accordance with his toleration edict, to reside in Brussels under the leadership of pastor Isaac-Salomon Anspach. Numerous représentants did move to Konstanz, the only settlement that proved permanent.[207] Clavière stated that politics at Konstanz, being monarchical, did not suit Genevan mores and that accordingly the settlement was not a true "new Geneva."[208]

The leaders of the représentants went first to the village of Péseux, in the Prussian protectorate of Neuchâtel, where they became acquainted with and employed Jacques-Pierre Brissot and Honoré-Gabriel Riquetti de Mirabeau.[209] The exiles were naturally concerned with self-justification. Two works stood out, being the product of the leaders of the représentants. The first was François d'Ivernois's *Tableau historique et politique des révolutions de Genève dans le dix-huitième siècle*, which had been composed before the collapse of the city. Indeed, d'Ivernois had visited Neuchâtel as early as January 1782 concerning the publication of the *Tableau*. When it finally appeared in November 1782, it "had a great impact in France and in Switzerland."[210] The *Tableau* was a response to Deluc's comment about the *Offrande à la liberté*, attacking it as a theoretical work ill-suited for the history of Geneva. In response d'Ivernois supplied a detailed history of eighteenth-century Genevan politics, enshrining exactly the theoretical platform outlined in the *Offrande* and revealing the full extent of the aristocratic "system calculated for subduing the citizens, and forcing them to silence by authority and fear." Vergennes attempted to have the work prohibited at Paris and to prevent the publication of works supportive of the représentants elsewhere.[211]

Perhaps the most striking fact about the work was that d'Ivernois included a dedication to Louis XVI. This was explained by his negative references to Britain. In the *Tableau* d'Ivernois deplored the fact that the British had refused to involve themselves in Genevan affairs when invited to do so during the mediation of 1768 by the Duc de Praslin: "England ought to have declared that she would watch over that independence, and cover the liberty of this small state with her powerful protection."[212] This was a prelude to the equally unhelpful behavior of the British in 1782. In such circumstances, all Genevans were forced "to plead the cause of liberty before a monarch, [Geneva's] patron, its protector, a monarch who since the beginning of his reign has been an object of veneration to true republicans." D'Ivernois's hope was that Louis XVI would accept that Geneva was naturally a democratic state in the sense that the sovereign, rather than the government, was the people. Industry could only ever be "grafted onto the tree of liberty" and would die in a regime dominated by "the intrigues of a few of our men in opulence."[213]

The work was also intended to influence the policy of Victor Amadeus III of Sardinia, whose father Charles Emmanuel III was praised by d'Ivernois as a "politic king" who had increased the population of Savoy by a tenth, and who had been wise in not intervening at Geneva in 1768. The policy of the son was "directly opposite" and self-defeating, as a destroyed Geneva with an impoverished populace would increasingly burden Savoy.[214] D'Ivernois argued that the origins of Geneva's government were democratic, in the sense of the people being the source of the legislative power within the state. Furthermore, "the more entire the species of democracy, the fewer jealousies and distrusts were perceived, external dangers kept alive the flame of patriotism, and continually cemented the general union." In 1738 the mediators "were wise enough to soar above the prejudices of their rank," laboring "not to destroy democracy or the assemblies of the people but to fortify them with dilatory formalities, fit to secure them against precipitation, too frequently the ruin of popular states."[215]

Against such principles, agreed upon by the French and the Swiss, a plot had been launched by Voltaire and his followers Crommelin and Hennin, acting in league with the magistrates, who wanted to usurp the power of the people.[216] They persuaded the duc de Choiseul to go against "the true principle of absolute monarchy, being the happiness of the majority," which meant that "the court of Versailles seemed to have no real interest in favouring the aristocratic views of the senate." But Choiseul's "most important object" became "the destruction of the two free governments which cardinal de Fleury had taken such pains to settle in 1738, Sweden and Geneva." Only the "cautious slowness" of the cantons in the course of the mediation prevented Geneva from Choiseul's "annihilation of the liberty of Geneva."[217] D'Ivernois revealed Necker's role in the negotiations of the 1760s and praised him as a "citizen distinguished for his virtues and abilities."[218] The *Tableau* amounted to the most detailed history of the negotiations that resulted in the compromise of 1768, and it fulsomely defended that settlement. A further volume promised to continue the story up to 1782, revealing the betrayal of the représentants and the rejection of the principles established in 1768. Once again, plotters at Versailles, now permanently linked to Geneva, were identified as responsible for the lamentable contemporary history of the city.[219]

The second justification of the leaders of the représentants was Brissot's *Le Philadelphien à Genève*. Like d'Ivernois, Brissot provided an overview of the history of Geneva in the eighteenth century; he too focused upon the growth of an aristocratic cabal in league with France, dedicated to removing popular liberties and favoring the rule of a francophone magistracy. Again following d'Ivernois, the magistrates were stated to be at odds with enlightenment, "the philosophical spirit" that had appeared across Europe during the final decades of the seventeenth century and which was a force for commerce, science, and popular education.[220] Rousseau was portrayed as a victim of a plot developed at Paris and Geneva to destroy advocates of liberty. The minister Choiseul was called "despotic in his mind and also in his heart," seeking to create a system of trade based on luxury that would impoverish the people. The full extent of the plot was revealed in the later 1760s, when Choiseul made clear his imperial designs upon the city, and, using trade as a weapon against the Genevans, "merchants were ruined, manufactures collapsed, artists suffered, and the workers died of famine." By contrast, the settlement of 1768 was described as a force for enlightenment, particularly when modified by the incorporation of the natifs into the citizen body. A new economic beginning for a city would have been the result of représentant success. Geneva's industries and politics thrived best where moderate wealth was the norm.[221]

Brissot's text differed from d'Ivernois's in that it dealt with the events of 1782 directly. It was notable for playing down the attacks on Vergennes, observing that he was consistently misinformed but that "his reputation for justice and probity remained intact." This was a completely different tone than that deployed by the leaders of the représentants after Du Roveray's *Fameuse Remonstrance* of 1780, and reflected the fact that the earlier strategy of shaming Vergennes or seeking his removal had failed. The représentants were now completely dependent upon the French foreign minister. Despite this, Brissot continued to blame France. The insurrection of 1782 was described as forced upon the représentants in response to the plot between the French and the négatifs, who were seeking to realize what they had failed to accomplish in 1768. Brissot described an ordered revolution within the city, calmly undertaken and respectful of persons, property, and religion; the General Council was deemed to have vetted every decision undertaken by the représentants. The locking up of the magistrates was an example, undertaken only to protect them from an angry populace. The tragedy was that Geneva was a weak state. This meant that a France that had respected the North American rebels, and had in an earlier century respected Cromwell, would seek to crush the représentants, being misinformed about both the nature of the rebellion and the treatment of the magistrates in its aftermath. So established was "the empire of slavery" that Genevan self-defense was presented as a "folly and a crime," whereas in actuality it would have been in the interest of France and Switzerland to support a représentant Geneva abundant in wealth. On visiting Bern, Brissot likened the despotism that he saw reigning there to the rule of a vizier. He accused the followers of

Cornuaud of being ready to enter the city to ensure that the magistrates' houses were safe while the rest were free to be pillaged.[222]

Brissot presented the leaders of the représentants as realists rather than cowards, calling them humane and cosmopolitan for not acting like the populace of Saguntum and sacrificing themselves before overwhelmingly superior invading forces. They had exercised their right to resist, which was enshrined in history, and most recently in the vaunted constitutions of the new North American states. But the right to resist did not entail the necessity of dying for a cause that could not be won in present circumstances.[223] Accordingly, Brissot wanted Vergennes to acknowledge the pacific nature of the représentant movement and to allow the exiled leaders to return to Geneva, where they could work with the magistrates to secure a lasting peace. He used the example of Rousseau, who had acted with pity when he heard of the condemnation of Helvétius's *De l'esprit*, throwing his own refutation into the flames rather than adding to the indictments of the author. A similar policy toward the exiles was recommended to Vergennes, rather than "pushing the dagger into the heart." If the exiles remained abroad, Geneva would sink into tyranny, having "lost her political identity, the sole force that maintained [Geneva]." The people would turn to luxury, pleasure, and the agreeable life, a life of indifference and necessarily without faith. Manners, the basis of every state, would be corrupted, and the veneration of wealth alone would become the religion of Geneva.

Brissot blamed the rich for corrupting the Genevan people and for persuading so many that a better way of life lay with France. He sought to prove that the représentants' ideas about democracy were not at all dangerous. In monarchies and in republics, the safety of the people remained the supreme law. At Geneva, the General Council determined what this meant. A distinction existed between sovereignty and government, and the resulting balance between legislative and executive powers had defined Geneva's stable democracy. Transforming Geneva into a tyranny, where there were no "asylums of liberty and of instruction, where the people were enlightened about the state of their country," and where the rulers governed in their own interests rather than in accordance with the common good, meant the end of its greatness.[224] Brissot presented the représentants as the inheritors of Calvin's mantle in their respect for pure manners and just laws. He praised their sumptuary laws and attempts by politicians such as Clavière to tax the rich and to prevent the police of grain from entailing unfair taxes upon the poor. Whereas the founder of the state had been damaged by his "Judaic fanaticism," the supporters of the représentants were almost all "deists or materialists," although the morals that were preached were "excellent."[225]

All of these works underscored the fact that Britain was deemed to be a secondary power with respect to Geneva, having let the représentants down in 1781, effectively giving notice to the French that this area of Europe was their domain, to do with as they wanted. This was obvious to Deluc from London. Even de Lolme, who disagreed with the widespread view that Britain was in decline, was of the opinion at this time that empire was more dangerous to Britain than to other states and that intervention to save small states such as Geneva was likely to be both futile and self-defeating. Brissot, before he completed the *Philadelphien,* wrote a work defining politics as "the cause of humanity" and noting that Rousseau "in politics was a guide whose notions are rather vague," which concluded that Britain should learn from its imperial misadventure and take its place behind France in a world governed by free trade, where economic power was in proportion to natural resources and size.[226] Such views corresponded with opinion at Paris among the physiocratic followers of Turgot and among the circles of Protestant dissenters and radical Whig reformers at London. The représentant exiles united with members of both groups, in seeking to alter both French and British policy between 1783 and 1787.

6

INTERNATIONAL CRISES AND PERPETUAL PEACE

THE EXILES IN BRITAIN

The Genevan représentants considered Britain largely unimportant as an ally before and during the events of 1782, having failed to persuade British leaders to become interested in the city since the 1760s. As d'Ivernois put it in his *Tableau historique et politique des deux dernières révolutions de Genève*, Britain in 1782 was perceived as a state "for the support of which all the free states of Europe must have some rights," but it had abandoned Corsica and was more interested in global war than in the protection of Europe's many notions of liberty.[1] From London there was sympathy but more pertinently a frank acknowledgment that Geneva was in the French sphere of influence. George III may personally have been opposed to the représentants.[2] In any case, Britain was losing a war against France that had significant implications for European policy, and it had neither the resources nor the desire to intervene. Intervention by Britain would, it was everywhere recognized, signal a very different stance with regard to the balance of power on the European mainland. Involvement in Genevan affairs would complicate relations with Savoy, Prussia, and the Swiss cantons. The inevitable expense might push Britain into a national bankruptcy. Other than in pockets such as Hanover or Holland, where dynastic or trading links dictated a more active policy, being embroiled in European politics was to be avoided, whatever the circumstances of a Geneva, a Corsica, or a Poland.[3]

Public opinion within Britain, as evinced by newspapers and periodicals, was unhappy with this stance. The press responded positively to the représentants in 1782. The contrast with British responses to previous upheavals at Geneva was marked. Possibly this was due to a recognition that French power had been restored and ought to be challenged. The change of tone was especially clear in responses to the expulsion of the leaders of the représentants. The works defending their cause were reported on widely. One review of d'Ivernois's *An Historical and Political View of the Constitution and Revolutions of Geneva*, appearing in John Farrell's translation, provided clear evidence of the change of perspective in condemning the fact that Geneva "was not only virtually, but formally, under the dominion of France." The Genevan experience had to be approached from the perspective of growing French power and the gradual loss of liberty in Europe's small states.

> Poland was dismembered; Geneva is ratified by France; and Switzerland yet possesses a doubtful and suspicious liberty. The time is probably not far distant, when more neighbouring states may be divided among their powerful protectors. . . . The work before us is entitled to considerable praises: though it contain the private dissensions of one little republic, yet it should be remembered, that they are the struggles of freedom against the worst of despotism, aristocracy. . . . When these luxuriant weeds have destroyed the useful plants, and introduced a general confusion, an ambitious sovereign will always be at hand to meditate and to protest, but in reality to conquer. The states of Greece were thus subjugated by Rome; England was, in this way, subdued by the Saxons: we need not add more modern instances, we fear they will be yet more numerous.[4]

Another review pronounced a similar verdict, although it condemned d'Ivernois's dedication of the book to Louis XVI, accusing the author of "supplicating the protection of a neighbouring despot," which "reminds us of the states of Greece imploring the protection of the Romans against the Macedonians, and of the Macedonians against the Romans, both, in their turns, the most oppressive of tyrants."

> The history of Geneva illustrates in a very forcible manner the truth of the political maxim, that all small republics are destined to perish either through internal dissentions or by foreign conquests. The Senate, in whose hands executive government was placed, made gradual encroachments on the liberties of the people. The people, high spirited, and impatient almost of the necessary and just restraints of government could not brook multiplied, and increasing acts of usurpation. Altercations and disputes were followed by violence. An appeal was made to neighbouring states: and an armed mediation put a period to the existence of the Genevese republic.[5]

Reviews of Jacques-Pierre Brissot's *Le Philadelphien à Genève* took particular notice of the claim that a "league that was entered into by France, Sardinia, and

Bern, to destroy the independence of Geneva." Ten thousand residents were said to be seeking to leave "since they could not resist the military force brought against them."[6] Another review of the same work reported twenty thousand ready to emigrate in quest of peace and liberty in some other climate.[7] Such responses amounted to demands for a more moral foreign policy. They contributed to the decision of the government to "secure a favourable reception for such families as were determined to quit Geneva, and not only a favourable reception but such positive encouragement & support as might reimburse their expenses, & lay the foundation of an establishment in this country."[8] This was carried out despite the complaints of Geneva's reinstated magistrates.[9]

Etienne Dumont reported from Geneva in October 1782 that d'Ivernois was in London and "occupied with the project of a Genevan colony in Ireland, about which they have already agreed the essentials." Du Roveray had also left for England by this time. Dumont wrote to Roget that "the colony will rise, and will allow our people, who have been corrupted in our native soil, to re-establish their vigour on foreign soil."[10] Philip Stanhope, 2nd Earl Stanhope, was reputed to have offered the Genevan substantial lands in Derbyshire.[11] But a decision was then taken to move to Waterford in Ireland, with the full support of Prime Minister William Petty, then 2nd Earl Shelburne. Prominent statesmen were equally favorable, including the governor-general of Ireland George Nugent-Temple-Grenville, Earl Temple and later 1st Marquess of Buckingham (1753–1813), who, like Shelburne, was interested in the commercial development of Ireland, especially by foreign Protestants.[12] It was said that "the nobility and gentry of Ireland seemed to vie with each other in countenancing the settlement."[13] The expectation was that a second Huguenot diaspora might do for the Irish economy what the late-seventeenth-century emigration had done for English trade.

The Irish experiment was based on the Waterford colony's enjoying the benefits of free commerce. It promised to be an example of economic power that would show France the mistaken consequences of invading smaller neighbors and taking away the liberties of industrious citizens.[14] It was equally intended to show that free trade in Ireland would not undermine competitor mainland industries, and that Ireland's Catholic peasantry could enjoy the positive consequences of economic development led by Calvinists. New Geneva was "to resemble the old Geneva in every thing, except in having an upper and a lower town."[15] A "new country" was promised, because "the terrible burden of [the British] national debt did not touch Ireland." Even Geneva's Academy was to be reconstituted under a regime of political and civil liberty.[16] Clavière's straitened financial circumstances prevented him from carrying out the intention of purchasing a vessel to ship citizens to Ireland. He did, however, establish a factory to refine flax, hoping to take advantage of the cheap labor in the Waterford area.[17] Full of energy and dedicated to the Waterford experiment, Clavière anticipated both the withering and death of old Geneva because of the selfish and stupid culture engendered by the French-supported magistrates, and the glorious success of a new colony founded on good manners and free trade.[18]

Every aspect of the Waterford project, however, failed. This was despite the keenness of the British politicians involved, and especially Thomas Orde, chief secretary in Ireland between 1784 and 1787, to maintain for the Genevans "the friendly protection of a liberal nation."[19] Several représentant families did not follow their leaders to Ireland. Those who settled became discouraged after their main supporter, Lord Shelburne, and with him Lord Temple as viceroy, fell from power in the autumn of 1783. It was said that overall only six hundred représentants had emigrated. Many returned to Geneva to take an oath of fealty toward the new government:

> The Genevans seemed so greatly to deplore the diminution of that liberty to which they had long been accustomed, and to which they ascribed the late remarkable increase of their population and riches, that if we had judged from the discontents and consternation of the citizens, we might have concluded the change of government would have been followed by an almost general emigration. The event, however, has not justified this conclusion. Excepting the principal leaders, those of the popular party who were banished, and a few others who renounced their country in compliance with their political principles; the greatest part of the emigrants returned, and again settled in the place of their nativity. And perhaps it may be affirmed with truth, that the late revolution has scarcely driven six hundred persons from Geneva.[20]

The British government did act to have one of the représentants, Amy Melly, released from prison at Geneva, where the magistrates had placed him for reputedly seeking to encourage emigration to Ireland.[21] The reason for intervention was because Melly, like Du Roveray, d'Ivernois, Clavière, and others, had become an Irish subject, taking an oath to George III at Dublin in 1783. Clavière wrote to Brissot advising him to make a new life in Ireland and to write a book about a state "which is not barbarous but which appears to be barbarous because of the evils it has suffered."[22] Before long, however, he was blaming the British for failing to support the colony, and he was certain that French ministers putting pressure on their British counterparts lay behind this.[23]

The Waterford experiment was tied to an initiative that defined political and economic thinking in the early 1780s: the establishment of perpetual peace by an alliance between Britain and France. The Genevans' involvement in this project was signaled in Brissot's *Philadelphien à Genève*. The "politics of all the cabinets of Europe," he declared, were changing. This was because "the enlightenment of philosophy" was revealing what public happiness entailed. In both monarchies and republics, public felicity meant peace first and foremost. The experience of America had made this evident: "The Americans have written in blood the axioms of their liberty. European governments can consecrate these very maxims, not in changing their form of state, but in addressing the welfare of their people." Opponents of this movement, such as Simon-Nicolas-Henri Linguet's "open war against philosophers, modern politics, and against all republicans," needed to be combated by underlining the evils of reason of state and of empire, which destroyed peace and industry. Brissot identified Mallet du Pan's writing on Geneva as being "French" in its apology for immoral politics.[24] By contrast, peace and liberty generated wealth, and any states that opposed such values were irrational and would ultimately be impoverished. The chance to banish immoral politics forever came with peace in North America. Brissot greeted the news with joy but added that it was "the signal for a universal peace."[25] This was a direct reference to Shelburne's initiatives at Paris in 1783 and his hopes that an Anglo-French alliance would be followed by a commercial treaty, to bring down all mercantile empires and restore peace to the large and small states of Europe in perpetuity. His aspiration was written into the treaty as section 18 of the Peace of Paris, which promised a commercial treaty between the nations by the end of 1786. Shelburne wrote to his friend Abbé André Morellet that "the great principle which pervades the whole [of the peace treaty] is a general freedom of commerce."[26]

The représentant exiles came to know Shelburne through the Waterford experiment, and the links became much stronger in future years after Etienne Dumont, in 1785, replaced Joseph Priestley in Shelburne's household as the resident philosophe. Shelburne was renowned for gathering a political circle around him to advise on reform policies, including a number of leading dissenting ministers such as Andrew Kippis and Richard Price, and occasionally physiocrats such as Morellet and libertines such as Mirabeau.[27] This was often referred to as the "Bowood circle" because of Shelburne's use of Bowood House in Wiltshire, although Shelburne House in London was equally frequented.[28] In the early 1780s they attempted to prevent the usurpation of Geneva and other small states by France by asserting the need for continued peace across Europe and the consequent respect for all existing national boundaries. By advocating the return of Europe to an economic growth path based on natural liberty, they hoped that the independence of the existing states of Europe could be protected, particularly since so many were, like Poland, falling prey to their larger neighbors in search of a British-style mercantile empire.

Shelburne, following Dean Tucker, discounted the fears about the poorer states of Europe being able, because of lower wage costs, to undercut the prices of richer states such as Britain. The argument that rich states would decline in conditions of natural liberty was widespread, made famous by Hume's essay "Of Money" in his *Political Discourses* of 1752. The belief that controls over trade would prevent or delay economic decline was one of the main tenets of the mercantile system.[29] Shelburne, by contrast, held that in conditions of free trade each state would specialize in particular branches of trade and thereby reap the rewards of greater commerce and wealth, untroubled by threats to national independence that had become illogical because they ruined trade. Between 1783 and 1787 he united physiocrats, philosophes, dissenters, natural philosophers, and the Genevan exiles of 1782 in advancing particular policies to establish the foundations for free trade and perpetual peace. The great benefit was seen to be maintaining Europe's existing multitude of small and large states, which defined the continent but were threatened by the growth of vast and antagonistic mercantile empires in Britain and in France and by the "barbarian" empires of Russia and the Far East.

SHELBURNE AND PERPETUAL PEACE

Shelburne owed his rise to the Seven Years' War, having so distinguished himself at Minden and Kloster Kampen that he was raised to the rank of colonel and appointed aide-de-camp to the king. Through knowledge of the court he became known to the prominent John Stuart, 3rd Earl of Bute, and was returned to the House of Commons as member for Wycombe. In 1762, before he could take his seat, he succeeded his father as Earl of Shelburne in the Irish peerage and as Baron Wycombe in that of Britain.[30] Shelburne's view was that Britain had become overextended despite its great victories during the Seven Years' War. The resulting soaring national debt and the successive controversies concerning the balance of constitutional powers in Britain and the role of Britain in European politics were all tied, because of the war, to the question of whether Britain ought to maintain and to extend its global empire, or to allow it to decline.[31] It was this question that Shelburne sought most ardently to address, and he persuaded others to follow him. He became prominent in national argument beginning in July 1766, when he served under William Pitt the Elder, 1st Earl of Chatham, as secretary of state for the Southern Department (until October 1768). His most significant memorandum foreshadowed later concerns, advocating giving the North American colonies much greater leeway with regard to setting their own western limits and trading policy, endowing them with greater self-governance, and reducing restrictions upon trade. At the same time, reform was envisaged without jeopardizing the integrity of the British Empire.[32]

Shelburne believed he was living in an age of domestic and international crisis. This, as discussed in chapter 3, was a commonplace view, neatly expressed by David Hume in a letter reporting that Shelburne had informed him personally of the Earl of Chatham's resignation: "Our administration is like a heap of loose stones, where, if you remove one, the rest will all tumble. This is the least of the numberless evils under which we labour. What do you think of our being such complete beggars as not to be able to subsist, and yet labouring under the jealousy and envy of all Europe, on account of our supposed power and opulence."[33]

Shelburne and his inner circle shared Hume's diagnosis of the evils of the day, epitomized by the likelihood of a debt-induced national bankruptcy, which was sometimes expected to prefigure a successful French invasion.[34] Unlike Hume, however, Shelburne and his friends believed that a solution could be found in the establishment of a sinking fund to deal with the debt, and the development of commerce in conditions of liberty domestically and internationally. Richard Price signaled such a prospect when he speculated about the true interest of Britain with respect to North America in 1776:

> Had we nourished and favoured America with a view to commerce, instead of considering it as a country to be governed: Had we, like a liberal and wise people, rejoiced to see a multitude of free states branched forth from ourselves, all enjoying independent legislatures similar to our own: Had we aimed at binding them to us only by the ties of affection and interest; and contented ourselves with a moderate power rendered durable by being lenient and friendly, an umpire in their differences, an aid to them in improving their own free governments, and their common bulwark against the assaults of foreign enemies: Had this, I say, been our policy and temper; there is nothing so great or happy that we might not have expected. With their increase our strength would have increased. A growing surplus in the revenue might have been gained, which, invariably applied to the gradual discharge of the national debt, would have delivered us from the ruin with which it threatens us. The Liberty of America might have preserved our Liberty; and, under the direction of a patriot king or wise minister, proved the means of restoring to us our almost lost constitution.[35]

With the advent of war with the North American states, free trade would succeed only when it was tied to a commercial alliance with France. The alliance was expected to bring peace to mainland Europe and to allow gradual and relatively untroubled reform at home. Price went as far as to advocate the establishment of an "umpire or senate" of delegates from all of the states of Europe, with the authority to maintain current national boundaries and to resolve disputes.[36] Britain's dangerous thirst for empire would not be tenable in conditions of free trade. Its trade would fall relative to that of rival states. Rapacious commercial companies would no longer control trade. Global politics would gradually recognize the relationship between peace and strength, by means of the clear link between peace and commercial development. In short, Britain would no longer be able to afford an empire and would no longer have a clear interest in sustaining one. This aspiration defined the politics of the Bowood circle and of the Genevan *représentants* in the 1780s.

Shelburne had real hopes in the early 1780s that, through peace with the United States, Spain, and France, and by signing commercial treaties to establish free trade among these nations, a means could be discovered to return European states to Adam Smith's vaunted "natural progress of opulence," which had been outlined as an ideal economic growth path in the third book of *The Wealth of Nations*.[37] Shelburne considered himself Smith's disciple.[38] He presented his friends with copies of *The Theory of Moral Sentiments*, persuaded Smith to tutor his younger brother at Edinburgh, and sought out Smith's opinion on particular issues of the day, such as Alexander Dalrymple's proposal for an expedition to the South Pacific in 1766–1767.[39] Smith had evidently preached the benefits of natural liberty with respect to trade, and Shelburne learned of what became one of the central themes of *The Wealth of Nations*: the comparison between a natural path of economic development, destroyed in Europe by feudalism, and the modern mercantile system, whose "unnatural and retrograde order" prevented the full development of commerce at the same time as it caused war. The mercantile system owed its origins to the fact that the urbanization of Europe, which was a legacy of the Roman Empire, had proceeded apace across the continent without any concomitant commercialization of agriculture. The promotion of natural liberty against the controls of the mercantile system was the solution.

Shelburne was ever a vociferous defender of commercial liberty, whenever peace could be guaranteed between states, and he favored neutrality during war as the surest way to the continued promotion of commerce. It was for this reason he attempted to persuade James Playfair to establish a journal called *The Neutralist* and praised William Thomson's proposed weekly paper *The Armed*

Neutrality, neither of which was ever launched.[40] While Smith was cautious and phlegmatic in his approach to practical reform, Shelburne believed in general moral principles "as may embrace the Turk or the Gentoo equally with the Christian."[41] He was in consequence smitten by Anne-Robert-Jacques Turgot's idea of "establishing certain fixed fundamental principles of law, commerce, morality and politics comprehensive enough to embrace all religions and all countries." Shelburne's close friend and secretary Benjamin Vaughan translated Marie-Jean-Antoine-Nicolas de Caritat, marquis de Condorcet's *Vie de Turgot* (1786), which outlined Turgot's project, and for which Condorcet had signaled his support in the same year, in his response to Raynal's essay competition addressing the question, "Has the discovery of America been beneficial or harmful to the human race?"[42] Shelburne wrote to Price that he wanted him to make a reality of Turgot's vision:

> It is to the inculcating [of] these principles I want you, my dear friend, to dedicate your whole time, to cry down war throughout the whole world, which nothing can ever justify, and to prove the advantages of peace, and the right which all countries have to require it of their sovereigns. If sovereigns are offended with each other, let them fight singlehanded, without involving their people in their silly quarrels. You have talents and character peculiarly adapted to give weight to these principles. Every one is sufficiently agreed about the existence of God and about his attributes, except some conceited men of letters, who are delighted to reason in the dark, and think themselves superior to the rest of the world, because they think they know what the rest of the world don't think worth knowing. I want you to keep better company.[43]

Shelburne continued to expound the principles he believed in until the end of his life:

> Providence has so constituted the world, that very little government is necessary. After the assembly at Philadelphia had sat a long time . . . considering what form of government they should adopt, Dr Franklin rose . . . to express his apprehension that if some plan was not speedily adopted, the people out of doors would learn a most dangerous secret, that things might go on very well without any positive form of government. How are all markets supplied? All the governments of Europe have been more or less occupied about the supply of their capitals, except London, which has never wanted. The grazier and the gardener know the amount of the demand ten times better than any legislator. What mischief has been done by legislating about corn, from which England even has not been exempt! Holland has left the corn trade entirely free, and has never felt what scarcity was. A negative government

will not do in order to make conquests or to keep distant governments in dependence. But is that intended, or what good purpose of any kind does it answer.[44]

In the early 1780s the similarity between the reform projects of Turgot's French and British admirers was marked. As his friend and biographer the physiocrat Pierre-Samuel Dupont de Nemours argued, Turgot had found a means of establishing peace by commercial treaties establishing free trade. One of the central questions for British writers was whether this would entail, as Dupont put it, such a prodigious economic superiority for France that "Britain would never be able to make war upon us in future."[45]

SHELBURNE AND THE PHYSIOCRATS

Such beliefs were the reason for Shelburne's friendship with the French physiocrat André Morellet, whom he met in Paris in 1771 and who visited Bowood in 1772 and in 1782.[46] Morellet was a disciple of the philosopher Claude Adrien Helvétius, who died at the height of his influence in 1772, and a member of Madame Helvétius's salon, which included the explorer Louis Antoine de Bougainville; the notorious atheist Paul-Henri Thiry, Baron d'Holbach; the soldier and philosopher François-Jean de Chastellux; Turgot; and Benjamin Franklin.[47] Neither Shelburne nor Morellet, who had met Smith at Paris in 1762, distinguished between Smith's politics and those of the second generation of French physiocrats associated with the reforming minister Turgot, whose short-lived ministry had become notorious for its bonfire of economic controls upon trade. Morellet's impact upon Shelburne was recalled three decades later: "I have not changed an atom of the principles I first imbibed from you and Adam Smith. They make a woeful slow progress, but I cannot look upon them as extinct; on the contrary, they must prevail in the end like the sea. What they lose in one play they gain in another."[48] It was from Morellet that Shelburne learned the "application of the principle of the liberty of trade to diverse questions of political economy."[49] When Shelburne presented Morellet with a copy of Smith's *Wealth of Nations* in 1776, he immediately set about translating it.[50] When Morellet was elected to the Académie française in 1786, a eulogy by the Marquis de Chastellux reiterated Shelburne's acknowledgment of Morellet's influence upon him: "Your writings and your conversation has done the most to enlighten me about the benefits of free commerce, a precious liberty which conciliates all the interests, which must one day become the shared and fecund source of the prosperity of nations."[51]

Chastellux's comment of 1786 is significant because it directly relates the liberty of trade to international relations. It was accompanied by the statement that Britain was now the imitator of France with regard to commercial principle, and that an era had been inaugurated that heralded peace between the two greatest commercial nations of the world rather than intermittent war and perpetual rivalry. Reference to the application of the principle of liberty to political economy as a whole meant addressing the issue of international strife. Morellet's letters to Shelburne confirm this. Morellet saw the counterpart to the liberalization of the French grain trade attempted by Turgot to be what he termed "cosmopolitan politics." These amounted to realizing the project for perpetual peace of Charles-Irénée Castel, the abbé de Saint-Pierre.[52] With respect to North America, Morellet constantly reminded Shelburne that "if Britain wants to restore relations with its former colony, it can easily do so, and, through the liberty [of commerce], would quickly recover all of the advantages enjoyed under monopoly [trade], which cost Britain so dear."[53]

If the first step for the Bowood circle was the domestic liberalization of trade and the application of commercial principles to agriculture, the second was to establish an international community dedicated to freedom of trade between nations. Despite Turgot's failure, this explains why Morellet went to London in 1782 to negotiate with Shelburne on behalf of the French foreign minister Vergennes. In the aftermath of the protracted negotiations, Morellet believed that he had helped to establish a new international order that rested upon mutual benevolence, itself founded upon enlightened self-interest, rather than upon egoism.[54] Shelburne served as secretary of state for home, colonial, and Irish affairs under Prime Minister Charles Watson-Wentworth, 2nd Marquess of Rockingham. After Rockingham's death, Shelburne served as First Lord of the Treasury from July 1782 to April 1783. Although Parliament was in recess for five months of this period, it gave Shelburne time to become directly involved in the diplomatic negotiations to end the North American war, aided by his emissary Richard Oswald and his private secretary Benjamin Vaughan. The new international order was inaugurated after a provisional treaty of peace was signed between Britain and the United States at Paris on 13 November 1782, and when on 20 January 1783 preliminary articles were signed with France and with Spain. The diplomatic work was deemed so significant that Shelburne persuaded Vergennes to give Morellet an annual pension after peace had been restored.[55]

From Morellet's perspective, the Treaty of Paris of 1783 put right the diplomatic wrongs of the Treaty of Paris (1764) that had ended the Seven Years' War and the Treaty of Aix-la-Chapelle (1748) that had put an end to the War of the

Austrian Succession. For Shelburne and his circle, in restoring peace between France and Britain he was working to end the post-1763 era of domestic crisis. In underlining the costs and dangers of an expansive empire, the treaty reminded the British that it was better to rely on trade rather than arms to sustain the state, and it represented a warning against future colonization. Above all it was a chance for Europe to return to the natural progress of opulence, by dealing a heavy blow against the mercantile system of controlled trade, as Shelburne's friend Andrew Kippis underlined.[56] In the House of Lords, Shelburne identified "the era of Protestantism in trade," the argument being that the new principle of commercial liberty was better suited to Protestant states and that the progress of trade would partner the progress of religion. Free commerce with North America was the best future for Britain:

> Monopolies some way or other, are ever justly punished. They forbid rivalry, and rivalry is of the very essence of the wellbeing of trade. This seems to be an era of Protestantism in trade. All Europe appear enlightened, and eager to throw off the vile shackles of oppressive ignorant monopoly, of that unmanly and illiberal principle, which is at once ungenerous and deceitful. A few interested Canadian merchants might complain; for merchants would always love monopoly, without taking a moment's time to think, whether it was for their interest or not. I avow that monopoly is always unwise; but if there is any nation under Heaven, who ought to be the first that rejected monopoly, it is the English. Situated as we are between the old world and the new—and between the southern and northern Europe—all that we ought to covet upon earth was free trade, and fair equality. With more industry, with more enterprise, with more capital than any trading nation upon earth, it ought to be our constant cry—let every market be open—let us meet our rivals fairly—and we ask no more. It is a principle on which we have had the wisdom to act with respect to our brethren of Ireland, and, if conciliation be our view, why should we not reach it out also to America.[57]

When Shelburne resigned, after being defeated in the House of Commons on a motion censuring him for giving too much to the North Americans, Benjamin Vaughan exchanged letters with Franklin. Vaughan noted that the imperative was "the overthrow of systems relative to English commerce" and that Shelburne had considered making the whole of England a free port, in a summary of the Bowood circle's hopes and expectations:

> You now see verified all that I said about binding down England to so hard a peace. It has put many good people into ill humour, and it has given a thousand pretexts to the bad people among us. But the overthrow of parties,

is nothing to the overthrow of systems relative to English commerce, which was intended to be placed on a footing that would have been an example to all mankind, and probably have restored England to her pinnacle again. America I am sure we should have had as much of, as could be expected, upon the proposed systems of liberality. But however the ministry shall finally arrange itself, I cannot but hope on all hands, that we shall be more or less cured of our fighting and monopolizing notions and look to an American's Friendship. The boldness of my friend's conduct therefore has done infinite service to men's minds, as his conversation has done to the royal mind. You will take pleasure in hearing that he talked of making England a free port, for which he said we were fitted by nature, capital, love of enterprise, marine, connections, and position between the old and new world and the north and south of Europe; and that those who were best circumstanced for trade could not but be gainers by having trade open. Indeed I may now say to you with courage that I have scarcely seen or heard any thing of what has passed already, or was meant to take place hereafter, that I do not approve and applaud, as conducted upon grand principles. In short, I think that at last England will mend, not her parties indeed, but the proceedings of those who remain in office, whoever they may be.[58]

Shelburne later argued that "the general system of the late peace" had extinguished "all mistaken ideas of rivalship." Looking back from the perspective of a more adversarial stance toward France, which he saw developing in the aftermath of the death of Frederick the Great, he claimed that "never was there a period when animosity so soon subsided, when so few subjects of discussion, much less of dispute, had occurred with France as subsequent to 1782."[59]

MIRABEAU AND THE CINCINNATI

D'Ivernois's *Tableau* and Brissot's *Philadelphien* were intended to foster Shelburne's cause in warning France that refusal to embrace free trade and to respect the independence of small states such as Geneva would result in rabidly democratic patriot rebellions or the dominion of a corrupt and servile aristocracy within a poor and economically collapsing state. As d'Ivernois put it: "If [Geneva] ever loses her liberty, industry will take its flight along with it: Geneva shall then be but a dungeon of slavery, and the court of some opulent and depraved men: no longer will it fix the attention of philosophers; and if it be still inhabited, no industry, no citizen, no Genevese will be found amongst its inhabitants."[60] More broadly, as both Brissot and d'Ivernois noted time after time, if the small states of Europe succumbed to external aggressors, commercial decline across the continent would be precipitate. Honoré-Gabriel Riquetti de Mirabeau made all of these points in a memorandum to Vergennes that he, or more probably Du Roveray, completed for the Genevan exiles in the autumn of 1782. This noted that the Genevan exiles, whom Mirabeau termed "the democratic party at Geneva," had been offered incentives to emigrate to other countries in the form of "a Genevan constitution, buildings, land and advances of money," and warned that the commercial consequences of a new Geneva in Hesse-Homburg or Prussia would be negative for France. Mirabeau also made Vergennes aware of the request from the British government to bring large numbers of Genevans to Ireland, raising the prospect of the transformation of a country "the least cultivated and most savage in Europe," being also "one of the most fertile and ideally situated for commerce." The British had offered the représentants political equality, minimal taxes, free trade, and cheap labor. Again Mirabeau warned Vergennes that Ireland might become "the most free country on earth and the most desirable abode for men who know the value of liberty." Britain, the "rich and calculating nation," would reap the rewards of a watchmaking establishment, as would advocates of civil liberty and of Protestantism.

Mirabeau's message to Vergennes in October 1782 was that it was not too late to restore the exiles to Geneva, where their economic impact would reverberate to the benefit of France. The price was an end of "the exclusive caressing of [Geneva's] aristocrats." Aristocracy was the worst of governments for trade, worse even than a monarchical despotism, in preventing emulation from leading to fit and proper rewards, because aristocratic ranks were closed to all but the most servile. In monarchies aristocracy masked the true national interest from the throne, erecting a barrier between monarch and people. The importance of Geneva to France was clear not only through Necker's extensive loans from the republic to the monarchy but also in its position linking so many European states and in governing the trade of all of them. Mirabeau was offering Vergennes a vision of a Geneva without aristocracy, governed by the représentants with the aim of economic development through free trade. Like Brissot, he drew a parallel between the image of France abroad as "the liberator of America" and the need to avoid "being called the destroyer of Geneva." In preventing the return of the exiles, Vergennes would see the area around Geneva become an economic desert, which risked Louis XVI's experiencing a similar economic disaster to that which followed the 1685 revocation of the Edict of Nantes.[61]

By the time of the failure of the Waterford experiment, the option of returning to Geneva had been ruled out for the exiles. In consequence, Du Roveray attempted to obtain a position teaching law at Trinity College Dublin, and he remained in Ireland as a tutor.[62] He also received a pension from the British crown for his endeavors at Waterford.[63] D'Ivernois was reputed in 1785 to have become "a great favourite" of Shelburne, who, with Charles Stanhope, was seeking to find him an official appointment.[64] Although he considered emigration to Canada, he served as tutor to the son of the banker Sampson Gideon between 1784 and 1786, while continuing to act as a lawyer. Until 1789 d'Ivernois continued teaching, accompanying his charges on the Grand Tour. He continued to be involved with the broader Shelburne circle and received an introduction from Richard Price to Thomas Jefferson, with whom he discussed the possibility of emigrating to the United States in 1785.[65] Du Roveray remained close to the exiled community of Genevans, and in 1788 or 1789 he returned from Ireland to live in London.[66] Du Roveray then became close to Dumont, who had arrived at Bowood in 1785. Du Roveray and Dumont maintained excellent relations with Clavière, who moved between Paris and Brussels throughout 1784 before finally settling in the French capital in December of that year. From June 1784 he rented a house from the playwright Beaumarchais on the rue Grange-Batelière. Relations between Clavière and d'Ivernois were less warm, as Clavière blamed him for the collapse of the Waterford experiment.[67]

At Paris Clavière's first goal was to further his personal commercial empire, restoring the fortune that had been sorely reduced because of the fluctuations in French government bonds. Since the establishment of the Caisse d'Escompte by Turgot in 1776, Clavière had sunk much of his wealth in the debts of the French state.[68] The expenses incurred by Britain in the war with America had convinced him that the French debt was more secure than that of her rival. When Henri-François-de-Paule le Fèvre d'Ormesson, the *contrôleur général des finances*, suspended payments on the bills of the Caisse on 27 September 1783, Clavière faced ruin.[69] It was Charles Alexandre de Calonne's elevation to the position of contrôleur général on 3 November 1783 that ultimately saved him from bankruptcy. Payments were resumed on 23 November, and it became clear that the French government was seeking to use speculation on the Bourse de Paris to promote commerce and improve the finances of the state.[70] Clavière was disappointed by Necker's refusal to lend him funds when he had been in dire straits. With Calonne's ascent, and with the participation of his compatriot Jacques Bidermann, Clavière quickly commenced speculation in the issues of the Caisse d'Escompte, in the shares of the Spanish Banque de Saint-Charles, and the Compagnie des eaux de Paris. In his schemes to influence share prices, Clavière was abetted by both Brissot and Mirabeau.[71]

Brissot had moved to London in mid-December 1782 in order to continue working for Clavière and to establish a club and a school in London for philosophers.[72] Still in London by August 1783, he ended up in a debtors' prison, only to be saved by funds from Clavière, before returning to Paris and spending time in the Bastille until 10 September 1784; he had been imprisoned on 12 July after being accused of spreading copies of a *libelle* critical of Marie-Antoinette, entitled *Le Diable dans un bénitier*.[73] It was from this time that Brissot became even more dependent on Clavière financially.[74] The relationship was one-sided because of this, but it is noteworthy that even when he became monetarily independent, Brissot acknowledged that his relationship with Clavière was that of master and student. Brissot believed that "Clavière knew more about mankind, about his country and his century than I did," had "sacrificed his fortune, his time, and his life to the cause of the people," and "had an unstoppable momentum that carried him toward revolutions and toward those who were able to influence them." Recalling the time when he was writing pamphlets to justify Clavière's share speculations, Brissot went so far as to argue that Clavière was ever motivated to oppose "immoral or false speculations, or those with adverse consequences for the public good."[75]

All the exiles were involved with Mirabeau, whom they met once again at London in August 1784.[76] With recommendations from Benjamin Franklin, whom he had become acquainted with at Paris, Mirabeau was introduced to Benjamin Vaughan and Shelburne, whom he saw a great deal of in London and visited at Bowood House. Shelburne introduced Mirabeau to Price and to d'Ivernois, who was one of the exiles Mirabeau had not become acquainted with at Neuchâtel in the autumn of 1782. D'Ivernois then introduced Mirabeau to Romilly.[77] Morellet was also visiting Shelburne at this time, and a circle of like-minded Genevans, French, Englishmen, and North Americans was established.[78] Mirabeau shared the view that Britain was a nation in decline. He called Britain's national character "ignorant, superstitious, headstrong . . . grasping and almost Carthaginian . . . melancholy and turbulent." The British people were "the most corrupt upon the face of the earth" and survived only because of the constitution and civil liberty. Lacking sociability, they could be termed the least free on earth. In terms of morals, a topic full of irony given his personal reputation, he considered Britain inferior to France. Despite the profound and ubiquitous animosity toward the French that Mirabeau found in Britain, the only hope for the future success and security of this nation lay in friendship with France, whose trade was thriving, and which was by nature the superior power.[79] Given such a perspective, and given his failure to complete a projected work directly comparing Britain and France, it was natural for

Mirabeau to want to foster the views of the Shelburne circle and to continue to defend the cause of the Genevan exiles.[80]

On arrival in London, Mirabeau was full of projects and severely short of funds. He was initially involved in d'Ivernois's completion of the *Tableau* by bringing up to date the historical account of Genevan politics that had not gone further than 1767. In the end d'Ivernois rejected Mirabeau's work on the grounds that he would steal his own thunder if Mirabeau were named the author of the further volume of the history of Geneva. When he did complete the *Tableau historique et politique des deux dernières revolutions de Genève* in 1789, he wrote to David Chauvet that Mirabeau would have ruined the exiles' project because of his personal reputation or by turning their arguments into the kind of general republican declamations characteristic of his writings about the Dutch, thereby weakening them. Afterward there was open antagonism between Mirabeau and d'Ivernois.[81] In consequence it was Romilly who was most directly involved with Mirabeau among the Genevan community at London. Romilly even began to sketch the characters of the leading Genevan exiles in order to contribute to the proposed history of Geneva, which he also offered to translate for Mirabeau or for Jean Roget, who was another putative author.[82] Romilly's character sketches were published in his later *Memoirs,* and he ended up translating a different composition. Franklin had encouraged Mirabeau to translate an attack on the recently established Society of the Cincinnati by the South Carolina politician and judge Aedanus Burke.[83] The society had been formed to unite the officers who had served in the Revolutionary War against Britain, and was named after the Roman dictator Lucius Quinctius Cincinnatus, who left his farm to save the republic and then abandoned military office to return to work on the land.[84] Mirabeau greatly expanded the pamphlet, abetted by Sébastien-Roch-Nicolas Chamfort, Gui-Jean-Baptiste Target, and others; the result, *Considérations sur l'Ordre de Cincinnatus, ou Imitation d'un pamphlet anglo-américain,* appeared in December 1784 in French.[85] Mirabeau persuaded Romilly to translate the work, and an English edition followed in the spring of 1785.[86] The *Considérations* was the first of his works to appear with Mirabeau's name on the title page. He wrote that "It is, of all I ever wrote, that with which I am the least dissatisfied."[87]

The focus of Mirabeau's political writings had hitherto been the regeneration of France. Both his *Essai sur le despotisme* (1776) and *Des lettres de cachet et des prisons d'état,* which was written in 1778 and published in 1782, contributed to the increasingly vocal jeremiad literature charting French decline into a form of absolutism akin to oriental despotism. In the story related in *Des lettres de cachet,* Mirabeau, following Gabriel Bonnot de Mably's *Observations sur l'histoire de France*, explained that France had been a democracy under the Franks and had then "been torn to pieces by anarchical aristocracy." The major cause was the "fatal effect of the union of civil and ecclesiastical powers" in ensuring that "sacerdotal despotism" led to "civil despotism." Mirabeau argued that religion "ought to give kings ideas of peace," refuting Montesquieu in particular for "capitulating to priests and to kings." Reform strategies, such as that of the physiocrats, were held by Mirabeau to have reinforced despotism by "comparing the sovereign authority to the paternal," rather than seeing the benefit of the counterpoises sustaining limited government. If decline could be charted in France, Mirabeau did not appear concerned by the likelihood of imperial aggression across Europe. All the princes "watch each other too closely to render any violent and sudden change of domination much to be apprehended," and "the progress of the arts" meant that "no nation of Europe has the advantage enough over another to subjugate it." At the same time, Europe was in decline because only the Dutch had solved the problem of the relationship between religion and politics, yet, like the British, were in a process of social unraveling because of the progress of luxury and of mercantile politics. The ancient republics could not serve as models for moderns, being tyrannies rather than free states. Democracy amounted to "the empire of the wicked over the good," creating "the most cruel of tyrants." Eclectic philosophy and stoicism alone were recommended as tools to guide Europe toward a tolerant and civilized future, the nature of which could only be guessed at.[88]

The argument of the *Considérations* was adapted to the more optimistic politics of the mid-1780s. Following a trend of the time, it called America "an asylum to mankind," having experienced "perhaps the first [revolution] that philosophy can approve of." The Society of the Cincinnati amounted to a "praetorian band," an "actual patriciate and a military nobility, which will, ere long, become a civil nobility." The stated aim of the *Considérations* was accordingly to prevent the United States from experiencing the kind of decline being experienced across Europe. More particularly, it was a warning to republics. The American states should not follow the course of republics such as Geneva by relying upon an aristocracy that would turn itself into a hereditary caste, in the process "overbearing the constitution" and creating a tyranny "a thousand times more dreadful and more formidable than a single tyrant." In turn, aristocratic oppression would cause domestic unrest. A caesar figure would then arise, who would restore order only at the cost of still greater oppression. Machiavelli had been right to call nobility "a species of vermin that insensibly consumes liberty." In Europe the growth of aristocracy was preparing states for a new feudalism, based on the ability of a small elite to "sell a people for a ribband." Republics were being infested by monarchical practices, which led to foreign intervention and the loss of independence.[89] In France the military nobility had united with a commercial elite, creating a "multitude of calculating leaches who suck the impoverished blood of twenty millions of Frenchmen":

> I observe that ferocity and pride have practised the rapine of avarice; and that the junction of power and wealth has united against the people the cruelty of a barbarous conqueror, and the rapacious industry of a speculator. It is not in me, alas, to venerate the result and offspring of this noble mixture. I have now and then some doubt, whether this really constitutes the most respectable part of the inhabitants of the earth, and when I see that it is, at least, the most respected, I sometimes feel a compassion for the human kind, and sometimes think they deserve, by their meanness and stupidity, a greater part of their misfortunes. That these ideas have a severe and gloomy cast, will be observed by fashionable writers, with all the amiable and easy grace of their native wit. But no matter, though they be severe, provided they be just, reasonable, and honest.[90]

Pessimism was a natural register for Mirabeau. Drawing a parallel between the excesses of the Roman nobility, their feudal descendants, and the mercantile aristocracies forming in modern Europe was becoming a common theme among radical critics of contemporary politics. Following the Shelburne circle, and going against his writings of the later 1770s, however, Mirabeau called Turgot "a sincere friend of liberty and of mankind," whose "sublime genius" was "actuated by the philosophy of a statesman." Turgot had "the heart of Fénelon, united with a much more comprehensive understanding," and was the closest of the moderns to Marcus Aurelius, although the descent of recent times was marked in the fact that Turgot stood for only two years as a minister.[91] This was why Mirabeau published for the first time Turgot's letter to Richard Price of 1778, following it with Price's own reflections upon America. These texts reiterated the pacific message of the Shelburne circle that European politics could be saved from political immorality by freeing trade and collapsing the mercantile systems of monopoly, which fueled war or raised the prospect of debt-induced bankruptcies. The alternative was "political liberty, religious liberty, liberty of commerce and of industry."[92]

Turgot, in his letter to Price, presented national pride as an especially British sin, leading to imperial adventures and an excessive role for the unstable voice of the people in national cabinets. He warned the North Americans that he was worried that both ideas played too great a role in their new politics. Against imperialism Turgot stated "that one nation can never have a right to govern another," and against democracy that "a tyranny exercised by a people is, of all known tyrannies, the most cruel and insupportable, and that which leaves the fewest resources to the wretches it oppresses." These were among the most important contemporary statements of the dangers of mercantile empire and of the need for free trade and peace between Britain and France. The greatest danger was that the United States would add to Europe's troubles by following the practices of the old country rather than the new principles of political morality:

> [America] is nothing more than a copy of the republic of Holland, though Holland had not, like America, to fear the possible increase of any of its provinces. The whole edifice, as yet, rests upon the unsolid basis of the old and vulgar system of politics; upon the prejudice, that nations and provinces may, as national or provincial bodies, have an interest different from what individuals have to be free, and to defend their property against robbers and conquerors; an imaginary interest to trade more extensively than others, not to buy merchandise from foreigners, to compel foreigners to consume the growth of their country, and the produce of their manufactures; an imaginary interest to possess a more extensive territory, to acquire this or that island or village; an interest to strike terror into other nations; an interest to surpass them in military glory, or in the sciences, and the arts.[93]

With opportunities for military expansion westward, and northward with the possible incorporation of Canada, Turgot worried that the rebelling American colonies could yet become "the counterpart of Europe, a mass of divided powers, contending together for territory, or for the emoluments of commerce, and constantly cementing the slavery of the people with the people's blood." For Britain, Turgot advised the "necessary amputation" of the colonies. Trade would decrease and national power would decline, but the result would be a nation more united and more peaceful, having removed "the canker of luxury and corruption."[94]

Turgot's message was seconded by the abstract of Price's *Observations on the Importance of the American Revolution*. This work contained the already well-known declaration that the American Revolution was of providential importance, in having the potential to lead the world to an era of peace: "The last universal empire upon earth shall be the empire of reason and virtue, under which the gospel of peace (better understood) shall have free course and be glorified; many will run, to and fro, and knowledge be increased; the wolf dwell with the lamb, and the leopard with the kid, and nation no more lift up a sword against nation."[95] Price indicted the mercantile system for causing wars that had "converted Europe into a theatre of devastation and murder." Fortunately, "the time, thank heaven! is now arrived when patriotism will cease to be a hatred of mankind; when the purpose of a free state will cease to be founded upon the lust of empire, as it was at Rome, or on the love of war, as it was at Sparta."[96] Mirabeau noted in his commentary that the traditionally celebrated plans for perpetual peace of Henry IV and of the Abbé de Saint Pierre—"with Rousseau's remarks"—needed to be read alongside Price's plan in his *Observations on Civil Liberty* and also Pierre-André Gargaz's *Conciliateur de toutes les nations d'Europe, ou Projet de paix perpétuelle entre tous les souverains de l'Europe & leurs voisins* (1782), which outlined a plan for a union between the major states of Europe and had been published in English at Franklin's request in 1782.[97] Price, like Turgot, opposed empire on the grounds that a state received "nothing but infection from foreign connections." As with Turgot, he replicated the long-standing argument, so often associated with Fénelon, that luxury, vice, and misery were resident in the great towns and seaports.[98] The only disagreement between Price and Turgot concerned the role of landed proprietors in politics. Turgot saw landowners as the only true citizens, while Price wanted to encourage the rule of those with moderate wealth, whatever its origin. Price's ideal was the distribution of wealth and industrious mores he found in Connecticut:

> The happiest state of man is the middle state between the savage and the refined, or between the wild and the luxurious state. Such is the state of society in Connecticut, and some others of the American provinces where the inhabitants consist, if I am rightly informed, of an independent and hardy yeomanry, all nearly on a level—trained to arms,—instructed in their rights—cloathed in home-spun—of simple manners—strangers to luxury— drawing plenty from the ground—and that plenty, gathered easily by the hand of industry; and giving rise to early marriages, a numerous progeny, length of days, and a rapid increase—the rich and the poor, the haughty grandee and the creeping sycophant, equally unknown—protected by laws, which (being their own will) cannot oppress and by an equal government, which wanting lucrative places, cannot create corrupt canvassings and ambitious intrigue. O distinguished people! May you continue long this happy; and may the happiness you enjoy spread over the face of the whole earth![99]

Mirabeau supported the general project he identified with Turgot and with Price in notes to the texts. The equality of fortune was "the sum of my admonitions." He attacked modern empire. He praised the proposal then popular in Shelburne's circle for balloons to be used to prevent the excesses of modern warfare, and possibly war itself, through the assurance of mutual destruction by employing them to drop bombs on armies or on towns. Like the other members of the Shelburne circle, Mirabeau anticipated, following Turgot, a Britain reduced in power and influence through the loss of commerce and of empire, but also a Britain whose people were happier and which had not collapsed as a state. This point was made against the Abbé Raynal's prediction in the *Histoire des deux Indes* that, should Britain be forced to abandon its empire by loss of war or loss of trade, it would become "insignificant and contemptible."[100]

THE SCHELDT CONTROVERSY, THE EDEN TREATY, AND THE DUTCH PATRIOT REVOLT

Mirabeau continued to speculate about the dangers to all states of continuing to develop international relations on the basis of the principle of reason of state and the desire for expanding commerce through empire. His next work, *Doutes sur la liberté de l'Escaut*, dealt with exactly this issue and, like the *Considérations*, was the product of his links with Shelburne and with the Genevans. *Doutes sur la liberté* was occasioned by the attempt by Joseph II, the Holy Roman emperor, in October 1784 to force the Dutch to open the river Scheldt, the closure of which since 1585 had prevented ships from reaching the ports of Antwerp and Ghent.[101] The issue was the first major challenge to the peaceful system of international relations established at Paris in 1783 and was seen in this light by members of Shelburne's circle.[102] Brissot's pamphlets on Joseph II's decision to forbid emigration from his territories, and in support of the right to resist in the case of the Transylvanian peasants of the Balkans, were one part of the response. With regard to Brissot's work, it is significant that a Genevan exile community existed at Konstanz, which was governed by Joseph II and subject to the laws of the empire. Written as an appeal to an enlightened despot capable of ruling for the good of his people and also of embracing "the language of ancient German despots," Brissot recommended Richard Price's writings, "unfortunately not yet translated into French," as the surest guide to modern politics—Locke's *Treatise on Civil Government* and Rousseau's *Contrat social* were also praised, alongside the first chapter of the Code of Pennsylvania.[103] Brissot warned Joseph II that commerce could be developed only where the populace was free in civil terms and where commerce was equally free: "Commerce and the arts have no country but are universal, and establish themselves where there are no shackles." Proof lay in the experience of the Genevans, who spent half of their lives amassing fortunes abroad and then returned to live and raise families at Geneva. Free emigration and free return were the keys to the success of the state.[104] Equally, Britain was bound to decline because it showed so little hospitality toward immigrants. As the age became more enlightened, following the progress of political and moral philosophy, "cosmopolitanism will replace this ridiculous patriotism or national honour, words invented by despots to keep their slaves loyal."[105] Learning from the experience of revolt was equally vital. Only in democratic republics, where the will of the people was the voice of the government, could rebellion be declared contrary to law. In all other states, and particularly in monarchies or aristocracies where the interest of the ruler would at some point become divorced from the public good, as in the case of Geneva in 1782, it was incumbent upon rulers to listen to their critics and respond positively to rebels. This was the advice of Price, Rousseau, Algernon Sidney, and Milton.[106]

Concerning the more international issue of the Scheldt, Mirabeau was advised by the Genevan exile and former pastor David Chauvet and by Clavière to write a pamphlet to help keep the peace. Benjamin Vaughan was the main author according to Samuel Romilly, which makes sense considering that the text reaffirmed the need to maintain the Anglo-French entente established in 1783.[107] Mirabeau's text, appearing within a month of Joseph II's actions and at the same time as the *Considérations*, praised commercial treaties as the surest means to peace and Shelburne as a model statesman. As Mirabeau's anonymous English translator noted, *Doutes* was "calculated to promote universal concord and harmony amongst the nations of Europe" with a policy derived from the maxim "love all men without distinction of nations."[108] Chauvet supported the Dutch on the grounds that, like Geneva in 1768, it was crucial to prevent a larger power from crushing a smaller, even if the price was opposition to free trade.[109] Clavière considered that the emperor's actions presented a danger so great to the Anglo-French alliance and to European peace that it would be better for the Dutch to be sacrificed to imperial reason of state in order to maintain the wider peace and the principle of free trade. If war broke out, supporters of liberty would have to embark upon "a vast emigration to North America." Mirabeau mischievously used Clavière's text to support the Dutch cause, adapting Clavière's opposition to war to argue against Joseph II. Clavière in consequence considered the pamphlet to be naive, it being foolish to presume that the philosophical and humanitarian ideas there proposed would have any effect upon governments.[110]

Mirabeau accused the emperor, styled "the sultan of Vienna," of fomenting a league of imperialist European states, including Prussia and Russia, which would reintroduce barbarism and war to central Europe by means of invasion by modern tartars, the "armed slaves vomited forth by despotism." As an "ambitious prince," Joseph was exhibiting "to Europe the most numerous and the most formidable legions that ever threatened its political liberty." Mirabeau warned against the rage for monarchical manners, the capacity of self-interested rulers to follow policies at odds with the true interests of the state, and the vile consequences of "confederacies of absolute sovereigns invested with great military power."[111] It was natural to fear armed despots, especially those who used the principles of free trade and armed neutrality to justify their imperial designs.[112] Joseph's actions were interpreted as an attempt to establish an Austro-Russian version of the mercantile system, which Mirabeau called "the Machiavellian system," by the subjugation of smaller states such as Poland, Venice, Hungary, and in this case Holland, whose commercial empire was expected to be divided between the aspiring mercantile powers. The emperor forgot that the closure of the Scheldt to imperial trade had its origins in the crushing economic consequences of the abandonment of civil liberties in the Hapsburg Netherlands by Philip II in the sixteenth century. The Dutch were correct to recognize that, once Joseph II had access to the Scheldt, he would easily be able to subject the entire country. The question was therefore whether to sacrifice "the whole nation to the prosperity of the traders of Antwerp." It was equally whether to risk the future of Europe by giving the Tsarina Catherine access to ports beyond the Baltic, allowing her to establish a militaristic navy with an aspiration to become "master of all the seas."[113]

The ideal means of dealing with such aspirations in Europe was "a solid, sincere, eternal alliance [between France and Britain]; an alliance founded upon a treaty of commerce, which should banish for ever all national jealousies, and indissolubly reconcile the interests of the two kingdoms." An Anglo-French alliance would, according to Mirabeau, "easily impose silence on all the rest of the world." France would exercise a "natural superiority" over the rest of Europe because of its size, resources, and position.[114] But the theme of the consequence of British decline loomed large in the work. Mirabeau called Britain "a power of the third order," having yet to resolve the question of having either "power abroad or liberty at home," and incapable of extensive involvement in continental Europe. The great danger was that the British would support Joseph II in order to divide France from an ally and in the hope of destroying Dutch competition. Blindness to the infinitely worse longer-term consequences of a rampant Austria and Russia dominating the globe was traced by Mirabeau to the corrupting effect of mercantile policies upon Britain's national character and national politics. The British had been "the enemies of mankind" since the creation of their navigation acts. They would "do eternal honour to the human species [only] from the moment that their wisdom represses their ambition, and subdues their pride."

Mirabeau stated that Shelburne was "the only statesman who understands the true interest of England and foreign politics, and who has extensive views, free from national prejudices." Having "saved [the nation] by the late peace," Shelburne was unfairly feared, mistrusted, and "little loved." Britain was simply too corrupt to accept him as redeemer. In consequence it "must suffer more calamities before she is cured of that mercantile intolerance, the natural and necessary effect of which is to multiply her enemies daily."[115] Mirabeau predicted the loss of India, which had discovered means of ejecting its oppressors, and that in the case of a war in which Britain supported Joseph II, the combined Dutch and French navies would vanquish the Royal Navy.[116]

With Britain sidelined and likely to face new calamities because of the national "violent and vindictive spirit," it was necessary to rely upon France to be "once more the protectors of liberty," and save the Dutch from "the situation of Damocles at the table of Dionysius the tyrant." The solution was a "prompt and vigorous war to preserve the republic." France, rather than aspiring to act in the manner of a Louis XIV, whose "grandeur grieves and dishonours humanity," had an interest in "universal peace." A liberated Hapsburg Netherlands, a new and independent republic, would contribute to the union of states favoring free commerce and peace. Mirabeau argued that a new republic in the Netherlands would have no need of a stadtholder, having no preeminent family or aristocracy to disturb the peace of the state. The German states would gain, as they would no longer have so much to fear from their larger monarchical neighbors. Toleration across the continent would benefit from the establishment of a Catholic republic. An impetus would be given to commercial treaties for Prussia, Britain, and Holland. France, "to whom the friends of humanity owe many thanks and eulogiums for having founded the United States of America, would complete its glory, by favouring the establishment of a Belgic confederacy." Mirabeau expressed as a maxim that "republics are the proper frontiers to monarchies." In circumstances where republics were unlikely to have the power to wage war against monarchies, France would only benefit from the establishment of the new state. The only argument against it, from the perspective of other powers, was France's overweening strength. Mirabeau reiterated an opinion associated with his father that a Europe in which France played the dominant role was a natural state for the continent. Proof of the benign nature of France was its respect for the integrity of Holland despite that country's evident collapse as a military power during the Fourth Anglo-Dutch War (1780–1784).[117]

In practice, the war over the opening of the Scheldt resulted in only a single shot being fired from an Austrian ship that traveled down the river. The French negotiated a settlement without the intervention of other European powers and without further war being risked. France appeared to be acting in accordance with the principles of the new system. The same could not be said, from the perspective of the Shelburne circle, of Britain. Rather than dismantling the mercantile system, which every member of the group argued was the correlate of the September 1783 Treaty of Paris, an Order in Council soon excluded all United States citizens from Britain's West Indies trade. Benjamin Vaughan, who was a member of the Committee of West India Merchants and Planters, failed to have the order rescinded and was warned by Franklin that "England will get as little by the Commercial War she has begun with us as she did by the Military."[118] Shelburne and Price in private were becoming increasingly pessimistic and shared their fears with both Franklin and Jefferson. Shelburne was anticipating the growth of French power and the further decline of Britain, especially when rumors emerged that Calonne was establishing free ports across France. Shelburne was concerned at having quickly moved away from the centers of national power, noting that "I know no more of what is passing in London than I do of what is going on at Constantinople." He could only hope that plans were being established to "check the disposition universally gaining ground to dissipation and corruption."[119] Price warned William Eden, 1st Baron Auckland, that "while the public debt continues such a monstrous load as it is, war is invited and rival powers are tempted to insult us."[120] He told Jefferson that Britain was on the brink of ruin because "there is, I fancy, no probability that Britain can be brought to consent to that reciprosity in trade which the United States expect."[121] Franklin was given the same argument, reiterating Shelburne's concern that France would be the victor if the economic and military antagonism between the two great European powers continued: "We may lose the trade and friendship of an increasing world, and throw it into the scale of France."[122] The positive aspect, especially for the Genevans, was that France had begun to behave as the protector of Europe's small states, at least in the case of Holland. A defensive alliance with the Dutch was signed on 10 November 1785. The natural expectation was that this might prefigure an altered attitude to Geneva. The worry was that what happened in Geneva in 1782 might also happen to the Dutch, in order to keep the peace.[123]

Despite the increasing pessimism in the Shelburne circle, the prospects for peace seemed to increase with the completion of an Anglo-French Commercial Treaty, signed by William Eden for the British government and Joseph Matthias Gérard de Rayneval for the French at Paris on 26 September 1786. It was intended to "adopt a system of commerce on the basis of reciprosity and mutual convenience, which, by discontinuing the prohibitions and prohibitory duties which have existed for almost a century between the two nations, might procure the most solid advantages, on both sides, to the national productions and industry."[124] Shelburne was reported to be far from happy with the treaty. George Wilson and James Trail wrote, "Lord Lansdowne sometimes says it is a pimping imitation of one of his great schemes—at others, that it is a very good treaty—and then, again, that it is a ruinous measure."[125] In fact Shelburne supported the treaty, which he considered "perfectly agreeable to my principles," and was pleased that Britain and France appeared to have adopted the principle of armed neutrality, following the model of the "Treaty of Amity and Commerce" between Prussia and the United States of 1785. Shelburne was concerned, however, that the public, being "so ignorant and so changeable," would reject the treaty as going against national principle. It was an irony that William Eden now supported free trade with France whereas before he had vehemently refused it to Ireland.[126] Shelburne admitted that he would be "vastly troubled if it fails, for prejudice will get a new lease, and we shall be drove so far back in error."[127] He realized that together the Treaty of Paris and the Anglo-French Commercial Treaty represented a transformed international world. The difficulties Eden faced in securing a treaty favorable to British ministers were extensive, exemplified by the horror at the prospect of the opening of the silk trade. John Baker-Holroyd, 1st Earl of Sheffield, an opponent of free trade and adviser to Eden, recognized that the treaty was hugely favorable to British interests and might result in France being flooded by British goods, which would never be acceptable to a French ministry. Indeed, the treaty proved controversial. It was significant that Charles-James Fox voted against the treaty in the House of Commons on the grounds that France was Britain's natural enemy.[128]

At Paris, Dupont de Nemours was making an identical argument that the Eden treaty "is alone the guarantor of peace between the great empires," and peace between Britain and France was vital if Europe was to survive as a civilized continent.[129] Jean-Louis de Lolme also wrote in favor of free trade and commercial treaties. With regard to the Eden treaty, he regretted that a more substantial treaty had been prevented, "since political jealousy proved too powerful for mercantile interest," but he welcomed "beneficial consequences from its opposition."[130] The major assumption of the group was that, if peace were maintained between Britain and France, free trade might gradually be introduced and would then mitigate the evils of empire and the mercantile system, restoring Europe to a natural system of international relations imitative of economic power, without being derailed by war. As late as 1788, Dupont de

Nemours was writing to Adam Smith (who probably considered him a dangerous utopian schemer), expressing the view that "the positive principles [of political economy] after having been concentrated for some time among the United
States of America, France and Britain, will spread out eventually to other
nations."[131] By this time, however, the Anglo-French alliance was all but dismantled because of the Dutch crisis and because of Calonne's establishment of
a French East India Company in 1785, despite Eden's efforts to conclude a
treaty to ensure peace in the Far East.[132]

When Prussia invaded Holland in support of the besieged stadtholder in
September 1787, a general war beckoned because of France's support for the
Dutch patriotic opposition. British prime minister William Pitt the Younger
was prepared to fight France once again if intervention against Prussia took
place. Pitt began arming to this end and promised British support for Prussian
arms. The background fear was that France had already taken possession of
Dutch trading posts and the infrastructure of empire in the Far East, and that
this prefigured a direct challenge to British interests in India.[133] Although
France did not intervene, the willingness of Britain to take action against France
ruined any sense of détente. The broader politics of Anglo-French relations
were undermining arguments based on longer-term commercial development.
Richard Price warned Shelburne that, in the wake of the Dutch crisis, "France
was likely to take measures to regain her weight which would open a new scene
in Europe," risking war between Britain, Prussia, and Holland on one side and
France, Russia, and Austria on the other.[134] Principled politics appeared impossible when short-term interests and domestic struggles for power were the norm.
As Benjamin Vaughan wrote to Franklin, "These late struggles have unhappily
shown however, how little any of these people [Pitt, Charles-James Fox, and
Richard Brinsley Sheridan] are capable of grand political ideas or plans. They
understand faction, and even that often but ill, but seem to know nothing of the
new systems of general politics."[135] Benjamin Vaughan, like Dupont de
Nemours, reiterated his commitment to free trade as a means to perpetual
peace. Equally, however, he blamed mercantile policies and the culture they
fostered as the reason for the breakdown of the commercial treaties project:

> It has certainly been the actual property of the narrow [mercantile] system
> to be devoted to wars of conquest and offence: while one of the chief objects
> of the free-trade system is to extinguish such wars, and to encourage such
> principles in our neighbours and in mankind generally, as shall lessen the
> frequency of the occasions even for wars of self-defence. There is scarcely
> one writer on free-trade, at the present day, who does not make this pacific
> turn more of a primary, than of a secondary, consideration. On the other

hand, there has been scarcely one of our latter ruptures with France, or other nations, which has not, directly or indirectly, originated from systems of trade or colonization founded in monopoly. In short, estrangement and jealousy, violence and revenge, by whatever cause they are set in motion, tend to war; while liberal intercourse and exchanges seem to make the corner stones of peace and concord.[136]

Britain, seemingly more mercantile than ever with respect to the rationale behind its policies, supported the Prussian invasion of Holland and the restoration of the stadtholder, and it prevented Denmark from supporting the Swedes after Russia invaded in 1788, while rearming for an anticipated outbreak of war against France. Britain might have been more involved in the diplomacy that governed European international relations, but it was less likely to support schemes for perpetual peace, to go to war on the basis of the need to maintain existing European boundaries, or to maintain the sovereignty of particular small states. By 1789 Jeremy Bentham had added his voice to the jeremiad chorus emanating from the Shelburne circle, attacking "Pitt's Machiavellian System" and plotting out his own scheme for perpetual peace in an unpublished essay.[137]

CLAVIÈRE AND THE RENEWAL OF FAITH IN FRANCE

Mirabeau's involvement with the Shelburne circle and with the Genevan exiles in London coincided with a revision in représentant policy with respect to France. In part through Mirabeau and also through Brissot, connections existed with Vergennes and with other members of the French court. With the failure of the Waterford experiment and the perceived decline of Britain relative to France as an economic power, the hope came to the fore once again that France might be persuaded to pursue its North American policy with respect to Europe's small states and republics, in anticipation of economic gains and the confirmation of its role as a global peacekeeper. As Clavière wrote, the key fact was that France was "altogether richer than Britain," and enjoyed "a fund of [economic] confidence."[138] The links between the French and the Dutch, as has been noted, were of fundamental importance as a signal of a new Genevan policy. The other major link with the French court was Jacques Necker, whose resignation from the French finance ministry in 1781 the exiles had lamented and who was widely perceived to be a friend to the exiles with respect to both international and economic policy. Necker, however, had had little contact with the exiles since the commencement of the diaspora, and the question arose as to whether he should continue to be trusted as someone in the mold of

Turgot, or whether others, such as Calonne or even Vergennes himself, ought to be supported in order to save Europe's small states from imperial designs. The key test for all parties was Necker's *De l'administration des finances de la France* (1784), published to "prove that France has lost a valuable servant, and that this same servant is extremely angry." Commentary on the appearance of this work revealed a caesura between the représentants and the former French minister. Mirabeau revealed this in a letter to Chamfort at the end of 1784. Here he attacked Necker as no lover of liberty, using the example of Turgot as a contrast and the abandonment of Geneva as an example of Necker's false politics and ill-will: "I know what to think of Necker's financial talents, and of his ministerial operations; and I am involved in preparing a work at present that will not present him in a positive light. He abandoned his country at the very moment he had the power to save it, and place it for ever out of the danger by which it is now surrounded, and such conduct shows him in his true light. Turgot was not a Genevese—a very different man indeed—yet he would have felt honoured and delighted in being called upon, in any way—and no trouble would he have spared—to save even a molehill where liberty might be endangered."[139]

Mirabeau's verdict was indicative of commentary from other exiles. Indeed, his letter to Chamfort was clearly copied in part from one of Clavière's, sent on the same date, to the natif Bérenger. Although partly inspired by financial disagreements, Clavière had become convinced that Necker could never be a Turgot, had failed to support Geneva, and suffered by comparison with true supporters of political principle and of liberty such as Price.[140] After reading Necker's *De l'administration des finances*, Clavière became convinced that Necker was more dangerous still, a supporter of mercantile systems of trade who envisaged turning France into an empire on the British model. The consequences for the small states of Europe would be disastrous, and Necker was henceforth deemed an enemy to the représentants and to enlightened economic and international policy. This judgment facilitated Clavière's development of new strategies for France.

Mirabeau returned to Paris in April 1785. He was soon laboring for Clavière on a series of stock speculation pamphlets. With the bankers Isaac Panchaud and Théophile Cazenove, among others, Clavière sought out overpriced companies on the exchange and pushed for the collapse of their share values, speculating on the fall of the price, by means of *marche-à-terme* (short-selling) agreements and opportunities to purchase shares at low prices before interested parties, and especially governments, took measures to raise them.[141] The language of the pamphlets was significant in that it employed the distinction between free and mercantile commerce that was key both to the Genevan exiles' arguments against aristocracy in government and in trade, and to the Shelburne circle's prescriptions for perpetual peace. Clavière portrayed himself as an honest broker, someone who had made many enemies because of his stance at Geneva but who had come to Paris because his fortune "is connected with that of this kingdom." Bankruptcy, he argued, following Turgot, was less likely in France because of the natural wealth of the country, because of the extent of French industry, because of the industriousness of the people, and because of the qualities of the good king Louis XVI.[142] It was vital that France not follow Britain and establish a mercantile empire based on corrupt commerce. It was equally essential that peace in Europe be maintained and commercial links based on free trade established as a means to the greater end. Politics had to be moralized, and the union of morals and politics forever adhered to.[143]

In the name of "disordered traffic," Calonne issued an *arrêt* to limit dividends on the shares of the Caisse d'Escompte on 16 January 1785. His actual agenda was to reduce interest payments on a government loan of 125 million livres. This was followed on 24 January by an arrêt making this retroactive, thereby annulling all fixed-term speculations on share movements. Clavière and Isaac Panchaud, as major speculators in the marche à terme of the bank, declared these acts to be a product of a secret cabal of government and shareholders, a supreme example of corrupt commerce.[144] *De la Caisse d'Escompte*, much of it written by Clavière, appeared in May 1785 in Mirabeau's name.[145]

According to the introduction, the work was inspired by the account in the London press of Calonne's intervention in the affairs of the Caisse, which had concluded that "the lack of public spirit in France makes the establishment of savings banks altogether impossible."[146] Declaring himself to be a patriot defending French culture against such accusations, Mirabeau sought to prove that certain forms of commercial activity were not only practical in France but were vital to her health and prosperity. The widespread argument expressed in the British press could be understood because France, and French philosophers in particular, had failed to recognize the difference between the ancient world and the modern. Where the essence of the former was war, creating forms of government whose first interest was security, in the modern world "the so called most noble art of war . . . which we have accorded so much glory . . . in fact merits as much infamy." Many of those who acknowledged the necessity of commerce made a second mistake in accepting the popular view that commerce was merely another way of conducting war. Although the introduction recognized that modern war was "a commercial speculation, for the politicians and the kings, who are the entrepreneurs, and for the soldiers, who are the agents and labourers," it emphasized the need to distinguish between such "political commerce" and "real commerce," the effects of which were very different:

> I know all that could be written against the universal mania for political, conquering, and sea-faring commerce, which infests the two hemispheres; but between this contagious madness and real commerce [*commerce propre-ment dit*], which exists everywhere men gather, there is doubtless an extreme distance. It is the principles, processes, and manners [of real commerce] with which I am concerned, the spirit of commerce envisaged through abstract and general exchange; it is the state of things which this produces, which it prepares for, which it necessitates, which must occupy our thoughts.[147]

De la Caisse d'Escompte called for the "ennoblement" of "real commerce" by educating people to distinguish between the two forms. Reflection would show that "political commerce" was the product of deadly passions, the "narrow and arid egoism . . . that exalts corruption." The tragedy was that in France this form of commerce was becoming dominant, as proved by Calonne's intervention in the market on behalf of the greedy shareholders of the Caisse:

> We know what the deadly system of financial speculation has cost the happi-ness and innocence of societies; we know what are and must be the results of exalted greed by the ease of making huge and excessive profits; we know the mania, or rather the fury, for gambling, which infests all ranks, troubles the repose [of society], pollutes morals, and isolates and withers men; we especially know that gambling on public funds, in facilitating the debt whose weight we bear, fuels the passions of administrators, exaggerates, intoxicates, and misleads their powers, foments, tightens, and confirms slavery, aggra-vates oppression and degrades the human species: because when man is no more than a commodity, it is impossible for him to be even the first.[148]

The pamphlet went on to distinguish between the "honourable sensibility," which could be found in the heart of every man, and the "cunning avidity" of "amour propre." Where the latter passions ruined lives and spelled disaster for societies, the former "renders [citizens] open, loyal, benevolent." It was respon-sible for "humanity and patriotism . . . a generous disposition to count among our earnings the sentiment which leads us to abandon some of our wealth for the public good." The only means to counter corrupt commerce, and keep the lid of Pandora's box firmly shut, was to allow governments to intervene in the marketplace to ensure that the rules of commercial morality were being adhered to. In the case of personal property, private immorality was not of public concern. But in the case of companies and institutions of interest to the health of society, regulation was absolutely vital to prevent "the errors which diminish the usefulness of the *Caisse d'Escompte*, or even make it dangerous": "An ordinary man, even a banker, has a right to ruin himself at will; the government has not the right to prevent this. A hospital, a municipal body, a public bank, have not the same right to ruin themselves, any more than a king can dispose of his wealth or the revenue necessary to support his nation and sovereignty, because these are of social institution, and made to fulfil a function that society has assigned to them, neither more nor less."[149] Fears of the example set by enthusiasts such as John Law ought not to prevent the policing of social institutions, since "the public has less to fear from government inspection than from the liberty of [private] administrators."[150] The principle justifying inspection stemmed from the fact that every authority had to be limited by another: "unlimited authority is arbitrary authority, the source of all evil, and the most redoubtable scourge of humanity." The Caisse had to submit to monitoring by public authorities, reduce its interest in government enterprises, and begin to provide low-interest loans to stimulate industry.

The second demand for honest commerce, this time wholly the work of Clavière and Brissot, attacked the bank of Saint-Charles, founded by François Cabarrus in 1782, which had lately become entwined with the financial interests of the Spanish government. Calonne paid for the work, having an interest in seeing the decline of the overly powerful Spanish enterprise.[151] On 13 June 1785 the pamphlet *De la Banque d'Espagne dite de Saint-Charles*, once more in Mirabeau's name, condemned the colonial monopolies that the bank exploited, and also avaricious speculators and capitalists—Cabarrus was likened to John Law—who made deals with governments desperate for revenue. Having examined the prospectus for the intended share issue of the bank, the pamphlet declared the bank to be not a source of investment for the stimulus of industry but a gold mine for privileged ranks and courtiers with interests in commercial monopoly and the maintenance of a standing army. The British argument about French culture was now turned against Spain, an economic backwater where the "mortal poison of superstition" reigned hand in hand with an indolence-inducing climate. The bank was powerless to stimulate Spanish commerce. Every investment would be wasted: "Capitals that leave a country to buy merchandise, or productions useful to a nation, do not impoverish the nation, because they yield an equal wealth; but the capital which flows to a foreign bank, to support paper money and equally illusory hopes [of wealth], inevitably impoverish a nation."[152] The attack proved so effective that the Spanish ambassador at Paris, the Marquis d'Aranda, perturbed by the falling price of shares, persuaded Calonne to proscribe the work on 17 July, inducing the wrath of Mirabeau in further pamphlets.

Clavière's campaign continued in October with an attack upon the Compagnie des Eaux de Paris, created to pump the waters of the Seine to the houses of Paris, a project that he claimed had been rejected by Turgot on the basis of information from London.[153] Clavière's preferred scheme was the redirection of the Yvette River into Paris. The controversy sparked a flurry of publications, pitting Clavière against his formidable former landlord Beaumarchais, who was a major shareholder and had long served Vergennes, and also against Calonne.[154] The Périer brothers, two engineers who had founded the company, were accused by Clavière, in Mirabeau's *Sur les actions de la Compagnie des Eaux de Paris* (London, 1785), of corrupt attempts to raise the value of their shares beyond their real worth. Clavière prophesied that three-quarters of Paris would have to be rebuilt to accept the water. Beaumarchais responded with the *Réponse à l'ouvrage qui a pour titre "Sur les actions de la Compagnie des Eaux de Paris"* (Paris, 1785), which branded the coterie of writers who were believed to be responsible for the pamphlets "the mirabelles." Although on 8 October Clavière was forbidden to write about these issues by the lieutenant of police, M. de Crosne, acting on the order of Calonne, this did not prevent the December publication, in Mirabeau's name, of the *Réponse du comte de M. à l'écrivain des administrateurs de la Compagnie des Eaux* (Brussels, 1785).[155] The work acknowledged Clavière to be the author of *De la Banque d'Espagne*. A second edition of Mirabeau's writings against the Périer brothers appeared in 1786 entitled *Recueil de divers écrits du comte de M. sur les Eaux de Paris* (London, 1786). In all of these pamphlets Clavière demanded honest and open commercial practices, the real foundation of "bonnes mœurs" and successful trade.

The Clavière-Mirabeau partnership, so crucial to the popularization of these ideas, was temporarily suspended in December 1785. Having been reviled in some of the pamphlets, Calonne responded by buying off some of his critics.[156] A diplomatic mission to Berlin was the price of the cessation of Mirabeau's involvement; he left Paris for Berlin in December 1785 and remained there until February 1787.[157] Another reason was Mirabeau's desire to publish under his own name, or perhaps to sell to Calonne, on a return to Paris in May 1786, Dupont de Nemours's *Mémoire sur les municipalités*, which he had copied while in the prison of Vincennes. The publication might in turn have confirmed Mirabeau in a more prestigious and more permanent diplomatic position. These expectations caused Mirabeau to try to prevent publication of Brissot's study of provincial assemblies, which included Dupont's *Mémoire*.

Since Brissot's work expressed his own views, and because the work underscored the abyss between Turgot and Necker, Clavière refused to stop the publication, opening up a rift with Mirabeau.[158] This forced Clavière to use Brissot's name, and he did so against the new Compagnie des Indes, created by Calonne on 14 April 1785, the Compagnie d'Afrique, and the Compagnie d'assurances contre l'incendie.[159] These were responsible for bringing the terms *agiotage* and *agioteurs* into popular parlance, representing the corrupt practices of privileged speculators who, as Mirabeau put it, "cheat by turn the government, the public, and their accomplices."[160] The pamphlets made Clavière rich. He was certainly hypocritical in many of the accusations leveled against other financiers. For example, when he created companies involved in the provision of water and life assurance, between 1786 and 1787, he sought privileges from the government identical to those he had vehemently condemned when solicited by others. But the pamphlets served to show that Clavière had taken completely to heart the views of the Shelburne circle that Britain had declined and that the future, in economic terms, belonged to France. By June 1786 he was anticipating war between Britain and France, noting that Louis XVI's visit to Cherbourg Harbor signified a willingness to fight "the Pitt system."[161] He was committed to solving the Genevan problem by the reform of France. One of the forms of support he believed he and his financial partners, in this case led by Pierre Stadnitsky, could give to France, in the summer of 1786, was a substantial payment in return for taking over the United States' debt to France, which involved Clavière in negotiations with Thomas Jefferson.[162]

CLAVIÈRE'S PROJECTED REFORM OF FRANCE

Clavière's view of France as the state most likely to save Geneva was set out fully in three books written in 1787 and published between April 1787 and January 1788: *De la France et des États-Unis*, *Point de banqueroute*, and *Observations d'un républicain*. All of them were written in conjunction with Brissot, to whom they are usually ascribed. The first, *De la France et des États-Unis*, appeared in Brissot's name in April 1787, but the introduction made clear the joint nature of the enterprise and its indebtedness to Clavière's "commercial philosophy." In his *Mémoires* Brissot stated that "all of the commercial part belonged to this profound man [Clavière]." According to Brissot, Calonne opposed its argument, in what must have been the final days of his ministry: "His [Clavière's] merit was not acknowledged; but it will be when peace has consolidated liberty and allowed commerce to repair her losses and extend her speculations. The minister's fear was so great in seeing the development of the philosophy of commerce and the prosperity of a free people, that he raised a thousand obstacles to the sale of this work. Journalists were advised to greet it with absolute silence."[163]

When a second edition appeared in 1791, both authors were named. Clavière also founded the Société Gallo-Américaine on 2 January 1787, formed to propagate the view that "the moral and political welfare of [France and the United States] must be the goal and principal outcome of commercial relationships."[164] Meetings were held at Clavière's residence between January and April 1787 to discuss the argument of *De la France*. One important source of information about America came from J. Hector Saint-John de Crèvecœur, the noble Norman turned New World adventurer who had returned to Paris in July 1785, and whom Clavière had met at the salon of Comtesse Sophie d'Houdetot. Crèvecœur became an active member of the Société. Clavière agreed with Crèvecœur's claim that the example of the United States could serve to illuminate the corrupt manners of the French people. This was the central argument of Crèvecœur's popular book, *Lettres d'un cultivateur Américain*, several editions of which had appeared since 1782 and which were followed by a greatly expanded edition in 1787.[165] The argument of *De la France* was also influenced by Brissot's own researches into North American life. These appeared in July 1786 as a critique of Chastellux's portrayal of American manners in his *Voyages de M. le Marquis de Chastellux dans l'Amérique septentrionale, dans les années 1780, 1781 et 1782* (1786), published only two months previously. Brissot's work contained a ringing attack on the economic and moral arguments for slavery, a condemnation of the mercantile system that fostered such immoral institutions and a description of the Quaker communities of New England as ideal with respect to manners and morals.[166] Brissot praised the Quakers for having "reduced divine worship to the greatest simplicity, to disconnect it from all its superstitious ceremonies, which gave it the appearance of idolatry; and particularly not to give their priests enormous salaries, to enable them to live in luxury and idleness; in a word to restore the evangelical simplicity. They have succeeded."[167] Such evidence led Clavière and Brissot to the conclusion that the United States could be used to create a new international axis for reform policies by creating two hugely powerful allied economies, confirming the decline and ultimate collapse of Britain's mercantile system and restoring France to preeminence in Europe.[168] A preeminent France could be trusted to respect the liberties of the small states, thereby securing the "happiness of humanity." The plan could be realized only if France's "ancient liberty" was restored.[169] The point was that at Geneva an economy based on moderate wealth existed and could be maintained through a political system in which the *représentants* were dominant. At France a luxury-based economy had been established by allowing the noble class to dominate trade. From this perspective, present-day France resembled a future Geneva, corrupted and controlled by magistrates turned aristocrats. With respect to contemporary France, however, the key was to use economic and political reform to return the country to a natural economic growth path, creating an economy more akin to that of Geneva and a political system more akin to that planned by the représentants, with an Estates General providing the monarch with reform policies.

The central argument of *De la France* derived from a belief that the American Revolution had altered the French intellectual world. This was not because America's federal constitution or republican culture could be transplanted to Paris. Such facile claims were rare because of the evident social and political abyss that divided the New World from the Old.[170] Rather, the American union was significant because its governments, although victorious in war, were facing bankruptcy. The crucial point was that, in the midst of financial crisis, the nation was becoming more stable and its politics more effective. In America public credit, rather than destroying the state, had become a force for commerce and a symbol of social union. The liberation of America, "so favourable to the people," had "underlined the importance of commerce to power, the necessity of public credit, and consequently the public virtues."[171] The last point was imperative. Public credit was sustained by public confidence, which in turn depended on virtuous popular manners. Behind such manners lay wealth, because without wealth the populace would become impoverished and prey to corruption. But wealth had to be generated by honest means and never be excessive, because the commerce that created wealth could easily produce inequalities and luxuries, both inimical to virtuous manners and credit. France could imitate American practices, but with crucial differences.[172] For France was a state similar to the United States in terms of natural resources and therefore had "all the means to procure a great commerce." The problem was that France had failed to fulfill its economic potential. This was compounded by the costs generated by France in war, which had inaugurated an era of crisis.[173]

To Clavière, the fetters on the French economy were evident to any independent observer; central features of French culture were anticommercial and immoral, making impossible any commercial renascence to resolve the debt crisis. French philosophers remained fascinated by the world of antiquity. Like Mably, they were "too enthusiastic for the [ancient] Greek republics," entailing study of the "vulgar politics of the balance of power." Such politics could provide no solutions to modern problems. French culture was shallow and flippant. The branch of the "science of civil relations" most neglected in France was political economy, whose "good principles" had been nurtured in Britain and had proved of enormous economic benefit: "The theoretical science of commerce is truly perfected in Britain; the practical science is truly valued. In France . . . the science of commerce is almost ignored, because its practice is deprecated by prejudice."[174] Clavière wanted to make explicit his conviction that ignorance of political economy in particular explained French military inferiority. This was manifest in dealing with public credit, which the British had studied for almost a century, and which the French had disregarded since the time of Law, with devastating commercial repercussions. While the British nobility had realized that a civic language sustained credit, the French nobility used an anticommercial language to maintain their social position. The relative weakness of France had a cultural cause: the French had allowed the passions free reign, dedicating themselves to "futile sciences, frivolous arts, fashions, luxury, the art of pleasing women, and the loosening of manners."[175] This had created an extensive market in luxury goods. One consequence was the spread of ignorance and debauchery. French workers were less efficient than their British counterparts in part because they were less skilled and less educated. The fundamental source of France's economic weakness was the power of the aristocracy within the state. Aristocrats encouraged the consumption of luxury products. They promoted the passions and gave altogether a negative example to the orders of society below them. Above all they prevented French politicians from recognizing the public interest, which accorded with true self-interest, that mass markets and the provision of basic necessities were the key to a thriving economy.

Clavière was fascinated by British civil liberties. So egalitarian were the British by comparison with the French that healthy moral practices were encoded in the language. One example he identified was that when "a man is accused of the greatest crimes, and of the most impoverished appearance, [he] is called 'Sir' when he is interrogated by his judges." In Britain moderate affluence was valued above excess. Individuals considered themselves equals before the law and therefore independent and "freeborn" rather than downtrodden and servile. In short, unlike France, British culture valued commerce and equality:

> Now do you wish to know the cause of the general affluence so widespread in Britain? Independently of the soil, of the [geographical] position, and the advantages of the liberty which reigns, affluence results from the importance accorded by public opinion to industry; it results from the protection assured by law to all individuals, against *all* government agents; it results from this that the pride, the *hauteur*, and the insolence which men are carried toward,

because of the effect of power on the uneducated, are continually quelled, and cannot debase the [manners of the] loyal citizen . . . [who] does not blush to be a merchant, an artisan, a laborer, etc. etc.[176]

By contrast, the French were so confused about good morals and the real nature of the economy that they called the United States an empire rather than a free republic.[177] The chief object of *De la France* was to sketch a political economy that explained the backwardness of French culture and revealed means to its speedy modernization, to make it compatible with the kinds of commerce and credit befitting a cosmopolitan state that valued peace, moderate wealth, and liberty.

Clavière's strategy was threefold, with civil, economic, and political aspects. The civil means to the cleansing of French culture was modeled on British political life, in which public credit was founded upon public opinion. If public opinion was constrained by oppressive laws, dominated by ignorance, or influenced by prejudice, then public credit would be weakened. Civil liberty was therefore not simply the institution of certain freedoms, but rather a culture that valued truth and virtue. The first steps were to safeguard freedoms of speech, thought, and expression and to abolish excessive physical constraint, slavery, and religious coercion. Liberty, rather than corrupting itself, actually destroyed fanaticism and tyranny (in Clavière's words, "enthusiasm and despotism").[178] Civil liberty would create a public able to discern and condemn the actions of financial speculators, mercenary politicians, and trivial artists and philosophers. Illustrations of the former transgressors were drawn from the *agiotage* of the Indies companies, of the Caisse d'Escompte, and of Calonne himself. The supreme example of literary crime was *Le mariage de Figaro*. Beaumarchais's comedy, libeled as "frivolous literature," was held responsible for the insensitivity of the masses to "profound truths."[179] Such cultural forms destroyed public credit where a truly commercial culture would sustain it: "This liberty is a powerful means to establish, to fortify, to maintain public credit; this credit has become ever more necessary to large nations, since borrowing is vital to them. . . . As long as the attacks of personal interest are made formidable by the secrecy which obscures them, public credit is never strengthened, and is never raised to its true height."[180]

Civil liberty was never sufficient to establish public credit. The necessary cause of public credit was flourishing commercial activity, which in turn depended on an economic strategy that nurtured forms of commerce natural to France. Clavière argued that a nation with a wide range of natural resources would gradually move from specialization in agricultural production to simple manufactures and ultimately complex manufactures, which demanded a dense urban population. The latter development would pose no danger to society so long as the agricultural sector was sufficiently large to feed the towns and markets were extensive enough to employ the rising population. The tragic neglect of these simple truths was responsible for the dire condition of the French economy. Rather than allowing freedom to reign, successive governments had attempted to use commerce as a weapon of war and thereby had set France upon a path of unnatural growth, classically resulting in the mercantile system as defined by Smith's *Wealth of Nations*. Clavière claimed to be drawing upon "the profound Smith" in his indictment of this "bad social organization," and from Smith's "proof" of the existence of a just realm of free economic relationships, consistently identified by Clavière as "la nature des choses."[181] Yet there was hope in the continued ability to identify what was natural in the economic world and to contrast it with the "exclusive system" that nature condemned: "Nature wishes to make brothers of men and families of nations; nature, which, in order to tie men by the same cord, has shaped their needs and made them mutually dependent; wise nature, by the distribution of her goods, counteracts, condemns, the exclusive system."[182]

To return France to her natural growth path, it was necessary to diagnose the effects of the "exclusive system" and prescribe an ameliorative strategy. In Clavière's eyes, action by ministers for over a century had created industries for luxury goods protected by laws proscribing competition. These industries had attracted labor from the countryside to the towns and ultimately created centers of poverty and disease because the markets, being supported by the demand of the noble classes, were unable to expand and employ the artificially increased urban population. In short, France had developed a protected urban manufacturing sector before her markets and income levels were able to support it. The prices of goods were beyond the reach of the ordinary citizen; the protected industries were parasites feeding on the coffers of the state; laborers were trapped because their numbers reduced wages to the absolute minimum; and product markets in luxury goods were incapable of expansion to increase demand. The natural movement toward industries producing complex manufactured goods had been interrupted by the control of trade by a selfish elite, whose desire for luxuries had been considered prior to the general interest of society. The people had been sacrificed to the nobility and the court. This was a symbol of "a bad social organization, which forces industry from necessary, free, and useful labor, to work which is a product of fantasy, coerced, and pernicious. It is a result of this, that the more manpower is cheap in a country, the more poverty is great and far-reaching."[183] The parallel was obvious between the selfish nobles of France and the arrogant magistrates at Geneva seeking to turn themselves into aristocrats wielding power permanently. Indeed, Clavière was transferring to France his analysis of the consequences of magisterial oligarchy for the Genevan economy. His view of the effects of aristocratic government for the economy and politics appeared to be confirmed in the commentary of travelers such as William Coxe: "During my subsequent visits to Geneva, in 1785 and the following year, I found an almost general discontent prevailing among all parties; many of the Negatives disaffected; all the Representants submitting in silent and sullen despair; and the people without spirit and energy. The wisdom of many of the regulations passed in 1782 was overlooked, or forgotten; those only which annihilated the first principles of liberty were remembered; and almost the only sentiment which prevailed, was the sentiment of degradation, arising from the subjection of a free people to a military government."[184]

Cheap goods were the secret of commercial success, but Clavière took pains to prove that such goods did not necessitate cheap labor. In adhering to the exclusive system, French ministers had assumed this to be the case, justifying poverty on the ground of economic necessity. Forcing wages down for the provision of luxury markets was self-defeating because the ability to supply low priced goods ultimately belonged not to the country that impoverished its workforce but to the country that had more natural resources and developed them in free markets; in this respect France was at once the most blessed country and the most tragic. Escape from this predicament necessitated the stimulation of commerce in manufactures and other goods that were natural to France, which would thereby yield enough profit to provide higher wages. Higher wages would in turn invigorate domestic markets, spread wealth, and further commercialize the culture. Ultimately, the commerce generated by such measures would solve the problem of state debt and address the issue of national poverty. Since France could not initially rely on the demand of domestic consumers to expand markets for indigenous products, it was essential to rely on foreign consumers. Foreign commerce was therefore the most important branch of national industry. Its development required the destruction of the nobility in France, whom Clavière also blamed for the excessive size of the national debt. But the first step was to abandon the control and direction of trade, since "favoring industry means leaving her to herself."[185] This significant step would be facilitated by entering into direct commerce with America, to initiate a mutually auspicious commercial division of labor: "If [France] opens her eyes to her real interests, if she delivers her domestic commerce from its fetters, she will not neglect her foreign commerce, and in particular that which the United States wishes to open with her. The products of her soil and industry are suitable [to American needs]. In exchange, she can receive the primary goods which she needs from America."[186]

Proof of this claim was manifest in the number of goods that might be the subject of trade. Most of the book was concerned with a detailed examination of these products and a justification of their proposed exchange. The first consideration was for America to "conserve her republican manners." To Clavière this required the development of agriculture and simple manufactures rather than complex industries, since the latter would create ranks and corrupt manners if introduced before wages were sufficient to counter any danger. France would therefore specialize in manufactures whose production demanded heavy capital investment and the concentration of labor. Examples ranged from smith work in iron and steel to the production of paper, books, hats, glassware, linen, cloth, silk, woolen goods, saddles, boots, shoes, and furs. France could also furnish America with primary goods in which she abounded, including wines, oils, olives, dried fruit, and salt. In return, America would supply France with primary goods, including rice, cotton, wool, raw indigo, linseed, wood, tar, wax, and fish, and simple manufactures such as candles. More important, America could solve the problem of high bread prices in France by ensuring the provision of cheap imported grain. Similarly, the vast French tobacco monopolies could be dismantled in favor of their American equivalents. The single complex industry that Clavière expected America to develop was shipbuilding, which underpinned the navy so vital for defense. He advised the Americans to stimulate the production of these goods by abandoning slavery in the sure knowledge that free labor was both superior and less costly. This section of the book ended with a ringing call to entrepreneurs in both countries to initiate a commercial revolution.

Clavière expected the ordinary people of France to become more involved and interested in commerce through this division of labor with the United States. This was indeed essential for the establishment of a self-sustaining commercial culture. If it was not popular, then it would not survive in an uncorrupted form. Additional steps had to be taken to ensure this outcome, the most important of which was the creation of a paper currency, which Clavière held to be an agent of commercialization. If the plan was backed by the promise of payment in tangible goods and was issued in small units by local banks, and if the government did not force it on the people, then there would be no danger of inflation or speculation-induced collapses of confidence.[187] Clavière passionately believed that counterarguments to his strategy, based on the acknowledgment of Britain's commercial superiority or the necessity of low wages, were products of the failure to examine the true cause of British success, which could be traced to a popular commercial culture. Proof came from countries such as Ireland, which were abundant in natural resources but had negligible markets because the people were not commercial and lacked the culture-generated affluence to ensure buoyant domestic markets and high wages for labor. Moderate affluence that, if it became widespread, would limit the establishment of ranks and luxuries was of acute concern. It made citizens proud to be involved in commerce and secure from corruption.[188]

At the end of the work, a constitutional framework was sketched that was deemed vital for the implementation of Clavière's plan. The threat to counter was the influence of the nobility, who in the court and the *parlements* would unquestionably inhibit the natural path of economic growth. Noting the falsity of Montesquieu's claim that monarchy necessitated aristocracy, Clavière and Brissot argued that the French nobility had to be sacrificed on the altar of the public good, the common interest shared by every uncorrupted citizen.[189] The political means to this end rested on the introduction of provincial assemblies into every locality, allowing the involvement of "the people" in government and administration. Without the involvement of the masses in politics, French culture would remain narrow and frivolous. Only the accession of "the people" to political life would vanquish the aristocratic prejudices that hindered progress and were ultimately responsible for the current threat of bankruptcy. Provincial assemblies would introduce "truly productive industry" into France, compatible, indeed inseparable from, "public spiritedness." The appearance of small banks in every district would ensure that commerce was never hindered by want of credit or money. The idea of civil equality would gradually permeate French culture, corroding the established nobility and allowing all individuals to consider themselves valuable citizens. Ultimately, the economic culture to be found in Britain and America would take root in France. French people would recognize *"that each of them is something*, and this idea, this sentiment of self-worth, alone makes the citizen, and, consequently, the prosperity and greatness of states."[190]

One French minister said that *De la France* "exalted the British nation."[191] Exactly the opposite was the case. Clavière envisaged the work as the great refutation of Necker's *De l'administration des finances* and of all other justifications of mercantile systems. Lord Sheffield, who had called free trade a "rash theory" and a system akin to "the wildest sallies of imagination," by comparison with the proven fact that the Navigation Acts were "the guardian[s] of the prosperity of Britain," was clearly particularly in mind.[192] Clavière saw himself as following the insights of the third book of the *Wealth of Nations* with respect to European history and the unnatural progress of opulence. He was certain, however, that

Smith had neglected the political dimension of economic reform, which could be used to restore European states to a natural state of peace and gradual development—something that Smith believed to be impossible. Clavière never claimed, in the manner of Emmanuel Joseph Sieyès, that he was completing Smith's work by applying the principle of the division of labor to politics, but he was doing something similar in working out the political means to economic peace.[193] Dupont de Nemours praised *De la France* as "among the classics of the science of government" on the grounds that it combated the view that France was in decline and "that we are a nation full of ignorance, corruption, and the worst governed in the world." On the contrary, Dupont claimed, France was "the nation the most enlightened and that has produced more than any other good books on all the aspects of the physical and moral sciences which contribute to rendering the people happy." The British constitution was imperfect yet superior to France's, but as the British did not know the true principles of finance and of commerce, and while their books and especially their parliamentary debates are "narrow, in favor of regulation and monopoly and oppression," a good administration would lead France to commercial supremacy.[194]

De la France was important to the Genevan exiles because it described an international system based upon the rejection of empire and upon an alliance between the oldest monarchy and the newest republic. A France allied to the United States and respectful of the principle of free trade could not but fail to renounce the aristocrats at Geneva, once it was recognized that the nobility of France were responsible for the failure of France to realize its economic potential. Accordingly, *De la France* amounted to a logical extension of the Shelburne circle's vision of the economic and international world, in circumstances where Britain had declined but where Britain's mercantile system needed to be forced to collapse completely by economic competition with France, and where France might be ruled by a new Turgot rather than by a Necker, a Vergennes, a Calonne, or a Pitt. Clavière and Brissot had some hopes that their influence over policy might become far greater with the rise of the duc d'Orléans's "chancellor" Charles-Louis Ducrest, who had been offered a position in Brienne's ministry and who appointed Brissot to a place in the Orléans household in June 1787.[195]

THE POLITICS OF PHILANTHROPIC COMMERCE

De la France did not specify a means of putting its proposals into practice. This was undoubtedly because the detested Calonne remained in power until April 1787. Equally, Vergennes had only recently died (in February), making influence dependent on appeals to members of the court with radical ideas. The campaign for an Estates General provided Clavière with opportunities to give his ideas a wider airing. During the six months after May 1787, Clavière and Brissot published two further books that underlined their opposition to current politics and further refined their proposals in response to the upheavals of late 1787. The first, *Point de banqueroute*, was completed in August and comprised letters to an owner of government bonds who was fearful of the possibility of a national bankruptcy, the gravest threat to Clavière's endeavors against mercantile empire and aristocratic control over trade. In response to advocates of bankruptcy, then attracting the rising courtier Etienne-Charles de Loménie de Brienne in particular, Clavière and Brissot reiterated the argument of *De la France*: a general bankruptcy would mean the collapse of trust both domestically and internationally, the end to treaties of peace and commerce, and a commercial depression that would bring misery to innumerable French citizens.[196] Further details were given of their constitutional program. Popular representation was not to include women, whose natural role was the cultivation of domestic virtues. Nor were "the ignorant" included; they were to be filtered out of the electoral process by instituting provincial assemblies in which candidates for an Estates General, to be held "three years hence," would serve, proving their wisdom and probity.[197] The Estates General, full of able men, would then be able to reconstitute the administrative system of the state and secure credit with the full support of the sovereign nation. France's superiority to Britain would be underlined, and the vast economic potential of the state would be realised.[198]

Clavière and Brissot believed it was imperative to stress the need for a form of popular sovereignty in France. The *Observations d'un républicain* had been completed earlier in 1787 and appeared alongside Dupont's *Mémoire* on provincial assemblies, but it was published as a separate work at the end of the year.[199] Necker's *De l'administration des finances* was taken to task for defending the excessive powers of the monarch and his ministers. Necker's hidden agenda, it was argued, was to rid the king of the *parlements* by creating assemblies of the rich and propertied, which were nevertheless wholly dependent upon the *intendants* serving the monarch.[200] By contrast, Turgot was described as an enlightened genius who had perceived the real problem of France to be the lack of a constitution; he had opposed the growth of egotism and the loss of the rights of the people. Following Condorcet's *Vie de Turgot*, Clavière and Brissot argued that the great man "belonged, by the liberty of his principles, to a Republic."[201] However, their notion of a well-constituted republic was singular. Clavière and Brissot stated that Turgot had never been a "true republican," because he had failed to recognize the need to combat directly the amoral qualities of the French populace. In France most of the people lived beyond the pale of government and morals, feeling no allegiance to their country because they were impoverished. As a consequence, Turgot's educational schemes to instill patriotism were derided as monarchical fantasies: it was necessary to establish a republic where all of the people owned a moderate amount of property and were protected in their use of it. Since Turgot supported the powers of the *intendants*, the bastion of tyrannical monarchy, the people could never be free in his system. He had been tainted by physiocratic ideas about citizenship that instituted social hierarchy and oppression, condemning in the political sphere what they valued in economic life: "Perhaps M. Turgot, in his economic system, had not tasted these republican ideas. He was persuaded, with the physiocrats, that Kings must govern according to evidence, that the people must submit themselves to it, that every counterweight was an obstacle and an abuse."[202]

Despite these errors, Clavière and Brissot believed that Turgot would have changed his mind had he lived to see the functioning of the constitution of the United States. This had shown the worth of a genuinely representative assembly, an estates general uniting the interests of the nation, with the power to return to the populace those *droits primitifs* that had been lost with the rise of aristocracy and ministerial powers. The means to the end lay in Clavière's commercial strategy and the proposals with which the *Observations* closed: the enfranchisement of "all the people." Clavière and Brissot acknowledged that such measures entailed sacrifice and insurrection, but were essential for the survival of the nation: "The Estates General, that I have just portrayed, neither resembles historic examples, nor those proposed by Necker and Turgot. Its institution would necessitate a great upheaval; and this is the objection which will be made: here is my response: a man who has been bitten by a rabid dog, consults his doctor, who replies: 'Quickly, apply a burning iron to your wound, and you will heal' — 'But, I will suffer.' — 'Then die, if you do not wish to suffer.'"[203]

A revised edition of *Point de banqueroute* published in October 1787 addressed the crises in French foreign policy provoked by the Netherlands revolt and the Russo-Turkish War. A policy based on nature was recommended, at odds with a lust for empire dictated not by reason but by the selfish ambition of ministers in the mold of Richelieu. Unfortunately for France, ministers like Calonne were followers of Richelieu, and this explained the present indebtedness of the state and the temptation to opt for a war or a bankruptcy in response to the lack of public credit. David Hume's metaphor of indebted states that fought wars being akin to gaming with cudgels in a china shop was the epigraph to *Point de banqueroute*, and it was used again in the conclusion, which conjured an image of a Europe addicted to war, causing the death of both public credit and nation states.[204] In its place was projected a world founded on peace and commerce, rather than on war, luxury, and monopoly. As France was in crisis, the only policy to be recommended was that of neutrality and avoidance of the turmoil that accompanied the schemes of Europe's empire builders. One result of the argument was that Brissot was forced to flee temporarily to London in November 1787, after Calonne's successor, Loménie de Brienne, dispatched a *lettre de cachet* against the author of *Point de banqueroute*.

Brissot and Clavière, in language redolent of Price and other members of the Shelburne circle during the conflict with the United States, condemned Britain's support for the reign of successive stadtholders, and the decision of Prussia to go to war for a presumed slight against the monarch's sister. With a stadtholder seeking to become a dictator and an aristocracy seeking to make itself hereditary, Holland was ceasing to be a republic, since a republic did not exist "if distinctions between men are admitted." Frederick II's *Histoire de mon temps* (1746) was praised for likening the policies of Europe's great states to the trade of the butcher, the consequence being that the lives and liberties of the people in all of Europe's states, small and large, endlessly suffered. The contrast between Frederick II's expressions of support for peace and the practice of the new Prussian monarchy of his nephew Frederick William II was highlighted, traced in turn to the self-interestedness of princes and to the mercantile system of Britain seeking to usurp the place of the Dutch in the Far East, thus encouraging Prussian aggression.

Although Clavière and Brissot expressed willingness to die for republican liberty, peace was more important for France. Accordingly, they advised French ministers to oversee the reestablishment of peace until Britain had exhausted her resources supporting the stadtholder. At such a time France would be able to unite with Dutch democrats and American republicans (identified as the commercial and industrious members of the polity) and mount a defense of liberty against the destructive system of aristocratic and monarchical war. Britain in particular was condemned for maintaining the mercantile system. It was also condemned for continuing the age-old antagonism toward France that was supposed to have been abandoned in 1783. The French were warned not to be concerned about alliances between Britain, Holland, and Prussia. As long as France avoided war, the country would become more powerful. Despite their activity in international relations, Britain and Prussia were portrayed as declining. Prussia, it was claimed, would rapidly collapse because its strength was due only to the military genius of Frederick II. In the longer term it lacked an economy capable of sustaining its military ambition. The Dutch, in turn, were advised to avoid luxury, because "the free man who loves luxury is already a slave," and to fight for their own liberty and not to trust aristocrats, who would always have an advantage in diplomacy with kings. The lesson of Geneva's experience in 1782 was stated to be that aristocracy had to be unmasked and destroyed the world over.[205]

In the case of the declaration of war by Turkey on Russia in 1787, French interests appeared to be at stake because of the historic alliance with the Sublime Porte. British ministers were reputed to be involved in the conflict. There was a threat to relations with Russia, with whom Vergennes had arranged a commercial treaty shortly before his death. Clavière and Brissot stated that "peace is the only policy that suits France." If the Turks were defeated, there would be no threat to the commercial links with France. If military losses led to the establishment of a less despotic government, trade would naturally increase. Clavière and Brissot claimed that this was the view of the most significant traveler across the Ottoman Empire, Constantin-François de Chasseboeuf, comte de Volney, whose *Voyage en Syrie et en Égypte, pendant les années 1783, 1784 et 1785* had appeared in a revised edition at Paris in 1787.[206] If Russia was victorious, France would equally be the victor in terms of trade, particularly because of the commercial treaty. France had nothing to fear from Russia because that state, as the travels of William Coxe and others proved, was not especially advanced commercially and lacked strength in military terms because of the servitude of the people.[207] France was by far the stronger nation: "True force is only real wealth, and real wealth comes only from the soil. Insofar as France conserves her land, the strength of the state will be maintained." France was advised to pursue the ideas about trade specified in *De la France* because this work stated "the true principles of philanthropic commerce" in favor of moderate wealth and against luxury and monopoly. France could not lose by being neutral in the Russo-Turkish War, and could defend its national interests against any state if peace continued. The only legitimate war was deemed to be a war in defense of liberty, and accordingly France ought to work to keep the peace in Europe, something that would make the state the most powerful on the continent.[208]

While Volney was a recent recruit to Clavière's group, advocating free trade and peace for France, and a France grown sufficiently powerful to defend Europe's small states, a more familiar contributor to the debate in 1787 was Mirabeau. At the end of 1786 Mirabeau had traveled to Berlin, reputedly on a diplomatic mission in the service of Calonne. He remained until February

1787, observing the alteration of the regime after Frederick II's death. In the aftermath he published under his own name Major Jakob Mauvillon's *De la monarchie prussienne sous Frédéric le Grand* (London, 1788), which, like *Point de banqueroute*, charted the decline of Prussia since Frederick II's death. Of this work Dumont later wrote that it was "an illustration, by facts, of Adam Smith's principles of political economy."[209] On his return to France, Mirabeau once more became involved with Clavière and continued to articulate and to popularize the notion of a cosmopolitan France devoted to free trade and to peace. Clavière supplied Mirabeau "with the subject matter" of the *Lettre remise à Frédéric-Guillaume II, roi régnant de Prusse*, which appeared in 1787. This advised the new monarch to abandon monopolies and to sustain the state by the development of free commerce and an alliance with a similarly reformed France.[210] In his biweekly periodical *Analyse des papiers Anglais*, which appeared for twelve months from November 1787, Mirabeau had Brissot and Antoine-Marie Cerisier, a former diplomat, compose a series of articles urging the Dutch to continue to maintain republican liberty, but without the involvement of France.[211] This argument was followed up in Mirabeau's *Aux Bataves sur le stathouderat* (London, 1788), written by the lawyer de Bourges, the pastor Paul-Henri Marron of Leiden, and Brissot himself.[212] Brissot's involvement ensured that it restated the views of *Point de banqueroute* concerning the need for the Dutch to defend their republican liberties alone. The great hope was that the Dutch would invigorate the capacity of weak states to stand up for themselves against imperial bullies, just as the North Americans had done.

Clavière jointed Brissot in London in November 1787.[213] On their return to Paris, in February 1788, Brissot and Clavière founded the Société française des amis des noirs, which replaced the Société Gallo-Américaine as the means of propagating their projects. It derived from the principle that "prosperity will constantly follow principles conforming to the rights of humanity."[214] The spreading of "general enlightenment" (*lumières générales*) to the friends of humanity, rather than the members of particular states or societies, was the specified goal.[215] Seeking the universal abolition of slavery and, as an essential corollary, the development of free trade and free labor, it promoted further attacks upon the mercantile system that was increasingly perceived to be Necker's vision for France. The Société attracted prominent members, including Charles-Maurice de Talleyrand-Périgord, soon to become bishop of Autun, and the Marquis de Lafayette. It also brought Clavière, Brissot, and Mirabeau together once more with Dupont de Nemours, Morellet, and Condorcet.[216] Equally the Société helped to place Clavière at a center of reform policy before the opening of the Estates General.[217] Elected president of the Société on

19 February 1788 as part of a system of rotation every three months, Clavière corresponded with members of the British Society for Effecting the Abolition of the Slave Trade, established in May 1787 by Quakers and Anglicans including Thomas Clarkson.[218]

Anticipating a revolution in France, Clavière wrote that those who shared "peace as a principle, and work as a habit, were the true benefactors of impoverished humanity."[219] He was establishing himself as a Genevan Shelburne at Paris. In June 1788 he underlined his commitment to France by purchasing a large property at Suresnes. Calling himself a person who belonged "to no other society than that of the entire world," he claimed that his mission was the propagation of "useful and beneficent truths, to all men, without distinction between nations."[220] Such truths of course meant a world purged of reason of state and made safe for small states. To Mirabeau, on 25 April 1788, Clavière wrote that the key to reform was to raise the poor to be full citizens, having sufficient wealth and education to contribute to the state both politically and militarily.[221] Such work was acknowledged to be a labor of generations, a point also made by Brissot in his *Plan de conduite pour les députés du peuple aux Etats-généraux de 1789*, which attacked, among other things, aristocracy at Geneva as having created an overpowerful government antagonistic to liberty.[222] Dumont charted Clavière's aspirations to the French finance ministry from this time. One sign of this was that Clavière began to publish in his own name through *De la foi publique*, which appeared at the end of 1788 and campaigned for a "monetary constitution," embodying an economic strategy for the commercialization of the populace, to underpin any political innovations. Clavière wanted to avoid bankruptcy, which Rousseau, "the immortal, the father of the happiness of children," would never have sanctioned, in order to prevent the return of France to brutal absolutist politics. At the same time he expressed great faith in Louis XVI. As the father of his people and "supreme administrator," Louis could be trusted to respect the sociable nature of humanity, furthering public education, the right to labor, a fair distribution of taxation, and the union of morality with politics. France, Clavière proclaimed, was superior to Britain economically, and was in the best economic health in its history. The revenues generated from commercialization would be sufficient to pay off the debt and reform the state. An era of peace and prosperity could be looked forward to once the example of Calonne had been banished, alongside the selfish machinations of priests and kings. Clavière claimed that the industrious could be trusted in politics. Their suffrage should never be feared, because the artisans, the poor, and the laborers would always support the rich and the prominent. Without a vast electorate, politics would begin to be dominated by cabals, prefiguring the reestablishment of aristocracy. On the back of such reform, France would become the preeminent state in Europe, superior to Britain and far stronger than despotic states such as Prussia or Austria. Necker was not personally attacked, although his policy of excessive use of loans and high interest payments was criticized in notes appended to the work.[223]

Whatever his aspirations to a ministry, Clavière's influence was more likely to be indirect, perhaps through the ascent of Mirabeau. Given such uncertainty, other projects continued to be embraced. Brissot left for America to pursue Clavière's land-purchase and related commercial schemes in May 1788. He returned in January 1789. Should the alteration of European politics prove impossible, both men continued to consider emigration to America, and did so until 1789. Dumont later wrote that Clavière was planning to establish a community of like-minded republicans somewhere in the United States; Brissot's task was to lay the foundations. But Clavière equally continued to see Paris as the place where he would rise, having reputedly had a premonition of becoming a French minister as early as 1780.[224]

The first step was to remove Necker, who was once more named *directeur général des finances* at Versailles in August 1788. Clavière was now unstinting in his antagonism toward the minister who, he claimed, supported the mercantile system and refused to make a break with historic policy on international relations and domestic politics. In private he attacked Necker as selfish and self-obsessed, uncertain about policy, circumspect to the point of inactivity, and incapable of recognizing that the Third Estate had to be brought into political life if France was going to be reformed.[225] As Dumont later said, the problem was that Necker, refusing to fall from power, instead slid.[226]

7

REVOLUTION AND EMPIRE

THE COMING OF REVOLUTION

With the commencement of the French Revolution, the Genevan exiles reached the height of their influence and contemporary fame. This occurred in part through their relationship with Mirabeau, risen to become the National Assembly's greatest orator and aspiring puppet master. After Mirabeau's sudden death in April 1791, the prominence of Genevan ideas in French politics was due more directly to Clavière, who served in the Girondist ministries under Jean-Marie Roland before becoming, in September 1792, the first finance minister of the new republic. Clavière's belief in the necessary transformation of France did not preclude friendly relations being established with Louis XVI.[1] So healthy were they that Clavière supplied his own coach for *citoyen* Louis Capet's lengthy journey to the guillotine on 20 January 1793. Dumont and Du Roveray were initially involved at Paris with Clavière.[2] London, however, remained for them a campaign arena of equal importance to Paris. With events in France always in the background, and working alongside Du Roveray, Dumont continued to push the Genevan cause through Shelburne and through William Pitt the Younger. With d'Ivernois they returned to Geneva to seek to reverse the debacle of 1782 in the spring and summer of 1791, during which time Du Roveray established a new constitution for the republic, the *Edit du 22 Mars 1791*.[3]

After they failed in both Paris and Geneva, the hopes of the exiles centered on Britain alone. D'Ivernois became one of Pitt's most indefatigable propagandists, and he continued to work as a diplomatic agent for Britain both before and after Pitt's death in 1806.[4] Du Roveray and Jean-André Deluc became spies for Britain. The story of the exiles' involvement with Mirabeau has been told before, and classically in Jean Bénétruy's *Atelier de Mirabeau*. Much evidence suggests that, rather than forming a group of aides for Mirabeau, the Genevans were frequently directing his labors prior to his arrival at the atelier of the National Assembly; in short, that he was as much a part of their workshop as they were of his. A debate has subsequently developed about the nature of Mirabeau's political thought. It is clear that, concerning Geneva and the maintenance of small states more generally, Mirabeau was in accordance with, and happy to follow the lead of, his Genevan friends. The same could be said of Shelburne, of Bentham, and, with less practical room for maneuver, of Pitt himself. More study should be devoted to the minutiae of the Mirabeau-représentant link, and that of Mirabeau with other authors who wrote speeches and articles for him. Equally, more research needs to be undertaken concerning the représentants' relationship with the vicissitudes of British foreign policy. The central concern of this chapter is rather the broader Genevan circle's attitudes to small states.

After Mirabeau's death, Clavière's rapid rise within the Girondist movement in the Legislative Assembly starting in October 1791 presented the exiles with their greatest opportunity to transform French policy permanently. Clavière's ascent, however, accompanied a growing dissatisfaction with events at Geneva, which had experienced its own revolution in January 1789.[5] A public revolt against the high price of bread there led the magistrates to acknowledge that the constitution of 1782 was no longer sustainable. More surprisingly, they sought a measure of national unity in offering clemency toward the exiles of 1782, initially by restoring political circles and by ruling that the exiles were welcome to return if they were willing to take an oath of allegiance to the state.[6] On 17 February 1789 matters went further. The Genevan General Council reversed the order of banishment, and the exiles were invited to resume their former membership of the executive councils. By the end of the month, the policies and constitution behind the *édit noir* of 1782 had been renounced, and a government much more attractive to the représentants established. D'Ivernois returned to Geneva briefly in February 1789. Du Roveray and Dumont began to participate in the city's politics in 1791.[7] Clavière, however, believed that reform at Geneva was insufficiently radical. As a self-professed "friend to humanity," he was unsure whether Geneva as presently constituted should continue without direct French guidance and involvement in day-to-day politics — with French "guidance" signifying support for the introduction of democracy. The great irony of the représentants' movement was that, as soon as they managed to get one of their own involved in the making of foreign policy at Paris, he began to act less like a représentant and more like Vergennes or Choiseul. The division of the exiles of 1782 into hostile camps followed, with some supporting Britain as the savior of Europe's small states, and others supporting France as the center of a republican empire. Although Clavière's activities in Paris between 1789 and 1792 have to be recalled in order to explain why he agreed to serve as Louis XVI's last finance minister, his policies to reform the French economy, which he perceived as midwife to a more profound social transformation, will be referred to only in passing. This chapter is primarily concerned with Clavière's continued involvement with debates about the future of Europe, and of Geneva above all else.

THE REPRÉSENTANTS IN LONDON AND PARIS

One of the most important changes within the Genevan exile community was the increasingly prominent role being played by the young pastor Etienne Dumont, who had returned from Russia to replace Joseph Priestley in Shelburne's household in 1785. Dumont had remarkable literary gifts, and his moderate and conciliatory character was deemed most likely to be successful in persuading French ministers to abandon their guarantee of Geneva's constitution. In 1788 Dumont visited Paris with Du Roveray in the hope of persuading Louis XVI, through their old associate Jacques Necker, once again director-general of finances at Versailles, to repudiate the guarantee.[8] The mission was unsuccessful, confirming to the London représentants that Clavière's verdict concerning Necker was correct: Necker was by inclination an advocate of absolute monarchy and to his very core an aristocrat.[9] Such a claim was also found in more neutral commentary at this time.[10] The later claims of Jean-Louis Soulavie and others that Necker's secret goal had been to make France more like Geneva was considered preposterous by the représentants.[11]

Necker, in *Du pouvoir exécutif dans les grands états* (1792) and *De la Révolution française* (1796), underscored his opposition to any form of democracy in a large state such as France, and claimed as a minister to have always been seeking a British-style government in France.[12] Critics called such statements "the bitter bread of banishment."[13] Necker's opposition was frustrating because British politicians appeared equally blind to the needs of Geneva.[14] Dumont was also now at the very heart of the Shelburne circle, with its interest in parallel political systems in each nation, a sentiment that became increasingly prominent in political argument.[15] D'Ivernois was reputed to have anticipated the collapse of France and the institution of a "limited monarchy like that of England" prior to 1789.[16] Samuel Romilly, after a visit to Paris with Dumont between August and September 1788, became sure that, amid the chaos of reformist ideas being canvassed at Paris, the French would be receptive to British constitutionalism, at least with respect to the conduct of political assemblies. On his return to London, Romilly quickly composed the *Règlemens observés dans la Chambre des Communes, pour débattre les matières et pour voter.* He also influenced Bentham in his decision to compose the *Political Tactics*, a work on parliamentary practice intended to help French legislators create peaceful forums for constitutional and legislative debate.[17] Dumont, soon to begin his long career as Bentham's editor and translator, published extracts from Bentham's work in Mirabeau's *Courrier de Provence* in 1789, in anticipation of its adoption in France.[18]

Dumont was also the author of the exiles' first published response to events in Geneva in 1789, the *Réclamation des Genevois patriotes établis à Londres.*[19] This text condemned the settlement of 1782 as having violated the most sacred ancient and modern constitutional edicts, including those of 1738 and 1767. Above all, 1782 had seen the entrenchment of aristocracy, a plant alien to Geneva, at odds with the national character of the city, its history and traditions. The aristocratic magistrates, not giving a fig for the independence of the republic, had sold it to France, with the consequence that morals and patriotic sentiments had collapsed, the economy had weakened, and politics had become fake, narrow, self-interested, and repressive. Geneva would become a free state again only if the French guarantee was abandoned. Geneva would remain a free state only if a government dominated by the représentants was established in the city. A democratic base needed to be created in political life, and regular elections instituted. Foreign troops had to leave the city, and a citizen garrison reestablished. Dumont advised the election of half of the Council of Twenty-Five and half of the Council of Two Hundred by the General Council. A tribunal would be established from among the citizens to decide whether to bring to the General Council représentations from more than two hundred citizens and bourgeois aged over forty. The edict of 1781 giving full rights to natifs was to be reinstated. The use of the new social class of those "domiciled" within the city was attacked as a means of maintaining an aristocracy that looked abroad for its preferred mode of governing. Geneva was being turned into a debauched Rome. Liberty had been lost. All the evils that Rousseau had predicted would accompany the installation of a theater in the city had come to pass.[20]

Nothing had altered représentant plans for Geneva since 1780. This said, there was now a stronger focus on the necessity of political reform to prevent the collapse of national manners. It was with regard to manners that Dumont expressed the greatest pessimism and concern about the future of the city. He explained his personal exile as a refusal "to submit to the chains of aristocratic servitude." The fact was that manners alone allowed the entrenchment of aristocracy and ensured the kind of popular misery that was so visible on any visit to Paris.[21] Manners at Geneva had evidently been corrupted since 1782. In turn the economy had declined as luxury had increased, and a sense of national lethargy was increasingly perceived externally. Geneva was losing its identity. In making such claims, the représentants were aligning themselves more directly than ever with the view that the corruption of manners was the key to recent Genevan history, and that only the restoration of national religiosity, in the form of a strict adherence to Calvinist duty, could reverse this. Dumont, like David Chauvet, Antoine-Jacques Roustan, and so many of the other représentant pastors or former pastors, continued to adhere to the published views of Jacob Vernes in defense of Calvinism against the challenge of the philosophes and Catholic or secular tyrants. Christianity was an egalitarian religion moved by the aspiration of "bringing all men together, allowing the spirit of equality to be born, and opposing every form of dependence and subordination."[22] Manners had to be reformed by the teaching of Calvinist duties. Individuals would thereby learn that from the basic love of God could be gleaned the duty to avoid pride, selfishness, and the correlatives of luxury and excessive wealth.[23] Labor, moderation, frugality, and temperance were recommended as central values capable of maintaining both pure morals and the traditions of Protestant worship into the modern world. The new generation believed that the modern Rome of France had to be countered, first and foremost, as a dangerous empire destructive of all that was free and good among human communities. The ancient Greek respect for a balance of power and for the independence of small states were the two key tests for moderns, a basis for evaluating their politics to ascertain the extent of their corruption.[24] Such ideas were shared with radical Protestants such as David Williams, whose plans for educational reform were called by Brissot a manifesto for the teaching of republican manners. Brissot's own justification of moral reformation cautioned that "without private morals, there is no public morality, no public spirit, and no liberty."[25]

In 1789 neither Dumont nor any of the exiles believed that Geneva's destiny could be separated from that of France. Accordingly, Dumont followed the publication of the *Réclamation* with a series of visits to Paris with a dual intention. The first was to foster peace between Britain and France, and to report to Lord Shelburne on events at Paris. The second, and for Dumont the goal closest to his own heart, was to remove the French guarantee of Geneva's constitution and in the process to ensure that in future Europe's small states remained safe from French intervention. Progress with regard to Dumont's first aim was recorded in a series of letters to Shelburne at London, which outlined a history of the French Revolution, strong traces of which could be found in Dumont's later *Souvenirs*.[26] Edited versions of Dumont's letters to Shelburne also saw print in an earlier guise in the form of the now little-known *Letters containing an Account of the late Revolution in France, and Observations on the Constitution, Laws, Manners, and Institutions of the English*, a hybrid work of which Dumont wrote the first twelve letters and Romilly the final ten, with the thirteenth letter authored by Romilly's friend the barrister John Scarlett. The book was completed after Dumont returned to England in March 1790 and was published at the end of 1792. The *Letters* appeared in the guise of a translation from German of the letters of "Henry Frederic Groenvelt." This conceit allowed Dumont, Romilly, and Scarlett to combine an interpretation of contemporary events in France with a guide to the constitution whose merits and flaws they believed ought to be dominating French discussion rather than Girondist or Jacobin republicanism.

While Dumont, Clavière, and Du Roveray were directly involved in French politics, d'Ivernois was in the process of publishing the culminating volume of his history of the représentants. This dealt with events at Geneva since 1767. He completed the writing of the work, entitled *Tableau historique et politique des deux dernières révolutions de Genève*, on 1 March 1789; it was published toward the end of the year. Following the *Réclamation*, this was another représentant manifesto intended to show that the exiles still had all of the solutions for the problems of Geneva. The historical sections of the work were much as might have been expected, following an epigraph from Tacitus condemning the involvement of princes in republican politics on the grounds that they led to the establishment of an aristocratic despotism even worse than the rule of a single tyrant.[27] Vergennes was accused of being the foreign prince, and the résident Hennin was accused of seeking to be the Solon of Geneva, governing a servile, corrupt, and Francophile nobility. The huge increase in the personal fortunes of some Genevans, on the basis of investment in French bonds, was identified as the root cause of the troubles of 1782. D'Ivernois accused the négatifs of backing the wrong horse in supporting aristocracy, having failed to realize that the trend of the times was against such a class, both in republics and in monarchies. Yet because of their close connections with the court of Versailles, where d'Ivernois identified Professor Paul-Henri Mallet as the négatif in chief, the aristocrats won through.

The result, according to d'Ivernois, was a collapse in republican manners. A fierce patriotism, sustained by military exercises and combined with a love of modesty and equality, was replaced by indolence, the love of frivolity and luxury, and the sentiment of pride. This was exemplified by the making of the city's main hill into an aristocratic citadel.[28] D'Ivernois accused Vergennes of seeking a series of aristocratic republics on France's borders, which he would be able to dominate, the wealth of which he could control, which he would always have the option of dividing up in the manner of Poland, or which he could transform into absolute monarchies such as Sweden. The latter, d'Ivernois emphasized, was ever Vergennes's political model.[29]

Although d'Ivernois claimed to have revealed the true depths of Vergennes's Machiavellianism, much of the rest of the *Tableau historique et politique* amounted to standard représentant argument since 1780. There was a significant difference, however, and one that drew criticism of d'Ivernois from within the exile community. It signaled a growing independence of mind.[30] D'Ivernois chose as the first epigraph to the book a passage from Polybius's *Histories*, which stated that the duty of the historian was to praise his enemies where necessary but equally to blame his friends when this was merited.[31] The epigraph followed a more general dedication to d'Ivernois's Genevan compatriots, which was linked to the culminating reform plan of the book. This demanded a commitment to national unity, minimal constitutional change, and the introduction of a scheme of public education to create citizens who were neither democrats nor aristocrats. D'Ivernois did not any longer want to see the rule of the représentants, but rather the generation of stronger forms of patriotism that moved beyond internal struggles for power.[32] Writing to David Chauvet and to Jacques Necker, he acknowledged that he was considered "half an aristocrat," and that his view of the necessary internal reforms had moved away from the position of his fellow exiles. Conflict with Dumont was anticipated, but d'Ivernois confessed that he was increasingly fearful both of enthusiasm and of the consequences of foreign dominion upon national manners.[33] For d'Ivernois a period of isolation followed, including no contact "even with the Genevans who worked on the *Courrier de Provence*." He spent most of 1789 in Italy and in the German states, returning to Geneva only in the spring of 1790.[34]

After d'Ivernois returned to Geneva and was elected to the Council of Two Hundred in September 1790, he attempted to put into practice the political vision of the final chapters of the *Tableau historique*, advocating a union of the représentants and the magistrates, and opposing regular democratic checks upon the magistrates. The French Revolution was altering the opinions of the représentants, as indeed it was those of almost all political writers. D'Ivernois's views began to chime with many of the attacks on popular government and of democracy hitherto uttered by his négatif and constitutionnaire opponents.[35]

DUMONT, DU ROVERAY, AND MIRABEAU

Having arrived at Paris with Du Roveray in March 1789, Dumont quickly became personally acquainted with the thirty or forty reformers who gathered at Clavière's residence or at the *maison* of the duc de La Rochefoucauld-Liancourt, and whom he considered to be in the vanguard of the movement for constitutional innovation.[36] Within a month he was concerned that, far from moving toward British constitutional forms, France was heading in a dangerously democratic direction. Commenting on the private meetings that were being held "to consider what steps the commons ought to adopt," prior to the gathering of the primary assemblies of the districts, he noted the prevalence of democratic ideas wrongly associated with Rousseau and the inevitable result of the loss of faith in the monarchy:

> I was present at two of these meetings, and I was astonished to observe what republican ideas prevailed in them, and how much the Parisians are weaned from their ancient love of monarchy. They seem to consider the principles of Rousseau's *Contrat social* as the only sound principles of government. . . . The people, universally, regard their representatives as their protectors and deliverers; all affection for the king appears to have diminished, in proportion as that for the [national] assembly has increased. If a Machiavellian republican had sought to degrade and ruin the court by his insidious counsels, he could not have suggested any more effectual measures than those it has pursued.[37]

Most of the perceived leaders of the Third Estate believed it to be necessary to foster certain kinds of patriotism in France. None of them, however, was fool enough to believe that Greek, Roman, Italian, English, or Swiss forms of republican patriotism could straightforwardly be established in France.[38] Attuned to the importance of political economy in modern states, Dumont and Du Roveray shared the near universal view, classically enunciated by David Hume and Adam Smith, that ancient republics rested on slave-based and agrarian systems of property, which for a variety of reasons made them both unjust and bellicose. In consequence, the history of such republics became largely irrelevant to those modern commercial societies that aspired to the establishment of a system of law based on justice and a system of trade based on sound morals.[39] To Dumont, those politicians who raised visions of ancient republicanism were wedded to passion rather than reason, and as demagogues used images of Rousseau and old republican glories in order to marshal popular support. This was fraudulent, given that republics rested on a fixed sense of who was and who was not a citizen, as Dumont had Mirabeau remind the National Assembly in a well-known speech.[40] Dumont called the people of Paris "extremely ignorant" and noted that in the primary elections to the Estates General "everything was settled by two or three persons who possessed a command of language." At the end of 1789 he noted of the popular politics then in the ascendance: "Falsehood is the constant and favourite resource of the cabals which prevail here. . . . The public is overwhelmed by lies and calumnies."[41]

The great tragedy of the Revolution was that so many of its authors had always been aware of the dangers of popular enthusiasm. When the people became political agents, the Revolution had become a different phenomenon than that conceived by any of its creators in the National Assembly, all of whom shared the aspiration of establishing a moderate and civilized monarchy. One of the points Dumont sought to emphasize was that moderates like himself, who considered themselves to be republicans when considering Geneva, were nevertheless the main enemies of democracy and republicanism in France. Dumont was mistakenly identified as a leading republican at Paris in 1792.[42] In fact, he had refused to become involved with Thomas Paine's journal *Le Républicain* and had earlier persuaded the publisher Le Jay to burn Mirabeau's edition of Milton's antimonarchical writings.[43]

The lurch toward popular politics was for Dumont an unintended consequence of the actions of leading figures in the court and the Estates General, who were each responsible for the failure to reach consensus about how to create a new constitution. Debate in 1789 centered on the presumed "Gothic" constitution France had experienced in feudal times, and the national character this was perceived to have embodied.[44] The factor that ultimately sustained the rift was Anglophobia, expressed as an expectation of the imminent collapse of the British state, in conjunction with the related belief that Britain's model of mixed government was the least likely to lead to political stability or national regeneration if adopted by France.[45] Dumont wrote to Samuel Romilly on 21 June 1789 that "the French have so much national vanity, so much pretension, that they will prefer all the follies of their own choosing to the results of British experience." Acknowledging that the British constitution was "repudiated as a reproach to human reason," Dumont had nevertheless expected French politicians ultimately to borrow from it if they were to maintain their commitment to a stable system protective of liberty and capable of fostering virtue.[46] He was shocked to find he was completely mistaken. From England Bentham seconded this view, confessing that he had expected to have to counter in France "too general and indiscriminate adoption of English law" and was surprised to find that in fact "a few English expressions, and of them too misapplied, compose nearly the whole of what France has drawn upon us for, out of so large a fund."[47] For Dumont, Anglophobia was the essential context for the decisions taken in the early months of the Revolution: "National vanity was wounded by the idea of learning from the wisdom of another nation, and [the assembly] would always have preferred to persist to the end with rules of procedure that were the worst possible and the most dangerous: the sitting of the 4th of August was proof of this."[48]

It was because the court rejected the British model, and was fearful of being forced into adopting British constitutional practice, that it refused to parley with the self-proclaimed National Assembly. In doing so, the court made the National Assembly dependent upon the variously expressed "will of the people" and thereby encouraged the emergence of the democratic politics that were fatal to the domestic stability of large states.[49] Equally, it was only because the members of the Third Estate within the Estates General were convinced that it was possible to create a constitution superior to that of Britain that they embraced Abbé Sieyès's script for national regeneration. The *Souvenirs*, with the benefit of hindsight, made clear that with every rejection of British parliamentary procedure, legislation concerning martial law, and above all constitutional law, France moved further away from liberty and further toward license.[50]

In the assembly, in the summer and autumn of 1789, Dumont's and Du Roveray's goals were first to establish a mixed constitution in which powers were limited and, as far as possible, balanced against one another, and second to introduce laws that would aid the process of establishing moderate manners supportive of liberty and order. Du Roveray had attempted, through Mirabeau, to establish a national guard based on the kinds of bourgeois militia he believed thrived in Britain; he was also behind the attempts to adopt British legislation on martial law and ministerial membership of the legislative assembly, in addition to Genevan legislation on the loss of political rights in cases of bankruptcy.[51] Together Dumont and Du Roveray sought to undermine the view espoused by Jean-Joseph Mounier, Pierre-Victor Malouet, and Trophime-Gérard de Lally-Tollendal, that the first constitutional act needed to be the restoration of royal executive power. This position was thought to be dangerous because it represented in practice a return to monarchy as traditionally conceived, entailing the restoration of government by "the thousand subordinate despotisms."[52] Although divisions existed on specific issues, such as the monarchical veto, and on the means of influencing the assembly, Mirabeau was content to advance Dumont's and Du Roveray's plans for a new constitution based on Britain's but with graduated elections and a clearer sense of civic identity.[53] With other leaders lacking, Mirabeau had to be the head of this putative movement. Romilly later stated in his memoirs that an English system had always been Mirabeau's secret goal.[54] Dumont was equally of the view that "he wished to give to France a Constitution modelled on that of England."[55] This view is supported by the testimony of Mirabeau's close friend at court, the Comte de La Marck, who accepted Mirabeau's willingness to act as a conduit to constitutionalism as a means of "saving the monarchy."[56] Mirabeau had earlier stated to Malouet, the great supporter of monarchy, that he was ready to use "all my influence to prevent the invasion of democracy which advances before us."[57]

DUMONT, SIEYÈS, NECKER, AND MIRABEAU

According to Dumont, it was Sieyès who had defined the Revolution, being responsible for its two fundamental elements: the transformation of monarchy from "a King by birth" to "a King by the consent of his people," and for the abolition of the aristocracy.[58] His three pamphlets, the *Essai sur les privilèges*, *Qu'est-ce que le tiers état?* and *Vues sur les moyens d'exécution*, "transport us beyond the sphere of our accustomed ideas and we discover in them that irresistible force, which enables them, unsubdued by prejudices, and unawed by established institutions, to conduct us to the most important truths."[59] While considering him a "deeply original thinker," Dumont was concerned that Sieyès had, with Necker, ultimately prevented the possible peaceful transition from absolute to Anglophone monarchy. Sieyès's worrying hatred of Britain was evident at an early meeting:

> I believed that this friend of liberty must certainly love the English, and in this I felt on my own ground. I was surprised, however, to find that he saw all the parts of England's constitution as fakery designed to be imposed upon the people. It appeared to me that he listened with pity when I described the elements of this constitution, the mutually-supporting balances, the veiled limits [upon power], and the masked but clear dependency upon one another of each of the parties that contributed to law-making. The influence of the throne was to his eyes only venality, and all the opposition merely a branch of the court. The only element of English practice that he admired was the jury system, but he did not understand it, and like all the French had come to false conclusions. It was manifest that he considered the English to be children in the matter of constitution-building, and was sure that he could give a much superior constitution to France.[60]

Having adopted Sieyès's form of national sovereignty in which the nation was defined as the collectivity of productive laborers, French legislators had been forced to remake social, political, and religious relationships within the state.[61] In reconstituting political society, they refused to take seriously the positive lessons to be derived from Britain's experience of mixed government, preferring to return to first principles of politics, while defining these principles in an ad hoc fashion.[62] Dumont believed Sieyès was correct with respect to the need for root-and-branch economic reform; together they were members of the Société française des amis des noirs and continued to advocate an end to slavery.[63] Yet Sieyès's constitutional projects, despite their genius, were ill defined, and the man himself useless when it came to providing leadership in the National Assembly.[64]

The problems with Sieyès's vision were twofold, according to Dumont. National sovereignty ("so bold a step has no example in history") had destroyed royal authority and in doing so vested too much power in a single assembly.[65] This was why Mirabeau and the Genevans favored the members of the assembly declaring themselves "deputies of the French people," in order to ensure a legislative process that operated in conjunction with the king.[66] Dumont wrote that Sieyès "had not dared to be a republican yet had continued to attack the weak remnant of royal authority."[67] Sieyès had too great a faith in the power of law to reshape popular manners, and too unyielding a confidence that rational laws could contain and ultimately withstand popular passions. In turn this could be traced to his implacable vanity; Sieyès was quintessentially French, Dumont contended, in believing that politics could become a science and that he himself had done exactly this in his writings.[68] In conjunction with national sovereignty, the declaration of rights, presented by Sieyès to the National Assembly on 29 August 1789, meant that he concurred with the expectation that no effective limits were going to be set on the theoretical power of the people over their legislators, which in practice opened the door to demagogues and generals.[69]

In all of Dumont's writings, the point was made that the court not only determined the initial course of the Revolution, but it also laid the foundations for the ultimate collapse into civil and international war. Dumont presented the king as un-French in terms of character, a man whose "weak mind" lacked the confidence, courage, and vanity to govern or to stand against his brothers the Comte d'Artois and Prince de Condé, who counseled a policy of maintaining monarchical sovereignty and threatening force against the members of the Third Estate.[70] Dumont's main criticisms, however, were directed at the most important of Louis XVI's ministers, Jacques Necker, whom he believed to be behind the inaction and vacillation that characterized the period up to August 1789. In failing to take a stand on the issue of the separation of the orders at the outset of the Estates General, Necker forced the members of the Third Estate to rely increasingly upon popular support.[71] Necker himself claimed in his account of the Revolution that he had consistently sought to establish the British constitutional model but had been thwarted by the court and more particularly by the king.[72]

Dumont refuted this account by arguing that Necker was, as Mirabeau reportedly said, "une horloge qui retarde," being "incapable of considering any subject from a grand point of view," having "seldom discovered any principles favourable to liberty" and having "never thought of the [e]states from any other view than that of finance."[73] Dumont damned Necker for failing to take advantage of a conciliatory *séance royale* to set up his own party in the assembly, as suggested to him by Du Roveray at the beginning of June, through the medium of Malouet, who had long been a friend to the représentants.[74] The conclusion was that Necker had always been an advocate of an unreflected union between the people and the crown ("la démocratie dans le cadre royal"), while in practice acting as the worst agent of aristocratic despotism in opposing the Third Estate.[75]

Mirabeau provided the Genevans with the prospect of an end to the French guarantee of Geneva's constitution through ministerial office and, in the interim, by vocal opposition to any movement in Geneva, whether overly democratic or aristocratic, that the représentants opposed.[76] Evidence of his continued support for the représentants occurred at the end of 1789, when Necker, having received a letter from Geneva's magistrates on 18 December, tried to persuade the National Assembly to accept 900,000 livres from Geneva's wealthy citizens in the form of a gift or patriotic contribution to France. On December 29 in the National Assembly, the Comte de Volney argued that the government of Geneva "does not owe its existence to the free consent of the nation" and stated that to accept the gift would be to support Geneva's aristocrats. He then read a letter received from Clavière, Du Roveray, and Dumont stating that Necker was offering the patriotic contribution in return for maintaining the guarantee that upheld their government. In a rhetorical tour de force, Mirabeau then proclaimed that the aristocrats at Geneva "have indefatigably endeavoured to suspend the sword of foreign interference over the head of their fellow-citizens," having usurped the state in 1782 and created a city "at present set in misery." He advised France to tell Geneva's magistrates to use their funds to reduce the price of corn, to "arouse the languid arts, support your manufactures, invite plenty into your laps, before you dream of offering us presents, which humanity would not suffer us to accept, unless with this condition, of showering them back with usury upon your famishing fellow citizens." Thunderous applause greeted his utterance that France had treated Geneva badly in 1766 and 1782, subjecting the city to the double yoke of civil and military despotism. France, he concluded, should not interfere in the politics of foreign states.[77]

The problem for the Genevans was that Mirabeau proved unable to turn himself into a minister or to control the National Assembly. Dumont always was convinced that, had Mirabeau lived, "the destinies of France would have followed a different course . . . [he] would have contained and possibly extinguished the Jacobins."[78] Yet for Dumont, Mirabeau had been incapable of dealing with the vanity of colleagues in the assembly and, despite his consistent general objectives, had lacked a precise plan of action until the time when he sought to unite supporters of monarchy against the Jacobins in the final six months of his life.[79] Such factors meant that he could never have headed a faction or a party, or acted as a force for national unity. Equally, Mirabeau's view that Britain remained the state that France had the most to learn from clashed with the Anglophobia of the time.[80] The implication of this stance was that no French politician could have successfully established mixed government.

Mirabeau was equally unsuccessful in removing Geneva's constitutional guarantee, although on 22 May 1790 France renounced offensive war and committed itself to peace. Dumont was increasingly concerned that events at Paris would be imitated at Geneva. By October 1790 he was complaining that there was no balance in Geneva's government, and he predicted that the "rule of the poor" would lead to disaster.[81] By the time of his death on 2 April 1791, both Dumont and Du Roveray had given up on influencing French politics. While notionally more democratic ideas about political rule were gaining authority through the Gironde in the Legislative Assembly at Paris, and through the actions of self-professed democrats at Geneva, Dumont spent six months in Geneva from January 1791 and three further months from February 1792.[82] United both with Du Roveray and with d'Ivernois, Dumont was involved in an attempt to reestablish political order. Seeing day-to-day politics becoming increasingly violent, and blaming the influence of France for the growth of democracy at Geneva, he increasingly put his faith in schemes for public education led by the pastors, who alone might restore the community to peace through the emulation of their behavior.[83] As such proposals came to nothing, and as a wholly popular government was instituted, Dumont arrived at the conclusion that democracy equated to rampant political Machiavellianism.[84]

CLAVIÈRE'S WAR ON NECKER

Clavière allied himself with Mirabeau in the hope of becoming chief adviser to a minister, and perhaps to facilitate his own ascent to office. In 1789 he began to publish in his own name, developing a political economy for France that was related to what he had once envisaged for Geneva: trade based on sound morals and on markets serving citizens who enjoyed moderate wealth. A France composed of right-minded représentants eschewing monopoly and aristocracy was the goal. This was the surest means of laying the foundations for a commercial system in France that would challenge Britain's mercantile system.[85] Convinced that economic conditions were the key determinant of order and ultimately the foundation of modern liberty, Clavière argued that the correlative of a moralized political economy in the domestic sphere was an international policy that eschewed empire building and promoted humanitarian causes, in part for sound economic reasons.[86] To this end Necker, deemed an advocate of exactly the opposite policies, had to be replaced as finance minister.

Necker was derided as an Anglophile and an advocate of the mercantile system justifying war and empire. In Clavière's view, Britain had succeeded in commerce because of an egalitarian public culture established after the Glorious Revolution. This had, however, been undermined by the growth of aristocracy in trade, which relied upon and was strengthened by the controls upon trade that lay behind the growth of Britain's empire. An example of an aristocrat-supporting institution was the Bank of England, which Necker wanted to imitate in France.[87] Necker's new loans and support for tax revenues generated by a *contribution patriotique*, proposed between August and October 1789, were condemned as palliatives. France needed credit and commerce to be stimulated, and Clavière advised the issue of a paper money backed by national property (*biens nationaux*), relying on Adam Smith's argument that "commerce is secure in proportion to the amount of effective legal-tender."[88] At the same time Clavière sought to stimulate commerce by the use of gold and silver plate to increase the circulating coinage. Smith had opposed such measures, but to Clavière's eye such a measure was worthwhile because it entailed the destruction of luxury goods made of such precious metals. Turning them into coin would give individuals the wealth necessary to purchase goods and to trade: "Sacrificing a luxurious fantasy will bring forth a source of general affluence: the public treasury, owners of gold and silver plate, creditors, the people, all will feel its beneficial effects."[89]

The point Clavière was making in all of his works, and which he had been making since the 1770s, was that trade was either moral or immoral. Immoral trade led to war in the form of the coercion of one individual by another; ultimately it led to nation fighting nation in order to dominate trade. Moral trade, by contrast, entailed all of the people becoming involved in commerce and establishing bulwarks against monopoly; bulwarks because the moderately wealthy and industrious individuals Clavière favored could overwhelm the power of the aristocrats in domestic markets. In short, if moral trade was fostered and popularized, demand for luxury goods would collapse along with the aristocrats who sustained their production.[90] To his old friend Jacob Vernes, Clavière described himself as an "errant and vagabond compatriot," devoted to peace but pursued by aristocrats, and hopeful that before long "the entire world will become a place of liberty," meaning that "the sacred rights of man will be the basis of every political association."[91] When the scheme for the conversion of silver and gold into coin failed, Clavière focused on paper money as the central means of getting the people involved in the economic life of the nation. He saw himself as the author of the *assignats* paper currency that he expected to do exactly this.[92] Until his fall from power in September 1790, Necker advocated the issue of treasury bills at interest, a revised tax system, and increased loans in order to pay the deficit. Clavière held the issue of assignats to be sufficient to resolve the financial problems of the state. By the summer of 1790 he was arguing that they had saved the Revolution. Alongside free trade, the assignats were key agents of the Revolution in fostering moral commerce.[93] Clavière considered himself to be establishing a "system of true liberty" based on the truth that "morality is the sole sure guide in politics."[94] Clavière envisaged the assignat paper-money scheme as an "old agrarian": with the depreciation of paper money, fortunes would become more equal, paving the way for the emergence of a citizen body of moderate property owners who could be trusted to act as political agents, inaugurating an era of liberty and political stability.[95]

MINISTER CLAVIÈRE AND PERPETUAL PEACE

After Mirabeau's death, Clavière set out his vision of a flourishing France in a publication for the Société française des amis des noirs. This countered Antoine-Pierre Barnave's decree of 15 May 1791 in support of the colonial sugar planters, who had refused to allow nonwhites to become citizens. Barnave argued that freeing the slaves would destroy France's empire and move the economy one step closer to ruin. He wanted to leave such decisions to the colonial authorities. The sugar planters initiated violent reprisals against the slave rebellions in Saint-Domingue and Martinique that they held had been fomented by the Société.[96] Against Barnave, Clavière reiterated the argument that slavery violated both the right of all men to political representation and the philosophical principle of human perfectibility. He added that the abolition of all slave traffic and the institution of means to educate former slaves would increase French commerce globally. Free trade, the abandonment of immoral commerce, and the involvement of all men in government, whatever their color, would best stimulate France's economy and ensure that newly won liberties could be enjoyed in the longer term. The alternative was the mercantile system, the lust for empire and concomitant war, and the governance of politics and the economy by corrupt aristocrats.[97]

In October 1791 Clavière entered the Legislative Assembly at Paris as a *député suppléant* for the Seine. Following the rules of the new constitution, he became French, taking the civic oath that rendered him a citizen. He helped Brissot, Condorcet, Armand Gensonné, Marguerite-Elie Guadet, and Pierre Victurnien Vergniaud to forge the party of the Gironde in the Legislative Assembly, and contributed to the Girondist journal, the *Chronique du mois ou les Cahiers patriotiques*, edited by Nicolas Bonneville.[98] As late as November 1791 Clavière invited Dumont to come to Paris to work on the *Chronique*.[99] Subsequently Clavière was elevated to the finance ministry, the position he had courted for so long.[100] He served as *ministre des contributions*, responsible for public finances, from March to June 1792 and from August 1792 until June 1793. Among the major questions facing the Girondist ministries was their relationship with foreign powers; war had been declared against Austria on 20 April 1792, after the foreign minister Charles-François Dumouriez listed French grievances at the bar of the assembly. Brissot had called for a new crusade in the name of universal liberty. The first step had to be taken against Austria as one of the most despotic of European states and as the state seeking to overturn the Revolution through the "Austrian committee" at Paris.[101] Prussia's declaration of war on France followed on 13 June.

During his second spell as a minister, Clavière saw the September massacres occur; the king's arrest, trial, and execution; the invasion of France; the victory over the Prussians at the Battle of Valmy; and the establishment of the First French Republic. Rumors abounded throughout 1792 of the desire of the French to create a greater republican empire, and more particularly to annex the Pays de Vaud and Geneva itself, restoring the ancient free county of Burgundy. Necker and Mounier leveled the accusation that the French were seeking the wealth of the Swiss.[102] Brissot was later deemed by Dumouriez to be the main advocate of a republican empire stretching from Italy and the Netherlands to the borders of Prussia and England. Brissot was certainly confident about the power of the republic to defend itself through the public passion for liberty, and to maintain extended wars if necessary: "Those kings of former times might perpetuate their wars. At this day, it is above the strength of all the powers to make a long war. Money is the sinew of it; and this sinew soon fails. Free citizens alone can, for their liberty, maintain long wars. The great interest of liberty, the interest which is self-nourished, supplies the room of money among them, which is easily spent."[103]

Clavière's views were more complicated. Contemporaries vilified Clavière as a wild republican whose true passion was self-regard, being "Cleondas" or "a misanthrope," "full of projects, of speculations, of critical views, and plans for reform . . . he is incapable of execution. The native of a free country, he professes principles, that are deemed visionary by the bigoted and the timid."[104] He was in fact more pessimistic about his prospects, more aware of the weaknesses of his fellow ministers, and more realistic about his limitations as a politician than others supposed.[105] This reputedly led him into later schemes to maintain the monarchy by establishing a regency under Louis XVIII.[106] Soulavie accused him of fomenting the disorders at Paris that led to the creation of a republic. This was said to be Clavière's goal, in order to make France like Geneva.[107] In fact Clavière had already come to the conclusion that Geneva ought to be following France's example, rather than the other way round. While supporting the ideals of the Revolution, Clavière more than ever believed that the economic transformation of France was the only means to their practical realization. The assignats, he was equally sure, were doing exactly this. Clavière's friend the banker Jacques Bidermann explained in the *Chronique du mois* of January 1792 that real incomes had risen, that capital was being drawn toward industry because labor was so cheap, and that the economic potential of France was finally being realized. New industries such as the production of cotton textiles could now be fostered through the use of imported English machines. Bidermann described Clavière as the author of the transformation and praised "the patriotism of his superior genius."[108]

The question for Clavière was always the identity of the political analogue to the success of the assignats. Their fall in value, he was certain, had a political origin. The "enemies of prosperity" were the opponents of the Revolution, who wanted prices to rise and liberty to be stifled through economic collapse. Clavière's plan to prevent this appeared early in 1792 as *De la conjuration contre les finances et des mesures à prendre pour en arrêter les effets* and at the same time was serialized in the January and February issues of the *Chronique du mois*. He reiterated his view that the assignats had allowed "the foundation of the constitution and its establishment." National resources, he declared, had never been so fecund. The national debt was being paid, and commerce was thriving. The assignats had become synonymous with the principles of the Revolution, being a force for patriotism and also for morality and moderate wealth as they gradually increased the numbers of the industrious. In doing so they underpinned the political equality at the heart of the revolutionary state.

Yet a "conspiracy against the finances" was being fomented. It was led by bankers, "the most perfidious speculators . . . born for the misery of humanity . . . [who] enrich themselves on our ruins," by "the embezzler Calonne," and by "the aristocrat Pitt." Through counterfeiting, and through gambling that the value of the currency would continue to fall, their collective aim was being achieved. The assignat was not recognized as an international currency, causing the value of French goods to collapse relative to those produced in the rest of Europe. Clavière argued that the value of the assignats would stabilize once the national land they represented was specified, allowing the paper money, becoming a deed of purchase, to be burned. France was not reenacting John Law's experiment, because the assignats were directly tied to the wealth of the state. Clavière called for a patriotic conversion of the assignats into landownership, arguing that this would amount to the regeneration of liberty once the people associated the assignats with the Spartan virtues of courage and devotion to the national cause.[109]

An additional step was necessary. The "first financial operation" had to be "a war against the coalition of princes." Clavière's war was to be paid for by a tax on inheritance, by the sale of forests and barren land, by a share issue from a short-term national bank, and by a tax upon stock market speculation.[110] The forces attacking the assignats could be found in the German states dominated by Austria and Prussia, in Spain, and in Savoy. Clavière stated that he wanted to see French-style revolutions commence in Vienna and Madrid. He argued that the war against the enemies of the Revolution would be defensive only — the territory and independence of the states involved would always be respected. The French economy would experience further stimulation when the values of the Revolution, against the monarchies and principalities that rested upon the old values of despotism and aristocracy, were exported abroad by force of arms. France could not, however, stand alone in undertaking this mission. An alliance of "free and industrious nations" was necessary to the success of the project. The most important was Britain.

Clavière claimed that Pitt was trying to bankrupt France in order to draw attention away from the state of Britain's public finances. Adopting a utopian register, Clavière predicted that Pitt would be removed from office once it was recognized that peace could be secured in perpetuity with a France that had renounced all aspiration to empire and was willing to write this clause into its constitution. The "national will" of the British favored "universal civilization." Clavière called the latter the "great enterprise, sacred to all honest men, which ennobles commerce." For practical reasons the British would be interested in developing their own commerce with France through a much more extensive commercial alliance than William Eden's and Gérard de Rayneval's. A cabal in Britain favored the mercantile system and its corollary in international relations, an alliance with Prussia and the support of the aristocracy in Holland, Ireland, and the Austrian Netherlands. But Clavière was convinced that a far larger proportion of the nation recognized that "free commerce between nations is as important as civil liberty."[111]

As a minister having good relations with Louis XVI, and believing that the economic reforms he had instituted could be relied upon to increase national wealth and public order, Clavière anticipated an end to the Revolution.[112] When the time came to declare war on Austria, Dumont reported that Clavière was initially opposed because of the state of the finances, although in the Legislative Assembly he voted for war.[113] The key, he believed, was to put into practice the view expressed in *De la conjuration* and to foster alliances with Britain, the Dutch, and the United States.[114] He probably had hopes of stimulating an opposition movement to Pitt, dedicated to economic and political reform and to international peace. This explains the length and content of his letter to Charles Stanhope, 3rd Earl Stanhope, of July 1792. Clavière here expressed the desire to return to private life. He equally made clear his complete dedication to the cause of France, defending the Revolution from the accusation that it was the rule of a violent mob by arguing that "there are, in great revolutions, movements of disorder and even of excess that it is impossible to prevent." Condemning the opponents of equality and the exponents of antipopular passion, he argued nevertheless that such antagonism was as necessary in the moral world as it was in the physical and ultimately served the cause of liberty. Such was "the love of liberty in the heart of the French" that no coalition of foreign powers was likely to put down the Revolution. The greater the challenge and the more extensive the war, the more intense that national devotion to the ideals of the Revolution became. Clavière noted that the same kinds of patriotism that had been generated to form Switzerland were having the same effect in France, necessitating war against Austria. Struggles for liberty could not be silenced, and French ideals would naturally spread to other states. France could go to war "for several years against the enemies of liberty, and sustain without cease its rights by its writings and by feats of arms." The transformative effect would be remarkable. Others would have to take a stand with regard to such "epidemic agitation." Clavière claimed that Stanhope was already aware that "the war that you made against the Americans has spread the idea of liberty across Europe, and especially within Britain, more than a hundred years of peace would ever have managed." The Genevan struggle against aristocracy had also paved the way for events in France.[115]

Clavière was not seeking to persuade Stanhope of the power of republican virtue in France. Instead he was pursuing the policy of political and commercial alliances, just as Shelburne had ten years before, in order to establish perpetual peace. Clavière claimed that the French would not trouble any of their neighbors if they were left in peace. Rather, an alliance would bring tranquility to Europe and farther afield. Contrary to the opinions of those in Britain who confessed themselves to be enemies of the Revolution in France, an Anglo-French alliance would restore calm to French domestic politics and above all "extinguish the hopes of an unruly faction" to extend disorder. In short, the Revolution would see itself "promptly terminated." Clavière stated that such views were more likely to be acceptable in philosophy than in political life, but he was equally certain that Stanhope shared them. The problem was that he was also sure that William Pitt did not.[116]

The urgency of finding means to an alliance with Britain had become a policy after Charles Maurice de Talleyrand was sent to London on 15 January 1792. He had letters for the foreign secretary, Lord Grenville, intended to extend the terms of the Eden Treaty and to follow it up with a more direct political alliance. Brissot gave vocal support to the proposed alliance in the *Patriote français*.[117] Free trade with France's colonies was offered in return for loans intended to bolster the assignat. On 19 March Talleyrand, accompanied by Dumont and Du Roveray, returned empty-handed, although they conveyed the message that neither Pitt nor Grenville was antagonistic toward France. High hopes were maintained of an alliance at a future date.[118] By July such hopes had been dashed, and a second diplomatic mission, in which Dumont and Du Roveray played a greater role, was also a failure.[119] Seen in this light, Clavière's letter to Stanhope was an exploration of the option of putting pressure on the British government from the ranks of the opposition for an alliance with France. The alternative was contained in a letter reputedly from Clavière to the Dutch at the outbreak of war in March 1792. This threatened the smaller state not to allow Prussian or Austrian forces into their territory, and that the French Republic would leave "neither truce nor repose in any quarter to her enemies either secret or open."[120]

CLAVIÈRE AND GENEVA

Geneva was of course the test case of Clavière's dual claim that France could not help but export revolutionary ideas about liberty but at the same time was not an imperial power. From the time that war was declared against Austria, he was accused of having particular designs upon the city of his birth.[121] When

French troops streamed into northern Italy in the autumn of 1792 as part of the war against Austria and its ally Savoy, both the Swiss and the Genevans were petrified that their traditional neutrality would be violated. Geneva called for armed support from the cantons. Over 1,500 troops arrived in the city. David Chauvet, having returned to Geneva in 1789, wrote to d'Ivernois that everyone was worried that "the new French Republic is preparing to destroy us, without a motive, interest or reason, and only to exercise the odious despotism that kings have directed against us since 1782."[122] Pressure was put on British ministers to demand an explanation of French conduct from Dumouriez.[123] Observers with less at stake equally acknowledged that the Genevan case was the great test of the new republic in international relations:

> Geneva is acknowledged by all the powers of Europe as an independent state: it seems contradictory to acknowledge sovereignty and independency in a state, and then complain of so natural an exercise of it as the calling in the aid of neutral powers to enable it to maintain strict neutrality. . . . This ill accords with the prudent and pacific tenor of the declarations which the National Assembly formerly made, and stamps credit on the assertions of the enemies of the Revolution, that the treatment which Geneva now receives from the new Republic is a specimen of what all the neighbouring states may expect. Although it may be thought natural that a monarch, particularly an arbitrary one, should from motives of vanity, avarice or ambition, endeavour to extend his dominions by war and conquest; yet the vanity or avarice of a private citizen of Paris, Lyons, Marseilles, or any other part of France, can be little gratified by the accession of new provinces. France, therefore, being now a republic, the ambitious and restless spirit of her kings, that fatal source to which the other states of Europe have imputed almost all the wars of the two last centuries, being now dried up, long peace and tranquillity is to be expected when this new form is acknowledged and established. This reasoning seems plausible *à priori:* — it is unfortunate, however, that the history of the world shows that republican states have been inspired with as violent a desire of conquest, and as restless an ambition, as any monarch from the age of Alexander to that of Louis XIV. And the spirit which the new republic of France begins already to manifest, gives no reason to expect that the philosophy from which she boasts her origin, has taught her more moderation than her predecessors.[124]

A controversy was initiated concerning the nature of Geneva's historic alliance with France and the clauses pertaining to acts of neutrality. A placard was placed on the frontier announcing the "neutral territory of Geneva."[125] For the *représentants* at London, calling upon Swiss troops in times of crisis was in accordance with all the treaties and presented no threat to the state of France of any kind. Brissot responded with the argument that the Genevans were challenging France and violating the terms of their alliance in asking for "foreigners" (the cantons) to defend the city against France.[126]

Clavière was then accused by his former friends of plotting to annex Geneva to France and of using his newfound powers as minister to orchestrate radically democratic republicanism in the city, in league with associates such as Frédéric-César de La Harpe.[127] Chauvet reported that Etienne-Salomon Reybaz had written to Clavière, urging him to do his duty as a Genevan. No reply had been received, and Clavière's views were clearly suspect. Chauvet also reported that Dumont, Du Roveray, and Reybaz had shown the utmost zeal and patriotism in urging the French ministers to be just toward Geneva. Du Roveray had lost his diplomatic position in consequence, and all three had urged Clavière to take action. The conclusion was that "the ministers of republics are as tyrannical as those who serve kings."[128] For Dumont, it was clear that Clavière's hatred of aristocracy was now directed at Geneva. This issue amounted to a parting of the ways for the exiled représentants, who had been so united since 1782.[129]

Clavière was, by the autumn of 1792, wholly committed to popular government abroad as well as in France. France was under threat from foreign powers and from the aristocracies, either domestic or émigré, that in his view controlled the policies of so many foreign courts. Despite the military victories, the assignats remained unstable. Something had to be done. Ensuring that external powers, and especially those on the borders of France, embraced the Revolution was a policy that not only promised to facilitate domestic stability in France and increase the security of its borders, but also offered larger markets for the industrious, as well as sources of wealth that France might draw upon in times of crisis. The populace of the foreign state would gain in terms of liberty from the establishment of democracy. Equally, its independence would be assured because France was no longer an imperial power. Furthermore, the economic reforms that accompanied the introduction of revolutionary laws would transform manners and promote moderate wealth. Clavière was clearly writing to a Genevan at the end of 1792 when he was ordering the end of aristocracy, the institution of a democracy, and the reform of manners by education.[130] He had begun to envisage a world characterized by "the empire of liberty." Agents such as Edmond-Charles Genêt were sent to the United States to develop commercial links with France and to persuade the new republic to join France in the war against Britain.[131] To the Swiss Clavière wrote that the goal of France was confraternity and an alliance of free peoples against "the coalition which is the enemy of every kind of liberty."[132]

While denying to his friends that he now opposed Genevan independence, Clavière was, as early as the end of 1791, actively encouraging the popular party at Geneva, attacking both Du Roveray and d'Ivernois in the process.[133] General Anne-Pierre de Montesquiou-Fézensac, who led the French army into Savoy, was deemed initially to be Clavière's agent when he brought his troops to the gates of Geneva in the autumn of 1792. On 8 October Clavière told the general to make Savoy "independent under the protection of the French Republic." At the same time he advised Montesquiou to maintain peaceful relations with the Swiss and to demand only the removal of troops from Geneva.[134] Rather than taking the city, Montesquiou became a hero to Genevans in agreeing to a compromise on 22 October, by which the garrisoned Swiss troops left Geneva, which remained independent. Clavière was subsequently horrified by reports that Montesquiou had chosen to negotiate with Geneva's magistrates and had not seen the Swiss soldiers leave, thereby jeopardizing the revolutionary movement within the city.[135] Clavière was further accused of plotting to have Montesquiou arrested for failing to invade, and of opposing initiatives for peace between Britain and France.[136] Having secretly entered Geneva on 2 November, Montesquiou abandoned his troops and fled into Switzerland. He accused Clavière of expressing the view that "I hope you will soon enter into Geneva: you must destroy that nest of aristocrats; and fish out from it the buried treasures." Montesquiou claimed to have replied that using violence against the Genevans would violate the law of nations and blacken the reputation of the French state.[137]

Dumont arrived at Paris in November 1792 at the request of Geneva's magistrates and the Genevan minister at Paris, Jacob Tronchin. He was alone rather than with Du Roveray because the latter had duties at the French embassy in London. By this time Montesquiou's initial attempt at a settlement had been rejected by the National Convention, and the threat of invasion still existed. Brissot attacked the Machiavellianism of Geneva's magistrates at the convention on 24 November.[138] Dumont reported that Clavière claimed not to have been involved in the threats directed against the republic and to be innocent of the accusations being widely leveled against him. Dumont used this claim to ensure that all the Girondist ministers took to the convention an agreement to respect the independence of the city republic, in return for the removal of the Swiss troops:

> Clavière told me that he had not concurred in the decree hostile to the Syndics of Geneva, as on the day it was determined upon, he had been prevented by ill health from attending the council. I seemed willingly to listen

to his excuses, and observed that a favourable opportunity now presented itself, of sheltering himself from all future reproach, by obtaining a ratification of the treaty. I also succeeded in bringing Brissot to the same way of thinking, although he had, in his *Patriote François*, been very violent against the Lilliputian republic, as he termed it. I represented to Vergniaud, Guadet, Gensonne, and Condorcet, the indignation felt in England at this attack made by republicans upon the weakest of republics; and one which had done the greatest honour to freedom. Others also contributed to soften the ministers and their party, and some consideration was still shown towards the Swiss. A few days after, the treaty was proposed at the legislative assembly, ratified without a dissenting voice, and the independence of the Genevese republic acknowledged by the most formal act.[139]

The republican patriotism of the Girondist ministers shocked Dumont because such sentiments appeared to him as being used to justify Machiavellian acts of policy. He was warned by the minister Pierre-Henri-Hélène-Marie Lebrun that a plot existed to make Geneva part of France, being promoted by the former exile Jacques Grenus, who was visiting Paris to advise the ministers at the same time as Dumont. Dumont then left Paris for Geneva, in the hope of preventing the purported coup d'état. It was clear that he ranked Clavière among the plotters. Geneva was the ideal base for a French attack on Savoy. The arsenal and riches of the state would be useful given the parlous condition of the French army.[140] Although Geneva was not annexed to France, an uprising that took place on 4 December brought to power a party of the followers of revolutionary France who called themselves *égalisateurs*. On 12 December all those born in the city, those who had Protestant parents, and those who had been granted residence, were henceforth considered equal citizens.[141]

The new constitutional politics at Geneva had genuinely revolutionary effects. Past political laws and judgments were annulled, including all the condemnations of rebels against the magistrates from Pierre Fatio to the exiles of 1782. Furthermore, all decrees against the person and writings of Rousseau were rendered null and void. Clavière had succeeded in seeing the Genevans imitate the French in launching a revolutionary movement dedicated to establishing moderate wealth and popular sovereignty, and abolishing aristocracy and the political culture it was deemed to have generated. On 19 November the National Convention decreed that France was willing to provide support for people anywhere seeking to recover their liberty. Savoy and Nice were annexed to France and the river Scheldt was opened. On 15 December the convention decreed that, wherever French troops were to be found, the sovereignty of the people was to be proclaimed and revolutionary institutions introduced. Brissot summarized these goals as "war to the castle and peace to the cottage."[142] Peoples everywhere had a right to liberty, and the French were merely facilitating this end.

The kinds of violence that were soon to become a political norm at Paris also scarred Genevan politics over the following three years. Many former représentants found the demand that they become revolutionary actors too much, and they especially objected to the oath of fealty to the new state.[143] Jean-Pierre Bérenger wrote that the Genevans had begun to misunderstand Rousseau, who had been an advocate of gradual reform and an enemy to social equality and democracy.[144] Clavière was often described as the author of Geneva's troubles, having encouraged the French résident to become involved in the popular war against the magistrates, and having bankrolled Grenus's schemes to turn Geneva into France's closest revolutionary ally. Clavière was now considered by many of his former représentant friends to be a traitor to his country, a hypocrite for having spent his life attacking French dominion at Geneva, and the vilest of political agents. Yet he was equally disparaged by the égalisateurs. Grenus later stated that Clavière let the opportunity slip to turn Geneva French, because of his friendship with "counterrevolutionaries" such as Dumont and Du Roveray.[145] Grenus was accused in certain quarters of seeking an end to Genevan independence from 1791, having been encouraged by Dumouriez and others to create an "Allobrogian" republic formed from Geneva, Savoy, the Valais, and the Pays de Vaud regions. A Société des Allobrogues was established to this end.[146]

Former représentants who continued to have faith in the old politics now combated the égalisateurs. In January 1793 Reybaz wrote to Dumont that independence had to be proclaimed and clung to, as the danger of it being lost was so great.[147] Dumont remained a member of the provisional government at Geneva, working to combat Grenus and to fight for independence. This took remarkable courage, as his response to the September Massacres at Paris underscored that he knew exactly the kind of government that might be established at Geneva. He revealed to Romilly that he was deeply pessimistic about the future prospects for liberty.[148] At the end of March 1793, he gave up and returned to London.[149] By February 1794 a new constitution had been adopted at Geneva based on direct democracy, in the form of the election of magistrates by all Calvinist male citizens over twenty-one who were willing to accept the civic oath. New taxes upon the wealthy, aimed to redistribute wealth and ensure the moderate wealth of all, were passed on 19 July 1794.[150]

Clavière's personal perspective was spelled out in a letter to his old natif friend Bérenger on 27 October 1792. Clavière stated that there was no need for further polemics concerning the Franco-Genevese alliance because Genevan independence was secure and France was removing its troops in accordance with Montesquiou's agreement. At the same time he underscored the fact that he considered himself devoted to the French revolutionary cause, noting that Geneva's magistrates had been foolish in requesting the return of France's artillery to French territory and the movement of troops at least ten leagues from Geneva. Geneva should remember that it was a dwarf and France a giant. He also called Bérenger a dupe of Geneva's aristocrats, attaching proof in the form of a letter from the government of Neuchâtel to Prussia. This revealed that the Genevan magistrates were turning to Prussia for succor in violation of all treaties with France. Clavière's country "was wherever true liberty reigns" and "wherever prejudice is fought to the death." Geneva remained dear to him, but his duty lay toward the free state that had placed its confidence in him as a minister. The French Republic did not threaten Geneva. It was preposterous to draw parallels with the old cause of independence, which had existed when Necker and his allies had continued to allow tyrants at Paris to dictate politics at Geneva. Clavière claimed not to be motivated by vengeance; he sought only the happiness of the people. This entailed the continuation of war against aristocracy, in France and beyond. Such were the only means to liberty, peace, security, and happiness. Genevans must learn to "live between two peoples [in Savoy and in France] who only recognized the equality of rights in the social system."[151] In short, Geneva had to accept that it was surrounded by states that had undergone the old représentant revolution and now valued moderate wealth, industry, and equality.[152]

From one perspective, Clavière was being consistent. The new regime of moderate wealth and austere republican morals needed to be fostered, and he believed he had found exactly the means to this end. The problem for fellow représentants was that it entailed the abandonment of the protection of small states. Clavière was allowing the economic element of représentant reform philosophy to trump the political support for the existing structure of Europe. The assignats needed large political and economic units to flourish. Clavière's dream became one of vast republics, united by free trade and the republican patriotism the Revolution had unleashed.

Clavière believed that he was being more consistent than any of his former associates, who had renounced their dedication to liberty. To see Dumont and Du Roveray ally themselves with the aristocratic magistrates at Geneva must have shocked him profoundly. He always maintained contact with Dumont, in spite of the latter's criticisms of Girondist policy. This may have been motivated by Clavière's view of Dumont's influence over Shelburne and his likely contact with other prominent figures in British public life.[153] Remarkably, he was continuing to seek an Anglo-French alliance just before the French declared war on Britain and the Dutch Republic, and at the time when Spain and Portugal had joined the First Coalition against France.[154] As a minister he continued to work on the economic transformation of France via the ongoing conversion of the assignats into the tangible wealth of land. Free trade was declared a principle of republican politics in December 1792.

The problem for Clavière, as for his fellow Girondists, was their failure to master the Jacobin Club. It was said of Clavière and of Jean-Marie Roland that they had little or nothing to do with the Jacobins before their ministry and most certainly not afterward. The same was said of other leading Girondists. In consequence, when Brissot and others attacked extremists within the Jacobin Club in October 1792, they were perceived to be outsiders attacking the true representatives of the people. Furthermore, it served to make leaders such as Maximilien Robespierre "more powerful and furious," having the support of the sans-culottes of Paris. As Dumouriez put it, the Girondists were "in the end assassinated by means of that very poniard of republicanism, which they themselves had sharpened and confided to their barbarous hands."[155] The treason of Dumouriez himself and the continued decline of the assignats also contributed. On 15 May 1793 Jean-Nicolas Pache, the mayor of Paris, presented a petition to the convention from thirty-five of the forty-eight sections of the city, demanding the arrest of the Girondist deputies. On the morning of 31 May an insurrection commenced in the streets of Paris, resulting in the arrest of Brissot, Clavière, and their associates on 2 June.

In the aftermath Clavière was vilified as a Machiavellian English agent who had taken up French citizenship only to undermine the state.[156] He continued to live at Suresnes under house arrest until September, when, with the war going badly, he was denounced at the Committee of Public Safety by Jacques Nicolas Billaud-Varenne as a corrupt spy and brought to the Conciergerie prison.[157] On 19 September he was interrogated about the supposed Girondist plot to make France subservient to Britain. Clavière had already published a self-defense stating that he had sent accounts to the ministers to prove his probity. Calling himself "a very old defender of liberty, a very old partisan of equality," he argued that manners were required to have a successful republic. Those of France were being destroyed by false calumny and accusation—forces more dangerous than plague or famine.[158] On hearing of his imminent appearance before the Revolutionary Tribunal, Clavière committed suicide in prison on 8 December 1793 by stabbing an ivory dagger into his heart, reputedly without uttering a sound.[159]

Clavière's death did not prevent him from being described as the source of the revolutionary violence that dominated Genevan politics by 1794. As the anonymous *Misfortunes of Geneva* put it, Clavière, seeking a French "world empire" with Brissot, espoused the doctrine that all sovereignty belonged to the people, that "perfect equality" ought to exist between individuals, and that "the will of the many, that is to say, of those who know how to seduce and to captivate the many, ought to be the supreme law." The consequence was the notion that "the authority of the magistrate ought to emanate from . . . the arbitrary pleasure" of those elected by the people. Pride began to characterize popular mores. The principles of order were called aristocratic and "cowardly." Genevan politics were transformed into scenes of dominion and massacre. In short, Clavière was blamed for causing Geneva's terror:

> The Republic of Geneva was not so guarded by her old constitution as not to be exposed to political convulsions. Her citizens, who, either from their own studious application, or from those public institutions which were open, in this city, to individuals of every class, had acquired the first principles of a good education, were eminently conspicuous for the foibles of speculative refinement. They had contracted the habit of expatiating on abstract subjects, and of making these, in their social circles, the constant topics of conversation. Every day gave birth to new systems, to unnatural jealousies, and exaggerated complaints against the magistrates; and these had not sufficient legal means to suppress, or to restrain such dangerous discussions. On various occasions, after their political debates, the people ran to arms, and tranquillity was re-established by the admission of such changes, or innovations, as were prejudicial to the authority of the state. However, the intestine commotions of Geneva had not, before the present period, been characterised by any strokes of cruelty. If, in the course of the five or six last revolutions, some individuals perished, they indeed perished, but were not assassinated by cowardly adversaries. Both parties had recourse to arms, and whoever fell, fell in the conflict. The crisis was always of short duration; and weeks of painful anxiety were succeeded by a general reconciliation of the citizens. It is not difficult to point out the causes of such moderation in the midst of discord. The people still retained some regard for the laws of justice and morality. The majority of the clergy enjoyed that influence which naturally arises from superior talents; and even those who courted popularity, had not yet dared to maintain that liberty consisted in throwing down, and destroying all those barriers, which are so necessary to keep men within the pale of duty—in exposing an ignorant multitude to the seductive arts of the ambitious, or of enthusiasts—and in making every citizen the slave of a few demagogues.[160]

Against this view, French politicians and ministers continued to claim that they respected the independence of small states such as Geneva, and were leading all peoples on the difficult journey from despotism to liberty.[161]

DU ROVERAY AND BRITISH POLICY

Du Roveray had remained at London after Talleyrand's second mission to London. Vilified by the popular party at Geneva, he was also identified as a friend to aristocracy in the French press.[162] After he lost his diplomatic position in the visiting French legation because of his stance on Geneva in October 1792, he changed his mind about any prospect for the enjoyment of peace or liberty, in any part of Europe, through France's revolutionary government. He began to develop a view of France as at odds with prior représentant policy as was Clavière's new position with regard to France. Du Roveray was equally against the policy of the Shelburne circle, or at least that of their leader. Like Dumont and Du Roveray, Shelburne had welcomed the Revolution and had great hopes of a return by Britain to its former policy of political and commercial alliances. Ideally this was to encompass the Dutch and the North Americans, as well as a France that had experienced its own version of 1688–1689.[163] As time passed, and events in Paris became more violent and caused riots at Birmingham and elsewhere, many former members of the Bowood circle began to consider reform impossible in Britain and France.[164] Some welcomed the war between Britain and France when it came in February 1793. Alongside Charles Stanhope, Shelburne consistently opposed war against the French Republic, forever seeing it as a barrier to free trade by entrenching aristocracies in the political and economic world.[165] He always looked back to the time between his brief premiership and the British rearmament that accompanied the Prussian invasion of Holland as a halcyon period for Europe, during which the Bowood circle's commitment to reform and international peace by means of free trade was articulated and ought to have been realized.[166]

Du Roveray in a sense moved from accepting the policy of Shelburne to the advocacy of the policies of Pitt. This was clear from what he believed to be his most important political work, *An appeal to justice and true liberty; or, an accurate statement of the proceedings of the French towards the Republic of Geneva,* completed in February 1793, and dedicated to one of the great supporters of the Waterford experiment, Thomas Townshend, 1st Viscount Sydney. Du Roveray sought to combat both the growing anarchy at Geneva and the French threat to the independence of the state, but his *Appeal,* rather than seeking to influence internal Genevan or French politics, was directed entirely toward Britain. The first and most significant argument was that Britain could not afford to ignore the plight of small states across Europe. The risk of French dominion to Britain's core interests was simply too great. There were also particular reasons for the British to be interested in Geneva's difficulties:

To such as form their judgment on political matters, from commercial or geographical considerations only, the concerns of a small inland state, which can neither affect the trade of Great Britain, nor be affected by her navy, will be rather unimportant. To those who are fond of diving into the bottom of political questions, the proceedings of the French, in regard to independent states, however small, as far as they are an immediate consequence of their avowed principles, and of their actual form of constitution, will not appear unworthy of notice. To the humane and sensible, to those who know Geneva, and have spent some time of their youth amongst its citizens, some degree of happiness must be derived from the sight of that *little seminary of virtue* (as it has been so justly called) defending its laws, its morals, its Helvetic connections, not only against the contagion of their principles, propagated amongst them by the foulest Jacobine artifices, submitting apparently for a while to their tenets, in order to save its independence; preserving an habitual order in the midst of visible anarchy; continually resisting the convulsive fits of a leveling system with patience, moderation, and composure; and ready to display, at the re-establishment of legal order, those same temperate virtues, from which alone may be expected, in such a small community, the return of true concord and of former happiness.[167]

Du Roveray praised Britain as the most honest and just state in international relations, the most respectful of treaties, and the most likely to carry out its duties toward fellow states. Britain was not an empire in the sense either of acting oppressively toward neighboring states or of seeking their territory. Rather, it treated weaker and less extensive states as its equal. It was accordingly the true friend to Europe's small states, and particularly states that shared Britain's mixed constitution.[168] Du Roveray was here moving beyond his countryman and friend de Lolme's distinction between monarchies such as Britain and republics such as Geneva, based on a fundamentally different attitude to the executive power. Rather, he was claiming that Geneva, like Britain, had always enjoyed mixed government and that this was being destroyed by France.

Du Roveray went on to describe what he termed the Jacobin plot, which he dated to 1791, to re-create old Burgundy. He castigated his former friend Clavière, who "is presumed to have nourished a strong and personal hatred, and a spirit of revenge against all the ruling powers in that republic." Clavière's antagonism manifested itself in bringing the French army to the gates of Geneva in 1792, which raised "several batteries, and with mortars, bombs, and red hot balls, threatened to reduce it to ashes, if its citizens did not immediately obey their summons." Aware of the echoes of 1782, Du Roveray praised the populace for deciding "to die rather than to submit." He also praised General Montesquiou for agreeing to terms of peace and for revealing Clavière's secret orders to take the city. Du Roveray stated that Clavière's likely plan, in addition to "direct plunder," was to reduce the French debt held by the Genevans and Swiss, by "butchering about two hundred young ladies, on whose heads that part of the French life annuities, which belong to Geneva and Switzerland, is placed."[169]

Du Roveray condemned the "wild system of liberty" entailed by "Jacobinistical sovereignty." Clavière's main agent was said to be Jacques Grenus, who had been "banished from Geneva in the year 1791 for his riotous and disorderly conduct" but had joined the Jacobins to become one of "those vile emissaries whom the French Jacobins vomited out on every surrounding country." Du Roveray accused Grenus of seeking to "avignonise" the Genevan state. This entailed bringing pro-French foreigners and Catholics into the city to overwhelm the loyal Protestant population when they were added to the citizen body. Elections that followed then resulted in the rule of a violent and corrupt committee. The fundamental problem was that the real desire of France was empire: "like the patricians of Rome, [they] have incessantly embroiled their country in war, in order to perpetuate their empire."[170]

Du Roveray's solution was for Geneva to become a canton. Stating that "for ages past" this "has been the constant object of every true Genevese to accomplish," he claimed that Britain had advocated exactly this in 1792, only to find that the cantons worked too slowly for it to be accomplished before the French armies entered Savoy. For Geneva to become a canton, two things had to come to pass. The first was the defeat of France. Du Roveray predicted that the French Republic could not stand against the united force of the rest of Europe, which detested leveling systems and "the delusive phantom of licentious liberty." Alternatively, France would collapse internally, because it was unlikely that a system devoted to anarchy, misery, immorality, and atheism would long remain stable. The second and more important route to the salvation of Geneva was for Britain to take the side of Europe's small states in its international relations policy. It was to Britain that Holland, the king of Sardinia, and the German princes looked for the restoration of their rights and invaded territories; from Britain that the Swiss needed "the preservation and improvement of her boundaries, and the strengthening of her union." Geneva required from Britain "her delivery." Writing in the mode of Vattel's *Droit des gens*, Du Roveray described Britain's capacity to keep the peace in Europe as a product of mixed government and as vital to prevent the Jacobin view, that "justice is abandoned among men," from prevailing:

> [Britain enjoys] the happiest system of constitution which human prudence could digest. A monarch is the maintainer of liberty, a free people the

supporter of royalty, and a nobility so intimately connected with both, as to be the sacred and mutual tie of their indefeasible union. On this noble basis, arises a legislature, under which both civil and religious laws are revered, property secured, industry encouraged, commerce and trade promoted, arts and sciences improved, and every comfort and blessing diffused through all ranks of society. Such, at home, are the fortunate effects of the British Constitution; abroad, they are no less conspicuous in a due and constant attention to the liberty of Europe, and the independence of its several states, in a manly and unwearied application to defeat those ambitious designs which, from time to time, have disturbed the general peace, or threatened that equilibrium of power, without which Europe would be a continual scene of war and oppression.[171]

After the publication of the *Appeal*, Du Roveray left London in October 1793 for Morges on Lake Geneva, then in Bernese territory. He had become a British agent with a brief to supply information about the French Republic and the activities of its armies across southern France, northern Italy, and Switzerland. He supplied Sir Evan Nepean, under secretary of state for war, with descriptions of French revolutionary policies and atrocities, particularly with regard to the city of Lyon.[172] Before the end of the year he was denounced by the Jacobin Club at Paris as William Pitt's leading spy in the region.[173] This did not prevent his involvement in the "Declaration des citoyens de Genève Anti-Anarchistes" of January 1794, which lamented the collapse of traditional politics, condemned the revolutionary threat to property and morals, and called for Geneva to be "Christian, Reformed, independent and neutral."[174] On 25 July 1794 he was among those "traitors and aristocrats" sentenced to death in absentia at Geneva.

D'IVERNOIS AND ASYLUM IN NORTH AMERICA

Du Roveray's was an impassioned appeal for Britain to act as the savior of Europe's small states and of the political traditions of Europe, in the face of the dire threat of French republican innovation. To his mind there was nothing in common between représentant politics or Genevan politics more generally and the new large-state republicanism that demanded upheavals not only in the social and economic structure of society but in religious and philosophical beliefs. Britain alone could challenge such revolutionary menaces. This view was seconded by David Chauvet, now returned to London, in his *Lettre d'un Genevois établi à Londres, à un de ses amis habitant du Pays de Vaud*, which took as its epigraph Horace's maxim, "You are also in danger when your neighbour's house is on fire."[175] Chauvet set out to prove that democracy, as it had been established at Geneva, led to violence, to the rule of the mob, and ultimately to the rule of a single individual capable of restoring order. The economy of Geneva, he stated, was on the brink of collapse. The populace, who believed they were enjoying the full exercise of sovereignty, were in fact dupes of arbitrary power.[176]

With the progress of revolution within Geneva, opposition to the regime of political equality increasingly fell into disfavor. D'Ivernois was condemned to death on 5 September 1794 for treason. By this time he had returned to London. He initially looked to the United States, proposing to move the Academy of Geneva to the New World.[177] To Thomas Jefferson, John Adams, and his former schoolfellow Albert Gallatin, he provided "a mournful recital of [Geneva's] expiring convulsions," and asked the Americans to "reflect on it with attention, and learn by the disastrous example of the most Democratical State that exists on the Continent of Europe, the extreme danger of foreign influence; and above all, how rapid and inevitable it is, to transgress the feeble interval which separates the abuse of liberty from its ruin!" Geneva, he advised them, had addressed its political problems after Vergennes's death and vanquished historical divisions through the establishment of the Code Du Roveray. D'Ivernois praised the period between 1789 and 1791 as the happiest in the history of the republic:

> Scarce had the Count de Vergennes expired, when with one accord and in the midst of universal joy, all parties united to overthrow the edifice of Government which his dictates had erected. Our fundamental Constitution was reestablished on all its Republican basis; its defenders were recalled and reinstated; and by an almost unanimous vote, every incident of the long litigation which had arisen for a century past betwixt the Assembly of the People and the Administrative bodies were definitively adjudged in favour of the former. This happy resurrection of liberty commenced in 1789, and consolidated in 1791 presents the most prosperous and brilliant period of our Republic. Every heart was reconciled, a harmony of principles reigned amongst us, trade and our manufactures flourished, and our Academy, that admirable establishment of the celebrated Calvin, our Academy, that nourishing vein of all our prosperity past and present, far from having interfered in, or suffered by the public dissensions, was solely devoted in directing the Genevese in their rapid advances towards the heights of science. So great have been its happy effects, that since the commencement of the present century, our population has been doubled, the fortunes of individuals have increased in an inconceivable ratio, and foreigners never failed to visit and to admire the prodigies of liberty and public education in a small state of 30,000

souls, in which the present generation had produced at once a greater number of men distinguished in the career of letters and of science, than the
three kingdoms of the North of Europe taken together.[178]

National unity was then destroyed by the intrigues of French ministers,
whose emissaries encouraged rebellion at Geneva with the active support of the
troops beyond the city gates. Jean-Louis Soulavie, the Jacobin and French minister resident in Geneva from June 1793 until his recall in September 1794, was
especially active in fomenting revolution.[179] D'Ivernois acknowledged to
Jefferson "the seducing effect of the intoxicating theory which the doctrine of
extreme equality inspires." As "the thunder of the French Revolution howled
over Geneva," administration collapsed, government by revolutionary committees was established, and terror became a national policy. For d'Ivernois the old
Geneva had been destroyed with the abandonment of proper government, the
respect for property, moderate manners, and the Calvinist faith:

> Geneva is entirely another town, which stands on the same spot as the for-
> mer: the spectacle it presents is that of crimes, pillage and desolation. Thus
> you see however, Sir, what the first step towards the Revolutionary Doctrine
> has been able to effect in so short a time, with a people, who in the midst of
> the most active civil dissensions had until then always preserved as in a
> sacred deposit, a horror at the effusion of human blood, and a respect for
> property! In a word Geneva is lost beyond resource and without hope of
> being restored to liberty and morality. For supposing even that the majority
> of its inhabitants being disarmed should succeed by a noble effort of despair
> in delivering themselves from the yoke of these Cannibals, yet the French
> soldiery are still at our gates to protect and revenge them, and to devote us to
> the fate of Lyons.[180]

D'Ivernois offered Jefferson a community of patriots who would bring to
America "republican morals, the love of enlightened liberty, the sacred habits
of equality in the sight of the Law, those of industry, respect for religion, and
above all things the dreadful experience of the numerous evils which are
involved by foreign influence and the first violation of the constitutional and
fundamental laws of liberty."

For d'Ivernois Geneva had become wholly dependent on France. He quoted
to Jefferson lines from the sixth book of Virgil's *Aeneid*, translated by John
Dryden: "The gates of hell are open night and day; Smooth the descent, and
easy is the way: But to return, and view the cheerful skies, In this the task and
mighty labour lies." The problem was that until the Revolution had exhausted
itself, Geneva would of necessity follow the same path. Any attempt at the

recovery of more modest forms of liberty would fail if radicals remained in control at Paris. As "Geneva is lost without resource in respect to Religion, to morals, to the sciences, to the fine arts, to trade, to liberty, and above all to internal peace," the only option remaining was exodus and the establishment of another "new Geneva."[181] Jefferson attempted to obtain support for the transfer of the Genevan Academy from legislators at Virginia.[182] He also petitioned President Washington, describing d'Ivernois as a "man of science" and the Genevan Academy as one of "the two eyes of Europe" with respect to learning.

Although Jefferson advised that a professorship in agriculture would be of the most use to Americans, he welcomed the prospect of the immigration of luminaries in natural philosophy, belles lettres, and modern and ancient languages. Due to a lack of suitable land, he argued, "we must give up the proposal of the colony of Genevan farmers." Instead he proposed a loan, to be repaid on the success of the venture: "the wealth of Geneva in money being notorious, and the class of moneyed men being that which the new government are trying to get rid of, it is probable that a capital sum could be borrowed on the credit of the funds under consideration, sufficient to meet the first expenses of the transplantation and establishment, and to supply also the deficiency of revenue till the profits of the shares shall become sufficiently superior to the annual support of the college to repay the sums borrowed."[183] By February the government of Virginia had decided against the transfer because of the cost, the lack of a common language, and the small population of Virginia: "the unprepared state of our youths to receive instruction through a foreign language, the expense of the institution, and its disproportion to the moderate state of our population, were insuperable objections."[184] To John Adams, Jefferson noted: "Our geographical distance is insensible still to foreigners. They consider America of the size of a garden of which Massachusetts is one square and Virginia another."[185] Washington's rejection of the project followed. One of the members of the Genevan Academy involved in d'Ivernois's scheme was Marc Auguste Pictet, then professor of philosophy. To Jefferson he wrote that "my name has been mentioned to you by a friend who was endeavoring to shelter us against the tempest which so destroyed Geneva in July last." The point was that "our situation is not however so desperate as it was at the time he wrote; no imminent danger is at the door, but a slow consumption is to be feared."[186]

THE *BELLUM INTERNECIUM* AGAINST FRANCE

After the collapse of the emigration project, d'Ivernois determined to remain at London and to labor to foster the destruction of revolutionary France. The first step was to reveal to the world the full story of the attempt to make Geneva part of a French revolutionary empire. His *Account of the late revolution in Geneva* appeared at the end of 1794 and comprised greatly extended versions of his letters to Jefferson, Adams, and others. The French plot, once again, was traced to Clavière—"Girondins, the revolution at Geneva is your work"— driven by the economic necessity of "plunder" to sustain the assignats. The central theoretical claim was that the revolutionary doctrine of "equalisation of rights" led "with systematic regularity, through all the intermediate stages of plunder, proscription, and murder, to their great object, the equalisation of property."[187] In making this argument, d'Ivernois conflated Jacobinism and Girondism. Soulavie, as résident, became the main instrument of Clavière's policy, which entailed the incorporation of Geneva into France and the loss of the republic's historic association with liberty, moderation, and good morals. Geneva had, d'Ivernois claimed, resolved its problems by 1791 and inaugurated a period of national unity and splendor. Due to the French Revolution, Europe had henceforth to be envisaged as a divided continent, into the old world of independent Christian states protective of property and liberty, and the revolutionary empire where government was ultimately dominated by the wild mobs of the poor and ungodly:

> The moral character of the most virtuous nation, affords no security whatever, that revolutionary doctrines, if suffered to be propagated in it, will have a less pernicious influence upon its manners, than upon those of any other nation. It is impossible that those doctrines can take root in any such nation, without producing a complete, and radical change in its character. It is barely two months since the Genevese deservedly possessed the reputation of a brave and humane people. One single night of revolution [19 July 1794], by putting the arms which had been wrested from the people of property, into the hands of those who possessed nothing, instantly changed the former into dastardly cowards, and the latter into ferocious beasts of prey.[188]

D'Ivernois concluded that Geneva, "that was once so distinguished among the cities of the earth . . . the seat of religion, of morality, of art and of commerce, but above all, of sacred liberty . . . is irrecoverably lost: peace, security, and happiness, have for ever abandoned her." Many Genevans were fleeing Europe for North America, because Europe appeared to be on the brink of a new dark age characterized by dreadful scenes of barbarism.[189]

D'Ivernois's lament for the condition of Geneva was followed up by more practical works. These were intended to direct British policy. The first was a response to Madame de Staël's call for peace across Europe in her *Réflexions sur la paix adressées à M. Pitt et aux Français*, which began to circulate early in 1795. De Staël's work was notable for its claims that France could stand against any coalition and that Pitt, portrayed as a warmonger, was destroying the British economy. By the end of May, d'Ivernois had published his *Réflexions sur la guerre, en réponse aux Réflexions sur la paix adressées à M. Pitt et aux Français*. Completed at the behest of the secretary at war, William Windham, it commenced d'Ivernois's direct work for Pitt's ministry. The argument was diametrically the opposite of that of Madame de Staël. D'Ivernois argued that, while Britain continued to be strong because of stable commercial resources, French power rested on the dubious foundations of the assignats, which would collapse unless peace and economy replaced democracy and conquest as the fundamental principles of revolutionary government.[190]

D'Ivernois became the leading exponent of the view that the future of Europe had to rest with a Britain directly involved in mainland politics. This necessitated the military defeat of the French Republic, or intervention in the wake of its internal collapse.[191] Perhaps inevitably, d'Ivernois was everywhere seen as a government hack. His prediction that the weakness of French finances would guarantee victory for Britain involved him in polemics with, among others, Thomas Paine and Alexandre Maurice Blanc de Lanautte, comte d'Hauterive.[192] His constancy in supporting the policy of war against France led to his being "dubbed a knight by the sword of a King," and he was named a Knight Bachelor on 11 May 1796 for such services.[193] Although he was widely condemned for his views, given that revolutionary France did not collapse economically or militarily, d'Ivernois later claimed that the financial crisis in France led to the rise of Napoleon Bonaparte, whom he portrayed as a monarch even during the Consulate of 1799–1804.[194] Bonaparte, he claimed, confirmed his view that French republicanism was unstable because it amounted to the rule of the mob, which history had always proved collapsed into one or other form of dictatorship. He equally held fast to the claim that France continued to seek to become "a new Rome." In international relations France sought empire. D'Ivernois explained Bonaparte's success solely on the basis of the continuation of republican policy in this respect. The "empire of the Gauls" was eating up the small states of Europe.

When the Cisalpine Republic was created in northern Italy in 1797 and when Switzerland was transformed into the Helvetic Republic in 1798, d'Ivernois considered his opinions to have been confirmed. The First French Republic, whether governed by a Brissot or a Bonaparte, could not be trusted. Britain had to keep leading a war against France in order to save Europe.[195] When France annexed Geneva in 1798, the three individuals not granted

French citizenship, on the basis of the threat they were held to pose to the interests of the new state, were d'Ivernois, Jacques Mallet du Pan, and Du Roveray.[196]
After 1798 d'Ivernois joined Mallet du Pan in the pages of the *Mercure britannique, ou notices historiques et critiques sur les affaires du temps* in condemning
French tyranny toward small states. The opinions of the former représentant
and former natif came together in portraying Britain as "the unwavering nation"
for true liberty. Mallet du Pan's *Essai historique sur la destruction de la Ligue &
de la liberté helvétiques* (1798) came to exactly this conclusion, stating that the
French destruction of Switzerland had left "only rocks, ruins, and demagogues."
The translation, published in 1799, appeared with a frontispiece drawn from the
Emblemata politica of 1618, showing a republic in the form of a leopard standing over the carcass of a once splendid stag, over the words, "Havoc and spoil
and ruin are my gain." Mallet du Pan reputedly called the French "the vilest
people in the history of Europe since the fall of the Roman Empire."[197]

For Mallet du Pan, as for d'Ivernois and all of the still exiled représentants,
the ultimate goal of revolutionary France's foreign policy was a continuation
of the Old Regime in bringing low the small states of Europe and transforming
the continent into a French empire. The irony was that, despite the language of
liberty deployed by the revolutionaries, the most oppressive client states were
being established that brooked no opposition and demanded the complete
dedication of the populace to the new revolutionary patriotism. Old beliefs and
manners were being washed away in the patriotic torrent, which also challenged Christianity and traditional ideas about social order and moderate liberty. Britain and the United States alone represented an alternative capable of
withstanding French ideas and leading Europe to a pacific and civilized future:

> Every Swiss who has defended his country, and who mourns for it, becomes
> criminal: to escape chastisement, it is not enough to have been insensible to
> the danger of the state, he must have joined in betraying it. Whoever hesi-
> tates to receive the laws of these sanguinary foreigners, is guilty of rebellion.
> To the very firesides of the first heroes of Helvetic liberty are their posterity
> pursued, except where the despair of the inhabitants has blocked up the
> entrance of those asylums with dead bodies. This is the fraternity of French
> republicans towards independent nations! Though, for a while, these
> destructive tyrants feigned to pardon kings, free states could find no favour
> from their despotism: it is for free states that they now reserve their schemes
> of extermination; and the spirit which has just entombed the Helvetic lib-
> erty, and enslaved Geneva, Bienne, and Mulhausen, will never be at rest
> while Britain preserves her constitution, and the United States of America
> support their laws.[198]

It is significant that the Anglophile représentants united with many of their former enemies in expressing the need for a "British" future for Europe. Joseph des Arts, the ardent négatif and major foe of 1782, united with d'Ivernois from the mid-1790s in opposing French initiatives. Jacques Necker was equally reconciled with his former critics.[199] Jean-André Deluc, like d'Ivernois and Du Roveray, entered the diplomatic service of Britain, undertaking missions in the German states to save Europe from France and to foster Protestantism.[200]

By 1800 the democratic turn at Paris had complicated inherited political ideas because the republican form of government was so evidently tied to the establishment of an empire. The identification of France with a new Rome was confirmed with the establishment of the Consulate. Optimists, including Shelburne and Stanhope, continued to imagine a return to the natural progress of opulence in the aftermath of an Anglo-French alliance, in turn preparing the way for reform in London and moderation in the revolutionary states of Europe. The signing of the Treaty of Amiens on 25 March 1802 was accompanied by exactly these hopes.[201] By contrast, Clavière's disciples at Geneva welcomed the transformation of Geneva into part of the Département du Léman. The French empire of liberty may have destroyed Europe's former republics, but as these were perceived to have been corrupt aristocracies, the new larger republics in Italy and Switzerland were seen to presage a republican future for Europe led by France. Because republican politics were so unstable in France, the imperative became the justification of a republic in a large state that would unite liberty with order. Benjamin Constant's work on a republican constitution in a large state was exemplary in this respect, as was Jean-Charles-Léonard Simonde de Sismondi's *Recherches sur les constitutions des peuples libres*, both of which were being written between 1798 and 1800.[202] Sismondi came from a négatif family exiled in England during the years of revolution. The fact that he was composing such a work, and working on the new French-Genevan *département* at the same time, underscored the transformation of political realities by the close of the 1790s.[203]

BONAPARTE AND THE FUTURE OF EUROPE

The ascent of Bonaparte to a dominant position in French politics with the coup of 9 November 1799 made work on the constitution of republics in the large states of Europe redundant overnight. This was why the writings of such authors as Constant and Sismondi remained in manuscript. Bonaparte is frequently portrayed as the person who confirmed the continuity between revolutionary and Old Regime politics, giving France imperial options unconsidered since the early decades of Louis XVI's reign. From the perspective of the small states of Europe, however, Bonaparte at first promised a return to the Europe of Charlemagne. His coronation on 2 December 1804 was modeled on that of Charlemagne, with a parade of virgins and the return of imperial regalia, including adoption of Charlemagne's symbol, the bee. Within the reconstituted *respublica Christiana*, communities were to be protected by an emperor devoted to religious and political diversity and toleration.[204] Even d'Ivernois acknowledged that Bonaparte supported civil freedoms, although he countered proposals to devolve power to the Helvetic republic and other imperial provinces, which Bonaparte offered during the short-lived peace between 1802 and 1803.[205]

Despite Bonaparte's military victories, d'Ivernois continued to argue that Britain alone had the power and authority to protect Europe's small states. The problems in the first decade of the new century were uncertainty as to whether Britain or France would win, what Europe would look like if one or the other did, or if they became so exhausted by war that another power might step into a vacuum. In 1802 d'Ivernois followed Deluc into diplomatic service, with missions across Germany, Scandinavia, and finally Russia in 1812–1813.[206] In publications he continued to predict the economic collapse of France, on the grounds that it was based on an unsustainable tyranny.[207] Such was the uncertainty of the times that in 1802 some exiled Genevans were concerned that d'Ivernois might turn Bonaparte against Geneva, to which he was held to be indifferent. David Chauvet in particular wanted to make Geneva much more Anglophile in terms of its culture, and in 1802 he sought to raise funds to support philanthropic ventures within the city.[208] D'Ivernois refused to help, on the grounds that Geneva was part of France, but he too supported the activities of Charles Pictet de Rochemont and others to develop links between Britain and Geneva. One of the most prominent examples of this policy was the journal *Bibliothèque britannique*, edited by Marc-Auguste Pictet and Pictet de Rochemont, which from 1796 brought information about British civilization, through commentaries and translations, to a Genevan audience.[209] So successful were such endeavors that by 1814 Sismondi was calling Geneva "an English enclave," linked by shared ideas about liberty, Protestantism, morals, and civilization.[210]

Bonaparte's empire crumbled at Geneva on 30 December 1813, when Austrian troops entered the city after the departure of the French garrison. D'Ivernois immediately left Britain and became part of the provisional government. He journeyed only briefly to Britain in 1814, resigning his government pensions in return for £10,000, and then returned permanently to the city of his birth with his new wife, Caroline Renée Frédérique Louise Bontems. Du Roveray, who was calling for a Genevan delegation to London to establish the foundations of the newly independent state, died just before he was able to return, on 24 June 1814. Since the mid-1790s, Du Roveray had had the least to do with politics of the exiled représentants. There is some evidence that he became a bookseller.[211] In his final letter to Dumont, he wrote of the need of Europe for an anchor if an international equilibrium was ever to reestablish peace.[212] With the former négatifs Joseph des Arts and Ami Lullin, d'Ivernois labored to put the vision first articulated by Du Roveray in 1793 into practice. Geneva had to become a canton in a Switzerland under the protection of Britain. D'Ivernois's particular role was to petition Lord Castlereagh to this end. Geneva, he promised the foreign secretary, could become a British base in Europe, one from which any attempts to rejuvenate French power could be combated.[213]

D'Ivernois and Pictet de Rochemont were named deputies for Geneva at the Congress of Vienna in 1814. The particular difficulty was to annex to Geneva territory in the Pays de Gex, which had hitherto been French, to establish a link by land between Geneva and the Swiss Pays de Vaud. Managing to defeat Talleyrand, who as France's delegate opposed this proposal, d'Ivernois was instrumental in establishing Geneva as a Swiss canton with a nonfragmented territory. In this he and Pictet de Rochemont were abetted by Dumont, who joined the delegation as someone who knew Talleyrand personally and who was also well connected with the British delegates, "our protectors."[214] D'Ivernois was subsequently directly involved in framing a new constitution, the first goal of which was to prevent the democratic upheavals that he now considered to have marred Genevan political life. He now expressed views of politics that would have been decidedly négatif had they been expressed between the 1760s and 1780s. The great difference, of course, was that the power the magistrates now looked to for support was Britain rather than France.

Britain's defeat of French aspirations to universal republicanism in the 1790s, and to universal empire in the older sense of territorial dominion between 1803 and 1815, had confirmed the shift of power toward Britain first speculated upon during Marlborough's wars. Although eighteenth-century writers had been obsessed with this shift and commented endlessly on its likely extent and implications, few had considered it more than a fleeting phenomenon, for the good reason that Britain was smaller, less civilized, and inferior in population and natural resources compared with France and other larger European states. British supremacy in the aftermath of its military successes was always recognized, but it was never accepted as a durable reality. This changed with the outcome of the Napoleonic Wars. In viewing its main goal as the prevention of future imperial designs across Europe, the Congress of Vienna acknowledged that the war for international supremacy that had raged between the English and the French since the 1680s had to end, and it sought to ensure that the struggle had in fact ended.

Espousing exactly this opinion, d'Ivernois served in the Conseil d'État at Geneva until 1824. During his retirement he became fascinated by the views of Thomas Robert Malthus and defended them in several publications against Sismondi. D'Ivernois died on 16 March 1842 at Geneva. During his long retirement, Britain continued to support the neutrality of Switzerland in times of European conflict, guaranteeing the independence of the republican confederation. Britain had become the ideal imperial ally for small states, and former représentants such as d'Ivernois now considered their past antagonism toward empire naive. The revolution in British foreign policy that d'Ivernois believed he had contributed to now provided a great protector operating on the European mainland and defending the small states. Although the map of Europe had altered irredeemably, for d'Ivernois the old représentant ideal of flourishing commercial centers supported by more powerful states, protective of liberty and of Christian mores, had become a reality. The controversy over imperialism that had raged throughout the eighteenth century had largely seen the European mainland as the arena of possible empires.[215] Concurrent or later controversies about empires farther afield largely followed the terms set by the intra-European debate. Europe had been seen as on the verge of being carved up by gigantic commercial powerhouses, and one or the other, Britain or France, had to win out. D'Ivernois believed that the dreadful vision of Europe as part of a military or commercial universal empire had been vanquished during his lifetime. The future was that of a liberal empire, respectful of independence and seeking commercial fraternity. With this vision in mind, opposition to empire could happily cease.

Part Four

EPILOGUE

8

THE LAST REPRÉSENTANT AND PHILOSOPHIC RADICALISM

I had hoped that Geneva was familiarized to such a degree of liberty, that they might, without difficulty or danger, fill up the measure to its maximum: a term, which though, in the insulated man, bounded only by his natural powers, must in society be so far restricted as to protect himself against the evil passions of his associates and consequently them against him. I suspect that the doctrine that small states alone are fitted to be republics will be exploded by experience with some other brilliant fallacies accredited by Montesquieu and other political writers. . . . It is unfortunate that the efforts of mankind to recover the freedom of which they have been so long deprived, will be accompanied with violence, with errors and even with crimes. But while we weep over the means, we must pray for the end.

—*Thomas Jefferson to François d'Ivernois, 6 February 1795*

The Senatus Romanus we know consisted of patricians originally of one order only. Perhaps we are not so well acquainted with the true formation of the Senate of Carthage. But since the Roman Ages we have Senates innumerable, & of so different natures & powers, that the name no longer indicates the powers. Not only every Republic, even the little Italian Republics of Lucia [Lucca] &c., but half the Cities of Germ[an]y., Holl[an]d. &c. have their Senates; & Universities & Colleges have their Senates. I have thought our familiar literary acquaintance with the Roman & Grecian Histories, have led us in America too much to adopt some of their republican titles &c., when by our limitations, descriptions & modifications, we render them totally different from any thing we can find in Antiquity. Even the term Republic, how different in America, in Holland, Geneva, Genoa, Venice, Switzerland, & at the head of the boot in Italy? How different all these from the Respublica Anglorum, which we know has always been monarchical from the days of Alfred, & of which Mr. Tho. Smith wrote so learnedly 200 years ago?

—*Ezra Stiles to William Samuel Johnson, 3 April 1789*, Correspondence [1st Federal Congress], vol. 15, First Session: March–May 1789, ed. C. Bangs Bickford and K. R. Bowling (Baltimore, 2004), 192–193

THE DISPUTED NATURE OF THE MODERN REPUBLIC

For Ezra Stiles the ancient and early modern republican legacy was profoundly uncertain for modern politics. Above all else, Britain appeared to be as republican as any other state. This fact had marked the nascent United States in a particular and enduring fashion. For Thomas Jefferson, by contrast, a new kind of republicanism was being engendered by the French Revolution. It promised the revitalization of communities that had suffered from aristocratic or monarchical degradation for centuries. Jefferson continued to have faith that the excessive popular enthusiasm at Paris would cease, despite its overturning established mores in religion and politics and the rising numbers of its victims. The French republican experiment would then become stable and, allied to the American republic, would inaugurate the new era of liberty and peace. This had been promised in 1789, when so many dreadful icons of the tyrannical past had been shattered. As long as Britain was prevented from establishing its own kind of commercial empire, the fate of the former colonies could be avoided across the globe, and a new anti-imperial age anticipated.

The dream of 1789 lingered in European consciousness. The ability to unleash the vitality of stifled communities, and realize the economic capacity of a commercial society open to the poor as well as to the rich, attracted adherents in the decades of British dominion that followed Bonaparte's final collapse. In the name of nationalism or inspired by the eternal revolutionary ideals of liberty, equality, and fraternity, utopian radicals, often termed "members of the French party," continued to imagine and sometimes to plot for a world from which injustice, war, empire, and poverty had been vanquished.[1] One difficulty was to explain how the ideals of the authentic French Revolution of 1789 might have avoided the subsequent terror. This was imperative if the vision of 1789, applied to another state, was not to result in another terror. To be convincing in political argument, it was vital to explain how a revolutionary state could put an end to empire and at the same time avoid the excessive power of a violent mob and the tendency of every popular state to end up being ruled by a caesar.

These were questions that Clavière and his acolytes addressed but failed to answer convincingly before their deaths. A common subsequent response, for those who held fast to the view that Europe would have been better off had the revolution continued unabated, was that of Clavière's secretary, the political economist Jean-Baptiste Say. For Say the involvement of Britain in French affairs, and the assertion of the mercantile system that accompanied British policy abroad, had caused the instability of the French Revolution and all of the resulting tragedies. Following so many eighteenth-century Jeremiahs, a rarer breed in the nineteenth century, Say predicted and hoped for the collapse of Britain, for the same reasons as had the aging Hume.[2] The challenge for nineteenth-century Anglophobe politics, inspired by 1789, remained an enormous one: to create a state that would avoid the route followed by every democratic polity in history, which had descended into disorder, imperialism, and ultimately forms of monarchy more repressive than any that had been replaced.

For so many former Genevan représentants and négatifs, this alternative future for Europe amounted to utopian claptrap. Individuals who had called themselves republicans before the French Revolution did not necessarily become democratic republicans in the 1790s. There was no straightforward route from eighteenth-century democratic politics to revolutionary democracy or nineteenth-century liberalism.[3] Either because of the generic nature of the human passions, or because of the peculiarities of the French national character, revolutionary ideals quickly translated themselves into reason-of-state arguments justifying a greater French empire. Democracies were, as Rousseau had written, governments for gods rather than for men. The need to appease the populace necessitated the establishment of negative communities, in the sense of groups of enemies perceived to be actively undermining the state both at home and abroad. Democratic societies needed the enemies defined by these negative communities, and this explained the frequent descent of democratic states into international war and domestic terrorism. From the perspective of political economy, it was equally the case that democratic polities were ill suited to modern trade, especially as they were associated with small communities that defined themselves by their patriotism and naturally placed their own narrow sense of self-interest above broader concerns, adopting beggar-my-neighbor policies rather than looking toward the cosmopolitan ideal of free trade.

The fundamental fact of modern politics was that commercial societies needed large markets, and large markets were best secured by large states respectful of the composite national elements and social groups that formed them. To many nineteenth-century observers, the successful creation of Britain by the Acts of Union in 1707, and the similar incorporation of Ireland in 1801, provided a model for commercial success and political stability that ought to be imitated everywhere.[4] Just as large farms and large companies tended to govern the economy, large polities ought to dominate political life. This was the lesson of the French Revolution as understood by d'Ivernois and a host of fellow Genevans. In embracing this point of view, they were acknowledging that the négatif critique of représentant democracy had been correct and that disorder would have been the eventual product of any représentant administration. They were equally rejecting the old Swiss or Dutch ideal of republican confederation being the surest route to peace. In addition, they were rejecting the politics of the balance of power that had characterized post-Westphalian life until the consequences of the second hundred years' war between Britain and France became clear. Ideas of a "federative system" or pacific league of states that had renounced empire, intended to attract most of the powers of Europe and capable of removing the "mutual jealousy" of international relations, appeared entirely fanciful in the postrevolutionary world.[5]

The significant fact about the position of Geneva and Switzerland was that they gave their political allegiance to Britain. They trusted Britain to act as arbiter in future international disputes. Neutrality rested on being allied with the dominant power of the day, and one that stood far above any historic European confederation or republic with respect to military might. The world of *virtus* as manliness was gone, and Britain was to be relied upon to prevent the modern version of virtue, patriotism, from causing similarly dangerous forms of political enthusiasm. Britain was also the fulcrum of the global economy. Trusting Britain economically was more difficult to justify. D'Ivernois had faith, without any scheme for a return to the natural progress of opulence redolent of the Shelburne circle and other radicals. For d'Ivernois, Britain's domestic politics and national character translated into moderation in international relations. By an imperceptible process, the evils of the mercantile system were ameliorated. In any case, Britain's mercantile empire was always to be contrasted with the more brutal imperial Bonapartist schemes of continental blockade.[6] D'Ivernois's politics had become négatif in Genevan terms, but the context was wholly different. While the eighteenth-century négatifs had relied on France to protect an aristocratic republic and therefore had to accept direct French involvement in city politics, because of the revolution in British foreign policy d'Ivernois could rather rely on a larger power uninterested in Genevan life but seeking to benefit from peace and from access to Europe's vast markets.

THE REPRÉSENTANT LEGACY FOR DUMONT

Etienne Dumont was as critical as any représentant of Clavière's vision of a Europe dominated by a republican France. He experienced what he perceived as authentically democratic politics first hand at Geneva. In the early 1790s he had made two visits to his native city: between February and June 1791, and between December 1792 and March 1793. His goal at Geneva was to counter the rise of revolutionary Jacobinism, which he believed used the veneer of anarchic popular politics to hide the real establishment of oligarchic despotism.[7] During his second visit, Dumont served on the executive Comité provisoire d'administration and was soon after elected to the Genevan National Assembly.[8] Recognizing that he was unable to prevent democratic fanaticism, he soon condemned the civic sermon demanded of all citizens as an affront to liberty, calling the leaders of the revolutionary party "Jacobin Tigers" who had compromised the independence of the state by selling muskets to France. He asked his sister and niece, "Have you learned of all the evils that afflict our poor Geneva? While some tranquility was expected under the new Constitution, there is in fact a conspiracy which takes as its stated object the destruction of an aristocracy that does not exist, but which in practice is motivated by the desire for indiscriminate pillage and private vengefulness."[9]

Disgusted by the violence at Paris and Geneva, Dumont lost any faith he had hitherto displayed in constitution-led reform. His fear of democracy intensified, as at Geneva and Paris he perceived it to be the form of government most open to manipulation by cabals of "scoundrels," whose dependence on the mob led to legally justified or politically inspired atrocity, always accompanied by the confiscation of property. To Bentham he wrote in August 1792 that "the evidence of popular cruelty makes me tremble."[10] In his *Souvenirs* of 1799 there was a direct correlation between the upheavals suffered by France and the growth of democracy.[11] A new imperative in states small and large was to prevent democracy from fostering extremism and from suffocating rational politics. Like d'Ivernois, Dumont rejected any projection of democratic ideas into the future.

At the same time, Dumont rejected the idea of a future dominated by aristocrats and monarchs in republics or in monarchies, guaranteed by the far from ideal British polity. Dumont was an Anglophile and fostered the links between Britain and Geneva as much as he possibly could from the mid-1790s onward. But he was equally an Anglophile who perceived the world from the perspective of Benthamism.[12] Dumont believed that this philosophy required evaluation by reference to its potential consequences both for domestic and for international stability. He considered the principle of utility to be a new voice in European thought, one that usefully responded to the opportunities presented by the great historical transformation that was seen to have occurred during the years of near-continual international war, coterminous with the inauguration of the First French Republic and the downfall of the First French Empire. Maria Edgeworth wrote of Dumont that "he loves Mont-Blanc next to Bentham above all created things." Sismondi recalled that Dumont considered Bentham "written reason . . . we have sometimes heard him say of what he most admired in other philosophers, 'it is convincing, it is truth itself, it is almost *Benthamic.*'"[13] By August 1792 Dumont was engaged in editing Bentham's manuscripts from the late 1770s, entitled "Plan of a Penal Code" and "Projet d'un corps complet du droit."[14] Whether this was perceived to be a short-term labor is uncertain, but it is clear that over the next years Dumont was converted to the view that Bentham's manuscripts held the key to future reform politics and amounted to a revolution in human knowledge of law and legislation.[15] As a philosophy, Benthamism was distinctly confident about problem solving and about creating a genuine moral and political science; the latter had the intention of guiding the learned while making the ignorant become habituated to reform. What reform meant was disputed, but it necessitated utilitarian evaluation of the prospects for Britain and acknowledgment of the significant fact that Bentham's writings had always been tied, in complicated and critical ways, to the ascendance of Britain as global economic power and international political arbiter.[16]

In the "Discours préliminaire" to the *Traités de législation civile et pénale*, which appeared in 1802 as Bentham's greatest work with Dumont as editor, Dumont concluded that too great a concern with liberty by legislators would produce bad laws. Bentham's work offered a means of calming the passions and establishing national characteristics that were capable of supporting liberty over time.[17] Supporters of the kinds of revolution that had occurred at France and at Geneva in the mid-1790s were described as "dogmatistes" in Dumont's edition.[18] Dumont had clearly jettisoned his belief in the necessary stabilizing effects of republican constitutionalism. In editing Bentham's work, he believed he was providing warnings against modern democratic impulses. Bentham revealed that civil liberty, independence, and domestic peace could be enjoyed without popular politics. A 1789-style revolution had not been necessary in France and needed to be avoided at all costs by other states. What attracted Dumont to Bentham in the 1790s was the notion that states of all kinds could be reformed. From this perspective, forms of government defending particular liberties as essential to citizenship mattered little. This was a view neatly summarized by Bentham himself on receiving the title "French Citizen" in October 1792:

> The different forms of the two governments [Britain and France] present no
> obstacle to my thoughts. The general good is everywhere the true object of
> all political action,—of all law. The general will is everywhere, and for every
> one, the sole external index by which the conformity of the means to the end
> can be decided. Professions the most opposed are conciliated—nay, they are
> prescribed by the varieties of position. Passions and prejudices divide men:
> great principles unite them. Faithful to these—as true as they are simple—
> I should think myself a weak reasoner and a bad citizen, were I not, though
> a royalist in London, a republican in Paris. I should deem it a fair conse-
> quence of my being a royalist in London, that I should become a republican
> in Paris. Thus doing, I should alike respect the rights and follow the example
> of my sovereign, who while an Anglican in England, is a Presbyterian in
> Scotland, and a Lutheran in Hanover.[19]

Aligning himself with Bentham did not mean that Dumont had become an enemy to republicanism in principle. He was rather an enemy to the kinds of French republicanism that had developed in the 1790s, signifying opposition to aristocracy, monarchy, and church in large states and supportive of democracy in every kind of state. Such doctrines, associated with Abbé Sieyès in France and Tom Paine in Britain, were deemed politically deadly when evaluated from the perspective of practical reform politics. Bentham's gift to humanity was the confutation of such authorities. Dumont, like Bentham himself soon after he composed his letter to Roland, began to despise the republicans at Paris.[20] Unlike Bentham, however, Dumont believed it to be vital to combat French republican attitudes ever after and to warn against their adoption in any state. Yet this was coupled with an acceptance of the need for a popular element in government, a belief in the need for the protection of civil liberties, and for a moral polity characterized by the acceptance and practice of austere republican manners. It was these elements that Dumont believed had to be salvaged from the old représentant cause, and could be propagated in the new century through Benthamism.

THE REPRÉSENTANT LEGACY AT GENEVA

Dumont's perspective on Bentham's message for small states was reiterated and extrapolated in the "Discours préliminaire" to the *Tactique des assemblées politiques délibérantes*, which was the third of Dumont's editorial works to be published, appearing at Geneva in 1816. Dumont argued that this work was "useful to all governments, even the most absolute," providing a guide to clear deliberation and an antidote to Machiavellian strategy and intellectual sophistry. The twin evils of oligarchy and anarchy must be avoided, and Bentham's procedural prescriptions were described as capable of preventing the excessive authority of aristocracy and the dangerous power of the demagogue-serving mob. Dumont repeated the view of the *Souvenirs* that the French Revolution had been doomed to failure because its assemblies had failed to imitate the orderly debates of the British Parliament. He reminded readers that when Mirabeau had presented Romilly's *Règlemens* to the relevant committee of the National Assembly, he had faced a chorus: "We want nothing from the English, we must imitate no one." Again following the *Souvenirs*, the "fatal night" of 4 August 1789 was described as proof that Parisians were experiencing the most misguided of revolutions. From that date, "the anarchical ascendance of the galleries of the Palais-Royal was carefully maintained to ensure that the majority of the assembly followed the will of a faction."[21] Democracy in modern states either led to or sustained oligarchy.

Part of the problem was that France had not been able to draw on an existing culture that fostered liberty and stability. To reinforce this claim, Dumont contrasted the ancient French Estates-General and the British Parliament. The former were "so weak and so feeble [because] they were incapable of establishing good discipline, a positive form of deliberation, and in consequence could never have created a true general will." By contrast, "the Parliament of England, less powerful originally than the Estates-General, but more regular in being convened, has known how to maintain itself through outrages and under the most despotic princes." This statement allowed Dumont to challenge an assertion he associated with Montesquieu, that France had originally learned to enjoy liberty "in the woods," as a Frankish kingdom governed by local assemblies. Rather, Dumont argued, it was the direct experience of particular rules, the product of reason rather than of history, and never any presumed or actual democratic history, which led to political moderation and justice. In Britain, where the lessons had been learned by 1688, these rules had been institutionalized and pursued ever since. Bentham's *Tactique* was accordingly seen as setting down the lessons of British history, having "observed the practices of the English Parliament, and having deduced in consequence his theory."[22] Bentham was, in Dumont's eyes, refuting standard apologists for the British constitution, having discovered the neglected source of Britain's constitutional success and the key to the notion of "balance" in the political system.

Dumont made clear that he was not seeking to return in every respect to the view he had articulated in the early 1790s that adoption of British constitutionalism would succeed in any state. Straightforward Anglophilia, in the sense of the advocacy of the immediate institution of British-style bicameralism, led to errors of reason:

Nothing would be so badly judged as to expect salutary effects from the British regime by its complete adoption. In politics, imitation is not always resemblance. The exterior conformity of government is only a machine which looks the same to the eyes, and which lacks the source of life. Those who talk of the prosperity of Britain in order to advocate her institutions as a universal model reason very badly. They assume equal prosperity under a regime which is actually different in a thousand respects; and they make the assumption without proof. In order to draw a legitimate conclusion, it is necessary to show that a definite link exists between an aspect of this regime and the prosperity of the country. Without this, such styles of admiration, so common and so facile, are not only frivolous but also dangerous declamations. Enthusiastic tones and absolute praise make for mistaken minds, and are conducive only to false imitation.[23]

Dumont here acknowledged the necessity of distinguishing between different forms of state when considering how to reform them. The central issue might be termed the transition problem, being the difficulty of improving a corrupt state with a view to making it capable of maintaining its reformed condition. Different degrees of reform were naturally required in different circumstances, measured by the extent of existing corruption and the extent to which corruption was grounded in an institutional framework and culture. From this perspective, many of the lessons Dumont wanted Bentham's writings to impart were negative. The *Traités* provided a guide to legislation for the good of all without the requirement of democracy, but they remained silent on the reform strategy required by particular states. Similarly, while the great benefit of the *Tactique* was that it revealed the secret of Britain's stability, it was silent about specific reforms for other polities—with one exception. For many readers, the significance of the *Tactique* lay in its central message for a British audience: that the source of British greatness was not directly traceable to monarchy, people, aristocracy, or church. Analysis of this constitution showed that laws had emerged that were in the main moderate and just, by following precisely a series of rules of procedure. In publishing the *Tactique*, Dumont was accordingly seeking to redirect interpretations of the advantages of the British constitution away from the loyalist Whig and Tory apologies

traceable to William Blackstone or to his fellow Genevan and friend Jean-Louis
de Lolme.

The *Tactique* was equally critical of Paineite views of Britain's constitutional
limitations when asserting that liberty and peace were not to be established by
democratic means. Dumont reaffirmed his antirevolutionary credentials and
argued against rapid political change in any state: "When things have taken a
certain course, it is better, in general, to maintain them, rather than to replace
them by other practices which might have been superior at the first establishment." At times of constitutional refounding, by contrast, every state should
choose "the best model available." In the last paragraph of his "Discours préliminaire," Dumont advised his readers to accept the message of Claude-
Carloman de Rulhière's *Histoire de l'anarchie de Pologne:* that however great
the virtues to be found in small republics, and however grand the civic characters formed in such states, they would always fall prey to anarchic democracy if
they were badly organized with respect to the forms of deliberation.[24] In advising the reading of an explicitly heterodox assessment of republican arguments,
and as such making a direct attack on republican constitutionalism as traditionally conceived in small states, Dumont was lending weight to the view that
standard republican doctrine required revision in the post-Napoleonic world.
He was also underlining the extent to which he had his Genevan contemporaries in mind. He considered himself to be editing Bentham for their direct
benefit.[25]

THE LESSONS OF LARGE STATES FOR SMALL STATES

It was in the hope of influencing Genevan legislators that the several texts
included in the *Tactique* amounted to an exact description of the necessary
transition process from Napoleonic despotism to peace, moderation, and liberty. Bentham was being employed to define forms of British constitutionalism
that could be adapted to secure domestically the independence of small republics. Dumont's intention was to save Geneva from repeating the constitutional
mistakes of the past by re-creating a city divided into aristocratic and democratic
factions. Avoiding this outcome had become especially urgent because of events
at Geneva since Napoleon's armies lost their grip upon their conquests. When
the French garrison abandoned Geneva at the end of 1813, a Provisional Council
speedily proclaimed national independence and in the following months
obtained guarantees of sovereignty from the allied powers. The council then
initiated the process of making Geneva into the twenty-second Swiss canton,
which was completed on 19 May 1815. The additional task was to establish a

new constitution for the republic. A commission of seven, including d'Ivernois, was appointed to undertake this labor from within the now Provisional Government. By 22 June a draft constitution had been sent to the Swiss Diet at Zurich. It was presented to Geneva's citizens on 17 August, with the request that they ratify the document six days later.

Dumont had returned to Geneva from London on 28 May 1815, and he was among the leaders of the opposition to the Provisional Government, alongside the Academy professors Sismondi, Jean-Marc-Jules Pictet-Diodati, and Pierre-François Bellot. Together they sought to prevent the passage of the new constitution. Their major concern was that the constitution, in reacting in too extreme a manner against the democratic movements of the 1790s, had once again institutionalized oligarchy, with a Council of State, whose members were elected for life, dominating a Council of Representatives, whose members in turn were elected from a highly restricted franchise. Dumont anticipated the return of old antagonisms. With the ratification of the constitution by the citizenry, the opposition leaders were vilified, although all of them were elected to the Council of Representatives in the following months.[26] In such circumstances, Dumont's goal became the revision of the new constitution. This was achieved in the main through his membership of a committee established to form procedural rules for the Council of Representatives.

Such events provided the setting for Dumont's publication of Bentham's *Tactique*. They explain why it was published at Geneva, why Dumont's own *Règlement pour le Conseil représentatif de la ville et République de Genève* was included as an appendix, and why the latter text was followed by Dumont's translation of Romilly's 1789 *Règlemens observés dans la chambre des communes pour débattre les matières et pour voter*. In several respects the *Tactique* was the work in which Dumont acknowledged the presence of his own authorial voice most directly. In the "Discours préliminaire" he asserted that Bentham had left him an incomplete manuscript, and that in consequence what Dumont presented to the public was not a translation; the manuscript text had been wholly modified. Bentham had originally composed *Political Tactics* with a didactic question-and-answer structure. Dumont abandoned this and rewrote it as a unitary discourse.[27] The same point was made in the "Discours préliminaire" to the accompanying *Traités des sophismes politiques et des sophismes anarchiques*, which criticized Bentham's original manuscript for its factional spirit, having "always in vue the British Parliament and British issues."[28] Dumont presented a different work, being applicable in principle to "nearly all political assemblies."[29]

Dumont's own *Règlement pour le conseil représentatif* appeared after Bentham's *Tactique* as a summary text, directly moving from general rules to a specific application of Benthamite ideas to Geneva. British members of Parliament were advised that they would recognize much: propositions being known in advance and in writing, no reading of speeches, no lists of orators, three distinct debates prior to the passage of a bill, similar rules of order, and the conversion of the assembly into a general committee for the scrutiny of proposed legislation. Making such links forced Dumont to state explicitly that in this instance there were no difficulties in advising a small state to follow rules devised for a large empire. Although the population of Geneva was said to be forty or fifty thousand and that of Britain fifteen or sixteen million, Dumont claimed that the sole difference with respect to the functions of political assemblies lay in the speed with which those at Geneva could operate, because its legislators had direct experience of events and circumstances in the locality.[30] In each state there was an identical need to protect the liberty of every assembly member, and especially minority voices; maintaining order was equally essential, as was methodical discussion, to arrive ultimately at what Dumont called "the general will."[31] One of the great virtues of Bentham's work to contemporaries was that it overcame this historic distinction between what was politically imaginable in small and in large states. This distinction had governed Dumont's own thoughts on politics from his earliest years. The measure of Bentham's impact on him was that he now abandoned it.

The central difference between Dumont's analysis of Britain and of Geneva was the division between the powers of the parliamentary assemblies. The Council of State at Geneva alone had the power of proposing legislation. Dumont justified this rule as the sole means of limiting the power of the other assembly, the Council of Representatives. If the latter council could propose law, the danger was that its members, being elected, and if in a large majority on a particular issue, would invoke the authority of the people, with dire consequences for domestic peace. While the Council of Representatives did not have veto powers over law, it had the right to amend legislation sent to it by the Council of State. Committees for the scrutiny of legislation were created from members of the elected council, and by a formal process they revised each piece of legislation by means of amendments carried by majority vote. The two chambers then formed a committee to accept or further revise the recommendations of the prior legislative committee. Members would sit not as councilors of state or as representatives of the people, but as citizens with the general will as their object and no personal office or position to defend. As Dumont put it: "By this measure everything is saved, with initiative [to propose legislation] on one side, and the right to amend on the other, and with the two councils sitting together with their different and rival prerogatives, but conserving between them a spirit of harmony which to me appears to have the mark of durability."[32]

The result was a system of balanced and interdependent powers, which followed the British example in seeking to institutionalize compromise in the aftermath of reasoned, orderly, and public argument. Dumont believed his version of the new Genevan constitution would prevent the eighteenth-century war between représentants and constitutionnaires from reemerging. He traced the source of historic unrest to the veto powers of the General Council. The old constitution, being too democratic, set the people against the magistrates by giving the assembled citizenry powers to reject legislation *tout court* and no alternative between acceptance or rejection of the laws proposed by the smaller councils. Dumont wrote of the ancient democratic Geneva that "acts of sovereignty themselves had the character of being weak and contradictory." Geneva was fortunate in not having "returned to being a democratic regime."[33]

The element that remained of représentant argument concerned the right of bringing grievances to the higher councils, which had of course originally defined the représentant movement. In Dumont's scheme all members of the councils had the right to bring to the attention of their assembly concerns about the infraction of law. The Council of State had to reply to any accusation. If this reply was deemed unsatisfactory by the individual who carried the grievance, with the support of a hundred votes it could be brought to the attention of the Council of Representatives, which would then rule on the nature of the infraction and its remedy. By such means, Dumont claimed that once again the new constitution incorporated means of removing the antagonisms that had characterized the pre-1782 constitution of the city. In doing so, he gave further evidence of the abandonment of his original political credo: "Here is another great advantage of our new constitution over the old. When the citizens used to carry a representation with great pomp to the small council, in order to plead that the law had been violated by the government, the government, being accused and judge, responded that it had not broken the law. The accused declared his innocence, the representation was repeated, and divisions became more heated and intense. There was no route out of this labyrinth other than insurrection or an appeal to foreign mediators."[34]

PHILOSOPHIC RADICALISM AGAINST DEMOCRACY

Taking the text of the *Tactique* as a whole, it is evident that Dumont's central intention remained the same as the one that inspired the publication of the *Traités* of 1802 and the revised edition of 1820. It was to employ Bentham to warn against overly democratic impulses in modern states, and more specifically against interpretations of the French Revolution that praised democracy and that drew the lesson from the 1790s of a democratic imperative for all states. Affirming this message led Dumont to append to the text of the *Tactique* Bentham's *Examen de la déclaration des droits de l'homme et du citoyen, décrétée par l'assemblée constituante, en 1789* and the *Examen partiel d'une déclaration des droits, proposée par un membre de l'assemblée constituante*, appearing under the general title *Sophismes anarchiques*. Dumont's "avertissement" to this work explained to readers the rationale, which some considered problematic, for linking the texts of the *Tactique* together.[35] While Bentham's notes on the declaration of the rights of man and the citizen were "a treatise on the subject of a contagious malady of which we no longer speak," they needed to be popularized because "the germ of this false theory of the rights of man is in the passions of the human heart, [which are] always the same, and which want only similar circumstances to reproduce themselves."[36] Noting that exactly this had happened in Caracas in Spanish America, Dumont warned that the French declaration "maintains a secret place in the democratic code of [current] opinion."[37]

Bentham's texts on rights and the Revolution were timely because they countered enthusiasm for democracy at the time when that movement was weak, while the experience of the 1790s proved that "it is too late when [enthusiasm] has strength." Dumont considered the sources of revolutionary ideas about rights and liberties to lie "in errors promulgated by the leading writers of the [eighteenth] century . . . Mably, Rousseau, Raynal, Condorcet, Diderot, Price, Priestley, and many others." While these authors had proposed false theories about individual action, the National Assembly had turned their ideas into positive legislation with general implications. In refuting both the foundational ideas and their practical application, Bentham's work was a model example "of the art of putting in its true place a dangerous falsehood."[38]

If the Bentham of the *Tactique* emerged negatively as an opponent of democracy, he was more positively in Dumont's view a rigid moralist. One of the major points Dumont wanted to make about the modern world was the danger sophistry and falsehood presented to individuals in their daily lives and, by extension, with far more damaging effects, to the actions and decisions of monarchs, ministers, statesmen, and legislators. Ideas about rights were tied to ideas about democracy in this respect. Like Bentham, Dumont considered all notions of universal rights to be straightforwardly mistaken and an obvious violation of rationality. He recalled that no member of the circle surrounding Mirabeau had taken rights seriously, describing the attempts of himself, Clavière, and

Du Roveray to put together a list of natural rights as "a stupid compilation."[39] That this attempt failed was for Dumont to have been expected, but what surprised him was the willingness of members of the National Assembly at Paris to follow the North Americans and seek to establish a set of rights as an objective moral standard and a permanent limit upon governmental activity.

While the United States Bill of Rights was manifestly false in that slavery continued to be the economic basis of a substantial portion of the polity, the French proved equally incapable of observing the rules they had imposed upon themselves; they followed rhetorical support for universal rights with the practical policy of the Terror. In the latter case, Dumont blamed the governmental form for exacerbating the fundamental problem of creating irrational laws. Democracy, and more particularly democracy in the context of rule-less assemblies of citizens, allowed the people to be deceived more easily than under other forms of government. This was in part because of the opportunities provided to skilled rhetoricians to turn themselves into demagogues. It was also because "the people," in following orators or in reading the writings of false reasoners, were easily convinced that utopian legislation to improve the world rapidly was the yardstick with which to evaluate actual government. This in turn led to a climate of permanent revolution, which France had experienced in the 1790s, or an arena of public argument in which governments had of necessity to deceive the people, because of the false expectations the people had about politics and the economic or moral limits upon it. In short, democracy created politicians who behaved like emperors without clothes, and the commonplace emphasis on rights as a potentially universal and definitive description of the appropriate morality for modern states provided the best illustration of the dangers of democracy as a form of government, political aspiration, or ideological value.

It was as one further illustration of his fear of democracy that Dumont attacked rhetoric as the pursuit of unreason and an example of belles lettres that scholars ought to treat with care and trepidation: "After so many *beaux esprits* who have indifferently taught the art of instruction and the art of seduction, the time has come to submit all rhetorical practices to scrutiny by reference to pure morals, in order to reveal all the means of artifice employed to mislead reason, and in order to ensure that political deliberation occurs with the dignity and utility that comes only from truth and virtue."[40] Dumont was personally concerned about two works that praised the rhetorical arts, and which he described as corrupting of British politics. The first was Bubb Dodington's *Memoirs* and the second William Gerard Hamilton's *Parliamentary Logic*.[41] Although in his edition of the *Sophismes* Dumont did not translate Bentham's comment on these books, they were published in *The Book of Fallacies* in 1824: "Of the self-written Memoirs of Bubb Dodington how much was said in their day! Of Gerard Hamilton's Parliamentary Logic, how little! The reason is not unobvious: Dodington was all anecdote; Hamilton was all theory. What Hamilton endeavoured to teach with Malone and Johnson for his bag-bearers, Dodington was seen to practise. Nor is the veil of decorum cast off anywhere from his practice. In Hamilton's book for the first time has profligacy been seen stark naked."[42]

Dodington's posthumously published *Diary* became notorious when it was edited by Henry Penruddocke Wyndham in 1784. It revealed political conduct "wholly directed by the base motives of avarice, vanity, and selfishness."[43] The prime example of this was Dodington's willingness to auction himself to rival factions in Parliament. Hamilton's *Parliamentary Logic* was less well known, as Bentham stated, but it concerned both Dumont and Bentham more directly because it consisted of a series of maxims intended to advise orators how to win debates by reference to rhetorical skill alone, employing deception where necessary and without reference either to reason or to truth.[44]

Dumont believed that Bentham's *Tactique* established proper rules of procedure within a constitutional framework that inhibited democracy and maintained order. The system was predicated on a political culture that valued truth, honesty, and virtue. This was why Dumont raised the issue of those authors he deemed neo-Machiavellian in their attitude to parliamentary rhetoric. It was also why another practice was retained from old Geneva: the oath at the beginning of each session, expressing before God fidelity to the constitution, to the independence of the state, to the Christian religion, and to good manners. The oath was followed by a prayer at the beginning of each session, which also closed with a further prayer. Religion thus remained the foundation of political virtue, despite Dumont having ceased to be a pastor.[45] In his concern with the propagation of truth and austere morals in political life, he remained true to the représentant connection with the Calvinist pastors who demanded the reformation of manners. Calvin had originally sought the transformation of society by austerity in morals and adherence to rigid codes of behavior in every social activity. Clavière had visions of a related austerity in economic life and similarly tied it to the idea of liberation from oppression: the latter in the form of the British mercantile system rather than the Catholic Church. Dumont remained faithful to the notion that the improvement of manners was the key to politics. Like Clavière and all of the leading représentants, the surest route to a sustainable moral culture was to make clear that good manners equated to individual and national self-interest. Preaching, instilling fear, and monitoring social life would all fail. Appeals to virtue would fail also, and would in any case be likely to lead to violence. Dumont's great achievement was to ensure that the name of Jeremy Bentham furthered the old représentant and Calvinist cause of a moralized politics. What Dumont did not make clear in his published works was the extent to which he was certain that a political economy for modern republics, and an international politics capable of establishing perpetual peace, could equally be found in Bentham's writings. Dumont's manuscripts reveal that he believed a Benthamite path might be charted to a world without war.[46] Such endeavors took Dumont further away from his représentant past, and require a different story.

NOTES

AdG   Archives d'État de Genève

AN   Archives Nationales de France

BdG   Bibliothèque de Genève

BFP   *Benjamin Franklin Papers*, Digital Edition, Packard Humanities Institute

BL   British Library

BN   Bibliothèque Nationale de France

CC   *Correspondance complète de Jean-Jacques Rousseau*, ed. R. A. Leigh (Oxford, 1963–1994), 51 vols.

KCRO   Kent County Record Office, U.K.

MW   Jean-Jacques Rousseau, *The Miscellaneous Works of Mr. J. J. Rousseau* (London, 1767), 10 vols.

NA   National Archives, U.K.

NLI   National Library of Ireland

OC   Jean-Jacques Rousseau, *Œuvres complètes* (Paris, 1959–1995), 5 vols.

PTJ   *The Papers of Thomas Jefferson Digital Edition*, ed. Barbara B. Oberg and J. Jefferson Looney (Charlottesville, Va., 2008)

RIV   Emile Rivoire, *Bibliographie historique de Genève au XVIIIème siècle* (Geneva, 1897), 2 vols.; *Bibliographie historique de Genève au XVIIIème siècle. Additions et Corrections* (Geneva, 1935)

CHAPTER 1. 1782 AND AFTER

1. In the following notes I have referred to bibliographic guides (such as Rivoire's *Bibliographie historique de Genève au XVIIIème siècle*) when they contain additional information concerning anonymous or obscure publications. In quotations from the

French, I have used contemporary English translations wherever possible. Unless specified, all other translations are my own. I have silently modernized spelling and grammar except in cases where the original contributed to my interpretation of the text. In using sources such as Dumont's *Souvenirs sur Mirabeau*, unless otherwise indicated I have used contemporary translations for quotations, and modern editions for citations (*Souvenirs sur Mirabeau*, edited by Jean Bénétruy, 1951, for example). I have sometimes used different editions of the same text in cases where the contents had altered. I have also, as in the case of references to de Lolme's *Constitution of England*, sometimes given the same reference in several editions, on the grounds that a particular point made in one edition rather than another can matter when making sense of the text and its author.

2. William Gordon, *A new geographical grammar, and complete gazetteer* (Edinburgh, 1789), 204–205.

3. Anon., *Lettres genevoises contenant les détails peu connus sur les derniers troubles de la République de Genève* ([Geneva], 1782), 6.

4. Andrew Le Mercier, *A geographical and political account of the republic of Geneva* (Boston, 1732), 1–5.

5. George Keate, *A Short Account of the Ancient History, Present Government, and Laws of the Republic of Geneva* (London, 1761), 129–132; Charles Borgeaud, *Histoire de l'Université de Genève, I. L'Académie de Calvin, 1559–1798* (Geneva, 1900); Gillian Lewis, "The Geneva Academy," in Andrew Pettegree, Alastair Duke, and Gillian Lewis eds., *Calvinism in Europe, 1540–1620* (Cambridge, 1994), 35–63.

6. Andrew Le Mercier, *The church history of Geneva, in five books* (Boston, 1732), 40–41.

7. Karl Ludwig, Freiherr von Pollnitz, *The memoirs of Charles-Lewis, Baron de Pollnitz. Being the observations he made in his late travels . . . In letters to his friend* (Dublin, 1738), 5 vols., V, 172.

8. Patrick F. O'Mara, "Geneva in the Eighteenth Century: A Socio-Economic Study of the Bourgeois City-State during Its Golden Age" (Ph.D. diss., University of Chicago, 1954), 94–97, 216–217.

9. For an overview, see Linda Kirk, "The Material Culture: Subsistence and Abundance," unpublished manuscript. I am grateful to Linda Kirk for allowing me to read her important study.

10. James Howell, letter of 5 December 1651, *Epistolæ Ho-Elianæ: familiar letters domestick and foreign, divided into four books: partly historical, political, philosophical* (London, 1737), 10th ed., 79–80.

11. Le Mercier, *A geographical and political account of the republick of Geneva*, 16.

12. Maximilien Misson, *A new voyage to Italy. With curious observations on several other countries: as Germany; Switzerland; Savoy; Geneva; Flanders, and Holland* (London, 1739), 2 vols., II, 657.

13. Jean-Baptiste de Boyer, marquis d'Argens, *Jewish letters: or, a correspondence philosophical, historical, and critical, betwixt a Jew and his correspondents* (Newcastle, 1739–1744), 4 vols., II, 95–96.

14. Ibid., 97.

15. Jean-Louis Soulavie, *Historical and Political Memoirs of the Reign of Lewis XVI. From his marriage to his death* (London, 1802), 6 vols., V, 200–207; the French original appeared as *Mémoires historiques et politiques du règne de Louis* (Paris, 1801).

16. Jacques-Antoine du Roveray, *Fameuse Remonstrance faite dans le magnifique Petit Conseil de la République de Genève, le 11 Décembre 1780* (London, 1781).

17. Soulavie, *Historical and Political Memoirs*, V, 210–217.

18. William Coxe, *Travels in Switzerland* (London, 1789), 2 vols., II, 356.

19. Soulavie, *Historical and Political Memoirs*, V, 218.

20. Coxe, *Travels in Switzerland*, II, 359–360; Pierre Mouchon to Samuel Romilly, 10 April 1782, and Jean Roget to Samuel Romilly, 13 April 1782, in F.-F. Roget, *Lettres de Jean Roget, 1780–1783* (London, 1911), 168–170, 177–179.

21. Etienne Clavière to Théophile Cazenove, 26 April 1782, in Jean Bouchary, "Etienne Clavière d'après sa correspondance financière et politique," *Les manieurs d'argent à Paris à la fin du XVIIIe siècle* (Paris, 1939), 3 vols., I, 21 (AN T646 [1]).

22. Clavière to Pierre-Marc Bourrit, 15 February 1782, and Bourrit to the Comte de Vergennes, 27 May 1782, cited in Edouard Chapuisat, *Figures et choses d'autrefois* (Geneva, 1920), 32–37.

23. Clavière to Lavabre Doerner & Co., 8 May 1782, AN T646 (1); Clavière to Etienne Delessert, 27 May 1782, and Clavière to Cazenove, 29 May 1782, in Bouchary, *Les manieurs d'argent*, 22–23.

24. Soulavie, *Historical and Political Memoirs*, V, 228. See also John Hardman and Munro Price, eds., *Louis XVI and the Comte de Vergennes: Correspondence, 1774–1787* (Banbury, U.K., 1998), 308.

25. Herbert Lüthy, *La banque protestante en France de la révocation de l'édit de Nantes à la Révolution* (Paris, 1959–1961), 2 vols., II, 742–743.

26. Vergennes to Bern, 9 June 1782, in Isaac Cornuaud, *Mémoires de Isaac Cornuaud sur Genève et la révolution de 1770 à 1795*, ed. Emilie Cherbuliez (Geneva, 1912), 371–372.

27. François d'Ivernois, *An Historical and Political View of the Constitution and Revolutions of Geneva in the Eighteenth Century*, trans. John Farell (London, 1784 [orig. pub. Geneva, 1782]), 303–304n; William C. Lowe, "Bertie, Willoughby, fourth earl of Abingdon (1740–1799)," *Oxford Dictionary of National Biography* (Oxford, 2004). See also John Wilkes, *The Speeches of John Wilkes* (London, 1777), 2 vols., I, 178, Soulavie, *Historical and Political Memoirs*, V, 228–235.

28. Anon., "British and Foreign History," *The New annual register, or, General repository of history, politics, and literature for the year 1782*, ed. Andrew Kippis (London, 1783), 63–64. John Payne later wrote that in the 1760s the Genevans, "to avert the evil which threatened them, sought the interposition of Great Britain, but the court of London declined to mediate in the dispute." John Payne, *An epitome of history; or, a concise view of the most important revolutions and events, which are recorded in the histories of the principal empires, Kingdoms, States, and Republics, now subsisting in the world: also their Forms of Government: Accompanied with short Accounts of the different Religions* (London, 1795), 2nd ed., 2 vols., I, 294.

29. Roget to Romilly, 20 June 1782, in *Lettres de Jean Roget*, 237.

30. Romilly to Catherine Roget, 20 May 1782, in *Lettres de Jean Roget*, 229, n. 1.

31. François d'Ivernois, *Tableau historique et politique des deux dernières révolutions de Genève* (London, 1789), 2 vols., II, 105.

32. BdG Ms. Suppl. 32, fols. 167–179, 187–189, 193–200, 213–215.

33. D'Ivernois, *Tableau historique et politique des deux dernières révolutions de Genève*, II, 103. On Mount Stuart, see Roland Thorne, "Stuart, John, first marquess of Bute (1744–1814)," *Oxford Dictionary of National Biography* (Oxford, 2004); online ed., January 2008.

34. Cornuaud, *Mémoires de Isaac Cornuaud*, 374–375.

35. Jacques-Pierre Brissot to Frédéric Samuel Ostervald, 14 June and 19 June 1782, in Robert Darnton, ed., *Correspondance de Brissot*, Letters-collection Database, Voltaire Foundation, University of Oxford.

36. Soulavie, *Historical and Political Memoirs*, V, 236–238; Coxe, *Travels in Switzerland*, II, 366.

37. D'Ivernois, *Tableau historique et politique des deux dernières révolutions de Genève*, II, 109–111.

38. Soulavie, *Historical and Political Memoirs*, V, 238–242.

39. Jean Roget to Romilly, 20 June 1782, in *Lettres de Jean Roget*, 235; Cornuaud, *Mémoires de Isaac Cornuaud*, 376–379.

40. Roget to Romilly, 11 May 1782, in *Lettres de Jean Roget*, 216.

41. Coxe, *Travels in Switzerland*, II, 365–368.

42. Roget to Romilly, 20 June 1782, in *Lettres de Jean Roget*, 250–253.

43. Jennifer Powell McNutt, "Church and Society in Eighteenth-Century Geneva, 1700–1789" (Ph.D. diss., University of St. Andrews, 2008), 268–269.

44. Albin Thourel, *Histoire de Genève depuis son origine jusqu'à nos jours* (Geneva, 1832), 3 vols., III, 297; Coxe, *Travels in Switzerland*, II, 370–373.

45. Catherine Roget to Romilly, 7 August 1782, in *Lettres de Jean Roget*, 257–259.

46. Cornuaud, *Mémoires de Isaac Cornuaud*, 390; d'Ivernois, *Tableau historique et politique des deux dernières révolutions de Genève*, II, 139.

47. Thourel, *Histoire de Genève*, III, 300.

48. Cornuaud, *Mémoires de Isaac Cornuaud*, 390–391; d'Ivernois, *Tableau historique et politique des deux dernières révolutions de Genève*, II, 124–147.

49. Thourel, *Histoire de Genève*, III, 310; "Letter of the Mediating powers to the government of Geneva, 21st November 1782," in Soulavie, *Historical and Political Memoirs*, V, 246–247.

50. Soulavie, *Historical and Political Memoirs*, V, 251.

51. Ibid., V, 254–255.

52. Jean-Marc Rivier, *Etienne Clavière, 1735–1793: Un révolutionnaire, ami des Noirs* (Paris, 2006), 38: "On dit que M. Clavière et ses compagnons de voyage s'étant arrêtés à Düsseldorf n'y ont rien vu qui doive partager l'attention de nos compatriotes. Le local est beau, il est vrai, les denrées à bon marché et la situation propre au commerce. Mais il n'y a pas parmi les principaux du lieu, le même empressement, tant s'en faut, à nous accueillir qu'a démontré la Régence de Mannheim. Et puis ces Etats avec qui il s'agirait de traiter . . . sont composés de gens entichés de leurs seize quartiers de

noblesse, et conséquemment très peu propres à favoriser les principes d'égalité et de popularité qui devraient faire la base d'une colonie d'artisans. Mrs Clavière et consorts se disposaient donc à continuer leur route et comptaient d'être le 16 (janvier) à Bruxelles et le 18 à Ostende."

53. Cornuaud, *Mémoires de Isaac Cornuaud*, 392.

54. Powell McNutt, "Church and Society in Eighteenth-Century Geneva," 271.

55. D'Ivernois, *Tableau historique et politique des deux dernières révolutions de Genève*, II, 121–135.

56. Thourel, *Histoire de Genève*, III, 295.

57. Catherine Roget to Romilly, 7 August 1782, and Jean Roget to Romilly, 11 September, in *Lettres de Jean Roget*, 260–261, 266–268; Cornuaud, *Mémoires de Isaac Cornuaud*, 386; d'Ivernois, *Tableau historique et politique des deux dernières révolutions de Genève*, II, 124–125.

58. Jacques-Pierre Brissot, *Le Philadelphien à Genève, ou lettres d'un Américain sur la dernière revolution de Genève, sa Constitution nouvelle, l'émigration en Irlande, &c. pouvant servir de tableau politique de Genève jusqu'en 1784* (Dublin, 1783), 56.

59. Josef Feldmann, *Die Genfer Emigranten von 1782/83* (Zurich, 1952); Marc Neuenschwander, "Les troubles de 1782 à Genève et le temps de l'émigration," *Bulletin de la Société d'histoire et d'archéologie de Genève* 19 (1989), 127–188.

60. Jean Roget to Romilly, 18 December 1782, in *Lettres de Jean Roget*, 288.

61. Cornuaud, *Mémoires de Isaac Cornuaud*, 402–404; Thourel, *Histoire de Genève*, III, 305–308.

62. See Vergennes's letter to his ambassador the Vicomte de Polignac (8 March 1781, CC, XLV, 13) on the action to be taken in the event of constitutional change in Geneva: "Il s'agit d'établir dans Geneve l'autorité légitime et de ne la pas laisser à la merci des mouvemens Populaires." Cornuaud argued that aristocratic states such as France and Bern had an obvious shared interest in preventing the development of democracy; *Mémoires de Isaac Cornuaud*, 411.

63. Jean Roget to Romilly, 18 December 1782, in *Lettres de Jean Roget*, 292–294.

64. Clavière to Cazenove, 29 May 1782, and Clavière to Roman l'aîné, 29 November 1782, AN T646 (1).

65. On Dumont's life, see Jean Martin, *Etienne Dumont, 1759–1829* (Neuchâtel, 1942); Jefferson P. Selth, *Firm Heart and Capacious Mind: The Life and Friends of Etienne Dumont* (Lanham, Md., 1997); and Cyprian Blamires, "Dumont, Etienne (1759–1832)," *Oxford Dictionary of National Biography*, online ed., May 2009.

66. Etienne Dumont, "Sermon sur la connoissance de soi-même," 28 March 1784, Dumont papers, BdG, Ms. 31, 70–82; d'Ivernois, *Tableau historique et politique des deux dernières révolutions de Genève*, II, 122; Cyprian Blamires, *The French Revolution and the Creation of Benthamism* (London, 2008), 126–127.

67. Dumont's friend the pastor Jean Roget, who had close connections to the Genevan expatriate community in London, wrote to Samuel Romilly, his brother-in-law, on 19 October 1782, stating that he was astonished at Dumont's eloquence as a pastor, and reported that Dumont was seeking to leave Geneva. Having neither money nor

patrons, Roget wrote, it was possible that Dumont would go as pastor to a Calvinist community in Greece. Roget asked whether it would be possible for Dumont to join Romilly in London (*Lettres de Jean Roget*, 272–275.)

68. On Dumont's relationship with Bowood, see John Neal, "Biographical Sketch of M. Dumont of Geneva" in his edition of Jeremy Bentham's *Principles of Legislation* (Boston, 1830), 148–157. Shelburne made Dumont financially independent by arranging the sinecure of chief clerk in the Pells Office from 1791 (*London Calendar*, 1791, 182).

69. Samuel Romilly, *Memoirs of the Life of Sir Samuel Romilly, Written by Himself* (London, 1840), 3 vols., I, 86–87; see also *The Speeches of Sir Samuel Romilly in the House of Commons* (London, 1820), 2 vols., I, xxv–xxvii.

70. Samuel Romilly, *Observations on a late publication, intituled, Thoughts on executive justice: to which is added, a letter containing remarks on the same work* (London, 1786), 100; see also H. F. Grœnvelt [Dumont, Romilly, and John Scarlett], *Letters containing an Account of the late Revolution in France, and Observations on the Constitution, Laws, Manners, and Institutions of the English* (London, 1792), 280.

71. Etienne Dumont, *Souvenirs sur Mirabeau*, ed. Jacob-Louis Duval (Paris, 1832).

72. On the reception of the *Souvenirs*, see Jean Bénétruy's introduction to his revised edition from the Dumont papers in the BdG (Etienne Dumont, *Souvenirs sur Mirabeau*, ed. Jean Bénétruy [Paris, 1951], 23–33); Henry Brougham, *Historical Sketches of Statesmen Who Flourished in the Time of George III* (London, 1839), 3 vols., II, 248; Jules Michelet, *Historical View of the French Revolution* (London, 1883), 104.

73. Jean Bénétruy, *L'atelier de Mirabeau: Quatre proscrits genevois dans la tourmente révolutionnaire* (Geneva, 1962), 166–227; Philippe Plan, *Un collaborateur de Mirabeau: Documents inédits* (Paris, 1874), 5–49; Chapuisat, *Figures et choses d'autrefois*, 1–119; Bouchary, "Etienne Clavière d'après sa correspondance financière et politique," 11–101; Robert Darnton, "Trends in Radical Propaganda on the Eve of the French Revolution (1782–1788)" (Ph.D. diss., Oxford University, 1964), 91–232, and "L'idéologie à la Bourse," in *Gens des lettres, gens du livre* (Paris, 1991), 86–98; Paul Waeber, "La parole ailée et les écrivains: Mirabeau, Clavière, Du Roveray, Etienne Dumont et Reybaz," *Musées de Genève* 118 (1971), 9–14.

74. Honoré-Gabriel de Riquetti, comte de Mirabeau, and Baudouin de Guémadeuc, *L'espion dévalisé* (London [Neuchâtel], 1784); Mirabeau, *Des lettres de cachet et des prisons d'état. Ouvrage posthume, composé en 1778* (Hamburg, 1782).

75. Mirabeau to Vergennes, 29 September 1782, in Alfred Stern, *La vie de Mirabeau* (Paris, 1895), 2 vols., I, 385–388.

76. Bénétruy notes the striking similarity between the original draft of Mirabeau's letter to Vergennes and Du Roveray's handwriting. See *L'atelier de Mirabeau*, 42–43. Otto Karmin had earlier stated that the author was Du Roveray; *Sir Francis d'Ivernois* (Geneva, 1920), 118.

77. Mirabeau to Vergennes, 4 October 1782, in *Mémoires biographiques, littéraires et politiques de Mirabeau, écrits par lui-même, par son père, son oncle et son fils adoptif*, ed. Gabriel Lucas de Montigny (Paris, 1841), 2nd ed., 8 vols., IV, 114–140. On the

crisis facing small states more generally in the eighteenth century, see Richard Whatmore, "'Neither Masters nor Slaves': Small States and Empire in the Long Eighteenth Century," *Proceedings of the British Academy* 155 (2009), 53–81; Whatmore, "Vattel, Britain, and Peace in Europe," *Grotiana* 31 (2010), 85–107; and Manuela Albertone, "Democratic Republicanism: Historical Reflections on the Idea of Republic in the Eighteenth Century," *History of European Ideas* 33 (2007), 108–130.

78. Between 1781 and 1782, Brissot planned to write about education, proposed an edition of Raynal's *Histoire philosophique*, having erroneously received information about Raynal's death, and contemplated an edited anthology of writings emanating from the Académie des Inscriptions et Belles-Lettres. See Brissot to Frédéric Samuel Ostervald, 5 November 1781 and 18 August 1782, in Darnton, *Correspondance de Brissot*. See also Robert Darnton, "J.-P. Brissot and the Société Typographique de Neuchâtel (1779–1787)," *Studies on Voltaire and the Eighteenth Century* 10 (2001), 5–47; and James Burns, "Jacques-Pierre Brissot: From Skepticism to Conviction," *History of European Ideas*, forthcoming.

79. Brissot to François d'Ivernois, 12 April 1782, BdG, Ms. Suppl. 1010, fol. 12.

80. Brissot, *Théorie des lois criminelles* (Berlin, 1782), 2 vols.; *Bibliothèque philosophique du législateur, du politique, du jurisconsulte* (Neuchâtel, 1782–1785), 10 vols.; *Lettres philosophiques sur St. Paul* (Neuchâtel, 1783); *Correspondance universelle sur ce qui intéresse le bonheur de l'homme et de la société* (London, 1783), 2 vols.; *De la vérité ou méditation sur les moyens de parvenir à la vérité dans toutes les connaissances humaines* (Neuchâtel, 1782).

81. Brissot, *Mémoires, 1754–1793, publiés avec Etude critique et Notes*, ed. Claude Perroud (Paris, 1912), 2 vols., I, 274, II, 28–29; Claude Perroud, ed., *J.-P. Brissot: Correspondance et Papiers* (Paris, 1911), 108; Brissot to Ostervald, 13 August 1782, reporting that he felt in a whirlwind because of the new ideas he had been exposed to (Darnton, *Correspondance de Brissot*).

82. Brissot, *Théorie des lois criminelles*, I, 221; *Bibliothèque philosophique du législateur*, III, 17, 23, V, 379, IX, 300; *Lettres philosophiques sur St. Paul*, 89; *Correspondance universelle sur ce qui intéresse le bonheur de l'homme et de la société*, I, 85, II, 27, 61–67, 85, 104–105; Brissot to Ostervald, 13 August 1782.

83. Brissot, *Mémoires, 1754–1793*, II, 28–29. See also Perroud, *Brissot: Correspondance et Papiers*, 108, and Brissot and Clavière, *De la France et des États-Unis, ou de l'importance de la révolution de l'Amérique pour le bonheur de la France; Des rapports de ce Royaume et des États-Unis, des avantages réciproques qu'ils peuvent retirer de leurs liaisons de commerce, et enfin de la situation actuelle des États-Unis* (Paris, 1788), 28.

84. Clavière asked his banker Cazenove at London on 20 October 1782 to pay Brissot, then at Boulogne, 100 pounds sterling; see Bouchary, *Les manieurs d'argent*, I, 24. Brissot asked Ostervald on 7 October 1782 to send copies of his *De la vérité* to Clavière, Du Peyrou, Jacob Vernes, Du Roveray, and Vieusseux.

85. Jan Willem Schulte Nordholt, *The Dutch Republic and American Independence* (Chapel Hill, N.C., 1982); Munro Price, "The Dutch Affair and the Fall of the Ancien Regime, 1784–1787," *Historical Journal* 38 (1995), 875–905.

86. Dumont, *Souvenirs sur Mirabeau*, ed. Duval, 53–54, 155; Etienne Dumont, *Recollections of Mirabeau, and of the two first legislative assemblies of France* (Philadelphia, 1833), 45.

87. Jeremy Bentham, *Traités de législation civile et pénale*, ed. Etienne Dumont (Paris, 1802), 3 vols. On their gestation, see Blamires, *The French Revolution and the Creation of Benthamism*, 233–253.

88. Jean-Charles-Léonard Simonde de Sismondi, "Notice nécrologique sur M. Etienne Dumont," *Revue encyclopédique* (October 1829); Augustin Pyramus de Candolle, "Notice sur la vie et les écrits de M. Etienne Dumont," *Bibliothèque universelle* (November 1829); Mirabeau, *Mémoires*, ed. de Montigny, VIII, 563–565, 578n.1; Jeremy Bentham, *The Works of Bentham*, ed. John Bowring (Edinburgh, 1834), 11 vols., X, 184–186; Elie Halévy, *The Growth of Philosophic Radicalism* (London, 1928), 515–521; Leslie Stephen, *The English Utilitarians* (London, 1900), 3 vols., I, 186–188, 191–193; Charles Milner Atkinson, *Jeremy Bentham: His Life and Works* (London, 1905), 91–94; Jean Martin, "Quatorze billets inédits de Mirabeau à Etienne Dumont et à Du Roveray," *La Révolution française* 28 (1925), 289–311, and *Etienne Dumont, 1759–1829* (Neuchâtel, 1942), 18–32; Charles Blount, "Bentham, Dumont, and Mirabeau," *University of Birmingham Historical Journal* 3 (1952), 153–167; William Thomas, *The Philosophic Radicals: Nine Studies in Theory and Practice, 1817–1841* (Oxford, 1979), 24, 33–34, 42; Blamires, *The French Revolution and the Creation of Benthamism*.

89. Jean Louis Eugène Lerminier, *De l'influence de la philosophie du XVIIIe siècle sur la législation et la sociabilité du XIXe* (Brussels, 1834), 204n.

90. Blamires, *The French Revolution and the Creation of Benthamism*, 283–288.

91. Dumont, *Recollections of Mirabeau*, xxxiii–xxxiv; Dumont, *Souvenirs sur Mirabeau*, ed. Duval, xvi–xvii.

92. Edouard Dufour, *Jacob Vernes, 1728–1791: Essai sur sa vie et sa controverse apologétique avec J.-J. Rousseau* (Geneva, 1898).

CHAPTER 2. GENEVA AND FRANCE

1. Jean Picot, *Histoire de Genève, depuis les temps les plus anciens, jusqu'à nos jours: accompagnée de détails sur les antiquités de la ville et de son territoire, sur les moeurs, les usages, le gouvernement, les lois, les monnoies, les progrès des sciences et des arts* (Geneva, 1811), 3 vols., III, 70–88; Pierre Bertrand, *Genève et la révocation de l'édit de Nantes* (Geneva, 1938), 23–28, 33–38, 46–50; Oliver Fatio and Louise Martin-van Berchem, "L'Eglise de Genève et la révocation de l'édit de Nantes," in Olivier Reverdin, ed., *Genève au temps de la révocation de l'édit de Nantes, 1680–1705* (Geneva, 1985), 159–312.

2. Jean-Pierre Bérenger, *Histoire de Genève, depuis son origine jusqu'à nos jours* (Geneva, 1773), 6 vols., III, 15, 23.

3. Picot, *Histoire de Genève*, III, 123.

4. Ibid., III, 2–5.

5. Ibid., III, 17.

6. Jérôme Sautier, "Genève et la France à la fin du XVIIe siècle," in Reverdin, *Genève au temps de la révocation de l'édit de Nantes*, 1–116.

7. Le Mercier, *Church history of Geneva*, 194.

8. Bérenger, *Histoire de Genève*, III, 11–14; Picot, *Histoire de Genève*, III, 51–62.

9. Marc Cramer, *Genève et les Suisses, 1691–1792* (Geneva, 1914), 1–55.

10. Maria-Cristina Pitassi, "Exemplarity to Suspicion: The Genevan Church between the Late Seventeenth and Early Eighteenth Centuries," *History of European Ideas* 37 (2010), 16–22.

11. Picot, *Histoire de Genève*, III, 90, 93–94.

12. Ibid., III, 98–99.

13. Christopher Storrs, *War, Diplomacy, and the Rise of Savoy, 1690–1720* (Cambridge, 1999), 122–171.

14. Picot, *Histoire de Genève*, III, 11–13; O'Mara, "Geneva in the Eighteenth Century," 212.

15. Abraham van Hoey, *Letters and negociations of M. van Hoey, ambassador from the States-General to His Most Christian Majesty* (London, 1743), 33–34; Richard Rolt, *An impartial representation of the conduct of the several powers of Europe, engaged in the late general war from 1739 to 1748* (London, 1749–1750), 4 vols., II, 92–93.

16. O'Mara, "Geneva in the Eighteenth Century," 201.

17. Picot, *Histoire de Genève*, III, 247.

18. Edouard Favre, "L'état du gouvernement present de la République de Genève [1721] par Antoine Tronchin," *Mémoires et documents publiés par la Société d'histoire et d'archéologie de Genève* 25 (1925), 203–234.

19. Abraham van Hoey to M. Fagel, 13 December 1741, in *Lettres et négociations de M. Van Hoey, ambassadeur à la cour de France* (London, 1752), 70–78.

20. Powell McNutt, "Church and Society in Eighteenth-Century Geneva," 48–53.

21. Hennin was the résident between 1765 and 1778. On Versoix, see Jean Louis Favier, Charles François Broglie, Charles Gravier Vergennes, Anne-Robert-Jacques Turgot, and Louis-Philippe Ségur, *Politique de tous les cabinets de l'Europe, pendant les règnes de Louis XV et de Louis XVI* (Paris, 1801), 2nd ed., 3 vols., I, 139; Soulavie, *Historical and Political Memoirs*, I, 107–108; Louis Simond, *Switzerland; or, a journal of a tour and residence in that country, in the years 1817, 1818, and 1819: Followed by an historical sketch on the manners and customs of ancient and modern Helvetia* (London, 1823), 2 vols., II, 340–342.

22. Abraham Stanyon, *An Account of Switzerland: Written in the Year 1714* (London, 1714), 230.

23. Louis Henry de Rouvière, *Voyage du tour de la France* (1713), in Jean-Daniel Candaux, ed., *Voyageurs européens à la découverte de Genève, 1685–1792* (Geneva, 1966), 24.

24. Edouard Favre, *Combourgeois. Genève/Fribourg/Berne 1526. Récit historique* (Geneva, 1926); Bérenger, *Histoire de Genève*, III, 177–178.

25. Anon., *The present state of Europe, or, The historical and political monthly mercury*, vol. 16, November (London, 1705), 413.

26. Stanyon, *Account of Switzerland*, 158–162.

27. Comte de Lautrec, *Discours prononcé à l'Audience du Petit Conseil de la République de Genève, le 2 Novembre 1737, par son excellence Monsieur Le Comte de Lautrec, Lieutenant-Général du Roi en la Province de Guyenne, Maréchal de ses Camps & Armées, Inspecteur-Général de son Infanterie, & Plénipotentiaire de sa Majesté Très Chrétienne, pour la Médiation des Troubles de cette République.*

28. Jean-Alphonse Turrettini, *De la part de nos Magnifiques & Très-Honorés Seigneurs Sindics, Petit & Grand Conseil* (1 November 1737).

29. Frederick II, King of Prussia, "Considerations on the present state of the body politic in Europe" [1736], *Memoirs from the peace of Hubertsburg, to the partition of Poland, and of the Bavarian war. Translated from the French by Thomas Holcroft* (London, 1789), 37–38.

30. De la Closure, *Discours fait par Monsieur De la Closure, Résident de France, Dans l'Audience qu'il a pris du Magnifique Conseil, le Samedi 21 Septembre 1737; Mémoire adressé par Monsieur De la Closure, Résident de la France, auprès de la Ville et République de Genève, au Magnifique Petit Conseil, le vendredi 4 octobre 1737.*

31. John Wilson, *The History of Switzerland* (Philadelphia, 1832), 225–233; Heinrich Zschokke and Emil Zschokke, *The History of Switzerland, for the Swiss People* (New York, 1855), 233–268.

32. Picot, *Histoire de Genève*, III, 101.

33. John Brown, *An Estimate of the Manners and Principles of the Times* (London, 1758), 2 vols., I, 90.

34. Ibid., II, 135–136.

35. Helena Rosenblatt, *Rousseau and Geneva: From the First Discourse to the Social Contract, 1749–1762* (Cambridge, 1997), 110, citing Fatio and Martin-van Berchem, "L'Eglise de Genève," 256. More broadly, see Gabriella Silvestrini, *Alle radici del pensiero di Rousseau* (Milan, 1993), and *Diritto naturale e volontà generale: Il contrattualismo repubblicano di Jean-Jacques Rousseau* (Turin, 2010).

36. Jean-Alphonse Turrettini, *Oratio III (Panegyrica in obitum . . . Gulielmi III. Magnae Britannicae Rex*, cited in John W. Beardslee, "Theoretical Development at Geneva under Francis and Jean-Alphonse Turrettini, 1648–1737" (Ph.D. diss., Yale University, 1956), 16.

37. Lüthy, *La banque protestante en France*, II, 749–789.

38. O'Mara, "Geneva in the Eighteenth Century," 207.

39. Keate, *A Short Account*, 63.

40. O'Mara, "Geneva in the Eighteenth Century," 128–134.

41. Jean-Jacques Rousseau, *Social Contract*, bk. I, chap. 6.

42. Sir John Talbot Dillon, *Historical and critical memoirs of the general revolution in France, in the year 1789: from the opening of the States General, on the 25th April* (London, 1790), 47–48.

43. Jean Bodin, *Les six livres de la république* (Paris, 1576), 267–268, translated from *The six bookes of a Comonweale* (London, 1606), second book, 233. See also Thomas Maissen, "Vers la République souveraine: Genève et les Confédérés entre le droit

public occidental et le droit impérial," *Bulletin de la Société d'histoire et d'archéologie de Genève* 29 (1999), 3–27.

44. Guillaume-Alexandre de Méhégan, *A view of universal modern history, from the fall of the Roman empire* (London, 1778), 3 vols., II, 166.

45. Le Mercier, *A geographical and political account of the republick of Geneva*, 44.

46. Jean P. Ferrier, "Une tentative de révolution à Genève en 1698 (le complot Gallatin)," *Revue d'histoire Suisse* 3 (1923), 322–355; Thourel, *Histoire de Genève*, I, 262–270.

47. Henri Fazy, *Les constitutions de la république de Genève* (Geneva, 1890), 293–300; André E. Sayous, "La haute bourgeoisie de Genève," *Revue historique* 180 (1937), 30–57. An additional Council of Sixty was composed of members of the Two Hundred who had held majors offices of state and could be called upon by the Council of Twenty-Five to provide advice on extraordinary matters.

48. Amédée Roget, "Les propositions de Jacques Boutilier, ou discussion constitutionelle à Genève en 1578," *Mémoires et documents publiés par la Société d'histoire et d'archéologie de Genève* 17 (1872), 60.

49. Edouard Mallet, "Conflit entre le Petit Conseil et le Conseil des Deux-Cents en 1667, ou épisode de l'auditeur Sarasin," *Mémoires et documents publiés par la Société d'histoire et d'archéologie de Genève* 1 (1841), 289.

50. François d'Ivernois, *Tableau historique et politique des révolutions de Genève dans le dix-huitième siècle dédié à sa majesté très-chrétienne Louis XVI* (Geneva, 1782), 5–6 (translation from *An Historical and Political View of the Constitution and Revolutions of Geneva in the Eighteenth Century*, London, 1784, 5–6).

51. D'Ivernois, *An Historical and Political View of the Constitution and Revolutions of Geneva*, 3–4n. This note does not appear in the original *Tableau historique et politique des révolutions de Genève*; the English translation states it was "added for foreigners."

52. Prior to the Edict of 1543, any citizen or bourgeois had the right to bring issues of concern to the General Council. The edict stated "Que rien ne soit mis en avant en Conseil des CC qui n'ait été traité au Conseil Etroit, ni au Conseil Général, avant qu'avoir été traité tant au Conseil Etroit qu'aux CC." See Fazy, *Les constitutions*, 50–52; pp. 289–335 reprint the edicts. See also Eugène Choisy, "La Réforme calvinienne," in Paul Guichonnet, ed., *Histoire de Genève des origines à 1798* (Geneva, 1951), 240–243.

53. Fazy, *Les constitutions*, 51–65; Jacques Courvoisier, "Théodore de Bèze et l'Etat chrétien," in Guichonnet, *Histoire de Genève*, 274.

54. Jacob de Chapeaurouge, *Lettre d'un Citoyen de Genève à un autre Citoyen de ses amis sur les mouvemens présens* (Geneva, 1707), 6–10; Jean-Robert Chouet, AdG, Registres de Conseil, 5 May, 1707, vol. 207, 327–345; Jean Barbeyrac, *Consultation en forme de lettre, adressés par M. Barbeyrac, professeur en droit à Groeningue, à M. le Capitaine Micheli du Crest*, 20 November 1731, BdG, Ms. Fr. 852.

55. Fazy, *Les constitutions*, 10–23; Louis Binz, "Le Moyen Age genevois," in Guichonnet, *Histoire de Genève*, 100. The représentants reprinted and distributed the franchises as *Coutumes, ordonnances, franchises et libertés de la Ville de Genève receuillies et publiés en l'année 1387 par Ademar Fabry, Prince et Evêque de l'Eglise et de la dite Ville de Genève* (1767).

56. Jean-Louis du Pan, *Edits de la République de Geneve* (Geneva, 1735), 1–15.

57. Keate, *A Short Account*, 69–71.

58. Ibid., 70–76.

59. Louis Henry de Rouvière, *Voyage du tour de la France* (1713), and Abraham Ruchat, *Les Délices de la Suisse* (1713) in Candaux, *Voyageurs européens à la découverte de Genève*, 18, 28. The contemporary historian Gregorio Leti wrote that at Geneva "le ménage du gouvernement a fini par se concentrer sur sept ou huit familles au plus qui forment comme une petite seigneurie ou dynastie. . . . On dirait que Genève prend à tache d'imiter Venise"; cited in André Corbaz, *Pierre Fatio* (Geneva, 1923), 63.

60. Keate, *A Short Account*, 101–102. See also Sayous, "La haute bourgeoisie de Genève."

61. Ferrier, "Une tentative de revolution en 1698"; Anne-Marie Piuz, "La politique du vin à Genève au XVIIe siècle et l'affaire de 1704," *Bulletin de la Société d'histoire et d'archéologie de Genève* 11 (1958), 259–290.

62. Marc Revilliod, *Dissertation sur la souveraineté et les droits du Conseil Général de la ville et République de Genève et sur la nécessité et grand utilité publique qu'il y a que le dit Conseil Général soit le seul souverain de l'État et que les autres Conseils en dépendent* (1704), in Marc Lahmer's edition, *Revue française d'histoire des idées politiques* 15 (2002); Bérenger, *Histoire de Genève*, III, 50.

63. Bérenger, *Histoire de Genève*, III, 81.

64. Pierre Fatio, *Propositions des citoyens*, BdG, Gf 315/179 (20).

65. Borgeaud, *Histoire de l'Université de Genève*, 406–418; Michael Heyd, *Between Orthodoxy and the Enlightenment: Jean-Robert Chouet and the Introduction of Cartesian Science in the Academy of Geneva* (The Hague, 1982).

66. Bérenger, *Histoire de Genève*, III, 60–66, 70–71; Thourel, *Histoire de Genève*, III, 5–17.

67. Thourel, *Histoire de Genève*, III, 13.

68. Bérenger, *Histoire de Genève*, III, 127; Joseph Planta, *The History of the Helvetic Confederacy* (London, 1800), II, 313; Rosenblatt, *Rousseau and Geneva*, 107–108, speech to the General Council by pastor Bénédict Calandrini, citing Romans 13 against the critics of magistracy.

69. Rosenblatt, *Rousseau and Geneva*, 103–105.

70. Bérenger, *Histoire de Genève*, III, 67.

71. Ibid., III, 150.

72. AdG, Registres de Conseil, 207, 5 May 1707, 334–335.

73. Ibid., 139–140.

74. Bérenger, *Histoire de Genève*, III, 111–119.

75. Ibid., III, 126.

76. Chapeaurouge, *Lettre d'un Citoyen*, 2–5.

77. Ibid., 7–14.

78. Ibid., 19–21, 30–31.

79. Bérenger, *Histoire de Genève*, III, 184–190.

80. Ibid., III, 167–168.

81. BdG, RC 207, 357–365.

82. Rosenblatt, *Rousseau and Geneva*, 106.

83. Bérenger, *Histoire de Genève*, III, 166; Planta, *History of the Helvetic Confederacy*, II, 315–316; Thourel, *Histoire de Genève*, III, 16.

84. Thourel, *Histoire de Genève*, III, 19–25.

85. Ibid., III, 30.

86. Planta, *History of the Helvetic Confederacy*, II, 325.

87. Ibid., II, 326.

88. Bérenger, *Histoire de Genève*, III, 272–277; Planta, *History of the Helvetic Confederacy*, II, 327; Thourel, *Histoire de Genève*, III, 34.

89. Brissot, *Philadelphien à Genève*, 15; Louis Simond, *Switzerland; or, a journal of a tour and residence in that country*, II, 377.

90. Vendramino Bianchi, *Relazione del paese de' Svizzeri* (1708), in Candaux, *Voyageurs européens à la découverte de Genève*, 27.

91. Vendramino Bianchi, *An Account of Switzerland and the Grisons* (London, 1710), 139–140.

92. Bérenger, *Histoire de Genève*, III, 277; Thourel, *Histoire de Genève*, III, 35.

93. See Rosenblatt's excellent account of Léger in *Rousseau and Geneva*, 108–125.

94. Powell McNutt, "Church and Society in Eighteenth-Century Geneva," 232–235, 237–239.

95. Picot, *Histoire de Genève*, III, 257–264.

96. Ibid., III, 253–255, 265–270, 275–276.

97. Thourel, *Histoire de Genève*, III, 101–103. More broadly see Jérôme Sautier, "La Médiation de 1737–1738: Contribution à l'histoire des institutions politiques de Genève" (Thèse de droit, Paris II, 1979).

98. On Micheli's life, philosophy, and politics, see Barbara Roth-Lochner and Livio Fornara, eds., *Micheli du Crest, 1690–1766: Homme des lumières* (Geneva, 1995); André Corboz, "Micheli du Crest, Polybe et Salomon: Examen du projet d'extension de Genève en 1730," *Genava* 28 (1980), 155–182; Paul Barbey, *Le discours politique de Micheli du Crest* (Geneva, 1992); Marc Lahmer, "Prolégomènes à Jean-Jacques Rousseau: Culture et débat politiques à Genève avant le Contrat social," *Revue française d'histoire des idées politiques* 15 (2002), 17–44; Dominique Micheli, "La pensée politique de Jacques-Barthélemy Micheli du Crest, d'après les 'Maximes d'un républicain,'" *Bulletin de la Société d'histoire et d'archéologie de Genève* 8 (1945), 165–176.

99. Picot, *Histoire de Genève*, III, 266.

100. Johann Heinrich Graf, *Des Leben und Wirken des Physikers und Geodäten J.-B. Micheli du Crest* (Bern, 1890); Martin Rickenbacher, "The Panoramic View of the Alps by Micheli du Crest: A Fruit of an Attempt to Survey Switzerland from 1754," *Cartographica Helvetica* 11 (1995), 21–34; Pirmin Meier, *Die Einsamkeit des Staatsgefangenen Micheli du Crest* (Zurich, 1999).

101. Micheli du Crest, "An Essay on the Observations which might be made respecting the Variations in the Atmosphere accompanying and preceding the different Seasons of the Year," *Foreign essays on agriculture and arts* (London, 1765), 88–98; Brissot, *Philadelphien à Genève*, 17; M. Bergerat, *Plaidoyer pour et contre J. J. Rousseau et le Docteur D. Hume, . . . Avec des anecdotes intéressantes relatives au sujet* (London [Lyon], 1768), 74.

102. Micheli du Crest, *Question politique, savoir s'il convient, en 1716, d'entreprendre un grand projet de fortification pour Genève*, AdG, Pièces historiques, 4563 bis no. 4; *Relation de tout ce qui c'est passé* (Cologne, 1731), 10, 20–21.

103. Micheli du Crest, *Mémoire pour le Magnifique Conseil des Deux Cents de Genève* (Strasbourg, 1728), 29.

104. Micheli, *Question politique; Mémoire pour le Magnifique Conseil des Deux Cents*, 5–6, 9, 25–26.

105. Micheli du Crest, *Discours en forme de Lettres sur le Gouvernement de Genève* (n.p., 1735), 94–97.

106. Micheli du Crest, *Supplication avec Supplément presentée aux Loüable Cantons de Zurich et de Berne* ([Basel], 1745), 5.

107. Micheli du Crest, *Maximes d'un républicain*, Archives d'État, Bern, Ms. BI 119, 1746, 11–13, 15, 42–43.

108. Micheli du Crest, *Maximes d'un républicain*, maxims 33, 32.

109. Micheli du Crest, *Maximes d'un républicain*, maxim 92.

110. Micheli du Crest, *Discours en forme de Lettres*, 138.

111. Micheli du Crest, *Discours en forme de Lettres*, 135; *Supplication avec Supplément*, 51, 75–76; *Maximes d'un républicain*, maxim 77.

112. Micheli du Crest, *Relation*, 17; *Maximes d'un républicain*, maxim 60.

113. Micheli du Crest, *Requetes, avertissement, plaçet et mémoire du Sieur Micheli du Crest* (n.p., 1735), 22.

114. Picot, *Histoire de Genève*, III, 252.

115. Barbey, *Discours politique de Micheli du Crest*, 16; Georges Werner, "La controverse Chapeaurouge–Le Fort," *Mémoires et documents publiés par la Société d'histoire et d'archéologie de Genève* (1931), 35, 181–322. On Lenieps, see R. A. Leigh, "Notes explicatives" in Rousseau, CC, II, 176.

116. Extrait des Registres du Conseil, AdG, Registres de Conseil, 230, 525–526, 533.

117. Micheli, *Requetes, avertissement, plaçet et mémoire*, 22.

118. Toussaint-Pierre Lenieps to Rousseau, 2 August 1763, CC, XVIII, 120–125; Lenieps to Du Crest, 20 April 1731, AdG, Procès criminels, 7602 bis; Micheli, *Supplication avec Supplément*, 21.

119. Micheli, *Supplication avec Supplément*, 21.

120. Toussaint-Pierre Lenieps, *A Très Illustre et Très Excellent Seigneur Monsieur le Chevalier Beauteville . . . tout ceux du Petit Conseil de la République de Zurich et . . . tout ceux du Petit Conseil de la République de Berne et ses ministres plénipotentiaires à Genève. Mémoire, pour Toussaint Pierre Le Nieps citoyen de Genève en apellant devant eux de la sentence rendue contre lui par le Petit Conseil de Genève et rend donc compte des fins qui il y en a donné lieu comme de la conduite qui a été rendue depuis par l'exposant afin qu'il plaise au seigneur médiateur le faire rentégrée dans tous ses droits, et lui faire allouer les dommages convenables aux torts que lui ont été faits* [1766], Lenieps papers, Archives de l'Arsenal, folio 16, 1–18.

121. Planta, *History of the Helvetic Confederacy*, II, 331–332.

122. Picot, *Histoire de Genève*, III, 266.

123. Lenieps to Jacques-François Deluc, 3 July 1736, in *A Très Illustre et Très Excellent Seigneur Monsieur le Chevalier Beauteville*, folio 16, 21–22.

124. Lenieps, *A Très Illustre et Très Excellent Seigneur Monsieur le Chevalier Beauteville*, folio 16, 23–26.

125. [Michel Léger], *Relation des troubles qui ont regné dans la Ville de Genève pendant l'année mil sept cens trente-quatre* (Rouen, 1736), 18.

126. Ibid., 124.

127. RIV I, 51 (327).

128. Jacob-Elisée Cellérier, "Du role politique de la Vénérable Compagnie dans l'ancienne république de Genève: Spécialement dans la crise de 1734 etannées suivantes," *Mémoires et documents publiés par la Société d'histoire et d'archéologie de Genève*, 12 (1860), 189–304; Powell McNutt, "Church and Society in Eighteenth-Century Geneva," 242–245.

129. Planta, *History of the Helvetic Confederacy*, II, 338.

130. Thourel, *Histoire de Genève*, III, 93–95.

131. Jean Barbeyrac, preface to Gerard Noodt, *The Power of the Sovereign and the Right to Liberty of Conscience* (London, 1708), xix.

132. Jean Barbeyrac, *Consultation en forme de lettre, adressés par M. Barbeyrac, professeur en droit à Groeningue, à M. le Capitaine Micheli du Crest*, 20 November 1731, BdG, Ms. Fr. 852, fols. 3, 6, 10, 12–13.

133. Ibid., fols. 8, 12, 16–17.

134. Jean Barbeyrac, "Discours sur la question, s'il est permis d'échaffauder en chaire le Magistrat, qui a commis quelque faute," *Recueil de discours sur diverses matières importantes* (Amsterdam, 1731), 253–255, 265, 276.

135. Petter Korkmann, introduction to Jean-Jacques Burlamaqui, *The Principles of Natural and Political Law* (Indianapolis, 2006). See also Silvestrini, *Diritto naturale e volontà generale*, and "Rousseau, Pufendorf, and the Eighteenth-Century Natural Law Tradition," *History of European Ideas* 36 (2010), 280–301.

136. Rosenblatt, *Rousseau and Geneva*, 132.

137. Jean-Jacques Burlamaqui, *Principes du droit naturel et politique* (Geneva, 1764), 97–100.

138. Jean-Jacques Burlamaqui, *Principes du droit de la nature et des gens, et du droit public general* (Paris, 1821), 656–658.

139. Ibid., 651–655.

140. Rosenblatt, *Rousseau and Geneva*, 133–140.

141. Picot, *Histoire de Genève*, III, 278; Lüthy, *La banque protestante en France*, II, 50.

142. Picot, *Histoire de Genève*, III, 283.

143. Ibid., III, 285: Gyleyn de Muelere, *Abrégé de l'histoire des papes, depuis St. Pierre jusqu'à Clément XII, avec un parallèle des cérémonies papistiques avec les cérémonies payennes, juives et mahométanes* (n.p., 1739).

144. Blamires, *The French Revolution and the Creation of Benthamism*, 105.

145. Lenieps, "Mémoire à Monsieur le Comte de Lautrec," Lenieps papers, folio 16, 32–36.

146. Micheli, *Supplication avec Supplément*, 75–76, 111–116.

147. Ibid., 34–51.

148. Micheli du Crest, *Maximes d'un républicain*, Maxims 7, 38.

149. Micheli, *Supplication avec Supplément*, 98.

150. Lenieps, *A Très Illustre et Très Excellent Seigneur Monsieur le Chevalier Beauteville*, folio 16, 9–12.

151. BdG, MS suppl. 1536, fols. 18–19; Jean-Louis Dunant to Jean-Jacques Dunant, 10 May 1738, E.-H. Gaullieur, "Une prise d'armes á Genève: Relation inédite des troubles de 1737 et de la Médiation de 1738," *Bulletin de l'Institut national de Genève* 7 (1858), 177.

152. Jacques-François Deluc, *Réfutation des erreurs de Mr. Micheli du Crest* (Geneva, 1766), 15, 22–23. In January 1766 Deluc's *Réfutation* was published by supporters of the magistrates hoping to reopen wounds among the représentants (RIV, 890).

153. Ibid., 6–12.

154. Planta, *History of the Helvetic Confederacy*, II, 343. Henzi's objective was "to revive the ancient municipal immunities; to remove the magistracy, and to appoint a new one in a general assembly of the burghers; to dismiss the seizeniers, and to elect for the future the magistrates in the tribes, in the same manner as was practised at Zuric and Basle; and lastly to appoint a dictator for the execution of this project."

155. Lahmer, "Prolégomènes à Jean-Jacques Rousseau," 17–44, and Lahmer's edition of the *Maximes*, 155–182.

156. Micheli du Crest, *Maximes d'un républicain*, maxim 66.

157. Théodore Rilliet to Etienne Clavière, 22 July 1767, BdG, Ms. Fr. 2475, fol. 115.

158. Anon., *Relation de ce qui s'est passé à Genève en 1749 au sujet du Traité avec la France* [Geneva, 1749]; Picot, *Histoire de Genève*, III, 295.

159. Gabriel Bonnot de Mably, *Œuvres complètes de l'abbé de Mably* (London, 1789–1790), 13 vols., VII, 313–320.

160. *Traité entre sa Majesté Le Roi de Sardaigne et la République de Genève* (Geneva, 1754); Picot, *Histoire de Genève*, III, 300–302.

161. Jacob Vernet, *Instruction chrétienne* (Neuveville, Switzerland, 1751–1754), 5 vols., V, 3–17.

162. As Voltaire rudely put it, "Of the dark synod, Vernet sits the head / Author of many books, but all unread / You know him not who buy—but they who sell / Know him, alas! Unhappily, too well! / The holy fathers he perus'd, when young / And thinks their manna dwells upon his tongue / Tho' Brown and Needham are not half such fools / Yet with affected piety, he rules." Voltaire, *The Civil War of Geneva, or, the Amours of Robert Covelle, an Heroic Poem, in Five Cantos* (London, 1769), 5–6; originally published as *La Guerre Civile de Genève, ou les Amours de Robert Covelle. Poème héroique* (E.-H. Gaullieur, 1768). Brown, a Scottish Presbyterian, and Needham, an Irish Jesuit, were fellow critics of Voltaire.

163. Anon., "Discours d'un Patriote Genevois," *Journal helvétique*, April 1756, 387–401.

164. Anon., "Essai sur les Sociétés Littéraires, établies à Genève, & sur l'origine & l'utilité des Académies," *Journal helvétique*, July 1759, 31–50.

165. Voltaire to George Bubb Dodington, Baron Melcombe, 4 February 1756, in Voltaire, *Correspondence and Related Documents, XVII: January 1756–March 1757,* ed. Theodore Besterman (Banbury, U.K., 1971), 55–56.

166. Anon., *Observations sur deux articles du journal Encyclopédique* (n.p., n.d.).

167. Jacob Vernet, *Lettres critiques d'un voyageur anglais sur l'Article Genève du Dictionnaire Encyclopédique; & sur La Lettre de Mr. d'Alembert à Mr. Rousseau* (Utrecht, 1761), 13; Graham Gargett, *Jacob Vernet, Geneva, and the Philosophes* (Banbury, U.K., 1994), 261–331.

168. Gargett, *Jacob Vernet,* 4–40.

169. N. Charles Falletti, *Jacob Vernet, théologien genevois, 1698–1789* (Geneva, 1885); Gargett, *Jacob Vernet,* 452–461; David Sorkin, *The Religious Enlightenment: Protestants, Jews, and Catholics from London to Vienna* (Princeton, N.J., 2008), 69–111.

170. Jean-Daniel Candaux, "D'Alembert et les Genevois ou l'enchantement rompu"; Pierre Speziali, "D'Alembert et les savants de Genève," in Monique Emery and Pierre Monzani, eds., *Jean d'Alembert, savant et philosophe: Portrait à plusieurs voix* (Paris, 1983), 120–132, 461–474.

171. Rousseau, *Lettre à d'Alembert sur les spectacles* (1758).

172. Rousseau to Jacob Vernes, 4 July 1758, CC, V, 1758, 106–107.

173. Vernet to Rousseau, 24 November 1758, CC, V, 239.

174. Voltaire to Vernes, ca. 10 December 1757, *Correspondence and Related Documents, XVIII: April 1757–March 1758,* 295–296.

175. Jean d'Alembert to Vernes, 17 December 1757, CC, V, 261; Théodore Tronchin to d'Alembert, 28 December 1757, CC, V, 262.

176. George Keate, *A Short Account,* 4–5.

177. Jean-Robert Tronchin, "Discours Prononcé au Magnifique Conseil du Deux-Cents de la République de Genève le 5 Janvier 1761," *Journal helvétique,* August 1761, 359–372. Similar sentiments were expressed in Tronchin's *Discours sur l'esprit de Parti, prononcé par Mr. Tronchin, Procureur-Général, dans l'Assemblée du Conseil des Deux-Cent de la République de Genève, au commencement de l'année 1762* (Neuchâtel, 1764).

178. Voltaire to Jean le Rond d'Alembert, 15 July 1762, in *Correspondence and Related Documents, XXIV: October 1761–May 1762,* 447–449.

179. Henry Temple, 2nd Viscount Palmerston to unknown [possible date 1763/1764], in Voltaire, *Correspondence and Related Documents, XXVII: October 1763–July 1764,* 138–139.

180. Planta, *History of the Helvetic Confederacy,* II, 340.

181. Le Mercier, *A geographical and political account of the republick of Geneva,* 50.

182. Jacques-François Deluc, "Représentations remises à M. le Procureur Général le 30 Décembre 1756," BPU, Ms. Cramer 81, 40–41.

183. Jacques-François Deluc to Paul-Claude Moultou, 8 August 1763, CC, XVII, 139; Jean-André Deluc et al., *Représentations des citoyens et bourgeois de Genève* ([Geneva], 1763), 70.

184. Jacques-François Deluc, "Projet de Réponse aux arrêtés des M. Conseils, tiré des Réflexions de divers Citoyens et Bourgeois sur cette matière," AdG, Ms. Hist. 84

(13 February 1757), 70–71; Jean-André Deluc, *Représentations des citoyens et bourgeois de Genève*, 61, 70.

185. Extrait des Registres du Conseil, 11 October 1763; Jean-André Deluc, *Représentations des citoyens et bourgeois de Geneve*, 132–133, 144–145.

186. Jacques-François Deluc, "Projet de Réponse," 70–71; Jean-André Deluc, *Représentations des citoyens et bourgeois de Geneve*, 61, 70.

187. Extrait des Registres du Conseil, 11 October 1763; Jean-André Deluc, *Représentations des citoyens et bourgeois de Geneve*, 132–133, 144–145.

188. This point was made to Jacques-François Deluc by Jean-Vincent Capperonnier de Gauffecourt in a letter of 19 July 1763, CC, XVII, 70–71.

189. Douglas G. Creighton, "Rousseau and the Delucs in 1754," *Diderot Studies* 19 (1978), 55–66; Douglas G. Creighton, *Jacques-François Deluc of Geneva and His Friendship with Jean-Jacques Rousseau* (University, Miss., 1982), chaps. 1–2.

190. Jacques-François Deluc to Rousseau, 23 June 1755, CC, III, 138–139.

191. Jacques-François Deluc to Rousseau, 9 February 1759, CC, VI, 23; Jacques-François Deluc, "Remarques sur le paragraphe de l'article Genève dans l'Encyclopédie qui traite de la Comédie et des Comédiens," *Journal helvétique*, May 1758, 504–509.

192. Jacques-François Deluc to Rousseau, 24 September 1762, CC, XIII, 105.

193. Jacques-François Deluc to Rousseau, 23 June 1755, CC, III, 138; Rousseau to Moultou, 6 July 1762, XI, 221–222.

CHAPTER 3. ROUSSEAU AND GENEVA

1. Béla Kapossy, *Iselin contra Rousseau: Sociable Patriotism and the History of Mankind* (Basel, 2006), 65–84; Michael Sonenscher, *Before the Deluge: Public Debt, Inequality, and the Intellectual Origins of the French Revolution* (Princeton, N.J., 2007), 222–253, and Michael Sonenscher, *Sans-Culottes: An Eighteenth-Century Emblem in the French Revolution* (Princeton, N.J., 2008), 134–201; Silvestrini, *Diritto naturale e volontà generale*.

2. Compare Bruno Bernardi, Florent Guénard, and Gabriella Silvestrini, eds., *La religion, la liberté, la justice: Un commentaire des "Lettres écrites de la montagne" de Jean-Jacques Rousseau* (Paris, 2006).

3. [Jean-Robert Tronchin], *Notes d'un membre du Petit Conseil de Genève au sujet de la condamnation des ouvrages de Rousseau*, 18 June 1762, CC, XI, 295–297. On 1 July the council at Bern decided to expel Rousseau from the canton, and by 10 July he had found refuge at Môtiers in Neuchâtel.

4. Jean-Jacques Rousseau, *Du contrat social* (Amsterdam, 1762), bk. II, chap. 1; bk. III, chap. 1.

5. Rousseau, *Contrat social*, bk. III, chap. 11, "De la mort du corps politique."

6. Planta, *History of the Helvetic Confederacy*, II, 347–348.

7. Théodore Tronchin to Jacob Vernes, 17 June 1762, CC, XI, 72–73.

8. Tronchin to Vernes, 20 May 1763, CC, XVI, 215.

9. Charles Bonnet to Albrecht von Haller, 15 June 1762, CC, XI, 85.

10. Jean-Louis Dupan to Abraham Freudenreich, 21 June 1762, CC, XI, 123.

11. Antoine-Jacques Roustan to Rousseau, 12 September 1761, CC, IX, 122–123. Roustan was referring to René Aubert de Vertot's *Révolutions de Portugal* (1689, 2nd ed. 1702), *Révolutions de Suède* (1695), and *Révolutions arrivés dans le gouvernement de la république romaine* (1719), and to Charles Rollin's *Histoire ancienne* (1730–1738).

12. Tronchin's *Lettres* appeared as three letters on 27 September 1763. In the last week of October a second edition appeared, quickly followed by a third, which divided the three original letters into four and added a fifth.

13. Jean-Robert Tronchin, "Conclusions du Procureur general sur deux Livres intitulés du Contrat social & de l'Education," CC, XI, 298–266, Appendix 19 June 1762.

14. Rousseau, *Émile, ou de l'éducation* (Frankfurt, 1762), 4 vols., IV, 195–199.

15. Rousseau to Nicolas-Bonaventure Duchesne, 23 May 1762, CC, X, 280–282.

16. Paul-Louis de Bauclair, *L'Anti-Contrat social* (Paris, 1764); Elie Luzac, *Lettre d'un anonyme à M. J. J. Rousseau* (Paris, 1764), 97; Guillaume-Francois Berthier, *Observations sur le contrat social de J. J. Rousseau* (Paris, 1789), 50.

17. Rousseau, *Contrat social*, bk. III, chap. 15. The translation is from Rousseau, *The Social Contract and Other Later Political Writings*, ed. and trans. Victor Gourevitch (Cambridge, 1997), 114.

18. Fazy, *Les constitutions*, 102; Edouard Rod, *L'affaire Rousseau* (Paris, 1906); Gaspard Vallette, *Jean-Jacques Rousseau, genevois* (Paris, 1911), 239, 294–326; Corbaz, *Pierre Fatio*, 67; Herbert Lüthy, "Rousseau the Genevan," *From Calvin to Rousseau* (New York, 1970), 251–269; Michel Launay, *Jean-Jacques Rousseau: Ecrivain politique* (Cannes, 1971), 36–42, 231–232; R. A. Leigh, "Le *Contrat social*, œuvre genevoise?" *Annales de la Société Jean-Jacques Rousseau* 39 (1972–1977), 93–111; Richard Fralin, *Rousseau and Representation* (New York, 1978), 143; Creighton, *Jacques-François Deluc*, 93; Pamela A. Mason, "The Genevan Republican Background to Rousseau's Social Contract," *History of Political Thought* 14 (1992), 547–572; Silvestrini, *Alle radici del pensiero di Rousseau*; Rosenblatt, *Rousseau and Geneva*.

19. Jean-Daniel Candaux, introduction to Rousseau, *Lettres écrites de la montagne*, OC, III, clix–cxcviii; Maurice Cranston, *The Solitary Self* (Harmondsworth, U.K., 1997), 77–78; Silvestrini, *Alle radici del pensiero di Rousseau*, 165–190; Rosenblatt, *Rousseau and Geneva*, 269–280.

20. R. R. Palmer, *The Age of the Democratic Revolution* (Princeton, N.J., 1959), 2 vols., I, 112–114, 129; Bénétruy, *L'atelier de Mirabeau*, 73, 92–142; Darnton, "L'idéologie à la Bourse," 85–98, and "Two Paths through the Social History of Ideas," in Haydn T. Mason, ed., *The Darnton Debate: Books and Revolution in the Eighteenth Century* (Banbury, U.K., 1999), 272–273, 291.

21. Rousseau, "Epistle Dedicatory," *Discourse on the Origin and Foundations of Inequality among Men* [1755], in Rousseau, *The Discourses and Other Early Political Writings*, ed. and trans. Victor Gourevitch (Cambridge, 1997), 118.

22. Rousseau's critics at Geneva often claimed that Rousseau had "adopted all of [Micheli's] ideas" and that both men were Hobbists. See Anon., *Lettre d'un citoyen de Genève à un autre citoyen. Le 15 Février 1768* [Geneva], 24, 73 (RIV, 1095, notes that the author may have been Jacob Vernet).

23. Rousseau, *Contrat social*, bk. 1, chap. 2.

24. Comte d'Antraigues, *Quelle est la situation de l'Assemblée nationale?* (Lausanne, 1790), 59–60.

25. Maurice William Cranston, *Jean-Jacques: The Early Life and Work of Jean-Jacques Rousseau, 1712–1754* (Harmondsworth, U.K., 1987), 27.

26. Patrick F. O'Mara, "L'affaire des lettres anonymes et l'agitation politique à Saint-Gervais en 1718," *Bulletin de la Société d'histoire et d'archéologie de Genève* 10 (1954), 261, and "Jean-Jacques and Geneva: The Petty Bourgeois Milieu of Rousseau's Thought," *The Historian* 20 (1958), 127–152; Rosenblatt, *Rousseau and Geneva*, 29–34.

27. Eugène Ritter, "La famille et la jeunesse de J.-J. Rousseau," *Annales de la Société Jean-Jacques Rousseau* 16 (1924–1925), 89–140.

28. Rousseau, *Confessions*, OC, I, 9.

29. See Rousseau's letter to his aunt Clermonde Fazy, which Leigh dates at the end of August/early September 1738, CC, I, 68–71.

30. Rousseau, *Confessions*, OC, I, 208–209, 216–218.

31. Rousseau, *Confessions*, OC, I, 393; *Lettres écrites de la montagne*, OC, III, 830–831.

32. Bérenger, *Histoire de Genève*, III, 7.

33. Rousseau, *Confessions*, OC, I, 395, nn. 2–3.

34. Rousseau, "Epistle Dedicatory," *Discourse on the Origin and Foundations of Inequality among Men* [1755], in Rousseau, *The Discourses and Other Early Political Writings*, 116–119.

35. AdG, RC, 18 June 1755, vol. 255, p. 326; Rousseau to Jean-Louis Chouet, 4 June 1755, CC, III, 132; Chouet to Rousseau, 18 June 1755, CC, III, 133–134; Jean-Louis Dupan to Rousseau, 20 June 1755, CC, III, 136–137; Rousseau to Vernes, 6 July 1755, CC, III, 141–142.

36. Rousseau to Lenieps, 12 July 1754, CC, III, 12–13; Rousseau to Vernes, 15 October 1754, CC, III, 42–3; Rousseau to Vernes, 6 July 1754, CC, III, 141.

37. Charles Bonnet to Albrecht von Haller, 19 June 1762, CC, XI, 115.

38. Extraits du Registre du Consistoire, 25 July 1754; and Leigh, "Notes explicatives," CC, II, 322–324.

39. Charles Bonnet, "Lettre de M. Philopolis," *Mercure de France*, October 1755, 71–76 (reprinted in CC, III, 151–154, and OC III, 1383–1386).

40. See Blamires, *The French Revolution and the Creation of Benthamism*, 112–115.

41. Jacques-François Deluc to Rousseau, 15 November 1758, CC, V, 224–226.

42. Théodore Tronchin to Rousseau, 17 November 1758, CC, V, 219–221.

43. Rousseau to Vernes, 25 May 1758, CC, V, 82–83; 4 July 1758, V, 106–107; 6 October 1758, V, 163–165; 22 October 1758, V, 183–186; Jacob Vernet to Rousseau, 24 November 1758, V, 239–240.

44. R. A. Leigh, "Rousseau's Letter to Voltaire on Optimism," *Studies on Voltaire and the Eighteenth Century* 30 (1964), 247–309, and "From the *Inégalité* to *Candide*: Notes on a Desultory Dialogue between Rousseau and Voltaire, 1755–1759," in W. H. Barber, J.-H. Brumfitt, et al., eds., *The Age of Enlightenment: Studies Presented to Theodore Besterman* (Edinburgh, 1967), 66–92. Voltaire caused Rousseau's falling out with Doctor Tronchin and Madame d'Epinay in 1757.

45. Henry Tronchin, "Rousseau et le Docteur Tronchin," *Annales de la Société Jean-Jacques Rousseau*, I (1905), 32–39.

46. Rousseau to Lenieps, 26 October 1758, CC, V, 188–190.

47. Rousseau to Jacques-François Deluc, 15 March 1758, CC, V, 68.

48. Vernes to Rousseau, 23 July 1759, CC, VI, 142.

49. André Gür, "Un précédent à la condamnation du 'contrat social': l'affaire Georges-Louis Le Sage (1752)," *Bulletin de la Société d'histoire et d'archéologie de Genève* 14 (1968), 77–94.

50. Tronchin, *Lettres écrites de la campagne* (Geneva, 1763), 49–52.

51. Ibid., 88–92.

52. Ibid., 105–106.

53. Ibid., 94–95.

54. Ibid., 98–100.

55. Ibid., 11–12.

56. Ibid., 113–115.

57. Ibid., 32–33.

58. Jean-Robert Tronchin, *Discours sur l'esprit de Parti, prononcé par Mr. Tronchin, Procureur-Général, dans l'Assemblée du Conseil des Deux-Cent de la République de Genève, au commencement de l'année 1764*, in *Deux discours sur l'esprit de parti* (Geneva, 1764), 39–42.

59. Jacques-François Deluc to Rousseau, 30 September 1763, CC, XVII, 289; Marc Chappuis to Rousseau, 11 October 1763, CC, XVIII, 34.

60. Jacques-François Deluc to Rousseau, 15 November 1763, XVIII, 139–140; Rousseau to Marc Michel-Rey, 9 June 1764; Rousseau to François-Henri d'Ivernois, 6 July 1764.

61. Rousseau to Jacques-François Deluc, 25 October 1763, CC, XVIII, 70.

62. Candaux, OC III, clxxxviii–cxc; Jean-André Deluc to Rousseau, 13 December 1763, CC, XVIII, 208.

63. François-Henri d'Ivernois to Rousseau, 6 September 1763, CC, XVII, 236; Paul Chappuis to Rousseau, 18 January 1765, CC, XXIII, 133–144.

64. Jean-André Deluc to Rousseau, 15 December 1764, CC, XXII, 241; Guillaume-Antoine Deluc to Rousseau, XXIII, 320. In his *Lettres sur l'histoire physique de la Terre* (Paris, 1798), xcvii, Deluc called Rousseau a theist, noting "il aurait été Chrétien, sans un penchant excessif pour l'indépendance, que lui fit chercher la Religion dans le coeur et l'esprit de l'homme."

65. François-Henri d'Ivernois to Rousseau, 21 December 1764, CC, XXII, 262.

66. Tronchin to Suzanne Necker, 18 February 1765, CC, XXIV, 41.

67. Vernet to Abbé N.-C.-J. Trublet, 9 January 1765, CC, XXIII, 70–71.

68. Vernet to Trublet, 9 January 1765, CC, XXIII, 72. Rousseau was sometimes later seen as "Turrettini's successor as a socinian"; see Anon., "Protestantism in Geneva: A Retrospect," *Blackwood's Edinburgh Magazine* 51 (January–June 1842), 162–172.

69. Déclaration de nos Magnifiques et très honorés Seigneurs sindics et Conseil [Geneva, 1765], CC, XXIII, 369–370.

70. Powell McNutt, "Church and Society in Eighteenth-Century Geneva, 1700–1789," 252.

71. Voltaire, *Sentiment des citoyens* [Geneva, 1765], 6. Voltaire had been offended by Rousseau's attack on him in the fifth of the *Lettres*. See also *A Letter from Mons. de Voltaire to Mr. Hume on His Dispute with M. Rousseau* (London, 1766), 10; Rousseau, *Réponse aux Lettres écrites de la montagne; publié à Genève, sous ce titre: Sentiment des citoyens* (Geneva, 1765).

72. Voltaire, *A Letter from Mr. Voltaire to M. Jean-Jacques Rousseau* (London, 1766), 9, 11.

73. Anon., *Le preservatif* (Bern, 1765), 2–3; Voltaire, *Lettre de Mr. de Voltaire au Docteur Jean Jacques Pansophe* (London, 1766), 10. Rousseau noted in the *Confessions* that the *Lettres* "was declared to be unworthy of being burned by the hands of the hangman, adding, with an address which bordered upon the burlesque, there was no possibility of speaking of or answering it without dishonour." *The Confessions of J. J. Rousseau, part the second* (London, 1790), 3 vols., II, 327.

74. It was only in March 1765 that Jacques Vieusseux was able to convince Rousseau that Voltaire rather than Vernes was the author of the *Sentiment des citoyens*; Vieusseux to Rousseau, 12 March 1765, CC, 4137, 209–210.

75. Rousseau to François-Henri d'Ivernois, 22 February 1765, CC, XXIV, 74.

76. Rousseau, *Lettres écrites de la montagne*, OC, III, 806–808. The translation is from *Letters written from the mountain*, MW, IV, 197–199.

77. Rousseau, *Letters written from the mountain*, MW, IV, 196: "Of the two books of mine which were burnt together, under the ordinary imputations, there is but one which treats of political law and matters of government. If these subjects are mentioned in the other, it is only by way of extract from the former." See also John S. Spink, "La première rédaction des *Lettres écrites de la montagne*," *Annales de la Société Jean-Jacques Rousseau* 20 (1931), 35, 58.

78. Rousseau, *Lettres*, OC, III, 809, MW, IV, 202–203.

79. Rousseau, *Rousseau juge de Jean-Jacques*, third dialogue, OC, I, 935.

80. Anon., *Lettre et remarques d'un étranger, Sur la Déclaration donnée par les Magnifiques & Très-Honorés Seigneurs, Syndics & Conseil de Geneve, le 12 Février 1765* (n.p., 1765), 4–6.

81. D'Ivernois, *An Historical and Political View of the Constitution and Revolutions of Geneva*, 177.

82. Anon., *Sentiment des jurisconsultes* (Bern, 1765), 2–8.

83. Rousseau to François-Henri d'Ivernois, 22 February 1765, CC, XXIV, 74.

84. Rousseau, *The Confessions of J. J. Rousseau, part the second*, II, 324–325 (OC, I, 623–624). On Rousseau's desire to play no part in Genevan politics, see the letter to François-Henri d'Ivernois, 22 February 1765, CC, XXIV, 74.

85. Rousseau to François-Henri d'Ivernois, 22 February 1765, CC, XXIV, 74.

86. Anon. to Rousseau, 26 February 1765, CC, XXIV, 98.

87. Rousseau to François Coindet, 9 February 1768, CC, XXXV, 91–97.

88. Rousseau to Jacques-François Deluc, 10 October 1762, CC, XIII, 191.

89. Pictet to Emmanuel Duvillard fils, 22 June 1762, CC, XI, 132–134.

90. Jean-François Rousseau and Théodore Rousseau to the Petit Conseil, and the latter's reply, 25 June 1762, CC, XI, 156–157.

91. Jacques-François Deluc to Rousseau, 24 September 1762, CC, XIII, 101–106.

92. Paul-Claude Moultou to Rousseau, 18 June 1762, CC, XI, 110.

93. Moultou to Rousseau, 18 June 1762, CC, XI, 108–110.

94. Moultou to Rousseau, 22 June 1762, CC, XI, 128–129.

95. Moultou to Rousseau, 10 May 1763, CC, XVI, 156–157.

96. Vernes to Moultou, 8 July 1763, CC, XVII, 35–36.

97. Moultou to Vernes, 5 July 1763, CC, XVII, 18–19.

98. Rousseau to Moultou, 17 February 1763, CC, 2489, 195–196; Moultou to Rousseau, 23 March 1763, CC, XV, 316–317.

99. Antoine-Jacques Roustan to Rousseau, 20 July 1762, CC, XII, 60–61; Roustan, *Offrande aux autels de la patrie, contenant la défense du Christianisme, ou réfutations du Contrat Social, etc.* (Amsterdam, 1764).

100. Jacques-François Deluc to Rousseau, 24 September 1762, CC, XIII, 102–104; Syndic Jean Cramer's account of a meeting with Deluc, 28 January 1763, CC, XV, 363–374; Jacques-François Deluc to Rousseau, 19 February 1763, CC, XV, 210.

101. Jacques-François Deluc, *Observations sur les savans incrédules et sur quelques-uns de leurs écrits* (Geneva, 1762), 275.

102. Moultou to Rousseau, 18 June 1762, CC, XI, 109.

103. Jacques-François Deluc to Rousseau, 10 November 1762, CC, XIV, 24; Rousseau to Jacques-François Deluc, 18 November 1762, CC, XIV, 66. AdG RC 263, 153, 29 April 1763.

104. Jacques-François Deluc to Rousseau, 23 November 1762, CC, XIV, 86.

105. CC, XVI, 2653.

106. Jacques-François Deluc to Moultou, 25 May 1763, CC, XVI, 244; Rousseau to Marc Chappuis, 26 May 1763, CC, XVI, 245–247.

107. Jacques-François Deluc et al., *Représentation des citoyens et bourgeois de Genève au Premier Syndic de cette République; avec Réponses du Conseil à ces representations* ([Geneva], 1763), 16–17, 125.

108. Ibid., 40, 47, 49.

109. Rousseau to Jacques-François Deluc, 25 June 1763, CC, XVI, 335; Rousseau to Moultou, 7 July 1763, CC, XVII, 24.

110. Rousseau to Moultou, CC, XIV, 101.

111. Rousseau to François-Henri d'Ivernois, 22 August 1763, CC, XVII, 171.

112. Rousseau to Moultou, 6 July 1762, CC, XI, 221; CC, XIII, 218; Rousseau to Moultou, 21 October 1762, CC, XIII, 233.

113. Rousseau, *Lettres*, OC, III, 687; MW, IV, 1.

114. Jacques-François Deluc to Rousseau, 12 September 1764, CC, XXI, 137.

115. Rousseau, *Confessions*, OC, I, 610.

116. Jacques-François Deluc to Rousseau, 12 October 1764, CC, XXI, 247; Rousseau to Jacques-François Deluc, 22 November 1764, CC, XXII, 105.

117. Jacques-François Deluc et al., *Réponse aux Lettres écrites de la campagne* (n.p., 1764), 184.

118. Rousseau to Jacques-François Deluc, 24 November 1764, CC, XXII, 110.

119. Rousseau, *Contrat social*, bk. III, chap. 4; *The Social Contract and Other Later Political Writings*, 90; *Lettres*, OC, III, 837–838.

120. Rousseau, *Letters*, MW, IV, 212–213.

121. Rousseau, *Letters*, MW, IV, 214.

122. Rousseau, *Lettres*, OC, III, 705; *Letters*, MW, IV, 30.

123. Rousseau, *Lettres*, OC, III, 866–867.

124. Rousseau to Jacques-François Deluc, 16 January 1763, CC, XIX, 36.

125. Rousseau to Lenieps, 18 March 1764, CC, XIX, 229.

126. Rousseau, *Histoire de Genève*, in *Œuvres complètes de Rousseau*, ed. Michel Launay (Paris, 1967–1971), III, 389.

127. Ibid., III, 396.

128. Rousseau, *Lettres*, OC, III, 698.

129. Ibid., OC, III, 704–705.

130. Ibid., OC, III, 717.

131. Ibid., OC, III, 801–802; *Letters*, MW, IV, 188.

132. Ibid., OC, III, 697.

133. Ibid., OC, III, 706.

134. Ibid., OC, III, 788.

135. Jacques-François Deluc et al., *Représentations des citoyens et bourgeois de Genève*, 42; *Réponse aux Lettres écrites de la campagne*, 30–32.

136. Jacques-François Deluc to Rousseau, 24 September 1762, CC, XIII, 102–105.

137. Rousseau to Jacques-François Deluc, 28 October 1754, CC, III, 78; Jacques-François Deluc to Rousseau, 24 January 1755, CC, III, 94.

138. Jacques-François Deluc to Rousseau, 2 May 1763, CC, XVI, 136; Rousseau to Jacques-François Deluc, 12 May 1763, CC, XVI, 171.

139. Jacques-François Deluc to Moultou, 18 May 1763, CC, XVI, 202.

140. Jacques-François Deluc et al., *Réponse aux Lettres écrites de la campagne*, 54.

141. Rousseau to Lenieps, 8 February 1765, CC, XXIII, 338–339.

142. Rousseau to Guillaume-Antoine Deluc and Jean-André Deluc, 24 February 1765, CC, XXIV, 87.

143. Guillaume-Antoine Deluc to Rousseau, 8 February 1765, CC, XXIII, 320–321; Guillaume-Antoine Deluc to Rousseau, 19 November 1765, XXVII, 279.

144. Rousseau to Lenieps, December 1751, CC, II, 175–178; *Confessions*, OC, I, 373–374. On Mussard, see Leigh, "Notes explicatives," in Rousseau, CC, II, 177.

145. Lenieps to Rousseau, 2 August 1763, CC, XVIII, 120–125; Lenieps to Du Crest, 20 April 1731, AdG Procès criminels 7602 bis.

146. AdG, Registres de Conseil, 237, 22–23.

147. Lenieps to Rousseau, 30 October 1766, CC, XXXI, 97.

148. Compare Jacques-François Deluc's *Réponse aux Lettres écrites de la campagne*, 18–19, 38, with his *Représentations des citoyens et bourgeois de Genève*, 59, and with Micheli's *Supplication avec Supplément*, 98–99.

149. Jacques-François Deluc to Rousseau, 6 December 1754, CC, III, 64–65; Rousseau to Jacques-François Deluc, III, 124.

150. Lenieps to Rousseau, 30 October 1766, CC, XXXI, 97.

151. Lenieps to Rousseau, 16 November 1762, CC, XIV, 57–58, and 24 May 1763, XIV, 237–240.

152. Lenieps to Rousseau, 9 June 1763, CC, XVI, 294.

153. Lenieps to Rousseau, 4 August 1764, CC, XXI, 5.

154. Lenieps to Rousseau, 27 July 1763, CC, XVIII, 94.

155. Candaux in Rousseau, OC, III, clxxxv–clxxxvii.

156. Toussaint-Pierre Lenieps, *Réponse aux cinq lettres écrites de la campagne dont le résultat est d'établir dans le Petit Conseil de Genève le pouvoir négatif qui anéantiroit la souveraineté des Citoïens & Bourgeois ou ce qui est le même les Assemblées Générales plus àpropos* (Ripaille, Savoy, 1763), 1, 6, 11, in Lenieps papers, Archives de l'Arsenal. On Bern, see Béla Kapossy, "Neo-Roman Republicanism and Commercial Society: The Example of Eighteenth-Century Berne," in Martin van Gelderen and Quentin Skinner, *Republicanism: A Shared European Heritage* (Cambridge, 2002), 2 vols., II, 226–247.

157. Lenieps, *Réponse aux cinq lettres écrites de la campagne*, 14, 16.

158. Rousseau to Lenieps, 23 July 1763, CC, XVII, 2837.

159. Lenieps to Rousseau, 24 May 1763, CC, XV, 239.

160. Rousseau to Lenieps, 26 October 1758, CC, V, 189.

161. Leigh, "Le *Contrat social*, œuvre genevoise?" and comments in CC, XIV, 241, and XVIII, 323.

162. Rousseau, *Lettres*, OC, III, 837.

163. Ibid., OC, III, 825–826.

164. Ibid., OC, III, 841.

165. Ibid., OC, III, 813.

166. Ibid., OC, III, 838.

167. Ibid., OC, III, 843.

168. Ibid., OC, III, 854.

169. Ibid., OC, III, 850.

170. Ibid., OC, III, 837–838.

171. Ibid., OC, III, 842; *Letters*, IV, 255.

172. Ibid., OC, III, 703–705.

173. Ibid., OC, III, 809.

174. Ibid., OC, III, 844.

175. Ibid., OC, III, 342.

176. Rousseau, *The Confessions of J.-J. Rousseau, part the second*, II, 324–325.

177. Ibid., OC, III, 843.

178. Paul Chappuis to Rousseau, 20 February 1765, CC, XXIV, 52–53.

179. Rousseau to Victor Riquetti, marquis de Mirabeau, 26 July 1767, CC, XXXIII, 238–242.

180. Vernet to Abbé N.-C.-J. Trublet, 9 January 1765, CC, XXIII, 72.

181. Moultou to Leonhard Usteri, 29 October 1763, CC, XVIII, 80.

182. Moultou to Rousseau, 6 March 1765, CC, XXIV, 149–150. Moultou noted that "Hume est un grand homme, mais entre nous, je le crois peu républicain."

183. Voltaire, *Civil War of Geneva*, 2–3.

184. Ibid., 15.

185. Ibid., 59. Cardinal Alberoni had tried to take the republic of San Marino in 1739.

186. Jean-Jacques de Chapeaurouge, *Projet d'arrangement et de conciliation* (Geneva, [22 February] 1768) (RIV 1054).

187. Voltaire, *Civil War of Geneva*, 63.

188. Voltaire to Pierre Michel Hennin, 27 February 1766 (letter D13185), *Correspondence and Related Documents*, XXX: *January–September 1766*, 113.

189. Charles Bonnet to Albrecht von Haller, 26 March 1765, CC, XXIV, 309–311; Leigh, "Notes explicatives," CC, XXVII, 280.

190. Etienne-Jean de Guimard des Rocheretz, baron de Montpéroux, to César-Gabriel de Choiseul, duc de Praslin, 29 December 1764, CC, 3084, 325.

191. R. A. Leigh, "Remarque," CC, 4153, 232.

192. Letter from Jean-Pierre Crommelin to Council of Twenty-Five, 28 February 1765, CC, 4100, 146–147.

193. D'Ivernois, *An Historical and Political View of the Constitution and Revolutions of Geneva*, 190–191.

194. Pierre Michel Hennin, *Discours de Monsieur Hennin, Résident de Sa Majesté Très-Chrétienne près la République de Genève, Prononcé au M. C. le Samedi 28 Décembre 1765* (Geneva, 1765), 2.

195. Pierre Michel Hennin to Choiseul, 6 January 1766, CC, XXVIII, 161–162; Hennin to Choiseul, 1 February 1766, CC, XXVIII, 264–265.

196. Hennin to Choiseul, 8 January 1766, CC, XXVIII, 169.

197. Jean-Pierre-François de Ripert, marquis de Monclar, to Jacques-François Deluc, December 1763/January 1764, CC, appendix 328, 268.

198. Anon., *Précis impartial de nos divisions* (Geneva, [December] 1765), 4.

199. [Jean-Robert Tronchin, Jean Cramer, Jean-Louis du Pan], *Lettres populaires ou l'on examine la Réponse aux Lettres écrites de la campagne* (Geneva, 1765); [Jean Cramer], *Lettre a l'auteur de la Gazette d'Amsterdam* (Geneva, 1765), 4–11; [Jean Cramer], *Suite des Lettres populaires* (Geneva, 1765); [Jean-Pierre Sartoris], *Observations sur le chef des représentations de l'année 1763 concernant les emprisonnemens* (Geneva, 1765); Antoine Charles Esmangart de Bournonville to Pierre de Buisson, chevalier de Beauteville, 10 June 1766, CC, XXX, 397.

200. Anon., *Sentiment des jurisconsultes* ([Geneva], [1765]), 1–4 (RIV, 813); Théodore Tronchin to Charles Bonnet, 21 August 1766, CC, XXX, 265–266.

201. D'Ivernois, *An Historical and Political View of the Constitution and Revolutions of Geneva*, 186–187, referring to Voltaire's letter to François-Henri d'Ivernois, 27 November 1765 (letter D13008), *Correspondence and Related Documents*, XXIX: *April–December 1765*, 421–422.

202. Bonnet to Haller, 22 July 1766, CC, XXX, 145. Bonnet was shocked that Hume had once placed Rousseau in the same rank as Grotius and Montesquieu; see Bonnet to John Turberville Needham, 5 September 1766, CC, XXX, 321–322.

203. Anon., *Réponses aux Lettres populaires. Seconde partie. Sur les emprisonnemens* ([Geneva], 1765), 265 (RIV, 865).

204. Anon., *Le Droit négatif* ([Geneva], [1765]), 2, 4, 19–20; Jean-André Deluc, *Les Représentations de 1763 et 1765 envisagées sous leur vrai point de vue* ([Geneva], 1765).

205. Jean-André Deluc et al., *Très-humble & très-respectueuse Représentation à Messieurs les Sindics, remise le Samedi 25 Janvier 1766* (Geneva, 1766), 3.

206. D'Ivernois, *An Historical and Political View of the Constitution and Revolutions of Geneva*, 193–194.

207. Council of Twenty-Five to duc de Praslin, 6 January 1766, cited in André Gür, "La négociation de l'Édit du 11 mars 1768, d'après le journal de Jean-André Deluc et la correspondance de Gédéon Turrettini," *Revue suisse d'histoire* 17 (1967), 166–217, n. 23.

208. Pierre de Buisson, chevalier de Beauteville, to Etienne François de Choiseul-Stainville, duc de Choiseul, 30 May 1766, CC, XXIX, 229–235.

209. Hennin to Voltaire, 1 March 1766 (letter D13191), *Correspondence and Related Documents, XXX: January–September 1766*, 114.

210. Voltaire to Hennin, [possible date: 12 July 1766] (letter D13408), *Correspondence and Related Documents, XXX: January–September 1766*, 309.

211. Anon., *Lettre d'un citoyen de Genève à un autre citoyen. Le 15 Février 1768*, 72–73.

212. Ibid., 14, RIV 1095.

213. Jean-Jacques de Chapeaurouge, *Exposé de la conduite des syndics et conseil de la république de Genève* (Geneva, 1767), 7–8, 17, 24–27.

214. Anon., *Adresse aux Augustes Puissances Garantes*, 2 (Geneva, 1766); Jean-André Deluc et al., *Très-humble & très-respectueuse Représentation à Messieurs les Sindics, remise le 15 Janvier 1766* (Geneva, 1766), 3.

215. D'Ivernois, *An Historical and Political View of the Constitution and Revolutions of Geneva*, 219.

216. Anon., *Traduction d'une Lettre de Leurs Excellences de Zurich du 16 Décembre 1765*, 3; *Traduction d'une Lettre écrite au nom commun de L. L. E. E. de Zurich & de Berne du 8 Janvier 1766*, 7.

217. Anon., *La Lettre d'acceptation du louable Canton de Berne* (9 January 1766); Beauteville, *Déclaration du 25 Juillet 1766*, 23.

218. Pierre de Buisson to Rousseau, 9 May 1766, CC, XXIX, 180–181.

219. Pierre de Buisson, Heinrich Escher, Jean-Conrad Heidegger, Karl Ludwig Ougspurger, Johann Rudolf Sinner, *Déclaration des Médiateurs du 25 juillet 1766*, CC, XXX, 400–401.

220. Pierre de Buisson to Etienne François de Choiseul-Stainville, duc de Choiseul, 21 June 1766, CC, XIX, 272–273.

221. Beauteville et al., *Projet de Règlement de l'Illustre Médiation, pour la pacification des dissentions de la République de Genève* (Geneva, 1768), 10–18, 32–33.

222. D'Ivernois, *An Historical and Political View of the Constitution and Revolutions of Geneva*, 224–227.

223. Voltaire to Pierre de Buisson, 19 January 1767 (letter D13865), *Correspondence and Related Documents, XXXI: October 1766–March 1767*, 274.

224. Choiseul-Stainville to Pierre de Buisson, 26 November 1766, CC, XXXI, 359; Pierre de Buisson to Choiseul-Stainville, 5 December 1766, CC, XXXI, 360–361.

225. Etienne Clavière to Jacques Roux, 13 October 1766, BdG, Ms. Fr. 2486.

226. State Papers Foreign, France: NA, PRO SP 78/271.

227. D'Ivernois, *An Historical and Political View of the Constitution and Revolutions of Geneva*, 258.

228. William Henry Nassau de Zuylestein, 4th Earl of Rochford, to William Petty, 2nd Earl of Shelburne, 19 November 1767, NA, PRO Secretaries of State: State Papers Foreign, France: SP 78/273.

229. Charles Bonnet to Antoine Charles Esmangart de Bournonville, 17 January 1767, CC, XXXII, 51.

230. Jean-André Deluc et al., *Très-humble & très-respectueuse remontrance des citoyens et bourgeois de Genève aux Magnifiques Seigneurs Sindics & Conseil. Remise à Messieurs les Sindics par la généralité des citoyens & bourgeois représentans, le 16 Octobre 1767* (Geneva, 1767), 3–21.

231. Clavière to Jacques Roux, 4 October 1766, BdG, Ms. Fr. 2486.

232. Voltaire to Hennin, 30 November 1766 (letter D13702), *Correspondence and Related Documents, XXXI: October 1766–March 1767*, 113.

233. Abraham Freudenreich to Jean-Louis Dupan, 14 July 1767, cited in Gür, "La négociation de l'Édit du 11 mars 1768," 182.

234. Jean-André Deluc to Jacques Necker, 1 May 1767, BdG, Ms. Fr. 2465, fols. 74–75.

235. Necker to Jean-André Deluc, 10 August 1767, BdG, Ms. Fr. 2465, fols. 82–84. Some représentants, and particularly Clavière, were skeptical about Necker's role: "Hier, je vis à la précipitée une lettre de N. Si cet homme a eu dessein d'agir & de ne rien faire, d'écrire & de ne rien dire, il a manifesté de grands talens. L'essentiel de sa lettre est une réflexion qu'il faut sur ce que la Cour voudroit se retirer. Il croit qu'en effet la Cour seroit charmée de se débarrasser d'une chose qui ne fait que lui donner des tracasseries sans profits." Clavière to Théodore Rilliet and Jean-André Deluc, 21 July 1767, BdG, Ms. Fr. 2486.

236. D'Ivernois, *An Historical and Political View of the Constitution and Revolutions of Geneva*, 245.

237. As the supporter of the magistrates Jean Cramer, put it, "C'est Cologny qui gouverne la Ville, là Rilliet, [Jean-André] Deluc, Clavière, Flournoy, et Vieusseux décident tous les soirs, ce que la Ville devra faire le lendemain." Ms. Cramer 97, journal, 30 May 1767, cited in Gür, "La négociation de l'Édit du 11 mars 1768," 216.

238. Jacques Vieusseux was the uncle of Pierre-François Vieusseux, who married Clavière's only daughter, and was the father of Jeanne-Pernette-Suzanne, who had married into the Rilliet family in 1761. Jean-André Deluc had married Françoise Vieusseux in 1752. See Théodore Rivier-Rose, *La famille Rivier (1595 à nos jours)* (Lausanne, 1916), 95–116. I would like to thank Jean-Marc Rivier for sending me a copy of this rare and useful work.

239. Jean Roget to Samuel Romilly, 18 February 1783, in *Lettres de Jean Roget*, 297–301.

240. Théodore Rilliet, *Solution générale ou lettres à Monsieur Covelle le fils, citoyen de Genève, pour servir de réponse aux observations* (Geneva, 1765), 30–48, 73–81.

241. [Jean-Louis de Lolme], *Lettre d'un Ami, traduite de l'Anglois* (Geneva, 1767).

242. Anon., *Mémoire. Pour servir de Réponse à la Patrie qui concerne le Droit Négatif dans celui qui fut adressé le 4e Avril à Mgr. le Duc de Choiseul par les LL. CC. de Zurich & de Berne* (Geneva, 1767).

243. D'Ivernois, *An Historical and Political View of the Constitution and Revolutions of Geneva*, 315.

244. Clavière to Roux, 1 October 1766 and 3 October 1766; Clavière to Rilliet, 11 July 1767, BdG, Ms. Fr. 2486.

245. Pierre de Buisson to Choiseul-Stainville, 26 June 1766, CC, XXX, 397–398.

246. Pierre de Buisson to Antoine Charles Esmangart de Bournonville, 2 July 1766, CC, XXX, 399–400.

247. Clavière to Roux, 8 October 1766, BdG, Ms. Fr. 2486; Jean-André Deluc to François-Henri d'Ivernois, Rilliet de Saussure, and Clavière, 14 July 1767, BdG, Ms. Fr. 2475, fols. 101–103.

248. D'Ivernois, *An Historical and Political View of the Constitution and Revolutions of Geneva*, 237.

249. Clavière to Rilliet and Jean-André Deluc, 17 July 1767, BdG, Ms. Fr. 2486.

250. Clavière to Roux, 6 October 1766, BdG, Ms. Fr. 2486. Clavière noted that Shelburne was unfortunately dining with Jean-Robert Tronchin in London.

251. Jean-André Deluc to François-Henri d'Ivernois, 16 July 1767; Rilliet to Clavière, 16 July 1767, BdG, Ms. Fr. 2475, fols. 105–107.

252. Rilliet to Clavière, 17 July 1767, BdG, Ms. Fr. 2475, fols. 108–109.

253. Ibid., fols. 109–112.

254. Rilliet to Clavière, 18 July 1767, BdG, Ms. Fr. 2475, fol. 113.

255. Rilliet to Clavière, 22 July 1767, BdG, Ms. Fr. 2475, fols. 115–118.

256. Jean-André Deluc to Jacques-François Deluc, 25 July 1767, BdG, Ms. Fr. 2475, fols. 118–119.

257. Rilliet to Clavière, 31 July 1767, BdG, Ms. Fr. 2475, fol. 124.

258. D'Ivernois, *An Historical and Political View of the Constitution and Revolutions of Geneva*, 291.

259. Pierre Michel Hennin complained to Charles Georges Le Roy, 18 April 1767, CC, XXX, 27: "Les Representans nous ont laissé fort tranquiles. Ils continuent à faire montre d'un orgueil sombre et ridicule dont sans doute ils seront dupes. Je voudrois bien que vous pussiez venir voir de près, ce que c'est qu'une Republique et ce peuple qu'un méchant fol [Rousseau] a exalté pour se targuer de n'être pas né sujet d'un Prince."

260. Clavière to Rilliet and Jean-André Deluc, 21 July 1767, BdG, Ms. Fr. 2486.

261. D'Ivernois, *An Historical and Political View of the Constitution and Revolutions of Geneva*, 315–324.

262. Jean-Pierre Bérenger, *Le Natif ou letters de Théodore et d'Annette* (Geneva, 1767), 53–53.

263. Clavière to Rilliet and Jean-André Deluc, 14 July 1767, BdG, Ms. Fr. 2486.

264. Jean-André Deluc, "Projet de conciliation pour la République de Genève," BdG, Ms. Fr. 2475, fols. 100–101.

265. Rousseau to François-Henri d'Ivernois, 29 January 1768, CC, XXXV, 62–65.

266. [Jean-André Deluc], *Journal de ce qui s'est passé d'intéressant à Genève à la fin de 1767 et au commencement de 1768, pour servir à l'histoire de l'Edit du 11e mars 1768* (Geneva, 1781), 2.

267. Ibid., 49–50, 104.

268. Bonnet to Haller, 4 February 1767, CC, XXXII, 98–99.

269. D'Ivernois, *An Historical and Political View of the Constitution and Revolutions of Geneva*, 346–347n.

270. [Jean-André Deluc], *Journal de ce qui s'est passé d'intéressant à Genève*, 46–48, 81–82, 105–110.

271. Ibid., 119–148.

272. Ibid., 60–66.

273. D'Ivernois, *An Historical and Political View of the Constitution and Revolutions of Geneva*, 238.

274. Jean-Jacques de Chapeaurouge, *Edit du 11 Mars 1768* [Geneva, 1768].

275. D'Ivernois, *An Historical and Political View of the Constitution and Revolutions of Geneva*, 363.

276. Beauteville, Escher de Keffiken, Heidegger, Ougspurger, Sinner, *Nous soussignés Ministres Plénipotentiaires . . . A Genève le 25 juillet 1766* (Geneva, 1766) (RIV 942).

277. Gédéon Turrettini to Friedrich von Sinner, 15 March 1768 and 22 March 1768, cited in "La négociation de l'Édit du 11 mars 1768," 203–208.

278. Anon., *Lettre d'un citoyen de Genève à un autre citoyen. Le 15 Février 1768*, 5–10.

279. Haller to Bonnet, 16 February 1768, CC, XXXV, 132.

280. [Jean-André Deluc], *Journal de ce qui s'est passé d'intéressant à Genève*, 283–285.

281. Jean-Louis Dupan to Abraham Freudenreich, 25 and 26 February 1765, XXIV, 101.

282. Rousseau, *Contrat social*, bk. III, chap. 6: in monarchies, "un homme d'un vrai mérite est presque aussi rare dans le ministère, qu'un sot à la tête d'un gouvernement républicain"; Rousseau to Moultou [February 1763], CC, XV, 192–193.

283. Rousseau to Pierre de Buisson, 23 February 1766, CC, XXVIII, 321–322.

284. François-Henri d'Ivernois to Rousseau, 5 January 1767, CC, XXXII, 21–22; Rousseau to François-Henri d'Ivernois, 7 February 1767, CC, XXXII, 116–117.

285. Rousseau to François-Henri d'Ivernois, 31 January 1767, CC, XXXII, 89–92.

286. Jean Jacques Rousseau to François-Henri d'Ivernois, 6 April 1767, CC, XXXIII, 11–12.

287. Rousseau to François-Henri d'Ivernois, 9 February 1768, CC, XXXV, 100–107: "Le P.C. tend fortement à la plus dure Aristocratie. Les maximes des Répresentans vont par leurs conséquences, non seulement à l'excés, mais à l'abus de la Démocratie: cela est certain. Or il ne faut ni l'un l'autre dans votre Rép[ubliqu]e; vous le sentez tous. Entre le P.C. violent aristocrate, et le C.G., Democrate effréné, où trouver une force intermédiaire qui contienne l'un et l'autre, et soit la Clef du Gouvernement. Elle existe, cette force; c'est le C. des 200. Mais pourquoi cette force ne va-t-elle pas à Son but? Pourquoi le 200, au lieu de contenir le 25, en est-il l'esclave? N'y a-t-il pas moyen de corriger cela? Voilà précisément de quoi il S'agit."

288. Rousseau to François-Henri d'Ivernois, 23 February 1768, CC, XXXV, 141–143; Rousseau to François-Henri d'Ivernois, 8 March 1768, CC, XXXV, 187–189.

289. Rousseau to François-Henri d'Ivernois, 24 March 1768, CC, XXXV, 220–222.

290. Rousseau to Moultou, 7 March 1768, CC, XXXV, 179–182.

291. Anon., *La Vérité, Ode à Mr. De Voltaire, suivie d'une dissertation historique & critique sur le gouvernement de Genève & ses révolutions* (London, 1765), iv, viii, 16, 143, 145.

292. Moultou to Voltaire, ca. 5 February 1768, in Voltaire, *Correspondence and Related Documents, XXXIII: January–July 1768*, 89–90.

293. Charles-Marie de la Condamine to Jean-André Deluc, 13 February 1765, CC, XXIV, 4. See also Jean-Robert Tronchin to Charles Pictet, 2 March 1765, CC, XXIV, 122–123, stating that the *Contrat social* was the most dangerous of books in challenging the basis of Geneva's settled constitution.

294. Jean-André Deluc, *Lettres sur l'histoire physique de la terre, adressées à M. Le Professeur Blumenbach, renfermant de nouvelles Preuves géologiques et historiques de la Mission divine de Moyse* (Paris, 1798), xcvii–xcix, cix–cxi.

295. Anon., *Lettre d'un citoyen de Genève à un autre citoyen. Le 15 Février 1768*, 16.

296. Anon., *Lettre d'un citoyen à Jean-Jacques Rousseau* (n.d. [1765]), 13; Anon., *Etat veritable de nos dissensions, ou letter à Mr. le B. De . . .* ([Geneva], [January] 1766), 13–14.

297. D'Ivernois, *An Historical and Political View of the Constitution and Revolutions of Geneva*, 161–163, 176–177.

298. [Jean Cramer], *Suite des Lettres populaires, où l'on éclaircit divers faits répandus dans la Réponse aux Lettres écrites de la campagne* ([Geneva], 1765), 5, 39, 78.

299. D'Ivernois, *An Historical and Political View of the Constitution and Revolutions of Geneva*, 294–295, 330–331.

300. [Jean-Louis de Lolme], *Purification des trois points de droit souillés par un anonyme ou réponse à l'Examen des trois points de droit traités dans les Mémoires des Représentans du 19 mai et 16 octobre* ([Geneva], [1767]); *Réflexions politiques et critiques, par un citoyen représentant, sur le Projet d'arrangement* ([Geneva], [25 January 1768]). On de Lolme's impact, see d'Ivernois, *An Historical and Political View of the Constitution and Revolutions of Geneva*, 250–252.

301. De Lolme, *Purification*, 30–48, 58–61.

302. Jacques-Pierre Brissot, *Mémoires, 1754–1793*, I, 296. Clavière was still anticipating repayment in 1774; see Clavière to Jean-André Deluc, 16 June 1774, BdG, Ms. Fr. 2463, fols. 96–99.

303. Brissot, *Philadelphien à Genève*, 220; citing Rousseau to François Henri d'Ivernois, 24 March 1768, CC, XXXV, 220–222.

304. William Constable to Rousseau, 1770, CC, XXXVIII, 82–84: "At Geneva I saw many people who did themselves the honour to call themselves your friends, all did justice to your merit, few spoke of you without tears, & [I] own I was surprised, what was become of your enemies. The greatest only gently suggested a difference in opinion."

305. Brissot, *Mémoires*, I, 277–279.

CHAPTER 4. GENEVA AND BRITAIN

1. Albin Mazon, *Histoire de Soulavie: Naturaliste, diplomate, historien* (Paris, 1893), 2 vols., I, 31–50.

2. Martin J. S. Rudwick, *Bursting the Limits of Time: The Reconstruction of Geohistory in the Age of Revolution* (Chicago, 2005), 129–131.

3. Raphael Melia, *A Treatise on Auricular Confession: Dogmatical, Historical & Practical* (Oxford, 1865), 90.

4. Soulavie, *Historical and Political Memoirs*, V, 183–186.

5. Ibid., 172.

6. Jean-Louis Giraud Soulavie to Benjamin Franklin, 20 May 1782, BFP.

7. Soulavie, *Historical and Political Memoirs*, V, 160–163 (citing the *Courier de l'Europe*, Friday, 3 August 1781, vol. X, 76). See also "Sur les anciens projets des anglais de changer en république nos provinces méridionales protestantes," *Journal de Paris*, 26 juin 1782, no. 177, 715.

8. Soulavie, *Historical and Political Memoirs*, V, 166–172.

9. Ibid., V, 173. Lucas de Montigny castigated Soulavie for having "made a practice of fabricating books and documents collected by all sorts of means . . . making up works . . . to which he affixed the names of pretended writers who never wrote a line of them." This was a nice irony coming from Mirabeau's biographer. Lucas de Montigny, ed., *Mémoires biographiques, littéraires et politiques de Mirabeau, écrits par lui-même, par son père, son oncle et son fils adoptif* (Paris, 1841), 2nd ed., 8 vols., IV, 73–74.

10. Soulavie, *Historical and Political Memoirs*, V, 190–191.

11. Ibid., V, 194–195.

12. Ibid., V, 197–198.

13. Ibid., V, 207. For the impact of Soulavie's interpretation, see the review of his *Historical and Political Memoirs* in Tobias Smollett, ed., *The Critical Review; or, Annals of Literature; extended and improved by A Society of Gentlemen* (London, 1802), vol. XXXV, 23–38.

14. Anon., review of Brissot's *Philadelphien à Genève* in *Correspondance secrete, politique et littéraire, ou Mémoires pour servir à l'histoire des cours, des sociétés & de la littérature en France* (London, 1787–1790), 18 vols., XV, 74–78, 27 August 1783.

15. Achille-Nicolas Isnard, *Observations sur le principe qui a produit les revolutions de France, de Genève et d'Amérique dans le dix-huitième siècle* (Evreux, 1789), 4, 6, 18.

16. François Rodolphe de Weiss, *A prospect of the political relations which subsist between the French Republic and the Helvetick body* (London, 1794), 43.

17. Abbé Augustin Barruel, *Memoirs illustrating the history of Jacobitism* (Hartford, Conn., 1799), 4 vols., I, 114.

18. Ibid., 115–119.

19. Albert Sorel, *L'Europe et la Révolution française* (Paris, 1885–1904), 8 vols., I, 142–143.

20. Joseph Addison to James Dayrolle, 17 May 1717; Addison to Thomas Crawfurd, 27 May 1717; and Addison to Francis Manning, 14 October 1717, in *The Letters of Joseph Addison*, ed. Walter Graham (Oxford, 1941), 359–360, 361, 471.

21. Thomas Gray to Philip Gray, 25 October 1739, in *Correspondence of Thomas Gray, Volume I: 1734–1755*, ed. Paget Toynbee and Leonard Whibley (Oxford, 1935), I, 123–125.

22. David Mallet to Alexander Pope, June 1735, in *Correspondence of Alexander Pope, Volume III: 1729–1735*, ed. George Sherburn (Oxford, 1956), III, 457–467.

23. James Waldegrave to Thomas Pelham-Holles, 12 and 23 September 1737 and 4 October 1737, NA SP 78/216; Reed Browning, "Holles, Thomas Pelham-, duke of Newcastle

upon Tyne and first duke of Newcastle under Lyme (1693–1768)," *Oxford Dictionary of National Biography* (Oxford, 2004); Philip Woodfine, "Waldegrave, James, first Earl Waldegrave (1684–1741)," *Oxford Dictionary of National Biography.*

24. Luke Schaub to Pelham-Holles, 31 March 1737, Schaub to Harrington, 26 January, 1738, NA PRO, SP 78/217; Michel Amelot de Chaillou, marquis de Gournay, to Waldegrave, 5 June 1738, NA, PRO SP 78/215; Philip Woodfine, "Schaub, Sir Luke (1690–1758)," *Oxford Dictionary of National Biography.*

25. Syndics and Council of Geneva to Waldegrave, 2 July 1738, NA PRO, SP 78/218.

26. Pelham-Holles to Waldegrave, 31 July 1737, NA PRO 78/218.

27. Jean-Pierre Crommelin to Charles Lennox, 16 June and 26 June 1766, NA PRO, SP 78/270; Henry-Seymour Conway to Lennox, 1 April 1766, NA PRO SP 78/269; Clive Towse, "Conway, Henry Seymour (1719–1795)," *Oxford Dictionary of National Biography*; William C. Lowe, "Lennox, Charles, third duke of Richmond, third duke of Lennox, and duke of Aubigny in the French nobility (1735–1806)," *Oxford Dictionary of National Biography.*

28. Conway to Lennox, 9 May 1766, NA PRO, SP 78/270; Crommelin to Conway, 16 June, 1766, NA PRO, SP 78/270; Lennox to Conway, 22 June 1766, NA PRO, SP 78/270; Lennox to Conway, 9 July 1766, NA PRO, SP 78/270.

29. Lennox to Conway, 23 January 1766, NA PRO, SP 78/269. Criticism of Pictet must have followed the letter from Pierre de Buisson, chevalier de Beauteville, to Etienne François de Choiseul-Stainville, duc de Choiseul, of 30 June 1766 (CC, XXX, 398–399), which complained: "Pictet cet agent amphibie d'Angleterre attire chez lui les principaux Représentans, et en les encourageant les excite à l'obstination. M. Northon, Ministre de Londres à Berne, intrigue en même tems."

30. Abraham Trembley to Lennox, 18 January 1766, NA PRO, SP 78/269.

31. James Hutton to Shelburne, 13 January 1767, CC, XXXII, 272–274. Others made similar appeals. See Jean Rodolphe de Vautravers to Shelburne, 12 February 1767, CC, XXXII, 283–284, writing that Shelburne was "known [for his] compassion for the oppressed assertors of their privileges and independence, in the ingenious, industrious, once flourishing protestant little republic of Geneva."

32. Hutton to Shelburne, 6 February 1767, CC, XXXII, 282–283.

33. Vautravers to Shelburne, 12 February 1767, CC, XXXII, 283–284.

34. Antoine-Jacques Roustan to Shelburne, 15 January 1767, CC, XXXII, 275–279.

35. Etienne Clavière to Jacques Roux, 6 October 1766, BdG, Ms. Fr. 2486; Pierre de Buisson to Choiseul-Stainville, 5 December 1766, CC, XXXI, 367–368.

36. Philip Stanhope to William Pitt, 3 September 1763, NA PRO 30/70/3/117; KCRO, copy of letters from Lord Stanhope to William Pitt (later Earl of Chatham) and one letter to Hon. Wm. Pitt, U1590/C18, 1757–1776; letters from Lord Stanhope to various correspondents, U1590/C19, 1740–1780.

37. Grizel Stanhope, Countess Stanhope, to David Hume, 12 September 1766, in *The Letters of David Hume, Volume II,* ed. J. Y. T. Greig (Oxford, 1932), II, 444–445.

38. Stanhope to Pitt, 18 April 1766, NA PRO 30/70/3/127.

39. Stanhope to Pitt, 2 February 1767, NA PRO 30/70/3/136.

40. Stanhope to Pitt, 19 December 1766, NA PRO 30/70/3/135.

41. Pierre de Buisson to Choiseul-Stainville, 30 May 1766, CC, XXIX, 229–235.
42. William Henry Nassau de Zuylestein, 4th Earl of Rochford, to Shelburne, 22 January 1768 and 11 February 1768, NA PRO, SP 78/274.
43. John Turberville Needham to Charles Bonnet, 16 August 1766, CC, XXX, 253–255.
44. James Boswell to John Wilkes, 13 July 1765, *Letters of James Boswell, Volume I: 29 July 1758–29 November 1777*, ed. C. Brewster Tinker (Oxford, 1924), 81–84.
45. Thomas Gray, *The poems and letters of Thomas Gray, with memoirs of his life and writings by W. Mason* (London, 1820), 299. See also Elizabeth Carter, *Memoirs of the life of Mrs. Elizabeth Carter, with a new edition of her poems; to whither are added, some miscellaneous essays in prose, together with her notes on the Bible* (London, 1808), 2 vols., I, 156–157.
46. David Hume to Comtesse de Bouffleurs, in *Private correspondence of David Hume with several distinguished persons, between the years 1761 and 1776* (London, 1820), 120: "I have read a great part of *Les Lettres de la Montagne*. The book in my humble opinion will not do credit to M. Rousseau though it might to another. I disapprove particularly of the seditious purpose of the last letters, which have succeeded but too well at Geneva: for the magistrates of that city, which the author had formerly celebrated with reason as one of the best governed in the world, are in mortal fear every hour of being massacred by the populace." Compare Arthur Young, *Letters concerning the present state of the French nation* (London, 1769), 357–359.
47. Arthur Young, *Political essays concerning the present state of the British Empire* (London, 1772), 21.
48. William Kenrick, "The Speech of Lord Lyttleton, on a motion made in the House of Lords for the Repeal of the Canada Bill, 17 May 1775," *London Review of English and Foreign Literature* (London, 1775), 384.
49. Ghita Stanhope, *The Life of Charles, Third Earl Stanhope* (London, 1914), 1–20.
50. Charles Stanhope, 3rd Earl, Miscellaneous political papers KCRO, U1590/C81 [n.d.]; Angela C. Bennett, "The Stanhopes in Geneva: A Study of an English Noble Family in Genevan Politics and Society, 1764–1774" (M.A. diss., University of Kent, 1992); G. M. Ditchfield, "Stanhope, Charles, third Earl Stanhope (1753–1816)," *Oxford Dictionary of National Biography*, online ed., January 2008.
51. Accounts of festivals etc. for Viscount Mahon as Commandeur du Noble Exercice de l'Arc and letter with diploma of Citizenship from Geneva, KCRO, U1590/C46, 1771–1795; Letters to the Earl of Shelburne regarding political matters, U1590/C56, 1778–1794; Letters and papers concerning Geneva, U1590/C66, 1774–1794; Copies of letters to M. le Sage at Geneva, U1590/C621776, 1786, 1795.
52. Adam Ferguson to William Robertson, 9 November 1774, in Voltaire, *Correspondence and Related Documents, XLI: June 1774–April 1775*, 192–194.
53. Ibid.
54. David Murray, 7th Viscount of Stormont, to Thomas Thynne, 3rd Viscount Weymouth, 11 September 1776, NA PRO, SP 78/299.
55. James Boswell, *The Scots Magazine* (Edinburgh, 1781), 605.
56. *The Annual Register, or a view of the politics, history, and literature, for the year 1782* (London, 1783), 208.

57. *British Magazine and Review* (London, 1782), 71.

58. Ibid., 463.

59. *The Town and country magazine, or universal repository of knowledge, instruction, and Entertainment, Volume XIV for the year 1782* (London, 1782), 665.

60. Jean Roget to Samuel Romilly, 18 May 1782, in *Lettres de Jean Roget*, 222. Romilly wrote about Geneva in the *Morning Chronicle* of 8 and 11 January 1782, and in the *St-James Chronicle* after 20 May; see *Lettres de Jean Roget*, 140, 237.

61. "British and Foreign History," in *The New annual register, or, General repository of history, politics, and littérature for the year 1782*, ed. Andrew Kippis (London, 1783), 63–64.

62. Thomas Robinson, 2nd Baron Grantham to John Stuart (Mountstuart, 4th Earl of Bute from 1794), 16 August 1782 (no. 7, draft), Bedfordshire and Luton Archives and Record Service, L 29/561/15.

63. Syndics and Council of Geneva to Thomas Townshend, 18 December 1782, PRO, FO 95/8/12; Syndics and Council of Geneva to George III, 18 December 1782, PRO, FO 95/8/12 f. 637.

64. John MacGregor, "Life of Jean Louis de Lolme," in De Lolme, *Constitution of England* (London, 1853), 2. De Lolme was reported by the Huguenot author Victor-Louis Dutens to have been secretary to the Abbé Mably, and in politics was associated with "Lord Lyttleton, Lord Abingdon, Lord North, Mr. Fox, Mr. Burke, and Colonel Barre." See Thomas Busby, *Arguments and Facts demonstrating that the Letters of Junius were written by John Lewis De Lolme . . . Accompanied with memoires of that "most ingenious foreigner"*(London, 1816), 12–13.

65. William Hamilton, "Observations on Mr. Rous' Claim Examined," *Intrepid Magazine* 1 (1784), 78: "Mr. De Lolme, originally of Geneva, long used to get his bread by writing, and finding no country where writing and printing are better trades, now living in this metropolis in the important character of editor of a newspaper, called *Le Courier de l'Europe*." This last claim was false.

66. Further French editions were published at Amsterdam (1774 and 1778), London (1785), Geneva (1787, 1788, 1789, 1790), Breslau (1791), and Paris (1819, 1822). German translations appeared in Amsterdam (1772), Leipzig (1776, 1848), and Altona [Hamburg] (1819), and a Spanish translation appeared at Oviedo in 1812.

67. Thomas George Western, *Commentaries on the Constitution and Laws of England, incorporated with the political text of the late J. L. De Lolme* (London, 1841), iii ("The excellent treatise of M. De Lolme upon the constitution of England, has long been acknowledged as the best written work upon that subject; indeed, some have gone so far as to say, that it deserved to be written in letters of gold"); Jean-Pierre Machelon, *Les idées politiques de Jean-Louis de Lolme* (Paris, 1969); Edouard Tillet, "La place ambiguë de Jean-Louis de Lolme dans la diffusion du modèle anglais de l'Ancien régime à la Révolution française," in Valérie Cossie, Béla Kapossy, and Richard Whatmore eds., *Genève lieu d'Angleterre, 1725–1814* (Geneva, 2009).

68. De Lolme, *Constitution of England* (London, 1775), 3.

69. De Lolme, *Constitution of England* (Dublin 1776), 262 (*Constitution of England*, London, 1817, 301–302).

70. De Lolme, *Constitution of England* (London 1778), 10 (1817, 250).

71. Ibid. (Dublin, 1776), 135 (1817, 249).

72. Ibid. (London, 1781), 100 (1817, 96).

73. Ibid. (London, 1775), 223 (1817, 238–239).

74. Ibid. (London, 1775), 230 (1817, 243–244).

75. Ibid. (Dublin, 1776), 134 (1817, 248).

76. Ibid. (London, 1775), 237 (1817, 251).

77. Ibid. (Dublin, 1776), 127 (1817, 240–241).

78. Ibid. (London, 1778), 100 (1817, 193).

79. Ibid. (London, 1775), 174 (1817, 194).

80. Ibid. (London, 1817), 192–193.

81. Ibid. (London, 1777), 231 (1817, 270).

82. Ibid. (London, 1775), 259 (1817, 270).

83. Ibid. (London, 1775), 348 (1817, 280).

84. Ibid. (London, 1775), 311 (1817, 315–316).

85. Ibid. (London 1777), 55 (1817, 59).

86. De Lolme, *A parallel between the English constitution and the former government of Sweden* (London, 1772), 30.

87. De Lolme, *Constitution of England* (London, 1778), 5 (1817, 239).

88. Ibid. (London, 1817), 325.

89. Ibid. (London, 1775), 8–12.

90. Ibid. (London, 1817), 159.

91. Ibid. (London, 1817), 36–38.

92. Ibid. (London 1775), 43 (1817, 42–43).

93. De Lolme, *A parallel between the English constitution and the former government of Sweden*, 8–18.

94. Ibid., 19–20.

95. Ibid., 23.

96. Ibid., 31–34.

97. Ibid., 24–25.

98. De Lolme, *Constitution of England* (Dublin, 1776), 35 (1817, 54).

99. Ibid. (London, 1775), 99 (1817, 84).

100. Ibid. (London, 1775), 95 (1817, 48–49, 80–81).

101. Ibid. (London, 1778), 37 (1817, 52).

102. Ibid. (London, 1817), 60–61.

103. Ibid. (Dublin, 1776), 9 (1817, 16).

104. Ibid. (London, 1777), 30 (1817, 28–29).

105. Ibid. (London, 1775), 27 (1817, 24).

106. Ibid. (London, 1817), 15–17.

107. Ibid. (London, 1775), 23 (1817, 19–20).

108. Ibid. (London, 1775), 25 (1817, 21–22).

109. Ibid. (London, 1777), 26 (1817, 25).

110. Ibid. (London, 1817), 33–34.

111. Ibid. (London, 1817), 44.

112. Ibid. (London, 1775), 285. De Lolme then noted, "I feel a kind of pleasure, I must confess, to observe on this occasion, that though I have been called by some an advocate for Power, I have carried my ideas of Liberty farther than many Writers who have mentioned that word with much enthusiasm" (1817, 288).

113. Ibid. (London, 1817), 57.

114. Ibid. (London, 1777), 62 (1817, 59).

115. Ibid. (Dublin, 1776), 173 (1817, 309).

116. Ibid. (London, 1775), 80 (1817, 64–68).

117. Ibid. (London, 1817), 85.

118. Ibid. (London, 1775), 86 (1817, 73).

119. Ibid. (London, 1775), 170 (1817, 191–192).

120. Ibid. (London, 1775), 176 (1817, 197).

121. Ibid. (London, 1775), 176 (1817, 198–199).

122. Ibid. (London, 1775), 188 (1817, 206–207).

123. Ibid. (London, 1775), 179 (1817, 199, 208).

124. Ibid. (London, 1775), 358 (1817, 205–209).

125. Ibid. (London, 1817), 280–281.

126. Ibid. (London, 1775), 108 (1817, 93).

127. Ibid. (London, 1775), 91 (1817, 77).

128. Ibid. (London 1775), 201 (1817, 219).

129. Ibid. (London, 1817), 253, 271, 329.

130. Ibid. (London, 1817), 60, 263.

131. Ibid. (London 1777), 326 (1817, 266).

132. Ibid. (London, 1817), 428–432.

133. Ibid. (London, 1817), 457–458.

134. Ibid. (London, 1777), 280 (1817, 319).

135. Ibid. (Dublin, 1776), 186 (1817, 330).

136. Ibid. (London, 1775), 333 (1817, 335–336).

137. John Lind, *Defence of Lord Pigot* (London, 1777), 234.

138. De Lolme, *Constitution of England* (London, 1775), 412 (1817, 459).

139. Ibid. (Dublin, 1776), 237 (1817, 460).

140. Ibid. (London, 1775), 434 (1817, 483).

141. Ibid. (London, 1817), 508.

142. MacGregor, "Life of Jean Louis de Lolme," 3.

143. De Lolme, *Essay on Constitutional Liberty, wherein the necessity of frequent elections of parliament is shewn to be superseded by the unity of the executive power* (London, 1780), 4–13.

144. Ibid., 10.

145. Ibid., 34.

146. Ibid., 53.

147. Ibid., 43–44.

148. Ibid., 53.

149. Roget to Romilly, 19 August 1781, in *Lettres de Jean Roget*, 58.

150. Ibid., 74.

151. Ibid., 82–84.
152. De Lolme, *An Essay containing a few strictures on the Union of Scotland with England; and on the present situation of Ireland* (London, 1787), 92; see also 19.
153. Ibid., 24.
154. Ibid., 42–43, 63.
155. Ibid., 62.
156. Ibid., 85.
157. Ibid., 85, 92.
158. Ibid., 81.
159. A list of de Lolme's varied publications, including some recently ascribed to him, can be found in the edition of de Lolme's *Constitution of England* edited by David Lieberman (Indianapolis, 2007).
160. De Lolme, *The Present National Embarrassment considered; containing a sketch of the political situation of the heir apparent, and of the legal claims of the parliament now assembled at Westminster* (London, 1789), 17, 38, 48, 67.

CHAPTER 5. COSMOPOLITAN VERSUS MERCANTILE EMPIRE

1. Jean-André Deluc, *Lettres sur quelques parties de la Suisse et sur le climat d'Hières* (The Hague, 1778), 156–157.
2. On the role of duties in Protestant natural-law thinking more broadly, see Knud Haakonssen, *Natural Law and Moral Philosophy: From Grotius to the Scottish Enlightenment* (Cambridge, 1996).
3. Jean-André Deluc, *Examen de la doctrine des Ecritures touchant la personne de Jésus-Christ, le rédemption et le péché originel, suivi d'un dissertation sur la religion naturelle* (Geneva, 1830), v–xii; *Lettre sur l'essence de la Doctrine de Jésus-Christ* (Brunswick, U.K., 1803).
4. Charles Bonnet, *Recherches philosophiques sur les preuves du christianisme* (Geneva, 1770), new ed.
5. Etienne Clavière to Jean-André Deluc, 3 February 1773, BdG, Ms. Fr. 2463, fol. 85.
6. Members of Jean-André Deluc's family had been visiting England since the 1750s (Jacques-François Deluc to Rousseau, 15 November 1758, CC, V, 225), but in 1773 Deluc had not learned the language, and problems were anticipated. See Clavière to Jean-André Deluc, 3 March 1773, BdG, Ms. Fr. 2463, fol. 87.
7. Joseph Priestley, *Experiments and observations on different kinds of air* (London, 1774), 219.
8. Theodore S. Feldman, "Deluc, Jean-André (1727–1817)," *Oxford Dictionary of National Biography*; Paul A. Tunbridge, "Jean André Deluc, FRS, 1727–1817," *Notes and Records of the Royal Society* 26 (1971), 15–33; Clavière to Jean-André Deluc, 21 December 1773, BdG, Ms. Fr. 2463, fols. 92–93. On Deluc in England and the court, see Clarissa Campbell Orr, "Queen Charlotte as Patron: Some Intellectual and Social Contexts," *Court Historian* 6, no. 3 (2001), 183–212, and "Charlotte of Mecklenburg-Strelitz, Queen of Great Britain and Electress of Hanover: Northern Dynasties and the

Northern Republic of Letters," in Clarissa Campbell Orr, ed., *Queenship in Europe, 1660–1815: The Role of the Consort* (Cambridge, 2004), 368–402.

9. Jean-Rodolphe Sinner, *Voyage historique et littéraire dans la Suisse occidentale, Volume 2* (Neuchâtel, 1781), 101–104.

10. Jean-André Deluc, *Lettres physiques et morales, sur les montagnes et sur l'histoire de la terre et de l'homme* (The Hague, 1778), 80–85, 163–180, 195–205.

11. Reviews of Deluc, *Lettres physiques et morales,* in *The Monthly review; or literary journal,* vol. 62 (London, 1780), 527–540, vol. 64, 481–492.

12. Jean-André Deluc to Jacques-François Deluc, 12 November 1768, BdG, Ms. Fr. 2461, "Sur la politique genevoise," fols., 23, 29.

13. Roget to Romilly, 14 July 1780, in *Lettres de Jean Roget,* 15–17.

14. Clavière to Jean-André Deluc, 3 March 1773, BdG, Ms. Fr. 2463, fol. 87.

15. D'Ivernois, *An Historical and Political View of the Constitution and Revolutions of Geneva,* 294–295.

16. Pierre de Buisson, chevalier de Beauteville, to Etienne François de Choiseul-Stainville, duc de Choiseul, 2 May 1766 (letter D13282), in Voltaire, *Correspondence and Related Documents, XXX: January–September 1766,* 205–207.

17. D'Ivernois, *An Historical and Political View of the Constitution and Revolutions of Geneva,* 22, 150, 294, 359.

18. Thourel, *Histoire de Genève,* III, 200.

19. [Jean-André Deluc], *Journal de ce qui s'est passé d'intéressant à Genève,* 163–168.

20. Pierre-Michel Hennin to César Gabriel de Choiseul, duc de Praslin, 25 May 1770 (letter D. app. 325. III), in Voltaire, *Correspondence and Related Documents, XXXVI: February–December 1770,* 484–485; Cornuaud, *Mémoires de Isaac Cornuaud,* 10–21.

21. Hennin to Voltaire, 16 February 1770 (letter D16151), *Correspondence and Related Documents, XXXVI: February–December 1770,* 29–30; Hennin to Voltaire, 17 June 1770 (letter D16421), *Correspondence and Related Documents, XXXVI: February–December 1770,* 259–260.

22. Jean-Pierre Bérenger, *Mémoire justificatif, pour les citoyens de Genève, connus sous le nom de Natifs* (n.p., 1770), 142–144.

23. Voltaire to Hennin, 16 February 1770 (letter D16155), *Correspondence and Related Documents, XXXVI: February–December 1770,* 32–33. See also Albert Choisy, "La prise d'armes de 1770 contre les natifs," *Étrennes genevoises 1925,* 47–77.

24. Hennin to Voltaire, 21 February 1770 (letter D16175), *Correspondence and Related Documents, XXXVI: February–December 1770,* 49–50.

25. *Journal des sçavans* 48, no. 2 (Amsterdam, October 1770), 292.

26. Cornuaud, *Mémoires de Isaac Cornuaud,* 53.

27. Thourel, *Histoire de Genève,* III, 207.

28. Jacques Mallet du Pan, *Compte rendu de la défense des citoyens bourgeois de Genève, adressé aux commissaires des citoyens représentants par un citoyen natif* (Geneva, 1771). Cornuaud called this work "the Bible of the Natifs." Appearing on 15 February 1771, it was burned before the end of the month as a seditious publication (Cornuaud, *Mémoires de Isaac Cornuaud,* 113).

29. Voltaire to Hennin, 19 May 1770 (letter D16349), _Correspondence and Related Documents_, XXXVI: _February–December 1770_, 202.

30. Voltaire to Hennin, 26 February 1770 (letter D16181), _Correspondence and Related Documents_, XXXVI: _February–December 1770_, 54–55.

31. Shelburne to Richard Price, 22 November 1786, in _The Correspondence of Richard Price, Volume III: February 1786–February 1791_, ed. William Bernard Peach (Durham, N.C., 1994), 86–87.

32. Anne-Robert-Jacques Turgot, "Réflexions rédigées à l'occasion du Mémoire remis par M. le Comte de Vergennes, sur la manière dont la France et l'Espagne doivent envisager les suites de la querelle entre la Grande-Bretagne et ses Colonies" (April 1776), in Ségur et al., _Politique de tous les cabinets de l'Europe_, III, 172–177; Turgot to Price, 22 March 1778, in Price, _Observations on the importance of the American Revolution_ (Dublin, 1785), 109–120: "The glory of arms is nothing to those who enjoy the happiness of living in peace."

33. Turgot, "Réflexions rédigées à l'occasion du Mémoire remis par M. le Comte de Vergennes," 190.

34. Ibid., 173.

35. Ibid., 174–180.

36. Ibid., 188–191.

37. Pierre-Samuel Dupont de Nemours, review of Gaillard's _Histoire de la rivalité de la France & de l'Angleterre_, in _Éphémérides du citoyen, ou bibliothèque raisonnée des sciences morales et politiques_, no. 1 (1771), 150; "Mémoire sur l'administration des finances de l'Angleterre depuis la paix," _Éphémérides du citoyen_, no. 4 (1769), 135–173; "Suite de l'histoire abrégée des finances de l'Angleterre," _Éphémérides du citoyen_, no. 5 (1769), 135–168; "Suite de l'histoire abrégée des finances de l'Angleterre," _Éphémérides du citoyen_, no. 7 (1769), 64–105; _De l'origine et progrès d'une science nouvelle_ (London, 1768), 25–30; review of Dickinson's _Lettres d'un fermier de Pensylvanie_, in _Éphémérides du citoyen_, no. 10 (1769), 97–98.

38. Dupont de Nemours, "De la république de Genève, & des troubles qui l'agitent," _Éphémérides du citoyen_ 1 (1770), 226–232, 239.

39. Ibid., 233–235.

40. Ibid., 242–252.

41. Hennin to Voltaire, 13 December 1775 (letter D19791), _Correspondence and Related Documents_, XLII: _May 1775–February 1776_, 286.

42. Hennin to Charles Gravier, comte de Vergennes, 19 December 1775 (letter D19803), in Voltaire, _Correspondence and Related Documents_, XLII: _May 1775–February 1776_, 295–296.

43. Victor de Riquetti, marquis de Mirabeau, _L'ami des hommes, ou Traité de la population_ (Avignon, 1758), 2nd part, new ed., 156–168.

44. Istvan Hont, "The 'Rich Country–Poor Country' Debate in Scottish Political Economy," _Jealousy of Trade: International Competition and the Nation-State in Historical Perspective_ (Cambridge, Mass., 2005), 267–324, and "The Rich Country–Poor Country Debate Revisited: The Irish Origins and French Reception of the Hume Paradox," in Margaret Schabas and Carl Wennerlind, eds., _David Hume's Political Economy_ (London, 2007), 222–342.

45. Roget to Romilly, January 1782, in *Lettres de Jean Roget*, 124.

46. Jacques-Antoine du Roveray, *Traduction des thèses philosophiques sur la patrie* (Geneva, 1767), 5–9, 19, 22.

47. Ibid., 10.

48. Ibid., 11, 16–17, 21.

49. Jacques-Antoine du Roveray to Gamaliel Benjamin Jaïn, 21 July 1769, CC, XXXVII, 115–116.

50. Powell McNutt, "Church and Society in Eighteenth-Century Geneva, 1700–1789," 211–225.

51. Bouchary, "Étienne Clavière d'après sa correspondance financière et politique," 13–20.

52. Clavière to Jean-André Deluc, 10 September 1773, BdG, Ms. Fr. 2463, fols. 90–91.

53. James Hutton to Shelburne, 6 February 1767, CC, XXXII, 282–283.

54. Clavière to Jean-André Deluc, 6 March 1774, BdG, Ms. Fr. 2463, fols. 96–99.

55. Clavière to Jean-André Deluc, 16 June 1774, BdG, Ms. Fr. 2463, fols. 105–106.

56. Clavière to Jean-André Deluc, 6 March 1774, BdG, Ms. Fr. 2463, fols. 96–99; Clavière to Jean-André Deluc, 17 April 1774, BdG, Ms. Fr. 2463, fols. 100–104. See also André Gür, "Quête de la richesse et critique des riches chez Etienne Clavière," in Jacques Berchtold and Michel Porret, eds., *Être riche au siècle de Voltaire: Actes du colloque de Genève, 18–19 juin 1994* (Geneva, 1996), 97–115.

57. Vergennes, "Mémoire de M. de Vergennes, à Louis XVI (Mars 1784)," *Politique de tous les cabinets de l'Europe*, III, 198–221.

58. Ibid., 201.

59. Ibid., 211–214.

60. Ibid., 201, 216–218; "Observations de M. de Vergennes, Sur le Coup de canon tiré sur l'Escaut (14 Novembre 1784)," 224–229.

61. Coxe, *Travels in Switzerland*, II, 349.

62. Etienne Clavière, *Reflexions politiques sur l'impôt proposé au Conseil Général* (26 December 1775), 14–16.

63. Clavière to Jean-André Deluc, 16–19 June 1774, BdG, Ms. Fr. 2463, fols. 106–108.

64. Clavière to Jean-André Deluc, 31 December 1775, BdG, Ms. Fr. 2463, fols. 110–111.

65. Thourel, *Histoire de Genève*, III, 221–222.

66. Anon., *Diverses pièces relatives aux délibérations du magnifique Conseil des Deux Cent depuis le 20 août au 3 septembre* (Geneva, 1779), RIV 1765; [J.-J. Gautier], *Mémoire instructif sur les dispositions actuelles de la République de Genève* (Geneva, 1779), RIV 1780.

67. Vergennes, *Lettre de monseigneur le comte de Vergennes . . . à monsieur Gabart de Vaux . . . le premier Septembre 1779* ([Geneva], n.d.), 1–4.

68. Hennin to Vergennes, 26 December 1774 (letter D19255), in Voltaire, *Correspondence and Related Documents*, XLI: *June 1774–April 1775*, 264–265.

69. Jean-Pierre Bérenger, *Mémoire justificatif pour les citoyens de Genève*.

70. Jean-Pierre Bérenger, *Histoire de Genève*, VI. Cornuaud said that Bérenger hated both the rich and the great, and called the history "inconsequential"; *Mémoires de Isaac Cornuaud*, 119.

71. Cornuaud, *Mémoires de Isaac Cornuaud*, 155–158.

72. Isaac Cornuaud, *Lettre d'un Natif à un Bourgeois de ses amis* (Geneva, 1777); *La famille divisée* (Geneva, 1777); *Examen politico-patriotique des cinq questions suivantes* (Geneva, 1777); *Le vrai Natif ou réponse à l'auteur de La Justice humblement réclamée* (Geneva, 1777).

73. Isaac Cornuaud, *La Voix publique, ou le peuple de Genève* (Geneva, [13 April] 1780).

74. Cornuaud, *Mémoires de Isaac Cornuaud*, 87–89, 139, 151–152.

75. Isaac Cornuaud, *Confession de foi patriotique de la partie du people de Genève, connue sous le nom de Natifs, adressée à tous les amateurs de la patrie et du bien-public* (Geneva, [22 November] 1779); *Les Aveugles devenus occulistes* (Geneva, [27 December] 1779); *Lettre d'un Natif aux auteurs du mémoire des membres Représentans du Mag. Conseil des Deux-Cent* (Geneva, [8 February] 1780); *Mémoires de Isaac Cornuaud*, 142–145, 174–176, 181, 189.

76. Isaac Cornuaud, *Le Natif encore interrogé, ou suite de la confession morali-politique d'un patriote de Genève* (Geneva, [8 April] 1780); *Histoire de la neutralité des natifs* (Geneva, [12 December] 1780); *L'heureuse position des Natifs dans le moment présent* (Geneva, [24 November] 1780).

77. Cornuaud, *Mémoires de Isaac Cornuaud*, 167–174, 193–195.

78. Clavière, "Lettre à son excellence monsieur Le Comte de Vergennes, Du 21 Février 1780," *Pieces justificatives pour messieurs Du Roveray & Clavière* ([Geneva], 1780), 7–11, 19–20, 29–30, 38–39, 51–54.

79. Cornuaud, *Mémoires de Isaac Cornuaud*, 234–240.

80. Thourel, *Histoire de Genève*, III, 230–239.

81. Cornuaud, *Mémoires de Isaac Cornuaud*, xxix–xxx, 257–258.

82. Ibid., 217–219.

83. Ibid., 222–231.

84. Roget to Romilly, 19 May 1780, in *Lettres de Jean Roget*, 8.

85. Johannes von Müller, "Tableau des troubles de la République de Genève, depuis leur origine jusqu'à nos jours," *Essais historiques* (Berlin, 1781), 101–109.

86. Romilly to Roget, 27 October 1780, in *Lettres de Jean Roget*, 24.

87. Jean-André Deluc to Jacques-François Deluc, 12 November 1768, "Sur la politique genevoise," BdG, Ms. Fr. 2461, fols. 8–13.

88. Ibid., fol. 16.

89. Ibid., fol. 20.

90. Jean-André Deluc to Jean-Jacques Vieusseux, 4 March 1777, Ms. Fr. 2461, fols. 33–41.

91. Théodore Rilliet, *Lettres sur l'emprunt et l'impôt* ([Geneva], 1779). On Rilliet's politics and political economy, see Béla Kapossy, "Genevan Creditors and English Liberty: The Example of Théodore Rilliet de Saussure," in Cossie, Kapossy, and Whatmore, *Genève lieu d'Angleterre*, 169–184. Rilliet in 1773 had married Ursule de Planta. Elected a member of the Council of Two Hundred in 1775, he was deposed in 1780 following his scandalous divorce proceedings against his wife, whom he accused of an incestuous relationship with her brother, which led to a pamphlet war; he was successfully sued for libel by his wife and his brother-in-law, Frédéric de Planta. Despite the loss of office and reputation, Rilliet refused to back down and defended himself in *Correspondance, ou Défence fondamentale contre l'ordonnance du conseil de Genève* (1782).

92. Cornuaud, *Mémoires de Isaac Cornuaud*, 140, 317.

93. Roget to Romilly, 22 November 1780, in *Lettres de Jean Roget*, 26.

94. D'Ivernois, *Tableau historique et politique des deux dernières révolutions de Genève*, II, 30–31.

95. Jean-André Deluc, *Mémoire remis le 21 août 1781, à monsieur le Comte de Vergennes par J.-A. Deluc, comme étant le sommaire de ce qu'il avoit eu l'honneur d'exposer à son excellence dans des audiences précédentes* (Geneva, 1781), 5–11.

96. Ibid., 12–16.

97. Gédéon Turrettini, *Considérations d'un patriote* (Geneva, 1781) (RIV 2235).

98. Cornuaud, *Examen du mémoire remis à S. E. M. le comte de Vergennes, le 21 août 1781, par M. J.-A. Deluc, ancien demagogue de la Bourgeoisie* (Geneva, [15 September] 1781); *Mémoires de Isaac Cornuaud*, 318.

99. [Jean-André Deluc], *Journal de ce qui s'est passé d'intéressant à Genève*.

100. Roget to Romilly, 13 January 1781, in *Lettres de Jean Roget*, 34.

101. Jacques-Antoine du Roveray, *Très-humble et très-respectueuse représentation, remise aux seigneurs sindics et à monsieur le procureur-général, le 20 Octobre 1780, par les citoyens & bourgeois représentans* (Geneva, 1780), 1–6, 16, 20, 27, 30–31, 35, 44, 51.

102. Du Roveray, *Remonstrance faite dans le Magnifique Petit Conseil, le 15 Novembre 1780, par monsieur le procureur général, au sujet de la représentation remis aux seigneurs sindics & à lui . . . le 20 Octobre 1780*, 6, 9, 12.

103. Ibid., 14–16, 24, 34, 48–50, 52–55.

104. Jean-Jacques Rousseau, *Seconde partie des confessions de J. J. Rousseau, citoyen de Geneve. Edition enrichie d'un nouveau recueil de ses letters* (London [Neuchâtel], 1790), 10 vols., VI, 174–178.

105. R. A. Leigh, *Unsolved Problems in the Bibliography of J-J. Rousseau* (Cambridge, 1990), 114–146.

106. Roget to Romilly, 23 January 1782, in *Lettres de Jean Roget*, 136.

107. D'Ivernois, *Lettre à son excellence le Comte de Vergennes* [Geneva, 1780], 4.

108. Ibid., 9–12.

109. D'Ivernois, *Considérations d'un citoyen de Genève, Sur la Garantie, accordée, en 1738, à la République de Genève, par la France & les L. L. Cantons de Zurich & de Berne* [Geneva, 1780], 20 21.

110. D'Ivernois, *Lettre à son excellence le Comte de Vergennes*, 5–8, 16–18.

111. D'Ivernois, *Lettre à Madame* *** [Geneva, 1780], 1–9; *Réflexions impartiales, Sur l'Etat actuel de la République de Geneve* [Geneva, 1780], 34–37; *La Loi de la réélection* [Geneva, 1780], 53–55.

112. Du Roveray, *Fameuse Remonstrance faite dans le magnifique Petit Conseil de la République de Genève, le 11 Décembre 1780*, 13–14, 27–29.

113. Ibid., 6–13.

114. Ibid., 12–19.

115. Ibid., 14–15.

116. Ibid., 11.

117. Ibid., 30.

118. Ibid., 32–36.

119. Du Roveray, *Fameuse Remonstrance*, 24–25, 38–40. See also, on the need for a représentant-governed state, Roget to Romilly, 23 January 1782, in *Lettres de Jean Roget*, 132.

120. Du Roveray, *Fameuse Remonstrance*, 20, 40–45.

121. Roget to Romilly, 27 December 1780, in *Lettres de Jean Roget*, 29–32.

122. [Reybaz or Du Roveray], *Lettre à l'auteur de la Réponse aux Deuxième, troisième & quatrième Lettres à un Négatif modéré. Contenant une courte description de la Fête du 15e du courant* (Geneva, [12 December] 1780), 2, 12 (RIV 2029).

123. Cornuaud, *Mémoires de Isaac Cornuaud*, 323.

124. Registres du Petit Conseil, 23 October 1780, 164.

125. Thourel, *Histoire de Genève*, III, 270; Clavière to Batistaire & Co., 23 August 1781, AN T646 (1).

126. Anon., *Lettres genevoises*, 98.

127. Vergennes to the Cantons of Zurich and of Bern, 24 December 1780, BdG, Ms. Fr. 2476, 105–106.

128. Vergennes to Gabard de Vaux, 30 December 1780, BdG, Ms. Fr. 2476, 107.

129. Thourel, *Histoire de Genève, depuis son origine jusqu'à nos jours*, III, 245–249.

130. Cornuaud, *Mémoires de Isaac Cornuaud sur Genève et la Révolution de 1770 à 1795*, 256.

131. Extrait des Registres du Conseil du 17 Janvier 1781, BdG, Ms. Fr. 2476, 110.

132. Jean Roget to Samuel Romilly, 13 January 1781, Roget, *Lettres de Jean Roget*, 34–37.

133. Cornuaud, *Mémoires de Isaac Cornuaud sur Genève et la Révolution de 1770 à 1795*, 280–281.

134. Jean Roget to Samuel Romilly, 20 January 1781, Roget, *Lettres de Jean Roget*, 39–44.

135. Thourel, *Histoire de Genève*, III, 260.

136. Coxe, *Travels in Switzerland*, II, 357–358.

137. Cantons of Zurich and of Bern to Vergennes, 17 February 1781 and 31 March 1781, BdG, Ms. Fr. 2476, 116, 134.

138. Vergennes to the Cantons of Zurich and of Bern, 8 March 1780, BdG, Ms. Fr. 2476, 123–124.

139. Vergennes to the Comte de Jallatin, 23 March 1782, BdG, Ms. Fr. 2476, 130.

140. Cornuaud, *Mémoires de Isaac Cornuaud*, 322–325.

141. Roget to Romilly, 2 March and 4 April 1781, in *Lettres de Jean Roget*, 46–57.

142. Frederick the Great to the Cantons of Zurich and of Bern, 30 January 1781, BdG, Ms. Fr. 2476, 125.

143. Vergennes, *Lettres de son excellence Monsieur le Comte de Vergennes, Ministre & Secrétaire d'Etat au département des affaires étrangers. Aux Sindics et Conseil de la Ville & la République de Genève* (Geneva, [10 April] 1781), 1–2.

144. Roget to Romilly, February 1782, in *Lettres de Jean Roget*, 140.

145. Cornuaud, *Adresse aux membres du Comité des Représentants* (Ferney, [31 October] 1781); *Mémoires de Isaac Cornuaud*, 290–292, 326–327.

146. Roget to Romilly, 3 October and 6 October 1781, in *Lettres de Jean Roget*, 70–73; Cornuaud, *Mémoires de Isaac Cornuaud*, 295–298.

147. Vergennes to the Cantons of Zurich and of Bern, 28 February 1781, BdG, Ms. Fr. 2476, 117.

148. Cornuaud, *Mémoire adressé à l'Illustre Médiation, par les Natifs de Genève* (Geneva, [15 June] 1781); *Mémoires de Isaac Cornuaud*, 277, 287, 305, 310, 314–315.

149. Coxe, *Travels in Switzerland*, II, 361; Roget to Romilly, 20 October 1781, in *Lettres de Jean Roget*, 82–86.

150. Du Roveray, *Très-humble et très-respectueuse représentation des citoyens et bourgeois représentans. Remise aux Seigneurs Sindics, & à Monsieur le Procureur Général, le 24 Octobre 1781* (RIV 2216).

151. Roget to Romilly, 1 December 1781, in *Lettres de Jean Roget*, 98–104, 106.

152. Bénétruy, *L'atelier de Mirabeau*, 19.

153. Cornuaud, *Troisième adresse aux membres du Comité des Représentants* (Ferney, [15 November] 1781); *Cinquième adresse aux membres du Comité des Représentants* (Ferney, [15 January] 1781); *Septième adresse aux membres du Comité des Représentants* (Ferney, [17 February] 1782).

154. Cornuaud to 1st syndic Barthélemy Rilliet, 1 March 1781, BdG, Ms. Fr. 2476, 120–122.

155. Roget to Romilly, 14 November 1781, in *Lettres de Jean Roget*, 90–93; Mallet du Pan, "Genève," *Annales politiques et littéraires* 2, no. 12, reprinted by Cornuaud with an "avis de l'éditeur" (*Mémoires de Isaac Cornuaud*, 327).

156. Roget to Romilly, 22 December 1781, in *Lettres de Jean Roget*, 112.

157. *Déclaration des Représentants du 28 mars 1781*; *Requisitions des Citoyens & Bourgeois Représentants à Mess. Les Sindics Bernoise le Samedi 14 Avril 1781*, BdG, Ms. Fr. 2476, 132, 138–140.

158. D'Ivernois, *Tableau historique et politique des deux dernières révolutions de Genève*, II, 51–52.

159. Jean Roget to Samuel Romilly, 27 April 1782, Roget, *Lettres de Jean Roget*, 204.

160. Roget to Romilly, 10 August 1781, in *Lettres de Jean Roget*, 64.

161. D'Ivernois, *Offrande à la liberté et à la paix, par un citoyen de Genève; ou idées de conciliation adressées à Mr. J. A. De Luc, en réfutation Du Mémoire qu'il remit le 21 Aoust [sic] 1781, à Monsieur le Comte de Vergennes* (Geneva, 1781).

162. Ibid., 18–24, 28–33, 38, 50–56, 67–69.

163. Ibid., 39–48.

164. Ibid., 99–105, 115–119, 137–141. D'Ivernois praised Brissot's work as distinguished "par sa théorie des loix criminelles" (157n).

165. Ibid., 77–84.

166. Jean-André Deluc "à l'auteur d'une brochure qui a pour titre *Offrande à la liberté*," BdG, Ms. Fr. 2476, 150–156.

167. Roget to Romilly, 18 December 1782, in *Lettres de Jean Roget*, 292.

168. François-Joseph Rey, Jacques-Antoine du Roveray, and Jean-Pierre Raccaud, *Lettre d'un membre de la communauté de Fribourg en Suisse* ([Geneva], 1781) (RIV 2266).

169. Clavière to Henry Ziegler, 14 December 1781; Clavière to [Jacques?] Diodati, 14 January 1782, AN T646 (1).

170. *Très-humble et très-respectueuse représentation des citoyens et bourgeois représentans, dans laquelle on réfute la partie de la Déclaration des Négatifs du 29e 8bre 1781, qui traite De la Prise d'Armes & de l'Edit du mois de Février 1781. Suivie De Notes essentielles sur la Souveraineté du Conseil Général. Remise aux Seigneurs Sindics et A Monsieur le Procureur Général, par la Généralité des Citoyens et Bourgeois Représentans, le 18 Mars 1782* (Geneva, 1782), 14, 38–39, 44, 50 (RIV 3333, 3334).

171. Coxe, *Travels in Switzerland*, II, 358.

172. Anon., *Lettres genevoises*, 48.

173. Anon., *Très-humble et très-respectueuse déclaration des citoyens et bourgeois représentans, remise aux Seigneurs Sindics et A Monsieur le Procureur Général, le 31 May 1782 par la Généralité des Citoyens et Bourgeois Représentans* (Geneva, 1782), 7–11 (RIV 2409).

174. Clavière to Théophile Cazenove, 26 April 1782, AN T646 (1).

175. Jacques Vieusseux to Mme. Vieusseux-Larguier, 4 June 1782, in Rivier-Rose, *La famille Rivier*, 103.

176. Anon., *Traduction D'une Lettre du Louable Canon de Berne, adressée aux Seigneurs Syndics* [Geneva, 10 May 1782]; Coxe, *Travels in Switzerland*, II, 362–363; Roget to Romilly, 27 April 1782, in *Lettres de Jean Roget*, 195–196.

177. Thourel, *Histoire de Genève*, III, 288–289.

178. Vergennes, *Lettre de S. E. M. le comte de Vergennes à S. E. M. l'Ambassadeur de France à Soleure* (Versailles, [2 May] 1782). Cornuaud later praised Vergennes for having combated Necker's "principes républicains," calling him in consequence the last faithful minister of Louis XVI (*Mémoires de Isaac Cornuaud*, 349).

179. Bénétruy, *L'atelier de Mirabeau*, 26.

180. Roget to Romilly, 20 June 1782, in *Lettres de Jean Roget*, 236.

181. Vergennes, *Lettres de son excellence Mr le Comte de Vergennes, ministre des affaires étrangers aux sindics et conseil* (Geneva, [15 April] 1782), 1–6.

182. Roget to Romilly, 27 April 1782, Catherine Roget to Romilly, 4 May 1782, in *Lettres de Jean Roget*, 202, 207.

183. Powell McNutt, "Church and Society in Eighteenth-Century Geneva, 1700–1789," 267–268.

184. Cornuaud, *Relation de la conjuration contre le gouvernement et le magistrat de Genève* (Geneva, [18 April] 1782), 18–23; *Mémoires de Isaac Cornuaud*, 350–358.

185. Cornuaud, *Mémoires de Isaac Cornuaud*, 362–363, 382–386.

186. Roget to Romilly, 17 April 1782 and 18 May 1782, in *Lettres de Jean Roget*, 192–194, 219.

187. Anon., *Lettres genevoises*, 2–5, 99–102.

188. Anon., *Précis historique de la dernière révolution de Genève; Et en particulier de la Réforme que le Souverain de cette République a faite dans les Conseils Administrateurs* (Geneva, 1782), 3 (RIV 2367).

189. Ibid., 2, 6–7, 9, 11.

190. Roget to Romilly, 20 July 1782, in *Lettres de Jean Roget*, 254.

191. *Lettre des très illustres & très excellens Seigneurs les Ministres Plénipotentiares de leurs Majestés très Chrétienne && Sarde & de la République de Berne, aux Magnifiques*

Seigneurs les Syndics & Conseil de la République de Genève (Geneva, [21 November] 1782).

192. Coxe, *Travels in Switzerland*, II, 380–383.

193. Cornuaud, *Mémoires de Isaac Cornuaud*, 406–410; Jean-Louis Mallet, *Tableau historique des dissensions de la République de Genève et de la perte de son independence* (Geneva, 1803), 46–47, 50. Both men blamed Clavière for transplanting the ideas of the représentants from Geneva into France after 1789, and in consequence held him responsible for the subsequent terrorist excesses in both states. Cornuaud called Clavière and Necker "monstres"; Paul-Henri Mallet to Hennin, 22 December 1782, in Karmin, *Sir Francis d'Ivernois*, 638.

194. Paul-Claude Moultou, "Lettre de M. Moultou sur la dernière révolution de Genève" in Grimm, Diderot, et al., *Correspondance littéraire, philosophique et critique*, ed. M. Tourneux (Paris, 1880), XIII, July 1782, 173–175.

195. Bénétruy, *L'atelier de Mirabeau*, 32.

196. Thourel, *Histoire de Genève*, III, 335.

197. Rivier-Rose, *La famille Rivier*, 104–105.

198. Cornuaud, *Mémoires de Isaac Cornuaud*, 418–419, 424–426.

199. Ibid., xxix–xxx, 407.

200. Madame de Gauthier, *Voyage d'une Française en Suisse* [Paris, 1790], 90.

201. Albanis Beaumont, *Travels from France to Italy* (London, 1800), 66–67.

202. Marie-Jeanne Roland, "Tour through Switzerland," *The works (never before published) of Jeanne-Marie Phlipon Roland, wife of the ex-minister of the interior; containing her philosophical and literary essays, Written Previous To Her Marriage; Her Correspondence, And Her Travels. To Which Are Annexed The Justificative Documents Relative To Her Imprisonment And Condemnation. The whole preceded by a preliminary discourse, interspersed with notes, illustrative and explanatory, by L. A. Champagneux. Translated from the French* (London, [1800]), 225.

203. Linda Kirk, "The Church in Eighteenth-Century Geneva," unpublished manuscript.

204. Roget to Romilly, 18 February 1783, and Catherine Roget to Romilly, 4 September 1782, in *Lettres de Jean Roget*, 262–263, 297–301; *Mémoires de Isaac Cornuaud*, 388–390; d'Ivernois, *Tableau historique et politique des deux dernières révolutions de Genève*, II, 138.

205. Thourel, *Histoire de Genève*, III, 332.

206. Brissot, *Philadelphien à Genève*, 195.

207. Coxe, *Travels in Switzerland*, II, 384: "The emigrants have principally established themselves at Brussels and Constance; where they have introduced manufactures of printed linens and watch-making."

208. Thourel, *Histoire de Genève*, III, 336.

209. Bénétruy, *L'atelier de Mirabeau*, 38–42.

210. Roget to Romilly, 23 January 1782 and 23 November 1782, in *Lettres de Jean Roget*, 136, 286.

211. Bénétruy, *L'atelier de Mirabeau*, 28–29.

212. D'Ivernois, *An Historical and Political View of the Constitution and Revolutions of Geneva*, 238–239, 370.

213. Ibid., vi–xvi.

214. Ibid., 277.

215. Ibid., 6–7, 118–120.

216. Ibid., 211–234.

217. Ibid., 235–237.

218. Ibid., 322–323.

219. Ibid., 372–374.

220. Brissot, *Philadelphien à Genève*, 10–11. The work appeared with Tacitus's declaration of neutrality as an epigraph: "mihi Galba Otho Vitellius nec beneficio nec iniuria cogniti."

221. Ibid., 22–39. Brissot likened the aristocrats at Geneva to the despots within the Paris order of barristers, for reasons to do with his personal career (27).

222. Ibid., 40–51, 98–99.

223. Ibid., 54–60, 75–79.

224. Ibid., 63–68, 108–113, 122, 152–156, 165, 174–175, 199–205.

225. Ibid., 163–167.

226. Brissot, *L'Indépendance des Anglo-Américains démontrée utile à la Grande-Bretagne. Lettres extrait du Journal d'Agriculture, Avril & Mai 1782* (n.p., n.d.).

Chapter 6. International Crises and Perpetual Peace

1. D'Ivernois, *Tableau historique et politique des deux dernières révolutions de Genève*, II, 107–108.

2. Karmin, *Sir Francis d'Ivernois*, 106.

3. W. F. Reddaway, "Great Britain and Poland, 1762–1772," *Cambridge Historical Journal* 4 (1934), 223–262; H. M. Scott, "Sir Joseph Yorke, Dutch Politics and the Origins of the Fourth Anglo-Dutch War," *Historical Journal* 31 (1988), 571–589; Daniel A. Baugh, "Withdrawing from Europe: Anglo-French Maritime Geopolitics, 1750–1800," *International History Review* 20 (1998), 1–32; Baugh, "Great Britain's 'Blue-Water' Policy, 1689–1815," *International History Review* 10 (1988), 33–58; Richard Pares, "American versus Continental Warfare, 1739–1763," *English Historical Review* 51 (1936), 429–465; Brendan Simms and Torsten Riotte, eds., *The Hanoverian Dimension in British History, 1714–1837* (Cambridge, 2009).

4. Review of d'Ivernois's *An Historical and Political View of the Constitution and Revolutions of Geneva*, in *The Critical Review* for October 1784.

5. Review of d'Ivernois's *An Historical and Political View of the Constitution and Revolutions of Geneva*, in *The English Review, or, An Abstract of English and Foreign Literature*, vol. V (London, 1785), 162–165.

6. Review of Brissot's *Philadelphien à Genève*, in *The European Magazine, and London Review*, vol. V (June 1784), 436–439.

7. Review of Brissot's *Philadelphien à Genève*, in *English Review, or, An Abstract of English and Foreign Literature*, vol. IV (London, 1784), 129–133.

8. Thomas Robinson, 2nd Baron Grantham, to John Stuart (Mountstuart, 4th Earl of Bute from 1794), 16 August 1782 (no. 7, draft), Bedfordshire and Luton Archives and Record Service, L 29/561/15.

9. Syndics and Council of Geneva to Thomas Townshend, 18 December 1782, NA PRO, FO 95/8/12; Syndics and Council of Geneva to George III, 18 December 1782, NA PRO, FO 95/8/12 f. 637.

10. Roget to Romilly, 19 October 1782, in *Lettres de Jean Roget*, 277–278. D'Ivernois had in fact met Lord Temple on 27 September 1782; see Brissot, *Philadelphien à Genève*, 149.

11. Brissot, *Philadelphien à Genève*, 150.

12. John Cannon, "Petty, William, second earl of Shelburne and first marquess of Lansdowne (1737–1805)," *Oxford Dictionary of National Biography*, online ed., January 2008; R. W. Davis, "Grenville, George Nugent-Temple-, first marquess of Buckingham (1753–1813)," *Oxford Dictionary of National Biography*, online ed., January 2008.

13. Coxe, *Travels in Switzerland*, II, 385.

14. Karmin, *Sir Francis d'Ivernois*, 113–159.

15. Romilly to Roget, 25 October 1782, in *Memoirs of Romilly*, I, 242–245.

16. Brissot, *Philadelphien à Genève*, 148–150, 210–211. Brissot reported to Ostervald on 12 August 1783 that all was going well in Ireland (Darnton, *Correspondance de Brissot*).

17. Bouchary, *Les manieurs d'argent*, I, 25–38.

18. Etienne Clavière to Roman l'aîné, 29 November 1782, Clavière to Amy Melly, 6 December 1782, AN T646 (1).

19. Thomas Orde to Jacques-Antoine du Roveray and d'Ivernois, 24 May 1784, 1st Baron Bolton Papers, NLI, Ms. 15914, fols. 1–5; Orde and Du Roveray to d'Ivernois, 18 April 1784 and 28 and 29 May 1784; d'Ivernois's memorandum on the settlement of the Genevans, 1st Baron Bolton papers, NLI, Ms. 15, 913–914.

20. Coxe, *Travels in Switzerland*, II, 384, 386.

21. Thourel, *Histoire de Genève*, III, 332–336.

22. Clavière to Brissot, 10 April 1783, AN T646 (1).

23. Clavière to Alexander Jaffrey, 6 August 1783, AN T646 (1).

24. Brissot, *Philadelphien à Genève*, 132–143.

25. Ibid., 178.

26. Andrew Stockley, *Britain and France at the Birth of America: The European Powers and the Peace Negotiations of 1782–1783* (Exeter, 2001), 111–113, 135–138, 204–208.

27. On Morellet's early opposition to Necker, see Kenneth Margerison, "The Shareholders' Revolt at the Compagnie des Indes: Commerce and Political Culture in Old Regime France," *French History* 20 (2006), 25–51.

28. Derek Jarrett, "The Bowood Circle, 1780–1793: Its Ideas and Its Influence" (B.Litt., University of Oxford, 1955); *The Begetters of Revolution: England's Involvement with France, 1759–1789* (London, 1973); John Norris, *Shelburne and Reform* (London, 1963), 82–98; Albert Goodwin, *The Friends of Liberty: The English Democratic Movement in the Age of the French Revolution* (London, 1979), 101–105; Andrew Hamilton, "Atlantic Cosmopolitanism and Nationalism: Benjamin Vaughan and the Limits of Free Trade in the Eighteenth Century" (Ph.D. diss., University of Wisconsin,

Madison, 2004); Edward G. Andrew, *Patrons of Enlightenment* (Toronto, 2006), 170–181.

29. Hont, "The Rich Country–Poor Country Debate Revisited"; Richard Whatmore, "Adam Smith's Contribution to the French Revolution," *Past and Present* 175 (2002), 65–89.

30. Norris, *Shelburne and Reform*, 1–17.

31. Richard Price to the Earl of Chatham, 9 February 1775, in *The Correspondence of Richard Price, Volume I: July 1748–March 1778*, ed. William Bernard Peace (Durham, N.C., 1983), 186–187.

32. Shelburne to the Lords of Trade, 5 October 1767, in *Trade and Politics, 1767–1769*, ed. Clarence Walworth Alvord and Clarence Edwin Carter (Illinois, 1921), Western Policy, Collections of the State Historical Society, XVI, British Series, vol. III, 77–81. Richard Price summarized Shelburne's views and argued that they could have restored peace between Britain and North America as late as 1776; see Richard Price, *Observations on the nature of civil liberty, the principles of government, and the justice and policy of the war with America* (Dublin, 1776), 101–110.

33. David Hume to William Mure, Baron Mure of Caldwell, 18 October 1768 (letter 422), in Greig, *The Letters of David Hume: Volume II*, 187–189. See also John Burnby, *An address to the people of England, on the increase of their poor rates, dedicated to the earl of Shelburne* (London, 1780), ii–iii.

34. Benjamin Vaughan to Benjamin Franklin, 3 July 1778, BFP: "We are certainly shockingly weak at this moment, and I believe it probable that the French may land and stay here for a season or so, though not permanently." More broadly, see Istvan Hont, "The Rhapsody of Public Debt: David Hume and Voluntary State Bankruptcy," in *Jealousy of Trade*, 325–354.

35. Price, *Observations on the nature of civil liberty*, 98.

36. Ibid., 7–10.

37. Istvan Hont, "The Political Economy of the 'Unnatural and Retrograde' Order: Adam Smith and Natural Liberty," in *Jealousy of Trade*, 354–388.

38. Shelburne to Dugald Stewart, 1795, in *The Collected Works of Dugald Stewart*, ed. Sir William Hamilton (Edinburgh, 1858), 10 vols., X, 95.

39. Adam Smith to Shelburne, 21 February 1759 (letter 28) and 12 February 1767 (letter 101), in *The Correspondence of Adam Smith*, ed. Ernest Campbell Mossner and Ian Simpson Ross (Oxford, 1987), 28–29, 122–124.

40. Shelburne to Price, 25 November 1786, in *Correspondence of Richard Price, Volume III*, 90. The benefits of neutrality were pressed upon Benjamin Vaughan by John Adams during the peace negotiations of 1783. Vaughan's cautious reply underlined the complicated relationship between support for a principle and contemporary reason-of-state politics; see John Adams, diary 39, 1 January 1783, *Adams Family Papers: An Electronic Archive*, http://www.masshist.org/digitaladams/aea/cfm/doc.cfm?id=D39.

41. Shelburne to Price, 29 September 1786, in *Correspondence of Richard Price, Volume III*, 64. Smith considered Price "a factious citizen, a most superficial Philosopher and by no means an able calculator": Adam Smith to George Chalmers, 22 December

1785, cited in Donald Winch, *Riches and Poverty: An Intellectual History of Political Economy in Britain, 1750–1814* (Cambridge, 1996), 125.

42. Durand Echeverria, "Condorcet's *The Influence of the American Revolution on Europe*," *William and Mary Quarterly* 25 (1968), 85–108.

43. Shelburne to Price, 22 November 1786, in *Correspondence of Richard Price, Volume III*, 86–87.

44. Edmond George Petty-Fitzmaurice, *Life of William, Earl of Shelburne, First Marquess of Lansdowne, with Extracts from His Papers and Correspondence* (London, 1912), rev. ed., 2 vols., I, 81.

45. Dupont de Nemours, *Mémoires sur la vie et les ouvrages de M. Turgot, ministre d'état, première partie* (Philadelphia, 1782), 171, 196.

46. Fitzmaurice, *Life of William, Earl of Shelburne*, I, 429–433.

47. André Morellet to Shelburne, 8 January 1772 (letter 676), in *Correspondance générale d'Helvétius, Volume III, 1761–1774, Lettres 465–720*, ed. David Smith, J. A. Dainard, Marie-Thérèse Inguenaud, Jean Orsini, and Peter Allan (Toronto, 1991), 386–387; André Morellet to Shelburne, 18 February 1777 (letter 727), in *Correspondance générale d'Helvétius, Volume IV, 1774–1800, Lettres 721–855, suivies de lettres relevant des périodes des trois premiers volumes et découvertes depuis leur parution*, ed. David Smith, J. A. Dainard, Marie-Thérèse Inguenaud, Jean Orsini, and Peter Allan (Toronto, 1998), 13–17. On the politics of Helvétius and his disciples, see Sonenscher, *Before the Deluge*, 266–282.

48. Shelburne to Morellet, 1802, in Fitzmaurice, *Life of William, Earl of Shelburne*, II, 430–431.

49. André Morellet, *Mémoires inédits de l'abbé Morellet . . . sur le dix-huitième siècle et sur la révolution* (Paris, 1822), 2nd ed., 2 vols., I, 277–279.

50. Morellet's translation never appeared, as publishers would not print it on the grounds that there was already a translation in circulation by the Abbé Blavet: see Morellet, *Mémoires inédits*, I, 243–246, II, 371.

51. François-Jean de Chastellux, *Discours prononcés dans l'Académie françoise, le jeudi 15 juin 1785 à la réception de l'Abbé Morellet* (Paris, 1785), 40–43.

52. Morellet to Shelburne, 12 March 1776, 102, and 30 December 1777, 130–135, in André Morellet, *Lettres de l'abbé Morellet de l'Académie française à Lord Shelburne, depuis marquis de Lansdowne, 1772–1803*, ed. Edmond George Petty-Fitzmaurice (Paris, 1898).

53. Morellet to Shelburne, 1 April 1783 (letter 788), in *Correspondance générale d'Helvétius: Volume IV*, 97–99.

54. Pierre-Edouard Lemontey, "Eloge," in Morellet, *Mémoires inédits*, I, ix.

55. Fitzmaurice, *Life of William, Earl of Shelburne*, II, 264; Morellet, *Mémoires inédits*, I, 27.

56. Andrew Kippis, *Considerations upon the provisional peace treaty with America and the preliminary articles of peace with France and Spain* (London, 1783), 2nd ed., 5, 79–81.

57. Shelburne, *The Speech of the Right Honourable the earl of Shelburne, in the House of Lords, on Monday, February 13, 1783, on the Articles of Peace* (Ipswich, 1783), 4.

58. Vaughan to Franklin, 25 February 1783, BFP. Franklin had plans for treaties of commerce and friendship between the United States and all of the major powers of Europe, including the Holy Roman Empire. See Thomas Jefferson to John Jay, 27 January 1786, PTJ. On Franklin's position, see Alan Houston, *Benjamin Franklin and the Politics of Improvement* (New Haven, Conn., 2009), 187–191.

59. Shelburne, *The Substance of the Speech of the Marquis of Lansdowne, in the House of Lords, On the 14th of December, 1790; on the subject of the Convention with Spain, which was signed on the 28th of October, 1790* (London, 1790), 7.

60. D'Ivernois, *An Historical and Political View of the Constitution and Revolutions of Geneva*, xviii.

61. Mirabeau to Vergennes, 4 October 1782, in *Mémoires biographiques, littéraires et politiques de Mirabeau*, 2nd ed., IV, 114–140.

62. It has been claimed that Du Roveray was given a chair in law at Trinity College Dublin, but this is unsubstantiated. See Bénétruy, *L'atelier de Mirabeau*, 10; Karmin, *Sir Francis d'Ivernois*, 155.

63. Bénétruy, *L'atelier de Mirabeau*, 53–54.

64. David Chauvet to Clavière, 15 April 1785, cited in Bénétruy, *L'atelier de Mirabeau*, 90.

65. Price to Jefferson, 2 July 1785, and the reply of 7 August 1785, in *Correspondence of Richard Price, Volume II*, 289–290, 299.

66. Dumont, *Recollections of Mirabeau*, 43.

67. Clavière to d'Ivernois, 28 October 1783, AN T646 (1).

68. Lüthy, *La banque protestante en France*, II, 420–469.

69. Clavière to Du Roveray, 17 November 1783, AN T646 (1).

70. Marcel Marion, *Histoire financière de la France depuis 1715* (Paris, 1914), 3 vols., I, 348–385; George Taylor, "The Paris Bourse on the Eve of the French Revolution, 1781–1789," *American Historical Review* 67 (1961–1962), 951–977.

71. Bouchary, *Les manieurs d'argent*, I, 38–55.

72. Brissot to Ostervald, 2 December 1782 and 18 September 1783, in Darnton, *Correspondance de Brissot*. On the broader context, see Simon Burrow, *Blackmail, Scandal, and Revolution: London's French libellistes, 1758–1792* (Manchester, 2006).

73. On Brissot's activities during these years, see Eloise Ellery, *Brissot de Warville: A Study in the History of the French Revolution* (Boston, 1915); Jean-François Primo, *La jeunesse de J.-P. Brissot* (Paris, 1932); Robert Darnton, "The Brissot Dossier," *French Historical Studies* 17 (1991), 191–205; Frederick A. de Luna, "The Dean Street Style of Revolution: J.-P. Brissot, Jeune Philosophe," *French Historical Studies* 17 (1991), 159–190; Richard Whatmore, "Commerce, Constitutions, and the Manners of a Nation: Etienne Clavière's Revolutionary Political Economy, 1788–1793," *History of European Ideas* 22 (1996), 351–368; Leonore Loft, *Passion, Politics, and Philosophie: Rediscovering J.-P. Brissot* (Westport, Conn., 2002), 85–110; and Simon Burrows, "The Innocence of Jacques-Pierre Brissot," *Historical Journal* 46 (2003), 843–871.

74. The Société typographique de Neuchâtel wrote to Clavière on 7 November 1784 as part of an investigation into Brissot's great indebtedness toward his publishers. Clavière replied that Brissot was continuing to write and might be able to pay his debts through a lucrative government appointment. On 26 December 1784 Brissot wrote similarly to

the Société to confirm his dependence upon Clavière; see Darnton, *Correspondance de Brissot.*

75. Brissot, *Mémoires, 1754–1793,* I, 293; II, 30, 348.

76. The best account of Mirabeau's projects and activities is François Quastana, *La pensée politique de Mirabeau (1771–1789): Républicanisme classique et régénération de la monarchie* (Aix-en-Provence, 2007), 328–385.

77. Franklin to Price, 7 September 1784, and Price to Shelburne, 27 November 1784, in *Correspondence of Richard Price, Volume II: March 1778–February 1786,* ed. D. O. Thomas (Durham, N.C., 1991), 226, 250; Mirabeau to William Temple Franklin, 19 September and 30 September 1784, BFP. See more broadly Rachel Hammersley, *The English Republican Tradition and Eighteenth-Century France: Between the Ancients and the Moderns* (Manchester, 2010), chap. 11.

78. Shelburne to Price, 7 October 1784, and Price to Henry Beaufoy, 22 December 1784, in *Correspondence of Richard Price, Volume II,* 229, 250.

79. Mirabeau to Sébastien-Roch-Nicolas Chamfort, 10 November 1784, in *Œuvres complètes de Chamfort,* ed. Pierre-René Auguis (Paris, 1824–1825), 5 vols., V, 409–410.

80. Mirabeau to Chamfort, 13 October 1784, in *Œuvres complètes de Chamfort,* V, 405.

81. D'Ivernois to Chauvet, 6 July 1789, cited in Bénétruy, *L'atelier de Mirabeau,* 90–91 (more generally on the history of the proposed *Histoire,* see 75–90), in turn citing Karmin, *Sir Francis d'Ivernois,* 161. See Dumont, *Recollections of Mirabeau,* 46–48: "In London [Mirabeau] fell in with D['Ivernois], who was writing a history of the Revolutions of Geneva, the first volume of which he had already published. D['Ivernois] wished to be an author without its being known, and seemed to blame himself for writing this work. He pressed Mirabeau to take his manuscripts and compose a History of Geneva. In less than a week, Mirabeau showed him an extract he had made from the volume already published. It was done in a masterly style; was energetic, rapid and interesting. I know not what made D['Ivernois] change his mind, but, on a sudden, he withdrew his manuscripts from Mirabeau. The consequence was a coolness, and something worse, between them." Quastana's *La pensée politique de Mirabeau* defends Mirabeau's independent knowledge of Genevan history (383–385).

82. Romilly to Roget, 7 January 1783, in *Memoirs of Romilly,* I, 257–262; Roget to Romilly, 18 February 1783, in Roget, *Lettres de Jean Roget,* 297–301.

83. Aedanus Burke, *Considerations on the Society or Order of Cincinnati. lately instituted by the major-generals, brigadier-generals, and other officers of the American army: proving that it creates a race of hereditary patricians, or nobility: interspersed with remarks on its consequences to the freedom and happiness of the republic. Addressed to the people of South Carolina and their representatives* (Charleston, 1783).

84. Markus Huenemörder, *The Society of the Cincinnati: Conspiracy and Distrust in Early America* (Oxford, 2006), 129–146.

85. Mirabeau, *Considérations sur l'ordre de Cincinnatus, ou imitation d'un pamphlet anglo-américain. Par le comte de Mirabeau. Suivies de plusieurs pièces relatives à cette institution; . . . d'un pamphlet du Docteur Price, intitulé: Observations on the importance of the American Revolution* (London, 1784); Pierre-Louis Ginguené, "La vie de Chamfort," *Œuvres de Chamfort* (Paris, 1794), 4 vols., I, 41; William Doyle, *Aristocracy*

and Its Enemies in the Age of Revolution (Oxford, 2009), 121–128; Quastana, *La pensée politique de Mirabeau*, 368–369. Target was campaigning for civil rights for French Protestants, which resulted in his *Mémoire sur l'état des Protestants en France* (1787), the year in which toleration was secured.

86. W. R. Fryer, "Mirabeau in England, 1784–1785," *Renaissance and Modern Studies* 10 (1966), 34–87.

87. Mirabeau, *Memoirs of Mirabeau: Biographical, Literary, and Political*, ed. Gabriel Lucas de Montigny (London, 1836), III, 28. Lucas de Montigny, on the basis of the writing style, attempted to refute Ginguené's claim that Chamfort had cowritten the work (130), but Chamfort's letters confirm the joint nature of the translation (Mirabeau to Chamfort, 22 June 1784, in *Œuvres complètes de Chamfort*, V, 385).

88. Mirabeau, *Des lettres de cachet et des prisons d'état*, 7, 134–141, 184–185, 190–200. Citations are from *Enquiries concerning lettres de cachet, the consequences of arbitrary imprisonment, and a history of the inconveniencies, distresses, and sufferings of state prisoners. Written in the dungeon of the castle of Vincennes, by the Count de Mirabeau* (London, 1787), 2 vols., I, 12–16, 73–76, 90–92, 196–196, 247–249, 276–285, 329–334, II, 332–336.

89. Mirabeau, *Considérations sur l'ordre de Cincinnatus*, 1–26, 62–66, 73, 83–84, 145.

90. Ibid., 85–86.

91. Ibid., 107, 154.

92. Ibid., 166–169.

93. Turgot to Price, 22 March 1778, in ibid., 155–157, 163.

94. Ibid., 170–172.

95. Price, *Observations on the importance of the American Revolution, and the means of making it a benefit to the world* (London, 1784), 7 (citing Isaiah 11:6, 2:4).

96. Mirabeau, *Considérations sur l'ordre de Cincinnatus*, 194–197.

97. Ibid., 182–183n. Pierre-André Gargaz was a former galley slave whose *A project of universal and perpetual peace* was printed at Passy in 1782. See Ellen R. Cohn, "The Printer and the 'Peasant': Benjamin Franklin and Pierre-André Gargaz, Two Philosophers in Search of Peace," *Early American Studies: An Interdisciplinary Journal* 8 (2010), 146–172.

98. Mirabeau, *Considérations sur l'ordre de Cincinnatus*, 191–193, 201–208.

99. Price, *Observations on the importance of the American Revolution*, 69; Price to Jonathan Trumbull, the Elder, 8 October 1784, and Price to Ezra Stiles, 15 October 1784, in *Correspondence of Richard Price, Volume II*, 233, 236.

100. Mirabeau, *Considérations sur l'ordre de Cincinnatus*, 171–172, 212–214, 217–218, 238, 274, 283–284.

101. Simon-Nicolas-Henri Linguet was employed by Joseph II to attack the Treaty of Münster, part of the Treaty of Westphalia (1648), which had justified the closing of the Scheldt. See especially Linguet's *Nouvelles considérations sur l'ouverture de l'Escaut* (Brussels, 1784) and Darlene Gay Levy, *The Ideas and Careers of Simon-Nicolas-Henri Linguet: A Study in Eighteenth-Century French Politics* (Urbana, Ill., 1980), 225–237.

102. Price to Franklin, 21 March 1785 (BFP): "We are just now alarmed here by the news that a war must take place on the Continent. I have hitherto been disposed to admire the [Holy Roman] Emperor; but I now execrate his conduct."

103. Jacques-Pierre Brissot, *Un défenseur du peuple à l'Empereur Joseph II. Sur son règlement concernant l'émigration, ses diverses réformes, &c.* (Dublin, 1785), 1–15; *Second lettre d'un défenseur du peuple à l'Empereur Joseph II. Sur son règlement concernant l'émigration, et principalement sur la révolte des valaques; Où l'on discute à fond le droit de révolte du Peuple* (Dublin, 1785), 16–19.

104. Brissot, *Un défenseur du peuple à l'Empereur Joseph II*, 35–38.

105. Ibid., 45–50.

106. Brissot, *Second lettre d'un défenseur du people à l'Empereur Joseph II*, 17–22, 38–39, 43–51, 80–81.

107. According to Dumont, "[Mirabeau] wrote his *Doutes* from a letter by M. Chauvet, which gave him the first idea of the work"; *Recollections of Mirabeau*, 44. For Romilly's claim about authorship, see *Memoirs of Romilly*, III, 111.

108. Anon., preface to Mirabeau, *Doubts concerning the Free Navigation of the Scheld claimed by the Emperor, And the probable Causes and Consequences of that Claim. In which the Views of his Imperial Majesty, and of the Empress of Russia are clearly pointed out, and the characters of those great Potentates are exhibited in a new, and interesting light* (London, 1785), i–vi.

109. Quastana, *La pensée politique de Mirabeau*, 376–382.

110. Chauvet to Clavière, 15 April 1785, cited in Bénétruy, *L'atelier de Mirabeau*, 71. On the *Doutes* as a whole, see Bénétruy's brilliant analysis, 56–70.

111. Mirabeau, *Doutes sur la liberté de l'Escaut réclamée par l'empereur* (London, 1785), 30–34, 56–57; citations are from *Doubts*, 27, 29, 30, 34, 57–58, 66.

112. Isabel de Madariaga, *Britain, Russia, and the Armed Neutrality of 1780* (New Haven, Conn., 1962).

113. Mirabeau, *Doutes*, 22, 63–64, 75–76; *Doubts*, 24–28, 66, 68, 76–77.

114. Mirabeau, *Doutes*, 19–22, 87–89; *Doubts*, 7–8, 17–22.

115. Mirabeau, *Doutes*, 77–80; *Doubts*, 76–80.

116. Mirabeau, *Doutes*, 81–86; *Doubts*, 81–87.

117. Mirabeau, *Doutes*, 160–167; *Doubts*, 127, 152–153, 156–168.

118. Franklin to Vaughan, 26 July 1784, BFP.

119. Shelburne to Price, 7 October 1784, in *Correspondence of Richard Price, Volume II*, 228–229.

120. Price to William Eden, 15 June 1785, in *Correspondence of Richard Price, Volume II*, 289.

121. Price to Jefferson, 21 March 1785, in *Correspondence of Richard Price, Volume II*, 268–269.

122. Price to Franklin, 5 November 1785, in *Correspondence of Richard Price, Volume II*, 319.

123. Jefferson to Vaughan, 2 July 1787, PTJ. See also Jefferson to James Maury, 2 July 1787, PTJ.

124. William Eden and Gérard de Rayneval, *Treaty of Navigation and Commerce between his Britannick Majesty and the Most Christian King. Signed at Versailles, the 26th of*

September, 1786 (London, 1786), 3. See also William Eden, Lord Auckland, *The journal and correspondence of William, Lord Auckland, with a preface and introduction by the Bishop of Bath and Wells* (London, 1861), 2 vols., I, 86–171, and Marie Donaghay, "The Maréchal de Castries and the Anglo-French Commercial Negotiations of 1786–1787," *Historical Journal* 22 (1979), 295–312.

125. George Wilson and James Trail to Jeremy Bentham, 26 February 1787 (letter 587), in *The Correspondence of Jeremy Bentham, Volume 3: January 1781 to October 1788*, ed. Ian R. Christie (London, 1971), 526–527.

126. William Eden, *Four letters to the Earl of Carlisle, from William Eden: on certain perversions of political reasoning, and on the nature, progress, and effect of party spirit and of parties. On the present circumstances of the war between Great Britain and the combined powers of France and Spain. On the public debts, on the public credit, and on the means of raising supplies. On the representations of Ireland respecting a free-trade* (London, 1779).

127. Shelburne to Price, 22 November 1786, in *Correspondence of Richard Price, Volume III*, 87–88.

128. Eden, *Journal and correspondence*, I, 164–171.

129. Dupont de Nemours, *Lettre à la chambre du commerce de Normandie, Sur le Mémoire qu'elle a publié relativement au Traité de Commerce avec l'Angleterre* (Rouen, 1788), 74–75.

130. De Lolme, *An Essay containing a few strictures on the Union of Scotland with England*, 81.

131. Dupont to Adam Smith, 19 June 1788, in Robert Prasch and Thierry Warin, "*Il est encore plus important de bien faire que de bien dire*: A Translation and Analysis of Dupont de Nemours' 1788 letter to Adam Smith," *History of Economics Review* 49 (2009), 67–75. On Smith's view of projectors, see Winch, *Riches and Poverty*, 90–93.

132. Price, "The Dutch Affair and the Fall of the Ancien Regime, 1784–1787"; Frederick L. Nussbaum, "The Formation of the New East India Company of Calonne," *American Historical Review* 38 (1933), 475–497; G. C. Bolton and B. E. Kennedy, "William Eden and the Treaty of Mauritius, 1786–1787," *Historical Journal* 16 (1973), 681–696.

133. Eden, *Journal and correspondence*, I, 169–185; J. Holland Rose, "Great Britain and the Dutch Question in 1787–1788," *American Historical Review* 14 (1909), 262–283.

134. Price to Shelburne, 10 November 1787, in *Correspondence of Richard Price, Volume III*, 152–154.

135. Vaughan to Franklin, 4 March 1789, BFP.

136. Benjamin Vaughan, *New and old principles of trade compared, or, A treatise on the principles of commerce between nations* (London, 1788), 2–3.

137. Stephen Conway, "Bentham versus Pitt: Jeremy Bentham and British Foreign Policy 1789," *Historical Journal* 30 (1987), 791–809.

138. Clavière to Batistaire & Co., 23 August 1781, AN T646 (1).

139. Mirabeau to Chamfort, 30 December 1784, in *Œuvres de Chamfort*, V, 424–425.

140. Clavière to Jean-Pierre Bérenger, 30 December 1784, in Rivier-Rose, *La famille Rivier*, 259–260.

141. J.-M. Rivier, *Etienne Clavière*, 45–69.

142. Clavière to Pierre Stadnitsky, 13 January 1786, in Bouchary, *Les manieurs d'argent*, I, 74–75.

143. Clavière to unknown, 18 April 1785, BdG, D.O. Autograph 1923/152 F 1189: "Je n'ai jamais distingué l'homme politique de l'homme moral: je fais profession de croire qu'ils doivent être étroitement unis, que la conduite du dernier est la pierre de torche qui détermine la valeur de l'autre; que l'homme politique estimable est celui qui met en action les devoirs de l'homme moral."

144. Isaac Panchaud, *Dialogue sur la Caisse d'Escompte entre un Parisien et un Lyonnais* (December 1784), and *Caisse d'Escompte: observations relatives à la fixation du prochain dividente* (6 January 1785). The best account of Panchaud's activities is Lüthy, *La banque protestante*, II, 420–425.

145. Bénétruy, *L'atelier de Mirabeau*, 92–104. Dumont later claimed that "Clavière wrote on every issue concerning finance: he was the author of the financial aspect of almost all of the works of Mirabeau"; Dumont, *Recollections of Mirabeau*, 327. For a list of publications, see Bénétruy, *L'atelier de Mirabeau*, 477–479. Brissot revealed the authors of the pamphlet in his *Mémoires* (II, 31), stating that he gave Mirabeau the seventh and eighth chapters, that another chapter was written by Dupont de Nemours (probably the first given the content), and that the rest was by Clavière.

146. Mirabeau, *De la Caisse d'Escompte* (n.p., 1785), v.

147. Ibid., viii.

148. Ibid., 83.

149. Ibid., 48–50.

150. Ibid., 61.

151. Brissot, *Mémoires*, II, 31, 348; Bénétruy, *L'atelier de Mirabeau*, 104–108.

152. Mirabeau, *De la Banque d'Espagne* (n.p., 1785), 108–109.

153. Clavière to Marc Lieutaud, 1 August 1785, in Bouchary, *Les manieurs d'argent*, I, 54–55, and, more generally on Clavière's speculations, 48–74.

154. On Beaumarchais, see Gunnar and Mavis von Proschwitz, "Beaumarchais et le *Courier de l'Europe*," *Studies on Voltaire and the Eighteenth Century* 273 (1990).

155. Bénétruy, *L'atelier de Mirabeau*, 108–116.

156. On Mirabeau's relationship with Calonne, see Quastana, *La pensée politique de Mirabeau*, 389–428.

157. Henri Welschinger, *La mission secrète de Mirabeau à Berlin* (Paris, 1900).

158. Mirabeau had read Dupont's *Mémoire* while in the prison of Vincennes and made copies of the manuscript for later publication in his own name. He gave a copy to Clavière in 1782 that was passed on to Brissot. For Brissot's account of the affair and the exchange of letters with Mirabeau, see *Correspondance*, 94–103, and *Mémoires*, II, 35–38. Brissot's edition appeared in 1787 as *Œuvres posthumes de M. Turgot, ou: Mémoire de M. Turgot, sur les Administrations provinciales, mis en parallèle avec celui de M. Necker, suivi d'une Lettre sur ce Plan, & des Observations d'un Républicain sur ces Mémoires; & en général sur le bien qu'on doit attendre de ces Administrations dans les Monarchies* (Lausanne, 1787). See also Bénétruy, *L'atelier de Mirabeau*, 118–126.

159. Brissot, *Dénonciation au public du nouveau projet d'agiotage* (July 1786); *Sur un nouveau projet de Compagnie d'Assurances contre les Incendies à Paris* (London, 1786); *Seconde lettre contre la Compagnie d'Assurances* (London, 1786).

160. Mirabeau, *Dénonciation de l'agiotage* (Paris, 1787), 29. Ironically, Mirabeau was here attacking not only Calonne and Necker but also Clavière's own plans for a life assurance company—having been paid to write on behalf of Panchaud. On the battle over life assurance companies, see Lüthy, *La banque protestante*, II, 711–715; on Mirabeau's involvement, see Bénétruy, *L'atelier de Mirabeau*, 128–132.

161. Clavière to Théophile Cazenove, 7 June 1786, in Bouchary, *Les maniers d'argent*, I, 78.

162. Jefferson to John Jay, 26 September 1786, PTJ. Jefferson recalled this to Washington on 6 June 1793 (PTJ). See also the pathbreaking article by Allan Potofsky, "The Political Economy of the French-American Debt Debate: The Ideological Uses of Atlantic Commerce, 1787–1800," *William and Mary Quarterly* 63 (2006), 489–516.

163. Brissot, *Mémoires*, II, 52–53. Clavière wrote to the Pastor Mouchon at Geneva on 5 June 1787 that the work was a product of each of their labors and that the truths it contained were relevant to Geneva (Chapuisat, *Figures et choses d'autrefois*, 66).

164. Clavière and Brissot, *Prospectus de la société Gallo-Américaine*, March 1787 (PTJ).

165. J. Hector Saint-John de Crèvecœur, *Lettres d'un cultivateur Américain* (Paris, 1787), 2nd ed., 3 vols., III, 116.

166. Brissot, *Examen critique des voyages dans l'Amérique Septentrionale, de M. le Marquis de Chatellux, Dans laquelle on réfute principalement ses opinions sur les Quakers, sur les Negres, sur le Peuple, & sur l'Homme* (London, 1786), 33–44, 61–62; *Mémoires*, II, 46–51.

167. Brissot, *New Travels in the United States of America* (London, 1794), 2nd ed., 77–78. Brissot went on to state that all the ministers were "men of talents, or at least, men of learning," and praised the fact that they were paid "by collections and rent of pews," before supporting an argument he ascribed to Clavière: that priests should marry even if their income was small, as fathers would want to marry their daughters to them because of their learning and good morals.

168. The review of *De la France* in *The English Review, or, An Abstract of English and Foreign Literature* (London, 1789) made the latter point, interpreting the text as French Machiavellianism directed against British commercial interests in the hope of bringing North America into a permanently French sphere of economic interest (14). See also Paul Cheney, "A False Dawn for Enlightenment Cosmopolitanism? Franco-American Trade during the American War of Independence," *William and Mary Quarterly* 63 (2006), 463–488.

169. Clavière and Brissot, *De la France et des Étas-Unis*, 106, 116, 130, 133.

170. Richard Whatmore, "The French and American Revolutions in Comparative Perspective," in Manuela Albertone and Antonino De Francesco, eds., *Rethinking the Atlantic World: Europe and America in the Age of Democratic Revolutions* (London, 2009), 219–238.

171. Clavière and Brissot, *De la France*, 24.

172. Jefferson to Brissot, 16 August 1786, PTJ: "Were I to select any particular passages as giving me particular satisfaction, it would be those where you prove to the United States that they will be more virtuous, more free & more happy emploied in agriculture, than as carriers or manufacturers. It is a truth, and a precious one for them, if they could be persuaded of it."

173. Clavière and Brissot, *De la France*, 80–81.

174. Ibid., 13.

175. Ibid., 5, also 8n, 32.

176. Ibid., 92.

177. Ibid., 8f.

178. Ibid., 13.

179. Ibid., 18.

180. Ibid., 20.

181. Clavière was also drawing on James Steuart: see Sonenscher, *Sans-Culottes*, 323–324.

182. Clavière and Brissot, *De la France*, 80–81, 403.

183. Ibid., 45.

184. Coxe, *Travels in Switzerland*, II, 411.

185. Clavière and Brissot, *De la France*, 47.

186. Ibid., 82.

187. Ibid., 74.

188. Ibid., 92.

189. Ibid., 13.

190. Ibid., 410–412.

191. Brissot, *Correspondance*, 177.

192. John Holroyd, Lord Sheffield, *Observations on the Commerce of the American States* (London, 1783), 2nd ed., 1–4, 120–122. Holroyd later opposed Jefferson's negotiated reduction of duties upon U.S. goods in 1794, identifying them as dangerous to the survival of the British Empire and unnecessary because of the cheapness of British products. See further Holroyd, Lord Sheffield, *Strictures on the Necessity of Inviolably Maintaining the Navigation and Colonial System of Great Britain* (London, 1804), 22–27.

193. On Sieyès's claims and their relationship with Clavière's, see Michael Sonenscher, "The Nation's Debt and the Birth of the Modern Republic: The French Fiscal Deficit and the Politics of the Revolution of 1789," *History of Political Thought* 18 (1997), 64–103, 267–325; Introduction to Emmanuel Joseph Sieyès, *Political Writings* (New York, 2004); and *Sans-Culottes*, 315–324.

194. Dupont de Nemours to Clavière, 1787, Dupont papers, Hagley Museum, Winterthur Manuscripts Group 2 Series A, DPDN, W2-292.

195. Brissot, *Mémoires*, II, 66–70.

196. Clavière and Brissot, *Point de Banqueroute, ou Lettre à un Créancier de l'État, Sur l'impossibilité de la Banqueroute National, & sur les moyens de ramener le Crédit & la Paix* (London, 1787), 5–7.

197. Ibid., 14f, 29–33.

198. Ibid., 3–7, 38–40.

199. Clavière and Brissot, *Observations d'un Républicain Sur les diverse systèmes d'Administrations provinciales, particulièrement sur ceux de MM. Turgot & Necker, & sur le bien qu'on peut en espérer dans les Gouvernemens monarchiques* (Lausanne, 1788).

200. Ibid., 114, 117, 123, 127, 133.

201. Ibid., 114f.

202. Ibid., 155.

203. Clavière and Brissot, *Observations*, 166–168.

204. Clavière and Brissot, *Point de banqueroute, Ou lettres a un créancier de l'état, sur l'impossibilité de la banqueroute nationale, & sur les moyens de ramener le crédit & la paix. Nouvelle édition, augmentée de trois autres lettres sur la dette nationale; considérée relativement à la révocation des deux impôts, à la guerre de Hollande, & à celle de Turquie* (London, 1787), 135–139.

205. Ibid., 48, 60–62, 69–75, 78–87, 89, 92, 98, 102–109.

206. Volney's later *Considérations sur la guerre actuelle des Turcs* (London, 1788), came to the same conclusion as the *Point de banqueroute* (1787).

207. William Coxe, *Travels into Poland, Russia, Sweden, and Denmark* (London, 1784).

208. Clavière and Brissot, *Point de banqueroute* (1787), 120–133.

209. Dumont, *Recollections of Mirabeau*, 50.

210. Mirabeau [Clavière], *Lettre remise à Frédéric-Guillaume II, roi régnant de Prusse* (Berlin, 1787); Dumont, *Recollections of Mirabeau*, 53.

211. Jeremy D. Popkin, "Dutch Patriots, French Journalists, and Declarations of Rights: The Leidse Ontwerp of 1785 and Its Diffusion in France," *Historical Journal* 38 (1995), 553–565.

212. Brissot, *Mémoires*, II, 171; Bénétruy, *L'atelier de Mirabeau*, 138–139. On all of these works, see Quastana, *La pensée politique de Mirabeau*, 429–495.

213. Bénétruy, *L'atelier de Mirabeau*, 134.

214. Brissot et al., *Lettre de la Société des Amis des Noirs, à M. Necker, avec la réponse de ce Ministre* (July 1789), 4.

215. Brissot to Jefferson, 8 March 1787, PTJ.

216. Brissot, *Correspondance*, 134–135, 166–175; *Mémoires*, II, 71. See also Claude Perroud, "La Société française des Amis des Noirs," *La Révolution française* 69 (1916), 122–147; Léon Cahen, "La Société des Amis des Noirs et Condorcet," *La Révolution française* 50 (1906), 481–511; David P. Resnick, "The Société des Amis des Noirs and the Abolition of Slavery," *French Historical Studies* 7 (1972), 558–569.

217. Dumont, *Recollections of Mirabeau*, 63.

218. Thomas Clarkson, *The History of the Rise, Progress, and Accomplishment of the Abolition of the African Slave-Trade by the British Parliament* (London, 1808), 2 vols., I, 446–451.

219. Chapuisat, *Figures et choses d'autrefois*, 70–71.

220. Clavière, "Procès-verbaux de la Société gallo-américaine," 9 January 1787, published in Brissot, *Correspondance*, 105–136. Clavière questioned the name of the society as he aspired to universal improvement rather than any reform limited by national self-interest: "N'ayant plus de patrie où les droits de naissance imposent des devoirs

particuliers, il ne lui convient pas d'appartenir à d'autres Sociétés qu'à la Société universelle; que sous ce point de vue, il ne saurait s'attacher à aucun corps ou Société ennemie par état ou par principe d'aucune autre." Brissot, *Correspondance*, 108.

221. Clavière to Mirabeau, 25 April 1788, in Bénétruy, *L'atelier de Mirabeau*, 139–141.

222. Brissot, *Plan de conduite pour les députés du peuple aux États-généraux de 1789* (Paris, [April] 1789), 234–235.

223. Clavière, *De la foi publique* (Paris, 1788), xxviii, 30–32, 53–58, 92, 72–74, 76–81, 91–92, 100, 106–108, 145–148, 174–176.

224. Dumont, *Recollections of Mirabeau*, 326–327.

225. Clavière to Jacob Vernes, 31 November 1788, BdG Ms. Fr. 299.

226. Dumont, *Recollections of Mirabeau*, 327–328.

CHAPTER 7. REVOLUTION AND EMPIRE

1. Dumont, *Recollections of Mirabeau*, 328, 331.

2. Bénétruy, *L'atelier de Mirabeau*, 172.

3. Marc Cramer, *Genève et les Suisses, 1691–1792* (Geneva, 1914), 194–198; Eric Golay, *Quand le peuple devint roi: Mouvement populaire, politique et révolution à Genève de 1789 à 1794* (Geneva, 2001), 240–244.

4. As the *Monthly Magazine* (London, 1799), 510, put it, "Sir Francis d'Ivernois is known to be a party writer." The *Monthly Review* (1795), 559, noted, on the publication of d'Ivernois's *Réflexions sur la guerre* in response to Madame de Staël's *Réflexions sur la paix adressées à M. Pitt et aux Français*, that he was "well known for his struggles for liberty."

5. André Gür, "L'Émeute Genevoise de Janvier 1789 avait-elle un caractère insurrectionel?" in Bronislaw Baczko, Louis Binz, Roger Durand, Olivier Labarthe, and Marc Neuenschwander, eds., *Regards sur la Révolution genevoise, 1792–1798* (Geneva, 1992), 39–67.

6. D'Ivernois, *Tableau historique et politique des deux dernières révolutions de Genève*, II, 270–309.

7. Marc Peter, *Genève et la Révolution: Les Comités provisoires, 28 décembre 1792–13 avril 1794* (Geneva, 1921), 41–47.

8. Dumont, *Souvenirs sur Mirabeau*, 40; Jarrett, *The Begetters of Revolution*, 260–264; Dumont to Romilly, December 1789, *Memoirs of Romilly*, 383.

9. D'Ivernois emphasized Necker's political impotence after the events of 1782 (*Tableau historique et politique des deux dernières révolutions de Genève*, II, 178) and argued against Soulavie in a draft letter of 1801 that any notion of an identity of opinion between Necker and the représentants had become preposterous long before 1789. See also Dumont to Necker, 7 December 1789, in Jean Martin, *La polémique Necker-Dumont en 1789* (Geneva, 1926), 10–14.

10. For example, the anonymous *Principes positifs de M. Necker, Extraits de tous ses ouvrages* stated that Necker was an advocate of absolutism and the employment of

foreign troops to protect the crown in times of disorder, and was an opponent of the right to resist ([Paris, 1789], 1–4).

11. Anon., *La vie privée et publique de Louis XVI, roi de France* (London, 1800), 101: Necker sought to render France "heureuse qu'en rapprochant son gouvernement de celui de cette petite république."

12. Jacques Necker, *Du pouvoir exécutif dans les grands états* (Paris, 1792), 2 vols., I, 52–66; 325–342; *De la Révolution française* (Paris, 1796), 2 vols., I, 261, 299–312.

13. [Jacques-Louis] De [la] Latocnaye, *Les causes de la Révolution de France* (Edinburgh, 1797), 164–165.

14. Dumont to Pierre Mouchon, 21 June 1788, BdG Ms. Fr. 496, fol. 232–233.

15. Richard Price to the Duc de la Rochefoucauld, in *Correspondence of Richard Price*, III, 305–311; James Mackintosh, *Vindiciæ Gallicæ* (London, 1791), 2nd ed., 326–335; Helen Maria Williams, *Letters Written in France* (Oxford, [1790] 1989), 68–69.

16. Anon., "Biographical Sketch of Dr Archibald Maclane," *Gentleman's Magazine* (London, 1818), 110.

17. *The Correspondence of Jeremy Bentham, Volume 4, October 1788 to December 1793*, ed. Alexander Taylor Milne (London, 1981), 17–18n; Bentham, *Political Tactics*, ed. Michael James, Cyprian Blamires, and Catherine Pease-Watkin (Oxford, 1999), Introduction.

18. Summaries of Bentham's related reform projects, including his *Draught of a New Plan for the Organisation of the Judicial Establishment in France* (n.p., March 1790), were translated by Dumont and published in the *Courrier de Provence* (from I, no. X, 8–9 [7–12 June 1789]).

19. Dumont, *Recollections of Mirabeau*, 42–43: "The councils had yielded some of their usurped powers, but had managed to retain several. The Genevese residents in London were by no means satisfied with this arrangement, and the clause which they reprobated the most, was the one which provided that the exiles, though recalled, should not resume their offices and honours. Meetings had been held on this subject; and, as I had not been banished, but was only a voluntary exile, it was considered that I could plead the cause of the exiles with much more propriety than themselves. My notions of liberty had been strengthened by my residence in England, and by the liberal spirit of the writings published, at that period, in France. I was one of the most active at our Genevese meetings; and I undertook to write a pamphlet containing all the observations we had made upon the new Genevese code. My work was well received; and it was proposed to address it to our fellow citizens. Du Roveray, who had just arrived from Ireland, persuaded me that the work would prove more effective if published at Paris; and that it was necessary to prevent a ratification of the treaty by the powers, otherwise the imperfect state of things then existing, might be rendered permanent and conclusive." See also Dumont to Mouchon, 16 February 1789, BdG Ms. Fr. 496, fol. 233–234.

20. Dumont, *Réclamation des Genevois patriotes établis à Londres* (Paris, 1789), 1–23, 25–48, 53, 63–65, 76–77, 82–85.

21. Dumont to Mouchon, 12 February 1788, BdG Ms. Fr. 496, fol. 229.

22. Jacob Vernes, *Confidence philosophique* (London, 1771), 337–338, 376–378.

23. Vernes, *Abrégé du Catéchisme* (Geneva, 1779), 43–81.

24. Antoine-Jacques Roustan, *Dialogues entre Annibal et Tite-Live* (Geneva, 1789), 18–36, 42–57, 63–81. As per http://www.hls-dhs-dss.ch/textes/f/F26130.php.

25. David Williams to Brissot, 13 March 1789, in James Dybikowski, "David Williams (1738–1816) and Jacques-Pierre Brissot: Their Correspondence," *National Library of Wales Journal* 25 (1987–1988), 167–197; Brissot, *Nouveau voyage dans les Etats-Unis de l'Amérique septentrionale, fait en 1788* (Paris, 1791), xii.

26. Shelburne correspondence, Dumont papers, BdG MS 33.

27. D'Ivernois, *Tableau historique et politique des deux dernières révolutions de Genève*, I, i: "Le Conseil de la ville de Séleucie est composé de trois cents personnes choisies pour leurs richesses ou leur capacité; & le peuple y a une part considérable aux affaires. Quand tous les Ordres de cette République sont unis, elle n'a rien à craindre des Parthes: mais quand la division se met parmi ses citoyens, le Prince étranger, que les uns ne manquent jamais d'appeller à leur secours contre les autres, les opprime tous également. Et c'est ce qui leur était arrivé sous Artabane, qui, pour son seul intérêt, livra le peuple aux Grands: car l'influence du peuple approche fort de la liberté, au lieu que l'aristocratie est plus conforme au despotisme d'un seul." Tacitus, *Annals*, bk. VI.

28. D'Ivernois, *Tableau historique et politique des deux dernières révolutions de Genève*, I, iv–xiii, 1–49, 188–200, II, 207–208, 217–219.

29. Ibid., II, 106, 111, 261–264.

30. On d'Ivernois's demand for national unity, and the danger of supporting aristocracy thereby, see David Chauvet to d'Ivernois, 15 January 1790, BdG, Ms. Fr. fols. 25–26.

31. D'Ivernois, *Tableau historique et politique des deux dernières révolutions de Genève*, I, i: "Le devoir d'un historien est de louer ses ennemis, lorsque leurs actions sont vraiment louables, et de blâmer sans hésiter, ses plus grands amis, lorsque leurs fautes le méritent."

32. Ibid., II, 317–341.

33. D'Ivernois to Necker, 12 March 1789; d'Ivernois to Chauvet [Spring] 1789, BdG Ms. Suppl. 979, fols., 15, 20–26.

34. D'Ivernois, "Ma réponse aux Mémoires de Soulavie," [1801], BdG, Ms. Fr. fols. 194–197.

35. Otto Karmin, "Un mémoire inédit de Francis d'Ivernois, sur la situation politique á Genève au début de 1791, et sur les moyens d'y établir un gouvernement stable," *Bulletin de l'Institut national genevois* 42 (1917), 73–95.

36. Dumont, *Souvenirs sur Mirabeau*, 6–7.

37. H. F. Grœnvelt [Dumont, Romilly, and John Scarlett], *Letters containing an Account of the late Revolution in France, and Observations on the Constitution, Laws, Manners, and Institutions of the English* (London, 1792), letter 1, 11; letter 11, 179.

38. For criticisms of classical republics, see Emmanuel Joseph Sieyès, *Qu'est-ce que le Tiers-état?* 3rd ed. (n.p., 1789), 31, and Jean-Paul Rabaut St. Etienne, *Considérations sur les intérêts du Tiers-état, adressées au peuple des provinces* (n.p., 1788), 10–11.

39. Dumont papers, BdG, Ms. 51, "Mélanges d'Économie Politique," fols. 143–217.

40. Dumont, "Motion pour l'inscription civique," Dumont papers, BdG, Ms. 64, pièce 26, "Mélanges historiques," cited in Martin, "Quatorze billets inédits de Mirabeau," 294.

41. Grœnvelt [Dumont], *Letters*, 8–10, 209–210. Dumont later identified the Jacobins as "un État dans l'État" (*Souvenirs sur Mirabeau*, 147) and was horrified when he heard about the massacres from England: "des details d'une férocité qu'on trouve à peine parmi les nations les plus sauvages de l'Amérique"; letter to Mme. Duval, 22 October 1792, in Jean Martin, "Achille du Chastellet et le premier mouvement républicain en France," *La Révolution française* 80 (1927), 129–131.

42. *The Annual Register, or a view of the history, politics, and literature, for the year 1792* (London, 1798), part 1, 171: "The republicans . . . planned and advertised a new paper, under the title of 'The Republican,' which was principally to be conducted by M. Dumont, a Genevese, with the assistance of Brissot, Condorcet, and our country-man Thomas Paine." See also Anon., *Biographical anecdotes of the founders of the French Republic, and of other eminent characters* (London, 1797–1798), 2 vols., I, 105.

43. Dumont, *Souvenirs sur Mirabeau*, 111, 176; Martin, "Achille du Chastellet," 104–132.

44. Guy-Jean-Baptiste Target, *Les États-généraux convoques par Louis XVI* (n.p., 1789), 28; Sieyès, *Qu'est-ce que le Tiers-état?* 3rd ed. (n.p., 1789), 57, 71; Sieyès, *Vues sur les moyens d'exécution dont les représentans de la France pourront disposer en 1789* (n.p., 1789), 39.

45. Frances Acomb, *Anglophobia in France, 1763–1789* (Durham, N.C., 1950).

46. Romilly, *Memoirs of Romilly*, I, 355.

47. Jeremy Bentham, *Essay on political tactics* (London, 1791), vi–viii.

48. Dumont, *Souvenirs sur Mirabeau*, 108.

49. Ibid., 95.

50. Ibid., 131.

51. Ibid., 83, 123–124, 140. Dumont noted that Mirabeau took Du Roveray "en quelque façon pour son Mentor, et consultait avec lui sur toutes les démarches de quelque importance"; ibid., 60.

52. Dumont, *Letters*, 172.

53. Dumont, *Souvenirs sur Mirabeau*, 61, 102–103.

54. Romilly, *Memoirs of Romilly*, I, 109.

55. Dumont, *Souvenirs sur Mirabeau*, 160; see also 51, 149, 171.

56. Mirabeau, *Correspondance entre le Comte de Mirabeau et la Comte de la Marck*, ed. Adolphe Fourier de Bacourt (Paris, 1851), 3 vols., I, 91–92, 102–104.

57. Pierre-Victor Malouet, *Mémoires de Malouet* (Paris, 1868), ed. Baron Malouet, 2 vols., I, 311–322, 373–381, II, 471–483. See also William Clarke, *Interesting letters on the French Revolution, extracted from the celebrated works of Mr. Malouet* (London, 1795), 52–53, 91–92. See further Munro Price, *The Road from Versailles: Louis XVI, Marie Antoinette, and the Fall of the French Monarchy* (London, 2004).

58. Dumont, *Letters*, 7, 169.

59. Ibid., 76.

60. Dumont, *Souvenirs sur Mirabeau*, 65–66.

61. Istvan Hont, "The Permanent Crisis of a Divided Mankind: The Contemporary Crisis of the Nation State in Historical Perspective," *Political Studies* 42 (1994), 166–231; Sonenscher, Introduction to Sieyès, *Political Writings*.

62. Dumont, *Souvenirs sur Mirabeau*, 104–105.

63. Clavière and Brissot, *Règlemens de la Société des amis des noirs* (n.p., 1790), 3; Brissot, *Adresse à l'Assemblée nationale pour l'abolition de la traite des noirs* (Paris, 1790), 15.

64. Dumont to Romilly, 1 June 1789: "L'abbé Sieyès . . . point de voix, timide, incapable de percer dans une assemblée aussi nombreuse, mais du génie, de la médiation, d'excellents principes: s'il a du caractère, il mènera les meneurs." In J.-M. Paris, "Lettre inédite d'Étienne Dumont sur quelques séances du Tiers État (May 1789)," *Mémoires de la Société d'histoire et d'archéologie de Genève* 19 (1877), 16.

65. Dumont, *Letters*, 52.

66. Dumont, *Souvenirs sur Mirabeau*, 71–73, 151.

67. Ibid., 179n.

68. Ibid., 92, 65. Dumont noted on 18 March 1792 that "s'il [Sieyès] en avait seulement mesuré les contours, s'il avait seulement conçu l'étendue et les difficultés d'une legislation complete, il n'aurait pas tenu ce language: la presumption en ce genre comme en tout autre est le signe le plus sûr de l'ignorance"; cited by Bénétruy in Dumont, *Souvenirs sur Mirabeau*, 65.

69. Dumont, *Letters*, 232.

70. Dumont, *Souvenirs sur Mirabeau*, 127, 184–185; *Letters*, 19, 83–85, 101, 109–111.

71. Dumont, *Souvenirs sur Mirabeau*, 47.

72. Jacques Necker, *On the French Revolution* (London, 1797), 2 vols., I, 123.

73. Dumont, *Letters*, 17–18; Dumont, *Souvenirs sur Mirabeau*, 165.

74. The negligible result was that Necker offered Mirabeau the post of ambassador to Constantinople (Dumont, *Souvenirs sur Mirabeau*, 61, 79, 121–122, 187). Bénétruy dates the meeting at 11 June 1789 (*Souvenirs sur Mirabeau*, 264). On Malouet's link with the Genevans, see *Mémoires de Malouet*, I, 179, 276; on the meeting with Necker, I, 276–284.

75. Dumont, *Souvenirs sur Mirabeau*, 74–75.

76. Jean-Gabriel Peltier, *Les Actes des apôtres, commencés le jour des Morts, et finis le jour de la Purification*, cited in Martin, *La polémique Necker-Dumont en 1789*, 12–13.

77. Mirabeau, *Speeches of M. de Mirabeau the Elder, pronounced in the National Assembly of France* (London, 1792), 2 vols., II, 65–78.

78. Dumont, *Souvenirs sur Mirabeau*, 158–161.

79. Ibid., 148–149.

80. Mirabeau, Speech of 16 July 1789, *Collection complète des travaux de M. Mirabeau l'aîné à l'Assemblée Nationale*, ed. Etienne Méjan (Paris, 1791), 5 vols., I, 336–340.

81. Dumont to Mouchon, 5 October 1790, BdG Ms. Fr. 496, fol. 238.

82. Dumont, *Souvenirs sur Mirabeau*, 145, 173, 292, 299.

83. Dumont to Mouchon, 1 August 1791 and 25 June 1792, BdG Ms. Fr. 496, fols. 240–214, 242–243.

84. Dumont to Mouchon, 19 July 1793, BdG Ms. Fr. 496, fols. 244–245.

85. Clavière, *Réflexions sur les formes et les principes auxquels une Nation libre doit assujétir l'Administration des Finances* (Paris, 1790), 159, 174.

86. Clavière, *Observations sommaires sur le projet d'une refonte générale des Monnoies* (Paris, 1790), 6, 24, 41; *Adresse de la Société des Amis des Noirs à l'Assemblée National* (Paris, 1791), 122, 124–155.

87. Clavière, *Opinions d'un Créancier de l'État, sur quelques matières de Finance importantes dans le moment actuel* (Paris, 1789), 30–45.

88. Ibid., 119.

89. Clavière, in *Courrier de Provence*, 17–18 August, 1789, no. 27, 17.

90. Ibid., 12–13.

91. Clavière to Vernes, 10 April 1790, BdG, Ms. Fr. 299.

92. Clavière and Brissot, *De la France*, 2nd ed. (1791), viii; Rivier, *Etienne Clavière*, 85–97.

93. Jacques Necker, "Contre l'émission de dix-neuf cents millions d'assignats," *Œuvres complètes de M. Necker* (Paris, 1820–1821), 15 vols., VII, 430–447; Clavière, *Réponse au Mémoire du M. Necker, concernant les assignats, et à d'autres objections contre une création qui les porte à deux milliards* (Paris, 1790), 13, 86, 125, 200; Clavière, *Réflexions adressées à l'Assemblée National, sur les moyens de concilier l'impôt du Tabac avec la liberté du Commerce, et les rapports que la France doit entretenir avec les Américains libres; sur l'usage des licences ou patentes qui permettent de fabriquer ou vendre* (Paris, 1790).

94. Clavière, *Réflexions sur les formes et les principes auxquels une Nation libre doit assujétir l'Administration des Finances*, 159–174.

95. Clavière, *Lettres écrites à M. Cerutti* (Paris, 1791), 5–6; *Pétition faite à l'Assemblée National par E. Clavière* (Paris, 1791), 3; *L'État actuel de nos finances* (Paris, 1791), 34.

96. Clavière and Brissot, *La Société des amis des noirs à Arthur Dillon, Deputé de la Martinique à l'assemblée nationale* (Paris, [10 March] 1791). On the broader context, see Paul Cheney, *Revolutionary Commerce: Globalization and the French Monarchy* (Cambridge, Mass., 2010), 195–228.

97. Clavière, *Adresse de la Société des Amis des Noirs à l'Assemblée Nationale, à toutes les Villes de Commerce, à toutes les Manufactures, aux Colonies, à toutes les Sociétés des Amis de la Constitution; Adresse dans laquelle on approfondit les relations politiques et commerciales entre la Métropole et les Colonies etc.* (Paris, [10 July] 1791), 22–55, 58–102, 123–155: "Abolition de la traite, liberté sagement préparée pour les esclaves, égalité des droits entre tous les hommes libres, quelque soit leur couleur, liberté de commerce, et confiance entière dans nos avantages naturels, et dans les résultats nécessaires de la totale destruction de l'ancien régime; tels sont les points que nous serons toujours prêts à défendre par les armes de la raison" (151). On Clavière's continued involvement with Thomas Clarkson and the British section of the movement, see Clarkson, *The History of the Rise, Progress, and Accomplishment of the Abolition of the African Slave-Trade by the British Parliament*, II, 132–156.

98. Gary Kates, *The Cercle social, the Girondins, and the French Revolution* (Princeton, N.J., 1985).

99. Clavière to Dumont, 26 November 1791, in Otto Karmin, "Trois lettres inédites de Clavière à Etienne Dumont (1791–1792)," *Revue historique de la Révolution française* 5 (1914), 5.

100. Dumont, *Recollections of Mirabeau*, 326. Earl Gower noted on 16 March 1792 that Clavière, "still a member of that [Jacobin] society and the intimate friend of Mr. de Condorcet and Mr. Brissot," was to be appointed minister and was considered

Necker's "rival in abilities and knowledge of finance." See Oscar Browning, *The Despatches of Earl Gower, English Ambassador at Paris from June 1790 to August 1792* (Cambridge, 1792), 162, 178–179.

101. Brissot, in *Le Moniteur universel*, 19 January 1792; Dumont, *Recollections of Mirabeau*, 335. See further Hans Alfred Goetz-Bernstein, *La diplomatie de la Gironde: Jacques-Pierre Brissot* (Paris, 1912); Ellery, *Brissot de Warville*, 250–256.

102. Anon., *An historical sketch of the French Revolution from its commencement to the year 1792* (London, 1792), 513–514: "Very recently, a fugitive from the Pays de Vaud, a M. Constant de Rebecque wrote in a journal called *Le Moniteur Universel*, to invite the French to seize the Pays de Vaud as part of the ancient kingdom of Burgundy, even as Avignon was part of the ancient country of Provence. The great question is not, what right have such or such countries to rebel; but what right have the French to interfere or to profit by it?"

103. Brissot, A *Discourse upon the question, Whether the King shall be tried? Delivered before the Society of the Friends of the Constitution, at Paris, at a Meeting, July 10th, 1791* (London, 1791), 27; *Le Patriote Français, ou Journal libre, impartial et national, par une Société de Citoyens, & dirigée par J. P. Brissot de Warville* (1139), 22 September 1792.

104. Anon., *Gallery of portraits of the National Assembly, supposed to be written by Count de Mirabeau* (Dublin, 1795), 2 vols., I, 262–265. Of Brissot it was said that nothing was new in his works, which could be read with pleasure, but "your head is converted for a moment into the bucket of the Danaides" (273–274).

105. Clavière to Dumont, 9 July 1791, in Bénétruy, *L'atelier de Mirabeau*, 419–420, and in Chapuisat, *Figures et choses d'autrefois*, 108–112; BdG, Dumont papers, Ms. 33, 376–377.

106. René de Batz, *Les conspirations et la fin de Jean, baron de Batz, 1793–1822* (Paris, 1911), 65–68, 103–107.

107. Soulavie, *Historical and Political Memoirs*, V, 109–110, 270–293.

108. Jacques Bidermann, "D'un Commerce National," *Chronique du mois*, January 1792, 83–88.

109. Clavière, *De la conjuration contre les finances et des mesures à prendre pour en arrêter les effets* (Paris, 1792), 5–11, 19–28, 33–35: "L'ami du genre humain, le philosophe qui consacre ses veilles à la recherche de la vérité, croit voir la face du monde changée, une régénération universelle prouver enfin, à tous les hommes, que les prérogatives de l'égalité politique, sont l'unique source où il faille chercher la perfection du système social" (28).

110. Ibid., 57–82. Clavière promised a detailed work proving that a single tax on inheritance was the key to good manners and economic well-being, should his ministerial duties allow him the time: "Je ne connois qu'un système où toutes les objections importantes, relatives à la politique et à la morale, soient résolues en prenant pour juges la liberté, la justice et la philosophie. C'est un impôt unique sur la généralité des successions; c'est de donner à l'état une part déterminée, dans tous les héritages; en telle sorte que la citoyen ne paye l'impôt que sur la fortune qu'il laisse à ses successeurs" (62n).

111. Ibid., 37–46.
112. Dumont, *Recollections of Mirabeau*, 323; Jeanne Marie Roland de la Platière, *An Appeal to Impartial Posterity, by Citizenness Roland, wife of the Minister of the Home Department, or A Collection of Pieces written by her during her Confinement in the Prisons of the Abbey and St. Pelagie, Part I* (London, 1795), 2 vols., I, 12: "As soon as he had appointed patriotic ministers, he made it his sole study to inspire them with confidence; and so well did he succeed, that for the first three weeks, Roland and Claviere were enchanted with the good disposition of the king. They dreamt of nothing but a better order of things, and flattered themselves that the revolution was at an end. 'Good God!' I used to say to them, 'every time I see you set off for the council with that wonderful confidence, it seems to me that you are about to commit a folly.' 'I assure you,' would Claviere answer, 'that the king is perfectly sensible, that his interest is connected with the observation of the new laws; he reasons too pertinently on the subject not to be convinced of that truth.'"
113. Dumont, *Recollections of Mirabeau*, 336, 341.
114. Thomas Jefferson to James Madison, 3 July 1792, PTJ: "A letter received yesterday, from Mr. Short gives the most flattering result of conversations he had had with Claviere & Dumouriez. Claviere declared he had nothing so much at heart as to encourage our navigation, & the present system of commerce with us. Agreed they ought immediately to repeal their late proceedings with respect to tobo. & ships, and receive our salted provisions favorably, and to proceed to treat with us on broad ground."
115. Clavière to Charles Stanhope, 9 July 1792, BdG Ms. Fr. 917, fols., 202–206: "Les intrigues de l'aristocratie pour en maitriser les Citoyens, le rôle que la cour de Versailles n'a pas rougi de jouer dans ce système suivi d'oppressions, ont donne lieu a une multitude d'écrits qui ont été lus en France. Les idées de justice publique, de droits politiques, de liberté, d'égalité se sont mêlées aux faits historiques; tout cela n'a pas peu contribué a monter les têtes françaises, et a préparer la révolution."
116. Ibid.: "La conséquence naturelle de ces observations relativement au peuple anglais, c'est que son alliance avec la France serait le plus sur moyen, en consolidant notre contribution, de nous donner la paix, de rétablir le calme dans les esprits, & de vous mettre a couvert de toutes les atteintes politiques que vous pourriez redouter de notre part. . . . Une telle alliance assurerait sans contredit le bonheur des deux états. Elle influerait puissamment sur le sort de l'Europe & sur la tranquillité générale."
117. Brissot (citing Condorcet), in *Le Patriote Français* (895), 22 January 1792, 85–86.
118. Charles-Maurice, duc de Talleyrand-Périgord, *Mémoires du prince de Talleyrand*, ed. duc de Broglie (Paris, 1891), 5 vols., I, 221–222; Charles-François du Périer Dumouriez, *The Life of General Dumouriez* (London, 1796), 3 vols., II, 200; William Edward Hartpole Lecky, *A History of England in the Eighteenth Century* (London, 1887), 8 vols., VI, chap. 22; Dumont, *Recollections of Mirabeau*, 300–303.
119. Dumont, *Recollections of Mirabeau*, 340–352.
120. Lord Auckland to George Nugent-Temple-Grenville, 27 November 1792, cited in William Edward Hartpole Lecky, *The French Revolution: Chapters from the Author's History of England during the Eighteenth Century* (London, 1904), 471.

121. Charles-François du Périer Dumouriez, *Lettres which passed between General Dumouriez and Pache, Minister of War to the French* (Perth, 1794), 111. Dumouriez to Clavière, 23 November 1792: "I address to you, Protestant Minister, the papers in the process raised against the Carthusian monks. To me Calvin and St. Bruno are alike. The republic will, I hope, be the gainer. I have time only to make my compliments." Dumouriez, *Memoirs of General Dumourier. Written by himself. Translated by John Fenwick, Part I* (Dublin, 1794), 83–86: "Brissot boasted of his plans for the conquest of Spain and Italy; but the general easily detected the folly of his calculations. . . . the malignity of Clavière had been lately gratified, in compelling General Montesquiou to become an exile . . . and in disorganizing Geneva, his native country. Brissot and his adherents maintained, that it was necessary to compel the Swiss Cantons to abandon their neutrality; or, in case of refusal, to attack them."

122. Chauvet to d'Ivernois, 21 October 1792, BdG, Ms. Suppl. 1010, fol. 116. Chauvet reported, "Vous pouvez imaginer dans quelles allarmes nous sommes sur les suites de cette affaire; depuis le moment où nous avons su ce qui préparoit, nous nous sommes employés de notre mieux à conjurer l'orage; j'ai écrit pour cela plusieurs lettres, Dumont a mis en jeu toutes ses rélations, Du Rouveray a envoyé un mémoire signé au Ministre des Affaires étrangères, ce qui peut être lui coutera la place qu'il occupe ici pour le Gouvernement françois; Reybas a écrit deux puissantes lettres à Clavière dans lesquelles il a remué tous les ressorts pour l'engager à faire son devoir. Jusqu'à présent tout cela n'a rien produit, & on va faire de nouveaux efforts pour que le temps que l'on emploie à la négociation produise quelque bon effet."

123. Browning, *Despatches of Earl Gower*, 190–193. Gower further reported that Dumouriez wanted to take the king south, and had information that Clavière was using six million livres of secret service money to raise value of paper money, because he had over a million livres invested himself.

124. John Moore, *A journal during a residence in France, from the beginning of August, to the middle of December, 1792. To which is Added, an Account of the most Remarkable Events that Happened at Paris from that Time to the Death of the Late King of France* (London, 1793), 2 vols., II, 144–146.

125. Anon., *Territoire neutre de Genève* (RIV 3551); Anon , *Très-humble et très-respectueuse représentation, remise à Messieurs les Syndics, et appuyée par un grand nombre de citoyens et bourgeois, les 8 et 9 octobre 1792* (RIV 3566); *Lettre du ministre britannique à la République de Genève, écrite de Berne le 11 octobre 1792, extraite de la Gazette Nationale de France, no 230 (signé) le lord Robert Fitz Gerald, ministre-plénipotentiaire de Sa M. B. près le Corps Helvétique et la République de Genève* (RIV 3575); Bérenger, *Lettres à M. Clavière, ministre des contributions publiques* (RIV 3579) and *Réponse à M. Condorcet* (Geneva, [20 October] 1792).

126. Brissot, *Le Patriote Français* (1153), 17 October 1792, 391–392. See also Sorel, *L'Europe et la Révolution française*, III, 122–126.

127. Cramer, *Genève et les Suisses*, 236–273; Henri Fazy, *Genève de 1788 à 1792: La fin d'un régime* (Geneva, 1917), 407–489.

128. Chauvet to d'Ivernois, 28 October 1792, BdG, Ms. Suppl. 1010, fols. 18–25.

129. Dumont's response to Reybaz's letter of 11 January 1793, in Bénétruy, *L'atelier de Mirabeau*, 423–424: "Je l'ai toujours aimé bien tendrement, et ce qu'il a fait pour nous dans ce moment-ci me fait aller plus en avant que je ne l'avais rétrogradé dans le temps de sa poursuite contre l'Aristocratie, qui me paraissait mettre en danger la patrie elle-même."

130. Clavière to unknown, 14 December [1792], BdG, Ms. Fr. 916, fol. 168: "Ecrivez à nos aristocrates, demis ou quarts. Qu'ils s'exécutent & qu'on ait le courage de faire un petit chef d'œuvre de Constitution démocratique. Répétez leur sans cesse que les bonnes loix vise l'éducation, & qu'il est insensé, parce qu'on a pas de bonne éducation, d'avoir de mauvaises lois qui sont une éducation très mauvaise."

131. Paul Mantoux, "Le Comité de Salut public et la mission de Genet aux États-Unis," *Revue d'histoire moderne et contemporaine* 13 (1909–1910), 5–29; M. J. Sydenham, *The Girondins* (London, 1961), 20–28.

132. Clavière to Nicolas-Frédéric de Steiguer ("avoyer de la ville et république de Berne"), in *Le Patriote français* (1162), 15 October 1792, 428–429.

133. Dumont, *Souvenirs sur Mirabeau*, 229–236; Clavière to Dumont, 26 November 1791: "L'enfance de la liberté le choque parce que l'Assemblée nationale n'est pas comme le Deux cent de Genève, pédantesquement politique; il [Du Roveray] ne veut voir que des polissons dans cette assemblée. Elle est très patriotique, et si c'est du *plebs* tout pur, elle prouvera que le plebs est ce qu'il y a de meilleur" (Karmin, "Trois lettres inédites de Clavière à Etienne Dumont, 1791–1792," 11).

134. Clavière, *Correspondance du ministre Clavière et du général Montesquiou: Servant de réponse au libelle du général contre le ministre* (Geneva, 1792), 14: "Il n'y a pas à hésiter sur le sort de la Savoie. Elle doit être libre et indépendante sous la protection de la République Française. Hâtez-vous d'y proclamer cette première loi; c'est justice et convenance tout à la fois. Mais que ferez-vous de Genève? Vous voudriez bien, et je pense comme vous, qu'on n'entrât pas en querelle avec la Suisse. Cela serait facile, si elle entendait bien ses intérêts. Q'ils retirent les troupes qui sont entrées dans Genève & les Suisses seront en paix avec nous? Nous n'avons aucun besoin de loger chez eux, pour garantir nos frères de Savoie contre leur Roi, notre ennemi commun."

135. Clavière to Montesquiou: "Je reçois des plaintes de plusieurs Genevois sur l'abandon où ils seront, lorsque vous serez éloignés de Genève. Ils pensent que l'on vous a prévenu contre eux. Ils sont désarmés, sans chef, & ont contre eux une aristocratie bourgeoise, qui a su se rendre redoubtable."

136. Karmin, *Sir Francis d'Ivernois*, 222–242; Herbert Marsh, *The History of the politicks of Great Britain and France* (London, 1800), 2 vols., II, 195–196.

137. Clavière to Montesquiou: "J'espère que vous entrerez bientôt à Genève: il faut détruire ce nid d'aristocrates et y pêcher tous les trésors que nous y avons enfouis." Marquis de Montesquiou, *Mémoire justificatif pour le citoyen français A.-P. de Montesquiou, Ci-devant Général de l'armée des Alpes, Précédé et suivi de Pièces importantes*, November 1792, 41, 47–48.

138. Brissot, *Rapport fait à la Convention nationale, sur la négociation entre Genève & la République de France, & sur la transaction du 2 novembre 1792* (Paris, [21 November] 1792).

139. Dumont, *Recollections of Mirabeau*, 359–360.

140. Ibid., 360–365.

141. *Édit consacrant l'égalité politique, sanctionné le 12 décembre 1792.* See Golay, *Quand le peuple devint roi*, 636–637.

142. Ellery, *Brissot de Warville*, 310–312.

143. Golay, *Quand le peuple devint roi*, 79–96, 293–343, 587–604.

144. Bérenger, *Lettre du citoyen Bérenger à ses concitoyens* (Geneva, 1793), 4–5.

145. Golay, *Quand le peuple devint roi*, 320–323, 449–450.

146. Jean Desonnaz, *Correspondance de Grenus et Desonnaz, ou État politique et moral de la République de Geneve* (Geneva, 1794), 3 vols., I, 1–4, 11–13; Desonnaz, *Histoire de la conjuration de Grenus, Soulavie, &c. contre la république de Geneve, faisant suite à la correspondance de Grenus et Desonnaz* (Geneva, 1794), 3 vols., III, 5–12, 52–56, 61–63.

147. Etienne-Salomon Reybaz to Dumont, 26 January 1793, in Golay, *Quand le peuple devint roi*, 103–104.

148. Dumont to Romilly, 11 September 1792: "Je me promène la moitié du jour dans une agitation extrême, et par l'impossibilité de rester en place, en pensant à tous les évènements malheureux qui découlent d'une source d'où nous nous sommes flattés de voir sortir le bonheur du genre humain. Brûlons tous les livres, cessons de penser et de rêver au meilleur système de législation, puisque les hommes font un abus infernal de toutes les vérités et de tous les principes. . . . Le passé est affreux, mais ce qu'il y a de plus affreux encore, c'est qu'on ne peut rien attendre, rien espérer pour l'avenir. Nous ne verrons que déchirement et massacres. . . . Je sens bien que le peuple est jeté dans cet état de fièvre par l'approche des ennemis; je me rappelle l'état de colère et de douleur frénétique où j'ai été moi-même, quand j'ai vu trois armées environner Genève pour nous soumettre à un gouvernement odieux. Je comprends que dans une grande ville comme Paris où tant de passions fermentent, elles ont dû s'exalter jusqu'à la fureur contre les aristocrates, qui ont attiré ces fléaux d'Autriche et de Prusse sur leur patrie." Bénétruy, *L'atelier de Mirabeau*, 428, citing Romilly, *Memoirs of Romilly*, II, 4.

149. On Dumont's role at Geneva, that of Reybaz working from Paris, and the aftermath, see Peter, *Genève et la Révolution: Les Comités provisoires (28 décembre 1792–13 avril 1794)*, and *Genève et la Révolution: Le gouvernement constitutionnel, l'annexion, la Société économique, 1794–1814* (Geneva, 1950). Du Roveray noted, in *An appeal to justice and true liberty; or, an accurate statement of the proceedings of the French towards the Republic of Geneva* (London, 1793), 55n, that Dumont, "after having written from London several strong remonstrances to many eminent characters in France, in favour of his country, was requested by the lawful magistrates of Geneva to hasten to Paris, in order that he might support, by his influence, the independence of the republic, and from thence proceed to Geneva, where his preference and abilities have been universally acknowledged by all the well-meaning citizens, as having contributed greatly to the public peace and safety."

150. Karmin, *Sir Francis d'Ivernois*, 253–254.

151. Clavière to Bérenger, 27 October 1792, BdG Ms. Supp. 363.

152. Mallet du Pan's verdict was that Clavière "may be forgiven his zeal for mobocracy, as he has lived in the midst of republican dissensions; but such is the calibre of his judgment, that he will not hesitate to try upon an empire of twenty-five millions of souls a form of government to which, at Geneva, he could not bring even the popular party to conform." *Memoirs and Correspondence of Mallet Du Pan*, ed. André Sayous (London, 1852), 2 vols., I, 275, from the *Mercure de France*, March 1792.

153. Clavière to Dumont, 19 July 1792. Dumont attacked the Gironde (and particularly Brissot) in letters to Romilly at this time (*Memoirs of Romilly*, II, 33). For his later assessment of Clavière, see Dumont, *Souvenirs sur Mirabeau*, 207, 212, 232.

154. Clavière to unknown [the intended recipient was surely Lord Stanhope], 24 January 1793, BdG, D. O. Autographe.

155. Dumouriez, *Life of General Dumouriez*, II, 182: "Dumouriez, Roland, and Clavière, were three very studious, and laborious men, who lived at home, assisted but very seldom at the debates of this [Jacobin] club previously to their entrance into the administration, never afterwards; and who considered it as a dangerous assembly, which it was necessary either to suppress, or lull asleep, in order to render it less hurtful."

156. Joseph-Marie Belgodère, *Supplément aux éclaircissements, pour servir de base à l'opinion qu'on doit avoir sur le citoyen Lamarche, Directeur de la confection des Assignats, & sur le Ministre Clavière qui en à la surveillance* (Paris, 1793).

157. Rivier, *Etienne Clavière*, 161–179.

158. Clavière, "E. Clavière à ses concitoyens" ([Paris], [12 July] 1793).

159. Antoine-François Bertrand de Molleville, *Histoire de la Révolution de France . . . tome douzième* (Paris, 1803), 254–255; Anon., *Hints; or, A Short Account of the Principal Movers of the French Revolution* (London, [1794]), 48: "CLAVIERE was also eminent for his republicanism and hatred of kings. A decree has been passed against CLAVIERE, and he is now an obscure wanderer under proscription, with the axe of the guillotine suspended over him. CLAVIERE deserves no pity, for he showed none."

160. Anon., *The misfortunes of Geneva; or, A Picture of the calamities that threaten, in the present crisis, the most moderate governments of Europe* (London, [1795]), 3–5, 27–32, 63–66, 69, 75.

161. Pierre-Auguste Adet, "Speech of Citizen Adet, the Resident of the French Republic, at the Republic of Geneva" (September 1794), *A collection of state papers, relative to the war against France now carrying on by Great-Britain and the several other European powers, containing authentic copies of treaties, conventions, proclamations, manifestoes, declarations, memorials, . . .* (London, 1794–1802), 11 vols., II, 378: "Fear not, then, citizens, that France will break the ties which bind her to Geneva. . . . It is not to make slaves, to trample upon states less powerful than their own, to change, as kings do, cities into tombs, and peopled countries into deserts, that the French have armed. . . . I assure you that the French people will never do any thing to the prejudice of your independence."

162. The *Gazette nationale* for August 1792 (London, 1797, 4 vols., III, 290) noted that the "fameux genevois . . . est répute servir ici chaudemont le parti de l'aristocratie."

163. Fitzmaurice, *Life of William, Earl of Shelburne*, II, 373–396.

164. Joseph Priestley, *The present state of Europe compared with antient prophecies: a sermon preached at the Gravel Pit meeting in Hackney, 24 February 1794* (London, 1794) 3rd ed., 1–3, 21–29.

165. Shelburne, speech to the House of Lords, 17 February 1794, in *The Annual Register, or a view of the politics, history and literature, for the year 1794* (London, 1799), 220–226; Charles Stanhope, *The Speech of Earl Stanhope, in the House of Lords, On Thursday the 20th of February, 1800, In support of his motion for Peace with the French Republic; Wherein he shews the ruinous tendency of the war* (London, 1800). For a sense of the altered times, see Thomas Skinner, *A refutation of Mr. Pitt's alarming assertion, made on the last day of the last session of Parliament, "that unless the monarchy of France be restored, the monarchy of England will be lost for ever": in a letter, addressed to the Right Hon. Thomas Skinner, Lord Mayor of the City of London: contents, Brissot's reasons for recommending to France a war with England* (London, 1794).

166. Fitzmaurice, *Life of William, Earl of Shelburne*, II, 429–433.

167. Du Roveray, *An appeal to justice and true liberty*, vi–vii.

168. Ibid., 2: "[Britain is] a country where the voice of truth and reason is still heard, a nation at all times distinguished for its good faith and generosity, and whose government has ever held treaties to be sacred and inviolable. Sensible of the invaluable blessing of its own independence, it has constantly respected that of other nations. In the eyes of such a government, the rights of a small state are as respectable as those of the most powerful. The facility of oppression has never sanctioned the secret projects of aggrandizement, nor have the disgraceful motives of revenge or retaliation, when even the plainest occasion offered, ever diverted it from the strict rules of national faith and impartial justice. To such a nation, and to such a government, the conduct of the enemies of Geneva cannot fail to appear in its true light."

169. Ibid., 4–17, 89–91, 106–110.

170. Ibid., 34–51, 77.

171. Ibid., 74, 79–80, 81–83.

172. Du Roveray to Evan Nepean, 18 October 1792: "I have just now got a copy of the Decree of the National Convention concerning Lyon; it is in every respect worthy of an assembly of Caligula. 1st An extraordinary Commission of 5 Members shall be named to punish in military way and without delay the counter revolutionists of Lyon. 2nd All the inhabitants of that city shall be disarmed & their arms given to the defenders of their country and to the oppressed patriots. 3rd Lyon shall be destroyed, the house demolished, reserved only those belonging to the poor, to the patriots, & the establishments of instruction or charity & of manufactures. 4th The name of Lyon shall be erased from the *tableau* of the cities of the Republic—The remaining houses will be called *ville affranchie*. 5th A pillar shall be erected on the ruins with this inscription *Lyon made war against liberty. Lyon is no more*. 6th All the goods possessed by the wealthy of Lyon in the whole extent of the Republick shall be confiscated & employed to indemnify the persecuted patriots." NA, Foreign Office Papers, Series 95, cited in Rivier, *Etienne Clavière*, 179.

173. Jean Desonnaz, *Histoire de la conjuration de Grenus, Soulavie, &c. contre la république de Geneve*, III, 52: On 2 December 1793 Desonnaz reported to the Jacobin Society at Paris that "Pitt has agents in Switzerland and at Geneva," that their chief was named Du Roveray, that he had been a friend of Brissot's, and that he should be arrested.

174. [Du Roveray], *Declaration des citoyens de Genève anti-anarchistes. Du 6 Janvier 1794* ([Geneva], 1794), 4. See also Bénétruy, *L'atelier de Mirabeau*, 454–458.

175. David Chauvet, *Lettre d'un Genevois établi à Londres, à un de ses amis habitant du Pays de Vaud* (London 1794), i: "Nam tua res agitur paries cum proximus ardet" (Horace, *Epistles*, Book I, epistle xviii, line 84).

176. Ibid., 8–11: "Toute constitution bien réglée doit assurer à chaque individu la conservation de ses droits & de sa liberté; elle doit maintenir la seule égalité possible, la soumission de tous & du Prince même, à la lettre de la Loi . . . dans les temps de révolution la volonté général n'est rien."

177. Karmin, *Sir Francis d'Ivernois*, 273–292.

178. D'Ivernois to Jefferson, 22 August 1794, PTJ.

179. Mazon, *Histoire de Soulavie*, I, 229–294.

180. D'Ivernois to Jefferson, 22 August 1794, PTJ.

181. D'Ivernois to Jefferson, 23 September 1794, 2 October 1794, and 26 February 1795, PTJ; d'Ivernois to John Adams, 22 and 30 August, 4 October, 11 November 1794, 24 February, and 28 March 1795, John Adams Papers, Massachusetts Historical Society; d'Ivernois to Gallatin, 22 August, 5 and 23 September, 4 October 1794, and 5, 12, and 16 March 1795, Albert Gallatin Papers, New York Historical Society.

182. Jefferson to Wilson Cary Nicholas (one of Albemarle County's two representatives in the Virginia House of Delegates), 23 November 1794, PTJ: "I take the liberty of inclosing for your perusal and consideration a proposal from a Mr. D'Ivernois, a Genevan, of considerable distinction for science and patriotism, and that too of the republican kind, though you will see that he does not carry it so far as our friends of the National assembly of France. While I was at Paris, I knew him as an exile for his democratic principles, the aristocracy having then the upper hand, in Geneva. He is now obnoxious to the Democratic party. The sum of his proposition is to translate the academy of Geneva in a body to this country. You know well that the colleges of Edinburgh and Geneva as seminaries of science, are considered as the two eyes of Europe: while Great Britain and America give the preference to the former, all other countries give it to the latter." See also Nicholas Hans, "The Project of Transferring the University of Geneva to America," *History of Education Quarterly* 8 (1968), 246–251.

183. Jefferson to Washington, 23 February 1795, PTJ: "The revolution which has taken place at Geneva has demolished the college of that place, which was in a great measure supported by the former government. The colleges of Geneva and Edinburgh were considered as the two eyes of Europe in matters of science, insomuch that no other pretended to any rivalship with either. Edinburgh has been the most famous in medicine during the life of Cullen; but Geneva most so in the other branches of science, and much the most resorted to from the continent of Europe because the French language was that which was used."

184. Jefferson to John Adams, 6 February 1795, PTJ.
185. Jefferson to John Adams, 27 May 1795, PTJ.
186. Marc-Auguste Pictet to Jefferson, 1 January 1795, PTJ.
187. D'Ivernois, *La Révolution française à Genève: tableau historique et politique de la France envers les Genevois, depuis le mois d'Octobre 1792 au mois de Juillet 1795* (London, 1795), v, 6–22, 63, 82–88, 93.
188. Ibid., 95–96. The translation is from d'Ivernois, *An account of the late revolution in Geneva; and of the conduct of France towards that republic, from October, 1792, to October, 1794; in a series of letters, to a citizen of Philadelphia* (Philadelphia, 1798), 66.
189. D'Ivernois, *La Révolution française à Genève*, 165; *An account of the late revolution*, 41, 53, 61–67. A sense of the response to the work in Britain can be gleaned from Anon., "Review of new publications," *Gentleman's Magazine*, February 1795, vol. 77, 146–147; regarding the response at Geneva, see Karmin, *Sir Francis d'Ivernois*, 257–269.
190. D'Ivernois, *Réflexions sur la guerre, en réponse aux Réflexions sur la paix adressées à Mr. Pitt et aux Français* (London, 1795), 30–89, 144–157; Karmin, *Sir Francis d'Ivernois*, 295–310.
191. D'Ivernois, *Histoire de l'administration des finances de la république française au 1er janvier, 1796* (London, 1796), 132–133; *Historical and political survey of the losses sustained by the French nation in population, agriculture, colonies, manufactures and commerce, in consequence of the revolution and the present war* (London, 1799), 34, 260, 466.
192. Thomas Paine, *The decline and fall of the English system of finance* (Paris, 1796); Comte d'Hauterive, *De l'état de la France à la fin de l'an VIII* (Paris, 1800); Anon., *A vindication of Europe and Great Britain from misrepresentation and aspersion; extracted and translated from Mr. Gentz's answer to Mr. Hauterive* (London, 1803); Karmin, *Sir Francis d'Ivernois*, 322–396; Murray Forsyth, "The Old European States-System: Gentz versus Hauterive," *Historical Journal* 23 (1980), 521–538; Emma Rothschild, "Language and Empire, c. 1800," *Historical Research* 78 (2005), 208–229; Marc Belissa, *Repenser l'ordre européen (1795–1802): De la société des rois aux droits des nations* (Paris, 2006); Isaac Nakhimovsky, "The 'Ignominious Fall of the European Commonwealth': Gentz, Hauterive, and the Armed Neutrality of 1800," in Koen Stapelbroek, ed., *Trade and War: The Neutrality of Commerce in the Interstate System* (Helsinki, 2011).
193. Anon., *Biographical anecdotes of the founders of the French Republic*, I, 103–105.
194. D'Ivernois, *Des causes qui ont amené l'usurpation du général Bonaparte, et qui préparent sa chute* (London, 1800). On the broader context, see Simon Burrows, *French Exile Journalism and European Politics, 1792–1814* (Suffolk, 2000), 196–222.
195. D'Ivernois, *The Five Promises. Conduct of the Consular government toward France, England, Italy, Germany, and especially Switzerland* (London, 1803), 65–127, 164–170.
196. Félix Desportes, "Politique. Affaires étrangères," *La Décade philosophique, littéraire et politique par une société de républicains* (Paris, 1798), no. 26, 20 prairial de l'an VI,

502. See also Marc Peter, *Le syndic Butin et la réunion de Genève à la France* (Geneva, 1914).

197. Blamires, *The French Revolution and the Creation of Benthamism*, 123.

198. Mallet du Pan, *The history of the destruction of the Helvetic union and liberty* (Boston, 1799), v, 15–16.

199. Jacques Necker, *Du pouvoir exécutif dans les grands états* (n.p., 1792), 2 vols., I, 58–59; *De la révolution françoise* (Paris, 1797), 3 vols., II, 21–76; *Dernières vues de politique et de finance* ([Paris], 1802), 105, 146–167, 270–293.

200. Jean-André Deluc to George III, 28 November 1797; Deluc to Lord Grenville, 21 December 1797; Deluc to Lord Grenville, 27 February 1798; Deluc to Lord Grenville, 3 March 1798; Deluc to George III, 4 April 1798; and Deluc to Lord Grenville, 1 July 1798, in *Historical Manuscripts Commission Report on the Manuscripts of J. B. Fortescue, Esq., preserved at Dropmore* (London, 1905), IV, 21–25, 30–37, 109–117, 119–120, 160–166, 524–527, 240–243, 524–527.

201. J. Holland Rose, "The Secret Articles of the Treaty of Amiens," *English Historical Review* 15 (1900), 331–335.

202. Benjamin Constant, *Fragments d'un ouvrage abandonné sur la possibilité d'une constitution républicaine dans un grand pays*, ed. Henri Grange (Paris, 1991); Jean-Charles-Léonard Simonde de Sismondi, *Recherches sur les constitutions des peuples libres*, ed. Marco Minerbi (Geneva, 1965). More broadly see Sonenscher, *Before the Deluge*, 356–371, and Helena Rosenblatt, *Liberal Values: Benjamin Constant and the Politics of Religion* (Cambridge, 2008).

203. Sismondi, *Statistique du Département du Léman*, ed. Helmutt Otto Pappe (Geneva, 1971); Pappe, "A Biography of the Early Years of J.-C.-L. Simonde de Sismondi," Pappe papers, University of Sussex.

204. Biancamaria Fontana, "The Napoleonic Empire and the Europe of Nations," in Anthony Pagden, ed., *The Idea of Europe from Antiquity to the European Union* (Cambridge, 2002), 116–228.

205. D'Ivernois, *Five Promises*, 2–7.

206. Karmin, *Sir Francis d'Ivernois*, 427–467, 483–521.

207. D'Ivernois, *Effets du blocus continental sur le commerce, les finances, le crédit et la prospérité des Isles Britanniques* (London, 1809); *Histoire des décrets commerciaux de Bonaparte et de leurs effets sur l'agriculture, les manufactures, le commerce et les finances de la France* (London, 1811); *Exposé de l'exposé de la situation de l'Empire français, et des comptes des finances publiés à Paris, en février et en mars 1813* (Reichenbach, 1813).

208. David Chauvet to d'Ivernois, 11 January 1802 and 22 September 1802, BdG, Ms. Fr, fol. 198, 204–207; Chauvet to d'Ivernois, 18 July 1802, fols. 200–203.

209. David M. Bickerton, *Marc-Auguste and Charles Pictet, the Bibliothèque Britannique (1796–1815), and the Dissemination of British Literature and Science on the Continent* (Geneva, 1978).

210. Sismondi, *Considérations sur Genève dans ses rapports avec l'Angleterre et les états protestants; suivies d'un Discours prononcé a Genève sur la Philosophie d'Histoire* (London, 1814).

211. John Barrett (librarian, Trinity College Dublin), undated book list with prices, mentioning Du Roveray, the bookseller or agent (Trinity College Dublin, MUN/LIB/10/188). I am grateful to Professor M. A. Stewart for this reference.

212. Du Roveray to Dumont, 24 August 1813, in Bénétruy, *L'atelier de Mirabeau,* 458–459; Karmin, *Sir Francis d'Ivernois,* 559; BdG, Dumont papers, Ms. 33, I, 420.

213. D'Ivernois to Lord Castlereagh, 12 April 1814, in Karmin, *Sir Francis d'Ivernois,* 548–549, 608–609.

214. Lucien Cramer, ed., *Genève et les traités de 1815; correspondance diplomatique de Pictet de Rochemont et de François d'Ivernois, Paris, Vienne, Turin, 1814–1816* (Geneva, 1914), 2 vols., I, 54–78; Lucie Achard and Edouard Favre, *La restauration de la république de Genève* (Geneva, 1913), 2 vols.; Irène Herrmann, *Genève entre république et canton: Les vicissitudes d'une intégration nationale (1814–1846)* (Geneva, 2003).

215. Recent work, such as Sankar Muthu's *Enlightenment against Empire* (Princeton, N.J., 2003) and Jennifer Pitts's *A Turn to Empire: The Rise of Imperial Liberalism in Britain and France* (Princeton, N.J., 2005), should be read from this perspective.

CHAPTER 8. THE LAST REPRÉSENTANT AND PHILOSOPHIC RADICALISM

1. Gareth Stedman Jones, *An End to Poverty* (London, 2006), 64–132, 194–224.

2. Richard Whatmore, *Republicanism and the French Revolution* (Oxford, 2000), 194–204; J. G. A. Pocock, "Hume and the American Revolution: The Dying Thoughts of a North Briton," *Virtue, Commerce, and History* (Cambridge, 1985), 125–142.

3. This is a weakness in the argument of Jonathan Israel's *A Revolution of the Mind: Radical Enlightenment and the Intellectual Origins of Modern Democracy* (Princeton, N.J., 2009), and *Democratic Enlightenment: Philosophy, Revolution, and Human Rights, 1750–1790* (Oxford, 2011).

4. Colin Kidd, *Union and Unionisms: Political Thought in Scotland, 1500–2000* (Cambridge, 2008), 211–256.

5. Louis-Philippe Ségur, "Examen du Système fédératif qui peut être le plus convenable à la France, et le plus utile au maintien de la Paix et de l'Équilibre en Europe," *Politique de tous les cabinets de l'Europe,* 367–383; Sonenscher, *Sans-Culottes,* 407–423.

6. D'Ivernois, *Les quatre époques du crédit public: et de l'administration des finances de la Grande Bretagne* (London, 1807); *Bonaparte administrateur; ou, Tableau du commerce extérieur et intérieur de la France, à l'epoque où son gouvernement déclara les Isles Britanniques en état de blocus* (London, 1808).

7. Dumont, *Souvenirs sur Mirabeau,* 145, 173, 292, 299; Blamires, *The French Revolution and the Creation of Benthamism,* 219–232.

8. Du Roveray, *An appeal to justice and true liberty,* 55n.

9. Etienne Dumont to Lisette Duval and Jeannette Soret-Duval, 19 July 1793 and 30 September 1794, in Jean Martin, *Etienne Dumont,* 48–49.

10. Dumont to Bentham, 23 August 1792, in *Correspondence of Jeremy Bentham, Volume IV,* 387–388. Dumont was referring to the death of Stanislas Marie Adelaide, comte de Clermont-Tonnerre, whom a mob had thrown from a window.

11. Dumont, *Souvenirs sur Mirabeau*, 95, 108.

12. The term "Benthamism" is employed, rather than "the writings of Jeremy Bentham," because Dumont was most interested in the implications of Bentham's principles, while recognizing that Bentham's thought was disparate, evolving, and all too often incomplete. Bentham, accordingly, was seen not as the chief of a unified sect but as the author of a new science with uncertain and extensive social applications. "Benthamite" and "Benthamism" were used as terms of abuse by contemporaries. See, for example, Thomas Moore, "Ode to the Sublime Porte," *Odes upon Cash, Corn, Catholics, and Other Matters, Selected from the Columns of the Times Journal* (London, 1828), 23; T. Perronet Thompson, *The Article on Parliamentary Reform, Republished from the Westminster Review no. XXVIII, for April 1831* (London, 1831), 16; and Thomas Carlyle, "The Hero as Man of Letters," *On Heroes, Hero-Worship, and the Heroic in History* (London, 1841), 270, 288. John Neal and John Stuart Mill were more usefully distinguishing between Bentham and Benthamism from the early 1830s: John Neal, "Biographical Notice of Jeremy Bentham," *Principles of Legislation from the Ms. of Jeremy Bentham* (Boston, 1830), 45; Mill to Carlyle, 11–12 April 1833, in *The Earlier Letters of John Stuart Mill, 1812–1848*, ed. F. E. Mineka (Toronto, 1963), *Collected Works* XII, 148–152.

13. Maria Edgeworth to Mrs. Frances Edgeworth, 10 August 1820, in Christina Colvin, ed., *Maria Edgeworth in France and Switzerland* (Oxford, 1979), 210; John Neal, "Biographical Sketch of M. Dumont of Geneva," *Principles of Legislation from the Ms. of Jeremy Bentham*, 162.

14. Bentham to Dumont, 16 August 1792, *Correspondence of Jeremy Bentham*, IV, 385.

15. Dumont, "Préface," in Bentham, *De l'organisation judiciaire, et de la codification* (Paris, 1828). See also Blamires, *The French Revolution and the Creation of Benthamism*, 181–199, 233–253.

16. Philip Schofield, *Utility and Democracy: The Political Thought of Jeremy Bentham* (Oxford, 2006), 198–247.

17. Bentham, *Traités de législation civile et pénale*, ed. Dumont (Paris, 1802), 3 vols., I, "Discours préliminaire," xv–xvi, xvii–xviii. "Il pense que le bonheur est l'unique but, l'unique objet d'un valeur intrinsèque, et que la liberté politique n'est qu'un bien relative, un des moyens pour arriver à ce but. . . . Le vice fondamental des théories sur les constitutions politiques, c'est de commencer par attaquer celles qui existent, et d'exciter tout au moins des inquiétudes, et des jalousies de pouvoir. Une telle disposition n'est point favorable au perfectionnement des lois. . . . Il ne dit point aux Peuples, 'Emparez-vous de l'autorité, changez la forme de l'État.' Il dit aux Gouvernemens: 'Connoissez les maladies qui vous affoiblissent, étudiez le régime qui peut les guérir. Rendez vos législations conformes aux besoins et aux lumières de votre siècle. Faites de bonnes lois civiles et pénales. Organisez les Tribunaux de manière à inspirer la confiance publique. Simplifiez la procédure. Évitez dans les impôts la contrainte et les non-valeurs. Encouragez votre commerce par les moyens naturels.'" Dumont used almost the same words when writing on Bentham for the *Bibliothèque britannique* (V, 1797, 163).

18. Bentham, *Traités de législation civile et pénale*, "Discours préliminaire, xxxiii: "Ils ont des professions de foi, des mots magiques; tels qu'Égalité, Liberté, Obéissance passive,

Droit divin, Droits de l'homme, Justice politique, Loi naturelle, Contrat social. Ils ont des maximes illimitées, des moyens universels de gouvernement, qu'ils appliquent sans égard au passé et au présent, parce que du haut de leur génie, ils considèrent l'espèce et non les individus, et qu'un système sublime ne doit pas être mis en balance avec le bonheur d'une génération. Leur impatience d'agir est en proportion de leur impuissance à douter, et leur intrépide vanité les dispose à mettre autant de violence dans les mesures qu'il y a de despotisme dans leurs opinions."

19. Bentham to Jean-Marie Roland de la Platière, 16 October 1792, in *Correspondence of Jeremy Bentham*, IV, 401–402.

20. J.-H. Burns, "Bentham and the French Revolution," *Transactions of the Royal Historical Society* (Fifth Series), 16 (1966), 95–114; Burns, "Jeremy Bentham: From Radical Enlightenment to Philosophic Radicalism," *Bentham Newsletter* 8 (1984), 4–14; Philip Schofield, Catherine Pease-Watkin, and Cyprian Blamires, introduction to *Rights, Representation, and Reform: "Nonsense upon Stilts" and Other Writings on the French Revolution* (Oxford, 2002); Schofield, *Utility and Democracy*, 78–108, esp. 100–104.

21. Dumont, "Discours préliminaire" to the *Tactique des assemblées politiques délibérantes* (1816), in *Oeuvres de Bentham* (Brussels, 1840), 3 vols., I, 348.

22. Ibid., 346.

23. Ibid., 347.

24. Ibid., I, 349, citing Claude-Carloman de Rulhière, *Histoire de l'anarchie de Pologne et du demembrement de cette république* (Paris, 1807), 4 vols., IV, 1–134.

25. Dumont, *Règlement pour le Conseil représentatif de la ville et République de Genève* (1816), in *Oeuvres de Bentham*, I, 413: "Après avoir lu cette théorie, on verra peut-être avec intérêt comment et avec quel succès elle a été mise en œuvre dans le conseil représentatif de la république de Genève."

26. "By the end of the day we were spoken of as public enemies, and some persons formerly well-disposed towards me were saying I had been used by ambitious men whose anti-patriotic objectives I had unwittingly furthered." Pierre-François Bellot, "Notes sur le constitution de 1814," cited in Selth, *Firm Heart and Capacious Mind*, 186.

27. Dumont, "Discours préliminaire," *Tactique des assemblées politiques délibérantes*, in *Oeuvres de Bentham*, I, 348.

28. Ibid., I, 437. Peregrine Bingham noted in his preface to the English edition that "the original papers contain many applications of the writer's principles to British institutions, and British interests; which, with a view to continental circulation, have been judiciously omitted by M. Dumont." *The Book of Fallacies, from Unfinished Papers of Jeremy Bentham* (London, 1824).

29. Dumont, "Discours préliminaire," *Traités des sophismes politiques et des sophismes anarchiques* (1816), in *Oeuvres de Bentham*, I, 437.

30. Dumont, *Règlement pour le Conseil représentatif de la ville et République de Genève*, in *Oeuvres de Bentham*, I, 414.

31. Dumont, "Discours préliminaire," *Traités des sophismes politiques et des sophismes anarchiques*, in *Oeuvres de Bentham*, I, 436.

32. Dumont, *Règlement pour le Conseil représentatif de la ville et République de Genève*, in *Oeuvres de Bentham*, I, 415.

33. Ibid., I, 413.

34. Ibid., I, 415.

35. Peregrine Bingham did not include the examination of the Declaration of the Rights of Man in his edition of *The Book of Fallacies*, on the grounds that "this forms no part of the present volume, to the subject of which, indeed,—Fallacies employed in *debate*,—it is not strictly pertinent" (*Book of Fallacies*, preface).

36. Dumont, "Avertissement" to *Sophismes Anarchiques* in *Oeuvres de Bentham*, I, 507.

37. Dumont was referring to the national congress of the Venezuelan independence movement, led by Simon Bolívar, which drafted a constitution in Caracas in March 1811 and in July declared the country independent.

38. Dumont, "Avertissement" to *Sophismes anarchiques* in *Oeuvres de Bentham*, I, 508.

39. Dumont, *Recollections of Mirabeau*, 112–113.

40. Dumont, "Avertissement" to *Sophismes anarchiques* in *Oeuvres de Bentham*, I, 508.

41. George Bubb Dodington, 1st Baron Melcombe (1691–1762), was a member of the Prince of Wales's entourage under George II and became a baron on the accession of George III. William Gerard Hamilton sat in Parliament from 1754 to 1796, holding office in Ireland, and becoming known as "single-speech Hamilton."

42. Bentham, *Book of Fallacies*, 23.

43. Dodington, *The diary of the late George Bubb Dodington, Baron of Melcombe Regis: from March 8, 1749, to February 6, 1761* (Dublin, 1784), viii.

44. Hamilton, *Parliamentary logick: to which are subjoined two speeches, delivered in the House of Commons of Ireland, and other pieces* (London, 1808), 48–49: "Sooth, flatter, and alarm. . . . Either overrate and aggravate what is asserted against you, and then you will be able to shew that it is not true; or under-rate it, and then admit it in a degree, and with an apology."

45. Dumont, *Règlement pour le Conseil représentatif de la ville et République de Genève*, in *Oeuvres de Bentham*, I, 416; "La Possession des colonies est-elle un avantage pour les métropoles," *Annales de législation*, vol. I, no. 2, 315, 346.

46. Dumont papers, BdG, Ms. 60, "Matériaux pour un traité de droit international"; Bentham MS boxes 177, 178, University College London; for the views of Dumont and Bentham, see David Armitage, "Globalizing Jeremy Bentham," *History of Political Thought* 32 (2011), 63–82.

INDEX

Abauzit, Théophile, 67, 72
Abingdon, Willoughby Bertie, 4th Earl of, 7–8, 111, 112
Adams, John, 261, 263, 264, 340n40
Alembert, Jean Le Rond d', 26, 27, 50–51, 59, 63, 76, 109
American Revolution, 15, 144–48, 158, 174, 187, 194, 223, 247
Anglo-French Commercial Treaty (1786), xv, 15, 202–4, 248
Anspach, Isaac-Salomon, 9, 10, 146, 172
Argenson, René Louis de Voyer de Paulmy, Marquis d', 165, 166
Aristocracy: and Bentham, 280; and Bodin, 27–28; and Brissot, 173; in Britain, 242; and Etienne Clavière, 250, 251, 254; and François d'Ivernois, 158, 159, 165–66, 172, 173; and Dumont, 277; and Dupont de Nemours, 144; and Jacques-Antoine du Roveray, 257; entrenchment of, 231, 232; in France, 194–95, 214, 219, 220, 227, 238, 240, 246, 247, 254; and Genevan constitution, 277; Genevan exiles' arguments against, 207, 213, 217, 224, 226, 227, 233–34; as hereditary caste, 166, 194; and Le Sage, 60–61; and Micheli du Crest, 41, 42, 75; and public good, 199; and représentants, 83, 95, 169; and

republicanism, 47, 194, 274; and Rilliet, 89; and Rousseau, 79, 93, 94; and Shelburne, 257; and trade, 190, 221, 242
Atheism, 50, 139, 259
Athens, 11, 36–37, 41–42, 93, 101, 117, 127
Austria: and Britain, 23; and Etienne Clavière, 246, 247, 248; and France, 103, 204, 227, 244, 247, 248–49, 268; and Mirabeau, 200; and Vergennes, 148, 168

Baczko, Bronisław, xvi
Barbeyrac, Jean, 45–46
Barnave, Antoine-Pierre, 243
Barruel, Augustin, 98, 102
Bassompierre, Jean-François, 157
Beaumarchais, Pierre-Augustin, 191, 210, 215
Beaumont, Albanis, 170–71
Beauteville, Pierre de Buisson, chevalier de, 84–85, 86, 88, 89, 96, 106, 323n29
Bellot, Pierre-François, 283, 369n26
Bénétruy, Jean, xvi, 229
Bentham, Jeremy: and British-French relations, 236–37; and colonialism, 142; and Dumont, xvii, 15–17, 231, 236, 277–82, 283, 285–88, 289, 368nn12 and 17; and French-Genevan relations, 229; and perpetual peace, 205; and Romilly, 231; and Shelburne, 13

371